BEHAVIOR OF

Norris G. Haring, editor
University of Washington

EXCEPTIONAL CHILDREN **Second Edition**

An Introduction to Special Education

Charles E. Merrill Publishing Company
A Bell & Howell Company
Columbus Toronto London Sydney

Published by
Charles E. Merrill Publishing Company
A Bell and Howell Company
Columbus, Ohio 43216

This book was set in Avant Garde and Helvetica.
The production editor was Frances Margolin.
The cover was prepared by Will Chenoweth.

Photos: *Tom Hutchinson,* cover; *Valentine Dmitriev,* 61–65; *Dr. Ronald B. Berggren,* 280, reproduced by permission; *Richard M. DeMott,* 337, 340, and 345 top; *Penny Musante,* 350 upper left; *J. Mark Rainez,* 350 lower left, 382 bottom; *Marvin L. Silverman,* 350 upper and lower right, 366, 367 bottom, 370 top and bottom right, 371, 377 bottom right, 382 top, 383 top left and right; *Paul M. Socha,* 368 top and bottom; *John Stripeika,* 374 top; *Joseph Dirickx,* 374 bottom; *Charles E. Merrill Publishing Co.,* all other photos. Color inserts: Insert 1, p. 2, *Nils Lindquist;* Insert 3, p. 2 (center right), *Dennis Kelleher* ; Insert 4, p. 2, (center right) and p. 4 (bottom two), *Dennis Kelleher;* and Insert 4, p. 3 (bottom), *Nils Lindquist.* All others by *Charles E. Merrill Publishing Co.*

Library of Congress Catalog Card Number: 78-53511

International Standard Book Number: 0-675-08398-2

2   3   4   5   6   7   8   9   10—85   84   83   82   81   80   79   78

Printed in the United States of America

Contents

Contents

This book has two aims: to introduce you to exceptional children and to the field of special education. In editing this second edition, some of my tasks have proven to be easier than I anticipated, and some were much tougher than I might have liked. One of the more difficult tasks was deciding how to organize all of the diverse information about special children we have collected over the last few decades. We know more today about children than any civilization ever has.

But the more you learn about exceptional children, the less neatly does all the information fit together. Simple black and white outlines lose their sharpness: you begin to see shades of gray. Categories are a perfect example. On the surface, the traditional categories of handicaps seem simple and useful. This child is mentally retarded. That one is emotionally disturbed. The next is visually impaired, and so on.

The problems with these labels are that the classifications often are *not* very accurate or even especially useful. For one thing, labels don't really refer to a set of distinct characteristics in children. Nor do they tell you very much about how to identify what a given child's greatest needs are, what his present level of development is, or how extensive the programs and services to help him must be. For these reasons, it has become common in recent years to criticize traditional categories of exceptional children. But criticism by itself isn't very productive, either. We need to make sense out of the mass of facts, not simply to argue with the past.

The early stages of planning this edition, then, consisted of a lot of list-making. How best could we organize the information we had, to make it both understandable and useful? Besides reviewing the traditional categories of handicaps, we wanted to communicate the role of delays in a child's normal development from infancy to childhood to adolescence to adulthood. And beyond that, we wanted to focus on the vast differences in levels of severity across all the kinds of handicaps. And that brought up a related concern for educators—the differences in programs and services needed to meet the very different and individual needs of special children. The table of contents shows the compromise we came up with to reflect those many lists and many shades of gray.

One other thing came out of all the lists we made. We saw that no one list is enough. You cannot fairly categorize children, only facts about them. To describe a child fairly, you must rely on all the variables . . . his level of development, the degree of severity of his handicap, the programs and services he needs. And critical to all that informaton, you must focus on his behavior—what he does, the ways he moves in response to the world around him. In short, we cannot give a realistic or useful understanding of exceptional individuals without giving you all of the lists—all of the ways of looking at children. In fact, that may be the most important outcome of learning about special education: to see a child from every perspective you can.

Interspersed throughout this book are four "Perspectives" sections. They are offered to eliminate some of the overlap that comes in trying to explain the same thing from several points of view. They are meant to give you a chance to touch base occasionally, whenever we move from one way of looking at children to another. I hope that these short transitions, along with the opening and concluding chapters, will help you see some continuity in all of the information presented here.

That information, of course, is not the result of my efforts alone. The seventeen other people whose names appear on the chapters deserve much praise. Their individual expertise and careful efforts have resulted in the latest and, I believe, the best information we can offer for a first course in special education.

Beyond these professionals, the many people who reviewed the manuscript merit recognition. Five instructors, Bill Heward at Ohio State University, David Herr at Madison College, Robert Harth at the University of Missouri, Anne Langstaff Pasanella and Cara Volkmor at the California Regional Resource Center, each reviewed the entire manuscript. In addition, individual chapters were reviewed by Patricia Looney, Lewis Brown, Patricia Cegelka, Gary Yarnell, Mary Lynn Calhoun, Ann P. Turnbull, Barbara Clark, Cecil Mercer, James Kidd, and Ghiselda Manifesto.

Schools and individuals graciously permitting us to photograph include: Marilyn Kilian, Marilyn A. Brown of East Whittier City School District, Dr. Judy Grayson of the Lincoln Development Center, Jady von der Leith, Will Carey of the Santa Monica Unified School District, Etta Fisher of Oralingua School, Dr. Edgar Lowell of the John Tracy Clinic, Sandy Sanborn, Mr. and Mrs. Bruce Clement, Mrs. Lois Moore of Santa Barbara School District, Sande Upright of Santa Barbara County Schools, Dr. and Mrs. Dennis Kelleher, Dr. and Mrs. Elliot Brownlee, Linda Kelly of the Santa Barbara County Schools, Frank LeVita of WORK, Inc., Joanne Freeman of Harding Elementary School, Louise De Rose of La Cumbre Junior High School, Joseph Pasanella of the Educational Assessment Service, William Berger of Dos Pueblos High School, Nella Gross of Santa Barbara County Schools, Deanna Kellogg-Robbins of El Rancho School, Jackie Anderson of Santa Barbara County Schools, Beth Staiger of Community Services in Santa Barbara, Mrs. Tejeda, Mr. and Mrs. Joiner, and Dr. Ronald Berggren of the Ohio State University Hospital.

Finally, our primary objectives in preparing this second edition were to greatly improve the continuity and coherence of the book, and to make it more even in level, more readable, and more understandable for readers not familiar with the concepts and terminology of the field. While the first and last chapters and the short perspectives sections are efforts to accomplish these objectives, the work of several others was critical. Claire Hill and Connie Pious double checked and added to the glossary of terms, a new feature of this edition. Ms. Hill also helped to proof the galleys.

Special thanks are due Madelon Plaisted and her staff, who spent more than 600 hours on the manuscript, eliminating redundant and repetitive information, cross-referencing material, simplifying language, and improving continuity and style in general. Without Mitzi's efforts, the book would not read as well as I believe it does. Finally, Tom Hutchinson, Merrill administrative editor, and Francie Margolin, Merrill production editor, designed and edited the book, took photos, and worried over it with us until it became the book you have now. Many thanks to all of these fine people. Together with them, I hope you find this second edition worth the investment you will give it.

BEHAVIOR OF EXCEPTIONAL CHILDREN Second Edition

An Introduction to Special Education

1

Introduction

Norris G. Haring

WHO ARE EXCEPTIONAL CHILDREN?

The exceptional child is different from his or her peers: different in the way he looks or the way she moves her body; different in the way he responds to the world around him; different in the way she learns or fails to learn. But everyone is different in some way from everyone else. So the exceptional child is not merely one who is different, but one who deviates so far from the average (or "normal") that he or she requires special attention—special services, facilities, curricula, instructional materials or educational procedures, and special teaching skills. It is important to realize that this deviation may be either higher or lower than the norm—both the gifted, higher-achieving child and the slower learning, lower-achieving child may be regarded as exceptional. In other words, exceptional individuals differ *significantly* in what they need to succeed in the world. They are *individuals with special needs,* a phrase that is becoming more and more popular as a description of these members of our society.

CATEGORIES OF HANDICAPS

In general, exceptional children are those having one or more of the following.

1. Sensory handicaps, including children with hearing and vision impairments.

2. Mental deviations, including the gifted as well as the mentally retarded.

3. Communication disorders, such as speech and language disorders.

4. Learning disabilities.

5. Behavior disorders.

6. Health impairments, including neurological defects, orthopedic conditions, diseases such as muscular dystrophy and sickle cell anemia, birth defects, and developmental disabilities.

It has been a practice in the past to further distinguish handicapped people, to make distinctions between "temporary" and "permanent" handicapping conditions. This notion is somewhat limiting, however, especially in light of recent breakthroughs and continuing research that may now help change the predicted futures of some children who might have once been considered permanently handicapped. In any case, the following distinctions are sometimes made between terms which might otherwise be taken as synonomous:

● *Exceptional* refers to any child who deviates from the norm, either by higher than average or lower than average performance or ability.

● *Disability* refers to the reduced functioning that results from any physical lack (the loss of a limb, the loss of hearing or sight, the presence of a disease, and so forth) or any significant behavioral characteristic (extreme difficulty in learning, antisocial or other highly inappropriate behavior, and so forth).

● *Handicap* refers to the difficulty which an exceptional or disabled person has in responding to the world because of the differences that set him or her apart from normal individuals. Thus, a blind person may be *actually* handicapped because he cannot hold certain jobs or take part in certain events that require eyesight (perhaps flying an airplane or being a photographer) or *socially* handicapped because people treat her as if she were unable to hold other jobs or participate in other events which do not really require eyesight (perhaps managing an airline or being a journalist).

For the most part, both professionals and lay persons tend to use these three terms interchangeably.

Unfortunately, we do not have an appropriate system for classifying handicapped individuals to better serve them. The effort to identify kinds of handicaps (for example, sensory handicaps, mental deviations, communication disorders, learning disabilities, behavior disorders, and health impairments) is fairly conventional, but it is hardly efficient for grouping people according to need. For example, the needs of those with unusually high mental deviations (the "gifted") are hardly similar to the needs of those with unusually low mental deviations (the "profoundly retarded"). A single program for educating both the gifted and the profoundly retarded under the same circumstances would hardly do justice to either group. The critical issue, then, is that we consider each child we teach as an individual with an instructional program based on his or her abilities and disabilities.

PROBLEMS OF LABELING

Placing a label on any human being does violence to that individual uniqueness which is the joy of humanity. Yet, we do it all the time because it is such a convenient communication shorthand. When we say a person is a halfback, or a Baptist, or an executive, or a campus radical, we have stripped him or her of some unique features, but have also conveyed some of the essence of that person's characteristics or functions. Educational labeling is no different. Whether we refer to a "good student," underachiever, behavior problem, gifted, or retarded child, we do so to quickly communicate part of the essence of that student. (Gallagher, 1972)

The effort to define and classify handicapping conditions is both necessary and plagued with problems. The wide range of differences among exceptional children does not allow a single definition to explain their social and educational problems. Many of the labels and categories now used in education are the result of an attempt to distinguish various handicaps through research in medicine and psychology. But their use has not been so much to help children learn more efficiently or adjust better to the world around them as it has been to simplify information for administration of services, for placement or grouping of individuals, and for legislation. Unfortunately, these generalizations about children, problems, and handicaps often hide more than they reveal. The individual differences and strengths of a child have too often been obscured by the generalized traits the label suggests. Worse yet, the use of labels may predict or actually shape limitations or failure for a child—the so-called "Pygmalion effect" (Rosenthal & Jacobson, 1968). In this study, two researchers assigned children to one of two categories: slow and late bloomers. Teachers were told that the "slow" children might never catch up, while the "late bloomers" would. And that is just what happened, even though the groups were really no different from one another at the start of the study. Though the adequacy of

the experimental procedures have been criticized (Elashoff & Snow, 1971), other studies support the notion that, to some degree at least, children will perform much as their teachers expect them to perform (Beez, 1969; Fine, 1970).

Research has not demonstrated how many handicapping conditions are created within the home or school environment, but behavioral research has shown that the environment is at least as responsible for creating and maintaining handicaps as are individual genetic or intellectual capabilities. Placing children in instructional programs on the basis of medical or psychological categories reflects a style of thinking that puts the problem "within" the child. Thus, if the child is failing, it is the child's fault. Fortunately, assumptions of

Perhaps the best label for Michael is "determined."

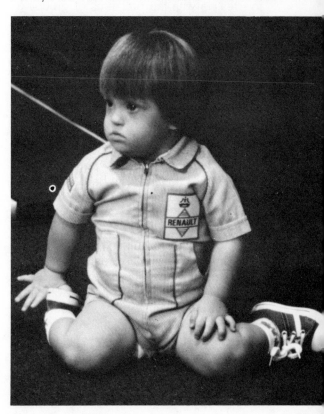

this kind have not fared well in recent years. As Reger, Schroders, and Uschold state (1968):

> We are saying that grouping children on the basis of medically derived disability labels has no practical utility in the schools. Children should be grouped on the basis of their educational needs, and these needs may be defined in any number of ways. The notion that simple labels, applied by high-status authorities from outside the school, should serve as a basis for grouping children is basically nothing more than a refusal to accept responsibility for making educational decisions. It is educational laziness.

Historically, as many as a dozen different categories of handicaps have been used, although some learning problems nevertheless could not be placed neatly into any of them (the area of "specific learning disabilities," most notably). One suggestion for dealing with the problems of grouping and classification is to use two broad categories that more accurately indicate those who are receiving special education and those excluded from it—the mildly handicapped and the severely handicapped (Haring, 1972). The new federal law for all handicapped children (P.L. 94–142) uses nine separate categories: mentally retarded, hard of hearing, deaf, speech impaired, visually handicapped, seriously emotionally disturbed, orthopedically impaired, other health impaired, and those with specific learning disabilities. But the significance of P.L. 94–142 in regard to labeling (and we examine the other important aspects of the law in greater detail later in this chapter) is not the categories it uses, but the demands it makes on how children shall be grouped and placed in educational settings. All handicapped children, according to the law, must have available to them "a free appropriate public education which emphasizes special education and related services designed to meet their unique needs." More specifically, a child is to be placed in educational services not according to the label he or she may be given, but in the "least restrictive environment" that will allow the child to succeed.

> To the maximum extent appropriate, handicapped children, including children in public or private institutions or other care facilities, are [to be] educated with children who are not handicapped, and that special classes, separate schooling, or other removal of handicapped children from the regular educational environment occurs only when the nature or severity of the handicap is such that education in regular classes with the use of supplementary aids and services cannot be achieved satisfactorily. (P.L. 94–142, Sec. 612, 5, B, 1975)

This principle of placing the child in the least restrictive environment suggests a "cascade" of services and options for placement (see Figure 1.1), with the regular classroom as the most natural and therefore least restrictive of all options. Of all remedies offered to change the traditional system of labeling and categorizing children, the least restrictive environment offers perhaps the best answer to the problems of labeling. We cannot avoid classifying children—by grade, by age, by nationality, by level of achievement, by height, weight, sex, or by nature or severity of handicap. But we can distinguish between the value of such generalizations for administrative or legal purposes (for instance, for appropriating funds for the category of children called "gifted") and the very limited usefulness they have for deciding what a child needs to grow and learn and succeed in the world.

The Incidence of Exceptionality

An accurate count of the number of exceptional children in this country is difficult to get because local school districts use varying criteria when reporting to state departments of education. The most reliable in-

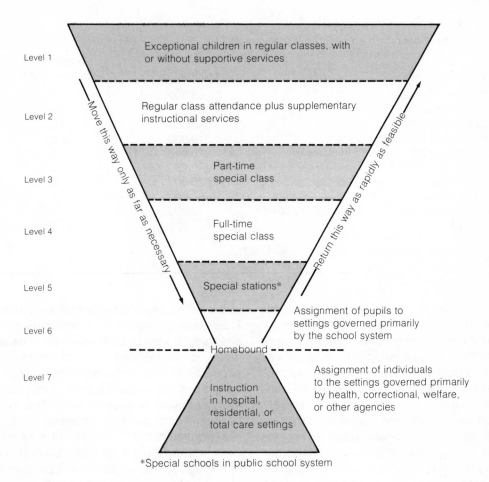

Level 1 — Exceptional children in regular classes, with or without supportive services

Level 2 — Regular class attendance plus supplementary instructional services

Level 3 — Part-time special class

Level 4 — Full-time special class

Level 5 — Special stations*

Level 6 — Homebound

Level 7 — Instruction in hospital, residential, or total care settings

Move this way only as far as necessary

Return this way as rapidly as feasible

Assignment of pupils to settings governed primarily by the school system

Assignment of individuals to the settings governed primarily by health, correctional, welfare, or other agencies

*Special schools in public school system

Figure 1.1
The Cascade system of educational placement

formation available comes from the Bureau of Education for the Handicapped, a part of the U.S. Office of Education under the Department of Health, Education and Welfare. With the implementation of P.L. 94–142 and its requirements for identifying handicapped children, this information will change and should become more accurate. The reported number of handicapped children will increase because the law increases the population of school-age children to include those from 3 to 18 years old, and by 1980 to include those from age 3 to age 21. In addition, because the law provides for money to come through the state department of education to the local education agencies based on average pupil costs, districts should become increasingly more accurate in their reporting.

The most recent information available on the number of handicapped children in the United States and its trust territories is shown below in Table 1.1. The category of learning disabilities is the most variable; the incidence may range of 1% to 3%, depending on the criteria used. In the fiscal year 1969, for example, only 761,817 learning disabled children (less than 1%) were reported by the states; in 1976, they reported 1,966,000 (3%).

Chapter one

Table 1.1
Incidence of handicapped children, fiscal year 1976

Type of handicap	Number of children	Percent of all children in U.S.
Speech impaired	2,293,000	3.5
Mentally retarded	1,507,000	2.3
Learning disabled	1,966,000	3.0
Emotionally disturbed	1,310,000	2.0
Crippled and other health impaired	328,000	.5
Deaf	49,000	.075
Hard of hearing	328,000	.5
Visually impaired	66,000	.1
Deaf-blind and other multiply handicapped	40,000	.06
TOTAL	7,870,000	12.035

From Bureau of Education for the Handicapped, 1977.

The severely and profoundly handicapped, which includes all categories of children with severe handicaps regardless of medical or psychological cause, represents less than one-tenth of one percent (.001%) of the total population. This estimate includes children who are severely emotionally disturbed (autistic), severely mentally retarded, deaf-blind, deaf and retarded, blind and retarded, and all other multiple handicaps (for detailed information on these children, see chapters 8 and 9 on the Severely and Profoundly Handicapped, and chapter 13 on the Physically and Multiply Disabled).

WHAT IS SPECIAL EDUCATION?

Throughout the history of civilization, societies have responded differently to their handicapped members. In chapter 5 of this book, Jim Payne and Carol Thomas trace the history of the treatment given the mentally retarded through several eras: from the view that the handicapped should be exterminated to our present belief that all handicapped children have the moral and legal right to an appropriate education. These eras are helpful in understanding the changing points of view taken towards all handicapped persons. Other chapters give accounts of the treatment other specific categories of handicapped individuals have received in more recent times, particularly in this country. In general, though, it is useful to note that our own treatment of (and frequent discrimination toward) the handicapped has largely been a product of our view of them as deviant from the normal people who make up the mainstream of our society.

Dr. Samuel Kirk (1972), one of the leading proponents and crusaders for federal legislation for exceptional children, writes that there have been three stages in the development of attitudes toward the handicapped—persecution, protection, and acceptance (Frampton & Gall, 1955)—in our own country. Until the early decades of the nineteenth century, the mentally subnormal were relegated to attics, back wards of hospitals, or the role of village idiots. Early in the nineteenth century, however, people like Horace Mann, Samuel Gridley Howe (profiled in chapter 12), and Dorothea Dix began providing services to the handicapped by establishing residential schools for the deaf, blind, orphaned, and others. Often the protection afforded by these schools was as important to the person's well-being as the education received. With the rise of the public school movement at the close of the nineteenth century, the education of the handicapped increased too, so that the public schools eventually developed programs for most kinds of handicaps. Special education, then, became the special efforts provided to help handicapped children learn despite their handicaps. In general terms, special education has the distinguishing characteristic of focusing greater attention on the individual differences among children than regular education. On the basis of those differences—both strengths and weaknesses—the special educator carefully arranges the educational environment and the instructional cues, materials, activities, and rewards specifically and individually for each child.

The development of compulsory education for all children did help bring education to many handicapped children who had never received it before. But many others, particularly the more severely handicapped, continued to be excluded from educational services of any kind. And the attitudes toward the placement of children in special classes, while far more humane than persecution and far more enriching than simple protection, still had the effect of excluding handicapped persons because they were different. As Dr. Leo Connor (1968) reflected, the traditional definition of special education had the central theme of "accepting children unable to fit into the regular school program." More than ever before, the last 10 years have seen a careful examination of the relationship of special education to regular education. Lloyd Dunn (1968), in an article written as he left the presidency of the Council for Exceptional Children (see the profile of this group on page 102), urged special educators to look at their own attitudes and to question the justifications for special programs and services.

> Regular teachers and administrators have sincerely felt they were doing these pupils a favor by removing them from the pressures of an unrealistic and inappropriate program of studies. . . . However, the overwhelming evidence is that our present and past practices have their major justification in removing pressures on regular teachers and pupils at the expense of the socioculturally deprived slow learning pupils themselves.

The effect, according to critics, has been to make special education a "dumping ground" for problem students. Dr. John L. Johnson (1969) writes:

> Special education is part of the arrangement for cooling out students. It has helped to erect a parallel system which permits relief of institutional guilt and humiliation stemming from the failure to achieve competence and effectiveness in the task given to it by society. Special education is helping the regular school maintain its spoiled identity when it creates special programs (whether psycho-dynamic or behavioral modification) for the "disruptive child" and the "slow learner," many of whom, for some strange reason, happen to be Black and poor and live in the inner city.

Ms. Annie Stein (1971) lists three central "strategies for failure" that operate in our public school system: (1) controlling through containment, including tactics of segregation and decentralization; (2) training teachers to fail; (3) institutionalizing mechanisms for failure, including labeling, tracking, and lack of administrative accountability. It is obvious that the handicapped and exceptional children are not alone in trying to get a quality education from the regular system. All too many children both physically or mentally handicapped and nonhandicapped have been frustrated in participating in the educational mainstream. Current critics writing for general public consumption assert as givens charges which as little as a decade ago would have been regarded as sacrilege by professional educators and their tax-supporting constituency, who considered the place of education unassailable in the roster of means to the good life (Deno, 1970).

Special education's function in the traditional system has been one of "fix and return." Evelyn Deno (1970) calls this the "statue of liberty" philosophy, that is, "Give me your defective, defeated, and unwanted and I will love and shelter them." Research has provided an abundance of data (Simches, 1970; Lily, 1970) that show the futility of this approach. Special education tends to provide a scapegoat that reinforces regular education's failure to provide equal opportunities for children to develop their potentials. By so doing, special educators work at maintaining the status quo of a system that ought to be challenged to change.

Special educators have generally been motivated by basic humanitarian interests to serve the needs of those children with

Feeding the bear is a reinforcer for Reyna and her classmates when they do especially well on an academic task.

severe physical handicaps, mental retardation, emotional disturbance, and learning problems that make successful growth and development an extremely difficult and painful task. One great problem that the special educator has faced is the lack of flexibility in structuring and programming in regular education classrooms and the accompanying inability of regular classroom teachers to handle children with various mildly handicapping conditions. The problem has intensified as more categories of handicapping conditions have been distinguished and as more children have been referred to special education classrooms for specific remedial help.

But one other development is important to note. Special education has, in the last dozen or so years, become the one component of the overall educational system that relies most heavily on the scientific method and experimental research to improve instruction and to provide ways to change developmental, learning, and behavior problems. Basic research and applications in learning, instruction, social reinforcement, behavior modification, and curriculum analysis and sequencing have evolved from attempts to find the best methods of teaching handicapped persons. Fortunately, they are now being generalized and carried over into other areas of education. Thus, as regular educators begin to recognize individual differences and develop the skills of teaching to these differences rather than to children's assumed similarities, they can make the regular classroom the "least restrictive environment" for many handicapped children.

The advance of special education in this country has been neither particularly long nor particularly smooth. For the most part, our exclusion of handicapped children from the mainstream of public school life went unchecked until the 1960s. Then determined parental advocacy on behalf of the rights of their handicapped children led to legal tests of those rights in many state courts. The combined force of parent advocacy and litigation in the courts led to greater awareness among lawmakers, which, in turn, led to laws written specifically to end the exclusion of handicapped children from an education.

Influence of Parent Groups

Parent groups have provided a powerful force for setting priorities and future directions for special education. The changing attitudes of parents toward their handicapped children after the second world war was a decisive factor in legislation benefitting the handicapped. Often parents of handicapped children refused to even admit the existence of such children in the home. Society's nonacceptance of handicapped children caused parents not to express their feelings about the daily problems they encountered. The parents' attitude, shaped by superstition and societal rejection, was one of sheltering the child from society or rejecting him. As long as attitudes like this prevailed, it is understandable why parents did little to seek better educational environments for their handicapped children. Feelings of guilt and shame resulted in an aura of secrecy.

Societal attitudes toward disability began to change as a result of World War II (Cruickshank & Johnson, 1967), apparently for two reasons. First, many men considered to be "normal" citizens were rejected for military service because of physical and mental defects. These men then returned to the local community to function once again as "normal" persons. Physical differences, as well as some psychological differences, were accepted as normal by society. The second force for changing attitudes was the return of the thousands of disabled war veterans. The attitude of the community towards disabled war veterans has generally been one of acceptance and

aid. This attitude fortunately has generalized to all types of exceptionality, providing an environment that is more receptive to the education and life possibilities of handicapped persons.

Local parent organizations began to appear as early as 1930, and by the 1940s national organizations were being created. Parents of cerebral palsied children were the first to begin organizing. Beginning on the local level, a national organization, the United Cerebral Palsy Association, began to push for research and treatment centers. This organization provided a forum for parents and professionals to work for legislation for research, professional training, and remedial programs.

About 1950, parents of mentally retarded children began to organize, demanding public education for their children. These parents argued that since they were taxpayers, laws excluding their children from public schools should be changed. The result was the National Association for Retarded Children. Local chapters of NARC have provided information for the community concerning the needs of the handicapped and programs for parents in attempts to overcome the social stigma and superstitions about mental retardation and the handicapped. Since 1950, parent groups, professional organizations such as the CEC and the American Association on Mental Deficiency (AAMD), and concerned state and federal officials have worked together to change public indifference and to work for service programs in public education. The historic federal legislation Public Law 88–164 began nationwide movements for training and research to improve both treatment and prevention of all types of handicapping conditions.

The effectiveness and success of parent and professional groups working for the mentally retarded prompted the organizing of parents with children suffering from milder forms of handicaps such as percep-

Chapter one

tual or neurological disorders, now commonly known as *learning disabilities.* In this field the growth has been almost incredible. By 1967 a national organization, the Association for Children with Learning Disabilities (ACLD), that began in the states of California, New York, Illinois, and Texas in the late 1950s, was functioning in 15 states with 200 local chapters.

During the 1960s the term *minimal brain dysfunction* became broadly acceptable in professional circles to describe children with certain perceptual and learning problems. These children, while handicapped, did not qualify for typical special education services. The learning disabled child seemed to hover between the poles of normal and retarded, but there were no remedial programs within the public education system to accommodate these special needs. The pressure of parent groups on state and local levels generated the creation in 1963 of a three-part task force sponsored by the Department of Health, Education and Welfare and the National Easter Seal Society.

Perhaps the most important results of the task forces and parental pressure were increased national interest and concern among educators about the specific and individualized instructional-management requirements of these children and increased awareness of the significance of precise educational assessment in addition to medical and psychological causes in planning remedial programs for learning disabled children. This activity and lobbying from parent groups and the Council for Exceptional Children was responsible for the Learning Disabilities Act of 1969, P.L. 91–320, signed into law in 1970.

Parent organizations have brought about change in both public attitudes and school programming. Special and regular educators now cooperate in working toward integrated programs flexible enough to facilitate individual differences. Public education is a service offered to the community and supported by it financially, and should be responsive to the needs of those it serves. Parent groups organized around special education services have been and will continue to be an important influence on changes in educational policy. And nowhere can we see clearer evidence of the effect of parental pressure on educational policy than in the passage of P.L. 94–142, the Education for All Handicapped Children Act (which we will examine later in this section).

Court Cases

Some of the recent reanalysis of the basic principles of special education has come from court cases brought against school districts over the issues of placement and labeling, techniques of psychological diagnosis, and the role of parents in the process of public education. Some think (Martin, 1972; Abeson, 1972) that full educational opportunities for exceptional children will be achieved mainly through establishing a strong legal basis. While federal and state legislation is one vehicle, certainly another effective way of getting increased services is litigation in the nation's court system.

Dissatisfied parents have brought both specific and class action suits against school districts or states based on the belief that the due process clause of the Fourteenth Amendment to the U.S. Constitution is being violated, depriving children of equal protection under the legal system. The landmark case that clearly articulated specific issues was Judge Skeelly Wright's decision in *Hobson* v. *Nansan* in 1967. Judge Wright ruled against the tracking system used to place children in special and regular classes. The tracking system is a method of assigning students to classes on the basis of their scores on standardized aptitude tests. Unfortunately, such group-administered tests are usually inappropriate for a large portion of the students in a school system. For instance, in Washington, D.C., which is predominantly black and working class, the tests used are standardized with white, middle-class students, and the test instruments are relevant only to that group. The results tend to show how a minority student would perform in the context of white, middle-class values and expectations. Classified according to the criterion of ability to learn in these terms, black and minority students are being classified according to racial and/or socioeconomic status, that is, "according to environmental and psychological factors which have nothing to do with innate ability" (269 F. Supp. 40, 1967).

Children forced in lower tracks because of poor performance on these achievement tests are often labeled anything from "slow learner" to "learning disabled" to "educable retarded." The Hobson decision also ruled that group tests used to diagnose children were rejected as invalid for placement or labeling. The tracking scheme is central to the issue of labeling we discussed earlier. In effect, **tracking** is an institutionalized form of labeling. As we have seen, labeling may be useful if it leads to increased or more carefully targeted educational opportunities. But if a label does not lead to successful remediation of the problem described by the label, why use it at all? The case of *Covarrubias* v. *San Diego United School District* sought damages for deprivation of equal protection under the law and an injunction against all special class placement until the procedures for placement were changed. This case and others represent the parental dissatisfaction with testing and placement that results in categorical labeling of students.

The problem of labeling and placement is complicated by the fact that much of the early legislation to provide funds for educating exceptional children was created under categorical labels. Those labels did not al-

ways change with our changing understanding of handicapping conditions, however. Often the labels were misused, as in cases of behaviorally disordered children being labelled "severely retarded" to remove them from the regular classroom. The use of categorical labels in public schools has too often excluded children who deserved admission to specific programs and placed other children according to single labels that did not lead to adequate services for the full range of their individual needs. The provisions of the Education for All Handicapped Children Act, P.L. 94–142, regarding procedural due process in labeling and placing children, and the requirement to place the child in the least restrictive environment, are specific legislative responses to these concerns.

Still another issue tested in the courts, and answered by P.L. 94–142, was the right of every child, *including all handicapped children regardless of their handicap,* to an equal opportunity for an education. That right was established in 1971 in the case of *Mills* v. *Board of Education of the District of Columbia.* Another widely publicized case that year, *Pennsylvania Association for Retarded Children* v. *the Commonwealth of Pennsylvania,* brought a class action suit to guarantee public support of education for all mentally retarded children. Not only did the court decide in favor of full educational opportunity for the retarded, but it also granted the right of the family and child to be notified and given legal due process before the child's educational status is altered. As we shall now see, the rights upheld in these and the other cases helped to stimulate legislation specifically written for the benefit of handicapped children.

Federal Legislation

Perhaps it was the civil rights movement and resulting civil rights legislation that provided the initial drive for changing views of education. The historic Supreme Court

Chapter one

decision, *Brown* v. *Board of Education of Topeka* in May 1954, began an intense questioning of the process providing equal opportunity for education across racial boundaries. The Court ruled that state laws that permitted or required segregated public schools violated the Fourteenth Amendment's equal protection clause. But perhaps more important, the Court used work of social scientists in demonstrating that theoretical work and research data presented by social scientists were relevant in developing and deciding public areas of educational and social priorities. This early civil rights decision set a precedent for change in programs of social equality. Special education as it exists today was essentially created by law. Beginning in the early sixties, state and federal legislation began to provide the structure and resources for the growth and development of special education.

One driving force behind legislation to aid special education and the education of handicapped children has been the Council for Exceptional Children. In 1958, CEC joined with NARC to support legislation to provide grants for training special education personnel. As a result of this effort, a policy statement that specified two basic needs for improving federal educational programs for exceptional children was drafted by a special ad hoc committee under the guidance of Leo Connor. First, the need for reorganization of the U.S. Office of Education to meet new demands was explained. Second, there was a need for improvement of scope and quality of services for exceptional and special children. As a result of this 1961 policy statement, a number of the objectives in the statement were realized by federal action during 1963. Perhaps the most significant was the creation of the Division of Handicapped Children and Youth (now the Bureau for Education of the Handicapped) within the U.S. Office of Education. Along with this came legislation, P.L. 88–164, that provided federal monies for scholarships, fellowships, and research funds in specific areas of special education.

The Elementary and Secondary Education Act (ESEA) of 1965 provided federal monies to state and local districts for developing educational programs for economically disadvantaged children and, for the first time, provided support for the handicapped. Edwin W. Martin, associate commissioner of the Bureau for Education of the Handicapped, described this legislation this way (1968):

> Of the many programs developed and approved by the 89th Congress and the Administration—programs aimed at the

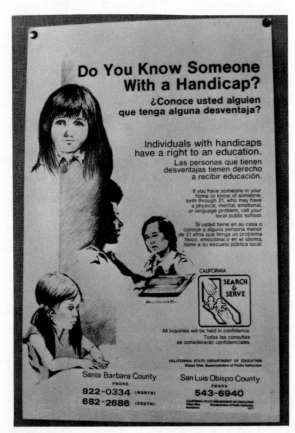

Both state and federal laws (like 94–142) have stimulated "child find" or "search and serve" efforts.

cities, at the aged ("medicare"), etc.—none outranked in brilliance the Elementary and Secondary Education Act of 1965, P.L. 89–10. Its final passage, with its programs of assistance to children in disadvantaged areas (including handicapped children), new instructional materials, centers for innovation and research, and support for strengthening state educational agencies, was precedent-shattering not only in its educational implication, but also in the brilliance of its legislative drafting and strategy which succeeded in overcoming the traditional barriers to federal aid to education.

Two points are important. First, for the first time federal legislation provided for money for research and program development. Second, the precedent was set for providing quality education for exceptional children of all types. The ESEA was a stepping stone for providing categorical aid to the handicapped. Resulting federal legislation advanced the basic 1965 laws.

But it was 1966 that was the banner year for special education. Administrative supervision at the federal level through the National Advisory Committee on Handicapped Children and the Bureau for Education of the Handicapped was created, and funds were especially earmarked for handicapped children. Other advances were matching funds to state departments of education for direct aid in developing programs for educating the handicapped, expanded services to state institutions and day schools, and extended services to the blind and deaf.

The 1966 legislation was the first step toward national programs to provide all children with the education they need and deserve. This legislation, however, only *began* to meet the needs of the handicapped. The National Advisory Committee on Handicapped Children advised Congress in 1966 that only one-third of the handicapped in the country were receiving necessary services. In 1969, P.L. 91–320, the Learning Disabilities Act, was passed. It

provided federal funds for service programs on a state level for learning-disabled children.

In 1970, P.L. 91–230, the Elementary and Secondary Education Act Amendments, were signed into law. With this package Congress began to see programs for the handicapped as a single, interlocking whole. Handicapped and exceptional children were recognized as a target population with specific needs. In addition, efforts of special educators to emphasize the need for human treatment and educational opportunities and to resist mechanical categorizations resulting from particular descriptions of disabling conditions were also recognized.

The early 1970s brought federal legislation recognizing the noneducational needs of the handicapped. Section 504 of the Rehabilitation Act of 1973 (P.L. 93–112) said that handicapped people could not be excluded from any program or activity receiving federal funds, simply on the basis of the handicapping condition. "Handicapped" was defined in terms of vocational opportunity, the intended focus of the act. The act was amended in December of the next year (Section 111a of P.L. 93–516) to have a broader base. It now applies across the board to any recipient of federal funds. No recipient can discriminate against the handicapped in employment or provision of services. In addition, the regulations mandate that employers make reasonable accommodations to the special needs of handicapped employees.

The next important landmark was the Education Amendments of 1974, P.L. 93–380. This legislation extended the life of several already existing laws, including the ESEA, and included several new provisions that indicated the federal government's growing awareness of the needs of exceptional children. The federal government authorized money to be spent by state and local agencies for planning programs for the gifted and talented. It also provided for money to be spent by the states for teacher and leadership personnel training and for research. In addition, it was a precursor to the Education for All Handicapped Children Act, noting that many handicapped children were not at the time receiving an education and setting a goal of correcting that defect. P.L. 93–380 also required the states to protect the rights of handicapped students and their parents at the time of any change in educational placement and to assure as much mainstreaming as possible. As we will see, these provisions became nationwide mandates with the passage of P.L. 94–142.

The Education for All Handicapped Children Act

Public Law 94–142, enacted on November 29, 1975, is clearly the most sweeping statement this nation has ever made about rights of handicapped children to full educational opportunity. Two aspects of the law are especially noteworthy. First, by assuring "a free appropriate public education" to all handicapped children between the ages of 3 and 21, the law rejects the practice of excluding exceptional children because of their differences from "normal" learners. Second, because of its highly specific provisions for the kind and quality of education handicapped children are to receive, the law establishes a new principle: the obligation to offer an *individually planned* education to meet the unique needs of each handicapped child. Because its specific provisions make the act a forceful mandate rather than a mere expression of hope for the exceptional child, let's examine those provisions more carefully.

All handicapped children, regardless of the severity of their handicaps, shall receive "a free appropriate public education which emphasizes special education and related services designed to meet their unique needs" (89 STAT 775). Those services must be provided at public expense, without charge to the child or parents; must meet the standards of the state education agency; must include an appropriate preschool, elementary, or secondary education; and must conform to the requirements of the individualized education program described below. Unless it has specific laws or court decisions that rule otherwise, each state must make such an education available to all handicapped children between the ages of 3 and 18 by September 1, 1978, and for all handicapped children aged 3 to 21 by September 1, 1980.

The act provides substantial increases in funding to compensate local school districts for the "excess costs" of educating handicapped children. Using a formula that gradually increases the amount of funding from an additional 5% to 40% of the average amount spent to educate each pupil, the act provides for an eventual federal contribution of over three billion dollars for education of handicapped children. In other words, the government's commitment is both legal and financial.

The focus on serving children who most need help is closely tied to the funding provisions. Thus, while the act defines handicapped children in terms of categorical labels, it demands that funds be spent on the basis of need rather than category. More specifically, it establishes two priorities of handicapped children: (1) the *un*served child, who currently receives no education, and (2) the *under*served child, who is not receiving all of the special education or services he or she may need to succeed. Among the unserved group are the severely and profoundly handicapped, most of whom have received no educational services at all in the past. Among the underserved group, priority is given to the most severely handicapped within each disability who are receiving an inadequate program. The effect of these provisions is to concentrate on individual needs rather than on categorical labels as the basis for service.

Consistent with the emphasis on needs rather than categories is the act's requirement to educate each handicapped child in the "least restrictive environment." As we saw earlier, the principle of the least restrictive environment is clearly a better rationale for the placement of children than is placement according to categories. With the new mandate to serve previously unserved children, the need to "return" mildly handicapped children to regular classes (mainstreaming) is even more critical. Placing these children in less restrictive settings like the regular class is necessary to free special education personnel to deal with the needs of "first priority" children. Of course, it is not yet clear whether the regular class actually becomes the least restrictive educational setting for the majority of mildly handicapped children. Much of the success of that effort will depend on the abilities of regular class teachers to become more flexible in planning for and meeting the individual needs of their pupils. And a large role in the development of those new skills may fall to special educators, who can share their systematic instructional procedures and experiences with regular teachers. In light of these needs, it is important to note that the act does call for a comprehensive system of teacher training and retraining, with special emphasis on inservice training of practicing teachers and special attention to promising new educational practices and materials.

Two other critical provisions of the act relate to the rights of the child and the parents. One is the extension and refinement of the requirements of P.L. 93–380 to observe legal due process in labeling and placing a child in special education. Among the specific guarantees is one that allows the parents to secure an independent evaluation of their child; another re-

quires that written notice of pending identification, evaluation, and placement of a child be given the parents in writing and in their native language. Still another sets up guidelines for prompt, unbiased appeal hearings in the event a parent disagrees with an evaluation or placement decision. A second major provision affecting parents is the requirement to involve them, to whatever extent possible, in formulating the **Individualized Education Program** (IEP) which must be written for their handicapped child.

The Individualized Education Plan

Of all of its provisions, one of the most specific and most significant is the requirement for an IEP for each child identified as handicapped. The IEP must be a joint effort of the child study team, which is comprised of a representative of the local education agency (other than the child's teacher), the child's teacher or teachers (regular and special), the parents, any other support staff (like speech therapists, school psychologists, physical therapists), and, whenever appropriate, *the child as well.* According to rules proposed to implement the act,

This IEP team includes a mother, teachers, an assessment specialist, and an administrator.

The individualized education program for each child must include;

1. A statement of the child's present levels of educational performance, including academic achievement, social adaptation, prevocational and vocational skills, psychomotor skills, and self-help skills;

2. A statement of annual goals which describes the educational performance to be achieved by the end of the school year under the child's individualized education program;

3. A statement of short-term instructional objectives, which must be measurable intermediate steps between the present level of educational performance and the annual goals;

4. A statement of specific educational services needed by the child (determined without regard to the availability of services), including a description of:

    a. All special education and related services which are needed to meet the unique needs of the child, including the type of physical education program in which the child will participate, and

    b. Any special instructional media and materials which are needed;

5. The date when those services will begin and length of time the services will be given;

6. A description of the extent to which the child will participate in regular education programs;

7. A justification for the type of educational placement that the child will have;

8. A list of the individuals who are responsible for implementation of the individualized education program; and

9. Objective criteria, evaluation procedures, and schedules of determining, on at least an annual basis, whether the short-term instructional objectives are being achieved. (Federal Register, Vol. 41, No. 252, p. 5692)

An example of a completed IEP is shown in Figure 1.2.

We stand at the beginning of a new era in education in this country—the "next civil rights movement," as some have called it. No longer is exclusion either justifiable or legal. No longer is our principal concern whether or not we *should* provide full educational opportunity to exceptional children; our concern now lies in determining how best we *shall* do it. The law tells us that we must now plan, in advance of placement, how, where, what, and how fast a child will learn. It tells us that the child has the right to be made aware of his performance and to be protected so that others will not judge him unfairly. It tells us that each exceptional child is to be considered an individual to the extent that he or she receives an individually planned program of instruction. And probably most important of all, it tells us that that program must be reviewed and evaluated regularly, on an annual basis at the very least.

Of course, the success of any law lies in the effectiveness with which it is put into practice and enforced. The Education for All Handicapped Children Act is no different. But we do have the resources and the knowledge, as we shall see in the next section of this chapter, to make full educational opportunity for exceptional children more than just a hopeful phrase.

HOW SHALL WE TEACH EXCEPTIONAL CHILDREN?

The impact of P.L. 94–142 on administrative and classroom teaching strategies is expected to be both lasting and profound. Using the mandate to place the handicapped child in the least restrictive environment that will allow him to learn successfully, state and local administrators, and individual communities as well, will have to reevaluate the settings in which children receive special help.

INDIVIDUAL EDUCATION PLAN (IEP)

IDENTIFICATION INFORMATION

Name	John Doe
School	Beecher Sixth Grade Center
Birthdate	5-15-65 Grade 6
Parents' Name	Mr. and Mrs. John Doe
Address	1300 Johnson Street
	Raleigh, N.C.
Phone: Home   none   Office   932-8161

CONTINUUM OF SERVICES

	Hours per week
Regular class	20 hours
Resource teacher in regular classroom	6 hours
Resource room	4 hours
Reading specialist	
Speech/language therapist	
Counselor	
Special class	
Transition class	
Others:	

YEARLY CLASS SCHEDULE

	Time	Subject	Teacher
1st semester	8:30-9:20	math	Franks
	9:30-10:20	language arts	Bambara (Resource)
	10:30-11:20	social studies	Bambara
	11:20-12:20	science	Franks
		lunch	
	1:10-2:00	art	Shaw
	2:10-3:00	P.E.	King
2nd semester	8:30-9:20	math	Franks
	9:30-10:20	language arts	Bambara (Resource)
	10:30-11:20	social studies	Bambara
	11:30-12:20	science	Franks
		lunch	
	1:10-2:00	art	Shaw
	2:10-3:00	P.E.	King

TESTING INFORMATION

Test Name	Date Admin.	Interpretation
PIAT	9-10-77	spell-1.7, math-5.7, read recog-1.2 read comp-N.A., gen info-6.3
test of initial consonants (CRT)	9-11-77	knows eight out of total-2.0 twenty-one initial consonant sounds
CRT Reading Checklist	9-12-77	oral comprehension - 6th grade reading skills - primary level
Carolina Arith. Inventory (Time)	9-2-77	Level IV
Carolina Arith. Inventory (Number concepts)	9-2-77	Level IV

CHECKLIST

9-1-77	Referral by Louise Borden
9-3-77	Parents informed of rights; permission obtained for evaluation
9-15-77	Evaluation compiled
9-16-77	Parents contacted
9-18-77	Total committee meets and subcommittee assigned
9-28-77	IEP developed by subcommittee
9-30-77	IEP approved by total committee

COMMITTEE MEMBERS

Teacher	
Other LEA representative	
Parents	

Date IEP initially approved 9-30-77

HEALTH INFORMATION

Vision:	good
Hearing:	excellent
Physical:	good
Other:	

Figure 1.2
An individualized education plan

Administrative Strategies—The Settings

In the recent past, the most widely used administrative strategy for public education of the handicapped was the self-contained day class for the so-called "educable mentally retarded." Teachers in these classes were normally trained to teach one type of exceptionality, but often the classes were filled with children with various handicapping conditions. In the last dozen years or so, special classes for the learning disabled were added in many schools.

In addition, school districts have employed special tutors and consultants to serve both regular and special teachers. Specialists such as visual, auditory, learning disabilities, and reading or language teachers and speech therapists provided extra instruction to children with specific problems. Other consultants trained in areas of behavior disorders or diagnosis and assessment have been available to the classroom teacher to help prepare remedial strategies and special materials and to suggest the best procedures to use.

Now, because of the least restrictive environment requirement of P.L. 94–142, the consultant plan for special services is certain to be more widely used than ever. To become proficient as such a consultant (or *resource specialist,* as some states call such a person), extensive graduate training in diagnosis, continuous evaluation, and individualized and systematic instruction is necessary. This plan will no doubt become a significant factor in the on-going inservice training of regular classroom teachers as they work with mainstreamed exceptional children.

Along with consultant services, special **resource rooms** and staffed instructional materials centers have gained popularity. Under the resource room plan, a child is enrolled in a regular class for part of the day, with special instruction in a separate, "resource" room during another scheduled part of the day. Ideally, a resource room is equipped with special equipment such as console teaching machinges, *Language Masters,* and equipment for recording academic responses. Often one or more instructional aides are there to assist the master teacher or resource teacher. The resource room provides a place to precisely assess entering behaviors and allows for the rapid acceleration of those children who can function for part of the day in the regular class. Again, as school systems act on the charge to place children in the least restrictive educational environments, the resource room will no doubt carry a heavy portion of the commitment to provide special education to children who are mainstreamed.

One of the clearest implications of P.L. 94–142 is the move to seek more appropriate and less restrictive settings for more severely handicapped children. Until recently, about 10% of the children receiving special education in this country were in **residential schools.** These schools have used a variety of names—training schools, hospital schools, detention homes, or boarding schools. Private boarding schools are still maintained throughout the country, offering services to the blind, deaf, emotionally disturbed, and learning disabled. Public residential settings traditionally served those with severe and multiple handicaps.

The increasing awareness of the rights of the severely and multiply handicapped has led to more careful examinations of public residential facilities in the last few years. As Neufeld (1977) points out:

> Some of the negative characteristics associated with these institutions are regimentation, lack of privacy, impersonal treatment, limited freedom and independence for the residents, and limited interaction between the residents and the "outside" world. The larger the institution and the larger the geographic area that it must

serve, the more difficult it is to normalize that environment for its residents. Activities aimed at improving conditions for residents in institutions can legitimately be called *deinstitutionalization.*

Instead of noncare, closed-door policies and back ward isolation for the severely handicapped, new programs are now being developed across the nation, emphasizing normal living in the community through use of hostels, foster homes, group homes, community training centers, day care, and community-based social services. Sailor and Haring (1977) describe two possible answers to the question, "Where should the class (for the severely handicapped) be located?"

> The "cluster" or self-contained school for special education students offers the advantage of high community visibility, concentrating parents, administrators, and resources—which are apt to be scarce in a community—in one central location. Staff and consultant communication and problem sharing are maximized under this model. Ancillary professional personnel spend less time in transportation and thus more time in service. Supervised practice teaching and inservice programs are easier to administer, and specialized support services, e.g., medical personnel, can be concentrated in one place.
>
> On the other hand, the "dispersal" model—or the spreading of classes for the severely handicapped throughout several, or many, schools in a district—offers the possibility of integration into community life and normalization (Sontag, Burke, & York, 1973). The students are apt to come into contact with the problems of the severely/ multiply handicapped child, and the possibilities for new approaches for remediation are increased.

Depending on the size and particular needs of a community, one or the other of these options may be more desirable. But the goal of returning as many institutionalized children to the community as possible is clearly backed by strong support. And as mildly and moderately handicapped children spend more time in regular school classrooms, more special educators can turn their attentions to working with the severely handicapped within the context of the public school system.

Teaching Exceptional Children— Systematic Instruction

In the last hundred years, as special education programs have been designed for handicapped children, the field has witnessed several philosophical swings and many new theories of how best to teach exceptional children. Not all of these efforts have contributed to better instruction, however; not all methods are equal. Today more than ever, teachers, both in regular and special education, need to develop and refine their best efforts to help exceptional children learn. More than that, they need to develop a view of themselves and of their profession that is compatible with the need to be effective for *every* child placed in their charge.

The focus of this book, as you will see in the remaining chapters, rests on that kind of view of teachers, of teaching, and of children. It views the function of the teacher as a manager and arranger of the information and resources and the total learning environment so that children acquire that information. More than that, it views the teacher as a *scientist.*

Because special education originally lacked adequate knowledge and procedures for educating children with various handicaps, the field began to use the scientific approach to build a basic body of knowledge. Over the years, certain refinements in this scientific approach have been developed, and the current best set of practices—systematic instruction and the application of behavioral principles in the classroom—are the subject of the rest of this chapter. Throughout the remaining chapters you will learn much more about systematic instruction and how it can benefit children with a wide range of handicaps at all levels of severity.

The view which the authors take toward children is nowhere better expressed than in the title of this book. Focusing on the *behavior* of exceptional children, or more correctly, the *behaviors* of each individual child, provides us with the best information about his or her abilities and needs. To use a more specific example, Dr. Sidney Bijou (1973) applies this view to the notion of retardation. He writes that

> In the teaching of the retarded child [we] conceptualize the retarded child not as one with symptoms of subnormal mental functioning, but as one with limited behavioral repertoires resulting from inadequate biological equipment and/or restrictions and limitations in his biological and sociocultural environment.

He goes on to say that we "*view teaching* not as communication, but as the arrangement of conditions to expedite learning."

What we are talking about is a technology of teaching, to use **technology** in the sense the ancient Greek meant it. P. Kenneth Komoski (1969) writes that "when the ancient Greeks introduced the concept technology or *technologia* into Western culture . . . *technology* had to do with *techniques for logically* arranging things, activities, or functions in ways that could be systematically observed, understood, and transmitted." The roots of the behavioral approach are deep and complex; but of all the models of learning, this approach focuses most directly on observable behavior and the relationship of a person's behavior to the environment.

> The specific curricula, materials, and instructional tactics which are required in teaching will vary with the needs of the pupil and the limitations of the situation in which instruction must take place. In order for teaching to be consistently effective, therefore, it must consist in part of procedures designed to determine and monitor the needs of the individual learner. Consistently good teaching is a process of learning—learning how to help others learn. . . . Unless the teacher is prepared to observe the behavior and learning patterns of each student carefully, noting particular needs and reactions to the instructional plan, some of the children will fail. A teacher must have the tools and skills necessary to learn from each child what best facilitates *that* child's growth. (White & Haring, 1976, p. 5)

Linda is using a toy phone to help assess Travis's expressive language.

Systematic instruction has grown out of the experimental analysis of behavior, which, as a scientific discipline, sought to find a systematic interpretation of human behavior based on generalized principles, or laws, of behavior. The goal of this search for laws of behavior was much the same as in any other branch of science—to make reliable predictions (Skinner, 1953). The development of behavior analysis has been rigorously scientific, beginning with basic laboratory research and slowly generalizing the results to social situations. Researchers have been careful in their work not to move too quickly in generalizing their data beyond the limits of the experimental situation.

The basic law of behavior, that is, that *the probability of a response is determined by its consequences,* was developed from B. F. Skinner's study of E. L. Thorndike's work. Dismissing the staunch all-or-none (Stimulus-Response) stance taken by earlier behaviorists such as J. B. Watson, Skinner held that behavior operates on the environment to generate consequences, as shown in this sequence:

Stimulus ⟶ Response ⟶ Reinforcement

In the actual classroom situation, the process of reinforcement and controlling reinforcement becomes a primary aim of research into the most effective classroom practices. Following the S-R-R formula, a stimulus is anything in the classroom that evokes a response, and a response is specified *observable* behavior. Reinforcement is the desirable or rewarding consequence for a response that increases the probability of that same response being made to that same stimulus in the future. If a child is reinforced by receiving free time for answering a series of math problems correctly, chances are that she will either maintain or improve her performance if it is contingent on the free-time reinforcer.

As its name implies, *systematic instruction* is an organized body of plans and procedures that leave nothing to chance—a technology for teaching. Moreover, these plans and procedures are supported by data gathered on the child as he or she progresses through the prescribed program. It is based on:

● Gathering objective data regarding the child's performance level at the start of the program,

● Establishing a priority of the skills the child needs to learn now and in the future,

● Identifying the prerequisite behaviors that are necessary to develop these skills,

● Carefully measuring and evaluating new skills as they are acquired.

Systematic instruction proceeds according to the phases of learning, in the same sequence by which you learned all of the skills you now have. First, you *acquire* a new skill (you learn how to hit a tennis ball). You may acquire this skill by observing and imitating others, or you may have an instructor who guides you physically through the motions. Next, in order to build *fluency* in that skill, you repeat it until you are proficient. (You develop the ability to hit a tennis ball until you have, say, 90% accuracy in returning the ball to the opposite court.) Now, if you do not continue to practice that skill, you will not *maintain* it (so you practice tennis regularly). Throughout this process, you are reinforced by the enjoyment or the exercise, the social component or your growing sense of mastery. As you become quite skilled in tennis, you find that you can transfer (*generalize*) the skills you have learned to other tasks and settings. (Your tennis-playing skills may cross over into ping-pong or badminton, and the eye-hand coordination and gross motor skills you have refined will cross over into other activities.) Finally, you may find yourself confronted with novel situations in which your new skills are required (you play racquet-ball for the first time), and you use them to meet the new situation (*application*). These phases—acquisition, fluency-building, maintenance, generalization, and application—become the basis for the teacher's plan to match the teaching procedure to the skill.

Teaching Procedures

Helping a child acquire a new skill is often difficult, particularly with the more severely handicapped. But systematic instruction provides a hierarchy of procedures for skill acquisition. Among these are the following:

• *Shaping,* or reinforcing successively better approximations of the target skill;

• *Molding* (prompting), or actually guiding a child through the physical movements involved in performing the task;

• *Demonstrating* (imitating), or actually performing the activity the child is expected to perform;

• *Modeling,* or providing the child with an example of the completed task;

• *Cueing,* or providing the child with a signal (like a verbal reminder) just before the desired response, in order to bring it out at the desired time (White & Haring, 1976).

Once the child has acquired the correct response, it must be strengthened. In other words, he or she must become more fluent in performing the skill. To build fluency, the teacher provides ample opportunity to repeat the skill (drill) and gives the child continuous reinforcement and feedback (for example, information on whether the response is correct or not). When fluency is attained, continuous reinforcement is changed to intermittent or less frequent reinforcement (perhaps on every third correct response), so the child will develop skill maintenance. To help the child generalize the skill, or transfer it to other tasks and situations, the teacher varies the events leading up to the desired response

(the *antecedent events,* as they are often called). The student then begins to learn that a given skill should be performed under a variety of conditions, and he learns that there are some conditions when the response is inappropriate. Finally, the teacher provides the child with as many novel situations as possible which require him or her to modify the skill (application) (White & Haring, 1976).

In addition to these carefully sequenced procedures for instruction in each phase of learning, systematic instruction offers several other refinements of the behavioral approach to teaching. Particularly important among these are task analysis, the use of direct observation and continuous measurement, and the use of daily planning sheets to implement instructional objectives.

Task Analysis

To guide the student from simpler to more complex responses, systematic instruction relies on breaking down a task into a series of small steps. Whenever a student cannot master a specific task, the teacher reduces it to smaller, more manageable units. This process also leads to a careful sequencing of learning tasks. The goal of teaching a severely handicapped child to feed herself may be reasonable, for example, but it is hardly precise enough to allow for carefully planned instruction. By dividing the skill into small instructional objectives, or *pin-points,* the teacher can sequence them so that one subskill builds upon another. Thus, if the student has difficulty in chewing food, the teacher knows not to begin the child's mealtime with instruction on how to use a spoon. The first step will be the most fundamental one. (An excellent, detailed example of one careful task analysis for a physically handicapped child is presented later, by June Bigge and Barbara Sirvis, in chapter 13.)

Observation and Measurement

One of the most significant features of systematic instruction, and the thing that keeps it from becoming a rigid set of inflexible procedures, is the dependence on continually updated information on how the child is progressing (or failing to progress). Rather than trying to measure psychological processes or abstract concepts such as intelligence, systematic instruction measures a behavior directly. In other words, the teacher specifies (pinpoints) a skill which the child must have in order to succeed in the world (for instance, adding simple math facts in first grade) and then measures the child's progress in terms of his ability to do that task. The information that comes from this direct observation is used to set up an instructional program for the child. The direct measurement of several pinpointed behaviors tells a teacher what the child can do and what he must learn. This information is organized into long-term and short-term objectives that help the teacher place the child in the curriculum and sequence instructional activities. In addition, the teacher continues to collect information and use that data to make any necessary changes in the instructional plan. By collecting the information frequently—even daily in many cases—the teacher can change a plan *before the child actually fails* (White & Haring, 1976). And when a child demonstrates mastery of a skill, the information tells the teacher to move the child to the next objective in the sequence. One very precise system of direct measurement and data recording is detailed in Tom Lovitt's discussion of precision teaching in chapter 7.

Daily Planning Sheets

To carry out such a finely tuned instructional program, the teacher will need to use individualized daily planning sheets that specify the program for each child, the steps within the program, the sequence of learning tasks, preparation and procedures, a record of correct and incorrect behavior, and criteria by which change may be measured. A daily planning sheet for each child also lets any person on the teaching staff, and parents, work with the child on a one-to-one basis. A sample of one kind of daily planning sheet is shown in Figure 1.3.

Conclusion

Thus, systematic instruction provides the classroom teacher with a precise tool for helping each student learn. By following the simple steps of assessing the child's performance, choosing the exact skills he or she needs to learn now and in the future, and measuring and evaluating the child's mastery of each of those skills, teachers can monitor each child's progress. Plans can be made, and modified, to provide meaningful successes for all children.

Two things must have seemed fairly obvious in this discussion of systematic instruction. First, the procedures of systematic instruction clearly offer an effective response to the requirements of P.L. 94–142 to provide every handicapped children with an appropriate, individually planned education based on his or her unique needs. Second, the procedures outlined here are just as applicable to teaching "normal," nonhandicapped children as they are to teaching severely handicapped youngsters. And it is this last point which is perhaps the most important of all. It has been our need to be more precise, more careful, and more effective in helping handicapped children learn that has led to the application of behavioral technology to the skills of teaching. Now we face a legal mandate to improve instruction for all handicapped children, and with it the return of many mildly handicapped children to

PLAN SHEET

ACCELERATE ➚ Reads words orally correctly TO 100 /min, BY 22 Nov	BEHAVER John ,age 11 ,grade 5 ,label L.D.
DECELERATE ➘ Reads words orally incorrectly TO 2 or less /min, BY 22 Nov	MANAGER Judy START DATE 10 Oct
target behavior rate date	ADVISOR Kathleen STOP DATE 27 Nov

SITUATION	EVENTS BEFORE/UNTIL	MOVEMENT CYCLES	EVENTS AFTER/ARRANGED
Room 5 Between 1:15 and 1:45 P.M. each day 6 other pupils present One aide monitors the other children while teacher works with John. Work at John's desk in a circle with 18 other desks. Read from Miami Linguistic Readers (whichever level is appropriate for the day). Other materials change with the activity, see plan at right.	Assessment Plan Teacher gives John his reader, opened to the appropriate page. Teacher says, "Read as fast and as carefully as you can. Ready. . .Begin." Teacher starts the stopwatch at the moment she says, "Begin."	reads words orally correctly	1:1 teacher counts correct movements on the right-hand side of a dual counter. first opportunity + 1' : 1 Teacher records correct count. John charts results. If the results are better than the day before, the teacher praises John.
		reads words orally incorrectly	1:1 teacher counts error movements on the left-hand side of a dual counter. first opportunity + 1' : 1 Teacher records error count. John charts results. If the results are better than the day before, the teacher praises John.
		correct and error together	first opportunity + 1' : 1 Teacher says, "Stop." If correct rate is at least 100, and error rate is less than or equal to two, then select next level reader for next day.
	During Instruction Teacher gives John his Miami Linguistic Reader workbook (level appropriate for day), opened to the page where he should begin work, then instructs John to work for 20 minutes.	circles correct answer	1 : 1, all on the next day, teacher returns corrected notebook.
		circles incorrect answer	1 : 1, all on the next day, teacher returns corrected notebook.
		circles either correct or incorrect	first opportunity + 20' : 1 teacher says, "Stop."
	Teacher sets timer for 8 minutes, then instructs John to say the word on each flash card which she will hold up. Teacher then holds up a flash card with a CVC word on it.	reads word orally correctly	1 : 1 teacher says, "Good," and then holds up next card.
		reads word orally incorrectly	1 : 1 teacher says sounds in word slowly, as in "c-a-t," and instructs John to read it fast.
		no movement, says nothing	10 sec. : 1 teacher treats the absence of movement as if it were an error (see "reads word orally incorrectly," above).
		any movement or no movement	first opportunity + 8' : 1 timer goes off, teacher says, "OK, now it's time for your timing " and proceeds with assessment plan (above).

Figure 1.3
A daily planning sheet

regular classes. When those children do return to their regular classes, they will take their own individual needs and skills with them. Regular teachers will have to meet those needs and build on those skills, so that more special educators can shift their priorities to helping the unserved, the more severely handicapped. Perhaps when the children return to their regular classes, they can also take back — through consultation from special educators and other, comprehensive inservice training efforts — the systematic instructional approaches which have been developed to help them. Perhaps instruction for all children can be made more systematic, and more effective.

FOR MORE INFORMATION

Most of these resources are textbooks that are readily available, many from Charles E. Merrill, the publishers of this text. Check your instructor, the education library, or the general library at your school.

Kirk, S.A., & Lord, F.E. (Eds.). *Exceptional children: Educational resources and perspectives.* Boston: Houghton Mifflin, 1974.

Kneedler, R.D., & Tarver, S.G. (Eds.). *Changing perspectives in special education.* Columbus, Ohio: Charles E. Merrill, 1977.

Pasanella, A.L., & Volkmor, C.B. *Coming back . . . or never leaving: Instructional programming for handicapped students in the mainstream.* Columbus, Ohio: Charles E. Merrill, 1977.

Payne, J.S., Kauffman, J.M., Brown, G.B., & DeMott, R.M. *Exceptional children in focus.* Columbus, Ohio: Charles E. Merrill, 1974.

Schwartz, L.L. *The exceptional child: A primer.* Belmont, Calif.: Wadsworth, 1975.

Turnbull, A.P., Strickland, B.B., & Brantley, J.C. *Developing and implementing Individualized Education Programs.* Columbus, Ohio: Charles E. Merrill, 1978.

Perspectives on Early Childhood

The three chapters that follow, by Alice Hayden, Val Dmitriev, and Jane Rieke, view exceptional children from a *developmental* point of view. They stress the early development of the child—from birth to school age—as the most crucial time of all. Delays in a child's development during this period are the most difficult of all to overcome. If we identify handicaps as soon after birth as possible, we can intervene to make development as close to normal as possible. Effective efforts can actually help reduce the serious effects of handicaps and prevent further delays that might result from inattention to the child's disabilities.

Early childhood education for the handicapped is the most rapidly growing area in special education. P.L. 94–142 mandates that by 1980 educational services be provided for all handicapped children starting at 3 years of age. Many state departments of public health are also recognizing the advantages of statewide screening programs for high-risk infants. This growing effort by the states will eventually allow us to identify the majority of severely handicapped infants and to begin early intervention programs for them.

Of those infant programs that are already in operation, many provide both home-based and developmental center services. The preschool developmental center offers a base for combining the expertise of professionals from several disciplines: pediatricians, pediatric occupational and physical therapists, communication disorders specialists, and special educators trained to work with young children. Home-based programs acknowledge the critical roles that parents and other family members play in the young handicapped child's growth and learning. Early learning is as important as proper nourishment and sensitive child care. The home is the child's natural environment, and the parents are his first and most frequent teachers. Thus, parent instruction is becoming a key responsibility of the early childhood special educator. No program of intervention can be effective without the parents' full cooperation and support.

As a discipline, early childhood education is establishing new strategies which are most promising. Continuous assessment from infancy to school age, new curriculum developments, and effective teaching procedures offer great promise for parents and all those who work with young handicapped children.

Chapter 2 gives an overview of these trends toward early identification and intervention. Chapter 3 then examines delayed development and how it can be dealt with in the preschool classroom. Next, chapter 4 explores the most critical facet of the young child's development—communication. Together, these three chapters take a careful look at handicapped children from the point of view of their early development.

2

Special Education for Young Children

Alice H. Hayden

These are the major topics in this chapter. You may want to use them as a checklist when you review.

- *Some of the early influences on public concern for young children.*

- *Ways in which the current focus on young children and young handicapped children affects programs for these children.*

- *Emerging trends.*

- *Some agencies and state or local sources of information about services for young handicapped children.*

- *Ways parents can learn to help their handicapped children.*

Chapter two

Early childhood education is not new. "The beginning is the most important part of the work," wrote Plato in *The Republic* (Book II, 377-B) and, through the centuries, others—Comenius, Rousseau, Basedow, Pestalozzi, Froebel—have echoed his interest in the abilities and needs of young children.

The twentieth century, which some regard as the "century of the child," has brought new insights and concerns for young children and for their education. There was evidence of a shift from philosophic to scientific teaching suggested, at least in part, by the publication in 1911 of G. Stanley Hall's *Educational Problems*. His concern for very young children is evident in the first chapter's title: "The Pedagogy of the Kindergarten." In his introduction to this basic work, Hall stated that at the turn of the century schools were stagnant and defensive, teachers were complacent, psychology of all kinds went unrecognized, and child study was unknown. He felt that although people were awakening to the fact that schools had lost touch with the child, much more remained to be done, and that considerations for the young child—whether in schools or in child welfare agencies—should become more professional and scientific.

Maria Montessori brought another experimental approach to early childhood education in the early part of the twentieth century. The first edition of the English translation of her book *The Montessori Method of Scientific Pedagogy, as Applied to Child Education in the "Children's Houses"* was published in 1912. On the book jacket, the publishers stated that "Dr. Maria Montessori's methods as practiced in Rome, Paris, New York, and elsewhere have created a sensation in the educational world, and will, perhaps, revolutionize child education." The book concentrated on the application of the principle and the method for educating children 3 to 6 years old. It is unfortunate that the well-known beginnings of Montessori's work received little attention until the work was "rediscovered" years later. But there were other emerging influences that were to affect early childhood education directly or indirectly in the early years of this century: agencies were concerned with child welfare and child labor; the employment of women in industry or in other work outside the home posed new problems.

HISTORY OF PUBLIC CONCERN FOR YOUNG CHILDREN

White House Conferences

The history of the American public's concern for young children needing special services is reflected in *The Story of the White House Conferences on Children and Youth* (1967). In each decade of the twentieth century, the United States has held White House Conferences which have been advisory to the American people as a whole and to their elected representatives in local, state, and national legislative bodies.

Each conference has been concerned with a problem typical of the particular de-

This 4-year-old attends a special preschool for the developmentally delayed.

cade. The first conference, in 1909, was on the Care of Dependent Children; the theme originated with James E. West, a young lawyer who was brought up in an orphanage from 6 years of age. Later he worked in an orphanage, and his deep interest in dependent children grew out of some of his personal experiences. In 1919, the White House Conference was on Child Welfare Standards; the topic in 1930 was Child Health and Protection; the 1940 conference subject was Children in a Democracy. Each conference's reports have been published; since most of the reports were several volumes long and represented the thinking of many different groups of people—from a few hundred participants in the early decades to more than 5,000 in 1970—the reports have also appeared in digest form. In the 1977 White House Conference, handicapped Americans had, for the first time, a voice in determining their own future. "The message from handicapped individuals and their families is very clear," said Dr. Henry Viscardi, chairman of the conference. "They want action. They want follow-through. They want commitment in both legislative and financial areas."

Some quotations from the digest of the 1930 White House Conference lend historical perspective to our interest in early childhood special education.

> The four sections of the Conference—medical service, public health service and administration, education and training, and handicapped children—were composed of specialists working in different fields but, with few exceptions, significantly similar threads were woven into the patterns of the reports presented. Among these were:
>
> **1.** The importance of individual rather than mass methods of dealing with children, in homes, clinics, schools, courts, and institutions.
> **2.** The child himself, the total child, as the unit for consideration—rather than the child

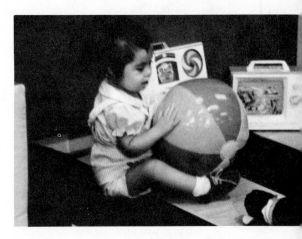

Like their nonhandicapped peers, children with handicaps learn through play.

as a patient, a pupil, a scholar, an athlete, or a "case."
3. The social aspects of the child's life—his home relationships and his relationships with those touching his life outside the home—as being equally important with his body and his mind in building up his personality and character.
4. The responsibility of society to provide a sound economic and social basis for family life and to conserve wholesome family life by every means at its command, whenever it is threatened by national or individual disaster.
5. The need for bringing to parents the most authentic information on child care and training, and for a foundation of all technical service to children in the understanding, support, and cooperation of individual fathers and mothers.
6. The establishment of specialized services upon the basis of adequate professional preparation and skill, sufficiently compensated and supported by the public.
7. National, state, and local cooperation in providing the information and the services required for translating into the lives of children the recommendations growing out of the conference.
8. The basic and transcendent importance of child welfare work to the future of the nation.

Chapter two

Some of these points can be illustrated further by examples from the reports and addresses. The report of the Section on Education and Training stated:

> Democracy demands universal education. Equality of opportunity has long been the ideal of the American child. There is grave danger, however, of confusing equality of opportunity with the sameness of educational training. No other type of government so much as democracy demands the adaptation of education to the individual differences which characterize her children. The danger of a dead level of mediocrity is more grave in a democracy than in any other form of government. Therefore, the first cardinal principle in the education and training for a democratic society is that each individual child should develop to his highest possible level of attainment.

Another section of the report's digest is important. The report of the Committee on the Physically and Mentally Handicapped declared:

> If we want civilization to march forward it will march not only on the feet of healthy children, but beside them, shoulder to shoulder, must go those others—those children we have called "handicapped"—the lame ones, the blind, the deaf, and those sick in body and mind. All these children are ready to be enlisted in this moving army, ready to make their contribution to human progress; to bring what they have of intelligence, of capacity, of spiritual beauty. American civilization cannot ignore them.
>
> The handicapped child has a right:
>
> **1.** To as vigorous a body as human skill can give him.
> **2.** To an education so adapted to his handicap that he can be economically independent and have the chance for the fullest life of which he is capable.
> **3.** To be brought up and educated by those who understand the nature of the burden he has to bear and who consider it a privilege to help him bear it.

> **4.** To grow up in a world which does not set him apart, which looks at him, not with scorn or pity or ridicule—but which welcomes him, exactly as it welcomes every child, which offers him identical privileges and identical responsibilities.
> **5.** To a life in which his handicap casts no shadow, but which is full day by day with those things which make it worthwhile, with comradeship, love, work, play, laughter, and tears—a life in which these things bring continually increasing growth, richness, release of energies, joy in achievement.

Many of the outcomes of the 1930 Conference seem fresh and modern enough to have been written today rather than over four decades ago. But what became of these ideals and concerns? The follow-up programs organized in many states frequently represented the first state-wide attempts to bring together different professional groups and agencies to review children's needs and to determine what services were available. One result was a great advance in the field of pediatrics and pediatric education.

However, this conference was held just prior to the Great Depression. The United States was still recovering from widespread drought and industrial depression and World War II was about to begin. Priorities—for families and for the nation—changed rapidly during that time. Mere survival, first economic survival and then wartime survival, became overriding concerns. Other national purposes were subordinated to these higher priorities. Yet when you consider the constraints operating during those decades, you must admire what was accomplished. Parents and educators did the best they could do with the available resources.

Increased Public Awareness

On December 10, 1948, the General Assembly of the United Nations adopted by resolution the Universal Declaration of

Human Rights. Eleven years later, the same body unanimously adopted and proclaimed a Declaration of the Rights of the Child. It set forth those rights and freedoms which the international community had agreed on for every child, among them the right to adequate prenatal and postnatal care, adequate nutrition and medical care, the right to special care for the child who is handicapped, to an education, to develop abilities, and to enjoy fully opportunity for play and recreation (p. 105).

Other expressions of concern for the young child and his rights are evident in the literature and through reports of groups such as the International Study Group for Early Child Care (Robinson & Robinson, 1973). Many books and articles have been written about the British Infant Schools, and visitors often make trips to England to study first-hand the procedures used in them. There are articles that discuss different patterns of programs for Chinese children who are 56 days to 7 years old; at 7, children enter primary school. Articles on Soviet life give interesting accounts of the kindergarten in Russia which serves many millions of children between the ages of 3 and 6. It is probably not possible to identify any specific ideologies, theories, or events that have stimulated the present international interest in and concern for young children. This interest has come slowly over a long period of time.

In the United States, many changes in society affect the health, the care, and the education of young children. R. A. Aldrich and R. J. Wedgwood (1970), two pediatricians, identify the forces of change as:

1. The vast advance in medical science; . . .

2. The heightened expectation of Americans that improved medical care can and should be available to them; . . .

3. The growing demand for a more efficient and extensive system for delivery of medical care to individuals and their families; . . .

4. The educational force which has begun to adapt to the changing nature and size of the demand for health personnel of all kinds; . . . and

5. The multitude of conflicting voices trying to resolve these complex issues. (pp. 110–111)

Professional and lay groups have worked together through a number of different organizations to serve handicapped children and to help make the public aware of their needs and their families' needs. (Many of these groups are discussed later throughout this book.) It soon became apparent to the leadership of some of these groups, however, that many children they sought to serve had not just one handicapping condition but associated handicaps as well. They realized the need to provide adequate special services and education for *all* handicapped children. Thus, some organiza-

These mothers bring their daughters to a special preschool and work with them there.

Chapter two

tions such as the American Association on Mental Deficiency, the National Association for Retarded Children, the President's Committee on Mental Retardation, and the Council for Exceptional Children and its Division on Early Childhood have not only helped to advance their own original purposes, but have also promoted the concept that appropriate assistance and programs should be provided for all handicapped children. It is encouraging to note the increasing number of efforts to coordinate the work of public and private agencies and University Affiliated Facilities at local, state, regional, and national levels.

Legislation

Most states have now enacted legislation to help fund and implement the programs

---

profile JANE DeWEERD

For her work as an administrator at the Bureau of Education for the Handicapped (BEH), Jane DeWeerd has a background of diverse service to handicapped children as well as dedication to these children, their families, and the professionals and others who work with them. Her hands-on experience with young handicapped children has given her a keen appreciation of the work and the needs of those who operate field programs, and she has strongly supported them. As coordinator of the Handicapped Children's Early Education Programs (HCEEP), administered by the BEH Division of Innovation and Development, she has facilitated the work of staff personnel in field programs by encouraging development, expression, and implementation of ideas, and she has continually encouraged new or novel approaches to working with young handicapped children.

Part of her own responsibilities in the bureau have involved working with other agencies concerned with young children in collaborative approaches to common problems. She has, in turn, emphasized the importance of collaboration and cooperation among agencies and organizations, making the point that the critical work on behalf of young children could be accomplished not only more efficiently but also more enjoyably through working together.

DeWeerd is widely recognized as one who listens sensitively to those in the field, who anticipates their changing needs, and who arranges programs to meet these needs. Long before outreach and technical assistance became part of many of the HCEEP demonstration efforts, and before the concepts achieved their current popularity, Jane DeWeerd understood and anticipated their importance, no doubt because she understood that the most urgent and important efforts would be those that take place in the grass roots of community programs, in settings away from the demonstration centers. She has been concerned about translating the findings from research and demonstration centers into real-world settings where there are different conditions and constraints.

Jane DeWeerd began her career in special education teaching preschool deaf children in public school programs and then at the Lexington School for the Deaf in New York City. There she was a demonstration teacher and supervised practicum training of students from Columbia University's Teachers College. Following this work, she developed programmed curriculum materials for young deaf children. The materials emphasized developing cognitive skills and language patterns. Since 1968, she has worked at BEH, at first as a program specialist in the Deaf/Blind Centers and Title III programs before coming to the HCEEP programs. DeWeerd has been honored and received recognition for her services to handicapped children and for her efforts to humanize government at the grass roots level.

mandated under P.L. 94–142. The parts of this law which pertain to early childhood education are:

● Parents must participate in the establishment of long- and short-term goals for their child; these are Individualized Education Programs (IEPs) for each child.

● The rights of children and their parents will be protected by confidentiality of all child records, nondiscriminatory testing, and due process.

● Parents must receive written notification in their native language prior to evaluation of their child or any placement change.

● A comprehensive system of teacher and other professional personnel preparation must be included in state plans and local policies.

● A special incentive grant to states will be aimed at encouraging the states to provide special education and related services to preschool handicapped children 3 to 5 years old.

Before 1975, the Handicapped Children's Early Education Assistance Act of 1968 focused attention on the needs of young handicapped children. Other legislation such as the Elementary and Secondary Education Act has included requirements that some money must be directed toward serving handicapped children. To date, the Bureau of Education for the Handicapped has helped to launch over 200 programs designed to serve young handicapped children.

The public has become increasingly aware of Head Start programs, initiated in 1965, and of Follow Through, which serves some of the "graduates" of Head Start as they move into the public schools. Head Start now has a mandate to integrate handicapped with nonhandicapped children in their programs—at least 10%. From its beginning, Head Start has helped to identify *early* any handicapped children in its population since these programs are designed to serve children 3 to 5 years old. Early identification of handicapped children provides a basis for determining the special service needs of a community and for seeking ways to provide services in rural as well as urban communities.

EMERGING TRENDS

Interest in early childhood education has prompted a reexamination of the basis of education of young children. Some considerations are:

1. Growth and development—normal and abnormal;

2. Relationship of the infant and young child to his environment;

3. Individual differences among children and individualization of instruction;

4. Curriculum development;

5. Educational methods or procedures;

6. Assessment of children's abilities and deficits; and

7. Placement of children in various types of programs based on assessment information.

Velma instructs Jennifer in familiar surroundings—the child's own living room.

Chapter two

The challenge to reexamine what is known and what is not known in some of these areas undoubtedly will help identify gaps in information and misconceptions. Reevaluation should help program evaluation and modification. When we consider the speed with which legislation has sometimes been enacted and programs have been initiated, it is little short of remarkable that these programs have been successful at all. Head Start, for example, was initiated with a 1-week training period for staff. The training varied from institution to institution across the country. Many of the staff members had backgrounds in elementary education, but few had much preparation for working with young children. It is clear now that the Head Start plan was oversimplified and that some of the premises on which it was based were relatively untested.

Further, it became obvious that many professionals—to say nothing of the American public—had misconceptions and stereotyped ideas about *the* poor, *the* blacks, *the* Indians and other ethnic minorities, *the* handicapped, and *the* gifted. While much was known about individual differences, few realized how wide those differences might be in every population and in every human characteristic. But a great deal has been learned through Head Start—the public has learned about the ill effects of poverty on children, about the need for improved health services, and about the need for *quality* education from the earliest years of growth. Head Start has provided a remarkable learning experience not only for the children and the families it serves but for Head Start staffs, other professionals, and the American public also.

profile JEFF

On the advice of their pediatrician, Jeff's parents enrolled him in preschool soon after he was 3 years old. The doctor encouraged them to find a small preschool because they were concerned about Jeff's apparent inability to play with neighborhood children and also because he had not begun to talk yet. The pediatrician knew that Jeff had not made many demands on his parents, but he wondered whether they had really enjoyed their son. Jeff was a handsome child and had not shown particular health problems. Still, the parents had brought Jeff to the doctor to have his hearing checked because he did not pay attention to them when they called him or tried to talk with him. Jeff's hearing was fine. Then the parents had asked the doctor to check the boy's vision since he seemed to stare at things for long periods of time and really did not focus his eyes on them. Jeff was hard to examine and his office

calls were difficult for the doctor. The mother explained that any new situation seemed to be especially stressful for Jeff. She expected it would take him quite a while to adjust to the preschool, but it would be worth the struggle if Jeff could learn to enjoy other children.

Jeff did fuss and whine most of the time during his first days in preschool. When any of the teachers tried to interest him in an activity or came near to comfort him, his fussing increased and he moved away. The teachers decided it would be best to leave him alone and let him get acquainted at his own speed. The teachers thought it was interesting that a child as young as Jeff seemed unconcerned when his mother left. His whining and fussing did not seem at all related to his separation from her.

To find a way to get Jeff to participate with the other children, the teachers decided to observe carefully to find out what he could do and what he liked to do. They found he spent most of his time wandering around. He did not interact with any of the

Some of the early studies of the effectiveness of preschool and Head Start programs questioned the long-term effects of such programs. More recent research (Preschool training pays off, June 7, 1977) reports that,

> A consortium of 12 early education scientists studied Head Start and other preschool children up to 10 years after they had left preschool and found they were significantly less likely to need special education or to be kept back a grade than other children from identical backgrounds. Further, at least one of the researchers found the money schools saved by not providing special education or more than 12 years of education for a child substantially exceeded the cost of preschool training.

Data from other studies which support preschool programs are building rapidly.

As we think about the successes and the failures of the past, certain trends emerge and point to future directions.

1. There will be an increasing awareness of individual differences and, with it, a recognition of the need for more individualized instruction.

2. Systematic observation of young children in different types of programs will permit on-going assessment and further identification of special needs for services and instruction.

3. The public will expect and demand accountability and competence on the part of all those who serve children and youth.

4. As communities require parental consent and approval before a child is placed in a program, Parent Advisory Councils will more carefully scrutinize these programs.

other children. He did not even like to play near them. In fact, Jeff did not play. If children approached him he moved away and often flapped his hands around his face. The teachers also noticed that Jeff tended to carry small toys around the room with him. He spent a lot of his time looking at lines and tracing the angles of objects. During snack time Jeff helped himself to food. When it was put out of reach, he whined. When the children gathered for a story, Jeff would not join the group so he had been permitted to wander quietly around the room. Jeff's mother asked almost every day whether or not he was beginning to play with the other children.

After Jeff had been in the program for nearly a month, the teachers met to review what they knew about Jeff in preparation for the usual first parent conference. They had already talked with each other about their concerns, but they decided it would be a good idea to make a list to help decide what to do. The first problem was that Jeff never looked at any of them—they never

knew what he was thinking. He seldom interacted with them and not at all with the other children. The teachers were concerned that Jeff had no play skills and they were especially bothered by the inappropriate way he used the materials that were available to him. They also wondered about his hearing since he seemed not to understand any of their directions. His whining was a poor substitute for words, and they thought he should be receiving therapy to teach him to talk. They completed a developmental profile to share with the parents.

On the basis of their observations the teachers found that Jeff was generally delayed in all developmental areas from 1 to 1½ years with obviously more significant delays in the language areas. The main problem, however, was his lack of interacting—his relating to people. Jeff will need intensive language therapy and a special program where he can benefit from the skills of teachers trained to work with children who do not interact.

This school takes infants as soon as they are identified as handicapped.

Their influence will help to deemphasize labeling and categorization of handicapped children.

5. Concerted efforts among professionals of various disciplines will result in new breakthroughs that will help prevent or remediate certain types of handicapping conditions.

6. Improved care and better delivery of health services before, during, and after birth will help reduce the number of handicapping conditions. (See chapter 3 for more on services for young handicapped children.)

7. There will be greater recognition of the need to provide programs for handicapped children from birth to 3 years of age. Recent studies report that 6.8% of handicapped children can be identified at or near birth (Beck, Adams, Chandler, & Livingston, 1976) but relatively few programs are available to serve these children and their families at the present.

8. The growing body of literature and knowledge in the area of infant research coming from many different disciplines and various parts of the world over the past decade will help focus a reexamination of earlier concepts and the need for greater

attention to the importance of the first 3 years of life (White, 1975; Kaiser & Hayden, 1977).

9. Emphasis on *prevention* of handicapping conditions will be directed toward early identification and treatment, maternal and child nutrition, effects of drug ingestion/drug abuse, effects of maternal age-related factors, effects of disease, effects of child abuse/neglect, importance of early and continuous prenatal care, accident prevention, and early and continuous intervention with handicapped children and their families (Hayden, McGinness, & Dmitriev, 1976; Hayden & McGinness, 1977).

10. There will be increasing emphasis on the improvement of the *quality* of programs for young handicapped children through studies of the characteristics of successful programs provided for young handicapped children. (McDaniels, 1977.)

INCIDENCE OF HANDICAPPING

State Departments of Education report on the number of handicapped children served with the assistance of State Handicapped Funds, but few states can provide information about the total number of children needing special education and special services in the birth to 5-year-old population. Information about 3- to 5-year-olds served is much more available than information about children from birth to 3 years old. Also, reports are based on children served and seldom provide much information about the *un*served and the *under*served children in the 0–5 age range.

State efforts to locate children who need special education (Child Find) should help provide some of the information that we presently lack. There is no national registry or handicapped individuals, and many states do not have a registry or do not fully use the registry they have. Physicians are sometimes reluctant to report handicapped children if programs are not available to serve these children and their families. Yet 6.8% of handicapped children could be identified at or near birth. Early and periodic screening could also do much to identify handicapped children, but some of these efforts are directed towards specific populations such as the disadvantaged. There is a need for more early and systematic screening for all children. Today there seems to be no routine or systematic examination of infants at birth, although practices vary considerably among physicians and hospitals in different parts of the country. An increasing number of assessment instruments are being developed, particularly for children from birth to 2 years of age.

Perhaps the best and most current estimates on the incidence of handicapping conditions in the birth to 5 population is provided in the 1976 Annual Report of the National Advisory Committee on the Handicapped in *The Unfinished Revolution: Education for the Handicapped*. The report contains a table on Estimated Number of Handicapped Children Served and Unserved by Type of Handicap. Projected estimates for 1975–76 for the total 0–5 population are 450,000 served, 737,000 unserved—a total of 1,187,000 served and unserved. The percentage of children served in this age range is 38%, and the percentage unserved is 62%. Although the figures for the served may seem to be discouraging, they represent an increase over figures reported earlier.

Efforts to identify and serve young handicapped children have not been too productive and effective, so it is little wonder that the handicapped and their families want action and commitment. Warren, in a recent article, "Early and Periodic Screening, Diagnosis and Treatment" (EPSDT) (1977), states that "in 1972, Congress made it mandatory that states set up screening programs, but by 1974, only

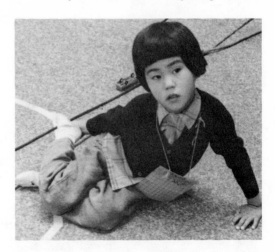

Each year, we identify a greater percentage of the preschool handicapped.

2,000,000 of the 13,000,000 eligible children had been screened, mostly through Head Start programs." Passing legislation is frequently easier than implementing it. The mandate on EPSDT is an example, according to John Meier, former director of the Office of Child Development.

> The major difficulty in effecting the program lay in implementation of the statutory requirement for an assessment of "mental" defects . . . . The inadequacy of available tests for predicting developmental disabilities in low income, minority group children; the necessity for assuring confidentiality and avoiding labeling; and a lack of personnel, facilities, and funds all proved to be obstacles to EPSDT . . ." Diagnosis seldom follows the screening, and when it does, intervention rarely occurs." (Warren, 1977)

THE NEED FOR PARENT EDUCATION AND INVOLVEMENT

Even in this modern age, little attention has been directed towards education for parenthood. This topic should be a part of every young person's formal education starting at least at junior high school. All too frequently, consideration of the responsibilities of parenthood begins with pregnancy and then more often educates the mother rather than both parents. Even though clinics and community services offer married or unmarried mothers' programs designed to teach planned parenthood, child development, and family living, too few pregnant women receive good prenatal care and assistance beneficial to both mother and child. It is difficult enough to provide all the care and attention a young child needs when the family is intact; it is even more difficult in one-parent families. We must deal with the problems of education for parenthood for the good of prospective parents, children, and society.

Parent Aid in Early Identification

Parents and others who are with children daily often notice behaviors that concern them. They are not always certain whether these are normal or abnormal behaviors. In

FOR MORE SUPPORT

Resources for meeting special needs of young children vary considerably from one community to another, yet some basic resources may be available in most large communities. (See the appendix for addresses of several of these organizations.) State Departments of Education and of Health and Social Services can usually provide information on available services. Representatives of the American Academy of Pediatrics, school districts, intermediate school districts, and community health and mental health centers are good sources of information. Universities, colleges, and community colleges may offer various types of services through clinics or training and service programs. Those institutions of higher learning which have an associated medical school frequently offer many different services, among which are clinics serving pregnant women and young children. Services are also available through county organizations and health departments; state and county chapters of many national organizations can frequently be of great assistance. Some further sources of information or help are:

Aid to Dependent Children
American Academy of Pediatrics
American Red Cross
Child development centers
Closer Look
Crippled Children's Association

Day care, nursery school, and preschool programs
The Easter Seal Society
Head Start, Home Start, and Homebound Programs
Mental health programs
Mental retardation programs
Public health and nursing services
School districts
State, county, and city organizations serving special groups such as those with cystic fibrosis, muscular dystrophy, cerebral palsy, and retardation
United Good Neighbors
University Affiliated Facilities

There may also be Planned Parenthood groups and Parent to Parent programs designed to provide information and to help families and children with certain types of handicapping conditions. All states should now have state and local groups concerned with developmental disabilities. Most community services, clinics, organizations, and school districts are eager to have the public know about the services they provide and are also eager to recruit community volunteers. They have public meetings and open houses to acquaint the public with their services; volunteers can often perform useful services in these programs as well as in others provided through state institutions and agencies.

In our mobile society, it is important for parents to know where to look for help if

too many cases, they tend to worry generally rather than specifically about certain child behaviors. An adult should pinpoint what he is worried about and then do something about it. Relatives and other well-meaning people may try to allay concerns by saying, "Oh, I wouldn't worry about that—the child will grow out of it." Such advice usually does little to reduce anxiety and may frequently delay needed services for both the parent and the child. There are

they move from one community to another. Many of the agencies and organizations mentioned here have national directories that list their members and services throughout the country. A number of governors' offices have established Child Development Offices, and many mayors' offices have shown interest in coordinating the services available in larger cities. There are also Regional Action Offices, Offices of Child Development, and Health, Education and Welfare Offices that provide information about available services. Community Action programs are growing in number. In addition there are national, state, and local groups interested in gifted children. (For more on the gifted, see chapter 14.) Much more should be done for the gifted; for history, replete with contributions made by gifted people in art, literature, music, politics, and science, to name but a few fields, tells us how much they can do.

There are frequent campaigns to urge business and industry to employ the handicapped. Many handicapped people are excellent workers and are eager to be independent and self-supporting. Society cannot afford to disregard the potential human resources of any group. There are areas in which most of the handicapped can function as independent or semi-independent workers, provided they receive the services and the training they need to do so.

many conditions that the child will not outgrow, but early action may help. Thus the parent should feel free to express his concerns and to seek professional advice on the specific problem of concern.

The parent also needs to be informed about actual or possible problems identified through medical examinations, screening, observation, and on-going assessment in various types of programs for young children. Families of children whose problems are identified early are fortunate in that the special needs of these children may be met, and the child may then function as normally as possible. It is important, however, to avoid conveying adult anxiety to the child. With understanding and appropriate care and treatment, the child may make a remarkable adjustment to a handicapping or potentially handicapping condition. The child may need special services over a considerable period of time, and it is important that he receive them. The family must always be an integral part of the team seeking to serve the child, and parents should be given training which will help the team attend to the child's needs in the home as well as in community programs.

Preliminary information from the Office of Child Development suggests that approximately 25% of the children served in Head Start need certain types of special services. As Head Start implements the mandate to integrate at least 10% of handicapped with nonhandicapped children in those programs, efforts to screen a larger number of young children should result in a more accurate estimate of the percentage of young handicapped children in all populations.

The early identification of handicapped children has profound implications for federal, state, and local agencies, as well as for children, parents, and professional and lay personnel working with young children. Mere identification, of course, is of little value unless there is follow-up and service for the child and his family. The handicapped population at any age level is too large to be regarded lightly. The problems of the handicapped and their families are problems of society in general, since handicapping conditions appear in all populations.

Chapter 3 gives more information on observation and assessment of young children.

Parent Understanding of Exceptional Children

Having a handicapped child can be a traumatic experience for parents, not only when they first learn of the child's disability but throughout the child's growing years. The recent movement to keep more handicapped children in the home instead of sending them to institutions has resulted in more parents who need special help and support. Some handicapped children are not easy to care for, and parents sometimes need relief care to fulfill their responsibilities to other family members. Parents must often walk a fine line between overprotection of the handicapped child and false expectations of the child's abilities. The psychological adjustment to a handicap takes time, for the parents, the child, and other family members. Teachers and health-care professionals can help parents and children make those adjustments.

As primary caregivers for their children, parents should be included in any plans that a teacher may have for the child. Parent involvement is a necessary part of every good preschool program. To work successfully with parents, the effective teacher must be sensitive to the parents' needs and hopes. A teacher who accepts parents as they are, and withholds criticism of the parents' child-rearing abilities, can make more successful changes in the parents' attitudes and behavior over time. Parents of handicapped children are coping with the many problems of raising such a child in the best way they know how. It is the

teacher's responsibility to help parents learn new, more effective ways of working with their children.

The passage of recent federal legislation requires parental involvement in their special child's school program. IEPs for each child must be designed with parental cooperation. And parents must sign short- and long-term goal statements for their child after parents, teacher, and any additional professionals have decided on the objectives for that quarter and year.

The teacher can encourage active parent participation in goal setting by asking the parents what behaviors of the child they would like to see change. The parent responses may range from specifics—like toilet training—to general desires such as "I want him to mind me." Parents' ideas are the first step in a teacher-parent effort to meet behaviorally defined goals for the child. When teachers show concern and acceptance of parental goals and needs, parents become more willing to cooperate with the teacher in programs for the child. Eventually, parents may be taught to record data at home, to run a home program parallel to the school program, and to revise their expectations and feelings about raising a handicapped child.

Teachers, then, must be compassionate and supportive toward parents. If teachers can set realistic goals for children and provide an atmosphere where parents can feel comfortable and productive, they are more likely to secure parent cooperation and participation.

Parent Education Programs

For those who are interested in parent education, there are excellent programs offered by public schools, community colleges, and other community organizations, as well as informative books and articles. Parents of exceptional children also find that there are many parent-to-parent programs sponsored by different organizations. Parents who have learned about services for different types of exceptional children can help other parents who have recently learned that their child is exceptional. The magazine *The Exceptional Parent* provides useful information for parents of handicapped children. Parent participation is particularly important in programs for very young handicapped children. The young child is usually in a program for a limited time each day, and parents need to understand and to carry on during the longer time at home the effective procedures used at school.

Such involvement also brings the parent in contact with other parents who are coping with similar problems, and their combined efforts have, in the past, been effective in promoting programs and services for handicapped children. Legislators and others who can provide funding for assistance more often heed parents' recommendations than those of educators and other professionals who also see the special needs quite clearly. The most effective efforts come from the cooperation of parents and professionals working together in behalf of handicapped children. It is obvious that *informed* parents can play an important role in their children's education; it should be equally obvious that in order to do so they need some preparation for parenthood.

FOR MORE INFORMATION

Most of these resources are textbooks that are readily available, many from Charles E. Merrill, the publishers of this text. Check your instructor, the education library, or the general library at your school.

Allen, K. E., Holm, V. A., & Schiefelbusch, R. L. (Eds.). *Early intervention — The team approach.* Baltimore: University Park Press, 1978.

Cooper, J.O., & Edge, D. *Parenting: Strategies and educational methods.* Columbus, Ohio: Charles E. Merrill, 1978.

Dardig, J.C., & Heward, W.L. *Sign here: A contracting book for children and their parents.* Kalamazoo, Mich.: Behaviordelia, 1976.

Fallen, N.H., with McGovern, J.E. *Young children with special needs.* Columbus, Ohio: Charles E. Merrill, 1978.

Hayden, A.H. (Guest Ed.). Education of the very young. *Educational Horizons,* 1972, *50* (2), 1–96.

Hayden, A.H., & McGinness, G.D. Bases for early intervention. In E. Sontag, J. Smith, & N. Certo (Eds.), *Educational programming for the severely and profoundly handicapped.* Reston, Va.: Division on Mental Retardation, Council for Exceptional Children, 1977.

3

Normal and Delayed Development in Young Children

Valentine Dmitriev

These are the major topics covered in this chapter. You may want to use them as a checklist when you review.

- *Optimal prenatal and postnatal experiences.*
- *Ways to identify handicaps in early childhood.*
- *Behavioral and functional definitions of handicapping conditions.*
- *Models for educating young handicapped children.*
- *Major developmental skills, to be considered in programming, that children acquire between the ages of 0 to 18 months, 18 months to 3 years, and 3 to 5 years.*

The first 2 years after birth are the most crucial, demanding, and dramatic of our lives. During this time a child grows from a horizontal, dependent infant to an upright, mobile toddler. This, at least, is what is supposed to happen in an optimal environment under optimal circumstances. To better understand the problems of abnormal development—handicaps which result from a damaged or deficient environment—consider the following basic requirements of the most desirable environment.

OPTIMAL ENVIRONMENT*

An optimal environment refers to the circumstances of a child's life both before (**prenatal**) and after birth (**postnatal**). An optimal prenatal experience is the birthright of every human being, and it should begin before conception. Among other things it includes the following:

Optimal Prenatal Environment

A Sound Genetic Endowment
In an optimal environment, a child has parents who are **genetically** healthy. Many physical and mental handicapping conditions are related to hereditary factors. Among these there are spina bifida, metabolic disturbances such as PKU (phenylketonuria), and some forms of Down's syndrome. Even if both parents are "normal," their risk of having a handicapped child is increased by 1.8% and 3.6% if either parent has one or more retarded brothers or sisters (siblings) (Reed & Reed, 1965). It is very important, there-

*Many of the specific conditions introduced here are discussed in more detail in later chapters. For instance, see chapter 5 for further discussion of the relationship of prenatal environment to mental retardation.

fore, that prospective parents who are themselves congenitally handicapped or who have close relatives with congenital disorders have genetic counseling before starting a family.

Prime Maternal Age and Birth Order
Statistics indicate that the most favorable years for childbearing are between the ages of 20 and 30. There is a greater risk for adolescent mothers—just as much as mothers in their late thirties and early forties—to have handicapped children. When deficits of all kinds are considered—low birth weight, prematurity, infant death, as well as undefined developmental and mental retardation—very young women and older women have more babies that fall into these categories.

The number of previous pregnancies and birth order may also affect development. In general, the first baby carries an extra risk, as do babies whose mothers are older and babies born in rapid succession. The latter have smaller birth weights and lower scores on developmental scales and IQ tests.

Good Maternal Nutrition and Health
Good nutritional health of the prospective mother is essential to provide an optimal prenatal environment. This means general good health long before pregnancy. Even if the mother does have a proper diet and medical supervision during pregnancy, some deficiencies in her previous diet cannot be remedied during the 9-month pregnancy period. Long-standing nutritional deficits are hard to overcome in the face of pregnancy's increased demands on the body.

Some young women enter motherhood nutritionally unprepared because of poverty and deprivation, dietary fads, ignorance. Unfortunately, malnutrition, both pre- and postnatally, produces physical and mental retardation. Healthy, well-nourished babies grow up to be healthy adults and, in turn, bear healthy children.

Protection from Harmful Drugs, Diseases, and Infections

After conception, an optimal prenatal environment protects the unborn child (fetus) from the harmful effects of nicotine, drugs, alcohol, and virus infection. For example:

1. Smoking increases the risk of a premature, low weight baby.

2. Heavy doses of barbituates can cause lack of oxygen (asphyxiation) and brain damage.

3. The tragedy of the tranquilizer thalidomide, which caused the birth of thousand of limbless babies in Germany, England, and Canada, is well-documented.

4. Heroin addiction affects the nervous system of the infant.

5. Recently, Fetal Alcohol Syndrome has been identified in babies born to alcoholic mothers. Alcohol, regularly imbibed, has been added to the growing list of agents that cause serious damage during pregnancy. Children with this syndrome suffer from hyperactivity and mental retardation. They are also noted for small stature and head size.

6. Diseases and infections can also threaten the unborn. German measles (rubella) contracted during the early months of pregnancy increases by about 50% the chance of having a miscarriage, a still-birth, or a handicapped infant. The possible results include profound hearing loss, mental retardation, cataracts, heart defects, and other organic and skeletal abnormalities.

Other diseases dangerous to the fetus are syphilis, smallpox, chicken pox, measles, mumps, scarlet fever, tuberculosis, and malarial parasites. In many cases these diseases can be prevented by immunization.

An optimal environment after birth includes the following:

Optimal Postnatal Environment

The Newborn (Neonatal) Period

The birth process can be hazardous for baby and mother. However, if care has been taken before birth, the risks are lessened considerably. The physical and emotional condition of the mother and the skill and sensitivity of the attending physician contribute to an optimal environment during and immediately after delivery. The medical profession is becoming increasingly aware of potential hazards at birth and is paying more and more attention to preventing brain damage that can result from too much medication, a lack of oxygen, and other causes.

Infancy and Early Childhood

The optimum environment as the child progresses from birth through infancy and into childhood is vast and complex. Briefly, the goal of this environment is to provide everything that a child needs to reach his maximum potential in the major areas of his physical (gross motor), fine motor/cognitive, social, and communicative development. To achieve this goal, the environment must provide not only good health but also a wealth of experiences and opportunities for practice, play, and learning as well as love, instruction, acceptance, and reinforcement.

At each age and at each stage of his development the child needs specifically different experiences, but the basic criteria for an optimal environment—whether at 3 months or 5 years—remain constant.

Health. An optimum environment is responsive to the child's health needs and insures:

1. Immunization and protection against

fatal and crippling diseases such as measles, smallpox, diphtheria, and polio;

2. Safety, protecting the child against injuries at home, on the playground, in the car, or on the street;

3. Protection from child abuse and exploitation;

4. Proper medical and dental attention not only for obvious illnesses or emergencies but routinely as a preventive measure. Physical check-ups should include eyes, ears, and teeth.

5. Good nutrition—diets that are deficient in protein, calcium, and other basic nutrients affect the physical growth of a child and his mental and emotional development.

Physical-gross motor development. Before the growing infant can reach the final goal of walking independently, he must master many physical skills ranging from lifting his head to turning, sitting, crawling, and standing. The normal infant spends many hours exercising his body, moving his arms, kicking his legs, twisting and turning to achieve these capabilities **(gross motor development)**. The optimal environment provides many opportunities for movement in different ways under different circumstances—in the crib, on the floor, or out of doors. As the child grows, he needs experiences with stairs, ramps, jungle gyms, tricycles, ladders, and other large toys.

Fine motor-cognitive development. The child learns through contact with the world which comes through seeing, hearing, and touching. The senses of taste and smell are also important. An optimal environment provides the infant and young child with many things to see, hear, touch, manipulate, and explore **(fine motor-cognitive development)**. The caretaking adult furthers this learning by providing approval and by structuring the child's daily life to maximize success and minimize failure.

Personal/social and communication development. An environment that provides optimal enrichment, stimulation, learning, and positive feedback for physical, fine motor, and cognitive development also benefits a child's social and communication skills.

If a newborn has a sound genetic endowment and a favorable environment, he can be expected to follow predictable patterns of physical, mental, and social growth.

HEREDITY AND ENVIRONMENT

Genetic and environmental factors can help or limit development. They are both independent of, and dependent on, each other. Combined, healthy heredity and a healthy environment promote optimal development. Yet many perfectly normal children fail to reach their genetic potential because of harmful environments. Poverty and malnutrition, hostile emotional climates, and cultural and intellectual deprivation delay physical and mental growth.

A child with a genetic handicap or a handicap acquired by illness or accident can be limited in his development. Poor environment hampers his accomplishments even more. In fact, it endangers his future as a functioning person. On the other hand, an appropriately nurturing and stimulating environment can encourage development by making up for the deficit. For example, a deaf child can exhibit severe retardation in social and academic functioning unless the deficit is compensated for by early training in total communication. Total communication is a system that combines manual communication (for example, fingerspelling) and the language of signs, with oral communication. Studies on hearing handicapped children who had early manual communication—as in the case of deaf babies born to deaf parents who used manual communication to interact with their children from infancy—show that these children do better in reading, math, writing, and on Stanford Achievement Test scores than deaf children of hearing parents who were matched for this study who did not use manual communication (Vernon, 1970). (See chapter 11 for more information on hearing handicapped children and the total communication system.)

How does a normal child learn from his environment? Why does a handicapped child experience difficulty? Why and how does abnormal development interfere with learning? Why is early identification of potentially handicapping conditions so crucial? What can parents, teachers, and other involved professionals do to compensate for the child's deficits?

These questions point out that learning involves the orderly development of the entire organism and that the environment can play a major role in maximizing achievement.

Actions and Responses

Every stimulus that reaches a child's senses tells her something about his world. For example, she discovers that some of his actions bring pleasure, warmth, food, companionship, stimulation, and novelty. Gradually she learns that by repeating certain actions, she can bring about specific pleasure-giving consequences. By moving her head to the side, a baby may discover that she can see something bright and fascinating on the wall next to her crib. A haphazard movement of her hand can bring her in contact with a rattle. The handle is smooth and round. As her fingers tighten around it, she has sensations of texture and form. She moves her arm harder, and the sound is louder. Accidentally she strikes the rattle against the side of the crib and hears a different sound.

In moments of stress, her crying may bring comfort, warmth, food. If this happens, the infant learns further that her actions can produce the results she wants. In this way random behaviors acquire meaning and purpose. Progressively they become established in the child's behavioral repertoire.

Other actions do not result in a pleasure-giving consequence, the child discovers. The results may be neutral, having no effect on the immediate environment; still other actions may bring discomfort or pain. Turning her head to a blank wall does not give the child the rewarding experience of visual stimulation. Lying face down against the pillow brings little pleasure and blocks breathing.

Sensory stimulation is reinforcing to the child. Increasingly she seeks out interesting objects and stops staring at a blank wall. She avoids behaviors which result in punishing consequences, such as pressing her head into a pillow. Instead, she learns new, rewarding behaviors. For example, the child learns to raise her head

Justin's special chair helps him sit up so he can interact with the world around him.

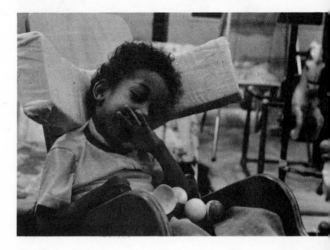

when lying on her stomach. This action in itself brings physiological rewards of new visual and muscular body sensations and further strengthens the child physically. Stronger neck, shoulder, and back muscles bring new motor and sensory rewards; they make possible new actions such as rolling, turning, squirming, crawling, with their new consequences—neutral, punishing, or rewarding.

In a loving situation, the powerful effect of the delight of others in response to a baby's activities adds an immeasurably important dimension to the learning process. The baby who coos alone in his crib is reinforced by this activity, because vocal exercises are fun for a child. If someone leans over the crib—smiling and cooing in return—it is even more rewarding for the

The first task of this boy's teacher is to get his attention.

infant. And so the normal baby learns and continues to learn for the rest of his life. He selects and perfects behaviors that bring desired consequences and abandons or avoids those that do not.

Parents, teachers, and society can aid learning and development by consistently attending to, praising, and rewarding the behaviors they want to establish and by consistently ignoring or punishing undesirable behaviors.

How a Child's Handicaps Can Interfere with Normal Learning

A normal child's activities result in consequences that shape his learning. One of the reasons learning does not occur readily may be that the handicapped child cannot receive normal physiological and parental/social reinforcement. A child whose movements are hampered by crippled or weakened muscles is less able to have rewarding interactions with his environment. A child with a visual or hearing handicap also does not have the stimuli and reinforcements which are part of the normal child's development.

Second, the handicapped child's progress may be slowed down by lack of reinforcement from his parents. He is often unable or slow to coo, grasp objects, to squirm, kick, reach, or do all the little things that delight parents. Grieved and discouraged by the birth of an impaired baby, parents may have such low expectations for their baby's development that they fail to recognize growth even if it occurs.

Sometimes, too, parents' overexpectations can have an equally harmful effect on the development of a child, whether handicapped or not. Realistically unable to live up to impossible goals, the child experiences failure as well as his parents' impatience and rejection. Thus the infant's feeble, but possibly major, accomplishments may go unnoticed. Unable to get reinforcement either from his environment or from his parents, the baby gives up his early efforts to acquire necessary developmental skills. Defeated, the child may become motionless and indifferent to his surroundings. Unless **intervention** begins, the gap between the child's abilities and his chronological age widens as each month passes.

Identifying Handicaps in Early Childhood

Before intervention can begin, you must be able to determine the child's problem. How can a parent, teacher, social worker, nurse, or pediatrician recognize a deficiency or defect?

The developmental status of a child can be determined by his **behavior**. *Behavior* is a term that can be applied to everything that a child does: reflexive behavior such as blinking, voluntary behavior such as reaching or grasping, spontaneous behavior such as laughing, or learned behavior such as reading and writing. We also know that developmental behaviors occur within a predictable age range and in a predictable sequence. What's more, when expressed as specific behaviors, development can be *observed, measured, compared, assessed, prevented,* and *remediated.*

Informal Identification

Most developmental observations begin informally. For example, a mother may notice that her 6-month-old daughter does not turn her head when someone approaches her crib or playpen. A father may begin to wonder why his 20-month-old child appears "slow." A kindergarten teacher may notice that one of the boys seems clumsy on the playground. Generally such informal ob-

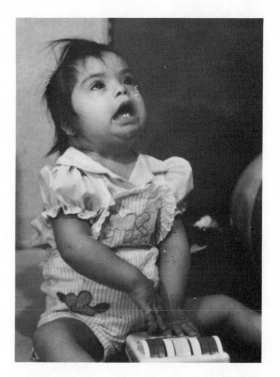

Children like Lucia who have Down's syndrome can be identified at birth and intervention can begin immediately.

servations have been made over a period of time before the observer begins to make mental notes of measurement or comparison.

Suspecting a hearing loss, the mother may begin a series of informal hearing tests, such as speaking to the child in varying tones and noting whether or not the child responds. The father may begin watching his child more closely to determine what the child does or does not do that expresses "slowness." The father may remember, for instance, that the child was almost 11 months old before he sat, or he may notice that the boy holds objects but does not play with them. After noticing the general awkwardness of his pupil, the kindergarten teacher may decide to determine exactly what it is about the child's behavior that makes him seem clumsy. Careful observation may show that the child does not alternate feet when walking up and down stairs or that he does not flex the knee of one leg when walking.

Once a *suspected problem* has been identified, the next step is to *observe this behavior in terms of what is considered normal* for the child's chronological age. Parents may compare their child's actions to those of their other children when they were the same age or to children of friends or relatives. The teacher may use his knowledge of growth expectations as a point of reference, although the first assessments probably are based on comparing behaviors of classmates. If these initial observations suggest a deviancy or defect, further evaluations can be made. These should include both medical and developmental assessments.

Medical Tests

Medical implications of a disorder are important. If a child's problem has not been medically diagnosed, or if she has not received treatment, referral to a competent physician is necessary. This is important if the child appears malnourished, overweight, spastic, or otherwise physically impaired. Medical attention is also required for poor vision, hearing, frequent colds, allergies, ear infections, and other chronic ailments.

Developmental Screening Tests

A developmental screening test helps a trained examiner evaluate a problem in relation to a child's total development. Standardized tests with standard materials and standard procedures are used. (See the appendix for a list of available tests.) Three frequently used tests are reliable predictors of future performance: the Bayley Scale of Infant Development, the Denver Developmental Screening Test, and the Gesell Schedules of Development (Bronfenbrenner, 1975). Although the tests may vary in

emphasis, all are designed to measure a child's performance in motor behavior, adaptive behavior, communication, and personal-social behavior.

Motor behavior refers to large body movements involving postural reactions, head control, sitting, standing, creeping, crawling, walking, running, jumping, and so on.

Adaptive behavior refers to eye-hand coordination, reaching, grasping, object manipulation, and problem solving. Sometimes it is referred to as *fine motor-cognitive development.*

Communication (including language and speech) refers to the whole spectrum of visual and auditory communication: facial expressions, gestures, sounds, words, phrases, and sentences. Chapters 4 and 10 discuss development of communication skills and language disorders in more detail.

Personal–social behavior refers to a child's reaction to his sociocultural environment. The level of a child's social interaction with adults and peers and his level of self-management and maturity, including bladder and bowel control, self-feeding abilities, independence in play, and responsiveness to training and social conventions, are examined. Although these behaviors may show many individual variations, there is a range of normalcy.

Teachers of young children should become familiar with some of the better known developmental screening instruments and learn how they are administered. According to Gesell and Amatruda (1969), a developmental diagnosis of behavior is important because:

1. Behavior can be assessed in terms of normal, delayed, or accelerated development.

stresses early intervention. The teacher puts peanut butter on the infant girl's mouth (upper left) in order to stimulate her to move the muscles that she will later need to speak. The parents are a child's first and most frequent teachers. To be truly effective, early intervention must involve parents. Preschoolers and their mothers join in this fun-filled activity with whipped cream (center left and right). Smearing the cream all over everything offers opportunity for fine motor, communication, and social development. Add a little food coloring and spoons (bottom), and the possibilities are greater than ever—both for fun and for learning.

Many successful early intervention programs are based, at least partly, in the home. This may involve a teacher who visits the home to work with both the parents and the handicapped child. Jennifer, who was born with hydrochephaly, is both developmentally delayed and visually impaired. She not only gets lots of the support and stimulation she needs from her mother, but also from her two brothers (one shown right) and from Dad (opposite page).

Early intervention for hearing handicapped children is offered at the John Tracy Clinic in Los Angeles. Missy, who was fitted with a hearing aid only 2 weeks ago, attends the Clinic regularly with her mother. Together they work with a teacher on language training activities they take back home with them. At Oralingua, a school for hearing handicapped in the same area, Sean and Jamie attend a preschool class where they receive intensive auditory training to overcome their hearing losses. All these children are in programs that use a strictly oral communication approach (described in chapter 11).

2. Problem areas, such as gross motor, personal/social, and others, can be identified.

3. Many mild or obscure forms of brain damage can be detected.

4. Social/emotional development and strengths and weaknesses in the parent–child relationship can be seen.

5. A child's development can be recorded over a period of time; this record can serve as a basis for an individualized program of intervention.

Measures for prevention or remediation can begin once the child's developmental status has been determined. The teacher has a major part but intervention can come from a number of professionals, including audiologists, ophthalmologists, psychologists, physicians, and physical therapists. They act as a resource or supportive team to the parents and teachers.

INTERVENTION AND MANAGEMENT

Methodical Observation

Once a teacher has noted something unusual in the child's appearance or behavior, it is his responsibility to approach the problem systematically. Casual recognition must lead to methodical observation through giving behavioral and, if possible, functional definitions of the disorder.

A **behavioral definition** should state precisely what the child does or does not do; for example, a 4-year-old child walks awkwardly, right foot turns in; or a 3-year-old child does not place pegs in a peg board, does not work a one-piece puzzle. Often the observed behavior can be recorded in terms of rate or duration; for example, the child takes 10 steps in 60 seconds—rate, or he lies passively, staring at the ceiling for 3 minutes at a time—duration. The more precise the information, the better.

A **functional definition** states in physical or genetic terms generally what the cause of the problem appears to be. This classification of a disorder is the result of a medical or psychological examination. Frequently an interdisciplinary team may be involved. P. L. 94-142 gives specific guidelines for classification which include parent permission. Although a teacher's prime concerns are with the exhibited strengths and weaknesses of a child's development, some knowledge of the functional basis of a disorder can be helpful. Program strategies frequently must take into account a child's particular handicap, such as hearing handicap, seizures, or poor vision. Table 3.1 illustrates how teachers might record this information for personal reference.

Sight, Hearing, and General Health Checklists

Other valuable assessment tools for teachers are checklists that are readily available or can be made. These lists can help teachers observe almost any aspect of a child's growth. Checklists for common behaviors that may indicate visual or hearing handicaps, poor health, and other problems relating to low performance are given below (Allen, Rieke, Dmitriev, & Hayden, 1972).

A doll is a good stimulus to use in assessing a small child's oral language.

Table 3.1

Behavioral and functional definitions of possible handicapping conditions

Child's name, age	Behavioral definition	Functional definition
John, 5 months	Head lag when pulled to sitting position; doesn't reach, grasp, or hold toys	Weak back, shoulders, neck; poor eye-hand coordination; Down's syndrome
Meg, 13 months	No eye contact with people or objects; eyes roll back; fixates only on lights	Visual impairment; brain damage
Bill, 24 months	Doesn't stand alone; legs scissor; legs extended and rigid	Physically retarded— cerebral palsy
Ann, 3 years	Poor articulation; high pitched voice	Impaired hearing

Severe sight or hearing loss is usually recognized before a child begins school. However, there are many problems of vision or hearing that are not dramatically apparent and go undetected until a child begins to show serious school problems. (See chapters 11 and 12 for more information on children with hearing and visual impairments, respectively.)

The following conditions and behaviors should be observed and noted as possible indications of visual impairment:

_____ **1.** Does the child have crossed eyes (strabismus)?

_____ **2.** How does a child use his eyes: tilting his head, holding objects close to his eyes, rubbing his eyes, squinting, displaying sensitivity to bright lights, rolling his eyes?

_____ **3.** Is the child inattentive to visual objects or visual tasks (looking at pictures, reading)?

_____ **4.** Is the child awkward in tasks requiring eye-hand coordination such as pegs, puzzles, and writing?

_____ **5.** Does the child avoid tasks that require close eye work? Does she prefer tasks that require distance vision?

_____ **6.** Are there complaints about inability to see?

Even the mildest hearing impairments may require attention. They may be the early warning signs of a progressive condition. Any hearing loss is frustrating to its victim in our verbal culture. A teacher should be quick to question any behaviors which might suggest hearing deficits:

_____ **1.** Does the child ignore, confuse, or not comply with directions?

_____ **2.** Does the child daydream to excess?

_____ **3.** Is he educationally retarded? Is he poor in speech for his age? Does he fail to attend to pre-academic tasks or stories read to him or does he fail to name objects?

_____ **4.** Is the child isolate in his social behavior?

_____ **5.** Does the child have a slight speech defect?

_____ **6.** Does the child appear dull?

_____ **7.** Does the child rub his ear frequently or complain of earache?

_____ **8.** Does the child favor one ear; does he always turn his head in one direction towards sound?

_____ **9.** Does the child breathe through his mouth?

_____ **10.** Does the child complain of noises in his head or dizziness?

_____ **11.** Does the child have too high, too low, or monotonous pitch of voice?

The teacher should be aware of fatigue, faintness, restlessness, tenseness, symptoms of allergies—rashes, running eyes and noses, coughing and wheezing—flushed cheeks, or paleness, and ask parents to refer children with these symptoms to a physician. The following behaviors and physical symptoms _may_ indicate a problem requiring medical attention.

_____ **1.** Does the child have excessive thirst, ravenous appetite (possible hypoglycemia or diabetes)?

_____ **2.** Are there symptoms of obesity, mental lethargy (possible hypothyroidism)?

_____ **3.** Is there loss of weight, irritability, fatigue (possible hyperthyroidism)?

_____ **4.** Does the child show signs of irritability (possible signal of a wide range of illnesses)?

_____ **5.** Does the child have a persistent cough (possible bronchitis)?

The sensitive teacher should be quick to notice and take steps to remedy the following items that may affect a child's well-being and performance:

_____ **1.** _Clothing:_ bulky, ill-fitting, too tight or too loose, too heavy or too warm for comfort, inadequate for outdoor play in cold weather, missing buttons, or broken zippers?

_____ **2.** _Shoes:_ sizes too small or too big, slippery soles, inadequate covering, or leather too stiff for gross motor activity?

In addition, a child with a facial blemish, protruding teeth, or some other disfigurement is as much in need of attention and remediation as the child with poor health or vision. Some of these seemingly cosmetic problems may have medical and dental implications as well as psychological ones.

Correcting Defects

One of the most notable developments in early childhood education has been the recent increase in programs for infants who, for socioeconomic, health, or genetic reasons, face developmental delay (**high-risk infants**). There are three major categories of early intervention efforts for these infants. The first category includes the greatest number of programs and children. It focuses on providing enrichment and education to normal children who have a high risk to be mentally retarded as a result of cultural and environmental deprivation. The second type of program provides services to homogenous groups of children who are considered high risk for physical or genetic reasons. For example, in this category we may find programs serving the mentally normal but blind and hearing handicapped. The third type of early intervention program is designed to help a heterogeneous group of multihandicapped youngsters who are developmentally delayed as well as severely involved.

The programs operate in a variety of settings. In a _home-oriented program_, a teacher trained in infant development visits a family weekly and teaches the parents how to interact with their baby in order to insure the best progress.

The emphasis generally is on creating desirable parent-child relationships by helping parents become effective as the child's teachers. Parents are encouraged to become aware of the child's growth in each of the key areas by learning to observe, recognize, and assess small gains in achievement. During visits the teacher observes, demonstrates the use of toys, instructs, and supports what the parents are doing with the child to promote desired skills in motor and cognitive development. The whole program is highly individualized to meet the specific needs of each parent-child unit.

Like the home-oriented program, *center-based intervention* focuses on child development and parent involvement. The programs are generally highly structured, with emphasis on the teacher as the prime instructor. In some cases the children are seen for 1 or 2 hours once a week; in other cases children attend school from 2 to 6 hours, 5 days a week. In some programs parents are actively involved as teacher assistants in the classroom. In others, parent education is a separate activity.

Most preschool children attend schools that are home-oriented, though some are center-based, and others use a combination of home and school settings. Usually the emphasis is not on special equipment but on how readily available traditional early childhood materials can be used in the programming.

Nationally Validated Models for Educating Young Handicapped Children

Since 1969 the Bureau of Education for the Handicapped has been funding projects to develop models for educating young handicapped children and to disseminate information. In November, 1975, seven of these projects were rated as highly effective for the young handicapped by the United States Office of Education Joint Dissemination Review Panel. The projects currently are being funded to provide training in duplicating their models. A brief description of these model programs follows.

Portage Project
Portage, Wisconsin
Susie Frohman, Coordinator

The Portage Project is a home-based educational program for handicapped children, birth to 6 years old. A home teacher visits the home 1½ hours each day to train parents to effectively teach their

profile MARK

Mark, a 2-year-old with Down's syndrome, was unable and unwilling to try to stand. He was also unwilling to take steps while holding on to the teacher's hands. Teacher effort was to be directed at training Mark to stand for 15 minutes during an hour period, to stand on verbal cue, and to walk with a teacher's assistance.

The teacher set up a small table with interesting toys and objects at a height which made it necessary for Mark to stand in order to reach them. She used a verbal prompt of "Stand up" and a physical prompt of pulling Mark to his feet, if necessary.

The first day, when pulled up, Mark drew his feet upward and refused to stand. The teacher then put light weights on his ankles, making it difficult for him to lift up his feet and legs. His standing time improved so greatly that it was only necessary to use the weights for 3 days. Ice cream and praise were used to reinforce his standing. Toys and ice cream were used as motivation and reinforcement for walking. The teacher placed the toy or food at a distance so that Mark was forced to walk while holding her hands in order to reach the desirable object. She gave verbal and physical prompts and praised his appropriate walking behavior.

own child. The model is a data-based, precision teaching program proven to be easy to duplicate.

Rutland Center
Athens, Georgia
Anthony Beardsley, Director

Developmental therapy is the psycho-educational curriculum for teaching young children who have severe emotional and behavioral disorders. The basic curriculum areas are behavior, communication, socialization, and preacademic. The curriculum provides a broad outline to guide the teacher in planning appropriate sequences of experiences to meet a series of developmental objectives for the disturbed child.

Comprehensive Training Program for Infant and Young Cerebral Palsy Children
Milwaukee, Wisconsin
Michael Murnane, Director

This program, developed at the Demmer-Kiwanis Children's Division of the Curative Workshop of Milwaukee, serves a target group of young multiply handicapped children with moderate to severe

The teacher recorded the number of prompts to stand and Mark's standing time—both the total time and the duration of each period of standing without sitting down. She also took data on his responses to walking prompts, the number of steps he took in a single attempt, and the total number of steps he took each week.

Figure 3.1 shows that after 5 days Mark responded 100 percent of the time to a prompt to stand up. It also shows that on the sixth day he stood two times voluntarily,

and on days nine, nineteen, and twenty, three times voluntarily.

Figure 3.2 shows an increase in Mark's total length of time standing from the first day, when he stood only for 90 seconds, to the twenty-second day, when he stood for 16 minutes. On the eighteenth day he stood for 35 minutes of the hour when data were taken. The large drop in time standing on days twelve, thirteen, and fourteen, and the sharp ascent following on the fifteenth and sixteenth days are due to the teacher's dis-

Figure 3.1
Mark—Stand Up

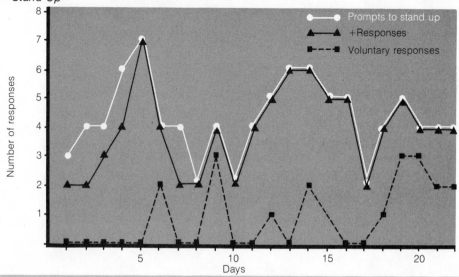

cerebral palsy. The children receive many types of service, including individual physical and occupational therapy. However, the major objective of the project is to help the child realize his full potential for speech and language development by means of early intervention—ideally under 12 months—and intense parent participation.

PEECH Project
Champaign, Illinois
Dr. Merle B. Karnes, Director

The PEECH Project provides a comprehensive language-based approach to the education of multihandicapped children, ages 3 to 5 years old. Components include screening, identification, classroom diagnostics, classroom management, curriculum, parent involvement, a learning playground, and inservice training for paraprofessionals. Outreach services are available to others establishing or maintaining similar programs.

UNISTAPS Project: Severely Disabled Children, 0-5
St. Paul, Minnesota

continuing and then reintroducing the table with desirable objects. Figure 3.2 also shows the length of time he stood in a single attempt—from 5 minutes on day five to as long as 19½ minutes on day eighteen.

Figure 3.3 shows a sample taken once each week of the number of steps Mark took—an increase in the total number of steps taken, 138 the first day to 300 the fifth day recorded. It also shows that the

number of steps taken in a single attempt increased from 40 the first day to 155 on the last day data were taken. Since the number of steps is also partly dependent on the frequency of prompts, the number of steps divided by the number of prompts is also shown in Figure 3.3. The large jump in the number of steps Mark took from February 29 to March 7 is due in part to the fact that during this time he began walking unaided

Figure 3.2
Mark—Length of Time Standing

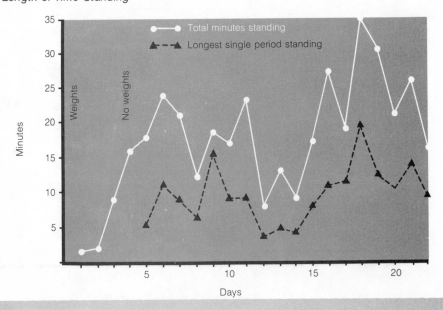

Dr. Winifred H. Northcott, Director

This is a family-oriented noncategorical preschool program for severely disabled children from birth to 4 or 5 years old. The State Department of Education received the program grant and the Special Education Preschool Program, Minneapolis public schools, is the laboratory. UNISTAPS has been expanded from the original program model for preschool hearing handicapped children to current service for a mixed population of the developmentally young. The program applies the new *State*

Guidelines for Preschool Handicapped in Minnesota.

Model Preschool Center for Handicapped Children
Communications Disorders Program
Down's Syndrome Program
Seattle, Washington
Dr. Alice H. Hayden, Director

The Model Preschool Center for Handicapped Children, including training, research, and service, is part of the Experimental Education Unit of the University of Washington's College of Education and

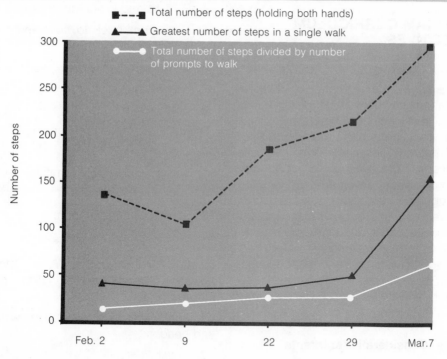

Figure 3.3
Mark—Gross Motor

by pushing a small cart.

The methods employed were effective in reaching the intended result. The weights seemed to be especially useful in helping Mark develop the initial behavior of putting his feet on the floor in the proper position for standing. By concentrating on the problem

and reinforcing the desired behavior, teachers helped him progress to the final goal of walking independently. On the twenty-second day of the program, he took three steps totally unaided. Spring quarter goal was for him to walk independently (Nicholls, Dmitriev, & Oelwein, 1972).

Child Development and Mental Retardation Center. Each year the Model Preschool Center serves approximately 190 children from birth to 6 years old, who have a variety of handicapping conditions ranging from mild to severe. The two largest programs within the Center—one serving children with communication disorders (see pp. 80-86 for a description of the curriculum used in this program) and another for children with Down's syndrome—have been validated for replication. Parent involvement is integral to all programs. Technical assistance and outreach are also prominent aspects of the Center's program.

PROGRAM CURRICULUM OBJECTIVES

The underlying goal of all intervention programs is to help the handicapped child develop as nearly normal as possible. Instruction must be individualized because children vary so greatly in their capabilities as well as disabilities. It is important to base instructional objectives on a sound curriculum for overall development. Following are suggested curriculum goals in motor, cognitive, and social growth for infants, toddlers, preschool, and kindergarten children. The items have been selected from the Down's Syndrome Performance Inventory (1976), which has been used successfully with a wide range of handicapped children.

Program Considerations: Infants

Between birth and the age of 18 months an infant has much to learn. The most noticeable growth occurs in the way he learns to handle his body and in his ability to coordinate his senses of sight, hearing, and touch with the intellectual awareness of his expanding world. Early social skills emerge. The child's prime developmental task is the increased mastery, management, and control of his environment; so a curriculum for infant enrichment should focus on achieving these goals. Patterned after the developmental sequence of normal infants, the training should meet the following objectives:

Goals for Motor Development: Birth to 18 Months

1. Lifts head—lying face down (prone) and lying on his back (supine);

2. Pulls to sitting position, head steady;

3. Head, chest up, arms extended, in supine position;

4. Pushes and kicks with legs and feet;

5. Rolls from back to front and front to back;

6. Creeps;

7. Sits without support;

8. Stands with support;

9. Pulls from sitting to standing;

10. Crawls;

11. Walks holding onto furniture;

12. Walks with adult help;

13. Stands without support;

14. Walks independently.

Goals for Cognitive—Fine Motor—Adaptive Development: Birth to 18 Months

1. Looks, follows moving object with eyes and head;

2. Grasps;

3. Reaches and grasps;

4. Releases;

5. Transfers object from one hand to another;

6. Picks up and holds two objects with both hands at the same time;

7. Places rings on a stick with help;

8. Uses thumb and index finger in pinching-type grasping;

9. Scribbles;

10: Builds tower with two cubes.

Goals for Social and Self-Help Development: Birth to 18 Months

1. Looks at faces;

2. Smiles responsively;

3. Smiles spontaneously;

4. In response, holds arms out to be picked up;

5. Resists having a toy pulled away;

6. Works to grasp toy out of reach;

7. Plays peek-a-boo;

8. Plays pat-a-cake;

9. Plays ball;

10. Imitates housework;

11. Plays with two or three simple toys appropriately;

12. Feeds himself finger food;

13. Drinks from a cup;

14. Uses spoon, spilling a little;

15. Eats foods of three different textures, for example, crunchy, chewy, lumpy;

16. Removes one garment.

Program Considerations: Toddlers

The age of 18 months to 3 years is the transition period between infancy and early childhood. The child is perfecting the emerging physical, mental, and social skills of infancy. Once again, curriculum objectives should approximate normal development. A toddler program at home, in preschool, or in a day care center should incorporate the following goals:

Goals for Motor Development: 18 Months to 3 Years

1. Walks with help;

2. Walks without help; stoops and recovers.

3. Walks across a board placed on the floor;

4. Walks a board that inclines from 6 inches to 24 inches;

Debbie, at 13 months, is developing eye-hand coordination by placing rings on a stick.

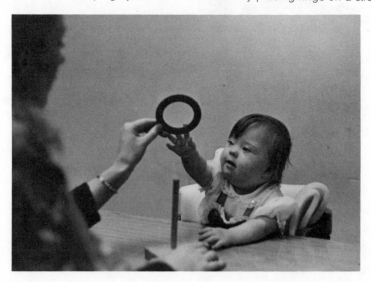

To improve her gait and balance, 3-year-old Christy walks across a board.

5. Uses slide;

6. Crawls up and down stairs;

7. Walks up and down steps with help;

8. Walks up and down stairs, holding on to rail, not alternating feet;

9. Jumps in place with help;

10. Jumps off from 6- to 12-inch elevation with help;

11. Kicks ball.

Goals for Cognitive—Fine Motor—Adaptive Development: 18 Months to 3 Years

1. Puts rings on a stick;

2. Puts pegs in a board;

3. Works a multiple shape puzzle-type board;

4. Does a one- to three-piece puzzle;

5. Points to pictures;

6. Matches and tells the difference among (discriminates) two to four colors;

7. Matches and discriminates two to four pictured objects;

8. Gives and takes objects, shapes, colors, and pictures when given the cue to give and take them;

9. Builds tower with four to eight cubes.

Goals for Social and Self-Help Development: 18 Months to 3 Years

Social.

1. Responds to:

　　a. "What is your name?"

　　b. Greetings.

2. Play skills:

　　a. Plays by himself (isolate);

　　　1) Entertains himself for 10 minutes;

　　　2) Initiates his own play;

　　b. Engages in similar type of play with his peers;

　　c. Engages in domestic make-believe play.

Self-help.

1. Locker skills:

　　a. Finds locker;

　　b. Takes coat off;

　　c. Puts coat in locker;

2. Eating skills:

    a. Speaks so that he can receive.

        1) Cracker;

        2) Juice.

    b. Eats cracker;

    c. Drinks juice from a cup;

    d. Feeds himself with a spoon;

3. Toileting:

    a. Tells his toilet needs;

    b. Pulls down outer pants at toilet;

    c. Sits on toilet;

    d. Uses toilet;

    e. Stays dry;

4. Dressing and undressing:

    a. Removes:

        1) Socks;

        2) Shoes;

        3) Coat;

        4) Hat.

    b. Puts on:

        1) Socks;

        2) Hat.

Program Considerations: Preschool through Kindergarten

From 3 to 5 years of age the normal child should complete the basics of his gross motor development. He should, by the end of this period, be well-coordinated and strong enough to move with ease, to run, skip, jump, and walk up and down stairs alternating his feet. In addition, much of his effort is directed towards perfecting extracurricular skills that not only have recreational values but play an important role in giving him competence and status in peer relationships.

Many handicapped children are noticeably delayed in their gross motor develop-ment and may never be able to achieve the physical competence of a normal child. This is equally true of the other skill areas. Nevertheless, it is important to set high expectations for achievement and to modify a program only to the extent necessary for the child to continue to be successful.

Within these limits, tricycle riding, ball-play skills, the ability to use playground climbing equipment, and the ability to swim are extracurricular physical activities with special recreational and social values for the handicapped child. Swimming is a particularly useful sport, even though it requires special facilities and instruction. First, the ability to handle yourself in water is important for safety. Second, swimming can help in treatment, as physical therapists and special educators know. And in many cases it is the only gross motor activity that a crippled child can perform with any degree of competency.

Steps and a climbing gym foster gross motor development in preschool children.

Chapter three

At the beginning of early childhood, the child begins to meet the demand for specialized academic learning (cognitive) and social skills. It is during these years that a child must master the fundamentals of writing, reading, and arithmetic and social interaction. His future success as a student and as a person depends on how well he is able to learn this knowledge in early childhood.

The suggested curriculum for the 3- to 5-year-old reflects these concerns for increasing physical, cognitive, and social competence. It is assumed that these children have had the benefits of intervention since infancy and are therefore ready for more advanced methods of learning. If any child entering a program lacks any of the necessary skills, his program must be individualized to meet the basic requirements.

Goals for Motor Development: 3 to 5 Years

1. Runs, gallops, hops;
2. Walks on an elevated board;
3. Walks across a balance beam;

4. Walks up and down steps, alternating feet;

5. Jumps in place;

6. Jumps over a bar from 6 inches above the ground;

7. Rides a tricycle;

8. Broad jumps 6 inches to 12 inches;

9. Climbs up and down a ladder, three to eight rungs;

10. Performs:

    a. Waist bends;

    b. Leg lifts;

11. Pushes, pulls objects;

12. Lifts, carries objects;

13. Rolls, throws a ball;

14. Bounces, catches a ball.

Goals for Cognitive—Fine Motor—Adaptive Development: 3 to 5 Years

1. Paints at an easel;
2. Pastes;
3. Strings beads;

At 39 months, Allison is performing a basic preacademic task: matching and pasting letters of the alphabet.

4. Uses crayons, pencils; scribbles; colors within lines;

5. Copies geometric shapes;

6. Completes 8- to 16-piece puzzles;

7. Makes representative drawings;

8. Matches, recognizes, sorts, names colors;

9. Matches, recognizes, sorts, names shapes and pictures;

10. Knows the parts of the body;

11. Imitates motor and verbal behavior;

12. Independently performs self-help tasks: washing, eating, toileting, dressing;

13. Performs household tasks;

14. Understands prepositions: *in, out, on, around, under, beside, in front, behind*;

15. Understands the numbers 1 through 4: concepts, sequence, and equivalence;

16. Understands size and quantity relationships;

17. Knows the alphabet;

18. Prints his name;

19. Reads 5 to 20 words by sight.

Goals for Social and Self-Help Development: 3 to 5 Years

Social.

1. Answers social questions:

    a. "How are you today?"

    b. "Where do you live?" (city).

2. Initiates a conversation with an adult or a peer;

3. Play skills:

    a. Cooperative play:

        1) Plays group games;

        2) Builds blocks, etc. with another child;

    b. Dramatic play:

        1) Combines cars and animals with blocks;

        2) Dresses up.

Two kindergarten students enjoy playing dress-up, an activity which helps develop the self-help skills of dressing and undressing.

Self-help.

1. Eating skills:

   a. Eats food with spoon and fork without spilling;

   b. Cuts with a knife;

   c. Drinks through a straw;

2. Toileting:

   a. Goes to the bathroom and uses the toilet, unaided;

   b. Washes hands afterwards;

3. Grooming and personal care:

   a. Brushes teeth;

   b. Washes and dries hands unaided;

   c. Covers mouth when coughs or sneezes;

   d. Blows nose;

4. Dressing:

   a. Zips open zipper;

   b. Snaps;

   c. Buttons four small buttons;

   d. Laces shoes;

   e. Fastens pants (sliding silver inside clasp);

   f. Buckles belt (with a single-prong buckle);

   g. Distinguishes front and back of clothing.

THE CLASSROOM AND THE TEACHER

The physical setting for an intervention program does not need to be different from any well-organized facility designed for normal infants and young children. The toys, materials, and furnishings of a quality nursery or school are purposefully selected to provide experiences appropriate for a particular age group. At the same time they are novel and challenging enough to stimulate experimentation and growth. Basically these are the same goals we maintain for the handicapped population. The major difference between a classroom for normal children and an intervention classroom for atypical children is the degree of structure and how the setting is used to achieve developmental objectives—not the physical setting.

The teacher of normal young children must provide supervision and a balance between formal and informal instruction. But that teacher does not teach directly as much and does not use task analysis, modelling, and physical assistance as much as the teacher of the handicapped.

Once an activity has been introduced, normal children usually are able to build and expand on the initial idea on their own. A great deal of social, physical, and cognitive learning occurs when normal children manipulate, explore, and share materials with their peers in a supervised but unstructured situation (free play). But unless the handicapped child has already been taught the spontaneous play skills of a normal child, he is rarely able to function well in free play. The atypical child has to learn to interact in a rewarding way with the environment.

A walking board placed on the floor of a nursery room prompts the normal 2-year-old to practice her walking skill. A timid child might hesitate, but after the first trial she is usually ready to continue the activity independently, walking and even running the length of the board with increasing delight at her success. A handicapped child, possibly hampered by perceptual difficulties and poor muscle coordination, may need many trials and a lot of teacher support and encouragement before she is able to undertake the same activity on her own. This may take days or weeks.

The Teacher

It is up to the teacher to provide the intervention. Sensitive to the individual needs of each child, the teacher must determine

Baer on a behavioral approach to child development (1961). Following a year of study with B. F. Skinner on an NIMH Senior Fellowship (1961–1962). Bijou has worked with and studied retarded children in different settings—first at the Rainier School in Buckley, Washington, and at the University of Washington's Developmental Psychology Laboratory when he was on that university's faculty; then at the University of Illinois; and now at the University of Arizona. His writings include several original studies that have inspired many duplications and extensions of the work by other investigators and several volumes in collaboration with Donald Baer that are regarded as classics in the field: Child Development: Readings in Experimental Analysis (1967) and three major volumes on child development—Child Development: A Systematic and Empirical Theory (with Baer, 1961); Child Development: Universal Stage of Infancy (with Baer, 1965); and, in 1976, Child Development: The Basic Stage of Early Childhood.

The major theme in his work is the question "What works best to facilitate learning?" He has focused on a method to use in studying behavior in natural settings, an individualized approach in work with young children, and a basic instructional pattern that can be used in any setting to teach any child any subject. The model includes these steps: specifying target behaviors, assessing the child's entering capabilities, planning and sequencing the teaching, assessing progress, modifying the sequence as called for by the child's progress data, and helping the child maintain or generalize the learned behavior.

Recently, Bijou has prepared a model of child development that extends his earlier examinations of environments. The model stresses the interaction between the developing child and the environment, pointing out how they have an impact on and change each other.

Sidney Bijou's work in early childhood education of handicapped children has helped us to work more effectively with these children. His ability to apply a theory to the practical, everyday problems of teaching has helped professionals realize that successful learning and achievement are the result of behaviors that can be defined, observed, measured, modified, and managed—first by the teacher and ultimately by the learner.

precisely which tools and activities best help develop a desired skill. Toys, materials, and equipment must be selected wisely, but the most sophisticated and special materials are useless unless the handicapped are taught how to interact with others and how to learn from their environment. It is the teacher who must be "special."

The role of the teacher of special children is not easy. It requires sensitivity, innovation, and a high degree of professional skill. A teacher must be able to cultivate a genuine feeling of caring and involvement not only towards specific children but towards all children who need special help. It may be difficult to relate warmly to a malformed, unattractive, or unresponsive child Under these circumstances it helps to recognize how deprived that child is and the great need of this child and his parents. The teacher who can approach a difficult problem with confidence and can find satisfaction from seeing small amounts of progress towards an objective will find this special work infinitely rewarding.

MEETING SPECIAL NEEDS

Every teacher of young handicapped children should keep in mind:

1. *Know and understand the sequence of normal development.*

2. *Remember that every child she sees is first of all a child. The fact that a child is handicapped is secondary. In spite of his disabilities, he may be more like a normal child than a handicapped person.*

3. *Even a severely handicapped, low functioning child has basic human needs for contact with other people and feeling a part of her environment.*

4. *The more limited the child is, the more sensory input she must have through whatever means available—sight, hearing, smell, touch, taste, and motion.*

5. *Know how to provide sensory input using as many pathways as possible. Even if a child is blind and deaf and paralyzed, the teacher must still find ways to bring the child in contact with his surroundings.*

6. *Too much enrichment—indiscriminate bombardment with noise, lights, confusing visual stimuli of shapes, colors, patterns, "busy" pictures, and physical activity—can be as harmful as not enough. Too much stimulation affects the nervous system and* can result in the child totally blocking out and withdrawing.

7. *Understand the importance of total communication. Eye contact, facial expression, gestures, and voice must be used in establishing communication.*

8. *Remember that all children are troublesome at times. Normal children also get into things, wet their pants, fuss, and cry.*

9. *Young children, especially infants, need to be held, stroked, rocked, and talked to. They need to be handled gently and lovingly.*

10. *Understand special problems and know how to deal with them.*

The following suggestions deal with some of the most common special problems:

1. Crying. *Young children cry. The younger they are and the less able they are to cope with stress, the more they cry. Occasionally you find a classroom full of crying children, which is not right. If it happens regularly, several things are probably wrong with the program: the scheduled activities, the number of children in the room, the staff, the room temperature, and so forth. However, even under ideal conditions a child may cry when:*

• *He is separated from his mother, father, or primary caretaker for the first time. Separation should be a gradual process. Allow at least 2 weeks. Take into account the child's age and emotional maturity.*

• *He is tired, hungry, sick, unhappy, or frightened. Don't be afraid to comfort the child. Comfort in moments of stress does not spoil a child; it has the positive effect of making a child more secure and outgoing.*

• *New demands are made of him. It does not help the child to learn, if all efforts are stopped at the first whimper, however. The teacher must be sensitive to the child's feelings and keep a fine balance between helping a child overcome his reluctance and not increasing his distress. Praise, a calm, positive, and comforting manner, and stopping the activity before it becomes a struggle of wills, are practical and effective ways of dealing with the situation.*

• *He has no other means of communication. Teach more acceptable ways. Help him communicate by touch, gesture, or sound. Be quick to respond to all attempts at noncrying communication.*

2. Throwing. *A common problem behavior among handicapped children is haphazard throwing of food, toys, and materials. Normal children around the age of 15 months also irresponsibly throw objects a lot. This behavior comes as a voluntary release which develops over a few months. If this throwing is not reinforced, it soon passes and the normal child goes on to stacking blocks and neatly placing objects into containers. A developmentally delayed child who tosses objects many months past the normal age for this activity has not progressed to more mature behavior. The best way to overcome the problem is to prevent throwing by stepping in before the action happens and physically helping the child place the object on the table, into a container, or wherever is appropriate. A consistent program of intervention with praise for the appropriate response—even when it occurs with teacher help—is generally effective.*

3. Biting and grinding teeth. *When either or both of these behaviors appear suddenly or increase in frequency, it is a good idea to have a physician see the child to rule out the possibility of a middle ear infection. If the biting is not related to an earache, watching the child and structuring her activities are the best ways of handling the behavior. Avoid placing the child near other children. Crowding and pushing increase the probability of biting. The biter as well as the hitter and pincher need to learn better ways of communication and social interaction. It is also important to structure the child's activities so that the behavior doesn't occur. A behavior that never has a chance to occur is never reinforced. Eventually the behavior ends.*

FOR MORE INFORMATION

Most of these resources are textbooks that are readily available. Check your instructor, the education library, or the general library at your school.

Allen, K.E., Rieke, J., Dmitriev, V., & Hayden, A.H. Early warning: Observation as a tool for recognizing potential handicaps in young children. *Educational Horizons,* 1972, *50* (2), 43–55.

Developing programs for Downs syndrome children. Reston, Va.: Council for Exceptional Children Institute, 1977.

Smart, M.S., & Smart, R.C. *Preschool children: Development and relationships.* New York: MacMillan, 1973.

White, B.L. *The first three years of life.* Englewood Cliffs, N.J.: Prentice-Hall, 1975.

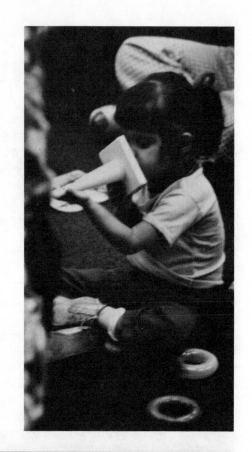

4

Communication in Early Childhood

Jane Rieke

These are the major topics covered in this chapter. You may want to use them as a checklist when you review.

- *Definitions of and the relationship among the terms* communication, language, *and* speech.

- *Initiating and responding behaviors in a child's communication development.*

- *Teacher behaviors which encourage and discourage continued communication interaction with students.*

- *A basic preschool communication curriculum.*

- *The team process as used to help a child develop communication skills.*

Chapter four

By the time a child enters first grade, he should be able to handle spoken language well enough to follow instructions, understand a detailed story, receive information, and use simple reasoning. He should also be able to express himself well enough to ask questions, give information, make his needs known, tell stories and events in proper order, describe scenes, choose, guess and pretend. In short he should be a verbal child, using speech and language to satisfy a variety of needs.

This statement from a Project Head Start Manual (*Speech, language, and hearing program,* 1973) describes our expectations for a typical 6-year-old's communication skills. Obviously these skills do not suddenly appear at the age of 6; rather, they develop over a period of years as the child hears and imitates other people in his environment. As LaBrant (1972) points out, "Language learning . . . is the responsibility of all who deal with the child through conversation or who are heard by the child."

We must recognize the critical nature of our interactions with young children, particularly as they affect language skills. All of us in early education and special education have a responsibility to know what normal language development is so that we can participate knowledgeably in its development. At the very least, we must recognize that much of the young child's understanding of language comes from what he hears us say.

In the preschool, it is much more appropriate to view language development as a continuing and constant process than as something to be taught at a certain time each day. Language programs are not ends in themselves; it is time to consider

I would like to acknowledge the contributions to this chapter of the staff of the Communication Programs at the Experimental Education Unit, University of Washington. Classroom teachers, speech-language pathologists, and students in training have participated in the development of these materials, and I am grateful for their contributions.—*J.R.*

language in the larger context of communication. We know that language competence is essential to academic excellence—a measure of success. If we also accept the premise that relationships with people (interactions) are important and may often be the measure of success for some of our less academically able children, then communication skills truly become extremely important for us all.

THE COMMUNICATION PROCESS

Young children develop language and speech skills through their communication with the people in their environment. Since this is so, we must first be sure that children are involved in interaction with others—for the sake of their learning. Once a child learns to interact, we can consider the refinements of language and speech.

What Communication Is

Communication can be defined as the exchange of ideas, of feelings, or of information. Communication involves giving and receiving; a "speaker" and a "listener;" a dialogue; an alternation of behaviors. We can define **language** as the written and spoken symbol system which we use in communication. We can define **speech** as the sounds we use to transmit language—the mode of producing and combining vowels, consonants, and the other sounds which allow us to communicate orally. (For a more complete discussion of our language and speech system, see chapter 10.)

The child who communicates—that is, who involves himself in the idea exchange—receives from the environment the kind of feedback that gives him the information, ideas, and experiences for learning that are denied the isolate or silent child. The child who is involved in the exchange also hears the speech and language models which he will use someday.

Because our society is so verbal, most of us tend to recognize communication only when it is verbal; that is, we pay attention when we hear and understand words. (Communication, however, is not limited to oral or to written words. Communication can occur on a completely **nonverbal** basis, by gestures and facial expressions.)Adults communicate many feelings and seek information nonverbally; and children do, too. Children who use no or few spoken symbols can still communicate.)

Just as nonverbal children can communicate, so too children who have verbal language skills are not always communicators. These children should concern the teacher as much as the silent, expressionless child does, for by their quietness they often remove themselves from the interaction where information is flowing.

Thinking of communication as all exchanges, verbal and nonverbal, between people directs our attention to *the* prerequisite for continued language development—**communicative interaction.** This is a pattern of exchange which gives children an opportunity to learn new words and new concepts. It also gives them opportunities to practice putting ideas into words in ever-changing situations. It provides practice for proficiency.

How Language Develops

Again, language develops through the child's interaction with the people around him. Some of the first communication behaviors we observe in an infant are nonverbal. The infant *turns* to look in the direction of a sound, *smiles* at a familiar voice, *reaches* for a toy. He cries when he is hungry and when he wants attention. Soon he is cooing and playing with new sounds. Soon, too, adults begin to respond to this vocal play. Their response encourages more vocal play, and in a short time the child adds vocalization and simple inflec-

tions to his looking, smiling, and reaching. In the expected course of development, sounds become the words for specific people (*mama, dada*) or events (*bye-bye*). In fairly rapid succession, the child's language progresses in a wonderfully human and little understood way from single words to phrases which he uses to make his wishes known. Finally, sentences and questions appear and, with these, more mature conversational exchanges.

Soon after he is 2 years old, the normal child is forming simple sentences; by the time he is 4, he astounds us by the questions he asks and the stories he tells. The language he uses is grammatically complex. He generally can be understood and is fun to talk with.

In a simple diagram, the developmental order of communication looks like Figure 4.1.

What is set out here as a sequence of communication behaviors reflects the order in which language skills develop. But the concept of developmental order, or sequence, for communication does *not* mean that advancing from one level to the next automatically eliminates continued use of earlier, nonverbal forms of communication. In fact, the process is one of *adding* communication behaviors—of enriching the repertoire.

The child's actual movement through the sequence is largely dependent on the way the adults in the environment respond to him. Communication takes at least *two* people. For a child to continue reaching and smiling, cooing and babbling, there

```
Nonverbal
   ↓
Vocal
   ↓
Verbal—words
     words together—phrases
     sentences—questions
```

Figure 4.1
Developmental order of communication

must be a person to reach for and smile to, and that person must respond. The infant who hears no verbal response from the people in his environment may *become* quiet.

When communication moves from non-verbal to vocal to phrases, its power increases. Adults other than parents usually enter into the exchange and the variety of reactions and responses he gets adds to the child's knowledge and to his information about language. He hears many ways to say things. He gets practice. His language repertoire continues to grow.

Communication Behaviors

When we look at a child's communication behaviors we look at two categories of behaviors: initiating behaviors and responding behaviors.

Tanya's normal development was interrupted by an accident. Now the staff at her preschool uses lots of one-to-one personal attention to stimulate her to express herself orally.

profile
BETTYE CALDWELL

Bettye Caldwell's extensive research and clinical work with young children has been widely recognized and honored among her professional colleagues and by the general public. In 1976, she received the Ladies' Home Journal award as "Woman of the Year" in the humanities category. She is the author of more than 80 publications.

Now a professor of education at the University of Arkansas, and director of the Center for Child Development and Education in Little Rock, Bettye Caldwell is continuing work begun in the 1950s on the impact of early experience on a child's development and on ways to make those early experiences as enriching and nurturing as possible, whether in the home or at school. Caldwell has been interested as well in children with delayed or atypical development, whether originating in the
child's social environment or from some organic condition.

Beginning in 1959, Caldwell collaborated with Dr. Julius Richmond in a longitudinal study of mother/infant interaction; Caldwell's responsibilities focused on the children's development. Her interest soon extended to children's cognitive development with attention to the effects of learning styles and environmental factors. In a study called "Infant Learning and Patterns of Family Care," Caldwell and her associates studied children from birth to age 3, enriching the experiences of those children in the sample who came from deprived environments. Their investigation was focused on whether or not these children could attain normal developmental patterns and avoid the decline in abilities that would have been expected without enriching experiences. As a result of her work, Caldwell was asked to help plan the federal Head Start project and convince the U.S. Congress of the urgent need for such a program.

Initiating Behaviors

Initiating behaviors are those which the child produces spontaneously and uses to gain the attention of another person. The behaviors may be either verbal or nonverbal. They occur when the child wishes to attract attention, to have some wish or need met, or to tell about something. The child also initiates an exchange when he wants information or has a question to ask. Figure 4.2 shows some of the initiating behaviors, arranged in a developmental sequence.

By the time the child is 3 years of age, he should be initiating conversation in short, simple sentences. These sentences become longer and more complex as the child's vocabulary increases and include adjectives, adverbs, prepositions, and conjunctions. The child should be asking questions.

Nonverbal	Watch, smile, beckon, touch, point to.
Vocal	Sigh, call, exclaim to attract attention.
Verbal	Words—"bye-bye," "look," "come," "cookie."
	Words together—"go bye-bye," "want cookie."
	Sentences—"I want to go." "I see the dog."
	Questions—"What's that?" "Where did it go?"

Figure 4.2
Initiating behaviors

After his fourth birthday, a child should be able to talk about what has happened and to relate experiences. He should be able to answer questions and ask many of his own. His sentences should be put together in an accepted way. He should show evidence that he is organizing his thoughts more carefully.

Caldwell is also well-known and respected for a preschool inventory she developed. This assessment instrument is widely used in Head Start and other preschool programs. Her device, called Home Observation for Measurement of the Environment, *for children from birth to age 3, is one of the few that looks at the home setting or any other setting where a child spends appreciable amounts of time; thus, the instrument is adaptable to day care settings.*

Caldwell's other main interest has been in developmental and educational continuity, that is, what happens to children when they leave the enriched preschool setting and how to help them maintain their early gains when they leave. In Little Rock, she has been associated with a center that provides an enriched early preschool program within a public school elementary program. The program offers day care to children from infancy to age 12 and opportunities for research and training in early childhood education.

Responding Behaviors

Responding behaviors are those with which a child responds to the questions or directives of another person. A very young child may respond to the words "good-bye" by waving. He may respond to the question "What do you want?" by reaching for the juice or by answering "More juice." We expect the child to respond to our directions by doing what he is told to do: stop fighting, come here, don't run. Responding behaviors develop sequentially from nonverbal to verbal behaviors in much the same way as do the behaviors in the initiating sequence—with the exception of nonverbal responses to complicated directions, such as finding a house in an unfamiliar part of town. Figure 4.3 shows some responding behaviors, arranged in a developmental sequence.

Chapter four

Nonverbal	Look at, smile, nod, come, get.
Vocal	Grunt, upward change in the voice (inflection) for questions, downward inflection for telling.
Verbal	Words—"yes," "no"; answering "What's that?" with nouns; answering "What's he doing?" with verbs. Words together—answering "In the closet," "On top," "Too fast," "Yes, more." Sentences—sentence responses occur naturally when questions are open-ended: "What did you do today?" Sentences are also used responsively following comments: "I thought he looked ill, too," in response to "John looked ill."

Figure 4.3
Responding behaviors

A Communication Model

At the point where a child uses sentences to initiate communication, he will also be able to respond to open-ended questions with sentences. The richness and complexity of his language is more evident when he is initiating than when he is responding to others' questions or commands.

Figure 4.4 shows that both initiating and responding behaviors develop in an orderly, sequential way. Again, the child should be initiating communication as well as responding to others. Adults who have engaged in a dialogue with a child can refer to this figure to find the developmental level at which the child is able to communicate most readily. It is at this level, regardless of the child's chronological age, that a child should first be encouraged to interact. Successful interaction helps him gain the proficiency he needs to move to the next developmental level.

Figure 4.4 can be made more useful by expanding it into a kind of working blueprint to look at more advanced communication

COMMUNICATION BEHAVIORS	
Initiating	**Responding**
Nonverbal ↓	Nonverbal ↓
Vocal ↓	Vocal ↓
Verbal	Verbal
words	words
words together	words together
sentences	sentences
questions	

Figure 4.4
Basic communication model

skills. It also can be used to help identify those behaviors which interfere with successful communication.

In Figure 4.5 we see that a child's maturity is marked in part by his ability to respond to increasingly complex question forms. The school-age child is asked to listen to and remember involved directions and then to carry them out. He is asked to independently follow directions given to a group. The older child is expected to tell us what happened. He should be able to describe events, which implies using adjectives and adverbs. The child should be able to explain, which means he should be able to use conjunctions and complex sentence forms. The expectation that the child is able to organize ideas in an orderly way involves memory and the ability to arrange ideas in a sequence. A child also needs to be able to ask a variety of questions as well as to answer them. The preschool teacher has the responsibility to see that the children in her classes have opportunities to develop these skills and to use them in a communicative way.

The Communication Model summarizes a good deal of what we have learned about the levels of language a child can use. That information can help a teacher understand children who do not have special needs and those who do. The model encourages

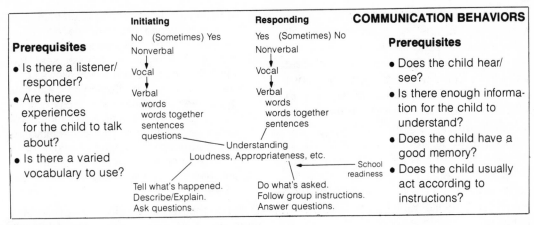

Figure 4.5
Communication model

teachers to look first for the place where the child can have some successful communicating experiences.

The expanded model in Figure 4.5 can also be used to help identify those children who show signs of not developing communication skills. There are questions a teacher can and should ask to help make the decisions about appropriate programs for children.

• *Does the child initiate communication?* No? Sometimes? Yes? If you can answer *yes*, the next question is: *At what level of communication?* Nonverbal (that is, reaching for)? Inflected sounds? Words? Phrases? Sentences?

• *Does the child respond?* No? Sometimes? Yes? If yes, *At what level?* Nonverbal (that is, nodding or doing)? Inflected sounds? Words? Phrases? Sentences? (Remember that your expectation of a sentence-length response should depend on the question preceding it.)

• Other questions deal with what interferes with communication and with what bothers or concerns us: Can't we understand him? Can't we hear him? Doesn't he always answer the question appropriately? Does he wander verbally?

If the answer to either of the first two questions about communication behaviors is *Yes, sometimes,* the questions become *When?* and *Under what conditions?* This is a time for the teacher to think about gathering information about what helps the child communicate more readily and more easily. And it is also a time to watch what happens following the child's communication behavior, to look for what continues or stops the communication exchange.

If the answer to either of the first two questions is *No*—if the child does not initiate at all or does not respond at all—the teacher should probably seek additional professional help. If the answer is *Not much— only sometimes,* the teacher might begin by referring to the lists of prerequisites listed in the Communication Model.

Prerequisites to Successful Communication and Language Development

As you've seen, a child's language develops as adults encourage him to listen and as they listen to him. The child's language improves as the adults provide models of good speech and language and as they encourage the child to express himself. Clearly, then, if a child's language is to continue to develop along the initiating sequence, he must have someone to talk with, experiences to talk about, and a varied vocabulary to use. And if a child does not initiate communication very much or if he is not developing variety of expression, you should look at these prerequisites for initiating communication. If a child is not responding consistently, the answers to *When?* and *Under what conditions?* might indicate a possible hearing loss. Other reasons might also be the child's lack of information on specific subjects, problems with following instructions, poor memory for instruction, habits of not answering, and so forth.

Some consistency of performance in both initiating and responding—at a level where the child can succeed—is a desired goal. Inconsistent performance demands that more questions be asked. Frequently a teacher arrives at a good solution by herself. At other times she calls in resource people to help. Her responsibility, however, is to identify that there is a problem.

What the Preschool Teacher Can Do

On the positive side, teachers who seek the answers to these questions can often adjust their expectations or their classrooms to give the child success. Sometimes the teacher finds the answer simply because she has taken time to ask the question. Sometimes a specialist who has been trained to observe communication behaviors and the variables which affect them is needed. If the observer records not only a child's communication behaviors but also the events or variables before and after the behaviors, she has a record of what deters or continues the communicative exchanges. Thus, the preschool teacher is in a unique position to help identify communication problems early. The teacher's vantage point is unique for a number of reasons.

The preschool teacher has been trained to work with young children; the children's parents may or may not have had such training. The preschool teacher sees the child in a social context which allows comparison of the child's development with that of his peers. Also, he or she sees the child for a longer period of time and in more various situations than others—a pediatrician, dentist, or psychologist, for example—who may deal only with discrete problems. (Allen, Rieke, Dmitriev, & Hayden, 1972, pp. 43-44)

But on the negative side, the person who unknowingly frowns because she does not understand a child discourages continuing communication. The person who frequently asks a child to "Say it better" discourages communication. The person who always pays attention to the most verbal child discourages the less verbal. The person who is always asking questions discourages the child's initiated communication.

The teacher of the child who is *developmentally* young is in the same advantageous position as one who teaches the *chronologically* young. By observing the various situations where communication is expected, she determines the child's level in the sequence of communication development. The habits of consistent initiating and responding are established over time through successful experiences in communicating. In the case of the child who is developmentally delayed, the expectations of adults for a level of performance consistent with her size or chronological age may not have been met. Repeated failure to communicate may discourage the child from further attempts. To maintain communicative interaction at a level where the child is successful is often difficult for adults.

The classroom teacher who identifies a communication development problem invariably adjusts his expectations so that he can have successful exchanges with the child. This is to be commended, but a warning must be added. Successful communication at one level is the first goal. But the child needs both many *different* opportunities at this level *and* the opportunity to progress to the next. Some children begin to improve their level of communication automatically once they are drawn into the communication exchange by success. For others, it is necessary to teach specific skills to change their level of language performance. Parents and teachers must adjust their expectations upward as children are able to meet new challenges. Further, they must show that they are especially pleased with the *new* skills in order for these more mature levels of language to become the child's habits.

COMMUNICATION GOALS IN THE PRESCHOOL

When a preschool program emphasizes communication, children's language delays, deviances, and disorders can be identified early and remedies sought. There are many places in the preschool curriculum where communication goals can be naturally and effectively combined with other education goals and activities. It is a matter of setting priorities. The teacher whose 8:30 to 9:00 A.M. priority is preparing snacks or mixing paint may not take time to listen to Susie tell what happened at breakfast, to encourage Mike to tell Scott about his dog, or to listen to Chris's response when he is asked about his sister. Both jobs need to be done and they can be combined. The schedule of activities can include not only general educational and developmental objectives but communication and language objectives as well.

Because of P.L. 94–142 and parallel state laws, any program that includes handicapped children is now held responsible for setting appropriate goals and objectives for the children. In this age of accountability, goals must be defined in terms of behaviors that can be observed and measured. Teachers are planning activities with these goals in mind. The teacher with expertise in child development and teaching and management procedures uses activities that give children opportunities to

After a "Good Morning" song, these aides and preschoolers remain sitting in a circle to discuss their plans for the day.

acquire developmentally appropriate motor, preacademic, self-help, social, and play skills. Teachers can also use these activities to help the child acquire communication and language skills appropriate to his development level.

A Basic Preschool Curriculum

Figure 4.6 shows a preschool day with some sample activities. It includes both activities directed by the teacher and activities directed by the child. The child's educational developmental goals associated with each activity reflect a concern for the development of the *total* child. Although only two suggestions are listed here with each activity, a teacher may have as many as four or five objectives planned. Examine Figure 4.6 and consider how communication/language goals could be incorporated. Figures 4.6a through 4.6e incorporate some sample communication/language goals.

Free Choice

In the sample schedule, the child's day begins with an opportunity to choose from a supply of different materials which have been set out in the room. The teacher expects the child to learn to play with the materials and to share. Reasonable communication objectives would be to encourage children to talk to each other about the materials or to describe the material. It is wise to start with one or two general goals.

Group Time

During the opening exercise, teachers often talk with youngsters about the calendar and weather, tell stories, or discuss the day's planned activities. It is an excellent time for children and teacher to practice communication skills at the children's level of competence. Possible communication objectives for opening exercises or group time would be to give each child the opportunity to answer questions and to comment on new information.

Classroom activity	Educational/developmental goals associated with activity
A. Free choice (Children play together with a choice of materials and activities)	1. To develop social skills (for example, cooperative play, sharing). 2. To explore new materials.
B. Group time: Opening exercise	1. To take turns in a group. 2. To be introduced to new information.
C. Snack time	1. To practice self-help skills. 2. To experience tastes and textures.
D. Special activity: Nonroutine projects: cooking, art, field trips	1. To learn to adapt to changes in routine. 2. To work cooperatively.
E. Transitions from one activity to the next.	1. To practice self-help skills (toileting, managing clothing). 2. To follow instructions given to the group.

Figure 4.6
Sample daily activity schedule

A.	Free choice		The child is:	The child is:
		1.	To develop social skills.	To interact with other children.
		2.	To explore new materials.	To tell what he found.

Figure 4.6a

B.	Group time		The child is:	The child is:
		1.	To take turns in a group.	To answer questions (responding).
		2.	To be introduced to new information.	To comment about the new information (initiating).

Figure 4.6b

Snack Time

Breakfast, a snack, or lunch is a part of every preschool schedule. Unfortunately this is often a time when staff members take their breaks. It is a prime time for language objectives and self-help skills to be worked on. This is a time when the teacher can help the child in his attempts to pour liquids, to cut food, to feed himself. It is also a time for adults and children to socialize. Objectives that might be realized during this time are opportunities to ask (initiating behaviors) and to hear new words—perhaps the names of foods and descriptive adjectives.

C.	Snack time		The child is:	The child is:
		1.	To practice self-help skills.	To ask for food.
		2.	To experience tastes and textures.	To hear the names of foods, tastes, and textures.

Figure 4.6c

Special Activities

Special activities give children a break from their usual routine. New experiences mean new words added to their vocabularies. A new experience gives a child something interesting to talk about or someone new to talk with. When he tells someone about his experiences, the child must organize ideas in a sequence.

Nonroutine activities also give a teacher an opportunity to see if the child is generalizing newly learned language behaviors to other situations or to other people. For example, to the other objectives in a cooking project we could add "to communicate in new situations" and "to retell what happened."

D.	Special activity		The child is:	The child is:
		1.	To learn to adapt to changes in routine.	To communicate in new situations.
		2.	To work cooperatively.	To retell what happened.

Figure 4.6d

Transitions

A good time to observe a child's nonverbal responding behaviors is during the transition from one planned activity to another. Does the child appear to hear the directions? Does he follow the directions given to a group? Does he follow novel directions? Does he follow long directions? Any *no* or *sometimes* answer needs to be investigated. Transition time, which is frequently left out in the teacher's daily plans, deserves to be planned as carefully as any other time, and to have objectives.

E. Transitions	The child is: 1. To practice self-help skills. 2. To follow instructions given to the group.	The child is: To listen To remember To do

Figure 4.6e

It is not always necessary to specify performance levels in the general goals for the preschool curriculum. Obviously a child may demonstrate responding behaviors by pointing, making a noise, using words together, or using long and involved sentences. What is important is that the *expectation* is written into the lesson plan and that opportunities for the behavior are provided. Establishing the developmental levels at which children can perform each task and setting different performance standards for each child are skills for a master teacher who has the resources to individualize programs for each child. Figure 4.7 is a summary plan which combines educational/developmental goals and the communication/language goals we've seen.

Developmental Assessment

A number of assessment tools have been designed to show or profile the development of skills in young children. Educators are especially interested in these tools since research has begun to show that some learning handicaps can be prevented, or at least their severity lessened, if they are identified early enough. The sample chart in Figure 4.8 shows some landmarks in language development as they relate to other areas of development. Such charts, which consider physical and mental growth, help us pinpoint specific problems as well as make judgments about overall skill development. From these observations, we can design an individualized program to fit the needs of each child.

A Sample Developmental Chart

Figure 4.8 shows four different areas of language development—receptive behaviors, expressive behaviors, grammar, speech—along with three other developmental areas—motor, feeding, and play. The four language sequences are taken from an assessment tool known as *The Sequenced Inventory of Communication Development* (Hedrick, Prather, & Tobin, 1975).

Classroom activity	Educational/developmental goals	Communication/language goals
Free choice	1. To develop social skills (for example, cooperative play, sharing). 2. To explore new materials.	1. To interact with other children. 2. To tell what he found.
Group time	1. To take turns in a group. 2. To be introduced to new information.	1. To answer questions (responding). 2. To comment about the new information (initiating).
Snack time	1. To practice self-help skills. 2. To experience tastes and textures.	1. To ask for food. 2. To hear the names of foods, tastes, and textures.
Special activity	1. To learn to adapt to changes in routine. 2. To work cooperatively.	1. To communicate in new situations. 2. To retell what happened.
Transitions	1. To practice self-help skills (for example, toileting, managing clothing). 2. To follow instructions given to the group.	1. To listen. 2. To remember. 3. To do.

Figure 4.7
Daily activity schedule

In their preschool, Lucia and Michael get the chance to play and share toys with each other.

Figure 4.8 *Developmental chart*

Years	a. Motor*	b. Feeding*	c. Play*	d. Receptive Behaviors	e. Expressive Behaviors	f. Grammar	g. Speech
1	Stands alone Uses finger-thumb grasp	Feeds self finger foods Drinks from cup with assistance	Bangs toys or objects together Plays interactive games (peek-a-boo)	Looks at people who talk Responds to simple commands accompanied by gestures	Says sound combinations that sound like words Responds to talking by "talking"		
2	Balances when walking Imitates vertical strokes	Begins to use spoon Lifts cup and drinks well	Throws objects and picks them up Enjoys pulling toys	Gets items of clothing on request Responds to simple commands without gesture	Asks for items by name Answers simple questions like "What's that?"	Combines 2 to 3 different words; some verb phrases	Uses initial *m, b, p, t, n, k, g, w* Final *n*
3	Pedals tricycle Imitates building a tower of 4 blocks	Inserts spoon in mouth correctly Holds small glass in one hand	Shows interest in manipulative toys Plays alongside another child	Selects big/little Puts items in or on, as directed	Relates immediate experiences Answers questions of choice like "Which one?"	Uses regular plurals Uses third person pronouns	Uses final consonants from above Uses *s, f, d, r* initial and final
4	Hops on 1 foot Draws a person in 3 parts	Serves self at table Pours well from a pitcher	Expresses imagination in play Begins sharing toys	Follows 3 action commands Puts items under or beside, as directed	Asks "Why?" and "How?" questions Answers complex questions like "What's it for?", "How?"	Uses past tense Says sentences of 4 words	Uses *th, ch, v, l,* and consonant blends (i.e., *st, sp, tr, bp*)

Note. a, b, c above selected from *The Washington Guide to Promoting Development in the Young Child,* by K. E. Barnard and M. L. Powell, University of Washington Child Development and Mental Retardation Center, Seattle, Washington. Copyright, 1972. d, e, f, g above selected from *The Sequenced Inventory of Communication Development,* by D. L. Hedrick, E. M. Prather, and A. R. Tobin, Seattle, University Press, 1975.
*Data from Kathryn E. Barnard and Marcene L. Powell, *Teaching the Mentally Retarded Child,* St. Louis, The C. V. Mosby Co. 1972.

Using the Developmental Chart

In each of the seven development areas, the chart shows those tasks which a child of a given age should be able to perform. By comparing the child's actual performance to the chronological age skills, it is possible to determine her functional age. If you were to mark with a colored pen those items which a child can perform with confidence, you would have a developmental profile of what the child can do. Patterns of uneven development could then be easily seen.

For example, a child whose chronological age is 4 years but who performs in all areas like a child of 2 years has an overall functional age of 2. He is developmentally delayed. A child of 4 who is functioning like a 4-year-old in all areas except that she is saying only a few isolated words has the language behaviors of a 1½-year-old. She has a specific problem in one of the expressive language areas. Programs for these two children will be different. Most screening or assessment tools which cover several developmental areas merely indicate the areas of concern for in-depth investigations. We have subdivided language functioning here, however, to look at several language areas. This helps us identify both strengths and weaknesses and helps us better differentiate abilities from disabilities (differential diagnosis).

Let us look more closely at the 4-year-old who is functioning generally at the level of a 2-year-old. If you draw a line just under the description of a 2-year-old's skills, your expectations for the child become more realistic. In the Receptive Behaviors column, you find that the child can be expected to get his shoes if asked to do so, but not to find the *little* hat. In expressive behavior, the child could be expected to answer "What's that?" with words, but not "How did it happen?" In grammar, he could be expected to combine two different words when he talks but not to say "He went to work." In speech, he could say *ba,* but not *ball.*

Now let us consider a child of 4 years with a specific language problem. She may be able to do what the average 4-year-old does in motor skills, feeding, play skills, and receptive behaviors. She may answer "How" questions at the 4-year-old level by pointing or gesturing, and she may ask "Why." However, she may only put two words together; she may not be able to speak in simple sentences, which is expected at age 2½ to 3. This is a deficit area. You can expect this child to perform differently in this one sequence when compared to her 4-year-old peers.

Or a child may perform all tasks at what appears to be a fairly even developmental level but use only the phonemes /b/, /d/, and /m/ with vowels to make words—to be so deficient in speech that you cannot understand him at all. Society tolerates some sound substitutions and errors in speaking clearly (articulation). But when a child is unintelligible, people cannot respond to him well and communication is unsuccessful. Special help is needed.

The child with a specific speech or language deficit is likely to fail repeatedly in communication, partly because of the expectation of the adults and peers around him that he will perform in *all* areas with the same ease. A specific speech or language deficit is often the cause of the child's withdrawal from the communication exchange. The adult who can find a place where successful exchange is possible is important to this child—and this person can be the teacher.

There will always be some developmental profiles where delays occur only in one of the language areas. On some of these profiles, the delays are slight and parents or teachers feel comfortable in attempting to help the child catch up. In other cases, of course, the problem is noticeable and professional help must be sought.

When a language remediation program is indicated for a child, the level of the child's receptive ability should always be considered. If a specific area or sequence of language behavior can be isolated, as suggested on the developmental profile here, then clinicians and teachers alike have some guidance as they seek helpful programs. There are a variety of commercial programs available which deal with one of the language sequences. Speech pathologists, speech-language clinicians, and communication disorders specialists are particularly trained to individualize a language program to remedy a specific deficit area.

Developmental screening devices are helpful in indicating (1) patterns that suggest delay, (2) patterns that indicate specific problems that need remediation, and (3) potential problems where progress should be watched. The developmental profile can be helpful in deciding how to establish priorities. It helps in making decisions about where remedial programs are needed and which are most critical or need to come before others. The developmental profile which shows sequential development indicates what the child *can* do now and where encouragement or teaching should be directed.

COMMUNICATION AND LANGUAGE HANDICAPS IN YOUNG CHILDREN

The Communication Model (Figure 4.5) and the various developmental screening tools available provide ways to determine

profile RITA

Rita, an only child, was enrolled in the neighborhood preschool when she was 4 years old because her parents wanted to be sure she would be ready for public school kindergarten the following year. The teachers found Rita to be a quiet child, easy to have around. She seemed to enjoy the other children and tried to do what they did.

After the first week the teachers noticed that Rita played only in the doll corner. Even though they invited her to other areas, she seemed to have no other interest and no other play skills. Outside she enjoyed pushing the tricycle but she had not yet mastered the pedals. During story time Rita lost interest before other children did. An aide sat beside her to keep her with the group. One thing Rita did enjoy was snacktime. She was always hungry and ate everything that was offered, but she was not as neat about eating as the others were. At first Rita seemed to fit into the group, but as time went on she appeared more and more immature.

As soon as Rita seemed comfortable in the preschool, the teachers expected her to talk more. During snacktime they managed the food so Rita would have to ask for something to eat or drink. Rita asked mostly by reaching. She did, however, say a few food names, and now and then she asked for "more." During the play times the teachers noticed that Rita seldom initiated a conversation. She was content to play by herself. Once in a while she would show a teacher what she was doing and say "dollie" or "bath" and sometimes "wash" or "eat." When Rita wanted something she could not reach, the teachers tried to encourage her to ask for it. When she did, she was often hard to understand. When the children were told to put the toys away, Rita could follow only the simplest of instructions by herself.

When the teachers discussed helping Rita fit into the group, they found they had several mutual concerns. The first of these was that Rita did not initiate communication very often. She seemed to be able to say

whether a child has a problem in the area of communication, language, or speech. If a child does not interact, does not initiate communication, or is not consistently responsive, he has a problem which should be investigated. Any inconsistency between a child's level of language or speech development and his functional age should be investigated. The many screening tools provide information about whether a child is functionally delayed in all or nearly all developmental areas or whether the delay is seen only in the language or speech sequences. Any language problem which interferes with communication interaction is certainly a handicap.

There are some communication and language problems found in young children which can be associated with specific

only a few simple words. Her understanding of what was said to her seemed limited to short, simple comments about familiar things. She was not able to pay attention in the group as long as she should.

When the teachers looked at their developmental assessment tools, they found that both Rita's understanding and oral language abilities were very much like those of a 2-year-old child. They also determined that her play skills, self-help skills, and motor skills were 1 to 2 years below her chronological age expectations.

Additional assessments confirmed the impression that Rita is a mentally retarded child. She is intellectually delayed as well as being delayed in many developmental areas, although her language and speech skills are not significantly more delayed. As a result Rita will be placed in a group for younger children. She will profit from language enrichment activities or a language emphasis of another kind, but speech and language therapy beyond these does not seem necessary.

Jeff, who is visually impaired as well as developmentally delayed, is allowed to choose between several toys during free time. He seems to have chosen a wide-eyed rabbit as a pal.

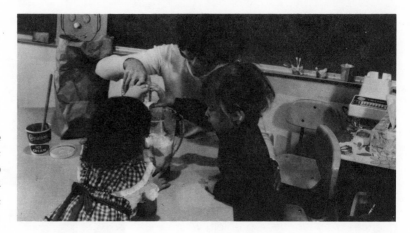

Making a malt is one way Linda teaches Jamie and Sean, who are both hearing impaired, to ask for things and follow directions.

physical or emotionally damaging circumstances. These circumstances include the following.

Delayed language development is often linked with *mental retardation*. The more severe the retardation, the poorer the child's communication behaviors, language, and speech. Most children who are mentally retarded do not communicate as frequently as the nonretarded. They begin to use words at a later age, use fewer words, talk in simpler sentences, and have more errors in grammar. They also have more problems with sounds that call for fine and rapid movements. Some children whose slow language development is associated with mental retardation have additional problems related to neurological damage, emotional problems, or environmental deprivation. (See chapter 5 for more detail on mental retardation.)

The child who has *cerebral palsy* does not have normal control over his muscles. Movement is often so constricted that the child cannot move himself into communicating situations. The lack of muscular control affects the child's breathing and his tongue, jaw, and throat. The child may have difficulty making speech sounds and sustaining sounds to form words and phrases. The difficulties some of these children have in coordinating breathing with vocalization

make oral language and intelligible speech virtually impossible. Some children who have cerebral palsy are also mentally retarded; some are intellectually gifted. (See chapter 13 for further discussion of the physically handicapped.)

Hearing loss can cause delays in the development of language and articulation skills. If the loss is severe, the child may be totally unresponsive to sound, and the problem will be recognized by adults. If it is a slight loss, the problem may go undetected during the child's early years, when she should be learning language. Some kinds of hearing losses make it difficult for the child to hear particular speech sounds. For instance a child who does not hear the /d/ and /s/ sounds has difficulty including them in her own speech. And these sounds are essential to the child's understanding of the past tense and the formation of many plurals. This kind of hearing loss can affect both speech and language. Some kinds of hearing losses make it difficult for children to hear when they are several feet away from the speaker or when the speaker turns away from the child. Some children's hearing is affected every time they have a cold.

The observant adult notices when a child does not pay attention to sounds. Poor attention, inconsistent responsiveness, lack of understanding, and limited vocabulary can frequently be attributed to hearing loss. The types of help provided to these children by the teacher can range from special training to rearrangement of the classroom. (Chapter 11 discusses hearing handicapped children.)

Neurological impairment, or "brain damage," can affect a child's language and speech development in a variety of ways. Some of these young children make so many mistakes in articulation and use such unusual speech patterns they can hardly be understood. Such severe problems are frequently called *articulation disorders,* and therapy is recommended.

Many children with neurological damage have trouble with grammar and syntax. This difficulty often appears while the child is still in preschool. In some instances, the language handicap may be related to auditory perception and discrimination difficulties which affect the child's ability to understand spoken language. As a consequence, the child may not be able to respond consistently or as quickly as the teacher expects.

Children who have suffered neurological damage may have problems in the areas of receptive language, expressive language, or speech—or in all three areas. These children are often acutely aware of their difficulties. They may stop trying to communicate because they have so much trouble saying words and putting them together. The teacher needs to give special attention to keep these children in the communicative interaction.

Autistic withdrawal is a communication or relating problem, involving four types of behaviors: unresponsiveness to social stimuli, gaze aversion, self-stimulation and fantasy, and language disorders (Kauffman, 1977). Many autistic children do not talk. Sometimes they echo what they hear. However, it is possible to teach some autistic children to use a few words. Occasionally, some develop a repertoire of stereotyped phrases, but even then they may not use the phrases to communicate with others in a meaningful way. These children require consistent training over a long period of time to improve at all. They are usually served in special, self-contained classrooms.

Environmental deprivation, usually associated with poverty, can be a cause of language delay in young children. A child who is not stimulated enough at home, who does not interact with his parents or other adults, may have trouble relating to others; he may have a limited vocabulary and be a poor listener. Frequently, the deprived child uses *this* and *that* in place of specific nouns. There is little variety in sentence structure, and the verbs are limited to little more than *need, have,* and *want.*

It is sometimes difficult to know whether a lack of language skills is due to environmental deprivation, mental retardation, or neurological damage. Children whose poor language skills are the result of deprivation usually make rapid progress when they are exposed to a stimulating environment, especially if some special strategies or language programs are used. The preschool teacher has a major responsibility to identify these children early before their lack of language becomes a major handicap for learning.

THE COMMUNICATION DISORDERS SPECIALIST

In the last 20 years, a growing concern about the retarded child has led us to study the language development of all young children. It is now recognized that language is an early indicator of educational problems. In addition to the *language improvement programs* which were once a part of kindergarten curricula and now are included in many preschools (sometimes called *language stimulation programs*), we have *language therapy* for young children. This therapy is provided by private practitioners, in clinics, and through school systems.

Interaction of Clinicians and Teachers

In many schools, therapy sessions are held outside the children's classroom. A disadvantage of this situation is that the teacher and clinician, or trained specialist, may not have a chance to work together. Often the specialist—an itinerant teacher—must divide his time among several schools, which makes meeting with the classroom teacher more difficult.

In some buildings, the clinicians are assigned a space, sometimes called a *resource room*. This has the advantage of making the specialist available for conferences with the teacher.

Many clinicians and teachers welcome the opportunity to work in the same room. The benefits of keeping each other informed about programs and progress and the bonus of sharing materials generally outweigh the inconveniences of arranging space and schedules.

The speech, language, and hearing services provided to children vary with state requirements, with professional certification requirements, and with the emphases of the various training institutions across the country.

Changes in Names of Specialists

Thirty to forty years ago the term *speech therapist* was used to identify those who had graduated from "speech correction" programs. Some of these specialists also helped elementary school teachers with "speech improvement" programs. "Language" work was largely done with adults who had suffered brain injury or with hearing handicapped children who had not learned

language well because they had not heard expressive language clearly.

Today the title *speech-language clinician* is replacing the title *speech therapist*. The field has so expanded that some clinicians are specializing in speech and language work with young children. The emerging term is *communication disorders specialist* or *communication specialist*. This title reflects our major aim—improved communication for the child. It is used in some states to indicate certification for a level of competence rather than for an academic degree. Some states expect the specialist to be able to help teachers with classroom programming and activities as well as to work with individuals and small groups of children outside the class.

This consultant role is particularly useful in early education settings, for several reasons, including the following:

1. Young children do not have long attention spans. Frequent short sessions are possible when the specialist is working within the classroom on a regular basis. It is also a more comfortable setting for the young child.

2. The language program must be directly related to the child's current level of communication. When teacher and specialist work together closely, it is easier to exchange relevant information about the child's skills.

3. The child needs many opportunities to practice newly learned behaviors if they are to become habits. The communication disorders specialist can help the teacher provide special opportunities for integrating new skills into day-by-day communication, within the regular classroom program.

Speech pathologists are now doing a lot of work with young children in the language area; work with infants is under way. This title is still used in private, university, and hospital clinics and is appropriate for all professional persons certified by the

American Speech and Hearing Association.

The Team Process

When members of different disciplines—in this case, teachers and communication specialists—work together on a regular basis, guidelines and procedures can define mutual expectations and reduce anxiety over roles.

Screening instruments can alert the teacher to any discrepancy between the child's development in language as compared with development in other areas. In some programs, the communication specialist customarily does the speech and language screening. Whatever the procedure, it is important for the teacher and communication specialist to compare their assessments of the child's development.

Using the Communication Model as a Team

The Communication Model (Figure 4.5) provides an excellent basis for teamwork. If the teacher identifies a problem in day-to-day classroom communications, he can relay the following important information to the communication disorders specialist: (1) the needs of the child in the classroom, (2) the types of communication opportunities already existing, and (3) the times and situations when the teacher can or does listen to the child.

The communication specialist can then identify the kinds of additional classroom data needed. The specialist may collect the data himself or supervise the collection. These data from the communicating environment help determine the child's communication behaviors, what factors may affect his communication in that setting, and what might be done to provide more and better communication opportunities.

Using Other Assessments

The communication disorders specialist may administer some speech and language assessments to determine (1) what the child is able to do in some specific tasks, (2) how she performs in an individual setting, (3) what her strengths are as well as her weaknesses, and (4) at what developmental level she is functioning for each task. This information is required for the child's individual educational plan. It probably also gives some clues as to the benefit of individual therapy. When specific deficiencies are discovered and teaching strategies are recommended, the team decides who does what.

Using Information from Other Professions

Sometimes the team needs information from other professions. Nurses, social workers, psychologists, psychiatrists, and nutritionists, to name only a few, may also be part of the team. Frequently the combined efforts of all are required to unravel the problems which started as a communication problem.

Following the Child's Progress as a Team

The teacher and communication specialist who work as a team to identify problems and work out programs are more likely to keep in touch about the child's progress. The teacher benefits from regular contact with the communication specialist as she helps the child use new skills.

Some communication deficiencies, once identified, can be easily corrected, and the child quickly adapts his newly learned skills to the classroom. For other children, particularly those in special programs, long-standing habits and years of failure make change more difficult. Special efforts may be needed to help them use their new skills.

PUBLISHED LANGUAGE PROGRAMS

The importance of speech and language skills, the growing recognition that early intervention is essential, and the mandating of programs for the handicapped have encouraged the publication of many language programs for young children. Some of these programs have been designed for parents but can be readily adapted for the preschool classroom. Some are written for use with groups of children; some that are written for individual work can be adapted to groups. Some of the programs include assessment forms and provide lessons related to the results of the assessments. Other published programs assume that assessments have been completed and that the teacher has made the appropriate selection of those programs based on the behaviors to be taught and on the specific needs of a given child.

It is important to recognize that published language programs differ in emphasis. When a program is selected, the teacher must know what skills the child needs to begin the program and what skills or behaviors the child can be expected to acquire. Some programs provide suggestions for checking the generalization of the speech or language behavior. If these are not included, the teacher must plan activities to show whether or not the new behavior occurs in the regular classroom program.

It is impossible to list all published programs. The following examples show the variety of programs available. The teacher or the communication disorders specialist who plans to use a published program should select the one which seems most appropriate and then make the adaptations necessary to assure the child's success.

Functional Speech and Language Training for the Severely Handicapped; I and II (Guess, Sailor, & Baer, 1976). This program contains 60 training steps to help a child develop language skills in six content areas: persons and things, actions with persons and things, possession, color, size, relation and location. The child should develop functional sentences. Generalization steps are included in the program. *Functional Speech and Language Training* is behaviorally written and the training goals, instructions, and procedures are clearly specified. The books include scoring sheets and instructions for keeping data. It would be helpful if the teacher is already familiar with behavior principles.

Non-Vocal Communication Techniques and Aids for the Severely Physically Handicapped (Vanderheiden & Grilley, 1976).

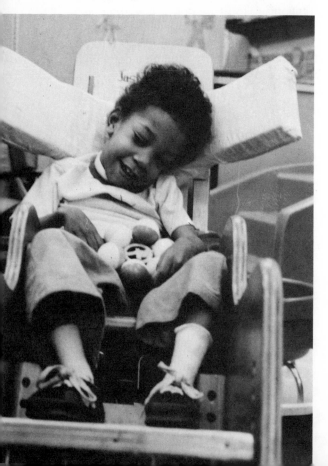

Justin, who has cerebral palsy, cannot talk yet. But with new aids and programs, he is learning to communicate with the world around him.

This material is an excellent compilation of alternate communication systems for children who are not able to use oral language. The systems include communication boards, simple graphic symbols to represent words and concepts (Blissymbolics), and descriptions of a variety of manual and electronic devices. Entry skills are specified for each of the communication aids. Many of these aids have been used with children with cerebral palsy and some have been used with the mentally retarded. There is helpful material on communication assessment with suggestions for adapting assessment forms. The reader will appreciate the diagrams in the book and the reference section which lists many communication aids, their publishers, and descriptions.

The Environmental Language Intervention Program (MacDonald & Horstmeier, 1978). This program was developed by James McDonald and the staff at the Nisonger Center at Ohio State University. Designed for the multiply handicapped, including those who have not yet developed verbal communication, the focus is on children under 6 years old. It has been successfully used with retarded children, cerebral palsied children who are capable of speech, and other language-delayed individuals. Goals are specified in terms of behavioral competencies, and the program relates language and speech behaviors to interaction strategies. The program includes prelanguage assessment material (*The Environmental Prelanguage Battery*), a language assessment tool (*The Environmental Language Inventory*), a tool for assessing the communication between a parent and a child (*OLIVER*), and a parent-training book (*Ready, Set, Go—Talk to Me*). The authors suggest that materials from the child's environment be used. In addition to the procedures for eliciting each of the prelanguage

or language behaviors, attention is given to generalization of the behaviors.

Teaching Aphasics and Other Language Deficient Children (DuBard, 1974). This publication presents a teaching method developed particularly for disorders of language which result from central nervous system dysfunction. It is suitable for children who are nonverbal but have normal intellectual potential. The program emphasizes visual presentation and includes reading and writing skills. It is more appropriately introduced to the older preschool child. The teacher will find training procedures in the manual, sequences of instruction, and many helpful sample lessons which emphasize sound production and grammar.

Teaching Makes a Difference (Donnellan-Walsh, Gossage, LaVigna, Schuler, & Traphagen, 1976). This program was developed in the Santa Barbara, California, County Schools and has been prepared for those who work with autistic children. The emphasis is on acquiring communication skills. One section deals specifically with procedures for teaching communication and language. It includes work on appropriate responses and eliminating echoing responses (*echolalia*). The material also gives suggestions for advancing from individual instruction to group instruction. The teacher's manual includes suggestions for generalization and a section on alternative systems of communication. The material is behavioral, and data-collection systems are explained.

DISTAR Language (Engelmann, Osborn, & Engelmann, 1969.) This is an instructional system which concentrates on the language skills of culturally disadvantaged children. The lessons are designed for small groups of children, preschool aged and older. The instructions for the teacher are specific, as are the responses expected of the children. The materials are easy to handle and tests are provided. The system addresses itself to the school readiness skills in the Communication Model (Figure 4.5).

FOR MORE INFORMATION

Most of these resources are textbooks that are readily available. Check your instructor, the education library, or the general library at your school.

Bloom, L., & Lahey, M. *Language development and language disorders*. New York: Wiley, 1977.

Cazden, C.B. *Child language and education*. New York: Holt, Rinehart & Winston, 1972.

Dale, P.S. *Language development: Structure and function* (2nd ed.). New York: Holt, Rinehart & Winston, 1976.

McLean, J.E., & Snyder-McLean, L.K. *A transactional approach to early language training*. Columbus, Ohio: Charles E. Merrill, 1978.

Rieke, J., Lynch, L., & Soltman, S. *Teaching strategies for language development*. New York: Grune & Stratton, 1977.

Schiefelbusch, R.L., & Lloyd, L.L. (Eds.). *Language perspectives—Acquisition, retardation and intervention*. Baltimore: University Park Press, 1974.

Perspectives on the Mildly Handicapped

As we've seen in the last three chapters, it is critical to consider handicapped children from a developmental point of view. Such a view allows us to begin as early as possible to prevent or overcome delays in the child's growth and learning. As we've also seen, though, this concern with the very young child is a new one for many special educators. Historically, special education in America has been concerned mainly with the school-aged child, and with activities to help "slow learners" succeed in school. Special education teachers traditionally have worked in separate classrooms set aside for "EMR" (Educable Mentally Retarded) children, for "ED" (Emotionally Disturbed) children, or, in recent years, for "LD" (Learning Disabled) children.

For the most part, we tend to think of education as *schooling,* and these handicapped children who were allowed to remain in the regular public schools were the ones with relatively mild handicaps. (As we will see in later chapters, school for other handicapped children—blind, deaf, or physically handicapped—very often meant a *separate* school.) Thus, these separate classes for children with mild handicaps—mild retardation, emotional disturbance, or learning problems—amounted to looking at them

from an *educational* point of view. And the labels they were given, *EMR, ED, LD* (and several others you'll soon read about), were more or less efforts to identify the *causes* of the educational delays the children experienced.

In many ways, this view of handicapped children is seriously outdated. This is due to the growing awareness that all children—no matter how severe their handicaps—*can* and *will* learn if programs are carefully arranged to meet their individual needs. In fact, the passage of P.L. 94–142 *guarantees* each and every handicapped child the opportunity for an education appropriate for him or her. Still, there are some advantages in looking at mildly handicapped children in terms of the educational programs and other services they need. For one, we can see that these children make up the majority of the handicapped who will be "mainstreamed," or integrated into regular public school classes. For most of these children, the law's demand for education in the "least restrictive environment" is a demand that they spend much of their time in regular classes with nonhandicapped children. And this situation presents some of the most pressing concerns we now face in both regular and special education.

While the Bureau for Education of the Handicapped has encouraged inservice training programs for regular teachers to gain skills to teach children, there are still problems. Not all teachers are adequately trained yet. Not all teachers are even convinced they want to deal with handicapped children, even if they could do so effectively. Not all parents, either of handicapped or nonhandicapped children, want mainstreaming. Not all principals and administrators fully understand or sympathize with the effort to mainstream these children. In addition, we must face the fact that teaching handicapped children in regular classes requires at least as much teaching skill and professional competence as teaching them in special education classes. And add to these the skills necessary to teach both normal and bright children, all in the same class. At the very least, then, success in integrating handicapped children in regular classes will depend on more training, more support from special educators, more carefully developed learning materials, and more flexibility in organizing programs and services than we have seen so far.

To achieve the goal of teaching the mildly handicapped child in the least restrictive environment, two resources will no doubt prove to be major assets. These are the use of systematic instruction and an increased reliance on the special education resource room.

Systematic instruction, as we noted in chapter 1, is a series of procedures for assessing each individual child's needs, for carefully arranging instruction to meet those needs, for monitoring progress, and for predicting failure before it has a chance to happen. Together with a number of related procedures for arranging and managing the classroom effectively, they offer teachers the necessary skills to help the mildly handicapped child learn successfully.

In addition, the special education resource room offers the mildly handicapped child a chance to get the highly individualized attention he may need to overcome his most serious learning difficulties. Staffed by a trained resource specialist, often with one or more instructional aides, the resource room can provide necessary special instruction, special materials and equipment, or other special arrangements and services that the regular classroom cannot be expected to offer. A child spends only part of the day in the resource room, for reading or math or language arts instruction, and then returns to the regular class to spend the rest of the day with his nonhandicapped peers. For many mildly handicapped children, the resource room is an important factor in allowing the regular classroom to be the "least restrictive alternative" for them to learn. (Be sure to note the special color photo essay on the resource room that appears in this next section.)

The next three chapters, then, describe exceptional children from the educational point of view we have examined here. Jim Payne and Carol Thomas introduce you to the study of mental retardation, its history and its current focus. Throughout their chapter, Payne and Thomas point out that retardation can vary in severity from mild to profound, but they concentrate on the mildly and moderately retarded. (These are the ranges of retarded children whom you can expect to see most often in public schools with nonhandicapped children.) Ron Reeve and Jim Kauffman introduce you to children with behavior disorders, pointing out the different theories about how best to help them overcome such problems. Finally, Tom Lovitt describes the newest "category" of handicapped children, those with learning disabilities. Besides describing the variety of learning problems grouped under this label, he gives you an expanded look at systematic instructional procedures (see his section on Precision Teaching).

5

The Mentally Retarded

James S. Payne
Carol Thomas

These are the major topics covered in this chapter. You may want to use them as a checklist when you review.

- *The four eras in the treatment of the mentally retarded.*
- *The currently accepted definition of mental retardation.*
- *The relevance of current legislation to working with the mentally retarded.*
- *Current management models for the mentally retarded.*
- *Some early intervention programs.*
- *The use of systematic instruction with the mentally retarded.*
- *The role of medical science in the prevention and treatment of mental retardation.*

Chapter five

HISTORY OF MENTAL RETARDATION

Although much attention is being given to mental retardation today, the condition itself is far from being new. Most probably mental retardation has existed for as long as people have inhabited the earth. Evidence has been found in early writings and in the form of skulls recovered from ancient graves. Papyrus writings of Thebes dating as early as 1552 B.C. refer to mentally retarded persons, as do passages from the Bible and literature of the Greek and Roman empires (Ellis, 1975). Archaelogical and anthropological studies have uncovered a microcephalic skull from an eleventh century Irish grave, evidence of mongolism in remains in an Anglo-Saxon burial ground, and a hydrocephalic skull from the Nile valley, dating from the period of A.D. 350–550 (Jordan, 1976).*

Kanner (1964) provides an interesting review of the terms used for the mentally retarded throughout literature. The earliest term found in the literature is the Latin *fatuus,* said to be a person "who understands neither what he says himself nor what others say" (p. 4). Persons in love were considered similarily afflicted, and the word *infatuation* appeared. *Amens* and *demens,* Latin counterparts of more recent terms, were referred to in the dictionary of Bishop Isidorus (560–636). The distinction between the two is that "the amens has no mind at all whereas a demens has retained part of his mind" (p. 4). The term *idiot* is derived from a Greek word meaning "a private person." It was used to describe "the unsophisticated layman without professional knowledge," and later, "an ignorant and ill-informed individual" (p. 5). Roman writers used the term *imbecillis* to mean "weak of mind," a less severe disability

than connoted by *idiot.* The term *dunce* has been used as a synonym for mentally retarded. This term has been traced to the fourteenth century scholastic theologian John Duns Scotus. In the sixteenth century his works were severely criticized and his followers called *Duns—Dunce.* The word *dunce* later took on the meaning dull, obstinate person not capable of learning. *Fool* and *jester* were the terms used in Rome for mental defectives who were kept to amuse the households of the wealthy.

Because of the long history of retardation, many writers have described specific time periods as being characteristic of typical feelings or attitudes toward the retarded (Hewett & Forness, 1974; Kauffman & Payne, 1975). One such conceptualization (Kolstoe & Frey, 1965) uses four treatment eras: extermination, ridicule, asylum, and education.

Era of Extermination

Survival was the goal of primitive human beings. The weak or physically abnormal were destroyed or abandoned because they could not contribute equally to the society. Those who did survive infancy faced a hostile natural environment demanding strength and courage.

Both the Greeks and Romans destroyed some weak members of society. The Roman father was given the power of life or death over infants who were deformed or female. In Sparta, defective infants were thrown from cliffs (Hewett & Forness, 1974). Plato (427?–347 B.C.), in Book V of the *Republic,* presents his views on the treatment of inferior children:

> The proper officer will take the offspring of the good to the pen or fold, and there they will deposit them with certain nurses who dwell in a separate quarter; but the offspring of the inferior, or of the better when they chance to be deformed, will be put away in some mysterious, unknown place, as they should be. (In Hutchins, 1952, p. 362)

---

*Microcephalus, mongolism, and hydrocephalus are all associated with mental retardation.

During this same era, there was an exception to this type of treatment in Egypt. According to Hewett and Forness (1974), the Egyptians believed in immortality and did not allow infanticide.

Era of Ridicule

A somewhat more humanitarian attitude followed as the struggle for survival became less pressing. While more defective people were spared, they were often abandoned. Some survivors became slaves; others were taken by beggars and deliberately maimed and used to solicit alms. Wealthy Romans kept *fools* or *imbeciles* to amuse their households and guests. Kanner (1964) relates a portion of a letter from Seneca (4 B.C.?–A.D. 65) describing such a situation.

> You know that Herpaste, my wife's fool (fatua), was left on my hands as a hereditary charge, for I have a natural aversion to these monsters. . . . This fool has suddenly lost her sight. I am telling you a strange but true story. She is not aware that she is blind and constantly urges her keeper to take her out because she says my house is dark. (pp. 5–6)

Later, a select few of the mentally retarded were employed as court jesters and as pseudocompanions of wealthy individuals. The majority of mental defectives, however, did not fare as well as those kept for entertainment in wealthy households.

Era of Asylum

Religion became the dominant force of change during the Middle Ages. Christianity brought with it more humanitarian treatment for the mentally defective—the retarded—while the mentally ill—the "mad"—were felt to be possessed by demons and often persecuted (Hewett & Forness, 1974). The mentally handicapped became wards of the church and were cared for in monasteries and asylums (Kauffman & Payne, 1975).

Era of Education

Very gradually concern for education evolved from concern for custodial care. Rather than simply housing the mentally handicapped, efforts were directed towards education and rehabilitation. English philosopher John Locke's ideas and theories allowed the possibility of changing the condition of mental retardation through instruction. In 1690 he attempted to distinguish between mental retardation and mental illness. In his essay *Concerning Human Understanding,* he says:

> In short, herein seems to lie the difference between idiots and madness: that madmen put wrong ideas together, and so make wrong propositions, but argue and reason right from them; but idiots make very few or no propositions, and reason scarce at all. (In Hutchins, 1952, p. 146)

Locke's *tabula rasa*—"empty tablet"—theory portrays a human being's mind as a blank paper upon which experiences are written. Since each person is a product of a certain environment, alterations of that environment could modify behavior. Followers of this point of view were called *sensationalists,* referring to the importance of the senses as the avenues by which the environment is experienced.

One sensationalist was Jean-Marc-Gaspard Itard, a French physician. When in 1799 a wild boy was captured in the forest of Aveyron, Itard was persuaded to work with the 12-year-old by a professor of natural history, Bonaterre. Bonaterre argued that finding Victor, as the boy came to be called, offered an exceptional opportunity for the sensationalists. If Victor's mind were an empty tablet, it should be possible to make impressions on it by appropriate sensory stimulation (Kolstoe, 1972).

Taking up the challenge, Itard determined five principal aims for Victor's mental and moral education: (a) developing an interest in social life, (b) awakening his nervous sensibility, (c) extending his range of ideas, (d) leading him to speak, and (e)

Chapter five

inducing him to use simple mental operations. After 5 years of intensive work, Itard abandoned his goals. Victor remained in the care of his governess, Madame Guerin, until his death in 1828. Although Itard felt that he had failed in his mission, Victor's behavior had greatly changed. He eventually was able to identify certain vowel sounds and to read and write a few words. Itard later published a detailed account of his work with Victor in the classic *The Wild Boy of Aveyron* (Itard, 1894/1962).

Edouard Seguin studied medicine and surgery under Itard. At the age of 25, he spent 18 months in a concentrated effort to educate a retarded boy. Because of his success, he began working with more children. After leaving France during the French Revolution, he settled in the United States, where he later founded the Pennsylvania Training School. The educational program for which he is known combines instruction of the muscle system, touch, hearing, speech, and visual abilities in a whole-child approach, rather than training each sense separately as Itard advocated. Furthermore, he developed a training sequence for basic to complex learning (Kolstoe, 1972).

Another pioneer in the field of retardation was Johann Jacob Guggenbühl, a Swiss physician. Guggenbühl became interested in the possibility of remediating mentally defective children from the Alps, known as cretins. He gave up his small practice and devoted his efforts to the establishment of an institution on the Abendberg, near Interlaken. He emphasized care of the body and development of sensory perceptions. Guggenbühl was highly praised for his work and became internationally famous. Unfortunately, conditions at the Abendberg deteriorated rapidly due to mismanagement, and it closed at about the time a number of other institutions patterned after it were beginning to flourish. While Guggenbühl has been severely criticized

for his failure to maintain standards of treatment and care, he is recognized as the originator of institutional care for the retarded. His work generated a great deal of interest and concern.

One of the early visitors to the Abendberg was Samuel Gridley Howe of Massachusetts. Howe had already taken an active interest in the education of blind and deaf children (see chapter 12 for a profile of Howe). His work with several blind children at the house of Colonel Thomas H. Perkins became the foundation for the Perkins Institute for the Blind. His broad interests included new instructional methods for the blind and deaf, educational reform, and emancipation of slaves. His untiring efforts on behalf of the mentally deficient led to the establishment of the first institution for the retarded in the Western hemisphere (Kanner, 1964).

As large residential facilities were constructed during the last part of the nineteenth century, responsibility for the mentally retarded and mentally ill shifted to the states. These state institutions rapidly became overcrowded and, in many instances, failed to provide adequate care and treatment (Farber, 1968). By the early 1900s, however, systematic release and parole systems began to be implemented. This change helped lead to the development of halfway houses and social service departments.

Models for Management

Today, the most common models for managing the mentally retarded may be broadly classified as residential institutions, regional facilities, community agencies, neighborhood services, and public schools (Leland & Smith, 1974).

Institutional Care

State hospitals, or schools or private institutions for those who can afford them, still offer 24-hour residential care. But these institutions are today being criticized as understaffed, with overcrowded and outdated facilities, and providing for only minimum health and educational needs.

Although institutions have played a vital role in the development of services for the mentally retarded, the current trend is towards a more normal setting. Wolfensberger (1972) defined this principle of normalization as "utilization of means which are as culturally normative as possible in order to establish and/or maintain personal behavior and characteristics which are as culturally normative as possible" (p. 28). Deinstitutionalization, as described by Wolfensberger (1976), is one of the major avenues towards accomplishing this goal.

> I can see no reason why small, specialized living units (mostly hostels) cannot accommodate all of the persons now in institutions. In turn, I believe that many persons who could be well served in hostels will be served even better in individual placements. . . . Furthermore, any feature of a residential service that is normalizing will increase the likelihood that the resident will either return to his family, move to a more advanced form of residence (e.g., from hostel to apartment or boarding), or be fully rehabilitated. (p. 420)

Regional Facilities

Regional facilities, in essence, are small institutions that accommodate all those needing institutional placement within a particular area or region. Because the patient remains in closer proximity to the family home, there may be less individualization for specialized needs.

Community Services

The development of community services has greatly increased the options open to parents for the care of their retarded children. Services available within a community might include clinics for evaluation and diagnosis, day-care centers, and sheltered workshops.

Neighborhood Services

Neighborhood services are local provisions for day-to-day health, education, and welfare services. These include contacts with private physicians or public health nurses.

Public Schools

When the retarded child enters public school, the traditional placement has been in self-contained classrooms either for the **educable mentally retarded** (EMR) or for the **trainable mentally retarded** (TMR). The trend towards normalization has returned many EMR youngsters to the regular classroom for the full day or for portions of the day; they spend the remainder of the day

Melinda lives in a group home where she cares for the bedroom she shares with one other retarded woman.

FOR MORE SUPPORT

American Association on Mental Deficiency (AAMD)

The AAMD is a national organization for professional persons as well as students and other individuals who are interested in the general welfare of the mentally retarded and in the study of cause, treatment, and prevention of mental retardation. Divisions of the AAMD include: Administration, Education, Medicine, Nursing, Physical Therapy, Psychology, Social Work, Speech Pathology and Audiology, and Vocational Rehabilitation, as well as a General Section and many subsections.

Committees include: International Activities; Joint Committee on the Deaf Retarded; Legislative and Social Issues; Non-White Affairs; Research, Terminology and Classification; and Use and Construction of Data Banks.

The AAMD publishes the American Journal on Mental Deficiency, Mental Retardation, Directory of Members, Directory of Residential Facilities, and varied monographs.

Council for Exceptional Children (CEC)

CEC's membership includes teachers, school administrators, and teacher educators who are concerned with children whose instructional needs require special services.

Divisions of CEC include: Association for the Gifted; Children with Learning Disabilities; Council of Administrators of Special Education; Council for Children with Behavioral Disorders; Mental Retardation; Physically Handicapped, Homebound, and Hospitalized; Teacher Education; Visually Handicapped; Career Development; and Partially Seeing and Blind.

Committees include: Canadian Affairs; Early Childhood Education; International Relations; Minority Groups; Professional Standards; and Research.

CEC publishes Exceptional Children and Teaching Exceptional Children. Each division also publishes its own journal and/or news bulletin.

National Association for Retarded Citizens (NARC)

with a resource teacher for individualized instruction. Paraprofessionals are also being increasingly used to provide additional help. Paraprofessionals help provide the individual attention that is so important in the teaching/learning process.

DEFINITIONS

One current concern in the field of education of the mentally retarded is defining the condition. Historically, as we have seen, the retarded have been called *idiots, dunces, fools, imbeciles,* and many other derogatory names. In this century, several definitions have been developed in the attempt

to dispel some of the confusion generated by vague, negative terminology. Tredgold (1937) and Doll (1941) wrote two of the most frequently quoted definitions. Tredgold refers to mental *deficiency* as:

> A state of incomplete mental development of such a kind and degree that the individual is incapable of adapting himself to the normal environment of his fellows in such a way to maintain existence independently of supervision, control, or external support. (p. 4)

Doll's definition reads:

> We observe that six criteria by statement or implication have been generally considered essential to an adequate definition and concept. These are (1) social incompe-

Parents, professional workers, and others interested in the mentally retarded work through NARC to promote treatment, research, public understanding, and legislation for the mentally retarded.

Committees of NARC include Architectual Planning, Early Child Care, Education, Governmental Affairs, International Relations, Poverty, Public Health, Recreation, Religious Nurture, Research Advisory Board, Residential Services, Vocational Rehabilitation, and Adult Services.

It publishes Mental Retardation News *and many documents primarily distributed to parents of retarded children.*

National Rehabilitation Association (NRA)

The membership of NRA includes physicans, counselors, therapists, disability examiners, vocational evaluators, and other individuals interested in the rehabilitation of the physically and mentally handicapped and the socially disadvantaged.

Publications of the NRA include Journal of Rehabilitation, NRA Newsletter, *and* Legislative Newsletter.

tence, (2) due to mental subnormality, (3) which has been developmentally arrested, (4) which obtains [is exhibited] at maturity, (5) is of constitutional origin and (6) is essentially incurable. (p. 215)

The most commonly used definitions in recent years have been those developed by the American Association on Mental Deficiency (AAMD). Under the direction of Rick Heber, in 1959 the AAMD published a manual on terminology and classification of mental retardation which was somewhat revised in 1961. Under the chairmanship of Herbert Grossman, a revised manual was published in 1973. These definitions are commonly referred to as the Heber and Grossman definitions. The Heber (1961) definition of mental retardation stated:

> Mental retardation refers to subaverage general intellectual functioning which originates during the developmental period and is associated with impairment in adaptive behavior. (p. 3)

In this definition, "subaverage general intellectual functioning" refers to earning a score on a standardized intelligence test of one or more standard deviations below the mean. Some of these tests are listed in the appendix of this book. "Adaptive behavior" refers to such behaviors as sensory-motor skills, communication, self-help, socialization, academic progress, and vocational skills. The "developmental period" encompasses the years from birth to age 16 (see chapters 1 through 4).

In 1973 Heber's definition was revised by Grossman to read as follows:

> Mental retardation refers to significantly subaverage general intellectual functioning existing concurrently with deficits in adaptive behavior, and manifested during the developmental period. (p. 11)

There are important differences between the earlier and the revised definitions which reflect the current trend towards a more conservative definition of mental retardation. In the Grossman revision "significantly subaverage" refers to earning a score on an individual standardized intelligence test of two or more standard deviations below the mean, as opposed to one or more standard deviations. The Grossman definition also extends the developmental period of 16 years to 18 years, thus covering the average period of public education. While "adaptive behavior" is included in both definitions, Grossman indicates that it must *coexist* with intelligence rather than merely be *associated* or connected with intelligence. This reflects the current movement away from classifying a child as mentally retarded solely on the basis of an intelligence test score. The importance of adaptive behavior is gaining universal acceptance. It implies that retardation may be situation-specific and that the condition is alterable. According to the two criteria then, a child who functions adequately within the community or in the school is not considered to be mentally retarded even though he scores within the retarded range on a standardized intelligence test. By the same token, an individual determined to be mentally retarded during school years may not be considered so after leaving school and functioning successfully on the job.

While the AAMD definition of mental retardation continues to be the most widely accepted, the search continues for other definitions. Dunn (1973), among other noted persons in the field, proposed that the term *mental retardation* be abandoned because it has negative connotations and because it does not relate to education. His suggested alternative is the term **general learning disabilities,** which he defines as follows:

> Pupils with general learning disabilities are those who require special education because they score no higher than the second percentile for their ethnic or racial subgroup on both verbal and performance types of individual test batteries administered in their most facile language. (p. 68)

While there may be some justification for developing a more positive and/or restrictive definition of mental retardation, the major professional organizations actively serving the retarded advocate the use of the AAMD definition. These organizations stress the need to work towards uniform adherence to the standards already set forth by AAMD for classification and placement.

Levels of Severity of Mental Retardation

The AAMD terminology manual (Grossman, 1973) also classifies retardation according to levels of severity. Table 5.1 gives the

corresponding IQ score for each level (as defined by Grossman) on the two most widely used individual standardized intelligence tests. Note that the levels of severity of mental retardation are identified according to intelligence test scores, and yet both the Heber and Grossman definitions contain dual criteria (subaverage intellectual functioning and impairment in adaptive behavior).

Table 5.1
Levels of retardation

Levels	Intelligence test	
	Stanford-Binet	Wechsler
Mild	68–52	69–55
Moderate	51–36	54–40
Severe	35–20	39–25
Profound	19 and below	24 and below

Mildly Retarded

Public schools usually refer to individuals at this level as "educable mentally retarded." Such a child can be effectively educated within the regular classroom at the elementary level with individualized instruction and with the help of specialists such as a resource teacher. In the upper elementary grades or at the junior high level, prevocational skills may be introduced, along with the essential and practical academics necessary for independent living. During high school, vocational training is emphasized, possibly with work-study programs, while academic classes continue teaching practical life skills. More and more, mildly retarded students are being incorporated into the regular vocational program offered by the junior or senior high school. A postschool follow-up program is important for providing continuing guidance for personal and job-related problems as well as for recreation and socialization.

Mildly retarded individuals are likely to be capable of handling semiskilled or unskilled jobs. They are able to care for their personal needs and have the communication skills necessary for independent or at least semiindependent living. Some can have satisfactory married lives (Robinson & Robinson 1976).

Moderately Retarded

The moderately retarded child is recognized early as being significantly delayed in development. Such children generally need a highly specialized program and are commonly placed in self-contained classes for the trainable mentally retarded. These classes concentrate on teaching the child to take care of her own needs and to get along with others. While she can generally care for her daily needs, such as dressing, preparing simple meals, and performing some household chores, she most likely will need much supervision throughout her life. While some may be capable of holding unskilled jobs, most moderately retarded adults who work do so in sheltered workshops where they are highly supervised. A sheltered workshop provides work that is usually uncomplicated and repetitious.

Severely and Profoundly Retarded

Robinson and Robinson (1976) characterize the severely retarded as likely to have sustained damage to the nervous system. Training for such individuals must be directed towards developing language and taking care of cleanliness and health needs. A highly supervised environment is considered necessary, as these people often show little independent behavior.(See chapter 8 also.)

Profoundly retarded individuals generally are not able to care for and protect themselves (see the discussion in chapter 9). Many are restricted to a bed or wheelchair

profile DANNY

Danny is a 17-year-old student at Roosevelt High School. He is enrolled in a work-study program where he is in school in the morning and works in the afternoon at a service station. In his special education math class, he is learning to count change; in reading class he is studying the importance of good grooming; in the regular gym class he is learning tumbling. His afternoon work site is six blocks from school, and he rides his bike to and from work. When asked what he likes most about working, he responds with a smile, "Getting out of school." His employer reports that he is doing satisfactorily, but he continues to make mistakes counting change and he can't handle a transaction using a credit card. He is liked by his coworkers and, if he learns to count change more accurately, he probably will be hired full-time after graduation.

profile ALICE

Alice is 10 years old and is in a class for the trainable mentally retarded. She has a tendency to drool and is being taught how to keep her tongue in her mouth, as well as to have proper posture, to look at the person she talks to, and to pay attention. She is somewhat overweight and is, in general, physically awkward. The teacher is concerned about her eating habits, coordination, finger dexterity, and poor language development. Her parents are beginning to question what will happen to Alice when she becomes high school age. All in all everyone seems concerned except Alice. She appears to be perfectly satisfied with her routine of getting up, going to school, going home, watching television, going to bed, day after day.

and require almost total supervision. Some may be able to learn to walk or feed themselves and respond to familiar commands (Robinson & Robinson, 1976).

While the severely and profoundly retarded certainly face limitations, recent
studies successfully using behavior management techniques offer some promise of
improved academic and social behavior.
Chapters 8 and 9 discuss these new pros-
pects in more detail.

RECENT RESEARCH ON ADAPTIVE BEHAVIOR

Since intelligence cannot be directly observed, it must be assessed indirectly
through testing and behavior to make descriptive, comparative, and/or predictive
statements about individual people. The
two tests most widely used for this purpose
are the Stanford-Binet Intelligence Scale
(Terman & Merrill, 1973) and the Revised
Wechsler Intelligence Scale for Children,
abbreviated WISC-R (Wechsler, 1974) (See
the appendix for a more extensive list of
intelligence tests.) Both are individual tests
tending to measure general mental
ability.

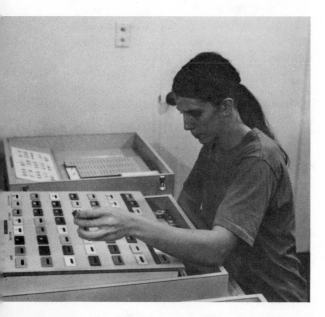

*Mindy's ability to sort by color and number is
assessed before she is given a workshop job.*

Tests have also been developed, however, to measure adaptive behavior. Adaptive behavior, according to the AAMD definition (Grossman, 1973), will be reflected in
the following areas according to age and
cultural group:

> During infancy and early childhood:
> **1.** Sensory-motor skills
> **2.** Communication skills
> **3.** Self-help skills
> **4.** Socialization
>
> During childhood and early adolescence:
> **5.** Basic academic and daily living skills
> **6.** Appropriate reasoning and judgment
> **7.** Social skills
>
> During late adolescence and adult life:
> **8.** Vocational and social skills. (p. 12)

While there are a number of scales for
measuring adaptive behavior, only two are
mentioned in the AAMD manual. These are
the *Vineland Social Maturity Scale* (Doll,
1965) and the *AAMD Adaptive Behavior
Scale* (Nihira, Foster, Shellhaas, & Leland,
1974). In the *Vineland,* basal and ceiling
ages are established and a social quotient
(SQ) is obtained. The purpose of the *AAMD
Adaptive Behavior Scale* is to provide objective descriptions and evaluations of how
effectively an individual copes with environmental demands. Another version of this
testing tool (Lambert, Windmiller, Cole, &
Figueroa, 1975) aids public school personnel in assessing adaptive behavior and in
specific areas for remediation.

One of the critical questions in testing
today is the evaluation of minority group
children. Jane Mercer (1971) conducted a
study in California and observed a dispro-
portionate number of Mexican-American
and black children obtaining IQ scores
below 80. The reason for this, according to
Mercer, is that clinical measures are interpreted from a culture-related perspective.
Her recommendation for minimizing the
vulnerability of minority children to being
labeled *mentally retarded* was to establish

This little girl has Down's syndrome, a chromosomal abnormality associated with retardation, often in the moderate to severe range.

separate norms for various sociocultural groups for current intelligence tests. An individual's score could then be interpreted with reference to the standard norms for his group to determine how well he might currently participate within the dominant culture. Interpretation of the individual's score within his own sociocultural group might indicate the probability of reaching a particular level in the dominant culture, given adequate education.

WHAT CAUSES RETARDATION?

It is difficult to discuss the causes of mental retardation adequately and accurately. Less than 6 percent of the cases of mental retardation have known causes, while 94 percent are unknown or unclassified. Jordan (1976) explains that the causes of mental retardation are "often unknown and when known are generally complex" (p. 448). Thus, when the cause is determined, the condition is often found to be the result of multiple interactions of agents or the absence of one or more crucial elements.

Basically, the problem of discussing cause in a realistic perspective is that the largest and most representative group of mentally retarded people—at least 80 percent—have only mild involvement and unknown causes. For the most part, the known causes are related to the less prevalent (moderate, severe, and profound) cases. However, the tendency in discussing "the causes of retardation" is to discuss the cases with established causes and ignore the bulk of cases which have unknown ones.

The majority of the mildly retarded are cultural-familial retardates (Dunn, 1973). *Cultural-familial* implies that the condition stems from a complex interaction of both environmental (cultural) and hereditary (familial) factors. Although there is no conclusive evidence concerning the causation of cultural-familial retardation, it is believed that the majority of cases are caused by early cultural and social inadequacies.

The terms *clinical* and *pathological* are now used in reference to brain damage as well as other commonly known causes of mental retardation. These pathological causes also include:

1. Infections and intoxication,

2. Trauma and physical agent,

3. Metabolism and nutrition,

4. Gross brain disease (postnatal),

5. Prenatal influence,

6. Chromosomal abnormality,

7. Gestational disorders,

8. Psychiatric disorders. (Grossman, 1973, pp. 36–37)

EDUCATIONAL TREATMENT

Trends in Methodology

A great variety of management techniques have been used with retarded children. As

Chapter five

profile **HERBERT GOLDSTEIN**

Herbert Goldstein has gained national prominence in the area of curriculum development and is particularly noted for his contributions in social and personal curricula. He became a public school teacher of retarded children after receiving his B.A. and M.A. degrees from San Francisco State College. In 1957 he received the Ed.D. degree from the University of Illinois, after which he became assistant and then associate professor at the Institute for Research on Exceptional Children, University of Illinois. In 1962 he became professor and chairman of the Department of Special Education at Yeshiva University, where he is now director of the Curriculum Research and Development Center in Mental Retardation, Ferkauf Graduate School of Humanities and Social Sciences.

Dr. Goldstein has been active in a number of professional organizations. He has been president of the Council for Exceptional Children. He has also chaired the research committee and has been a member of the Advisory and Management Service Committee of the American Association on Mental Deficiency. He has served as an adviser to the United Cerebral Palsy Research and Education Committee and consultant to Technical Assistance Development System in Early Education, University of North Carolina. Dr. Goldstein is also a former chairman of the Scientific Advisory Committee, National Program for Early Childhood Education.

Other accomplishments of Dr. Goldstein's include selection as a Fulbright scholar and lecturer in mental retardation and chairmanship of the Education Committee, Rehabilitation International, and of the Education Committee International, Association for the Scientific Study of Mental Retardation.

with any program or strategy, the effectiveness of a particular method relies heavily on the teacher's ability to use it as well as his personal feelings toward it.

Behavior Modification

Behavior modification is the most popular and common method used for teaching the mentally retarded. It has been used successfully with both retarded children and adults at various levels of severity. Behavior modification has been defined by Wallace and Kauffman (1978) as "any systematic arrangement of environmental events which produces a specific change in observable behavior" (p. 17). This principle has been successfully used with the retarded to decrease or do away with unwanted behaviors, reduce tendencies to maladaptive behavior, increase desired responses, and acquire complex behavior (Kauffman & Payne, 1975). Three trends in applying behavior modification methods with the mentally retarded are programmed instruction, contingency contracting, and token systems.

Programmed Instruction

Programmed instruction is commonly used with the retarded. The material to be learned is carefully sequenced and presented in small amounts. The student is able to work at his own pace, and response is usually immediate. Teaching machines and computerized programs are extensions of programmed instruction and have been successfully used with the retarded. While they do provide many of the same advantages as other methods of programmed instruction, they are considerably more costly.

Contingency Contracting

The use of contracts is a means of setting specific goals for the retarded student. They may be simple agreements between the student and the teacher concerning specific amounts of academic work, or they may concern complex behavioral changes. When the contract is fulfilled, the student gets a previously agreed-upon reward or activity. Figure 5.1 shows a sample contract.

Token System

Token economies have also proved useful in maintaining appropriate behavior and providing incentives for completing academic work. In a token economy the teacher gives the children tokens, points, check marks, poker chips, play currency, and so forth for certain previously specified behaviors. The tokens are later used as a medium of exchange for goods—for example, candy or toys—and services—for example, recess, tutoring help, or privileges.

This "menu" shows a first-grade class what they can buy with "worker points."

𝕮𝖔𝖓𝖙𝖗𝖆𝖈𝖙

I Will <u>*do twenty multiplications problems everyday during*</u>
<u>*my math period*</u>

<u>*Jerry Jeff Walker*</u>
(signed)

After successfully doing this I may <u>*play basketball outside for*</u>
<u>*fifteen minutes*</u>

<u>*Ms. L. Brooks*</u>
(signed)

Date signed <u>*January 6, 1976*</u>
Date completed <u>*January 7, 1976*</u>

Figure 5.1
Sample contract

Note. From *Strategies for Teaching the Mentally Retarded* by J.S. Payne, E.A. Polloway, J.E. Smith, Jr., and R.A. Payne, Columbus, Ohio: Charles E. Merrill Publishing Company, 1977, p. 77. Copyright 1977 by Bell & Howell Company. Used by permission.

Chapter five

Applied Behavior Analysis

Task analysis and the applied behavior analysis (ABA) approach have been applied to many areas of work with the mentally retarded. Three areas in which ABA has been effective are social behavior, language, and toileting.

In 1964 James Lent began his first experience with operant conditioning as a means of changing behavior of retarded persons. His concern centered around a number of retarded individuals working in various hospital jobs who were failing to do well for personal/social reasons. After talking with supervisors and making behavioral observations of what the workers did and said, Lent was able to determine certain observable behaviors that might be responsible for this failure. An example is the worker's avoidance of eye contact when a supervisor approached him, which was interpreted by the supervisor as resentment of authority. After determining such behaviors, Lent devised a plan to reward the workers for engaging in desirable alternative behavior. Selected workers were instructed that certain behavior was expected of them and, in turn, and that they would be paid for demonstrating the desired behavior. After a few weeks, the appropriate behaviors remained at a high, stable level. Lent's elation at his success is shown in his statement that

> the experience had a profound influence on my future career: not only had I been able to change behavior in ways that would benefit retarded people, but I knew exactly how I had done it, could do it again, and could even tell others how to do it. (p. 255)

Lent's experiment includes the main ingredients of ABA: direct measurement, daily measurement, replicable teaching procedures, individual analysis, and experimental control. This design has also been used with language training. One of the most recent programs done by William Bricker and Diane Bricker (Haring &

Schiefelbusch, 1976) was designed for young, developmentally delayed, language deficit children in a classroom setting. In an earlier program, the Autism Project, an applied behavioral approach to training receptive language was used with two autistic-like preschool age children. Each child was presented with an auditory clue—the name of the object—and then required to choose between two objects presented. If the child responded correctly, he found a reward under the object he had chosen. The children's correct and incorrect responses were continually assessed to insure that they were progressing through a sequence of more difficult tasks established for each goal. Bricker and Bricker stress the need to use specific tasks in developing assessment and training procedures not only for the autistic-like child but for the moderately and severely/profoundly retarded as well.

Foxx and Azrin (1973) have used behavior modification procedures for toilet training. Their procedure stresses "the importance of rewarding correct toileting, dealing with the toileting act one small step at a time, rewarding immediately and consistently, and eliminating unintended rewards for accidents" (p. 20). This particular approach uses devices to detect moisture on the pants of the person being trained and on the toilet. Each device emits a tone of a different frequency so that the caretaker knows if the elimination was appropriate (toilet) or inappropriate (pants). In this way, the trainer can give immediate praise or punishment. Foxx and Azrin developed a detailed sequential program with explicit instructions and forms to be filled in by the trainer.

In each of these examples, the researchers broke down a task or a desired behavior into very specific small steps. An exact sequence must be followed during training, and learning must be continuously assessed through observed behavior at each stage. This approach offers substantial hope for raising the level of functioning of many retarded people. See chapters 8 and 9 for summaries of some research studies using behavioral methodology with the severely and the profoundly retarded.

Imitation

Another technique used in educational management of the retarded is **imitative learning** or **observational learning** (Robinson & Robinson, 1976). This refers to patterning behavior after an observed model. Bandura (1969) has proposed a theory of observational learning that includes attention, retention of the observed behavior, and motoric response. The effectiveness of using modeling to change behavior has been noted by Altman and Talkington (1971). Some of the advantages they cite for using this approach over operant techniques are elimination of the necessity of breaking tasks into small steps and elimination of the use of reinforcers since the modeling itself is reinforcement. Turnure and Zigler (1964), among other researchers, have indicated that retarded individuals have a greater tendency than "normals" to look externally for clues as to how they are to behave or to perform ("outer-directed"). Reports of these studies offer support for the use of imitation (observational learning) as a tool for use with retarded.

A Major Issue and Need: Training of Special Educators

Over the last few years the question of how to train special educators has been developing into an important issue. Some institutions responsible for preparing teachers of the retarded are indicating a need for a competency-based approach.

Government interest in a systems approach to education and the current widespread emphasis on accountability have furthered a growing attitude that teachers should be responsible for children's learning and that teacher-training institutions should be responsible for developing effective and competent teachers.

The underlying assumption of performance-based teacher education is that learning is observable and therefore measurable. The teacher in training should be able to demonstrate a particular level of competency in bringing about and working with a learning environment that will result in altering specified student outcomes. One common problem with developing a **competency-based program** (Iannone, 1976) is the difficulty of agreeing upon the types and levels of competencies needed. Educators trained from a humanistic or psychoeducational viewpoint (see pp. 132–36) argue that by stating specific competencies, creativity and spontaneity are lost. They also argue that the social and emotional growth of the learner may suffer under a regimented competency-based program.

Because of this lack of agreement, most teacher-training institutions continue with traditional programs in which a student is awarded a degree after taking a certain number of courses. A survey conducted by the National Association for Retarded Citizens (NARC) of traditional programs for training teachers of the retarded found the most frequent components to be a survey course, a methods course, a curriculum-related course, and student teaching experience.

In October, 1973, the Education Committee of NARC adopted a position on teacher preparation and certification. The following recommendations were made:

1. A common terminology should be used by state departments of education and certification boards for levels and types of certification.

2. Standard minimal requirements for certification should be endorsed by all states.

3. Any teacher of the mentally retarded should meet minimum certification requirements and have completed a

Chapter five

bachelor's degree program. Provisional certification should be discontinued.

4. Any teacher of the mentally retarded should be competent in four basic areas: basic knowledge, methods and techniques for teaching the retarded, curriculum, and the demonstrations of teaching competence.

5. Teacher-training institutions should be responsible for judging the competency of students completing their programs.

6. Admission to teacher-training programs should be through formal application procedures including a personal interview. Satisfactory progress should be reflected in advancement. Retention or dismissal should be imposed for unsatisfactory progress. Due process should be observed in all instances.

A competency-based teacher preparation program mainly deals with item 4 of NARC's recommendations. The basic assumption behind the competency-based system is that, in addition to basic knowledge, certain teacher behaviors are directly, or at least indirectly, related to the performances of children. Tawney (1976) has listed measures of a teacher's competence with the mentally retarded:

1. The teacher interacts humanely with children.

2. The children work efficiently when asked to do so.

3. The children produce positive and observable changes in performance over time and over increasingly complex tasks.

Most individuals responsible for serving the mentally retarded agree with these three criteria. It is far more difficult to agree on how to evaluate whether or not a teacher has become competent by these three measures. For instance, someone with a behavorial background may interpret the first criterion ("interacts humanely with children") as appropriate *child* behavior 90% or more of the time, as measured by a teacher–child interaction scale. On the other hand, an individual with a psycho-educational background may avoid such precision in favor of the opinions of two or three experienced educators observing the teacher.

The major issue facing teachers of the mentally retarded today is to determine what competencies they need and how these competencies can be evaluated. At the same time, more facts are needed to evaluate competencies of retarded students. The time is rapidly approaching when the call of P.L. 94–142 for "an *appropriate* education" for the mentally retarded must be defined.

OTHER DISCIPLINES INVOLVED WITH THE MENTALLY RETARDED

Professionals in many fields other than education are closely involved with retarded persons and their families. The field of medicine—particularly disease research, genetics, chemistry, psychiatry, and surgery—currently has the greatest direct and indirect influence on mental retardation.

Classification of Causes

One indication of the importance of medicine in mental retardation is the etiological classifications listed on page 107 above from the AAMD *Manual on Terminology and Classification in Mental Retardation* (Grossman, 1973). Although it is estimated that there are known causes in only 6 to 15% of the cases of mental retardation (Dunn, 1973; Kolstoe, 1972), medical research has contributed a great deal towards the understanding of those causes and hypothesizing about others.

Virus Research

One example of such research deals with German measles (**rubella**). Krim (1969) has estimated that rubella, when contracted by mothers during their first three months of pregnancy, may cause severe damage to 10 to 40% of unborn children. In 1962 the virus causing rubella was isolated and a vaccine developed to prevent it. This illustrates the application of scientific research towards the prevention of mental retardation.

At the present time other viruses are the focal point of active research. The cytomegalo virus has been isolated from children who have been born with unusually small heads (microcephalus). The majority of lower-income families have immunity to this virus, while only 32% of those of more affluent backgrounds have such immunity. Research is also being conducted on a protozoan parasite called *Toxoplasma* which has been found in infants with such abnormalities as inflammation of the brain and spinal cord (encephalomyelitis) and unusually large, fluid-filled heads (hydrocephalus). Medical research also continues on congenital syphilis, poisonous substances, infectious diseases, and the effects of maternal malnutrition.

Chromosome Analysis

Chromosome analysis of potential parents today makes certain abnormalities more predictable, although they cannot be prevented. Chromosome abnormality also can be detected within a few weeks of conception through the analysis of fluid in which the embryo is developing. The fluid is drawn from the uterus of the pregnant woman.

Biochemical Analysis

Biochemical analysis of a newborn's body fluids like blood and urine has permitted large-scale screening programs for conditions such as phenylketonuria (PKU) and other genetic diseases (Krim, 1969). Jordan (1976) reports progress being made through controlling the body chemistry with drugs for certain conditions. Drugs are also being used to upgrade the functioning level of certain retarded people rather than as a cure for the condition. Certain tranquilizers also have been successfully used with some retarded children to raise their level of functioning and to control behavior.

Psychotherapy

Psychotherapy also has achieved some measure of success with retarded individuals. Both individual and group therapy as well as techniques such as sociodrama, sensitivity training, and the use of art, dance, and music have been used. Jordan (1976) points out, however, that while positive results have been reported, the most favorable outcome to be expected is increased adequacy, not normalcy. It appears that a positive behavior change can be produced through psychotherapy.

Surgery

Surgical procedures have long been used for certain conditions associated with mental retardation. Premature closing of the sutures of the skull (craniostenosis) can sometimes be avoided by the use of surgical techniques. Hydrocephalus has been treated by surgically diverting the cerebrospinal fluid from the brain. Some of the physical symptoms of cerebral palsy have been treated surgically (Jordan, 1976).

Another use of surgery that is currently receiving more recognition and acceptance is cosmetic surgery. Its purpose is to make the retarded person appear more normal. While this does not increase intellectual functioning, it can have a major influence on the retarded individual's self-acceptance and also on the way he or she is treated by family members and others within the community. There may be more work and job opportunities for the retarded individual whose facial features no longer create barriers in addition to his mental capabilities.

FUTURE CONSIDERATIONS

President's Panel on Mental Retardation

In 1961 President John Kennedy created the Panel on Mental Retardation and appointed Leonard W. Mayo chairman. One year later, the panel published *A Proposed Program for National Action to Combat Mental Retardation* (Mayo, 1962). Its recommendations were based on an intensive study and inquiry using task forces on specific subjects, public hearings, visits to facilities for the retarded in other countries, and a review of the literature. The panel's recommendations, which made a major impact, fell into the following broad categories: research, prevention, clinical and medical services, education, the law and the mentally retarded, and local, state, and federal organizations.

Research

Recommendations for research were centered around:

1. Federal leadership in research,

2. Expanding the total research effort in the neurol and behavioral sciences, including that which is specifically directed at mental retardation;

3. Increasing the statistical information on the incidence, severity, and the sociocultural manifestations of mental retardation;

4. Expanding the federal support of research on the learning process;

5. Better dissemination and application of the findings of research; and

6. Increasing the supply of scientific manpower in this field. (Mayo, 1962, pp. 21–22)

More specific recommendations included:

1. Establishing research centers to be affiliated with certain universities,

2. Doing population studies,

3. Increasing laboratory space,

4. Holding scientific conferences,

5. Granting additional fellowships, awards, and scholarships,

6. Initiating an extensive program of federal aid to education.

Prevention

Mayo refers to prevention as "our great hope and ultimate goal" (p. 47). Proposals included a strengthened program of maternal and infant care, particularly in high risk localities. Laws and/or regulations were endorsed for the use of x-rays and other radiation sources as well as for drug-testing procedures. Genetic counseling and extended diagnostic and screening services were emphasized. The panel proposed a domestic Peace Corps to help meet personnel shortages and other special needs in deprived areas.

Clinical and Medical Services

The recommendations for additional clinical and medical services emphasized community-based facilities. Also, the panel said that restrictions preventing retarded children from being served by certain state and local agencies should be lifted.

Education

The recommendations called for strengthening, expanding, and enriching specialized educational and rehabilitation programs for the mentally retarded to help "every individual to make the most of his potential for participation in all the affairs of our society, including work, no matter how great or how small his potential may be" (p. 100). Specific recommendations dealt with enriching the environment of deprived children, establishing instructional material centers, extending educational and diagnostic services, increasing leadership from the U.S. Office of Education, and adding 55,000 trained teachers of the mentally retarded. Most important, the panel recommended that appropriate educational opportunities be provided for all retarded children.

---

profile OLIVER P. KOLSTOE

Oliver Kolstoe is known primarily for his pioneering work in work/study and vocational programs. He also has gained national prominence for his texts Teaching Educable Mentally Retarded Children *(Rev. ed., 1975);* Mental Retardation: An Educational Viewpoint *(1972); and* A High School Work-Study Program For Mentally Subnormal Students *(with R. M. Frey, 1965).*

Dr. Kolstoe holds a B.A. degree from State College in North Dakota, an M.S. degree from the University of North Dakota, and a Ph.D. from the State University of Iowa.

He has held positions with public schools as a teacher, principal, and superintendent and has been principal of the Perkins School at Children's Hospital in Iowa City, *Iowa. He became an associate professor of education at the University of Illinois in 1952 and professor and chairman of the Department of Special Education at Southern Illinois University from 1956 until 1965. He joined the University of Northern Colorado as professor of Special Education and has, since 1971, remained there as professor and chairman of the Department of Mental Retardation.*

He is a fellow of the American Association on Mental Deficiency and a member of the Council for Exceptional Children and Phi Delta Kappa. Kolstoe has received many special honors for his work in the field of education, including an appointment by President Lyndon B. Johnson to the National Advisory Council on Vocational Education.

Law

The panel firmly stated that "like other citizens, the mentally retarded must be assumed to have full human and legal rights and privileges" (p. 150). It recommended that each state establish a protective service for the retarded to consult on social and legal problems and to supervise private guardians of retarded persons. The recommendations stated that a judicial hearing should be held before an adult is institutionalized except in cases of voluntary admission where the individual is deemed to be capable of making such a decision. Judicial review every 2 years for continued institutional care of all retarded adults was also suggested. A clarification of the theory of responsibility in criminal acts as it relates to the retarded was urged.

Organizations

A person, committee, or organization should be locally available to every retarded person to give advice or counseling, the panel said, and a person, office, or division of every health, education, and welfare agency should be responsible for services to the mentally retarded. A formal committee should develop and coordinate community-based programs for the retarded. It was further recommended that the Secretary of Health, Education and Welfare be authorized to make grants to states for planning programs for the mentally retarded and that the federal government take leadership in developing model programs.

The recommendations of the President's Panel on Mental Retardation were clear in their direction and broad in the scope of services they envisioned. Indeed, the panel was "ahead of its time." For instance, the panel recommended a free, appropriate education be provided for all handicapped children. Subsequent lawsuits, revisions of earlier legislation, parent efforts, and work by professional groups finally helped turn this recommendation into law in late 1975 with the signing of P.L. 94–142.

Current Shifts in Emphasis

While general goals in the field of mental retardation today are essentially unchanged from 1962, there has been some shift in emphasis.

Research

Many of the panel's recommendations in the area of research have been followed. Later legislation emphasized research and material centers and the importance of having knowledge available (Martin, 1968). Research has become an important facet in the training of special educators and is fostered through the availability of funds for students and professionals. Most authorities in the field emphasize the need for expanded **basic** and **applied research.** Basic research involves inquiry into sensory-motor development and aspects of cognition such as memory, attention, and orientation. The continuing need for and current emphasis on medical research in determining the possible causes of retardation are also aspects of basic research. The social and behavioral aspects of retardation must be investigated through applied research and the findings used to better control the influence of the condition. There is a great need for research into specific problem areas that can be interpreted, reported, and disseminated to allow others to benefit from the information from the study.

Prevention

Prevention of retardation is still an issue of the highest priority. A large reduction in the occurrence of mental retardation is a much more possible goal than it was a few years ago because of increased knowledge about the causes of retardation and expanded medical facilities available. The medical field must continue its active participation in the search for cause, cure, and treatment.

Education

Educational opportunities for the mentally retarded have greatly expanded since 1962. Not only has the quantity increased but so has the range of educational services now available. There has been a shift from self-contained classes for the retarded toward maintaining physical and emotional contact with nonretarded children. **Mainstreaming,** as this current trend is called, generally involves integrating handicapped children into regular classes and providing for their special needs through individualized instruction, tutoring, or a portion of the day spent with a resource or special teacher.

Coordinating Services

In 1962 the panel recommended a "continuum of care" which would blend and use, in proper sequence and relationship, "the medical, educational, and social services required by a retarded person to minimize his disability at every point in his lifespan" (p. 74). While this goal of coordinating services is still largely unrealized, services have been extended to a broader age range. For example, the trend today is for educational intervention to begin during the preschool years and to continue into early adulthood. Furthermore, increased awareness and the development of effective instructional techniques have assisted in aggressively seeking services for the severely and profoundly handicapped.

Law

Litigation and legislation have been particularly active in the field of mental retardation. Due to pressure from parent and professional groups and the influence of sympathetic and interested persons in influential positions, many of the panel's recommendations in this area have been met. The most significant, perhaps, is the passage of

Marty has been mainstreamed into a special education class of "learning handicapped" youngsters. Here he and his mother make oatmeal cookies—a fun lesson in following instructions.

P.L. 94–142, which mandates a free appropriate education for all handicapped children.

Future considerations in legal reform appear to be taking two directions. First, compliance is not necessarily assured by the passage of a particular piece of legislation. Individuals and groups must be aware of the civil and personal rights of the retarded and actively work for these rights to be carried out. Second, the adequacy of current state laws must be evaluated in the light of the latest knowledge on retardation. For example, the future of many institutionalized persons still appears grim, although there is now great hope for increasing the capabilities of the severely and profoundly retarded. Members of the President's Committee on Mental Retardation (Weinberger, 1973) addressed themselves to these issues when they stated that:

> Many mentally retarded citizens cannot organize themselves. They need others to speak with and for them. There must be litigation and legislation in their interest. We must not wait for them to demand their rights. For they are, indeed, the silent minority. (p. iii)

CURRENT TRENDS, ISSUES, AND NEEDS

Legislation and Litigation

Legislation on behalf of the handicapped is not new. Almost all states now have mandatory legislation requiring public education for at least a portion of their handicapped children (Abeson, 1974). Too often, however, such requirements have been ignored, standards not upheld, and services not provided. As Lawrence Kane stated in the preface to *Silent Minority* (Weinberger, 1973):

> Our founding fathers declared that "all men are endowed by their Creator with certain inalienable rights; that among these are life, liberty, and the pursuit of happiness." But a silent minority—America's six million retarded citizens—are often denied these rights. (p. vi).

The plight of the mentally retarded and of all handicapped individuals has greatly improved during recent years. One major reason for this is the increased use of litigation to clarify and secure certain rights. Most legal actions involving the mentally retarded can be grouped into one of the following categories: right to treatment, questions of standards, and right to education (Gilhool, 1973).

Right to Treatment

The case of *Wyatt* v. *Stickney* is characteristic of many current right-to-treatment cases. In this particular case it was ruled that residents of Alabama's institutions for the mentally retarded and the mentally ill have the right to humane physical and psychological treatment and to habilitation. Also, they have the right to individualized programs that are to be periodically reviewed and administered in the least restrictive setting (Gilhool, 1973).

Questions of Standards

Questions-of-standards cases deal with procedures related to identification, evaluation, and placement. Cruickshank and De Young (1975) cite *Hobson* v. *Hansen* as the first major case of this nature. As a result of this action the "educational tracking" practices in the District of Columbia were abolished as being in violation of the equal protection clause of the fourteenth Amendment to the Constitution. This approach was carried further in the case of *Diana* v. *Board of Education* in 1970 on behalf of nine Mexican-American children in California who had been placed in special education classes. While Spanish was the language spoken in the homes of the children, their placement was based on testing conducted in English. The court ruled that all children be tested in their native language prior to placement (Ross, De Young, & Cohen, 1971).

Right to Education

The case of the *Pennsylvania Association for Retarded Children* v. *Commonwealth of Pennsylvania* is perhaps the best known of the right-to-education cases. This class action complaint was filed in January, 1971, on behalf of retarded children who claimed that they were being denied an appropriate education at public expense (U.S. Department of Health, Education and Welfare, 1975). Gilhool (1973) mentioned that while initial action of this type was brought about for the mentally retarded, subsequent cases now involve all exceptional children. The final order in the *PARC* case granted access to a free public program of education and training to any mentally retarded child between the ages of 6 and 21 (Lippman & Goldberg, 1973). In *Mills* v. *Board of Education of the District of Columbia,* the plaintiff charged the District of Columbia with failure to provide training for exceptional children at public expense (Ennis & Friedman, 1973). The federal district court held that the school board acted unconstitutionally and stated in the judgement that:

> No child eligible for public supported education . . . shall be excluded from a regular public school . . . unless such a child is provided (a) adequate alternative educational services suited to the child's needs, which may include special education or tuition grants, and (b) a constitutionally adequate prior hearing and periodic review of the child's status, progress, and the adequacy of any educational alternative. (Phay, 1973, p. 52)

The influence of such litigation as well as pressure from parent and professional groups can be seen in current legislation. The most current is P.L. 94–142.

Trends in Government Action

Executive Order #11776 (Weinberger, 1974) was signed by President Richard M. Nixon on March 28, 1974; it continued and broadened the responsibilities of the President's Committee on Mental Retardation. Three major goals were proposed.

(1) Reduce the occurrence of mental retardation by one-half before the end of the century. While this might be an unattainable goal, there are many encouraging factors that point to great progress. There are 200 known causes of retardation (Weinberger, 1973), many of which can be diagnosed before birth. With the Supreme Court ruling on the legality of abortion, such pregnancies could in some cases be terminated. The importance of nutrition of the mother on the developing baby is receiving renewed interest. Proper care before birth could greatly minimize mental retardation. Legislation restricting the use of lead-based paint as well as local efforts to identify children with lead poisoning have drastically reduced this cause of mental retardation (Richardson, 1971). Early intervention and parent education programs are helping to provide good nutrition, health care, and a stimulating environment to large numbers of children.

(2) Return to the community one-third of the persons presently in public institutions. In some states this goal has already been met (Weinberger, 1972). In other states, however, retarded individuals remain on long waiting lists to enter institutions or are returned to the community before practical plans have been put into action for their reentry. Weinberger (1972) lists alternative placements for children and for adults who are returning to the community after institutionalization. For children under 18 years of age these include foster homes, group foster homes, child welfare institu-

tions, boarding homes, and temporary care homes. For the retarded adult, placement considerations include foster homes, group foster homes, boarding homes, short-term residential care, long-term residential care, and nursing home care.

(3) Assure retarded individuals full status as citizens under the law. While many retarded persons have been and are being denied such rights, public awareness on this issue has greatly increased through recent litigation and legislative action. Rights of the mentally retarded which are currently receiving attention are listed by Richardson (1971) as:

1. The right to training,
2. The right to medical treatment,
3. The right to psychiatric treatment,
4. The right to insurance,
5. The right not to be experimented upon in institutions,
6. The right not to be sterilized,
7. The right to privacy,
8. The right to marry. (p. 17)

In 1971 the United Nations adopted a resolution entitled "Declaration on the Rights of Mentally Retarded Persons." Among the seven rights listed by Woody (1974) are these:

- The mentally retarded person has, to the maximum degree of feasibility, the same rights as other human beings.

- The mentally retarded person has a right to proper medical care and physical therapy and to such education, training, rehabilitation and guidance as will enable him to develop his ability and maximum potential. . . . (pp. 46–47)

The United Nations charged that this resolution . . . "calls for national and international action to ensure that it will be used as a common basis and frame of reference for the protection of these rights." (p. 47)

The goals set forth in Executive Order #11776 appear overwhelming. However, the rapid increase in our knowledge of mental retardation and its causes, together with proper administration, legislation, and litigation, make these goals possible. Educationally one of the major ways to reach the three goals is through intervention programs.

In this sheltered workshop, retarded workers are paid to assemble medicine droppers.

MEETING SPECIAL NEEDS

1. Emphasize concrete, meaningful content in initial instructional presentations. You could, for example, introduce colors through three-dimensional objects. It is important to use examples taken from the child's environment, such as the color of the school bus, the grass, the chalk board, lollipops, and other readily available and recognizable items.

2. Insure mastery of new material through overlearning and repetition. For instance, after working with addition facts in a drill format, supplement the presentation with addition games (Guizmo, Concentration, dice), a tape program, and activities that require coloring pictures that have been subdivided into addition facts. This activity also requires the child to understand that a certain sum corresponds to a given color. These activities provide enjoyable means for overlearning and repetition.

3. Provide the learner with methods of verbal mediation, which is extremely beneficial for learning and recalling associations between pairs and items. One way to use verbal mediation is to embed the elements in a meaningful sense. For example, if a child was asked to learn the association between "pencil" and "writing," a sentence such as "The pencil is used for writing" might be appropriate. Often these associations can be increased through the use of music (e.g., "The hip bone is connected to the thigh bone").

4. Increase attention initially by highlighting relevant dimensions and by minimizing unnecessary stimuli. As the child develops skills in attending, gradually increase the outside stimuli to improve his complex attending skills. One effective procedure commonly used to reduce outside stimuli is to darken the room and present the instructional material on an overhead or opaque projector. As the concepts being taught are learned and the attending skills developed, the stimuli may be gradually and systematically increased. Venetian blinds and dimmer switches allow you to let more light into the room.

5. Promote an atmosphere of success on which to base future learning tasks. Go over facts the child already knows to insure some success and strengthen her self-confidence before embarking on new facts. Provide activities that the child can experience and demonstrate success in before proceeding to new, unlearned material.

6. Incorporate incentives into all learning arrangements. Good things should automatically happen to children as they learn, behave appropriately, and remember. These good things (incentives) may come in the form of food, toys, privileges, or pleasant activities. Incentives may be presented directly after the student learns the task, or they may be earned and subsequently presented after the child accumulates a previously agreed-upon number of points or tokens. For instance, you could allow the student to play a game after successfully completing a reading assignment.

7. Teach sequenced information from the easy to the difficult. For instance, in developing fine motor cutting skills, don't start off by requiring students to cut out irregular polygons. Start with cutting short straight lines, then move into cutting a longer straight line, and then increase the complexity by small increments.

8. Use a variety of methods to present material as well as to reinforce its acquisition. Use several methods to deal with sight word recognition. Sight words may be presented on flash cards, slide projectors, overhead projectors, a Language Master, or a tape recorder. Even a tactile presentation is possible; allow the student to trace the words in a sand box. Or present the words as a spelling list and require the students to write them on colored paper with attractive marking pencils.

FOR MORE INFORMATION

Most of these resources are textbooks that are readily available, many from Charles E. Merrill, the publishers of this text. Check your instructor, the education library, or the general library at your school.

Brolin, D.E. *Vocational preparation of retarded citizens.* Columbus, Ohio: Charles E. Merrill, 1976.

Jordan, J.E. *The mentally retarded* (4th ed.). Columbus, Ohio: Charles E. Merrill, 1976.

MacMillan, D.J. *Mental retardation in school and society.* Boston: Little, Brown, 1977.

Moore, B.C., & Moore, S.M. *Mental retardation: Causes and prevention.* Columbus, Ohio: Charles E. Merrill, 1977.

Payne, J.S., Polloway, E.A., Smith, J.E., & Payne, R.A. *Strategies for teaching the mentally retarded.* Columbus, Ohio: Charles E. Merrill, 1977.

Robinson, H.B., & Robinson, N.M. *The mentally retarded child* (2nd ed.). New York: McGraw-Hill, 1976.

Smith, R. *Clinical teaching* (2nd ed.). New York: McGraw-Hill, 1974.

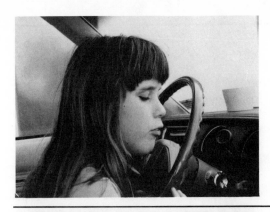

6

The Behavior Disordered

Ronald Reeve
James M. Kauffman

These are the major topics covered in this chapter. You may want to use them as a checklist when you review.

- *The six basic characteristics of mentally healthy children and the ways behavior disordered children do not have these traits.*

- *A functional definition of a behavior disordered child.*

- *Five major models for understanding and treating behavioral disorders.*

- *The characteristics of a good educational program.*

- *Four organizations which provide services for behavior disordered children, their parents, and professionals who work with them.*

Behavior disordered children,* unlike hearing impaired or learning disabled children, make themselves known through their actions and words. They upset the "system"—the family system, the school system, and the rest of their world. They make others angry towards them. Their behavior is deviant enough that they receive hostile responses from school officials, police, courts, and other authority figures. Typically they are unhappy with themselves, unpopular with their peers, and unsuccessful in their school work. They are indeed handicapped—not physically as are crippled or diseased children—but handicapped by their behavior, which is significantly different from social expectations.

Disturbed children are at odds with their surroundings because their behavior goes to some extreme. Their problems show up in different ways; they may be too agressive, striking out at others with little or no provocation, or they may be too withdrawn. Some live in their own, seemingly bizarre,

*In this chapter several terms, including **behavior disordered, emotionally disturbed,** and **psychologically disordered**, are used interchangeably to refer to the same kinds of children.

profile JASON: A SOCIALLY WITHDRAWN CHILD

Jason is an unobtrusive, average looking, quiet boy of 8. An outsider visiting the classroom would not likely pick him out of the group. But school officials and teachers know him—for sure.

Jason had transferred to the school earlier in the fall. When his mother registered him, she made vague reference to Jason having experienced some problems in his last school. At the urging of school officials, she agreed to allow the school psychologist to send for past records. Jason's career at the school began uneventfully enough. On his first day, he sat silently, head bowed and eyes to the floor. But the next morning, Jason's actions caused excited squeals and giggles among the children around him. He was sitting expressionless, eating a red crayon. When asked about it, Jason said nothing, and the teacher quickly diverted attention back to the lesson. Later in the day the teacher noticed an ugly mark on Jason's arm. Teeth marks could be seen on closer examination. Jason apparently had bitten himself. The teacher sent an emergency message to .the principal, and the principal immediately sent for the school psychologist, who placed a quick long distance call to Jason's previous school. Though he probably should have waited for written permission to release information, the principal of Jason's previous school told the psychologist that Jason had been in a special program for emotionally disturbed children because of his extreme social withdrawal and a series of bizarre behaviors.

After much deliberation, the staff at Jason's new school decided to try to keep Jason in a regular class with behavior management consultation for the teacher from the school psychologist and with help from the resource teacher. It was hoped that the models for appropriate behavior from other children in the regular class would have a positive effect on Jason. But his disruptive behaviors continue, pointing up that he is a very disturbed child. When asked to draw a picture of himself, for example, he either draws a monster or a turtle, always with "poop poop" coming out the back. When he is able to sneak off alone to the rest room, he invariably urinates on the walls. If he happens to have matches, he strikes them, then puts them out with his urine. His school work is average, but he remains a social isolate and a puzzle to the school's staff.

worlds. The accompanying profiles illustrate these behavioral extremes. These case studies also illustrate two common characteristics of behavior disordered children: they tend to be somewhat below average in tested IQ and are quite often seriously academically retarded. See Kauffman, 1977, for a review of research on intelligence and achievement of disturbed children.

DEFINITION

There is no generally accepted definition of the behaviorally disordered or emotionally disturbed child. A child is emotionally disturbed when someone with authority so labels him. And the labels are arbitrary because the definitions are not precise. People who have worked with disturbed children typically have had to make their own working definitions as they have proceeded. There are a number of reasons for the lack of clarity and agreement in defining *behavioral disorder*.

Reasons for Lack of Clarity

Measurement Problems
A visual handicap can be identified with reasonable accuracy through optometric testing. A child thought to be mentally retarded can be given an intelligence test and his IQ can be determined with a rela-

---

profile **DARRICK: AN AGGRESSIVE, ACTING-OUT CHILD**

Reared in a tough inner-city neighborhood, Darrick gives a first impression of being a street-wise, independent kid. He is neither. By the age of 6 he had been excluded from two Detroit schools for "uncontrollable outbursts." He had been sent to a state hospital for disturbed children at age 7, when his parents were divorced. The state took legal custody of Darrick after his parents left the state. By age 10, he was pronounced "cured" by the hospital staff, placed in a good foster home, and enrolled in public school. Considerable testing indicated that Darrick's IQ was in the low 60s and he was performing on a late first-grade level academically. He was placed in a special class for mildly mentally retarded children. The teacher of this class was trained in dealing with emotionally disturbed children and was willing to accept the challenges Darrick's presence brought.

The first week was a nightmare. Darrick first refused to go to his classroom; once there, he refused to stay. When the teacher tried to block his exit, Darrick pushed desks over, swore loudly, and threw things all over the room. The resource teacher's office became his refuge. This meant she had to devote all her attention to him, ignoring the rest of her caseload. After 2 days with Darrick, the resource teacher negotiated an arrangement: Darrick could earn 15 minutes of the resource teacher's undivided attention by working independently and without getting into trouble for 30 minutes in the class. Though meeting his end of the bargain was exceptionally difficult for Darrick at first, he did manage to make it through several calm half-hours the first day. After that, the situation slowly but steadily improved. As Darrick came to be more and more in control of his behavior, the length of peaceful, productive in-class time required in order to earn the resource teacher's time was increased—first to an hour, then to two hours, and eventually to half a day. Darrick still occasionally has outbursts of rage directed at the teacher or at other children, but progress clearly is being made. It now appears that Darrick will be able to remain in a public school setting.

tively small margin of error. His social behavior can be assessed. In contrast, there are no psychological tests that measure personality, anxiety, or adjustment precisely enough to be useful in defining behavior disorders. Attempts have been made with personality inventories, behavioral rating scales, screening tests, and "projective" tests of personality, but the reliability and validity of these tests are questionable and make them useful primarily for identifying children who *might* be disturbed. See the listing of standardized tests in the appendix for the names of some appropriate devices. Since we have no reliable formal tests to measure behavior and personality, the task of identifying disturbed children is left to "clinical" judgments by "experts."

The environment under which tests are given is another variable in measuring behavior. Psychological tests usually are given in an ideal situation—the psychologist's office, a mental health clinic, or at least a quiet room in the school. Such places are hardly typical of the child's everyday world. The child moves daily from an often chaotic home through a visually, auditorily, and socially stimulating school and an often incomprehensible community back to home again. Seldom during the day is the child in a quiet, one-to-one relationship with another person. The behavior and the emotional responses brought out by a psychologist in a testing situation therefore may not at all represent the manner in which a child responds to the rest of the world. More than traditional psychological measurement is essential to gain an adequate sample of a child's behavior.

Lack of a Clear Definition of Mental Health

Many assume that being emotionally disturbed is the opposite of being mentally healthy. Unfortunately, this assumption does not add much clarity to a definition

because there is no clear definition of *mental health,* either. Psychologists and other mental health professionals generally agree on the following characteristics as a partial description of a mentally *healthy* child:

1. Maintains a realistic understanding of self and an acceptance of self as a worthwhile person (a positive self-concept);

2. Builds and maintains positive relationships with other people (interpersonal or social skill);

3. Perceives reality accurately, including setting goals which are obtainable;

4. Organizes thoughts and actions appropriately;

5. Achieves academically at a level which is reasonable for the child's abilities; and/or

6. Generally acts the ways a person the child's age and sex is supposed to act and is able to function independently.

If it is true that a behaviorally disordered child is the opposite of a mentally healthy child, then we could describe a disturbed child as one who:

1. Possesses an unrealistic and/or negative self-concept;

2. Experiences serious interpersonal problems;

3. Distorts reality, including setting either unobtainable or unrealistically low goals;

4. Is disorganized in thought and in attempts to carry out meaningful actions;

5. Achieves academically below the level expected based on ability; and/or

6. Generally behaves inappropriately for his or her age and sex and is excessively dependent on others.

Using this approach possibly helps to communicate a clearer understanding of the types of children who are considered emotionally disturbed. However, none of these characteristics is objective. *Organized* and *disorganized,* for example, are hard to define. Further, all children exhibit some of these characteristics some of the time, so holding closely to the list could result in everyone being labeled *disturbed.* Thus, basing a definition on this, or any other, list is subjective rather than reliable and complete, and at best helps identify areas at which you may look.

Differing Conceptual Frameworks

There are a number of theories within psychology and special education which look at emotional disturbance differently; some of these theories will be discussed later in this chapter. Those who support a given theory or model use their own set of technical terms to describe disturbed children's behavior and the treatments they feel are appropriate. A definition offered by those of one view could be considered unacceptable by those of a differing view. As we shall see, differences in theory further compound problems of trying to define *behavior disorder.*

Differing Social and Cultural Expectations

Defining *emotional disturbance* is further complicated by the fact that expectations for behavior vary from one social and cultural group to another. Behavior considered normal and adaptive by one group often is viewed as deviant by another group. For example, poor children raised on the streets can be observed to fight more frequently than suburban middle-class children. Depending on which group's standard is used, the other group may be labeled as *disturbed.* Clearly, social and cultural expectations must be taken into account when defining *behavior disorder.*

Behavioral Aspects of the Disorder

In attempting to label a child behaviorally disordered, the authority should consider the child's actual behavior. One of the ways the behavior of people varies is how the behavior looks or the specific movements of the person (this is called *topography*). The behavior of disturbed children is topographically similar to the behavior of normal children. Nearly all healthy children, at some time or other, do most of the things that disturbed children do. They laugh, cry, do the opposite of what they are told, flap their arms, hit themselves on the head, stare into space, kick other children, and ignore adults. However, there are several ways in which the behavior of disturbed children differs significantly from the normal child.

Children are seldom considered disturbed on the basis of an isolated instance of behavior. *Disturbed children have longstanding problems.* Behavior problems that come and go or disturbances that are caused by specific situations may require brief intervention, but disturbed children demand intervention appropriate for a continuing problem.

The events surrounding a behavior and the location in which it occurs have predictable effects on how that behavior is evaluated. *The behavior of disturbed children is grossly inappropriate for the time and place in which it occurs.* Stimuli such as the presence of other people, directions or questions, facial expressions, gestures, touch, a toilet, toys, music, and pictures do not bring the same response from a disturbed child as they do from a normal child. The child seems unaware of his surroundings and established codes of conduct.

The severity of a child's behavior problem—indeed, the judgment of whether or not there is a problem—is indicated by how often the behavior happens in a period of time (rate), the force and determination with which the behavior is performed (magnitude), and the number of different behaviors involved (multiplicity). *Rate is the most important distinguishing feature of*

Eric's repeated withdrawal from enjoyable group activities indicates a behavior problem.

disturbed children's behavior. Disturbed children perform a given behavior much more often or much less frequently in a given amount of time than normal children. *The behaviors of the disturbed child tend to be of greater or lesser magnitude than the normal child.* He may bang his head harder, scream louder, clench his fists tighter, or talk more softly. *Also, disturbed children usually exhibit numerous problem behaviors* in more than one area of functioning.

Current Definitions

Despite the inherent difficulties, a number of attempts have been made to define *behavior disorders.* For example, Ross (1974) emphasized the importance of social norms and adult's judgments:

> A psychological disorder is said to be present when a child emits behavior that deviates from a discretionary and relative social norm in that it occurs with a frequency or intensity that authoritative adults in the child's environment judge, under the circumstances, to be either too high or too low. (p. 14)

Bower (1969) emphasized the context of the school in his definition. A child is considered to be behavior disordered if he exhibits one or more of the following to a marked extent over a period of time:

> **1.** An inability to learn which cannot be explained by intellectual, sensory, or health factors;
> **2.** An inability to build or maintain satisfactory interpersonal relationships with peers and teachers;
> **3.** Inappropriate types of behavior or feelings under normal conditions;
> **4.** A general, pervasive mood of unhappiness or depression; and
> **5.** A tendency to develop physical symptoms, pains, or fears associated with personal or school problems. (pp. 22–23)

Kauffman (1977) added the consideration that the child may be disturbed if he fails to meet his own expectations. His definition, in part, reads as follows:

> Children with behavioral disorders are those who chronically and markedly respond to their environment in socially unac-

ceptable and/or personally unsatisfying ways. . . . (p. 23)

All states now provide special educational programs for disturbed children. Definitions vary from state to state. Material from Michigan, for example, defines an *emotionally impaired child* as

> A person identified by an educational planning and placement committee, based upon a comprehensive evaluation by a school psychologist and social worker, a certified psychologist, a certified consulting psychologist, or a certified psychiatrist, and other pertinent information, as having 1 or more of the following behavioral characteristics:
>
> **a.** Disruptive to the learning process of other students or himself in the regular classroom over an extended period of time.
> **b.** Extreme withdrawal from social interaction in the school environment over an extended period of time.
> **c.** Manifestation of symptoms characterized by diagnostic labels such as psychosis, schizophrenia and autism.
> **d.** Disruptive behavior which has resulted in placement in a juvenile detention facility. (Michigan Department of Education, 1973, pp. 2–3)

Degree of Severity

In addition to the broad definition, emotional disturbance may be defined by levels or degrees of severity. Behavior disorders may range anywhere from the mild, transient problems exhibited by perhaps 30% of all children sometime during their development to the profound, chronic disorders known as childhood **psychosis**, childhood **schizophrenia**, or **autism**.

Children with mild and moderate behavior disorders typically are educated in regular or special classes in public schools. They are seldom described as

Glen and Via, who are in a program for autistic children, each spend most of their free time playing alone. To get them to interact, Jackie has set up a game that requires them to pass a tray of colored chips back and forth to each other.

"losing touch with reality," and the prospect of recovery for most of them is quite favorable. In fact, most of them will not be considered disturbed for more than a few years. They probably will become independent, relatively well-adjusted adults unless their behavior disorder is characterized by hostile, antisocial aggression and school failure.

On the other hand, severely and profoundly disturbed children usually are educated in special classes, day schools, or institutions. They are often described as "losing touch with reality," and the future for most of them is dismal. They are likely to be institutionalized as retarded or psychotic as adults, and they are seldom able to function independently in adult life. Their childhood years are characterized by intellectual retardation, lack of daily living skills, bizarre behavior, and extreme social withdrawal.

EXTENT OF DISTURBANCE AMONG CHILDREN

Since there is no generally accepted definition of behavior disorder, estimates of its extent (prevalence) vary tremendously. The range reported in various surveys was found to be from .1% to 30% by Morse (1975), depending on the criteria used in defining disturbance and on the age of the children being considered. An estimate of 2% is used by the U.S. Office of Education (1975). Based on extensive surveys of children in California schools, Bower (1969) suggested that two or three children in an average classroom (which would be roughly 10%) can be expected to show signs of emotional problems.

Juvenile delinquency may be considered to reflect a special kind of emotional disturbance, a clear demonstration of behavioral disorder which violates the law. In an average year, about 3% of the youth in America

are referred to a juvenile court (Achenbach, 1974; Cavan & Ferdinand, 1975; Kirk, 1976).

Factors Affecting Prevalence

Socioeconomic level

A higher incidence of emotional disturbance is reported among lower-class children than among middle- and upper-class children. Though there is no way to know for certain, this may be because middle- and upper-class parents can afford private treatment for their children, thus keeping them from coming to the attention of schools, courts, and so forth. It is clear that aggressive, acting-out behavior occurs more frequently among lower-class children (Graubard, 1973). Such behavior violates the standards set by middle-class authorities, who make the judgment that a child is disturbed.

Sex

Morse, Cutler, and Fink (1964) found that boys are considered to be disturbed much more often than girls. Among severely disturbed (schizophrenic or autistic) children, where statistics are more precise, boys outnumber girls by a ratio of from 2:1 to 5:1 (Hingtgen & Bryson, 1972; Morse, 1975). Among the disturbed, boys typically exhibit more conduct disorders and aggressive behavior patterns than do girls (Quay, 1972; Schultz, Salvia, & Feinn, 1974), while girls tend to be more anxious and withdrawn. Crimes involving aggression are typical of male juvenile delinquents, while females more often have been involved in sex-related offenses. There does seem to be a trend toward females committing more violent crimes, however (Cavan & Ferdinand, 1975).

Age

In their survey, Morse et al. (1964) found a relatively low incidence of disturbed children in early grades, with a peak of prevalence in the middle grades. By junior high school, there was a decline in reported incidence which continued through high school. As the boys grew older, they tended to show more conduct problems (disruptiveness, aggression) and immaturity, while the tendency for the girls was to show greater personality problems (withdrawal, shyness, anxiety) with increasing age. For juvenile delinquents, arrest rates increased sharply at junior high age, perhaps reflecting the relatively greater harm older children are capable of doing. A trend toward more violent crimes being committed by younger children than in previous years, however, was also apparent (Cavan & Ferdinand, 1975).

HISTORY

Education of disturbed children began with the dawn of special education for the mentally retarded in the early 1800s (Glavin, 1973; Kauffman, 1976, 1977; Lane, 1976). That is, the fathers of special education, including Jean-Marc-Gaspard Itard, Edouard Seguin, and Samuel Gridley Howe, dealt with disordered behavior as well as mental retardation and other handicapping conditions. Even in the special education literature of the 20th century, there are close conceptual ties among the fields of emotional disturbance, mental retardation, and learning disability (see Hallahan & Kauffman, 1976, 1977; chapters 5 and 7 in this book). It was not really until the early 1960s that special *education* (as opposed to therapy) for behaviorally disordered children became clearly separated conceptually, methodologically, and professionally, although there were a few special classes, schools, and trained teachers for disturbed children in earlier years (see Kauffman, 1977, chapter 2).

Some of the first classrooms for seriously disturbed children were those established at Bellevue Psychiatric Hospital in New York City in the 1930s. In the 1940s, Bruno Bettelheim opened the Orthogenic School at the University of Chicago and Fritz Redl and David Wineman operated "Pioneer House," a residential facility in Detroit for aggressive boys. These early classrooms and institutions were the source of much of the philosophy for the psychodynamic and psychoeducational models of educational intervention described in the next section of this chapter. Also in the 1940s, Alfred Strauss, Heinz Werner, Laura Lehtinen, and others at the Wayne County Training School in Northville, Michigan, experimented with a highly structured, directive approach to dealing with the classroom problems presented by children who today might be labeled *learning disabled, emotionally disturbed, brain-injured,* or *hyperactive.* The work at the Wayne County Training School provided the foundation for many present-day teaching methods and is consistent with the principles underlying the behavioral model of educational intervention. Thus, historical and philosophical roots of current models of intervention can be clearly identified in the 1930s and 1940s.

However, it was not until the 1960s that public school classes for disturbed children became common. And classroom applications of the psychodynamic model (e.g., Berkowitz & Rothman, 1960) and the behavioral model (e.g., Haring & Phillips, 1962) of education for disturbed children were not clearly expressed until the early 1960s. Since 1960, attention to the problems of disturbed children has increased dramatically, and programs of teacher training, research, and service have grown. There are now several professional organizations that play a major role in spreading information and working to improve special education and other services for disturbed children.

THEORIES TO EXPLAIN CAUSES AND CURES

There are many different theories which attempt to explain the cause, the nature, and the cure of behavior disorders in children. For example, Rhodes and his coworkers (Rhodes & Tracy, 1972 (a), (b); Rhodes & Head, 1974) in their project "A Study of Child Variance" dealt extensively with five major conceptual approaches—**psychodynamic, biophysical, sociological, ecological,** and **behavioral.** Another approach which became popular in the late 1960s is the humanistic model. Almost no one individual can be said to represent any single viewpoint perfectly. Most professionals borrow ideas from more than one conceptual approach. Yet, each model represents a rather complex system of thought, with its own assumptions and its own terminology.

The Psychodynamic and Psychoeducational Models

In a psychodynamically oriented approach, the emotional atmosphere in which the child is conceived and brought up is believed to be of primary importance. The at-

FOR MORE SUPPORT

American Orthopsychiatric Association

The American Orthopsychiatric Association is one of the oldest professional organizations concerned specifically with the behavior disorders of children. Founded in 1924, it is comprised largely of psychiatrists, clinical psychologists, and social workers, though educators also participate as members. "Ortho" prefixed to psychiatry denotes "corrective" psychiatry. The Association is concerned not only with correcting the child's behavior and its milieu, but with preventing the development of disorders. The American Journal of Orthopsychiatry, published under the auspices of the AOA, is one of the most important journals in the field.

Council for Children with Behavioral Disorders (CCBD)

The Council for Children with Behavioral Disorders, which recently began publishing its own journal, Behavioral Disorders, *was organized in 1964 as a division of CEC. It is the primary professional organization of special educators who are concerned with disturbed children. CCBD membership is available at reduced rates for student members of CEC.*

Association for the Advancement of Behavior Therapy (AABT)

The Association for the Advancement of Behavior Therapy also offers students memberships at reduced rates. AABT was founded in 1966 as a means of facilitating communication among individuals interested in the research or practice of behavior therapy and behavior modification. The association's journal, Behavior Therapy, *is one of the learning journals in behavior modification.*

National Society for Autistic Children (NSAC)

The National Society for Autistic Children was organized in 1965 to serve interested professionals and parents of severely disturbed children. NSAC is "dedicated to the education, welfare, and cure of children with severe disorders of communication and behavior." It publishes the Journal of Autism and Childhood Schizophrenia *and offers information and referral services to the public.*

Other journals that are particularly helpful to teachers of disturbed children include Behaviour Research and Therapy, Journal of Behavior Therapy and Experimental Psychiatry, *and* Journal of Applied Behavior Analysis.

titude of the mother and father toward the child—even during pregnancy—and the family atmosphere and traumatic events in the child's life are viewed as most important (Bettelheim, 1950; Finch, 1960). Bettelheim (1970) described a 4-year-old girl who "had become the terror of the neighborhood, violently attacking other children and adults and who had been declared an incurable psychotic" (p. 45). She had a peculiar liking for breaking people's glasses which Bettelheim accounts for as follows:

> She could not understand her mother's behavior. This is understandable because the mother often went into the worst kind of depression and was a borderline schizophrenic, and in and out of hospitals all her life. The mother wore glasses and she couldn't understand her mother's behavior, so we say she couldn't see what her mother was all about. But since the mother wore glasses to see better, she decided maybe she could understand the mother's behavior and with it the world, if she would wear glasses. So she got the glasses and put them on. But as she put the glasses on, she saw even less of the world, having normal eye sight, than she had before. And that infuriated her. What infuriated her was the injustice that other people see better and when she tried to see better she saw worse. (p. 45)

There are ample anecdotes said to support claims for the psychodynamic origin of severe emotional disturbance in children. However, there is extremely little, if any, scientific evidence that psychodynamic factors account for the appearance of deviant behavior (Lehrman, 1967; Skinner, 1967).

The psychological theories initally proposed by Sigmund Freud provide the basis for the explanations of behavior that use the word *dynamic*. Freud believed that mental life as well as overt behaviors are regulated by unconscious impulses. These impulses result from an interplay between the three major parts of the personality—the id, ego, and superego. Developmentally, a child progresses through a sequence of psychosexual stages which have both biological and psychological significance. Conflicts at any developmental stage can lead to distortions in personality which recur in various forms later in life. Freud's theories have created great controversy since he first put them forth, and therefore they have undergone major revisions by some psychodynamic thinkers. Many "dynamically"-oriented ego psychologists, for example, downplay the Freudian notion of the existence of inborn sexual and aggressive drives. However, the assumption remains that behavior is determined to a great extent by unconscious processes that go on within the self (and are thus called *intrapsychic*).

Treatment from a psychoanalytic viewpoint consists of attempting to find the underlying, intrapsychic problem that is the root of the present behavioral or emotional difficulty. Behavior is seen as a surface phenomenon which is important only as a clue to the psychic location of the real problem. The job of the therapist is to assist the patient in sifting back through the patient's developmental experiences until the source of the conflict is identified, to aid the patient in gaining insight into the way in which that area of conflict unconsciously influences present thoughts and behaviors, and then to work with the patient in restructuring the personality into a psychologically healthier person.

In a purely psychoanalytically oriented system, the child's school setting is a critical factor in uncovering and dealing with his underlying mental pathology. The classroom offers a relatively permissive environment in which the child feels accepted and therefore feels free to act out his impulses. The teacher's primary concern is not to change surface behavior (symptoms) or to teach academic skills. Rather, the focus is on discovering the unconscious and symbolic meaning of the child's behavior and on helping the child work through his conflicts.

A majority of psychiatrists and psychologists in the United States, especially among those trained in the first half of this century, have adopted psychodynamic orientations varying from classical Freudian to ego psychology. They have had considerable influence on early treatment programs in this country. Among the pioneers in the application of psychoanalytic thinking to the treatment of emotional disorders in children are Bruno Bettelheim (1950, 1967) and Pearl Berkowitz and Esther Rothman (1960).

The psychoeducational approach can be considered an offshoot of psychoanalytic theory. Those who developed this approach (e.g., Fenichel, 1974; Morse, 1974, 1975) have sought to balance psychiatric and educational concerns. Fenichel and Morse maintain that the child's problem involves both underlying pathology and surface behavior (including academic underachievement). Therefore they try for a balance between psychotherapeutic goals and academic and behavioral goals.

---

profile CARL FENICHEL

A Leading Proponent of the Psychoeducational Model

Carl Fenichel's work played a particularly significant role in clearly defining the psychoeducational approach. He is noted as the founder and director of The League School, the first day school in the country designed to meet the needs of severely disturbed children. Fenichel began his professional career as an elementary school teacher in the New York City Public School System, where he had graduated from City College in 1928. He taught for 15 years, gaining invaluable insight into the problems of the disturbed children in his classroom. Fascinated with these children, Fenichel later worked at Kings County Hospital, Psychiatric Division, from 1948 to 1952, dealing exclusively with severely disturbed children (see Fenichel, 1974).

By 1953, under Fenichel's guidance, The League School was established to provide an alternative to institutionalization for the severely disturbed child. Through constant exposure to these children, both Fenichel's and the school's philosophy changed dramatically. Fenichel's professional preparation included training in analytic psychotherapy techniques. Originally using a Freudian approach which permitted free and unrestricted expression of all impulses, The League School now depends on discipline and structure to help its students develop self-control and independence. The League School is able to help children with severe behavior disorders through an individualized curriculum which relies heavily on the services of a large and varied staff of professionals.

While devoting most of his professional time to the school and to the Home Training Program, an extension of the school that teaches parents how to deal with their disturbed children, Fenichel managed to earn a number of degrees. He held a masters degree in psychology from The New School (1951), a certificate in psychotherapy from the William White Institute of Psychiatry, Psychoanalysis and Psychology (1954), and a doctor of education degree in special education from Yeshiva University (1960). Fenichel was also a member of the faculty of Teachers College, Columbia University, and a professional lecturer at Downstate Medical Center.

Teaching activities typically are individualized, with emphasis on projects and the creative arts (such as art, music, dance). Thus while underlying causes of behavior are considered important, and present behavior is seen as being merely symptomatic of those causes, the psycho-educational approach recognizes the importance of academic achievement and the reality of demands for appropriate behavior in a child's everyday environment.

The Humanistic Model

Growing out of ego psychology and the humanistic psychology of Abraham Maslow (1962) and Carl Rogers (1969), the human-

istic approach to educating emotionally disturbed children became popular in the late 1960s. The humanistic approach, at least in part, developed as a revolt against traditional education. It is described by such terms as *open, nonauthoritarian, affective, self-directed, personal,* and *self-evaluative.* Children are felt to be disturbed because they are out of touch with their own feelings, and/or because they cannot learn best nor find self-fulfillment in traditional school settings.

In the humanistic approach, emphasis is placed on the teacher serving as a nonjudgmental friend, a resource for specific information, and a catalyst for children's learning, rather than as an authoritarian fig-

---

profile **PETER KNOBLOCK**

A Leading Proponent of the Humanistic Model

Peter Knoblock joined the faculty of Syracuse University in 1962 immediately after completing his formal education at the University of Michigan (Ph.D. in Education and Psychology). While at Michigan, Knoblock worked extensively at Hawthorne Center at Northville, Michigan, where he gained experience dealing with disturbed children. However, once involved in teaching others his philosophies and techniques, Knoblock became acutely aware of the existing gap between theory and practice. As a result, he became dedicated to creating learning environments that aid the growth of teachers as well as of students. In 1967 Knoblock received a 4-year training grant from the Division of Training, Bureau of Education for the Handicapped, U.S. Office of Education, which he used to develop a field-based teacher preparation model designed to give students practical experi-

ence in working with emotionally disturbed children in an urban setting.

Three years later, Knoblock founded Jowonio: The Learning Place. Based on open education principles, The Learning Place provides the opportunity for normal and severely emotionally disturbed children to learn together in an atmosphere of mutual care and affection. Operating on a 2:1 ratio—2 "typicals" to 1 "labeled"— the children are placed in "family groups" consisting of nine children of various ages and abilities. Activities are designed not only to encourage interaction among all children within the group but also to involve different levels of participation, thereby catering to the individual needs of each child. Children are encouraged to express their feelings and concerns, and specific problems are discussed openly. It is Knoblock's belief that this unique environment promotes healthy social development in all children, while providing those "labeled" children with an opportunity to learn from their healthy peers.

ure in control of the situation. Teachers are supposed to concentrate primarily on enhancing children's internal motivation, emotional involvement, and self-evaluation. Respect for individual dignity and encouragement of a person's individual interests are major themes.

For descriptions of the humanistic approach, see Dennison (1969) and Knoblock (1973).

The Biophysical Model

This conceptual approach offers a "disease" model for explaining the existence of emotional disorders. That is, supporters of the biophysical approach believe that the origin of the disease (pathology) is within the individual in the same sense that influenza or cancer or any other such disease is biophysically contained within the living being. This disease may exert its effects before birth, during labor and birth, or at any time after that. Some theorists who believe in the biophysical model feel that there must be deviant biological or chemical factors to explain emotional disorders (e.g., Rimland, 1969). Others believe that biophysical factors play a major role in the cause of disordered behavior, but that environmental stresses may be necessary to activate the individual's disturbance (e.g., DesLauriers & Carlson, 1969; Werry, 1972).

Intervention from a biophysical point of view follows a medical—rather than a behavioral or environmental—model. As with other "diseases," prevention is a major goal. When possible, there is treatment with drugs to bring the person into chemical balance. Those who believe that environmental stresses interact with biophysical tendencies to cause the disorder emphasize the discovery and elimination or control of factors in the surroundings that cause a disease.

Perhaps the most important contribution of the biophysical perspective has been to make mental health and special education professionals aware of the different assumptions that follow from biogenic and psychogenic concepts of causes of conditions. Accordingly, a teacher's attitudes toward, and responses to, a child can differ markedly. For example, the teacher can consider the child's misbehavior to be from physical causes as opposed to stubbornness or fear or hostility.

The Sociological-Ecological Model

Sociological approaches to emotional disturbance take two forms. In one approach, disturbance is compared across cultures and social classes (Eaton & Weil, 1955; Hollingshead & Redlich, 1958), or such factors as social change are examined to determine how they may contribute to disordered behavior (Lieghton & Hughes, 1959). This is an **epidemiological** approach. In the second, emotional disturbance can be viewed simply as social rule breaking, or deviance. The social deviance perspective is important because it makes clear the role of society's control in establishing norms for behavior with which everyone in that society is expected to conform. For example, in some cultures extensive sexual activity among adolescents is encouraged. If a member of such a cultural group happened to live in the United States and engage in this "normal" (for his cultural group) behavior, he would be considered deviant and might well be labeled *emotionally disturbed*. Thus it is important to examine the meaning a behavior has to the behaver before calling it "disturbed." While the sociological perspective has proven helpful in broadening our understanding of emotional disturbance, it offers little in the way of intervention, except for suggesting the need for major social change.

Closely allied to the sociological viewpoint is the *ecological* approach (e.g., Graubard, 1973; Hobbs, 1966, 1974;

profile **NICHOLAS HOBBS**

A Leading Proponent of the Ecological Model

Nicholas Hobbs is concerned with the educational alternatives offered to severely disturbed children. In 1956, while studying programs for retarded and disturbed children in western Europe, he was exposed to several programs very different from the psychoanalytically oriented programs which were currently popular in the United States. With the help of the observations Hobbs made while abroad, he developed the guidelines for Project Re-Ed, one of his most significant contributions to special education.

A residential school designed to alter the disturbed child's ecological system to the point where he can begin to learn more appropriate behavior, the Re-Ed school depends on its teacher-counselors for its success. Trained both clinically and educationally, these dedicated people live with the children on a day-to-day basis, preparing them to reenter their natural environments. Working to build a relationship of trust between themselves and the children, the teacher-counselors teach their students to control their behavior by creating a sta-

ble and predictable atmosphere. They help their children find joy in the world and supply incentive for future goals by advocating the philosophy that life is to be lived now. The Re-Ed schools prepare their students for a productive and healthy life outside of the residential community by gradually introducing them to elements within their natural environment and sending them home for weekends.

A 1936 graduate of The Citadel, Hobbs continued his education at The Ohio State University, earning an M.A. in 1938 and a Ph.D. in 1946. Currently he is on the faculty at Vanderbilt University. Most recently Hobbs coordinated the landmark Project on Classification of Exceptional Children, funded by the U.S. Department of Health, Education and Welfare. This project brought together the best of current thought regarding diagnosis and labeling of children, as well as recommended future directions. The resulting publications, Issues in the Classification of Children *(Vols. I and II) (1975b) and* The Futures of Children *(1975a) already are classics in the field.*

Rhodes, 1967, 1970) which borrows from biology, from the study of animal behavior (ethology), and from several other areas of inquiry. Ecology is the study of interactions between organism and environment. A child is an element in a complex ecological system, and every part of the system is intermeshed and in dynamic balance with every other part. A change in any part of the system is seen as having an impact on every other part. From this perspective it makes sense to consider a "behaviorally disturbed" child as one whose behavior is disturbing to the eco-system. The behavior is in ecological balance for the child, but other elements in the system are disrupted by what the child is doing. In order to be successful, an intervention strategy must take into account the entire social system of which the child is a part—family, other pupils in the classroom and school, physical environment, community, social agencies. The intervention must change the entire ecological system so that it supports the child's altered behavior. It is seldom enough to effectively teach the child in the classroom. An effective program from the ecological perspective also must intervene in the other parts of the child's environment.

The Behavioral Model

Based on the principles of learning clarified by B.F. Skinner (1953) and Albert Bandura (1969), the behavioral approach assumes that all behavior is learned. Disordered behavior, then, results from inappropriate learning. Observable and measurable behaviors are the focus for behaviorists. No underlying origins of a disease are assumed; rather, it is believed that the inappropriate behaviors themselves are the problem. A disturbed child can be helped by a modification of his inappropriate behaviors. This modification occurs by manipulating the child's immediate environment and especially by controlling the

consequences of the child's behavior. In order to be effective, behaviorists must specify precisely the behaviors to be altered and the consequences to be manipulated. Therefore, the observable problem behaviors are analyzed and measured before, during, and after the intervention. In the 1960s a number of individuals clearly stated an approach to the education of emotionally disturbed children based on behavioral principles (Haring & Phillips, 1962; Haring & Whelan, 1965; Hewett, 1968; Lovaas, 1967; Whelan, 1966).

SPECIFIC FACTORS THAT CAUSE BEHAVIOR DISORDERS

Each of the conceptual models discussed offers a different origin for disordered be-

profile FRANK HEWETT

A Leading Proponent of the Behavioral Model

Frank Hewett is among the most influential of the behaviorally oriented educators. As a clinical psychologist, he has devoted much of his professional career to the education of exceptional children. After receiving a Bachelor of Arts degree in theater arts from the University of California at Los Angeles in 1951, he remained at UCLA for his clinical psychology training, earning his M.A. in 1958 and his Ph.D. in 1961.

Through his personal experience as a teacher and supervisor in UCLA's Fernald School, Hewett came to view all exceptional children as learners who are to be described strictly in educational terms. Recognizing that the most important factor within the educational process is the teacher, Hewett expressed an early dissatisfaction with the numerous programs designed to help special educators cope with disturbed children, criticizing them for

their confused and contradictory orientations. Consequently, in 1964 Hewett developed what is now known as the engineered classroom. Based on behavioristic principles, Hewett incorporated learning principles and relied on systematic reinforcement to put this educational program into practice. Hewett's "critical levels of competence" represent gradual gains in educational functioning ranging from attention to mastery. The entire program is highly structured and designed to eliminate failure at the most elementary levels.

While best known for his work with the engineered classroom, Hewett also has been associated with various other clinical and educational facilities at UCLA and is presently Professor of Education and Psychiatry and Chairman of Special Education in the Graduate School of Education at UCLA.

havior. The fact that differing viewpoints still have serious and knowledgeable supporters suggests that no one really knows why a child becomes emotionally disturbed.

All theoretical models consider that *predisposing, precipitating,* and *contributing* factors are important. For example, a child may have a tendency—be predisposed—genetically to develop an emotional problem. However, a specific traumatic event such as the loss of a family member may actually trigger, or precipitate, the disturbance. More than one cause for an emotional disturbance can usually be identified. Three frequently cited factors that cause behavior disorders are examined here—biological factors, family factors, and school factors.

Biological Factors

All human behavior involves neurochemical and central nervous system activity. Given that fact, it can be argued that all behavior disorders result from a biological problem—either disease, brain injury or dysfunction, genetic accident, or biochemical imbalance. Attractive as that argument might be, it clearly ignores several facts. First, many behaviorally normal children have serious biological defects, while many disturbed children have no detectable biological problems. Second, it is certain that environmental factors interact with and modify the behavior which results from biological processes. Even genetically inherited traits are altered somewhat by the child's environment (McClearn, 1964; Restak, 1975; Scarr-Salapatek, 1975; Williams, 1967).

Temperament is an example of a biological factor which may be among the causes of emotional disturbance. All children are born with a biologically determined temperament or behavioral style. Though child-rearing practices may alter the initial temperament to some extent, it appears that children with "difficult" temperaments

Kelly, who is blind, also has behavior problems: she is disruptive in class, frequently talks out loud to herself, and often does not work or play well with other children.

may be predisposed to emotional disturbance (Thomas, Chess, & Birch, 1968). Properly managed, difficult children may develop normal behavior patterns, and children with easy temperaments may be handled so poorly that they become disturbed; so a prediction based on temperament is unreliable. However, the biologically determined behavioral style of a child appears to be an important factor in the child's emotional development and may help to explain the etiology of some emotional disorders, especially those which are mild or moderate.

The clearest evidence of biological causes which produce emotional disturbance is found in markedly disturbed children. Psychotic children, for example, often show signs of neurological defects (Des-Lauriers & Carlson, 1969; Werry, 1972). **Schizophrenia,** which is one type of **psychosis,** appears to have a major genetic component in many cases (Heston, 1970).

In early infantile **autism,** a neurochemical disorder likewise probably plays a role (Rimland, 1964, 1971). Even with schizophrenia and autism, however, the relationship between biological factors and resulting behaviors is unclear. No one can say whether the disorder itself is caused by biological factors, or whether the child is vulnerable or predisposed to the disorder but would not develop the disorder unless environmental factors were to trigger it (Werry, 1972).

An examination of the evidence available at this time suggests that it is unreasonable to assert that biological factors are the single root cause of emotional disturbance. However, for the severely disturbed, there is sound evidence suggesting that biological factors at least contribute to the condition. While biological factors can influence behavior, environment modifies the behavioral expression of physiological processes.

Family Factors

The nuclear family—mother, father, and siblings—obviously exerts a major influence on the child's early development. Until a child reaches school age, she is likely to spend most of her time interacting within this small unit. Therefore, it would be tempting to assume that the family is the source of emotional problems which develop. Many psychoanalytically oriented professionals (e.g., Bettelheim, 1967), in fact, believe that almost all emotional disturbance results from inappropriate early interactions between parents and the child. However, evidence does not support such a strong stance. Research so far has indicated that the influence of parents on their children is complex and is not all one-sided. In the last few years it has become clear that family members interact and transact with one another; that is, disturbed children may influence their parents' behavior as much as

parents influence their children's behavior. (Martin, 1975; Parke & Colmer, 1975; Sameroff & Chandler, 1975).

Considerable research has been done on the subject of parental discipline. Consistent findings are that love-oriented approaches to dealing with misbehavior, giving attention, praise, and other reinforcement for appropriate behavior, and sensitivity of parents to the needs of their children tend to foster positive behavioral characteristics in children. The opposite also is true. A generally lax approach to discipline, especially when misbehavior is dealt with in an inconsistent, cruel, rejecting manner, is more likely to result in aggressive and/or delinquent children (Becker, 1964; Martin, 1975). The homes from which juvenile delinquents are most likely to come are those which are broken or otherwise disorganized, especially if the parents themselves have arrest records (Cavan & Ferdinand, 1975; Robins, West, & Herjaniz, 1975).

A child's temperament apparently interacts in complex ways with the parents' child-rearing practices (Becker, 1964; Thomas et al., 1968). The environmental pressures with which the family must cope also have to be considered. The research results are inconclusive. Therefore, it is not scientifically defensible to place all the blame on parents for their children's emotional disorders. Professionals must realize that parents of disturbed children have experienced a great deal of disappointment and frustration and that they, too, want to see their children's behavior improve. Rather than blaming parents, it would be more productive to enlist their aid in altering the disordered behavior.

School Factors

Other than the home, the school is the place where children spend the greatest amount of time. Therefore, it probably is the second most powerful socializing influence on the child. Some children come to school already disturbed. Most disturbed children, however, become disturbed during their school years. Because the socializing influence of school is so great, it is reasonable to ask whether or not the classroom contributes to the development of emotional disorders. Evidence seems to indicate that it certainly can. However, as with biological and family factors, we can only state ways in which school experiences *may* contribute to the child's emotional problems.

The temperament, academic abilities, and social skills which a child brings to the classroom appear to be important elements influencing behavioral development (Glidewell, Kantor, Smith, & Stringer, 1966; Thomas et al., 1968). If a child enters school with a difficult temperament and lacks social and academic competence, he is likely to bring out negative responses from teachers and peers. This child runs a great risk of becoming disturbed, caught up in a spiral of negative interactions between his irritating behaviors and the irritating responses he gets from those around him.

Following are five rather specific ways in which the school can help avoid developing behavior disorders in children (Kauffman, 1977).

1. Have a fair attitude for individual differences in interests and abilities; do not force every child to fit a narrow mold.

2. Have appropriately average expectations for behavior and academic achievement. If too low, expectations become self-fulfilling prophecies; if too high, expectations frustrate a child.

3. Manage a child's behavior consistently; if the parents' being too lax or too rigid encourages disordered behavior, inconsistent school discipline can have the same negative result.

4. Include areas of study which have relevance to the child; not to do this invites truancy or misbehavior.

5. Reinforce desired behaviors and do not reinforce inappropriate behaviors; from a behavioral psychology viewpoint, not to do this is to contribute to disturbance.

SOME RECENT DEVELOPMENTS AFFECTING THE BEHAVIORALLY DISORDERED

Cognitive Behavior Modification: A refinement in treatment techniques

While behavior modification is a relatively new area of interest within the fields of psychology and education, its impact on clinical research and practice has been tremendous. Over the past 25 years, methods of **classical** and **operant conditioning** have proved to be empirically effective for altering observable behavior. However, only recently have conditioning techniques become associated with covert behavior. **Cognitive behavior modification,** as its name implies, deals with altering thought processes in much the same way that **behavior modification** alters overt behavior. Mahoney maintains that "private events"— thoughts, feelings, memories—are similar to observable behavior because they can be altered through conditioning techniques. In his book *Cognition and Behavior Modification* (1974), Mahoney states that behavioral science is presently restricting itself to a "relatively small fraction of human behavior" when it deals solely with observable events. He encourages empirical examination of significant events that can be observed directly only by the person experiencing them.

Within the past 10 years, many studies have been conducted which support cognitive behavior modification as an effective treatment tool for the purposes of self-control. Meichenbaum (1969) discovered that institutionalized schizophrenics who were taught to produce healthy talk in an interview setting spontaneously generalized their "learned" behavior to other situations. Building on this phenomenon, Meichenbaum and Goodman (1971) later demonstrated that "private speech"—semantic thought—can be directly taught by means of modeling and cognitive rehearsal. Many clinical populations (for example, schizophrenics, neurotics, impulsive children, test-anxious students) have since been helped through cognitive behavior modification techniques stemming from this concept of private speech or "self-talk."

Bornstein and Quevillon (1976) provide another example of successful use of cognitive behavior modification techniques. The children in their study were three 4-year-old boys enrolled in a Head Start program. The boys were serious behavior problems; they were aggressive and overactive, and seldom paid attention to the teacher's instructions or to the tasks they were to perform. Bornstein and Quevillon first observed the boys in the classroom daily to obtain a baseline level of appropriate, on-task behavior (i.e., paying attention to the teacher or performing the prescribed activity). As shown in Figure 6.1, the boys were usually behaving appropriately less than 20% of the time.

During intervention (the *B* phase shown in Figure 6.1, which was introduced after a different number of baseline days for each boy for experimental design purposes), the experimenters worked with each of the boys individually for 2 hours. During the intervention sessions the experimenters taught the children to ask themselves questions, for example, "What does the teacher want me to do?"; cognitively rehearse the answer, for example, "Oh, that's right, I'm supposed to copy the picture"; instruct

themselves in how to perform the task, for example, "OK, first I draw a line here"; and reinforce themselves for performance, for example, "How about that; I really did that one well!" The experimenters first demonstrated these steps for the children, then had the children practice the cognitive rehearsal and self-instruction, and so forth, aloud; then practice the four steps silently. After 2 hours of this kind of intervention, the children were returned to the classroom. As can be seen in the figure, their on-task behavior improved dramatically and remained high until the end of the study.

The most noteworthy aspect of the Bornstein and Quevillon study is that the intervention consisted of teaching the children self-instruction techniques which they were able to use covertly to modify their own behavior. The cognitive self-control techniques put behavior management in the hands of the children themselves rather than in the hands of an external agent.

Aggression: Advances in understanding one type of disordered behavior

Confronted with steadily increasing rates of violent juvenile and adult crime and alarmed by exposure of young children to violent acts via the media, legislators, teachers, and parents are all clamoring for stricter standards (Gallup, 1975) and for solutions (Wint, 1975) to the problem of violence. For the researcher, the issue is no longer an intellectual debate about what constitutes **aggression**. Rather, there is a growing demand to know what causes it, how to reliably observe and record its occurrence, and consequently, how to modify or eliminate it, while fostering alternative behavioral styles.

Four Theoretical Views

Traditionally, four theoretical viewpoints have been offered as explanations of ag-

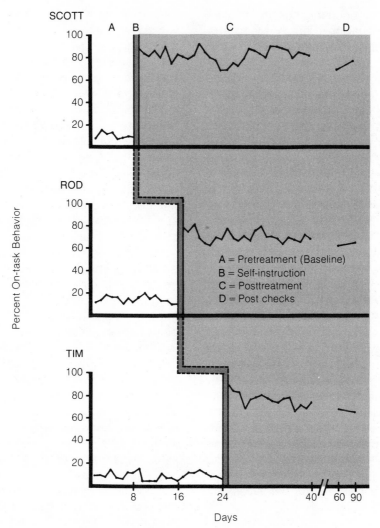

Figure 6.1

Daily percentage of on-task behaviors for three 4-year-old boys, Scott, Rod, and Tim, across experimental conditions.

Note. From "The Effects of a Self-Instructional Package on Overactive Preschool Boys" by P. H. Bornstein and R. P. Quevillon, *Journal of Applied Behavior Analysis*, 1976, *9*, 184. Copyright 1976 by Journal of Applied Behavior Analysis. Used by permission.

gression: biological, psychodynamic, frustration-aggression, and social learning. These viewpoints have been supported by varying amounts of experience and experiment.

The biological viewpoint incorporates three positions—a genetic/instinctual tendency, a hormonal/biochemical process; or electrical activity within the central nervous system. There is little support for the position that aggression is a consequence of genetic/instinctual control (Bandura, 1973; Montagu, 1968). There is some evidence that supports a biochemical-electrical

Chapter six

mechanism in encouraging or inhibiting aggressive behavior in humans and sub-human species (Delgado, 1969; Restak, 1975).

Psychodynamic explanations of aggression (e.g., Bettelheim 1970; Berkowitz & Rothman, 1960) have proved to be of limited value because they are based on empirically untestable hypotheses. In addition, psychodynamic intervention has not been a very successful therapeutic tool (Bandura, 1973).

The once heralded frustration-aggression hypothesis of Dollard, Doob, Miller, Mowrer, and Sears (1939) is no longer sacred. Recent research has indicated that aggression is not an inevitable outcome of frustration, nor is frustration the sole cause of aggressive behavior (Achenbach, 1974; Berkowitz, 1973).

Extensive reviews by Bandura (1973) and Mahoney (1974) have contributed an impressive foundation for a social-learning theory of aggression, helping explain how aggressive behavior is acquired and how it may be modified. A wealth of data exists from which we may conclude that socially aggressive behavior stems in large measure from the learning processes of imitation, punishment, and reinforcement as well as by what a child thinks, perceives, and feels.

Controlling Aggressive Behavior

The manner in which we control aggressive behavior is largely dependent on how we interpret its cause. For the advocate of psychodynamics, intervention involves channeling a child's aggressive impulses into socially acceptable activities (Berkowitz & Rothman, 1960). To date, there is no experimental evidence supporting the effectiveness of allowing a child to express his aggressive feelings and impulses either through sublimation, displacement, or fantasy (Bandura, 1973). It appears that en-

gaging in such experiences only aggravates the problem of aggressive behavior rather than relieving it. Bandura's (1973) and Berkowitz's (1973) comprehensive reviews clearly indicate that aggression promotes aggression.

Advocates of a psychoeducational approach (e.g., Fenichel, 1966; Long, 1974; Morse, 1975) tolerate the psychodynamic concepts of need, drive, and instinct as possible motivating factors. However, the psychoeducational advocate believes in the idea that behavior is also a function of our cognitive and affective interpretations of environmental interaction. So, intervention involves focusing on the cognitive and affective problems of a child to develop insight into his own needs and motivations. In this way, behavior will be changed (Fagen, Long, & Stevens, 1975). At this point it appears that the use of the insightful techniques of talking and experiencing as the only therapeutic treatment fails to promote behavioral change (Bandura, 1973; Hobbs, 1974; Mahoney, 1974).

The behavioral approach focuses its attention on the cognitive and affective problems of a child, but it also examines the stimuli which appear to elicit and maintain aggressive behavior. Here, the emphasis is on objectively measuring and defining situations which bring about and reinforce hostile behavior. From this point on, the task becomes one of structuring a nonaggressive environment for the child through one or more interventions, including modeling nonaggressive responses to aggression-provoking situations, practicing non-aggressive behaviors, reinforcing nonaggressive behaviors, extinction of aggressive responses by denying a child reinforcement for having engaged in such actions, and punishing, which might include presenting an aversive stimulus, withdrawing a child's favorite reinforcer, or allowing the child to experience a brief period of isolation from environmental reinforcers (Bandura, 1973;

Grieger, Kauffman, & Grieger, 1976; Kauffman & Hallahan, 1973; Patterson, Cobb, & Ray, 1972; Patterson, Reid, Jones, & Conger, 1975). Given these techniques, a teacher can influence a child to behave in more socially acceptable ways.

LOCATING AND PROVIDING HELP

Ideally, the process of locating children who need help because of emotional problems and providing that help should move from screening to assessment and diagnosis, then to classification, and finally to intervention and evaluation. But each of these apparently simple steps can prove to be very complex in practice.

Screening

Disturbed children do not usually escape notice, although occasionally they go undetected because they are especially quiet, or because teachers are not sensitive to their problems, or because they are relatively less disturbed than other children in the environment. Also, the younger the child, the more difficult it is to judge whether the behavior exhibited actually indicates an emotional disturbance. Children's behavior changes rapidly during the early years. A behavior that seems to be a major problem may disappear "spontaneously" over a period of a few weeks or months. But it is rare for disturbed children to avoid being identified. In fact, because school personnel so readily pick out disturbed children, very few districts now operate systematic screening programs.

Bower and Lambert (1962) developed a screening procedure which has been widely used for several years. It consists of teacher rating, peer rating, and self-rating scales appropriate for levels kindergarten through grade three, fourth through

seventh grades, and eighth grade through high school. At all levels, the teacher ranks each child in the class on a number of behavioral characteristics, such as "This pupil gets into fights or quarrels with other pupils more often than the others." The peer rating and self-rating scales are designed with each of the three levels in mind. Children in kindergarten through third grade rate each other by identifying the classmates they think would act like a child shown in a series of pictures showing adaptive and maladaptive behavior; they rate themselves by sorting pictures into "sad" and "happy" categories. For grades four through seven, children rate their peers by choosing the classmates that would be best cast in certain roles (for example, "A mean, cruel boss") in a class play; they rate themselves by checking items on a self-test, indicating whether they would like very much to be or would very much not want to be like a child who, for example, "daydreams a lot." The self-test is essentially the same for older children in grades seven through twelve, but the peer rating consists of a student survey in which children name the classmates they believe are best described by statements like "A student who is good in school work."

Recent research has shown that informal teachers' judgments are relatively reliable and valid for screening children for emotional problems (Nelson, 1971). Perhaps the best way to screen is a combination of teacher, peer, and self ratings.

Assessment and Diagnosis

The next step is to have a thorough diagnostic evaluation. Diagnosis should be a process which leads to a prescription for treatment (Linder, 1965; Menninger, 1963). Traditional diagnostic methods, which rely heavily on psychological tests, are often of minimal value in developing such a prescription (O'Leary, 1972). Some disturbed children are untestable and do not respond appropriately to interview techniques. Consequently, the diagnostician often must rely on interview data obtained from the parents or caretakers of the child and on behavioral data obtained from direct observation. Using interviews and observation it is possible to identify the specific behaviors which are most disturbing to others and debilitating to the child. Lovaas and Koegel (1973) have suggested that a diagnosis that specifies what behaviors the child does and does not have suggests treatment and a prognosis—when the variables controlling the child's behavior can be found—and simplifies communication among those who are interested in the child.

Psychiatric and psychological methods of assessments often do not sample the child's behavior in a variety of circumstances and under a variety of conditions. As a result, the diagnostician has a limited, vague, and often unrealistic picture of the child that does not accurately predict behavioral development. The child may exhibit certain behaviors only in certain locations or in the presence of specific persons or objects. Or the child may perform certain tasks only when cued, prompted, or reinforced. Adequate child study and assessment demand observation of the child over a period of time, in various settings, and under a variety of conditions.

Interdisciplinary efforts in diagnosis can be valuable. The educator, psychiatrist, psychologist, social worker, speech pathologist, audiologist, neurologist, and pediatrician should cooperate in assessment of the disturbed child whenever possible. However, seldom are *all* of these professionals available and ready to work together when a child needs diagnostic services. The educator should remember that other professionals may be able to identify conditions which may cause or increase a child's behavioral or educational difficulties. For example, neurological examination

of a child who "vomited every time an attempt was made to get him to go to school" showed a brain tumor which accounted for the vomiting (Menninger Foundation, 1969, p. 15). Nevertheless, the special educator must be *primarily* concerned with assessing how, when, and where the child responds in educational situations. The insights of other professionals can add to, but cannot replace, the teacher's insight into how the child learns.

Classification

It seems reasonable to expect that the emotionally disturbed could be classified according to the types of problems they exhibit. Unfortunately a generally accepted classification system has not been devised. This should not be surprising, considering the problems of arriving at a broadly acceptable definition for behavior disorders.

The most popular current classification system is in the second edition of the *Diagnostic and Statistical Manual for Mental Disorders (DSM-II)* compiled by the American Psychiatric Association (1968). The *DSM-II,* unfortunately, is typical of the problems with most classification systems. These problems include:

1. *Reliability.* In a reliable system, a disturbed child would not be classified one way one week and another the next; or one way by Dr. Green and another by Dr. Brown; or one way if seen at home and another at school.

2. *Treatment implications.* A child's placement in a certain category usually means little so far as treatment is concerned.

3. *Adult systems.* Most classification systems result from attempts to adapt preexisting systems, developed to apply to adults, to children; but the same type of behavior may have a different meaning for a child than for an adult. What is normal at one developmental stage for a child may be quite abnormal at another.

Because diagnostic categories typically do not lead to improved treatment, and because labeling a child may result in negative expectations, many feel that labels do more harm than good (e.g., Goldstein, Arkell, Ashcroft, Hurley, & Lilly, 1975). To replace labeling a child, leading psychologists and special educators have recommended thorough individual assessment of the child's specific behavior and competencies, including the situation in which the behaviors occur (Morse, 1975; O'Leary, 1972).

Both the *DSM-II* and the second most popular classification system—proposed by the Group for the Advancement of Psychiatry (1966)—were created by committees of psychiatrists who established the diagnostic categories through committee decision and through a poll of their colleagues. An alternative approach is an empirically based "dimensional" system. Several attempts to arrive at such a system have been made in the past few years (Achenbach, 1966; Quay, 1972, 1975).

Quay's system, using cluster analysis and factor analysis as the statistical tools, appears to be reliable but does not provide an adequate basis for intervention. Its usefulness is limited to describing the major types of disordered behaviors of children. Quay and his colleagues began with behavior ratings by parents and teachers, children's life history characteristics, and children's responses to questionnaires. Using these data, they identified four clusters, or dimensions, of interrelated behavior traits: *conduct disorder, personality disorder, immaturity,* and *socialized delinquency.* In the conduct disorder group are children described as disobedient, disruptive, fighting, destructive, having temper tantrums, irresponsible, impertinent, jealous, angry, bossy, attention seeking, and boisterous. Those in the personality disor-

der cluster are characterized by feelings of inferiority, including self-consciousness, social withdrawal, shyness, anxiety, oversensitivity, depression, guilt, and unhappiness. The third dimension, immaturity, includes children with short attention spans, clumsiness, and passivity and those who prefer younger playmates, daydream, and in general lag behind their agemates in social development. Children in the socialized delinquency group are associated with and loyal to bad companions, belong to and are active in delinquent groups, steal, are habitually absent from school, and take pride in having a social life within a delinquent subculture.

Intervention

Intervention involves educational and other treatment activities to which the behaviorally disordered child is exposed. It can be argued that intervention actually begins when the child is first singled out for concern. Many psychologists and special educators, for example, have found that some children need only to feel that someone cares about them. When singled out, as they must be when they are seen by resource teachers, consultants, or psychologists, a few children show remarkable and lasting positive behavior change. Unfortunately, such an intervention is effective for only a small percentage of children with behavior problems. More formal interventions are considered here.

Range of Interventions

Not so many years ago children with behavior problems were given only one option. In effect, they—and their parents—were told to "shape up or ship out." As special educational opportunities began to be made available, the possibilities broadened. Fifteen years ago, in a typical city and state, a disturbed child could be either in a regular class, a self-contained special class for the emotionally disturbed, a state or private institution, or at home. In recent years, especially since the passage of mandatory special education laws, most school systems of reasonable size offer a wide range of treatment options. (See chapter 1 for a more detailed discussion of recent laws and special education.) The philosophy should be that the least drastic intervention which works is the one which ought to be instituted.

From least to most drastic, the following are the possible treatment situations in which a disturbed child might be placed.

Regular class placement, with consultant support. A child should be kept in a regular class as long as possible and returned to the regular class as soon as possible for a least two reasons: normal peers have a positive influence on a child as models for appropriate behavior, and there is a stigmatizing effect when a child is removed from a regular class. Most regular class teachers, however, lack the training and/or the time to handle a disturbed child without support. Expert advice, necessary materials, and crucial moral support and encouragement can be provided by the school system's special education personnel or psychologists or by outside consultants. In addition, when possible administratively, the best kind of support for a regular class teacher who has behaviorally disturbed children in her class is to have a smaller class size.

Regular class placement, with resource or helping teacher support. Many school systems now employ specialists called "crisis teachers," "helping teachers," or "teacher-consultants." First developed by William Morse (1962, 1976), the idea spread quickly. These specialists usually are master's level teachers with training in emotional disturbance. Although functions differ, the helping teacher typically sees individual or small groups of disturbed children for varying lengths of time during the day. He is also available to provide direct assistance immediately in case a crisis erupts anywhere in the school. Instead of sending the child to the office for discipline, the helping teacher can deal with the child in a more therapeutic manner.

Split placement in regular and special class. Even those children who cannot learn best, or cannot be tolerated, in a regular class for the major part of the day often can spend a portion of the day in a regular class setting, provided that they get the support they need from a special class setting for the other part of the day. The split arrangement has the advantage of allowing the child to keep social ties with behaviorally normal children. This eases the reentry process when it is appropriate.

Special class placement in a regular school.

Placement in a special day school.

Special school or institutional placement. Occasionally a child's behavioral difficulties are sufficiently severe that she is dangerous to others in a regular school situation or simply cannot be taught effectively even in a special class. Also, it is sometimes important to control the entire environment of a child. This often is the case, for example, when the child's home situation is confusing and inconsistent. There are a variety of public and private schools for children who are this severely disturbed.

As a child's behavior improves it is usually wise to move her one step at a time back toward full-time regular class placement.

Initial Education Assessment
Regardless of the treatment situation chosen for the child, a good educational assessment is critical. Part of the assessment probably will occur before placement, but

part of it will most likely be left to the teacher or consultant after the child arrives in the selected intervention situation.

The traditional, psychoanalytically oriented approach to assessment placed primary importance on historical information which was collected in an attempt to uncover the cause of the child's problem and thereby resolve the conflict or dissolve the anxiety involved. Because historical data have not lived up to their expectations, many behavioral psychologists and educators criticize their use. Nevertheless, a detailed history of the child's development can become a valuable *part* of the teacher's initial assessment of a child. Specifically, information regarding the child's development and past treatment can serve the following purposes:

1. Inappropriate expectations and unnecessary errors can be avoided by noting the child's developmental characteristics and his past responses to specific situations and management techniques,

2. Probable reinforcers and high probability behaviors can be identified quickly by noting reports of the child's typical or preferred activities, and

3. Information regarding the child's past behavior provides a crude baseline against which to judge progress (see Gelfand & Hartmann, 1975).

Data obtained from formal tests, like historical data, have often been downgraded recently. Still, formal test data (from IQ, achievement, and personality tests, and so forth) can be useful when they are interpreted as a sample of behavior obtained under standardized conditions or when used as a means of identifying broad areas of deficit and strength. The astute teacher uses formal test data to narrow the universe of behavioral skills to those most *likely* (although not *certain*) to be appropriate for initial instruction.

Initial educational assessment should lead directly to an initial teaching strategy.

The teacher should use historical data, formal test results, and informal evaluation procedures to determine where and how to begin the child's educational program. An initial teaching strategy specifies those tools, materials, and methods that the teacher will first want to use because they have a high probability of success. Through adequate initial assessment, the teacher is able to zero in on the child's skills and deficits without floundering needlessly.

Goals and Objectives

The content of educational objectives and goals for disturbed children should be chosen carefully. Skills which humanize the child should have highest priority. These include self-help, communication, and basic social and academic skills which allow the child to function as independently and happily as possible. Unless objectives and goals are carefully chosen and precisely stated, the teacher may unknowingly waste the child's time in school, which is inexcusable for children who have waited too long for effective education.

Because disturbed children traditionally have been handled by psychotherapists, and many popular accounts of treatment of behavior disorders have romanticized play therapy and psychoanalysis, teachers have often confused their role with that of a therapist. But, as Wing and Wing (1966) have noted, "Teaching is not an inferior form of psychotherapy, and should not be confused with 'treatment' at all" (p. 196). The teacher's work is to help the child learn crucial skills and overcome her behavioral disabilities—not simply to find the cause of the child's problem and allow the child to "work through" her feelings—and to develop a meaningful relationship with peers, parents, and others. Skillful teaching is necessary to provide a basis for the development of a good teacher-child relationship (Wallace & Kauffman, 1978; Wing & Wing, 1966).

Curriculum Considerations

There is no generally accepted curriculum for disturbed children. Approaches to curriculum development range from child directed, open classroom, or free school models, to modification and adaption of standard curriculum materials for normal children, to individualized programs for teaching specific skills (see Kauffman & Lewis, 1974; Rhodes, 1963). The degree of severity of the disturbance determines the amount of curriculum modification necessary.

There appears to be general agreement among those who support a behavioral point of view regarding priorities of skills to be taught. Self-help skills, specifically toileting, feeding, bathing, and dressing, are of primary importance for severely and profoundly disturbed children who have not mastered these responses. Language is secondary only to acquiring self-help behaviors. If the child has acquired self-help and basic language skills, the priority should shift to appropriate social and affective responses—for example, play skills,

To teach Eddie, a severely emotionally disturbed adolescent, to make bags for seedlings, his teacher used task analysis (see chapter 1). Eddie was taught to pull out the plastic, tie a knot in the end, cut the other end, and put the finished bag aside.

cooperation, direction following, manners, pleasantries, and expressions of pleasure.

Basic academic skills, such as reading, writing, counting, and so on, should also be taught while language and social-emotional responses are being learned. If the child is far enough advanced academically, it is possible to adapt curricula for normal children to extend the learning of the disturbed child. Although many curriculum materials designed for retarded children or normal younger children are useful in teaching disturbed youngsters (see Hallahan & Kauffman, 1976),

> Teachers who enter this field should be willing to invent and make apparatus to suit the child they are teaching as well as making use of the great range of materials already available. (Elgar, 1966, p. 228)

There is no adequate substitute for a highly personalized curriculum when you are teaching a disturbed child.

Instructional Procedures and Programs

As in the case of curriculum, there is no consensus among experts in the field regarding the most effective approach to instruction. Instructional procedures range from the very nondirective and permissive (e.g., Bettelheim, 1950; Dennison, 1969) to highly structured and sequential (e.g., Haring, 1974; Hewett, 1968; Lovaas & Koegel, 1973; Wing & Wing, 1966). However, the effectiveness of a highly structured, directive approach is clearly indicated in the recent literature (Burchard & Harig, 1976; Kauffman, 1977; Kauffman & Hallahan, 1976; Lovaas & Newsom, 1976; O'Leary & O'Leary, 1976; Ross, 1974; Rutter & Bartak, 1973), especially for more severely disturbed children.

This directive, structured approach is particularly important for severely disturbed children because, contrary to popular opinion, most such children do not become productive or creative when left to their own devices. They desperately need direct help to organize their environments and to learn skills which will allow them to live happily at home, in the school, and in the community. Help for behavioral problems through directive teaching opens a new world for the child. In a nondirective, permissive, unstructured, or diversionary school environment, the severely disturbed child is not likely to make significant progress. On the other hand, when the child is consistently confronted with clear direction, firm expectations, and reinforcement of specific behaviors, his inappropriate behaviors most likely will subside, and he will acquire necessary skills.

Evaluation

Though evaluation is usually thought of at the end of a process, it should be continuous, and it should provide immediately useable information. This information should be used to make on-going modifications in the structure of the program. Evaluation is appropriate at each level of any program of intervention (see Gelfand & Hartmann, 1975).

Evaluation of the Student
As with the other program levels, evaluation of each pupil should follow naturally from the goals and objectives which have been specified for that child. For some general goals, such as raising the reading level or improving the self-concept, standardized educational and psychological tests may be somewhat helpful. More specific objectives in each area for each child are developed during the assessment and diagnostic process. If that procedure has been followed carefully, it is a relatively straightforward process to evaluate the child's progress in light of the specified objectives.

Evaluation of the Teacher
A major concern of all teachers, but particularly those of handicapped children, is measurement of the effectiveness of their instruction. In the past, teacher effectiveness has been assessed in vague, subjective terms. Attempts are now being made to measure teacher effectiveness on a sound empirical basis (Kauffman & Hallahan, 1975). This requires measurement of instructional time and teacher behaviors as well as measurement of pupil responses. To obtain a given level of pupil behavior, the effective teacher requires less time and less teaching effort than the ineffective teacher; effective teaching implies that the child's achievement increases in relationship to both time and amount of teacher activity. In the future, research may lead to methods of quantifying a teacher's effectiveness so that teachers can be matched to the combination of child, instructional method, and curriculum content with which they are most effective. However, until that time, we will continue to use relatively subjective techniques. These may include examining standardized or other test data to determine overall academic progress of individuals in the class or the class as a group, checking success in reaching goals and objectives, bringing in experts to give their opinions about the teacher's work, or simply providing a period of time during which the teacher can go through a self-evaluating and reorienting process.

Evaluation of the Program
The effectiveness of the overall program provided for disturbed children should be evaluated continuously. If goals and objectives have been developed for each part of the program, the evaluation simply involves comparing actual performance with objectives, and then examining areas where performance differed from the objective. Pro-

vus (1971) outlines this approach, called *discrepancy evaluation.*

Additional methods of program evaluation can also be used effectively. These may include obtaining measures of "consumer satisfaction," where children and their parents who are or have been participants in a program are asked to provide their opinions. Or outside experts may be asked to look carefully at the operation of the program.

TEACHER COMPETENCIES AND CHARACTERISTICS

Teaching disturbed children is intellectually and emotionally demanding. To be successful, you must first be an excellent teacher, able to adapt a normal curriculum to fit the academic learning needs of a classroom filled with unusually individualistic learners. Teaching academic skills to disturbed children is important because of the survival value that reading, writing, and arithmetic have for any child in our society. Without these skills a child's chances for successful adjustment are minimal. Yet it may be necessary to use novel teaching methods, for which there are no prepackaged materials, to teach basic academic skills to disturbed children.

A teacher of behaviorally disordered children also must be prepared to teach social skills and to expose children to affective experiences where they learn to manage their own feelings and behavior and learn to interact appropriately with other people. This is an important part of a curriculum for disturbed children. Without special instruction it is unlikely that they will learn these skills; the normal socialization processes clearly have failed.

On a personal level, the teacher of disturbed children must be stable and mature, able to tolerate rejection and aggressively hostile behaviors without responding in a rejecting or counteraggressive manner, and confident of his values and his teaching skills. Since these children do not respond conventionally, he must not expect that his kindness and warmth and generosity always will be given in return. He must be able to take satisfaction in small, positive increases in appropriate behavior, especially if the children with whom he is working are more severely disturbed. Hobbs' (1966) description of the type of teacher-counselors he was looking for in his Project Re-Ed is appropriate here:

> But most of all a teacher-counselor is a decent adult; educated, well-trained; able to give and receive affection, to live relaxed, and to be firm; a person with private resources for the nourishment and refreshment of his own life; not an itinerant worker but a professional through and through; a person with a sense of the significance of time, of the usefulness of today and the promise of tomorrow; a person of hope, quiet confidence, and joy; one who has committed himself to children and to the proposition that children who are emotionally disturbed can be helped by the process of reeducation. (pp. 1106–1107)

FUTURE CONSIDERATIONS

Areas of Needed Research

The "science" of human behavior and the "science" of special education are both in their infancy. Relatively little in these fields can be considered established, scientifically documented fact. Until quite recently professionals working with behaviorally disordered children have been forced either to use their best instincts or hunches based on experience or to follow the advice of "experts" who recommend practices based on *their* best instincts or experiences. We are now entering a time when scientific evaluation can be applied to educational practice to produce reliable information about the effectiveness of different approaches to the treatment of all exceptional children, including the emotionally disturbed (Haring & Schiefelbusch, 1976; Lovitt, 1977).

Within the past decade, behavioral research has indicated that disturbed children can be taught effectively. The greatest challanges now are to find the simplest, most efficient, and most humane ways of modifying children's maladaptive behavior, and to find the methods that produce the most generalized, long-lasting changes in behavior. To be most useful, behavior-change strategies must make the best use of the limited therapeutic resources available, have the widest possible positive impact on the child's characteristics, and be sustained over the longest period of time. The ultimate goal is to teach disturbed children self-control so that their desirable behavior becomes self-perpetuating. A great deal of additional research is needed to find the most effective and efficient methods of teaching self-management skills and to define more precisely just how people become self-controlled.

The Issue of Prevention

Special education and psychology traditionally have been concerned with solving existing problems. A child comes to the attention of professionals *after* her behavior is sufficiently excessive or deficient that she has called attention to herself. A much more efficient and humane approach would be to focus on causes of the problem and to work to lessen those. Though comparatively little is agreed on in terms of the causes of emotional disorders, enough is known to provide targets for preventative measures. Almost everyone agrees that poverty and malnutrition breed disturbance. Child abuse and neglect also are known to bring about major emotional difficulties. Our society must renew its commitment to wipe out these difficult but critical problems.

On a slightly less global level, it is generally admitted that failure in school at least makes emotional problems worse if it does not cause them. In addition, the longer the failure continues, the greater the probability of emotional difficulty for the child. It is vitally important that the "science" of education advance to the point that potential academic failures can be identified earlier and more reliably and that effective instructional techniques can be applied so that failure is avoided.

MEETING SPECIAL NEEDS

As the trend toward mainstreaming all types of mildly handicapped children continues, the probability increases that regular class teachers as well as special educators will come in contact with children who exhibit behavior disorders. Suggestions for teachers regarding appropriate approaches to managing behaviorally disordered children can be found in various publications (e.g., Goodwin & Coates, 1976; Madsen & Madsen, 1974). The local school psychologist or resource teacher also can often provide helpful hints. Here are some general principles which have been useful in classroom situations:

1. *Learn as much about the behaviorally disordered child as you can before the child arrives in your classroom. Talk to his previous teachers about management and teaching techniques which have proven to be successful. If the child has been receiving help from a mental health worker, ask for her suggestions about management.*

2. *Meet the child (and possibly the parents) before he comes into your classroom and observe the child in his previous setting. If possible, arrange for the child to visit your class before he formally becomes part of the group.*

3. *Beginning with your first meeting with the child, communicate clearly to the child* that you expect a reasonable standard of behavior to be maintained. Classroom rules for conduct should be spelled out in unmistakable terms. When you expect the child to perform some task, be certain that the directions are given clearly and firmly.

4. Consequences for the child's behavior should be given consistently. Reward desirable behavior by praising, smiling, or giving other signs of approval. Should inappropriate behavior occur, ignore it, or if necessary, give mild but firm punishment. Generally it is good practice to reward the child in full view of his classmates. However, reprimands and other punishments are best given quietly and privately, with the limits firmly repeated at the same time.

5. As quickly as possible, get to know the child's academic and behavioral ability level. It is important for the child primarily to have success experiences both in school work and in self-control. The expectations which you have for the child must be within his capacity. Generally tasks are too difficult if a child cannot succeed 90% of the time.

6. Remember that, although labeled behaviorally disordered, the child is a child. Basically you can expect him to respond as most of your other students do to your behavior management and instructional techniques. By making sure that your classroom is a place where children respect each other and take pride in themselves and their work, you are taking the best possible action.

FOR MORE INFORMATION

Most of these resources are textbooks that are readily available. Check your instructor, the education library, or the general library at your school.

Clarizio, H.F. & McCoy, G.F. *Behavior disorders in children* (2nd ed.). New York: Crowell, 1976.

Kauffman, J.M. *Characteristics of children's behavior disorders.* Columbus, Ohio: Charles E. Merrill, 1977.

Long, N.J., Morse, W.C., & Newman, R.G. (Eds.). *Conflict in the classroom* (3rd ed.). Belmont, Calif.: Wadsworth, 1976.

Ross, A.O. *Psychological disorders of children.* New York: McGraw-Hill, 1974.

7

The Learning Disabled

Thomas C. Lovitt

These are the major topics covered in this chapter. You may want to use them as a checklist when you review.

- *A brief history of learning disabilities, including five influential systems: perceptual, neurological, multisensory, psycholinguistics, and precision teaching.*

- *Definitions.*

- *Common characteristics of learning disabled children.*

- *Three alleged causes of learning disabilities.*

- *Four common treatment approaches.*

- *Who will teach the learning disabled and where they will be taught.*

- *Future needs in the field of learning disabilities, particularly in respect to mainstreaming.*

Learning disabilities is the newest of the categories in special education. Though public schools have had classes for many years for special children such as the mentally retarded, deaf, blind, and orthopedically handicapped, classes for learning disabled children date back only a dozen years or so. Further, college and university programs to train personnel, and federal funds for research and training programs, are of much more recent vintage in learning disabilities than in older, better established categories.

Although learning disabilities is the most recent category in special education, it has generated the most controversy—over such fundamental issues as an acceptable definition—not only from within the field but from outside it as well. Some people have complained that learning disabilities (abbreviated LD) is the category for the elite. They contend that only middle- and upper-class white children who have reading problems and are hyperactive qualify for placement in LD classes. The field has been criticized from time to time by legislators displeased with professionals' definitions of LD children. Occasionally they have threatened to withdraw or reduce funds.

Even though the LD category has been associated with controversy, it has had widespread appeal for parents. Parents across the land have banded together; they have lobbied and pressured schools and legislators in every state, and as a result, effected great changes. No other category has so many dedicated, militant, active, and knowledgeable parents.

LD has been an extremely popular category and receives much press coverage. Many articles have been written about famous people, including Nelson Rockefeller, Albert Einstein, and Thomas Edison, who were allegedly disabled or dyslexic as children. These and other articles on LD children stimulate parents and teachers to observe their children for similar "symptoms."

One of the fascinations with the field of LD is that it includes different views, approaches, and philosophies. It makes room for both beliefs and disciplines as varied as psychiatry, pediatrics, ophtalmology, neurology, nutrition, pharmacology, psychology, and education.

HISTORY

The LD movement began in 1963 at the Conference on Exploration into the Problems of the Perceptually Handicapped Child, when Samuel Kirk delivered an address to a group of parents. Many of their children had difficulty reading and were hyperactive. Nevertheless, they did not consider their children to be emotionally disturbed or mentally retarded. And they were not pleased with labels such as *dyslexia, strephosymbolia, perceptual handicap,* and *minimal brain dysfunction*—terms which had been used to describe their youngsters.

Therefore, when Kirk used the term *LD,* it became the accepted label. Interestingly, he did not suggest that the term *LD* should be used. He merely said that, "Recently, I have used the term 'learning disabilities' to describe a group of children who have disorders in development in language, speech, reading, and associated communication skills" (Kirk, 1975). The major point of his address was a straightforward plea to diagnose and describe children more behaviorally. He said, "I often wonder why we tend to use technical and complex labels, when it is more accurate and meaningful to describe behavior."

The parents, however, so readily accepted Kirk's term that they organized the Association for Children with Learning Disabilities (ACLD). Since its beginning in Chicago, the membership in this organization of parents has grown considerably; by 1976 there were chapters in nearly every state.

In 1963 there was another significant landmark in the history of LD. Three task forces, sponsored by several national agencies and headed by Sam D. Clements, were authorized to deal with matters of importance to LD. Several documents were written by those task forces which affected legislative and administrative decisions for years to follow.

Another milestone occurred in 1968 when the Council for Exceptional Children (CEC) established the Division of Children with Learning Disabilities (DCLD). In 1970 a congressional bill entitled the Children with Specific Learning Disabilities Act became law. That legislation included special programs for learning disabled children and authorized monies for research, training, and the development of model centers.

Five movements have significantly influenced the field of LD: perceptual, neurological, multisensory, psycholinguistics, and precision teaching.

Perceptual Disorders

Certain professionals believe that learning disabled youngsters cannot read or perform other academic subjects as well as others because they have *perceptual* problems. They claim that learning disabled children have deficits particularly in respect to visual or visual-motor perception. Visual perception generally refers to the ability to see an object or symbol and attach meaning to it. Visual-motor perception is the ability to see an object or symbol and move some part of the body in response to it.

Two significant contributors to this perceptual group are Alfred A. Strauss, a neuropsychiatrist, and Hans Werner, a developmental psychologist. They worked at the Wayne County Training School in Michigan during the 1930s and 1940s. Based on a series of investigations with mentally retarded children, they concluded that many of them had perceptual problems; the children had difficulty discriminating between a figure and its background. The retarded children were also easily distracted; they responded indiscriminately to many objects and people (Strauss & Werner, 1942). Several scholars, many of whom became prominent in the field of LD, studied with Strauss and Werner. Among them were William Cruickshank, Newell Kephart, and Kirk.

Cruickshank continued and extended the work of Strauss and Werner by studying a group of cerebral palsied children of normal intelligence. He reported that the youngsters had visual perceptual deficits in that they showed poor figure-ground relationships and were distractible (Cruickshank, Bice, & Wallen, 1957).

Since all of Cruickshank's subjects and some of Strauss and Werner's subjects were brain-injured and since they were inclined toward distractibility, Cruickshank and others concluded that brain injury and distractibility were related (for example, see Strauss & Lehtinen, 1947). Their reasoning prompted others to refer to children who were distractible as brain-injured and to assume they had perceptual disturbances, whether or not they were, in fact, brain-injured. Cruickshank's theories have been translated into practice by many schools. Comments about those efforts are provided in the section on treatments on pages 173–74.

Neurological Disorders

There are several researchers who maintain that learning disabilities are the result of **neurological** disorders. The most prominent and influential of those is Helmer Myklebust, who conducted considerable research at Northwestern University in the 1950s and 1960s. He proposed the term *psychoneurological learning disabilities,* which referred to children with language disorders (see chapters 4 and 10). That term reflected the behavioral characteristics of the children and the underlying central nervous system dysfunction (Boshes & Myklebust, 1964).

According to Tarver and Hallahan (1976), Myklebust's theory of language includes five levels of language acquisition:

> The first level, that of inner language, involves the formation of simple concepts. The development of inner language permits transformation of experience into verbal or nonverbal symbols. At the second level, auditory receptive language skills develop. Symbols and experience are associated, enabling the child to comprehend spoken words. Next, the development of auditory expressive language is evidenced in the child's speech. The fourth developmental level, that of visual receptive language, involves the comprehension of printed words, i.e. reading. At the last level of development, visual expressive language is evidenced in the ability to express oneself through writing. (pp. 27–28)

Myklebust and others state that the brain has two systems. Greatly simplified, they suggest that the left hemisphere is ordinarily used to process verbal signals, whereas the right side manages visual symbols. This belief has influenced some LD teachers to match modalities; that is, to determine whether a child learns better auditorily or visually and to instruct him by way of his "better" channel.

Children with learning disabilities benefit from individual attention and work on specific deficits. This student is working on spelling words with an aide.

Multisensory Disorders

Many LD specialists agree that several sensory channels should be used to instruct some youngsters. One of the most influential advocates of **multisensory** training was Samuel Orton, a neuropathologist. He devoted a large part of his life to studying children with severe reading problems (Orton, 1937). Lerner (1976) summarizes his therapeutic reasoning.

> Language function originates in the left cerebral hemisphere, and the left cerebral hemisphere is also the center for motor movement on the right side of the body; therefore, the language center in the left hemisphere should be strengthened and made dominant by strongly establishing the right-sided motor responses of the body. (p. 48)

Several well-known individuals trained under Orton. Monroe and Bender, notable in remedial reading and psychology, studied with him at the State University of Iowa. Hirsch and Gillingham, contributors in the fields of speech pathology and reading, received instruction from him at Columbia University.

Gillingham translated Orton's theories on functions of the brain into a multisensory technique for reading instruction. She developed a highly structured approach which blended the visual and kinesthetic senses (Gillingham & Stillman, 1966). Gillingham used these techniques with several reading disabled children on a one-to-one basis. Slingerland, who studied with Gillingham, adapted her methods and used them with groups of learning disabled youngsters (Slingerland, 1972). (See pages 174–75 for a discussion of the Slingerland method.)

Psycholinguistics

Several researchers have taken the position that learning to receive and express information (language development) is necessary before learning to read, write, and spell. Many of them subscribe also to the concept of modality diagnosis and modality matching. They believe that the diagnostician's first task is to determine the channel by which a child functions best, and then to arrange a curriculum accordingly.

The principal advocate of this approach is Kirk. Although he has made several contributions to special education and LD in particular, perhaps his most notable contribution has been his idea of **psycholinguistics.**

That plan can be explained most easily by describing the Illinois Test of Psycholinguistic Abilities (ITPA), which was developed in the early 1960s. Kirk, McCarthy, & Kirk (1968) designed a test based on the notion that language use involves certain psychological "information-processing" activities. The ITPA involves three dimensions of language functioning: levels of organization, channels of communication, and psycholinguistic processes. There are two levels of communication: the *representational level,* where the person uses language symbols, and the *automatic level,* where the person functions out of habit. The channels of communication are the input-output processes (or modes): auditory-vocal, auditory-motor, visual-motor, and visual-vocal. There are three psycholinguistic processes: receptive, associative (or organizing), and expressive. The test itself is made of 12 subtests, each of which involves a level of organization, a channel of communication, and a psycholinguistic process. The subject is evaluated on one or more of the subtests. The 12 subtest scores, plotted on a personal profile, show the subject's relatively strong and weak areas. Figure 7.1 shows the ITPA profile of a student with a visual channel disability. His chronological age (CA) scores are plotted for each subtest. These scores indicate that his lowest performances were in visual memory, visual association, visual reception and manual expression. Based on those scores, a program might be developed to focus on those deficit areas.

Chapter seven

PROFILE OF ABILITIES

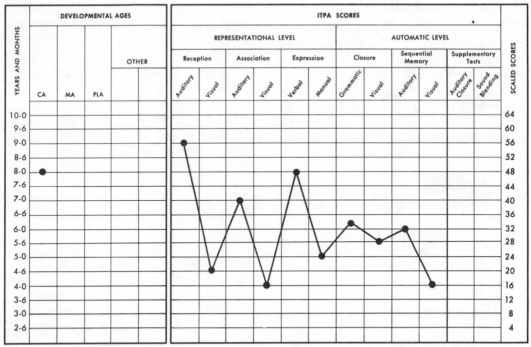

Figure 7.1
ITPA profile of abilities

From S. A. Kirk, J. J. McCarthy, & W. D. Kirk, The Illinois Test of Psycholinguistic Abilities (rev. ed.). Urbana, Ill.: University of Illinois Press, 1968. © 1968 by the Board of Trustees of the University of Illinois.

profile SAMUEL KIRK

Sam Kirk was born in North Dakota in 1904 and earned his Ph.D. in physiological and clinical psychology from the University of Michigan. He is currently a professor of special education at the University of Arizona. From 1952 until 1967 he was director of the Institute for Research on Exceptional Children at the University of Illinois.

His contributions to special education include the conceptualization and development of the Illinois Test of Psycholinguistic Abilities. Although not uniformly accepted, this test has been synonomous with the assessment of children with LD. Perhaps Kirk's most notable research effort was his preschool intervention study published in 1958 (Early Education of the Mentally Retarded).

Kirk will also be remembered because of the faculty he assembled at the University of Illinois and the dozens of outstanding students trained by that group.

Although Samuel Kirk and Winifred Kirk (Kirk & Kirk, 1971) designed treatment exercises which correspond to the ITPA subtests, Lloyd M. Dunn and James O. Smith have done more to translate the psycholinguistic concept into classroom practice (Dunn & Smith, 1965).

Precision Teaching

Since 1964, when O.R. Lindsley introduced **precision teaching** at the University of Kansas, dozens of researchers and teachers—many of them in the field of LD—have adopted this approach.

Those who subscribe to this method are not greatly interested in neurology. For example, they would not be overly concerned whether or not a pupil was brain-injured. This is not to say they are uninterested in the brain and its functions. But they do maintain that, since little can be done to aid a damaged brain, it is more important to direct attention to behaviors such as speaking, writing, and walking. Furthermore, precision teachers attach little importance to other presumed underlying causes of behaviors. If a child cannot read, for example, they would not say that that is from a visual-motor problem or from a poorly developed language system. Although they might speculate as to why he behaved in a certain way, they would tend to deal directly with the behaviors of concern.

Another characteristic of precision teachers is that ordinarily they do not endorse any exclusive treatment or remedy. Although some of them have used approaches which are strongly advocated by certain educators in LD—for example, the Slingerland method (Slingerland, 1964, 1971, 1972), the DISTAR materials (Englemann & Bruner, 1969; Englemann, Osborn, & Englemann, 1969), the materials developed by Marianne Frostig (Frostig & Horne, 1973; Frostig, Lefever, & Whittlesey, 1964), and the system founded by Maria Montessori (1912)—others have used different techniques. Not only has a great deal of research been conducted with this approach, but the system has been used widely in the public schools, particularly in certain sections of the United States. Most probably this system will, in the near future, greatly influence other schools throughout the country.

ISSUES IN THE FIELD

Since its beginning, LD has been a source of controversy. Even the name itself has created considerable disagreement. Many professionals argue that the term *learning disabilities* should be replaced by descriptions such as *minimal brain dysfunction, brain damaged,* or *perceptually handicapped.* Let's examine the most critical issues, including my viewpoints:

1. Several task forces and scholarly groups have grappled with *definition* over the years without finding one acceptable to the majority of professionals in the field.

2. There are arguments over the *characteristics* of learning disabled children.

3. Another issue relates to the *cause* of LD (etiology).

4. An issue which has always haunted the field is *assessment;* there has been little agreement on how best to evaluate LD children.

5. The field is often in disagreement over the most appropriate form of *treatment* for these children.

6. The issue of *who should teach* learning disabled children has brought great debates about territoriality in the past few years.

7. Many in the field disagree over *where should LD children be taught,* although current legislation has created a rush towards mainstreaming.

Definition

Finding an acceptable definition of LD has been a problem from the beginning. Although many have been written, all have been severely critized for one reason or another.

Perhaps the first definition of LD was written by Kirk. It was published in 1962.

> A learning disability refers to a retardation, disorder, or delayed development in one or more of the processes of speech, language, reading, spelling, writing, or arithmetic resulting from a possible cerebral

dysfunction and/or emotional or behavioral disturbance and not from mental retardation, sensory deprivation, or cultural or instructional factors. (p. 263)

A more recent definition was advanced in P.L. 94–142:

"Specific learning disability" means a disorder in one or more of the basic psychological processes involved in understanding or in using language spoken or written, which may manifest itself in an imperfect ability to listen, think, speak, read, write, spell or to do mathematical calculations. The term includes such conditions as perceptual handicaps, brain injury, minimal brain dysfunction, dyslexia, and developmental aphasia. The term does not include children who have learning problems which are primarily the result of visual, hearing, or motor handicaps, of mental retardation, or of environmental, cultural, or economic disadvantages.

Mercer, Forgnone, and Wolking (1976) analyzed the definitions from 42 states. To do so they identified several components which were featured in most of the definitions. According to the authors, the six most important were the intelligence, process, academic, exclusion, neurological, and affective components.

One of the most important reasons for defining groups is that a definition should lead directly to a form of treatment. To define a child as learning disabled, dyslexic, a poor reader, or whatever, should tell us how to treat him.

Another reason for defining children is for research purposes. It stands to reason that if several investigators similarly defined their populations they would be better able to repeat one another's findings. The results could then be readily and confidently put into action in the schools. An acceptable definition of LD, therefore, should be encouraged since youngsters will surely profit.

But attempts to define LD, in my view, will continue to be useless until those who de-

velop definitions stop using intelligence and achievement tests as the primary means for classifying children. There are three reasons for not using these instruments:

1. They do not always provide a *direct* measure of the behavior identified for instruction. They often measure behaviors which are not being taught and fail to assess other behaviors which are being taught.

2. They do not provide *frequent* measures of the identified behaviors; tests are given once or twice a year. If a child scored exceptionally high or low, any decisions based on those scores would, indeed, be shaky.

3. They do not reveal an index of *learning*. It is not possible to determine the rate at which a pupil learns, since only one or two measures of a behavior are obtained.

Direct, daily measurement should replace intelligence and achievement tests. More explanation will be provided later about this system.

In addition to changing assessment techniques, two other aspects of behavior should be explained in the definition. One of those features refers to the child's educational history. It is important to know how a child acquired some of her current behaviors. It is important also to know how long it took her to learn certain behaviors and the conditions which prevailed while she acquired those behaviors. Second, a pupil's current motivational state should be considered in the definition. Although difficult, it is necessary to determine the extent to which a child is motivated to learn a specific skill. Currently, these features are rarely included in the definitions of learning disabled youngsters.

Characteristics

Most textbooks agree on characteristics commonly associated with learning disabled youngsters. Tarver and Hallahan (1976) listed the 10 most often cited in the literature, in order of frequency: hyperactivity, perceptual-motor impairments, emotional lability, general coordination deficits, disorders of attention, impulsivity, disorders of memory, specific LD, disorders of speech, and equivocal neurological signs. Behavioral disparity should be added to this list.

Hyperactivity refers to constant motion. It is difficult for some children to sit at their desks; they prefer to glide aimlessly about the room. When they are seated, they often rock back and forth in their chairs, tap their fingers, and shuffle their feet.

Perceptual-motor impairments refers to an inability to identify or discriminate. Some youngsters have difficulty identifying visual or auditory symbols. Others are unable to discriminate among a series of letters, sounds, or shapes. Perceptual disorders are distinguished from sensory defects such as blindness and deafness; some children with perfect eyesight are unable to identify certain symbols or to discriminate between a set of symbols.

Emotional lability has to do with a child's emotional condition. Some children are high-strung and nervous. Some of them have low frustration thresholds; others have weak self-concepts.

General coordination deficits relates to the physical awkwardness of some children. Some youngsters cannot throw or catch a ball as well as their peers. Others cannot skip rope, play jacks, or throw a Frisbee. Some children are generally clumsy when they walk; they stumble and often fall.

Disorders of attention refers to an inability to stay on task. Keogh and Morgulis (1976) described three types of attention: the ability to attend initially to an object, the ability to switch from one symbol to another, and the ability to stay with a certain situation. Some children have problems with one or more forms of attention.

Impulsivity means that some youngsters react suddenly to a wide variety of events; they are unable to filter certain visual or auditory stimuli. Furthermore, their actions do not appear to be contemplated.

Disorders of memory relates to an inability to remember past experiences. Some youngsters are unable to remember over long periods of time; others cannot recall facts after a short period. Some children cannot remember visual symbols, whereas others cannot recall auditory messages.

Specific learning disabilities refers to an inability to perform in certain academic areas. Many youngsters have difficulty learning to say words, to read in context, or to comprehend. Others have problems with handwriting, creative writing, spelling, and mathematics.

Disorders of language are widely varied. Some youngsters have a very limited verbal repertoire; others are clumsy in arranging their words. Some children have problems with specific features of language—for example, correctly forming plurals. Others have articulation or voice

These junior high students are working on consumer math problems in their resource room.

problems, whereas still others use a language of their own invention.

Equivocal neurological signs means that some learning disabled youngsters may be brain-damaged. As discussed earlier, a few investigators learned that some brain-injured individuals were hyperactive and displayed other characteristics discussed here. Other investigators concluded that if youngsters displayed these behaviors, they were brain-injured.

Behavioral disparity refers to wide performance differences. Some youngsters are quite capable in mathematics and handwriting but have great difficulty with spelling and reading. Others can read orally very well but cannot comprehend. These discrepancies are sometimes as wide as three or four grade levels.

Etiology

Several causes of LD have been proposed. Some are organically based; others are biochemical or environmental in origin.

profile JOSH

Josh is 10 years old and attends the intermediate LD classroom at the Experimental Education Unit (EEU), University of Washington. There are 12 children in his classroom; they range in age from 10 to 12. Josh is one of the youngest.

This is his second year at the EEU; he spent last year in the primary LD classroom. Prior to coming to the EEU, Josh attended classes in a suburban Seattle school district. While there, he spent 2 years in kindergarten and 2 years in first grade.

The classroom is smaller than the average room. At one end, there is a small room with a one-way window, which often is used by visitors when they observe the pupils and by teachers when they work with one or two children. The head teacher's office also is adjacent to the classroom. Outside the classroom is a small patio which overlooks a canal and a lake.

The classroom is well-equipped; several basal reading series are available. There is also an ample supply of workbooks, arithmetic and phonics sheets, and science, social studies, and art materials. In addition there is a TV set, four small tape recorders, a Language Master, and a record player.

The class is managed by a head teacher who is assisted by an intern. Six graduate students, who work a few hours each day

on special projects, are also assigned to the class.

Josh is small for his age, about as tall as the average 7 year old. He is apparently healthy, however, and he hasn't missed a day of school in 2 years. He is a good-looking boy: large black eyes and dark hair cut in a page boy. He, like the rest of his classmates, wears a cotton shirt and pair of jeans every day.

Each morning Josh boards his bus at 7:30 and begins the 70-minute trip to the EEU. He rides the bus with six other youngsters, some of whom are in his classroom.

He arrived at 8:45. Immediately he ran to his classroom, swinging his lunch pail. When he entered the room he looked for Suzanne, the head teacher, and Jenny, the intern. He excitedly told them about Adam 12, the TV show he watched the night before. Josh also informed Suzanne that he and David (one of his classmates) had a fight on the bus coming to school.

By 9 A.M., the 12 class members had arrived. They took their seats and Suzanne began the preliminary exercises. While she talked, Josh sat on the back of his seat, pulled a sheet of paper from his desk, rocked back and forth on his chair, and then raised his hand. Suzanne noticed, but didn't acknowledge him. She continued talking about the calendar and the weather. She then mentioned that if they behaved

Organically based

For some years there have been many who claimed that the primary reason some children were learning disabled was because of a brain injury. One of the problems with this hypothesis is that the techniques used to detect brain injury are rather crude and insensitive. Commonly, two methods have been used. One has been to administer a battery of tests including the WISC and the Bender Visual-Motor Gestalt Test. Another method has been to administer an electroencephalograph (EEG).

Boshes and Mykelbust (1964) provided data on those examinations which suggest cautious interpretations of the findings. According to them, when 200 normal youngsters were given neurological examinations, 38% were classified as abnormal. When 200 learning disabled children were assessed, 49% were abnormal. Those youngsters were also classified according to EEG readings: 29% of the 200 normal

themselves until Friday they would take a field trip to the nearby fire station.

At 9:25 Josh began working on his story problems. He is assigned problems of the following type: "John needs 5 bird cages. He made 2 bird cages. How many more should John make?" Each day he is required to complete 10 problems. On some days his answers are all correct, but on other days he simply writes random numbers. When he finished, Jenny came to check his work. When she discovered all his answers were incorrect, she told Josh to draw pictures to represent the problems, for example, 5 birds and 2 more birds. She informed him that when he finished, using this method, he should signal her to recheck his work.

After 10 minutes or so he completed his problems and summoned Jenny. She checked them, and this time they were all correct. Josh then plotted his 100% score in a notebook. All the pupils plot their scores for their subjects. They each have notebooks which contain graphs, one for each subject.

At 9:40 Josh took out his reader, The Dog Next Door, a second grade reader from the Ginn reading series (Ousley & Russell, 1961). This is his second time through the book. Today he was expected to read about eight pages silently. As he read, he stuck his feet inside his desk, took out a

piece of paper, and scribbled something on it. Jenny came by and reminded him that he could play pool when he finished his work. This prompted him to read some more.

While reading he chewed a piece of paper and rocked back and forth in his chair. After he flipped a few pages, he was distracted by the conversation of two boys seated next to him. He listened for a few seconds, then sauntered over to them and joined in. In a few seconds he returned to his seat, flipped a few more pages, then summoned Jenny. They talked about the story and she was convinced he knew something about it.

Josh then read some of the story orally for 1 minute. As he read, Jenny wrote down his errors, corrected his mistakes, and told him words if he hesitated. His correct and incorrect rates were 65 and 4. After the reading session he plotted his rates.

Josh was then required to answer 10 questions about the story. They were factual questions like "Where did Bill live?" Josh read the questions and wrote his answers. It took him about 1 minute to complete the task, and once again he called for Jenny to correct his paper. She checked them all wrong and required him to redo them. This process continued five more times until he finally reached the required criterion of 80%. While Josh "worked" on

children were believed to be abnormal, whereas 42% of the 200 LD youngsters were abnormal.

Although more learning disabled than normal youngsters were classified as abnormal on the two measures, a direct relationship between brain injury and LD was not established.

According to Becker (1975), better methods for detecting brain injury are being developed. He said that Towbin, for example, has demonstrated dramatically that specific organic causes of minimal brain dysfunction exist and can be documented and demonstrated under some exacting neuroradiological and laboratory conditions.

Biochemically based

Several biochemical factors have been associated with LD. Cott (1972) reported that

the problems he continually fidgeted, squirmed, tugged, and pulled. He was never still.

From time to time Ritalin has been prescribed in an effort to control Josh's hyperactivity. Although data have not been obtained to determine whether the drugs are effective, his teachers are skeptical. According to them, he is just as hyperactive on some days when the drug is given as he is on certain days when the drug isn't used.

After the comprehension session, Josh went to the bumper pool table, a recent purchase of the class. All the children can earn time to play pool by performing up to a certain standard in their various subjects. When Josh played pool he was very impulsive; he rarely took time to aim. He lined up behind the ball and fired. Sometimes he hit the ball; at other times he chipped it. Amazingly, however, he beat Anne. His last ball ricocheted off three sides before it went in. Anne reacted by screaming indignantly, "Lucky, Lucky!" Josh then played Pat and nearly beat him; but in his haste to shoot, he knocked in Pat's last ball.

About 10:30 A.M. Josh began his math assignment. Problems of the type 47 + 26 = ___ were assigned. He had been working with carrying problems for only a few days. Josh finished the sheet of 25 problems in about 30 seconds and went to the checking area. One of the graduate students scored his paper and determined

he missed every problem. He simply wrote down random numbers. She gave him another sheet of problems and he returned to his seat.

After five visits to the checking area, he finally achieved the criterion of 92%. While he worked on the problems, between visits to the checking area, he stuck his feet in his desk, sat on the back of his chair, sat on both feet. He was a whirling dervish.

When Josh finally finished his math he played another game of pool, this time with Will. Throughout the game Will poked fun at him. He said, sarcastically, "Oh wow, some shot, Josh!" and, "Boy, Josh, you're really good!" Josh lost the game.

Will isn't the only one who doesn't like Josh; at best, his classmates seem to tolerate him. When I asked Josh who his best school friend was, he couldn't name anyone. According to him, he has several friends at home, however.

After the pool game Josh worked on his phonics program. He is assigned three phonics skills each day. One pertains to the long vowels; another, to the long a; the third, to CVC (consonant-vowel-consonant) words. Drill sheets are used for each skill; several words are printed on each sheet. For example, there are 50 words which feature the five long vowels on the first sheet.

Each day he is asked to say as many sounds or words as he can in 1 minute. His correct rates today on the three sheets

Vitale and Veler discovered that 95% of the children in a Colombian village who were normal at birth became retarded before they reached puberty. They suggested that the regression in intelligence was caused by a lack of essential amino acids in the children's diets.

Wunderlich (1973) suggested that some learning problems are associated with allergies. Others have linked learning and behavioral problems with protein, vitamin, and mineral deficiencies. Still other researchers have suggested that such biochemical irregularities as glandular disorders (Eames, 1962) and hypoglycemia (Roberts, 1969) are related to LD.

Perhaps the most controversial biochemical linkage with LD and hyperactivity has been artificial food colors and flavors. Feingold argued that his data, and those of others, suggest that additives such as preservatives, antioxidants, buffers, artificial

were 45, 30, and 55. Only two errors were made on the five-vowel sheet, but none were made on the other sheets. The phonics skills will be assigned until his correct rates are greater than 60 per minute and his incorrect rates are less than 3 per minute.

About 11:45, Josh began his spelling assignment. Each day he studies 10 words from the Hanna, Hanna, Hodges, and Peterson (1970) spelling program. His words were gave, cake, wait, made, rain, make, name, train, matches, *and* maps. *After studying the words for a few minutes, he requested that a teacher ask him the words. A graduate student read them to him. When finished, he checked his answers from a guide, crossed out the words he passed, and wrote down those he needed to practice.*

If he spells a word correctly for two consecutive days that word is dropped and a new one added. If he misses a word he must copy it several times. Spelling is Josh's best subject; he generally passes two or three words each day. Not surprisingly, this is his favorite activity.

After spelling, it was time for lunch. The children and the teachers ate at their desks. Josh brought a sandwich, an apple, and purchased a carton of milk at a nearby cafeteria.

After lunch Suzanne read to the class about Muhammed Ali. Today's episode was about Ali as a young man. All the youngsters, including Josh, apparently enjoyed the story; they all sat quietly and later talked about it.

About 12:45 P.M., they began their writing period. Frank, one of the older boys, passed out the folders. Each pupil's folder is a collection of blank sheets of paper with a construction paper cover. The covers are decorated by the youngsters; some have pictures of dogs, cars, and athletes. Josh's cover was decorated with pictures of scantily clad females.

Before they wrote, Jenny gave a brief lesson on the use of capital letters. She pointed out that cities like Seattle and the names of lakes and rivers should be capitalized. Today they were told to write on a topic of their choice. On other days they are given prompts such as story starters and pictures before they begin writing.

The writing period lasted for 10 minutes. During that time they raised their hands if they needed a teacher to spell a word for them. Josh asked for help eight times. The pupils were very quiet throughout this period. Most of them enjoy writing and compose rather interesting stories. Following is Josh's effort:

I spleept in the now haos Last nighe
It was fun sleeping thar to.
We movd sum of the stuff last night.
We took the stof up in pikup and car
and a voxwagan to. It was sow fun

food colorings, and flavorings are the cause of many cases of hyperkinesis and learning disability (1976).

Spring and Sandoval (1976) reviewed the current data on the relationship between food additives and hyperactivity. They concluded that the correlation between the two factors had not been conclusively demonstrated.

Environmentally based

Although some definitions of LD dismiss the association of environment associated with LD, it is absurd to think otherwise. In fact, there appear to be at least three environmental causes of LD: emotional disturbance, motivational deficits, and inadequate instruction. These causes and others are often interrelated.

---

that i laft a gegld. My sistr gegld and laft and laft. My mom laft

Later in the afternoon a graduate student took them to gym. First he asked the youngsters to line up at one end of the gym, then hop back and forth. Some of them couldn't do this, but Josh did quite well. Next, they did a few sit-ups. Josh positioned himself as far away from the other youngsters as he could while he did this exercise.

After a few more calisthentics, they chose sides and played whiffle ball. It was quite a challenge playing ball in the small area, for occasionally the ball bounced off three or four walls before it was retrieved. At one time a ball was hit to Josh in right field. He chased it wildly, having no idea where it was going. Finally, he picked up the ball and threw it to home plate. Later, when he came to bat, he got a double on the first swing. Surprisingly, he stayed on base until the next batter knocked him in.

After the children returned to class they had a science period. They discussed instruments which are used to measure various aspects of the weather. Suzanne prodded and hinted for several minutes before the children understood what she wanted. Frank and Art mentioned the weather vane, barometer, and weather balloon. Toward the end of the discussion Suzanne asked Josh how rain was measured. He immediately informed her that a

box was used.

When the science period ended, only a few minutes remained until they met the busses at 2:15. During this time the children were given free time; some played pool, others read. Josh and four others played Twister. A large mat with several squares was placed on the floor. Throughout the game the participants are required to place their hands and feet on various squares. As the game progresses, some awkward positions are noted. If a performer cannot maintain a position, he is eliminated. Josh was the first player to leave the game.

Recently, Josh was administered the Wechsler Intelligence School for Children (WISC). His full-scale score was 83; his verbal and performance scores were 75 and 92. His scores on a Wide-Range Achievement Test (WRAT) were as follows: Reading, 2.3; Spelling, 2.2; Arithmetic, 1.8. On the ITPA his scores ranged from 6–10 (visual motor and auditory memory) to 10–4 (verbal expression and manual expression).

Josh has a better-than-average family life. He has a younger sister who is not yet in school. His father works for Boeing and his mother is the homemaker. They both attend all the school conferences and are concerned about his progress. His mother is particularly anxious about Josh's ability to learn, but she is sympathetic to his teachers. She realizes it is demanding to work with such a fiesty boy.

Several researchers have claimed for some time that there is a relationship between emotional factors and learning. Morse, Cutler, and Fink (1964), for example, reported that the inability to learn was a frequent characteristic of children diagnosed as behaviorally disordered.

Several teachers have reported that some learning disabled children have motivational problems; they are not reinforced by the events and circumstances which appeal to normal children. Not only is it sometimes difficult to identify reinforcers for these youngsters; but when they are identified, they rapidly lose their effectiveness.

A third environmental condition which might contribute to a learning disability is poor instruction. Although many children are able to learn in spite of poor teachers and inadequate techniques, others are less fortunate. Some youngsters who have experienced poor instruction in the early grades never catch up with their peers.

There are no studies which demonstrate that any of the causes discussed here were individually responsible for a learning disability. There are people who are intellectually gifted despite extensive brain injury, and others who are intact neurologically, but function below average. Some are gifted despite poor diets, while some with healthful diets act intellectually below normal. *But despite all the variables, the cause-effect relationship is important and research should be continued and encouraged to find answers to the many puzzling questions mentioned here as well as others.*

Assessment

In special education, assessment has generally been synonymous with administering several tests. Hundreds of tests (several of which are listed in the appendix) have been developed to determine various behaviors of learning disabled children. Current practice is for teachers or psychometrists to assess children for classification or instruction at the beginning of school or when referred for special testing at a school or clinic. Both indirect and direct testing procedures are used.

Who Does the Assessment?

Children are assessed either by their teachers or certified psychometrists. Classroom teachers often administer achievement and diagnostic tests. Intelligence, aptitude, and projective tests are generally administered by psychologists or other accredited assessors.

profile **BARBARA BATEMAN**

Born in Medford, Oregon, Barbara Bateman obtained a B.S. degree in psychology from the University of Washington and an M.A. in special education from San Francisco State College. She earned a doctorate in special education from the University of Illinois and was awarded a law degree from the University of Oregon.

Bateman has taught the mentally retarded, emotionally disturbed blind children, and remedial reading. She has also worked as a speech correctionist, psychomotrist, and parent counselor. She was associated with the Institute for Research at the University of Illinois for several years and later was affiliated with DePaul University and the Henner Speech and Hearing Center in Chicago. In 1966 Bateman joined the special education staff at the University of Oregon, where she currently works.

Bateman has written several books, chapters, monographs, and articles on several special education topics. Her primary contributions to the field of learning disabilities have been her researches on reading, psycholinguistics, curriculum development, diagnosis, and assessment. And in addition, Bateman has become quite active in supporting special education legislation and working for the educational rights of all exceptional children.

Reasons for Assessing Children

Children are assessed to classify them or to aid in their instruction. A test or group of tests is sometimes given in order to categorize children as to type of disorder, such as emotionally disturbed or learning disabled. In some instances a child scoring below a certain score can be classified as a Type X child. Scores at or above another point can label the child a Type Y youngster. This kind of assessment has administrative value only. When children are so classified, administrators can count the numbers in each category and report those counts to state or federal agencies.

The second reason for assessment is for purposes of instruction. Some types of assessment lead directly to instruction; others are, at best, only indirectly related to instruction. When teachers study the results of some tests, they know the level at which to begin instruction. The tests tell them the instructional techniques to be used. By contrast, when teachers receive the results of other tests, they are at a loss. They are neither informed about what should be taught nor how it should be taught.

When Are Children Assessed?

Ordinarily, learning disabled children are assessed when they first begin school. Many school systems arrange screening procedures during the kindergarten or first-grade year. At that time a reading readiness test or tests such as the Developmental Test of Visual-Motor Integration (Berry & Buktenica, 1967) or the Developmental Test of Visual Perception (Frostig, Lefever, & Whittlesey, 1964) are administered to pupils. On the basis of these test scores the child is placed in one program or another.

The rationale for screening children is logical. If children with learning problems can be detected and assisted at an early age, fewer children should develop severe learning problems. There are, however, two common problems with many screening programs: (1) special programs for such children are not universally available, and (2) the tests used may not lead directly to instruction to lessen the disabilities. Thus, the children suffer in two ways. They are identified early as learning disabled and thus are burdened with a negative label; and they may receive irrelevant instruction which doesn't help them overcome the disability.

The other time some learning disabled youngsters are assessed is when they are referred for special testing. These requests for additional information may occur any time during their school careers. In most instances the child is referred by a classroom teacher. Occasionally, parents, guardians, physicians, guidance counselors, or psychologists request additional data.

Places where Children Are Assessed

Children are either assessed at their school or at a clinic. Probably 90% of learning disabled children are tested at their schools. The 10% clinic assessments are prompted either by parents who are dissatisfied with the evaluations provided by the school, by school personnel who wish to confirm or elaborate on their findings, or by physicians who have greater confidence in professionals at clinics than those at schools.

There are numerous public and private clinics in most cities which evaluate youngsters. Many diagnostic clinics are affiliated with universities, others with hospitals or special schools; some are free, others charge a fee. The waiting lists for most clinics, either public or private, are generally long.

Assessment Strategies

Either indirect or direct assessment is used. In indirect assessment, a child's ability to, for instance, discriminate shapes and sounds might be evaluated, although he is not being taught to identify these skills. The logic is that it is necessary to know about a child's performance on fundamental tasks which are related to more complex behaviors.

The other method of assessment is to measure directly those behaviors being taught. For example, if a first grader was being instructed to count to 10, to say the sounds of the short vowels, and to read some sight words, these behaviors would be measured. The child's performance with respect to behaviors presumed to be fundamental to those skills would not be evaluated.

The process of referring children for special assistance has become increasingly complex. A few years ago, a classroom teacher concerned about a youngster would chat casually with a specialist about the child. The specialist might administer a test or two and then, if the results so indicated, the child would be placed in a special education class. Referral procedures now are much more sophisticated. Parents are better informed than they once were; and the referral stages are carefully planned and followed.

The Referral and Assessment System
The following procedures are used by one of the school districts in the Seattle area. Their situation is typical of other districts and explains the referral and assessment system.

First, a child may be referred by a teacher or parent to a special educator, often an LD specialist. Notice of that referral is sent to the school psychologist. Next, a conference is scheduled for the parents of the referred child, the special educator, and the school psychologist. The meeting notifies the parents their child has been referred and explains the services available if she is placed in special education. The parents are then asked to sign a form which allows the school personnel to assess her. All along the way, the parents can stop the proceedings.

Next, the parents and school personnel agree to exchange information about the child. The parents will provide a medical history of their child, and the school will inform them about the assessment results. If the parents give permission to assess their child and agree to share information, the school psychologist and principal are informed that the assessment will start.

Next, the teacher who referred the child provides written information about the child's academic abilities. The teacher explains the child's abilities to read, comprehend, spell, write, and compute. He also describes her social and emotional development.

Next, several standardized tests are administered. (For descriptions of these and other tests, see the appendix.) The school psychologist gives the Wechsler Intelligence Scale for Children (Wechsler, 1974), the Bender Visual-Motor Gestalt Test (Bender, 1962), and the Goodenough-Harris Drawing Test. (Goodenough & Harris, 1963). Meanwhile, the special education teacher administers the Durrell Analysis of Reading Difficulty (Durrell, 1955), the Peabody Individual Achievement Test (Dunn & Markwardt, 1970), the Wide Range Achievement Test (Jastak & Jastak, 1965), the Pupil Rating Scale (Mykelbust, 1971), and the Gates-McKillop Reading Diagnostic Tests (Gates & McKillop, 1962). Data pertaining to the child's physical development are also noted. If they are incomplete, she will receive an examination.

After all this information has been assembled, an educational plan is developed. The plan specifies which behaviors are to be instructed, the extent to which they will be learned, who will teach the child, where she will be taught, and how long the process will take. If the child's parents agree to the plan, the new program will begin.

However, because of the expectations of parents, other teachers, and clinicians,

Chapter seven

While the other children study independently, Marilyn is working with Tony to assess his daily progress in add facts.

teachers must know the purposes and limitations of the many commonly used standardized instruments, even though they are seldom of much value in determining what to teach the child.

Assessment Recommendations

First, *all assessment should lead to instruction.* After a child's behavior has been assessed a teacher should know what to do next: whether to use a different technique, to teach a simpler behavior, or to shift instruction to a more advanced behavior. Second, *assessment should be direct.* Those behaviors a teacher wishes to teach should be assessed. Third, *assessment should, whenever possible, be conducted in the child's classroom.* That is her instructional forum; customarily she isn't taught in the psychologist's chambers.

Fourth, *the teacher should conduct as much of the assessment as possible.* He must know immediately and precisely about a child's performance, for he, not the psychologist, is ultimately responsible for the pupil's development. Finally, *assessment should be continuous.* Since assess-

ment should lead directly to instruction, the teacher should be advised daily about each child's progress in order to make periodic adjustments.

Treatment

Several teaching approaches are used with learning disabled youngsters, just as there are several viewpoints when it comes to the definition, the characteristics, and the causes of LD.

According to Myers and Hammill (1969), seven instructional approaches have been developed for children with LD: perceptual-motor, multisensory, language development, phonic, structural, test-related, and neurological organization. Tarver and Hallahan (1976) explained five instructional approaches: structured classrooms, behavior modification, perceptual-motor programs, linguistic approaches, and clinical teaching.

Based on my observations of several classrooms, I describe four approaches: remedial, perceptual, multisensory, and precision teaching.

Remedial

There are several instructional situations for learning disabled youngsters that are based on the remedial approach. They might be characterized as miniature regular classrooms. When this approach is followed—in either self-contained or resource situations—the materials are similar to those used in regular classrooms. The teacher uses one or two basal reading series and requires the children to read from those texts and perform the related workbook exercises and other assignments that accompany the series. Teachers of this type often use traditional spelling texts, handwriting programs, and mathematics books.

Scheduling activities is much like a regular class. Children are placed in reading and mathematics groups depending on their abilities. The teacher assists one group at a time while the others work independently at their seats. For example, while she helps one group in reading, the others work on their handwriting and mathematics assignments. Throughout the day a few recesses, free-time periods, art, music, and physical education are sprinkled in.

Occasionally, some data are obtained that reflect the children's progress. Each Friday, for instance, a spelling test is administered, the results of which are entered in the teacher's record book. When the children complete chapters or units in their mathematics texts, they take summary tests. From time to time the teacher gives reading diagnostic tests to find out, to some extent, about the word recognition, reading, or comprehension abilities of the students.

Perceptual

There are some teachers who feel that the reason some children are unable to read, write, spell, and compute as well as other children is that they have perceptual deficits. Many believe, further, that these youngsters have specific visual, motor, or auditory deficits. The teachers believe, therefore, that those perceptual deficiencies must be dealt with before the children can develop behaviors which are more complex.

Teachers of this orientation use worksheets, games, exercises, and tapes designed to develop one form of perception or another. Many of them use the Marianne Frostig materials (Frostig & Horne, 1973), which are designed to improve five components of visual perception: eye-hand coordination, figure-ground discrimination, constancy of shape, position in space, and spatial relations. When those materials are used, children are assigned worksheets which concentrate on the five areas.

profile **MARIANNE FROSTIG**

Marianne Frostig was born in Austria in 1906. She received her Ph.D. in 1955 from the University of Southern California. In 1947 she founded the Frostig Center of Educational Therapy in Los Angeles and directed it until 1972. She is currently a clinical professor in education at the University of Southern California.

Her most notable contribution to special education–learning disabilities in particular–is the Developmental Test of Visual Perception and the detailing of activities which focus on the components of that test.

Many other teachers of this type subscribe to the perceptual-motor notions of Newell Kephart. They use the Purdue Perceptual-Motor Survey (Roach & Kephart, 1966), designed to assess various aspects of motor development. Correspondingly, they use a set of techniques designed to improve specified deficit areas (Chaney & Kephart, 1968). According to this approach there are four components of motor development which should be taught: balance and posture, locomotion, contact, and receipt and propulsion.

The research on the effects of Frostig- & Kephart-oriented programs was reviewed by Hammill, Goodman, and Wiederholt (1974). They concluded that the results were unimpressive in 13 of the 14 studies which evaluated the effectiveness of the Frostig materials on reading. Of the seven studies which were concerned with reading readiness, only three reported positive data. Finally, of the eight studies concerned with stimulating visual-motor growth, only two were effective.

The research on Kephart and other perceptual-motor programs was nearly as unspectacular. Of the 15 studies which dealt with the effects of visual-motor training on intelligence, school achievement, and language functioning, only six reported

significant changes. Three of nine studies
interested in the effects of training on
school readiness showed significant improvement; four of 11 concerned with the
development of visual-motor performance
indicated significant changes.

Other teachers of perceptually designed
classes use materials supposedly designed to assist every perceptual channel:
games, tapes, cards, pictures, balls, puzzles, beads, boxes, stencils, designs, puppets. There is little, if any, research which
either supports or refutes the effects of
these materials.

Multisensory

There have been programs which use
multiple modes or channels to instruct exceptional children for many years. Perhaps
the most notable of these was the system
developed by Grace Fernald (1943). She
emphasized the visual, auditory, kinesthetic, and tactile modalities during initial
stages of learning.

Orton and Gillingham also advocated a
multisensory approach for instruction of
youngsters with reading problems. Slingerland (1971) translated their instructional notions to the extent they are used with
groups of children. Her method forms the
basis for instructing reading, spelling, and
writing.

When these procedures are used, the
regular consonants are initially introduced.
Then the vowels are taught; next, the consonants and vowels are associated.

The following process is used to teach
consonant and vowel sounds. A child says
the letter name, then a key word associated
with the letter, then the sound of the letter,
for example *a*, "apple," /a/. While he says
this sequence, he forms an "a" in the air
with his hand. The auditory, visual,
kinesthetic, and tactile channels are used
simultaneously.

When the Slingerland method is used,
spelling and writing are taught at the same
time as reading. Words the children learn to
read are used for these lessons. They practice the words by tracing and naming each
letter as it is formed. Initially, cursive writing
is used instead of printing.

Although the popularity of the Slingerland
method has increased significantly in the
past few years, as seen by the number of
workshops and classes which emphasize
the approach, only limited data are available to support its effectiveness. A group of
Slingerland advocates published a report
on the achievement of specific language
disabled children (A report . . ., 1974). They
claimed the actual achievement test scores
of youngsters enrolled in Slingerland programs were higher than their expected
scores.

A few years ago we conducted two research projects which featured the Slingerland technique (Lovitt & Hurlbut, 1974). The
data from the first study indicated that performance on several phonics tasks and oral
reading increased, presumably as a func-

tion of Slingerland instruction. In the second study, two pupils received Slingerland instruction while two others received instruction based on the Palo Alto reading program (Glim, 1973). Those data indicated the performances of all students improved on several phonics tasks and oral reading. Neither program, however, was more effective than the other.

We conducted a separate study with 14 youngsters. Seven received Slingerland instruction; the other seven used a technique derived from the Sullivan reading program (Sullivan, n.d.) The children's performances were assessed in regard to several phonics, whole word, and oral reading tasks. Those data revealed that both groups of pupils improved considerably. Again, both techniques were equally effective (Lovitt & Cardell-Gray, 1976).

Precision Teaching

Many classrooms throughout the country use precision teaching techniques. Although there is great variability from one classroom to another, five characteristics are apparent in the best of these situations.

1. The teacher or pupil must *pinpoint* each behavior of a child's program. If one goal is to increase his ability to read orally from a certain text, a situation would be arranged to deal directly with that behavior.

2. An *aim* must be determined for each identified behavior. In order to determine an aim, the teacher or pupil must decide the rate at which the selected behavior should occur and the date that criterion should be achieved. Lines of progress would then be drawn on a chart of that activity from the intersection of the current date and rate to the point the projected date and rate intersect.

3. Third, the teacher or pupil must *count* the number of times the behavior occurs. For reading orally, the pupil might be required to read from Lippincott's Book C

(McCracken & Walcutt, 1965) for 1 minute. While he did so, the teacher would count the number of correctly and incorrectly pronounced words.

4. The teacher or pupil should *chart* each day the number of times the pinpointed behavior occurred. In the example chosen here—oral reading—two entries should be charted each day. One should reveal the number of correctly pronounced words and another, the number of incorrectly pronounced words.

5. The teacher and pupil should *evaluate* the performance of each charted behavior each day. If the correct rate is above and the incorrect rate below the corresponding progress lines, the current instructional technique should be continued. If, however, the progress is not satisfactory, an instructional change should be considered.

For a more detailed description of these steps and others, consult White and Haring (1976).

1. Leslie is a resource teacher who uses precision teaching to monitor her pupil's progress. Here she pinpoints the desired behavior. After the youngster read from several books of various types and levels, they decided he should read orally from Lippincott's Book C.

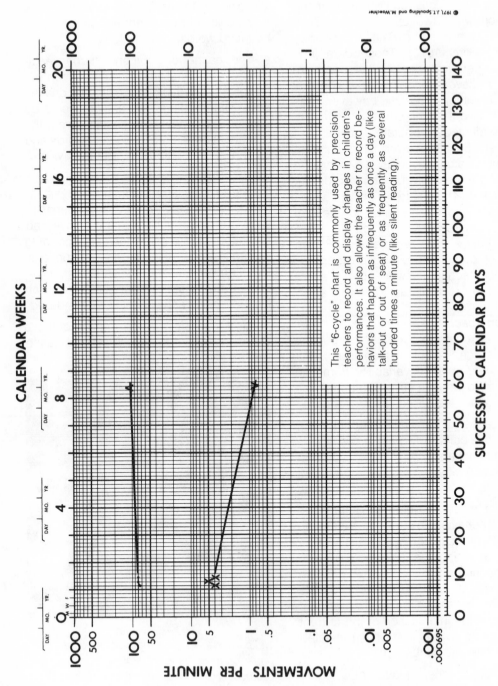

CALENDAR WEEKS

MOVEMENTS PER MINUTE

SUCCESSIVE CALENDAR DAYS

This "6-cycle" chart is commonly used by precision teachers to record and display changes in children's performances. It also allows the teacher to record behaviors that happen as infrequently as once a day (like talk-out or out of seat) or as frequently as several hundred times a minute (like silent reading).

© 1971, J.T. Spaulding and M. Woechter

2. They set correct and incorrect aims for 100 and 2 words per minute. Furthermore, the pupil is to achieve these rates in 8 weeks. Lines of progress are drawn to reflect these aims. The top line indicates the correct rate slope and the bottom line, the incorrect rate slope.

3. Leslie writes down each mispronounced and aided word as he reads orally for 1 minute. Following the reading, they count the total number of words in the passage and subtract the mistakes from that amount. Thus each day they obtain two counts: one for correct and another for incorrectly read words.

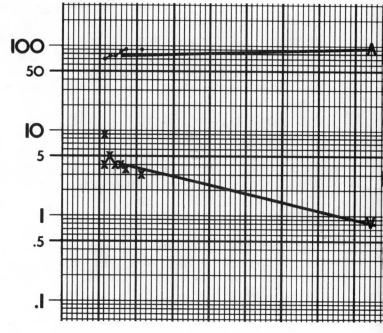

4. Each day the pupil plots his correct and incorrect rates, as shown on a portion of his chart.

5. Since his correct rates have fallen below the progress line for 3 consecutive days, some feature of the institutional program will be changed.

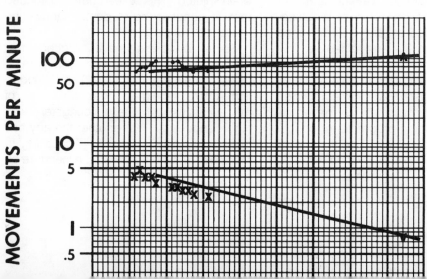

Chapter seven

Considerable research using precision teaching techniques with learning disabled youngsters has been conducted. A summary of several studies conducted at the University of Washington is included in a text by Haring and Schiefelbusch (Lovitt, 1976).

One study pertained to mathematics (Lovitt & Curtiss, 1968). In that report a boy was assigned 20 subtraction problems each day. In the baseline phase, during which no instruction was offered, his performance was very poor. During a second phase he was required to verbalize each problem and its answer before he wrote the answer. His performance was excellent throughout that period. Finally, throughout a third condition, he was no longer required to verbalize the problems; he simply wrote his answers. Although he no longer said the problems, his performance continued to be very good.

Techniques Recommended by Clinics

In addition to the treatments used in schools, there are others recommended by special clinics or physicians. Although some of these treatments are used in classrooms, they are ordinarily prescibed and directed by persons other than teachers.

The most widely used specialized technique is *drugs*. They are often prescribed to reduce hyperactivity, a condition believed by many to adversely affect learning. Sulzbacher, at the University of Washington, has conducted several well-designed drug studies with learning disabled children (1972).

Another treatment which is often scheduled for LD youngsters is *optometric vision training*. Several optometrists have arranged vision training programs for certain youngsters in order to enhance their reading skills. Keogh (1974) published a review of the effectiveness of those programs and concluded that the evidence was too limited to recommend their use.

A third treatment is the *neurological organization training program* developed by Doman and Delacato (Delacato, 1966). They claim that individuals pass through stages which parallel the evolutionary development of the human species and suggest training activities which correspond to those levels. Children are required to creep, crawl, and perform other exercises. They are often assisted to move by dozens of volunteers. Even though this approach is popular in many locations, some researchers have seriously questioned its credibility as a means of improving reading or other school-related abilities (Robbins & Glass, 1969).

Biofeedback is another technique sometimes advocated by clinicians. Braud, Lupin, and Braud (1975), for example, reported that a young "hyperactive boy was taught to reduce his muscular activity and tension through the use of electromyographic biofeedback." They claimed that his behavior improved in the classroom and at home as long as he used biofeedback techniques learned in the laboratory.

Relaxation training is another treatment suggested for learning disabled youngsters. Carter and Synolds (1974) used an audio-taped relaxation program with a group of children described as minimally brain injured. The researchers concluded that, in general, the students' handwriting improved.

Some clinicians have argued that megavitamins could assist certain learning disabled children. Cott (1972) and Wunderlich (1973) claimed that the use of megavitamins with these youngsters was highly successful. Yet another therapy has been the use of hormones. According to Marx (1976), who surveyed the literature on this topic, the prescription of certain hormones might aid the impaired memories of LD children.

Recommendation

Teachers of learning disabled youngsters should design instructional programs based on precision teaching techniques. Two ingredients of that system should certainly be used. Teachers should carefully pinpoint the behaviors they wish to teach and chart pupil performances. *Teachers should constantly survey the research in regard to teaching practices:* which behaviors should be taught, when, and how. If the evidence suggests approaches different from theirs, they must modify their programs immediately.

Not only should teachers of learning disabled youngsters evaluate the effects of their instructional techniques, *they must monitor the treatment recommended by physicians or other professionals.* They must determine whether drugs, relaxation training, or another therapy is, in fact, beneficial. If a teacher uses precision teaching techniques, he will be able to assess the effects of these nonschool scheduled therapies.

Who Will Teach Them?

Only in the area of LD do arguments rage as to *who* should teach the youngsters. Although supportive personnel such as speech therapists, occupational therapists, psychologists, and others assist mentally retarded, physically handicapped, and emotionally disturbed youngsters, it is clearly established in those areas that their teachers are the principal managers.

But in the field of LD there is some controversy about who will ultimately be responsible for the children. The reading people, through their organization, the

International Reading Association (IRA), and the speech people, through the American Speech and Hearing Association (ASHA) (see chapter 10), have challenged LD specialists for the privilege of managing learning disabled children.

There are at least three reasons which might account for these territorial rights issues: definitions, professional training, and state regulations. Each discipline—learning disabilities, reading, and speech—has its own definition for handicapped youngsters. It is little wonder that there is confusion, jealousy, and suspicion. When it comes to professional training, there has been little communication across the disciplines. Invariably, students in one program know little about the others.

There is little consistency from one state to another in certifying LD or remedial reading teachers. In this respect, the speech people can boast that their standards are more consistent and perhaps more rigorous.

These problems have unquestionably contributed to the fact that reading and speech people have challenged the sovereignty of LD specialists. The two primary factors which account for these attacks, however, are money and employment.

In recent years, state and federal funds have been provided to hire staff and supply classes for learning disabled youngsters. When monies became scarce for reading and speech programs and when their personnel were cut, they found a possible source of revenue in LD. Since LD professionals have always been at odds among themselves, they were indeed vulnerable.

The IRA, the most rigorous challenger, announced that monies were being used for LD specialists who were qualified to assist only a few severely handicapped youngsters. They suggested that some

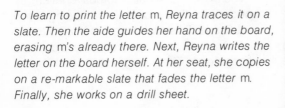

To learn to print the letter m, Reyna traces it on a slate. Then the aide guides her hand on the board, erasing m's already there. Next, Reyna writes the letter on the board herself. At her seat, she copies on a re-markable slate that fades the letter m. Finally, she works on a drill sheet.

the least restrictive environment that allows them to succeed in school.

basic skills—language, reading, math—and a reward area are the basic ingredients. And here are plenty of the right materials, carefully sequenced to promote step-by-step progress toward the annual goals of the IEP. For children who need to learn social skills appropriate to the classroom, the resource room can also be a place with clearly spelled out rules and consistently applied consequences for both appropriate and inappropriate behaviors.

Ways to get Marks

B - coming in quietly with school supplies only.
B - sitting down at own desk.
B - being ready to learn.
B - starting work on time.
B - raising hand for help.
B - working accurately.
B - completing work.
B - moving on to next task.

M - Math   W - Writing
S - Spelling   R - Reading
O - Order   AC - Activity Center

Two basic characteristics of any resource room are (1) a limited number of children present at any one time and (2) extra instructional assistance from teacher aides (left), parent volunteers (bottom), and special equipment or self-instructional materials (top right). And resource rooms can serve exceptional children of any kind...from learning handicapped (left and top right) to gifted (center and bottom).

funds should be used for reading personnel because they could assist more children, particularly those with mild problems. They resolved to vigorously support legislators who favored more equitable distribution of available funds.

About the same time, ASHA adopted a position statement concerned with instruction of learning disabled youngsters. The association stressed that language was central to communication and the primary means through which curriculum should be presented. The position statement also noted that many children do not have intact language systems, and it argued that language problems sometimes show up in poor reading and other academic areas (see chapter 10 for a more extensive discussion of communication disorders.) ASHA concluded that speech personnel should be included as members of every instructional system which interacts with learning disabled children.

In a special issue of the *Journal of Learning Disabilities* (JLD) devoted to the question of territoriality, Sartain (1976) wrote an

---

profile BEN

Ben is 7 years old and is in the second grade of a suburban school. His teachers have been concerned about his academic and social progress for the past two years; this is the first year, however, Ben has received special instruction in a resource room.

His school day begins at 9:15 in a regular class. There are 16 boys and 15 girls in the class. The room is equipped with an ample supply of books, workbooks, arts and crafts materials, and games. In addition, there is a TV set, overhead projector, and tape recorder in the room. The walls are richly decorated with children's art.

Today Ben's teacher took the lunch money from those who wanted to buy a lunch. The children then gave the flag salute. This ritual was followed by some news items. One girl told about a fire at another elementary school. Others commented on this. Ben didn't contribute to the discussion; he was busy rearranging and sorting the items in his desk.

The teacher is a young woman; she has taught for 8 years. She has control over the class but isn't harsh. Occasionally, when the youngsters get a bit out of hand, she mildly reprimands the violators by pointing out what they have done. If several children are unruly she simply turns off the lights. They immediately quiet down when this happens.

After the morning activities the children change rooms for reading. The youngsters in the three second-grade classes are grouped according to their abilities in reading and mathematics. During those periods they go to one room or the other.

Ben is assigned to the lowest class. In that class he is in the lowest of three groups; his group is the "banana splits." The first activity for all three groups was to work on singular and plural words. The teacher said a singular word like "pencil" and the children were expected to hold up one finger. She then said a plural word, "tables," and the children held up two fingers. This exercise continued for about 10 minutes.

Before the next activity, one boy gave each student a large sheet of construction paper. The children were then instructed to fold the paper until there were eight sections. The teacher gave the directions carefully and slowly; she had done this before. Most of the children, including Ben, successfully completed the task.

The youngsters were then told to look at the seven singular words on the chalkboard and write plurals for them in the spaces on their papers. The words were

article that represented the viewpoint of the reading specialists. He suggested several steps that might be taken by reading and LD specialists to reconcile their differences. His major point, however, was that the two disciplines should divide their efforts. According to him, LD specialists should assist youngsters with serious reading problems and reading specialists should deal with children who have moderate difficulties.

Stick (1976) presented the speech pathologists' point of view in the same issue of *JLD*. He contended that speech pathologists should concentrate on several aspects of language with learning disabled youngsters, among them the ability to use grammatical forms, the development of auditory perceptual skills, the development of linguistic abilities, and the ability to process information and express oneself.

Larsen (1976) presented the LD specialist's perception of the matter in that same issue. He contended that LD specialists should be the primary managers of learning disabled children, but conceded that reading specialists and speech personnel should be assigned important

"dress," "work," "pencil," "brush," "cup," "glass," and "pen." She told them to make up their own plural word for the eighth space.

Ben began this task as soon as the other children and finished at about the same time. His handwriting was not as good as his classmates', but his plural words were all correct.

The teacher then summoned the "banana splits" to the corner of the room. She was seated and the members of the reading group huddled around her. They sat on rugs or large pillows. There the first activity was spelling. The teacher pronounced 10 words, and the children wrote them in their workbooks. Ben missed only the words "pencil" and "glass." Next they completed a workbook exercise. The teacher gave directions such as, "Circle the word that is something to eat" and "Draw a line underneath something you wear." Ben gave his undivided attention to this activity; he answered all 10 directions correctly.

After reading, Ben went to the resource room. He goes there every day for a 30-minute session. There are two other second grade boys in Ben's group; reading is the primary target for all three. The resource teacher assists 12 other groups of children

throughout the day. They come to her in sets of two, three, and four. Each day, 35 children visit her class, the number required in Washington to obtain monies from the state.

She is an excellent teacher. She interacts calmly with the children, programs carefully for them, and liberally reinforces their appropriate behaviors. She also relates well to the regular teachers and to other school personnel: the building principal, director of special education, and the school psychologist. Furthermore, she has good relationships with the parents of children currently and previously assigned to her.

The resource room is a small area off the gym. There are two study carrels, a table with five chairs, and a teacher's desk in the room. There is also a cabinet in which the children's folders are placed.

Each day when the students arrive they select their folder, go to either a carrel or a chair, and begin to work. Ben pulled out his folder, dropped it, picked it up, and went to a chair. The resource teacher has an ample supply of phonics and arithmetic workbooks, beginning reading books, and ditto sheets for various phonics and word analysis activities. Today Ben had five activities, all related to reading. His first activity was to circle the correct word in a set of

instructional responsibilities.

In that same issue Wallace (1976) noted several factors which should be considered in efforts to foster interdisciplinary cooperation. He encouraged professionals in the three disciplines to arrange and conduct research studies in early childhood education. He believed further that they should establish interdisciplinary training programs.

Apart from the reading people, the speech pathologists, and the LD specialists, there are other contenders for the responsibility of managing learning disabled youngsters: optometrists, psychologists, pharmacologists, nutritionists, pediatricians, and psychiatrists, to name a few.

But *it is unimportant* who *serves learning disabled youngsters. The important issue is to determine* what *a child should be taught:* to read, to compute, to ask questions, or to spell.

The next task should be to identify the teaching skills of the personnel available to instruct those children. Finally, the pupils and their needs should be matched with staff competencies. Some schools may discover that some librarians, music

---

10 sentences. For example, "Judd dares Sue to ride his male/mule." Ben quickly and accurately completed this task. Next, he read the following story orally without an error:

> *Pete will toss his bean bag to Jean. Bam! Jean did not get the bean bag. The bean bag fell in Mini's tea. The tea fell at Mini's feet. Mom got mad. Pete ran.*

Ben's third activity was a vowel program. He was given a worksheet with several pictures. One of the pictures was a weather vane; another was a pin. Underneath the vane were two words: "van" and "vane." The words "pin" and "pine" were underneath the pin. His task was to circle the correct word. Ben completed all 10 items correctly in a few minutes.

Ben next read two word lists. One list contained regular, CVC words; the other list, words from his reading books, for example, "fell," "will," and "got." After Ben practiced the word lists for a few minutes, his teacher timed him for 1 minute. From the first list he said 82 words correctly and from the second list, 68. According to his teacher, those were record performances.

His final activity was to read a half-dozen stories orally from a linguistic reader. Once again Ben's performances were flawless. For this achievement, he was awarded a small tagboard circle. This meant his name and the date were written on the circle, and the circle was pasted on the wall with dozens of others, forming a bookworm chain. These bookworm circles are given to some students when they complete a book and to others, such as Ben, when they read a story perfectly.

When his 30-minute period ended, he returned to his regular class and took his seat. Although most of the children were seated in two clusters in the center of the room, Ben and a girl were isolated. The girl's desk was next to the teacher's, toward the rear of the room, and Ben's was off to one corner.

The first assignment after Ben returned was spelling. Ten words like "does," "done," "shoe," and "some" were discussed. The teacher described them as "snurk" words because they were irregular. After the discussion, she pronounced the words and the children wrote them.

During the spelling test Ben began to squirm. It wasn't a rapid movement, but a continuous engagement between his body, his chair, and his desk. He first sat on his feet, then stuck his feet out the back of the chair, then sat on his chair, then rocked.

teachers, and custodians are more competent instructors of learning disabled pupils than others who profess to be experts.

Where Will They Be Taught?

The controversy over where learning disabled youngsters should be taught is different from the other issues presented here. While debate on LD will continue, the issue of placement has largely been resolved.

The arguments over location for instructing learning disabled youngsters—whether in self-contained, resource, or regular classes—may have been decided when congress enacted the Education for All Handicapped Act, P.L. 94–142. One of the provisions of the act is that children must be educated in least restrictive environments. When that requirement is met, it will mean that most learning disabled youngsters will be assigned to regular classes (mainstreamed). While some of them will be assisted by specialists in regular classes, and others will receive instruction in resource rooms, few learning disabled children will be educated in self-contained classrooms.

Several reasons have been advanced for adopting the mainstreaming process. According to Birch (1974), one reason for supporting the system is that research failed to show that handicapped youngsters advance more quickly in special, rather than in regular, classrooms. Another

During this process he knocked his chair over several times. The teacher didn't attend to Ben throughout this period, even though she was aware of his activity.

After spelling, the children ate. Ben brought his lunch and ate in his room with the other children. Following lunch they went outside for about 30 minutes. The youngsters were not deterred by the typical Seattle drizzle.

Ben found a group of first graders and played with them. Their game consisted of chasing one another and stomping in water puddles. By the time recess had finished, Ben was a mess. He was soaking wet from his seat on down.

The next activity was math. Once again the children went to one of three rooms, depending on their levels. Ben stayed in his own class since his teacher worked with students in the lowest level. His group worked on expanded notations. The teacher wrote numbers like "426" on the board and the pupils told her how many hundreds, tens, and ones there were in the numbers. After a brief discussion they were required to add several problems of this type. Ben scooted and rocked constantly

throughout this activity. He was the last pupil to complete the assignment.

Ben and his desk in his regular class were a mess. Under his desk were three or four sheets of paper, several wads of paper, a couple of broken pencils, and small clods of dirt. I'd never seen anything quite like it.

Music was the next activity. The music teacher, with guitar in hand, entered the room and sang "There's a hole in the bucket." While she sang, the children were very attentive. Ben and the others laughed and clapped throughout the song. When she finished singing, the music teacher clapped some rhythms and asked the children to repeat the patterns. All of them, including Ben, complied; they seemed to enjoy the activity. Following the rhythm exercises, they were asked to sing a song. Now their interest lagged; only half of them sang. Many of the youngsters, Ben among them, only moved their lips, and several others didn't attend at all.

Later in the afternoon, they had an art period. Today they made Irish potatoes. Ben was asked to pass out strips of brown and green construction paper to his class

motive for its support is that normal interactions between handicapped and non-handicapped children can develop only if all pupils are educated together. A third reason for adopting the process is that many parents never wanted their handicapped children segregated from nonhandicapped youngsters in the first place. A fourth reason is that many people have rejected the notion of labeling children; they recognize the potential harm of classifying them as *mentally retarded* or *learning disabled*. Another reason is that recent court decisions have affirmed the

These boys attend a separate class for the language disabled, where they work on abstractions such as "over" and "below."

members. He was extremely pleased with this assignment.

Before they began, the teacher gave a few instructions, but she encouraged them to be creative as they made a brown potato with a green hat and tie. Ben stayed with the assignment for about 20 minutes. After a few futile attempts to complete the task, he gave up and again rearranged the items in his desk.

A few minutes before dismissal, Ben went to a kindergarten class to read a story. His teacher believed this motivated him to improve his reading. He and the teacher sat in the front of the class, and Ben began reading. The first sentence he read was "A pig danced a jig." Immediately, a boy said, "A pig danced a jig." Ben slammed his book down and said, "Don't repeat, kid!" He picked up his book and continued reading, however. While he read he occasionally stopped and reprimanded his audience if they didn't attend. In spite of the few interruptions, it was a good session; he read well and the children enjoyed the story.

Ben has been given several tests. His score on the WISC was 110; the performance and verbal scores were about the same. On the WRAT, his reading, spelling, and math scores were 1.6, 1.2, and 2.4. On the Durrell reading test his oral reading and word recognition scores were 2.0 and 1.0. On the Peabody Individual Achievement Test (PIAT) his spelling score was 2.2, and his math score was 1.8.

Ben's family life is not always pleasant. When he misbehaves, his stepfather often threatens to send him to his real father. Both his stepfather and his mother beat him from time to time. To add insult to injury he has a younger sister who is an angel; she is the perfect, bright, beautiful child.

According to his teachers, Ben has learned to manipulate his mother, stepfather, and to some extent, teachers. He keeps them on edge by behaving admirably for several days, and then suddenly his behavior deteriorates. He teases children, tears up papers, refuses to work, giggles, and ignores adults. On those days his parents and teachers are very frustrated. They know that he can behave adequately when he wants, but they can't determine what they, as adults, must do to maintain his appropriate behaviors.

rights of all handicapped children to a free and appropriate education.

Although the mainstreaming process is progressing at full speed, some eminent educators are skeptical about the system. Cruickshank (1974), for example, has expressed several complaints about mainstreaming. His first is that some teachers might be less than accepting when certain handicapped youngsters are enrolled in their classes. A second grievance is that many teachers are limited in their capacities to meet the wide needs of the returning handicapped children. A third dissatisfaction is that many handicapped youngsters will stand out as different from their nonhandicapped peers.

If handicapped children are to receive appropriate education in regular classes, teachers must modify their teaching styles. According to the National Advisory Council on Education Professions Development ("Mainstreaming," 1976), regular teachers must be proficient in six skills in order to manage handicapped youngsters:

- understanding the emotions of handicapped youngsters,

- recognizing handicaps and prescribing appropriate learning experiences,

- individualizing instruction,

- understanding the emotions of handicapped youngsters,

- using the services of supportive personnel to aid youngsters, and

- communicating effectively with parents of exceptional children.

I feel *it is unimportant* where *learning disabled youngsters are educated*. The first act should be to *define the behaviors which children should learn*. Then, a decision must be made about who should provide the instruction. Finally, it should be decided where the instruction will take place. It might be determined that some youngsters should be educated in regular classes,

profile JOE JENKINS

Joe Jenkins was born in 1942. He received his Ph.D. from the University of Minnesota in 1967. Jenkins was associated with the University of Delaware and New Mexico State University before moving to his current location at the University of Illinois, where he is a professor in special education.

Jenkins' research with learning disabled students, investigates peer tutoring, oral reading, arithmetic, and other topics. He has also written on such topics as resource rooms and mainstreaming, and has been a critic of the use of achievement tests as evaluative instruments.

At Illinois, Jenkins coordinates the resource/consulting teacher program. He is also associated with the recently funded Center for Research on Reading at that university.

others in special rooms, still others in music rooms or libraries.

The movement toward mainstreaming has been too rapid, with little research to support it. Mainstreaming has been promoted by legislators and administrators; regular teachers who must put the process in practice have generally not been consulted. Although plans have been made to provide them with inservice sessions and supportive assistance, they have not been considered about the major decisions of mainstreaming.

FUTURE NEEDS

Since LD is a relatively young field, its development hinges on future research. More information is needed on many of the issues we have discussed, including the classification of children. Neuropsychologists should be encouraged to determine the functions of various parts of the brain and the metabolic and environmental variables that might influence learning. Some research on biofeedback and other relaxing systems should be promoted. Effects of megavitamins, drugs, and various hormones on learning and hyperactivity need extensive and careful examination. And the effect of P.L. 94–142, particularly relating to the education of learning disabled youngsters in regular classrooms, will require much attention. Research and development in the six areas stressed by the National Advisory Council should receive the highest priority.

Expand Curricular Notions

If regular teachers are to serve learning disabled children, their ideas about materials should be altered. If, for example, they intend to teach all their handicapped and nonhandicapped children to read, they will have to use more than one basal series. They must greatly increase their knowledge of reading materials, and programs for teaching mathematics, handwriting, and spelling as well.

Since some learning disabled children are not as self-directed or as independent as their nonhandicapped peers—an LD child might not get out her math book when it is math time or hang up her coat without being told—some instruction must be devoted to self-management behaviors. Some programs designed to teach self-management skills to learning disabled youngsters have been conducted in the past few years (Lovitt, 1973).

Expand Repertoire of Techniques

As handicapped youngsters return to regular classes, their teachers must expand greatly their repertoires of instructional techniques. Since many of those returning are by definition disabled, slow, and academically retarded, regular teachers must be resourceful and creative. They must be able to draw on several techniques in order to teach the basic skills and other behaviors.

P.L. 94–142 provides additional encouragement for regular teachers to individualize their instruction. According to that law, teachers must design individualized educational programs (IEPs) for the handicapped children in their classes. Fortunately, a variety of instructional techniques are available. It has been our experience that when specific behaviors were identified for instruction, many simple, instructional techniques were extremely effective.

In a few projects we showed that verbal instructions can alter academic behaviors. For example, Lovitt and Smith (1972) reported that two aspects of a boy's verbal behavior were modified when he was asked to begin his sentences with different words and to use more words when he described pictures.

Other studies have been conducted which demonstrated that modeling techniques—providing children with partial or completed examples of a finished task—could change school behaviors. In one study (Smith & Lovitt, 1975), data revealed that *showing* learning disabled children how to compute various types of arithmetic problems was effective; the pupils learned to solve the problems which were modeled and similar types which were not modeled.

Another study (Gardstrom & Lovitt, in press) demonstrated that several forms of feedback can alter academic performance. After each writing period, a group of second graders were shown charts which gave the number of words and thought units they had written. The data from that study revealed that the performances of most youngsters improved.

In other studies it was shown that simple reinforcement influenced academic skills when the reinforcement was wisely scheduled. In one study (Smith & Lovitt, 1976), the speed with which learning disabled pupils computed arithmetic problems was positively influenced when model airplanes were given to them depending on correct rate.

Expand Management Systems

Just as there are teachers who use only one set of reading books and one instructional technique to teach reading, there are others who have limited repertoires for dealing with unruly youngsters. Since some learning disabled children returning to regular classes might display a wider range of deviant behaviors than the nonhandicapped youngsters, regular teachers must expand their capabilities for managing these behaviors.

In their efforts to establish environments which are relatively free from distracting and annoying behaviors—like children getting out of their seats, talking out of turn, and fighting with other children—teachers should consider the research on classroom management. Several studies, which took place in classrooms, demonstrated that when good behaviors were consistently praised they increased, and when deviant behaviors were consistently ignored they decreased (e.g., Madsen, Becker, & Thomas, 1968).

In addition to simply ignoring inappropriate behaviors, there is much research on approaches designed to decrease the frequency of specific behaviors of individual students. Among the techniques which have proved effective are:

- *Punishment* (presenting a negative consequence or removing a rewarding consequence if the student emits the undesirable behavior) to reduce talk-outs (O'Leary, Kaufman, Kass, & Drabman, 1970);

- *Satiation* (allowing the undesirable behavior to occur freely or requiring that it occur frequently) to reduce hoarding (Ayllon, 1963);

- *Differential reinforcement (DRO)* (reinforcing the child only if the undesirable behavior is not emitted during a specified time interval) to reduce fantasy play (Sloane, Johnston, & Bijou, 1967);

- *Differential reinforcement of low rate (DRL)* (reinforcing a child for not emitting the undesirable behavior more than a set maximum number of times during a specific interval) to reduce talk-outs (Dietz & Repp, 1973);

- *Time-out* (removing a child from any positively reinforcing situation immediately following the undesirable behavior) to reduce inappropriate talking or noise-making (Lovitt, Lovitt, Eaton, & Kirkwood, 1973);

- *Response cost* (removing earned tokens, points, or other rewards immediately after the undesirable behavior) to reduce crying (Hall, Fox, Willard, Goldsmith, Emerson, Owen, Davis, & Porcia, 1971);

- *Extinction* (removing all reinforcers for an undesirable behavior) to lessen whining (Williams, 1959).

These techniques and others are explained in more detail in Gardner (1977) and Wallace and Kauffman (1978).

In addition to the procedures used to reduce the deviant behaviors of individual

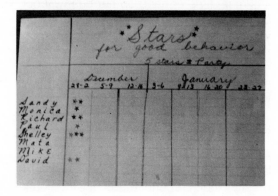

Displayed for all to see, stars are a strong reinforcer for many children.

children, some group-oriented techniques have been developed (Litow & Pumroy, 1975). One of these involves an event given to all members of the group on the basis of the group's performance. An example would be giving a recess to all the children if no one talked out of turn.

A second group-oriented procedure involves giving the same consequence to all group members, but whether or not the group receives the consequence depends on the performance of a selected member of the group. An example would be giving the group a few minutes of extra recess if a certain member didn't talk out of turn for a period of time.

A third approach provides the same contingency for all group members but is applied on an individual basis. An example would be taking tokens from each child who talks out of turn.

Expand Motivational Repertoire

Some teachers have limited ideas about the events and circumstances which reinforce children. They only know the use of recess, praise, grades, and stars. These events, if arranged appropriately, can be reinforcing, particularly for nonhandicapped children. Many returning handicapped children, however, might not be motivated by those events. Therefore, teachers must identify others.

A few researchers have demonstrated that dozens of classroom events are motivating for children if they are arranged appropriately. Walker and Buckley (1974), for example, provided an inventory of several activities and materials which were reinforcing for children. Those possibilities ranged from playing teacher and cleaning chalk, to finger painting and making puppets, to playing *Monopoly* and making jewelry.

The reason for locating potential reinforcers is to help children develop certain skills. If, for example, a teacher knew that a boy liked to build model airplanes, but his computation performance was erratic, she could associate those two. A contingency might be arranged which allowed him to work on an airplane if his computation performance reached a specified goal.

Other researchers have shown how to arrange token economies—systems in which a child earns tokens (beans, points, play money, checkmarks, gummed stickers on a chart) for desired behavior. Those systems have at least two advantages: teachers can give tokens any time, without interrupting a child to reinforce him while he is engaged in an activity. Also, tokens can be exchanged for a variety of events, so there is less probability that a child will tire of any one item. Several reviews of token economies have been published (e.g., O'Leary & Drabman, 1971; Kazdin & Bootzin, 1972).

Expand Delivery Systems

If regular teachers are to provide appropriate learning opportunities for their children, many of whom require different materials, techniques, and reinforcers, they will soon run out of energy if they attempt to do all the instructing themselves.

Teachers need to rely on others to assist with many instructional chores. They must learn, therefore, to instruct staff such as communication disorders specialists, psychologists, reading instructors, nurses, and music teachers to help with the children in their classes. Teachers should learn to train parents so they, too, might help with their children. Patterson and his colleagues have shown convincingly that parents can be taught to control certain deviant behaviors of their children (Patterson, 1971).

In addition to using staff and parents to aid with the education of children, teachers can use other children. In the past few years considerable research on this topic has been conducted (Devin-Sheehan, Feldman, & Allen, 1976). Children can also be taught to aid themselves. Some special education teachers have taught youngsters to time their performances, to check their responses, count the number correct and incorrect, graph those data, and inform teachers when they require special assistance. When children are taught these management skills and others, they free teachers for other instructional duties. Obviously, there are added benefits when children learn to manage their activities, for they learn to become independent to some extent.

Expand Communication Skills

When some handicapped youngsters reappear in regular classes, the teachers have to expand their abilities to communicate. They are required to interact with a wider range of individuals than they dealt with in the past. Many of the returning handicapped children receive care from pediatricians, psychologists, psychiatrists, and other specialists while they are in the classroom. Teachers must interact with those professionals.

In addition, many parents of returning handicapped youngsters are extremely knowledgeable about special education because they have been from one professional to another and from one special school to another. Many know so much they can be intimidating. Teachers must know special education terminology and must be comfortable with everyone with whom they deal.

MEETING SPECIAL NEEDS

1. *While emotional causes, motivational problems, and a history of poor instruction can all contribute to LD, there is no single factor responsible. Keep the whole constellation of possible causes in mind while you directly attack each specific learning problem.*

2. *Don't use standardized intelligence and achievement tests to classify children. Instead, pinpoint the behaviors you want to teach to each student and use direct daily measurement of those skills. By measuring the pupil's progress each day on specific tasks, you get a direct, frequent index of his learning—an index you can then use in making educational program decisions.*

3. *Conduct your assessment of each child in the natural classroom environment—the place the child is ordinarily required to learn.*

4. *Use the results of your daily assessments to chart each pupil's progress in the specified behaviors.*

5. *Keep up-to-date with current research on teaching practices, and be prepared to modify your programs as necessary.*

6. *With an eye on modifying your own programs to deal with changes, evaluate the effects of any treatment prescribed for a learning disabled child by a physician or other professional.*

7. *Be prepared to use the services of anyone, from cook to physical education teacher, who can help teach a needed skill to a learning disabled child.*

8. *Be flexible, too, about the setting for LD education. The media center or playground may be better for some programs than the regular classroom.*

FOR MORE INFORMATION

Most of these resources are textbooks that are readily available, many from Charles E. Merrill, the publishers of this text. Check your instructor, the education library, or the general library at your school.

Bryan, T.H., & Bryan, J.H. *Understanding learning disabilities.* Port Washington, N.Y.: Alfred, 1975.

Hallahan, D.P., & Kauffman, J.M. *Introduction to learning disabilities: A psychobehavioral approach.* Englewood Cliffs, N.J.: Prentice-Hall, 1976.

Kauffman, J.M., & Hallahan, D.P. (Eds.) *Teaching children with learning disabilities: Personal perspectives.* Columbus, Ohio: Charles E. Merrill, 1976.

Lerner, J.W. *Children with learning disabilities* (2nd ed.). Boston: Houghton Mifflin, 1976.

Lovitt, T.C. *In spite of my resistance . . . I've learned from children.* Columbus, Ohio: Charles E. Merrill, 1977.

Stephens, T.M. *Teaching skills to children with learning and behavior disorders.* Columbus, Ohio: Charles E. Merrill, 1977.

Wallace, G., & Kauffman, J.M. *Teaching children with learning problems* (2nd ed.). Columbus, Ohio: Charles E. Merrill, 1978.

Wallace, G., & McLoughlin, J.A. *Learning disabilities: Concepts and characteristics.* Columbus, Ohio: Charles E. Merrill, 1975.

Perspectives on the Severely and Profoundly Handicapped

As Payne and Thomas pointed out in chapter 5, mental retardation can vary from mild to profound. Likewise, while most children's behavior disorders are not severe enough to exclude them from public schools entirely, some do exhibit extremely bizarre or antisocial behavior that prevents them from functioning in any sort of normal environment. In other words, looking at the *levels of severity* or the *severity of involvement* of a handicap can tell us much about a child's needs and what we can do to meet them.

Historically, the severely and profoundly handicapped were kept at home, dependent on their parents and families for their total care. Or worse, they were relegated to institutions, often in conditions that allowed poor care and fostered no constructive learning. Only in the last few years, in fact,

have we begun to regard the severely and profoundly handicapped as at all capable of learning.

Almost for the first time in our history have we begun to concentrate our efforts on helping reduce the overwhelming deficits that keep the severely handicapped from reaching their full potentials. These "first priority" children, as we noted in chapter 1, are the first who must be served under the new Education for All Handicapped Children Act. To accomplish that goal, however, will require the most highly trained and dedicated professionals the field of special education has ever produced. Nor can special educators achieve the task by themselves. As the next two chapters will show, the effort can only be effective if it crosses over traditional discipline boundaries. What are needed are teams of professionals—physicians, psychologists, occupational and physical therapists, communication disorders specialists, and special educators—to work with parents in developing new programs for the severely handicapped. More than ever, these individuals will require our fullest attention and our best technology.

The next chapter (chapter 8) examines the severely handicapped, and chapter 9, which Judy Smith coauthored, describes the profoundly handicapped. In a sense, these chapters look at children from a *developmental* point of view, to the extent that they emphasize the serious delays in development each of these persons faces. In another sense, these children are looked at from an *educational* point of view, emphasizing the need for highly specialized programs and services, most of which will necessarily have to be implemented outside regular classrooms for nonhandicapped children.

Finally, these chapters present a *behavioral* view of severe and profound handicaps. You will note that the chapters cut across traditional categories (like blind, deaf, physically handicapped, retarded, disturbed) to concentrate on behaviors these individuals can perform and those for which they need special intervention—instruction, equipment, or arrangement of their environments. (You will note some overlap in these two chapters as you read them, again because they cut across traditional categories to examine the different levels of functioning of each group.) This behavioral point of view defines the severity of the individual's handicap in terms of his current level of functioning and the degree and kinds of programming and services needed to raise him to higher levels.

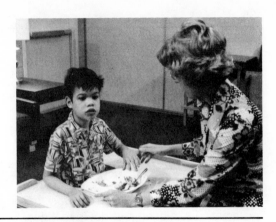

8

The Severely Handicapped

Norris G. Haring

These are the major topics covered in this chapter. You may want to use them as a checklist when you review.

- *A complete definition of severely handicapped.*

- *Diagnostic categories contributing to severe handicaps.*

- *Trends, problems, and concerns in providing appropriate services to the severely handicapped.*

- *A comprehensive approach to intervention, education, and performance measurement of the severely handicapped.*

- *Principles and procedures used by members of three disciplines involved in intervention with the severely handicapped.*

- *Instructional materials which appear useful in assessing or teaching the severely handicapped.*

- *Research studies which illustrate the technology of teaching the severely handicapped.*

Chapter eight

Education of severely handicapped children has been largely neglected until recently, partly because there has been a limited body of knowledge on the subject.

The severely handicapped were long denied the opportunity to receive an education because it was assumed that they could not learn. But many studies have shown that they can benefit greatly from systematic instruction and do, in fact, learn throughout their lives. Their learning potential and their right to education have only recently been emphasized vigorously by parents, the courts, legislators, behavioral scientists, and educators. As a result, since 1972 many state and federal laws have been passed mandating that the severely handicapped are entitled to an education.

The transition from no education to free, public education has been rapid and is a radically new effort for American education (Myers, Sinco, & Stalma, 1973). The task of teaching the severely handicapped has become perhaps the most challenging area of special education in terms of developing successful techniques and determining how these children may reach the long-range goal of contributing to society.

DEFINITIONS

Over the years we have described severely handicapped persons in ways that have matched our limited understanding of them. But they should be defined by their actual characteristics and potentials.

A Past Definition of Social Deviance

An earlier view was that the severely handicapped are disruptive or dangerous or

I would like to thank Judy Smith for her contributions to this chapter.—N.G.H.

hopelessly backward and unproductive and should, therefore, remain apart from society. So long as the primary approach to these people was to house them in back wards of large state institutions, it was common to classify them as idiots or imbeciles, call them vegetables, and consider then totally dependent, requiring 24-hour-a-day supervision. When people are described this way, they regress and often fulfill the negative labels given them (Kreger, 1971). The severely handicapped have many problems, but to describe them in ways that make them social outcasts can only intensify their problems.

Medical Definitions

Severe handicaps often require medical attention, explaining the long popular idea that these children should be treated by a physician without regard to help by educators. Medical classifications are concerned with causes and diagnosis. Some of the more common causes of severe handicaps are (Robinson & Robinson, 1976):

1. Chromosomal abnormality: Down's syndrome, Turner's syndrome.

2. Genetic disorders: tuberous sclerosis, neurofibromatosis, Sturge-Weber syndrome, myotonic dystrophy, Apert's syndrome, Albright's hereditary osteodystrophy, microcephaly.

3. Disorders of metabolism: phenylketonuria, maple syrup urine disease, histidinemia, homocystinuria, Hurler syndrome, Hunter syndrome, Tay-Sachs disease, Lesch-Nyhan syndrome.

4. Maternal infection: rubella, syphilis, cytomegalic inclusion disease, Herpes virus hominis (Type II) infection.

5. Neural tube closure defects: anencephaly, hydrocephalus, meningomyelocele.

6. Gestational factors: prematurity, postmaturity, Rh incompatibility, parental age.

7. Hazards at birth: perinatal asphyxia, neurotoxicity from hexachlorophene, direct injury to the head or brain. (See chapter 3 for a more complete description of some birth hazards.)

8. Postnatal hazards: head injury leading to cerebral palsy or seizures, brain tumors, meningitis, encephalitis, ingestion of lead or mercury or certain food additives.

9. Psychiatric disorders: infantile autism, schizophrenia.

10. Environmental influences: extreme sensory deprivation, malnutrition, physical neglect during critical developmental periods.

On the one hand, the medical profession is absolutely necessary to treat these problems of the severely handicapped, to clarify the multiple nature of the impairments, and to provide important advice concerning educational programs. On the other, there are disadvantages in relying on medical labels. They tend to give the idea of incurability, which contributes to the idea that it is futile to attempt education. Also, medical descriptions tend to give other professionals the impression that their expertise is not sophisticated enough to change the behavior of the severely handicapped. But, in fact, helping someone with learning and social behavior is distinctly different from medical treatment.

The trouble with such definitions is that they do not always represent a severely handicapping condition. A 13-year-old may not be toilet trained, may not be ambulatory, may be aggressive, and may have seizures, but these characteristics do not, in and of themselves, make him severely handicapped. In addition:

> All, most, or only one or two of the descriptors may apply to any individual labeled severely handicapped. However, there is not one educationally relevant characteristic that all share. Thus, it is difficult if not impossible to determine those behaviors a given severely handicapped individual may exhibit, on the basis of the label alone.

Second, the traditional static definitions do not meet validity requirements which useful categorization systems must meet. Static descriptor definitions do not communicate information to the educator concerning appropriate remedial programs. While similar remedial programs may apply to both self-mutilation and aggression toward others, it is doubtful that the same training would apply to toilet training or social awareness training.

> In addition . . . static definitions do not reflect changes in individuals. For example, an individual labeled severely handicapped who initially self-mutilates but does not do so following intervention may still be labeled severely handicapped, despite the change in behavior. No direction is given, under a static categorization system, of changes in the individual.[1]

Still another type of administrative definition was proposed by the Bureau of Education for the Handicapped, U.S. Office of Education, in 1974:

> A severely handicapped child is one who, because of the intensity of his physical,

[1]Haring, N.G., Nietupski, J., & Hamre-Nietupski, S. *Guidelines for effective intervention with the severely handicapped: Toward independent functioning.* Unpublished manuscript, University of Washington, 1976.

Jennifer, who is visually impaired, was born hydrocephalic and needed a shunt. Her brothers help her work on problems caused by these conditions.

mental, or emotional problem, or a combination of such problems, needs educational, social, psychological, and medical services beyond those which have been offered by traditional regular and special education programs in order to maximize his full potential for useful and meaningful participation in society and for self-fulfillment. Such children include those classified as seriously emotionally disturbed, schizophrenic or autistic, profoundly and severely mentally retarded, and those with two or more serious handicapping conditions, such as the mentally retarded-blind, and the cerebral palsied-deaf. Such severely handicapped children may possess severe language or perceptual-cognitive deprivations and evidence a number of abnormal behaviors including failure to attend to even the most pronounced social stimuli, self-mutilation, self-stimulation, manifestation of durable and intense temper tantrums, and the absence of even the most rudimentary forms of verbal control. They may also have an extremely fragile physiological condition. (USOE, 1974, Section 121.2)

The implication is that this definition is based on the previous exclusion of the severely handicapped from the public schools; it also presents a series of static descriptions. However, it does attempt to define the services that the severely handicapped need. It implies that diagnosing and labeling without treatment, service, or programs are futile.

Definition Based on Measured Intelligence

There have been other attempts to classify the severely handicapped as a homogeneous group; these definitions use the intelligence quotient (IQ) as the constant factor. When educable mentally retarded (EMR) children—whose IQs are estimated at between 55 and 70—and trainable mentally retarded (TMR) children—with IQs between 35 and 55—were included in public education programs, the severely handicapped were not included on the premise that their lower intelligence made them uneducable and untrainable in the traditional sense.

This means of classifying children does not take into account the difference between an intelligence test score and the person's ability to adapt.

> Though subaverage IQs unquestionably affect school achievement, they do not necessarily preclude adequate functioning in other behavioral realms. Thus, even very limited reading and number skills will not, in and of themselves, prevent an adult from achieving an independent adjustment. (Baroff, 1974, p. 5)

Moreover, any definition that isolates a group as uneducable reveals more about teaching practices than about learning problems.

> Traditionally, an individual who does not learn what is presented is considered to be incapable, indifferent, unmotivated, or lacking. The behavioral view, on the other hand, is that if the student does not learn, something is wrong or lacking in the teaching situation. (Bijou & Cole, 1975, p. 12)

Until recently, public schools have been unprepared to offer the programs required to educate the severely handicapped. Rather, they have been able to offer primarily standard teaching methods and long-standing self-instructional materials, which are ineffective with severely handicapped students.

> It is also popular to teach some skills that teachers do understand and believe in, like reading, but which some children will not need as badly as they will more mundane things, like toothbrushing and replying appropriately to common greetings. (Lent, 1975, p. 9)

Definitions which rely only on intelligence quotients preserve our educational practices. Worse, they do not acknowledge that some cases of severe retardation stem from intense physical, sensory, or behavioral deficits, rather than from irreversible brain damage. There is great variability among the severely handicapped in terms of their learning potentials and behavioral characteristics. With the proper educational opportunities, all of these children can make gains—and some will make spectacular advances.

Administrative Definitions

To meet federal funding requirements, some definitions are lists of observable characteristics that can distinguish severely handicapped individuals as a group. For example, they may be described as individuals having a number of physical defects that are often severe, unable to attain an upright or mobile position, partially or completely unaware of the environment, extremely infantile in behavior, unable to interact or communicate with people and surroundings, lacking speech development, lacking feeding and toileting skills, and unable to guard themselves against the most common physical dangers (Somerton & Myers, 1976). Other characteristics include self-mutilation, regurgitation, aggression toward others, rocking, handwaving (stereopathics), tantrums and seizures, extreme physical fragility, and lack of response to simple commands (Sontag, Burke, & York, 1973).

An Instructional Definition

None of the definitions reviewed so far lend themselves to developing specific programs that can assist in learning. A valid definition is both more basic and more complex. Basically, a person is severely handicapped if he cannot do even the simplest things that other people can do and if excessive inappropriate behaviors interfere with his acceptance and functioning.

Namely, if students do not speak, follow directions, play with peers, control their own behavior, etc., they are severely handicapped in their ability to function in society and need to be taught such skills to do so. (Brown & York, 1974, p. 4)

Here the focus shifts from the handicapped student to the instruction he needs. The most important part of the definition is change in the child's behavior. Through such a definition, instruction may be described as:

The creation or arrangement of an environment that produces specified changes in the behavioral repertoires of the students. This definition, of course, is an extreme oversimplification of a complex and dynamic construct and may have little if any utility for someone teaching poetry to gifted adolescents.

Such a definition has practical value for at least the following reasons:

1. The teacher is required to know exactly what responses are desired—the teacher determines what the instruction will be.

2. The teacher is required to know exactly what changes he or she will make in the student's environment to bring about the change that is desired—attention is focused on those aspects of the student's world which the teacher can actually change.

3. The teacher is required to prove that the student actually has changed. (Brown & York, 1974, p. 4)

The education of the severely handicapped might well be described as

The level of resources necessary to produce acceptable educational progress, an acceptable curricula, toward independent functioning—which greatly exceeds the level of resources provided in regular education.[2]

This statement implies that we must evaluate student performance by using a measurement system understandable to both

[2]Haring, Nietupski, & Hamre-Nietupski, 1976, p. 4.

Chapter eight

teacher and administrator. It also calls for criteria for assessing individual progress to determine whether program changes are necessary, and it requires that long-range curricula be developed which result in adaptive, independent functioning on the part of the student.

Six Behavioral Characteristics

The following behavioral characteristics of the severely handicapped, when taken together, amount to a kind of definition also. Their value over some of the other definitions we have noted, however, is that they describe severe handicaps in terms that are critical to the teacher.

Lack of compliance and excessive self-stimulation are related problems for the severely handicapped.

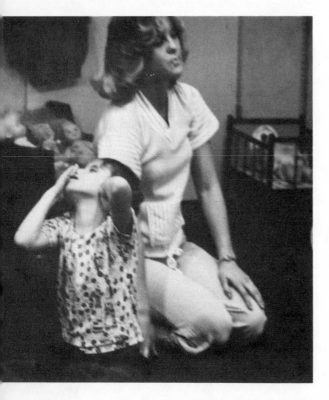

1. *Compliance problems.* When prompted to give their attention, whether to spoken or visual or even physical cues, severely handicapped individuals often do not comply. They may engage in self-stimulation, which we will discuss in a moment, or they seem not to respond at all. The effort to find ways to insure compliance has come to be a major area of research with the severely handicapped.

2. *High rates of self-stimulation.* The severely (and profoundly) handicapped, more than any other group, engage in self-stimulation, that is, recurrent, repetitive behavior that has no apparent functional effects on their environments (Foxx & Azrin, 1972). Such frequently recurring (stereotyped) behavior may be individual to a single child (like the child who sits for long periods on the floor twirling an ashtray with his finger) or may be typical of many children (like flapping one's hands, playing with one's hair, or rocking back and forth). Self-stimulatory behaviors often include self-destructive behaviors (like head banging or pinching or biting oneself), and they can be very dangerous to the child's own health and safety. The relationship between compliance and self-stimulation is generally clear: the more self-stimulation, the less compliance occurs.

3. *Slow response and development rates.* The severely handicapped generally are much slower to respond than mildly or moderately handicapped children, and this characteristic has important implications for teachers. With less severely involved children, teachers can often see change even through simple and informal observations. But it is often impossible to "eyeball" change in the severely handicapped person, because that change occurs too slowly for anything but the most careful and precise measurement.

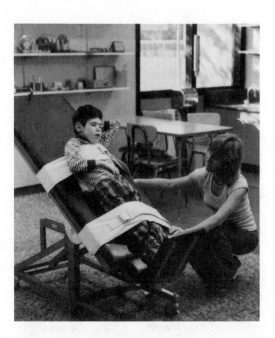

It requires precision to measure Bryan's progress in holding his head erect.

4. *Poor communication.* Severely handicapped children are limited not only in expressing themselves, but also in receiving information. They often have very limited language, are often completely without speech, and frequently have very few nonverbal communication skills before instruction takes place. This lack of communication limits the child's opportunities to experience pleasure and emotional satisfaction. Worse, it limits the effectiveness of instruction and thus requires special attention from everyone who works with the child. (For a more complete discussion of a range of communication deficits, see chapter 10.) Some theorists even suggest that the high rates of self-stimulation among severely handicapped result from this lack of interaction with their environments.

5. *Poor social skills.* The severely handicapped show tremendous deficits in the amount of interaction with peers and in so-

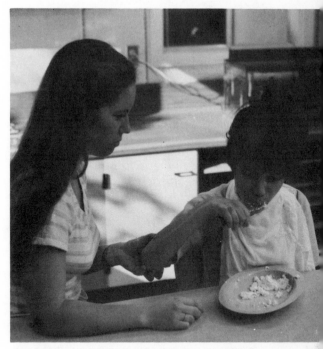

With the aid of an adapted spoon and dish, Nancy helps Mark learn to feed himself.

cial skills in general, at least partly because of their poor communication skills. Most of their behaviors are self-centered, and some are even self-destructive. In addition, they show poor personal care. A very large number of the severely handicapped have great difficulty with even the most basic self-help skills—feeding themselves, dressing themselves, toileting properly or even controlling bladder and bowels. Personal hygiene is a frequent problem of the severely handicapped.

6. *Poor health and physical or sensory impairment.* In chapter 13, June Bigge and Barbara Sirvis describe a wide variety of health and physical disabilities. Almost any of these, or even several of them, may combine with other impairments (like vision or hearing losses) to further handicap these individuals. Many of them have deficiencies

In addition to his severe learning and behavior problems, Frank has extremely limited vision.

in almost all of their physiological systems, including dental malformations.

TRENDS IN ACTION ON BEHALF OF THE SEVERELY HANDICAPPED

The current movement in educating the severely handicapped emphasizes developing an instructional technology to allow these people to learn. Accompanying this trend has been a movement to assure them their civil rights. Both factors have contributed to the current trend to prevent severely handicapped children from being placed in institutions and returning those already institutionalized to community settings.

The practice of institutionalizing the handicapped began in this country in the middle of the nineteenth century. This was also the beginning of the American Indus-

trial Revolution. Ever since, we have placed a premium on job skills, which has made it increasingly difficult for handicapped individuals to compete, to be productive in the marketplace, and to cope with their environments.

profile

BUREAU OF EDUCATION FOR THE HANDICAPPED and ED SONTAG

Before 1972, no federal government agency had focused on models of educational service for the severely and profoundly handicapped. In the fall of 1971, however, the Pennsylvania case was decided in favor of education for all handicapped children, and this and related developments eventually gave rise to P.L. 94–142. Against this background of rapidly changing attitudes and legal mandates, the Bureau of Education for the Handicapped (BEH) began to bring attention to the need for educational programs for severely and profoundly handicapped individuals and to the fact that much can be achieved with this population, and to make possible some personnel preparation programs and research projects.

Because there were only a few educational products and procedures to use with this group in 1972, the leadership and individual actions taken by such people as Ed Sontag, Paul Thompson, Josephine Taylor, Malcolm Norwood, and Jack Jones, with the full endorsement of Edwin Martin, Deputy Director of the Bureau, and Richard Whelan, then Director of the Division of Personnel Preparation, were critical. These people brought together the first panel ever to focus on educational programming for the severely and profoundly handicapped. A series of follow-up meetings was spon-

Although our earliest institutions focused on the "elevation of human functioning," after the turn of the century they became gradually more custodial, less educational, and less client-centered (Blue, 1970). As a number of commentaries have revealed, they became prisons of neglect (Blatt & Kaplan, 1966; Rivera, 1971). Professionals, legislators, and concerned citizens only recently have become involved again in raising the functional level of the thousands who are in institutions, and only recently

sored by Maynard Reynolds, through the University of Minnesota's Leadership Training Institutes, and participants included not only professionals determined to provide services and qualified personnel but also representatives of such parent groups as the National Association of Retarded Citizens.

This period of group problem solving and creative planning, initiated by BEH, created a sense of movement and inspired the interest of many professionals. Simultaneously, those same leaders began to identify people who were already working with the severely handicapped across the country, and to recognize and support those with special understandings who could contribute to research and development. This input from top people in the field, coupled with Bureau leadership, gave direction and cohesiveness to a professional movement that might otherwise have had little effect.

In November, 1974, Ed Sontag convened a consortium of training institutions in Kansas City, including 15 representatives who had been identified for their dedication to providing services for the severely and profoundly handicapped. During the proceedings, Sontag suggested that the group might consider forming a national organization whose keystone would be the education of those children for whom so many had chosen to be advocates. That consortium formed an ad hoc group and planned a conference for the following year. That conference, the initial meeting of the newly formed American Association for the Education of the Severely and Profoundly Handicapped, attracted more than a thousand people.

Ed Sontag's leadership at the federal level helped stimulate the profession to develop classroom programs and personnel preparation programs for the severely and profoundly handicapped. Today this is one of the highest funding priorities. All the divisions of the Bureau of Education for the Handicapped have meanwhile contributed significant impetus and leadership. The Division of Innovation and Development, under the direction of Garry McDaniels, has supported several research projects and now budgets $5 million annually for the demonstration of program effectiveness, including on early childhood programs. Since 1974, the Division of Assistance to States has also funded programs for the education of severely and profoundly handicapped individuals, and has administered five telecommunications projects for those who are homebound, funded by the Division of Media Services. The Learning Resource Branch of the Media Services Division has sponsored significant annual conferences focusing on providing services to the severely and profoundly handicapped in rural areas, and a number of conferences have also been held by the Research Divsion to determine crucial areas of research.

Thus, the Bureau of Education for the Handicapped has assumed a tremendous leadership role in working for the severely and profoundly handicapped. Particularly in the area of personnel preparation, Ed Sontag has made a significant contribution to professionals and pupils alike.

has there been commitment to help these individuals live in the best learning environment—their own communities, schools, and homes.

This evolution in thought about the handicapped, and particularly about the severely handicapped, developed during a time of revolutionary educational, scientific, and social progress. Behavioral research began to reveal the learning potential of the severely handicapped. It is both a paradox and a sign of caring that, although the technology of our culture has made many of the handicapped unable to complete, a part of that technology is now being applied to methods that will help them to be functional citizens.

The civil rights decision of 1954[3] led to increased public interest in the severely handicapped. This decision encouraged a series of actions across the country by minority groups who gained confidence in the possibility of ending discrimination against them. Among these were the parents of severely handicapped children, who sought the benefits of public education and the fundamental right of having their children at home.

Litigation and Legislation

By the 1960s, parents of the severely handicapped had begun to form strong organizations, such as the National Association for Retarded Citizens (see chapter 5, page 102), and to lobby for the educational opportunities that would help their children achieve what research was proving possible. Over the past few years, the work of parents, educators, and other professionals has resulted in a number of significant court actions. These cases have usually been class-action suits in which a small group of plaintiffs—children or young adults who have been considered ineligible

[3]*Brown v. Board of Education of Topeka*, 347 U.S. 483 (1954).

for public education—have represented all similar individuals in the state. The following descriptions of just a few plaintiffs in one of these actions may help to clarify the seriousness of denying educational rights.

1. N. is the 9-year-old daughter of Mr. and Mrs. C. G. She is an exceptional child suffering both from mental retardation and physical disability. She is presently hospitalized at the L. Hospital and Training School. The educational program at the hospital is inappropriate to her needs. This is primarily due to the fact that the hospital receives no public school funds as required by law and is therefore pitifully underfinanced. Furthermore, the program fails to comply with the defendant Department of Education's regulations and standards for special education.

2. L. is the 12-year-old son of Mrs. R. L. He is an exceptional child in that he is autistic, a condition first diagnosed when he was 3. While in attendance at the public schools of his city, L. has continually been educationally misplaced. He was first enrolled in the public elementary school. After two weeks, his mother was told to withdraw him because there was no program or teacher able to meet his educational needs. He was later enrolled in the public schools of another city in the fall of 1971. Although he was placed in a special education curriculum, he was able to attend only in the mornings. His teacher admitted that she did not have adequate time to spend with him, and his parents were required to provide his transportation because his school hours were different from [those of] other school children receiving public transportation. Because of the unsuitability of the public school curriculum, L. has now been sent by his mother to a private school in another state where tuition is more than $850 per month.

3. A. is the 14-year-old daughter of Mr. and Mrs. S. O. She is an exceptional child in that she is mentally retarded and her behavior is often hyperactive. She has been excluded and expelled from enrollment in the public schools. She was unable to attend public school until she was 10 years of age because of the unavailability of a suitable educational program. During this period of time, she was taught on a limited basis by a homebound therapist funded by the local Elks Club. When A. was 10 years old, she was allowed to enroll in a facility administered by the public school system. After 2 years at that school, she was expelled because school officials said her condition was such that she needed individualized instruction which they were not able to provide. As a result of this exclusion from public school, A. now attends a limited community program for the handicapped.

4. W. is the 22-year-old son of Mr. and Mrs. J. T. W. suffers from congenital mental retardation due to Van Reichlaush disease. For the period of time he was of school age, he was an exceptional child. W. has been consistently excluded from the public schools because of the system's lack of educational programs suitable to his exceptionality. As a consequence of this exclusion, W.'s educational development has been impaired. To compensate for their past wrongs, the defendants should be required to fund a compensatory program of education appropriate to W.'s needs.

Right-to-education cases in behalf of children such as these and others previously excluded from the public schools have been filed in more than half the states. Among these cases have been: [4]

1. *Pennsylvania Association for Retarded Citizens* v. *Pennsylvania.*[5] In May 1972, a three judge federal court approved a consent agreement assuring that all retarded children in Pennsylvania had the right to a publicly supported education appropriate to their needs. The consent agreement also required the state to locate all children who

had been excluded from school, and local school districts to evaluate all retarded children within their jurisdictions. The agreement further stated that all retarded children placed in special classes must be reevaluated every 2 years, that all retarded children must be placed in educational programs suitable to their capacity, and that the parents of these children must be given all rights of due process in connection with placement in educational settings.

2. *Mills* v. *Board of Education of the District of Columbia.*[6] In a 1972 decision that changed American education, federal court judge Joseph Waddy extended the right to education to *all* children previously denied the benefits of education. He ordered that not only the retarded but every school-aged child living in the District of Columbia must be provided a free and appropriate publicly supported education, no matter how severe the degree of the child's mental, physical, or emotional disability.

3. *In the Interest of G. H., a Child.*[7] In this 1974 litigation, the North Dakota State Supreme Court affirmed that the state constitution guarantees the right to a public school education. In addition, the court ruled that the residence of a child determines the school district that must educate him, and that placement of a child in a special program outside that district does not change his legal residence.

4. *Maryland Association for Retarded Children* v. *the State of Maryland.*[8] In a decision that clarified the meaning of public education, the Baltimore Circuit Court in 1974 stated that Maryland law provides for

---

[4] Bolick, N. Personal communication. Reston, Va.: Council for Exceptional Children, April 26, 1976.

[5] *Pennsylvania Association for Retarded Citizens* v. *Pennsylvania,* 334 F. Supp. 1257 (E.D. Pa. 1971) and 343 F. Supp. 279 (E.D. Pa. 1972).

[6] *Mills* v. *Board of Education of District of Columbia,* 348 F. Supp. 866 (D.D.C. 1972).

[7] *In the Interest of G. H., A Child,* N. D. Supreme Court, C.A. No. 8730 (1974).

[8] *Maryland Association for Retarded Children* v. *State of Maryland,* Equity No. 100–182–77676 (1974).

a free education to *all* handicapped children, and that mental retardation *does not* justify home teaching rather than classroom instruction. The court also outlawed placing any child in a private facility unless the facility provides an accredited educational program and can guarantee immediate admission to that program, rather than entry on a waiting list.

The thrust of these and other cases has been to end the automatic institutionalization of the severely handicapped by providing educational programs for them within their own communities. Judicial decisions have been accompanied by legislative decisions containing similar guarantees. The result of many of these court cases is federal legislation mandating a free and appropriate public education for *all hand-icapped children* (see the discussion of P.L. 94–142 in chapter 1).

Court rulings and legislation have established that public education is responsible for the severely handicapped and that teachers will be held accountable for the programs of these students, but rulings and laws will not carry out these charges. Translating these trends into action is neither simple nor rapid; it requires energy, creativity, and commitment on the part of the educational system and the community. It also requires the use of instructional procedures that will succeed with these children— procedures that are quite new to American education.

The Behavioral Technology

The term *educational technology* refers to the methods, processes, tools, and instruments developed from scientific research that let us create instructional programs, develop intervention strategies, and evolve step-by-step procedures that apply to children's learning needs. Traditionally, these methods and tools have been based

primarily on verbal interaction. Children are ordinarily expected to hear what is said to them, interpret and understand it, process the message, and then respond appropriately to what they have been told. The inability of the severely handicapped—and many other less disabled children—to learn through traditional instructional methods led many people to believe that they could not learn at all. In the past few decades, the technology of applied behavior analysis has shown repeatedly that, when any child fails to learn something that he should potentially be able to learn, the fault is not within the child but more likely within the instructional procedures or environment that have failed to produce change. (See chapter 1 for a full discussion of systematic

profile **THE PARSONS RESEARCH CENTER**

During the decade between 1959 and 1969, the goals of the Parsons Research Center in Parsons, Kansas, were concentrated on conducting basic research aimed at understanding behavior, especially communication, and demonstrating the effectiveness of behavioral principles by applying them with retarded children and adolescents in daily living situations. Jointly sponsored by the Parsons State Hospital and Training Center and by the Bureau of Child Research of the University of Kansas and directed by Joseph E. Spradlin, these research activities had three major thrusts.

The first thrust was the development of a strong laboratory research program to determine whether certain general principles of behavior would be applicable to the retarded. Two early researchers, Fred Girardeau and John Hollis, focused on searching for effective reinforcers, shaping behavior, and placing behavior under stimulus control in the laboratory—and they became convinced that severely retarded

instructional procedures which have been derived from applied behavior analysis.)

The severely handicapped do not learn as easily or as automatically as most of us. They are difficult to teach; they do not learn rapidly; they make small changes slowly. Therefore, their instruction must proceed in minute increments based on each child's developmental level, and precise techniques must be used to help the severely handicapped student acquire new skills. Equally important is the constant measurement of progress so that even the smallest behavioral gain—which may be quite significant—will be recognized. It is also necessary to build one small skill on another through correct sequencing, and to repeat correct execution of a skill over and over beyond what is ordinarily required to remedy the deficit (overcorrection).

To achieve the precise programming that the severely handicapped require, these elements of behavior analysis are particularly important.

Observation and Continuous Measurement

At first glance, many severely handicapped children may appear to have no skills at all. But if you look for small incremental skills and fragments of skills, you can find a number of strengths on which to build. You will also discover the competencies the child needs to learn and the skills she can learn immediately. By using observation and assessment, the teacher can pinpoint

children could be more effectively and humanely managed and educated if reinforcement principles were systematically applied in the natural environment.

These observations led to the second thrust, the development of experimental cottages in which reinforcement principles were systematically used. The Mimosa Cottage Project, a highly structured program for 80 retarded adolescent and preadolescent girls, operated on a token system in which specific behaviors (including personal grooming and the development of social, academic, and occupational skills) were reinforced. There were several long-term effects of the Mimosa Project. The girls' performances in personal grooming and some aspects of social development clearly improved, but they showed no systematic improvement in verbal abilities as a function of the program, which reflected the project's lack of emphasis on language instruction. Another evaluation concerned whether the girls of Mimosa Cottage ad-

vanced to a higher cottage level or to the community, or regressed to a lower cottage level. During a 2-year period, most advanced: eleven went into the community, seven advanced to a higher level cottage, and four moved to a lower level cottage. These data are quite important in that they represent a time when people in institutions did not often move from one setting to another, before the current emphasis on deinstitutionalization.

Some reinforcement practices developed for the Mimosa Cottage girls were used in other cottages at the Parsons State Hospital, and the project also stimulated other institutions throughout the nation to apply reinforcement procedures to the management and education of the retarded. However, when funds for the project were discontinued in 1970, some unresolved problems remained. For example, while the program was generally reinforcing to the research staff and was effective for the girls in the cottage, it was not rein-

targets for behavior change to lead to developing gross motor, fine motor, self-help, communication, and social interaction skills. Through continuous measurement of sequenced developmental behaviors, the special educator can determine what the child needs to learn, what she is ready to learn, and how she learns.

Task Analysis

Task analysis is particularly important with the severely handicapped because they need small, carefully sequenced tasks presented systematically. For example, it may be a major goal of the instructional program to expect a child to learn to feed herself. While this goal is reasonable, it is not precise enough to lead to skill building for a severely handicapped child. Dividing such a task into small, sequenced instructional ob-

jectives (pinpoints) is necessary so that one skill is built on another. If the student has difficulty chewing food, you know not to begin her mealtime training program with instruction on the use of a spoon. The first step should be the most fundamental one.

Daily Planning Sheets

Seldom does a teacher work in isolation with a handicapped child. As we discuss in the next section on the interdisciplinary team, the teacher may need the assistance of a psychologist, social worker, vision and hearing specialists, physical and occupational therapists, administrators, paraprofessionals, and, of course, parents. In addition to all of the other benefits of daily planning sheets (see Figure 1.3), they help anyone work with the severely handicapped child on a one-to-one basis.

forcing to the permanent aides who worked there. This problem prevails with the primary core and training staff of many programs for the severely and profoundly retarded, and manifests itself in staff preoccupation with activities such as folding clothes and doing paperwork, as well as in absenteeism and a high rate of personnel turnover. The problem of making the job reinforcing to those people who work directly with the severely retarded is critical for future researchers and behavioral engineers.

The third thrust of the Parsons project was developing a speech and hearing clinic based on operant principles. The early development of the clinic program was carried out by Ross Copeland and Ed Leech, and expanded by Jim McLean, Lyle Lloyd, and Bob Fulton. McLean developed procedures for improving the articulation of the retarded and any other child with articulation problems (see chapter 10). His procedures involved modeling the correct

articulatory responses, and then shifting stimulus control over these correct responses to pictures of verbal contexts. Procedures for evaluating the auditory processes of the severely and profoundly retarded were developed by Lloyd and Fulton, and were also based on laboratory-derived principles of reinforcement and stimulus control. Data indicated that operant procedures yielded reliable measures of hearing sensitivity in 85 to 90% of the children for whom standard audiometric tests (see chapter 11) had failed to produce reliable results.

A major hope for the research and demonstration programs at Parsons was that they would provide models and results that could have a national impact on the management, education, and rehabilitation of retarded citizens. This work has become a very credible part of the evidence that procedures based on behavioral management are most effective in the education of the severely handicapped.

Instructional Procedures

The sequence of procedures outlined in chapter 1 for acquisition, fluency, skill maintenance, generalization, and application can be effectively used with the severely handicapped. Experience and additional research in shaping, imitating, prompting, and cueing are giving us more information about matching the correct procedures to each phase of learning.

Prosthetic Environments and Equipment

The techniques of applied behavior analysis lend structure and precision to the teaching/learning situation. Prosthetic environments and devices have similar benefits that make it possible for children with severe sensory or motor deficits to learn.

Ogden Lindsley (1964), operating on the belief that "children are not retarded; only their behavior in average environments is sometimes retarded" (p. 62), suggests techniques for designing *prosthetic environments* to increase the behavioral efficiency of children who have difficulty adapting in average surroundings. The prosthetic environment includes **prosthetic** response **devices** that help a child make appropriate responses (for example, voice-operated telephone dials, arm-operated faucets, response-feedback systems that correct errors before they actually occur) and prosthetic consequences (for example, exaggerated social reinforcers such as clowns and cartoons).

The devices used in the prosthetic environment change the severely handicapped individual or his surroundings to the extent that he can do things that he would otherwise not be able to do. Adaptive and prosthetic equipment can also help correct or prevent physical deformity and can help in learning almost any skill, including:

1. Positioning, through the use of pillows, wedges, sandbags, special chairs, supports, standing boards, adapted tables;

After Olga makes her way through the wheelchair obstacle course, her teacher rewards her with a smile and a sign—"Good!"

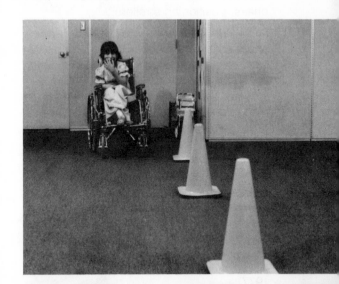

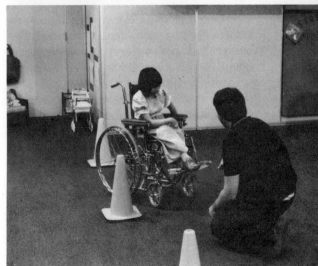

2. Developmental gross motor skills, through the use of walkers, crawlers, adapted scooters and bicycles, wheelchairs, positioning strollers;

3. Developmental self-help skills, through special equipment for dressing and eating, overhead feeders, specially built toileting equipment.

4. Responding to academic cognitive tasks, by means of head pointers, arm splints, electronic communication boards (Campbell, Green, & Carlson, 1977).

5. Communication, via letterboards, wordboards, pictureboards, expanded or recessed keyboards, scanning aids, encoding aids, plexiglas panels with numerals or other symbols indicating elements of messages, symbol vocabulary systems (Harris – Vanderheiden & Vanderheiden, 1977).

Some prosthetic devices may require architectural changes, large expenditures, special training, and constant supervision. Many, however, may be created by the teacher, parent, or volunteer with the guidance of a physical therapist, physician, and other members of the educational team.

The Interdisciplinary Team

The work of the teacher of the severely handicapped goes beyond the instruction necessary in a regular classroom. For example, if students are nonverbal, nonimitative, and unresponsive to social stimuli, teachers must be able to teach the students to communicate, imitate, and relate to the social environment. Teachers must work with temper tantrums, escape and avoidance behaviors, or self-multilation. Students must be taught to feed themselves, dress themselves, move around, play with materials, read, write, and so forth. (See Haring, 1977, p. 3 ff.)

To accomplish these goals, teachers need to be familiar with the basic principles

of such fields as medicine, occupational and physical therapy, speech and language, and physiological psychology. They might work with professionals in these areas as well as social workers, nutritionists, other school personnel, and parents. Teachers of the severely handicapped need to be able to communicate and work with all of these possible members of an interdisciplinary team.

Educational Synthesizer

Bricker (1976) has developed the concept of the *educational synthesizer* to describe the teacher as a coordinator of special services. In order that the team has the most practical educational value to the severely handicapped, the educational synthesizer is the key person who translates all information into daily learning experiences for each student.

Medical Specialists

Pediatricians, nurses, pediatric neurologists, and other medical specialists are necessary to describe the medical importance of some educational activities. They must also teach personnel about the dosage and effects of various medications and guide the handling of medical crises, including seizures. In these and other matters, the medical profession can have life-and-death importance. Also, medical prognosis can serve as a guide to development of long-term educational objectives for severely handicapped students. On the other hand, data and discussions supplied by other team members can be of great value to the physician in the student's ongoing treatment plan.

Psychologists

Psychologists also play a major role, supplying information on the functional level of the student as well as interpreting test results. The psychologist's advice also is valuable to structure the learning experience for the child's psychological development, and to clarify the dynamics that occur among teacher, student, and other team members. The psychologist can be involved in parent counseling, and a behavioral psychologist may be of great help relating the principles of applied behavior analysis to instructional techniques.

Social Workers

The social worker is a liaison between the educational team, the family, and community agencies. He has specific understandings of family dynamics and can be a key in creating consistency between classroom and home. The social worker also assists and counsels the family, helps with long-range planning, and secures community services for the severely handicapped child and his family. The social worker's unique role may be as liaison between institution and community, to prepare a severely handicapped individual to leave a residential facility and adjust to his home, public school, and community.

Vision and Hearing Specialists

Specialists in vision and hearing are necessary to evaluate the sensory capacities of the severely handicapped, to recommend activities for the use of what limited hearing and sight the student has (residual sensory acuity), and to help the educational staff use and understand prosthetic devices. Communication disorder specialists participate in program planning, evaluation, and direct therapy. They can also familiarize the staff with various communication methods and devices and instruct educators on procedures for carrying out skill development in language and communication.

Physical and Occupational Therapists

Physical therapists apply techniques gathered from a knowledge of neurological and motor development to problems of feeding, positioning, moving around (ambulation), and the development of other **gross motor** and **fine motor skills**. Their work with the child contributes to his independent functioning, and their work with the staff clarifies the use of procedures that are beneficial, rather than damaging, to the fragile health of many severely handicapped children. The contribution of the occupational therapist includes developing practical activities that aid the general growth of the student, while leading him to productive prevocational and vocational activities. This specialist also plays an important role as liaison between the educational agency and sheltered workshops and other potential employers in the community.

Nutritionists/Researchers

Because the severely handicapped child's eating skills and habits may be far from ordinary, the help of a nutritionist prevents malnourishment or gross overweight. Another suggested member of the team is a researcher who gathers data that adds to

FOR MORE SUPPORT

The American Association for the Education of the Severely/Profoundly Handicapped.

Founded in 1974, this organization is made up of teachers, researchers, parents, physicians, nurses, and other professionals and lay people interested in the severely and the profoundly handicapped. It has grown in a few years from a handful of concerned individuals interested in exchanging ideas to a membership of several thousand. AAESPH holds an annual convention and publishes a monthly newsletter, a quarterly journal, the AAESPH Review, *and an annual volume of research and current practices,* Teaching the Severely Handicapped.

our information about the severely handicapped and who helps others who work with these children on a day-to-day basis to learn the skills necessary to do applied research.

School Administrators

The school administrator is ultimately responsible for the education of the severely handicapped; therefore, his understanding and support are essential. His contributions to educational planning in terms of finances, logistics, transportation, and planning are most valuable.

Paraprofessionals

The interdisciplinary team should also include the paraprofessional—a new and important part of the educational staff. This

staff member may be a parent, volunteer, teacher's aide, vocational specialist, physical therapy aide, or other support person who helps provide effective, individualized instruction. The paraprofessional may do many of the procedures listed on the daily planning sheet for each student; his intimate knowledge of the child's day-by-day development is significant.

Parents

Parents are important members of the team, not only because of the due process guarantees of P.L. 94–142 but also because they have many insights about their handicapped children. They vitally need a full understanding of the problems, plans, and progress related to their children if they

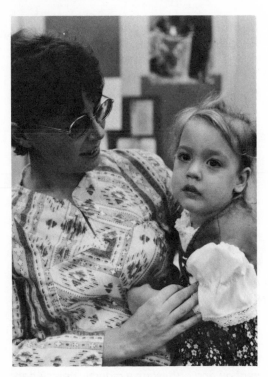

Kim and her mother go to school together to help Kim overcome her delays in development.

profile MICHELLE

Michelle was a normal 5-year-old when she was hit by a car on her way home from school 4 years ago. She suffered severe head injury and quit breathing and was revived three times in the first hour after the accident. She had extensive head surgery, developed hydrocephalus, and required several months of hospitalization and convalescence.

Subsequently Michelle returned to school, where she exhibited no behavior. She was essentially quadraplegic, although she had some slight movement in the right limbs. Her vision and hearing were questionable but could not be assessed. She could not sit without support or engage in any self-help skill. She did not react to visual or auditory stimuli. She was totally lethargic and would sleep any time she was left unattended. She also was on heavy medication for control of seizures.

Initially, the teacher selected as a target any task that would establish an observable response. Because there was some

are to effectively follow through with procedures at home. Parents should also be involved in the classroom teaching processes as much as possible, so that they learn the techniques that work best with their own children. As parents become teachers, they often have an extremely positive influence on the management of their children.

Through exchange of information and skills, members of the interdisciplinary team can create comprehensive services for the severely handicapped that incorporate the principles of applied behavior analysis into all aspects of therapy, treatment, education, and training. This kind of service assures the right of public education and the privileges of community living to the severely handicapped.

ISSUES TO RESOLVE

The education of the severely handicapped is a young and developing field of service. As part of this continuing progress many issues must still be resolved.

What Is the Proper Setting for the Severely Handicapped?

Although the current national trend is to keep severely handicapped young children from entering institutions, many parents or guardians are still being advised to commit their children to large residential institutions far away from their homes. A number of factors may account for this.

The movement from no educational services to full educational services for the

movement in the right arm, the teacher chose reaching to touch an object, with the eventual goal of self-feeding. Once this was established, Michelle was taught to reach and grasp a spoon, and then finally to bring it to her mouth. Currently, she is able to feed herself with little assistance.

The teacher and therapist determined that Michelle could sit with some support. Over a period of time they were able to teach her to sit without support for periods of 15 to 20 minutes. When she first entered school, Michelle cried or whined when she was touched or moved (extreme tactual defensiveness). She has now become willing to be moved and touched. The teachers also established a program to strengthen head control so that Michelle can now sit without her head falling down, although she still has some weakness in her neck muscles. She was also taught to roll over as a first step in increasing her mobility.

The classroom staff has had only moderate success in teaching Michelle to re-

spond to her name. She turns to the person who is managing the learning only about 70% of the time when her named is called. It is unclear whether this results from a hearing deficit or some "processing" dysfunction.

Another significant program for Michelle has been drinking. Initially, she would not take liquid but only pureed food. Through a program of gradual thinning of pureed food, she has been taught to accept water and other liquids.

The major strategies with Michelle have been the use of large amounts of prompting and physical assistance, accompanied by direct reinforcement with food. This prompting and feeding have been gradually reduced, so Michelle performs many of her tasks with minimal adult assistance.

Michelle is still severely handicapped but she now engages in many behaviors that make her more interactive with her environment and less dependent on others for feeding.

severely handicapped has taken place so quickly that many school districts may not begin programs for these children until the mandatory date of 1980. Part of this delay is because people do not understand how to set up these programs. Another problem is the short (but steadily increasing) supply of trained professionals. Still another cause for delay is public and even professional apprehension. Some parents believe that the severely handicapped may harm or influence their normal children; some administrators and educators insist that their presence in the public schools will have detrimental effects on the total educational endeavor; and some parents of severely handicapped children are afraid that their children will become objects of ridicule or be treated badly by people in the public school and community. Some professionals have not seen what these children can accomplish, and continue to have very low expectations for them.

These attitudes toward mixing normal and handicapped children interfere with the phasing out of institutionalization. Moreover, these concerns have led some school districts to build self-contained facilities for the severely handicapped or to renovate old buildings especially for them. This violates the basic goal of deinstitutionalization, which is to return people into normal society. It also resembles the institutional environment which causes the severely handicapped to regress because they have little or no contact with people

profile THE JOINT TRAINING, SERVICE DELIVERY, AND INFORMATION DEVELOPMENT PROGRAM

The joint program of the University of Wisconsin-Madison and the Madison Metropolitan School District is designed so that all severely handicapped children from birth through young adulthood who live in the district receive a free public education in a public school that contains nonhandicapped age peers. The program has evolved from the belief that all children, regardless of functioning level, should be educated in desegregated public schools. This service delivery model could not have been realized without a good working relationship between the university and the city school district, sensitivity to community attitudes and values, long-range curriculum planning, and a productive relationship that has developed between parents and university and public school personnel. These key people have collaborated on many projects since the beginning of the program in 1969.

One major objective of the program is to train preservice and inservice teachers who want to work with severely handicapped students, to train doctoral level students who want to, in turn, train teachers of the severely handicapped, and to train school administrators from around the country who need information on and experience with educating the severely handicapped in desegregated public schools. A second objective is to evolve a model of a public school system that offers the least restrictive educational environment to severely handicapped students. The program is also concerned with generating longitudinal curriculum sequences for this group. A final objective is to provide technical assistance to public school systems and universities developing programs for the severely handicapped and to spread information on instructional programs, teaching techniques, service delivery models, and so on.

This program tries to provide each child with continuous multidisciplinary evaluation and individualized planning. It is staffed by teachers who have been specifically trained to work with the severely handicapped. The teachers are the basic unit for

who are different from themselves and too narrow a range of activities. Also a few so-called "nurturing" programs still exist. These programs focus on a loving atmosphere for the child, on meeting his physical demands and needs, and on providing cognitive experiences rather than structure. They offer little serious intervention, few requirements for advancing through skill sequences, and no systematic instruction. While these programs may gratify the children and offer relief to parents during the day, they do not make many changes in the behavior of the severely handicapped. On the contrary, they contribute to the idea that these children cannot learn.

Even those parents who do not want to place their children in institutions often find that keeping them at home becomes a great burden because they cannot rely on community services and support systems. Parents often report that they have not spent an evening away from home in years because they could not find anyone to supervise their handicapped child for a few hours. Parents also find that the task of providing for the physical care and well-being of their handicapped child is so exhausting and time consuming that the general care of home and family are undermined. It is often difficult to take a severely handicapped child to a public place, enroll him in programs and activities in the community that benefit normal children, or find a doctor or dentist who will treat him. Many parents have no prospect of relief,

the development of curricula, materials, and techniques, many of which have been used in other areas of the United States. A constantly expanding parent program that includes counseling, training, and participation in all levels and kinds of services is emphasized.

Perhaps the most unique aspect of the program, however, is that it has closed all local segregated or self-contained facilities. All severely handicapped students, regardless of functioning level, attend classes in buildings with their nonhandicapped age peers at public high schools, middle schools, and elementary schools as close to their homes as possible.

One part of the program serves severely handicapped children under 5 years of age in classrooms with less handicapped and, in fact, some normal children. The goal is to prevent the progressive developmental delays that can occur when severe handicaps are not treated from an early age. In Madison, children are served from birth; where possible, potential handicaps are identified

and parents can be counseled even before the children are born.

The secondary level program is one of the few of its kind in the country. Severely handicapped individuals up to age 25 participate in educational programs that take them into the community, in some cases more than half the time. This program is guided by "the criterion of ultimate functioning"—the premise that the severely handicapped must be prepared to function in settings where they are capable of living, settings that might become their natural environment when they have finished school. This is translated into "schools with small walls"—learning essential skills in the places where those skills will be used instead of in simulated artificial settings. The success of this program has been due in part to the care taken to arrange precise learning experiences and in part to excellent cooperation between public schools, university personnel, and the community of Madison. Severely handicapped students are hired, for example, to deliver advertis-

even for a day, from the constant care of their child, and have no one to turn to for solutions to the personal problems and marital difficulties that can result from the burdensome task of raising a severely handicapped child with no outside help (Kenowitz, Gallagher, & Edgar, 1977). Finally, most parents are deeply worried about the future of their severely handicapped child and how he will get along when the family is no longer able to care for him.

All of these problems—misinformation, negative attitudes, lack of services, improper services—prompt some professionals to advise institutionalization and some parents to seek it. As time goes on and as we work to raise the functioning level of these children, many of these prob-

lems will diminish, and it will be clear that there is really no issue at all about the proper setting for the severely handicapped. Those who are cared for at home generally reach a higher level of mental ability than those placed in institutions at an early age, and it is now known that even the most severely handicapped profit immeasurably by growing up with parents who care for them and stimulate whatever abilities they do have (Apgar & Beck, 1972).

What Should the Severely Handicapped Be Taught?

The severely handicapped have so many behavioral deficits that the selection of skills to teach them would seem at the out-

ing circulars, to work in laundries, and to wash dishes. A local motel has offered the program at least one room so that students may learn motel room maintenance on a daily basis under actual work conditions. Students are also taught to eat in restaurants, use public recreational resources, use public transportation, shop in supermarkets, and purchase clothes and personal items. In addition, a large segment of the program is devoted to teaching home living and adult self-help skills in actual group and natural homes.

Still another component of the program is the development of curricula. Teachers, parents, administrators, students, and professors decide together which curriculum areas to address each year and how to devote resources within each area. Since 1969, the program has generated nine major curriculum products. It is currently developing curricular strategies that can be used in other communities that want to integrate their severely handicapped students into regular schools.

Curriculum sequences, task analyses, instructional programs, position papers,

and other materials useful to teachers, ancillary professionals, administrators, and parents have been produced. In fact, the project honors approximately 6,000 requests for information each year.

Staff members visit other communities and school systems to offer technical assistance. Formal workshops and learning experiences have also been provided in Madison.

The Madison program has demonstrated that severely handicapped students can be served without expensive new facilities but with quality teaching and the consultation of related professions. Moreover, the Madison model allows nonhandicapped students to grow up with severely handicapped students, hopefully minimizing their ignorance, rejection, and intolerance.

Finally, the program has not only brought children out of institutions, but has also made sending them there unnecessary. And, significantly, it produces approximately 45 trained teachers, and trains from 10 to 12 professionals in summer workshops each year.

set to be easy. But they learn slowly and their educational needs are tremendous. Thus, curriculum must be developed systematically, and logical skill sequences must be taught in a standardized manner according to each child's readiness.

A common approach to curriculum development has been to assess and teach according to the developmental patterns of normal infants and young children. This approach has advantages.

> **1.** The developmental approach serves as a uniform basis for arranging experiences at least for the first 72 months of development. We believe that once a child has reached a developmental age of 72 months, he can no longer be considered *severely* handicapped. That is, a person with the level of skill development expected of the normal 6-year-old—the mobility, cognitive, social, self-help, and communication skills—has a fairly wide range of capabilities and many other options for curriculum experiences are available to him.
>
> **2.** The developmental approach is based upon an observed record of many children from many cultures developing from birth to early childhood; therefore, arranged experiences and interventions on the basis of the sequence typically followed by developing children have a certain logic.
>
> **3.** The developmental approach serves as the basis for treatment by several other management disciplines, such as child development specialists, communication disorder specialists, nurses, occupational therapists, physical therapists, and pediatricians. This, of course, increases communication among the disciplines and provides a common base among disciplines for measuring the child's progress. (Haring & Cohen, 1975, p. 44)

However, the severely handicapped population is heterogeneous. Some children have severe physical limitations, other have gross neurological damage, and still others have sensory deficits; some have combinations of these problems. Thus, the question

is whether the curriculum should be based on a normal child's development and, if not, what is an appropriate basis?

The problem is compounded by the fact that a number of current curricula do not provide a rationale for the content they recommend or for the sequencing of skill development they describe.

Among the curricula guides available are the *Portage Guide to Early Education* (Shearer, 1972); the *Right to Education*

---

profile **DOUG GUESS, WAYNE SAILOR, AND DONALD M. BAER**

Since the early 1970s, Drs. Guess, Sailor, and Baer have been developing, field-testing, and revising a speech and language training program for use with severely handicapped children and youth. The program is based on remedial logic; it uses the children's immediate environment and their most urgent coping needs as the basis of intervention. The curriculum includes 60 individual training steps. This sequence is divided into six content areas: Persons and Things (steps 1–9); Action with Persons and Things (steps 10–29); Possession (steps 30–35); Color (steps 36–42); Size (steps 43–49), and Relation/Location (steps 50–60). Each step includes a description of the training goal, the training materials needed, a discussion of the procedures and instructions to be followed, and recommendations for increasing generalization to other persons, settings, and materials. Each step also includes individual scoring forms and summary forms for assessing progress of each student across time.

The program is also being adapted and tested for use in nonoral communication modes, including signing for students with hearing problems and communication boards for students with severe motor impairment.

Child (Myers, Sinco, & Stalma, 1973); the *Basic Skills Screening Test* and the *Basic Skills Remediation Manual* (Schalock, Ross, & Ross, 1974); the *Perceptual Motor Development Curriculum Guide* (Ronayne, Wilkinson, Bogotay, Manculich, Sieber, & McDowell, 1974); the *Zero Reject Project Curriculum,*[9] and *Systematic Instruction for Retarded Children: The Illinois Program* (Chalfant & Silkovitz, 1972).

The content of these curricula appears to have been based on practical experience and includes relevant behaviors. However, if our procedures are to be systematic, it is necessary to validate an open-ended curriculum that does have a rationale and sequence specific to the population of children being served.

Developmental Pinpoints

One approach to this problem is the Developmental Pinpoints (Cohen, Gross, & Haring, 1976). The **pinpoints** are descriptions of skills that are listed in many existing developmental scales, but that have been adapted and made specific to classroom use with the severely handicapped child. They are expressed as measurable behaviors and are arranged in a format that enables the teacher to trace the development of one skill or another. Therefore, the teacher does not need to search through dense clusters of developmental skills to follow the sequence of those she is actually teaching a particular child. The pinpoints provide guidelines for program development as well as ready reference material, in the areas of preacademic skills, leisure time skills, social interaction, self-help, communication, motor skills, and rein-

forcement activities (activity preferences of the child which may serve to increase desired behavior).

Criterion of Ultimate Functioning

Another approach is a curriculum rationale called the **criterion of ultimate functioning** (Brown, Nietupski, & Hamre-Nietupski, 1976). Briefly, this rationale states that the teacher should try to determine what will be required of each severely handicapped individual at the end of his educational experience, determine the skills he will need to become as independent as possible, then teach those skills. The younger the child, the less accurate the prediction. If a child begins education at the age of 15, there are relatively few years remaining until he should become independent or semi-independent. In this case, it may be possible to make predictions about his ultimate functioning, based on his own characteristics and on the features of the environment he will be in. Moreover, with a child of this age, it is also necessary to proceed rapidly and practically with skill training. With very young children, however, a curriculum based on normal development may be far more appropriate.

Measurement

In addition to a practical and comprehensive curriculum for the severely handicapped, tools for measuring change are needed. These help compare initial performance from program to program and effectiveness of one program with another. One of the greatest needs expressed by professionals working with these children is the need for more materials and training in measurement and evaluation techniques (Lynch, Shoemaker, & White, 1976). The development of a comprehensive curriculum will contribute greatly to the development of the tools and methods of measurement.

[9] Brown, L., Scheuerman, N., Cartwright, S., & York, R. The design and implementation of an empirically based instructional program for young severely handicapped students: Toward the rejection of the exclusion principle. Unpublished manuscript, Madison, Wisconsin, 1973.

What better way to begin to function independently than to learn your way around a kitchen, making a salad for lunch?

When Should Education for the Severely Handicapped Begin?

Severe handicaps can be detected at birth or very shortly afterwards, and the disabilities of the severely handicapped child interfere significantly with his development from the very beginning of his life. Research on both normal and handicapped children has led to the conclusion that the first 3 years of life are crucial to later development and should receive a great deal of professional attention (Hayden & McGinness, 1977; White, 1975). However, P.L. 94–142 specifies education *beginning* at age 3, and, although some state statutes call for education and training from birth, infants and toddlers have seldom been considered candidates for public education and are currently being served in very few school districts. Uniform procedures are not being used to examine infants so that their handicaps can be detected at the earliest possible time.

To put off intervention for several years delays the opportunity to deal with developmental problems when they are least complex (Bricker & Iacino, 1977). Because many severely handicapping conditions are progressive, the child's developmental status becomes worse in comparison with other children as she grows older; failure to help her at an early age also leads to atrophy of her sensory abilities and to general regression (Hayden & McGinness, 1977). Because early intervention is usually more effective than later intervention, it is also more economical.

The effects of early intervention on later performance of children have been shown to be quite positive. Early results in programs for Down's syndrome (mongoloid) children, such as programs at the University of Washington and at Milwaukee, have

Feeding her doll in a toddler-sized kitchen helps Teresa develop fine motor and language skills.

provided convincing evidence that early detection and intervention, including infant instruction and parent training, significantly improves the later performance of handicapped children. On the basis of the results of these programs and many other studies, well-planned, systematically implemented infant intervention and parent instruction programs can reduce the effects of handicapping conditions, and increase the future abilities of these individuals.

Is Vocational Education Appropriate for the Severely Handicapped?

While there are relatively few early intervention programs, there are even fewer public school programs directed towards severely handicapped adolescents and adults. P.L. 93–112, the Rehabilitation Act of 1973, provides increased funding for vocational rehabilitation programs for these individuals,

but this training is being carried out largely by state and local rehabilitation agencies. At issue is the public schools' responsibility to prepare handicapped students with the prevocational, vocational, and community living skills they need to enter these programs, as well as to equip them with the social skills necessary to succeed in training and on the job. Also at issue is the question of what to expect vocationally from the severely handicapped.

The use of behavioral technology in vocational and prevocational training has shown that the severely handicapped can perform complex manual tasks such as putting together a drill machine (Crosson, 1969), assembling bicycle brakes (Gold, 1972, 1973), assembling circuit boards (Merwin, 1974; Levy, 1975), packing and storing merchandise (Spooner & Hendrickson, 1976), and accomplishing various workshop tasks (Brown et al., 1972a,

1972b). Programs are also being developed to teach the severely handicapped the grooming, dressing, and domestic skills that can lead to independent functioning (Hamre, 1974; Horner & Keilitz, 1975; Nietupski & Williams, 1975).

Under the proper conditions, the severely handicapped should be able to learn a variety of work tasks that would make them employable and should be able to perform with gradually less supervision. However, the question of their actual employment remains unanswered. Few programs have shown that the severely handicapped can reach competitive production rates. Also, the handicapped vocational trainee often is emotionally unprepared for the frustrations of job training and may lack the social skills needed to get along on the job. These factors contribute to the rejection of the severely handicapped as employees but, even when they are well-prepared for all aspects of employment, it is not easy to place them in jobs. There must be intensive cooperation between school, rehabilitation agency, and community, and possibly government subsidies to employers who are willing to employ severely handicapped workers (Wheman, 1976).

All of the issues related to vocational training for the severely handicapped are important to the total effort to educate and reintegrate them. If the public, parents, and the handicapped themselves cannot see any possibility of independent or semi-independent living at the end of the vocational program, deinstitutionalization will be greatly undermined. It is a responsibility of the public schools to provide effective programs for adolescents and to provide continuing education for severely handicapped adults so that they may succeed in independent living. It is also the responsibility of the schools, community agencies, and businesses to work together to integrate the severely handicapped into the work force.

What Further Needs Are There?

Effective services for the severely handicapped require continuous, applied research and development designed to study all aspects of intervention and management. In 1975 the Bureau of Education for the Handicapped identified critical research needs which are still valid. [10] First on the Bureau's list of priorities was study of prevention, including systems of early identification, determination of risk factors, and programs of parent counseling. In early intervention, work is needed to set up more comprehensive case-finding systems, to develop assessment tools for diagnosis and

[10] Bureau of Education for the Handicapped. Proceedings of the conference on research needs related to education of the severely handicapped. Unpublished report, 1975.

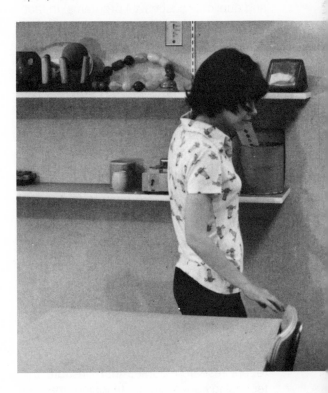

Learning to find her way around is important for Denise, who was born totally blind.

screening, and to get information on the social and economic factors that apply to the earliest possible discovery of handicaps in children.

Equally important is the development of uniform and systematic procedures for directly measuring behaviors and for assessing overall child progress. Research and development must focus on using measurement systems to determine how well intervention programs produce desired learning outcomes and the total effect of education on improving the life of the severely handicapped after formal schooling is over.

Finally, as our technology is refined and as new methods and strategies are discovered, it will be vital to measure the effect of flow of information on pupil gains and teacher behavior and to find ways to use and duplicate successful programs. In fact, evaluation and dissemination should become part of the total research and development effort so that new discoveries will be put into action while also being evaluated to determine their effectiveness.

In addition to research and development needs, there are a number of other needs that must be met to refine and expand comprehensive programs for severely handicapped children and young adults. These pressing needs include adequate personnel preparation, parents and members of helping professions learning how to work together, and adjustments within the community to help the severely handicapped.

REVIEW OF SELECTED RESEARCH

The following summaries are a few of the recent research studies that illustrate the technology involved in teaching the severely handicapped, the precision with which this technology must be applied, and

the potential of these individuals if the proper procedures are used in their education.

Autism Reversal: Eliminating Stereotyped Self-Stimulation of Retarded Individuals (Azrin, Kaplan, & Foxx, 1973). Autisms are repetitive, nonfunctional, self-stimulatory behaviors such as body rocking, head weaving, hand gazing, paper flipping, and cloth rolling. Such behaviors are a primary characteristic of autistic children and also exist in two-thirds of retarded persons in institutions. These activities interfere with socialization and also divert the individual from learning more productive behaviors.

In this study, a ward procedure was developed for continuously reinforcing outward-directed behaviors, which are thought to be incompatible with autistic behaviors, and for evaluating the effect of such a program on decreasing these behaviors in severely and profoundly retarded adults.

Nine subjects' autistic behaviors were recorded by means of time sampling; every 15 minutes an observer viewed each subject and recorded whether or not he or she was engaging in autistic behavior at that time. Three intervention procedures were used: nonreinforcement, reinforcement, and combined reinforcement plus autism reversal (based on the overcorrection principle).

The nonreinforcement procedure consisted of having the subjects seated at large tables in a day room with various materials such as toys, crayons, coloring books, puzzles, blocks, and talking toys. Staff members observed the subjects during their daily 6 hours in the day room but did not interact with them except to prevent them from injury.

During the reinforcement program, the subjects received smiles, praise, hugs, and the offer of candy or other desirable foods each time they engaged in outward-directed activities by using the materials in appropriate ways.

In combined reinforcement plus autism reversal, the subjects continued to be reinforced for outward-directed activities but, in addition, autism reversal procedures were used. For example, if a subject were self-stimulating, he was reprimanded, required to move to another part of the room, and then required to move the body part used in self-stimulation in a manner opposed to the original behavior (for example, if the subject had been gazing at his hand, he would be required to hold his hands up for 20 minutes). As the self-stimulatory behaviors diminished, the autism reversal procedure was shortened in duration (faded) from 20 minutes to 10 minutes to 5 minutes, and so on.

Results of this program indicated that subjects continued to self-stimulate about 75% of the time during the nonreinforcement procedure. The reinforcement program, on the other hand, reduced these behaviors by 75% or more for five of the subjects but only by 50% or less for the other four. Moreover, when the reinforcement program was discontinued, autistic behavior increased significantly. The combined reinforcement plus autism reversal program reduced autistic behavior significantly on the very first day; by the third day and for 66 succeeding days, these behaviors were virtually absent.

These findings suggest that negative reinforcers are effective in reducing autistic behaviors and also support the theory that autisms emerge when there is not enough environmental stimulation.

Effects of Reinforcement and Guidance Procedures on Instruction-Following Behavior of Severely Retarded Children (Whitman, Zakaras, & Chardos, 1971). Although the ability to follow instructions is important for establishing and maintaining behavior, the severely handicapped often have difficulty incorporating verbal instructions into their motor responses. This study was designed to determine the usefulness of a physical guidance procedure, used with positive reinforcement, for producing appropriate motor responses to 22 verbal instructions. The subjects were two severely retarded children enrolled at the Logan School for the Mentally Retarded in South Bend, Indiana. One was a 4-year-5-month-old boy with the verbal skills of a 1-year-old; the other was a 7-year-old girl whose language level was between 2 and 3 years.

To assess each child's ability to follow instructions before training began (that is, to establish a baseline), the experimenters prepared a list of 22 instructions that their teacher felt the children were capable of learning to respond to correctly (for example, "Sit down," "Stand up," "Look at me," "Point to your nose," "Pick up the jacket," "Come here," "Hold my hand," "Give me the cup"). During each baseline session, the entire set of 22 instructions was presented to each child twice, and each child was given 15 seconds to respond.

After the operant response level had been established, a 30-minute training session was conducted each day for 20 consecutive school days. In the initial sessions, only half of the 22 instructions (the training set) were used. Training involved physical guidance, positive reinforcement (Fruit Loops, chocolate bits, verbal praise), and fading procedures. Even when the child's response had to be physically guided by the trainer in early sessions, reinforcement was given and later reduced by gradually withdrawing physical guidance and immediately reinforcing the child's increased independence in responding. During training, each session began with the trainer's working on an instruction to which the child had already consistently and correctly responded; then a new instruction was presented. After each training session, a new operant level was established by presenting the child with the entire list of instructions without any type of reinforcement or guidance.

At the end of 20 days of training, the operant level of each subject's response to social commands was again assessed during a 5-day baseline period. After this second baseline was completed, training was reinstituted for 15 days, along with daily measurement of the operant response level.

In both subjects, there was a pronounced increase in the frequency of correct responses during the first training period, followed by a decrease during the second baseline period, and a subsequent increase in the second training period. Also, extensive generalization occurred in that the subjects learned many of the second 11 instructions (the generalization set), although their responses to these instructions had never been reinforced.

The Use of Positive Reinforcement in the Control of Self-Destructive Behavior in a Retarded Boy (Peterson & Peterson, 1968). Changing self-destructive behavior can be accomplished by *discontinuing reinforcement for a self-destructive response* (extinction), by aversive stimulation, or by positive reinforcement of behaviors that are incompatible with self-injury. This study examined the effects of positive reinforcement on eliminating self-injury in an 8-year-old severely retarded boy whose behavior problems included slapping the side of his head or leg with either hand, hitting his hand against his teeth, banging his forehead against his forearm, and striking his head and hands against walls and pieces of furniture.

The subject was seen in 15-minute sessions that coincided with mealtime so that food could be used as a reinforcer. During the baseline period, data were gathered on the usual rate of self-destructive behavior in 12 observations on the ward. During these observations, the boy manifested 21.6 to 32.8 self-destructive responses per minute (mean 26.6).

In the first experimental phase, the subject received food and the trainer response "Good" whenever there was a 3- to 5-second interval with no self-destructive behavior. When such behavior did occur, the trainer removed the food from the table, turned away from the boy, and began counting silently. If no self-destructive behavior occurred during the next 10 seconds, the trainer turned back, said "Good" and gave the subject a bit of food. The trainer also attempted to lengthen the interval between self-injurious responses. This procedure continued for 10 sessions.

During the second experimental period, reinforcement continued following a brief interval of any behavior other than self-destructive behavior, but the time between responses was not increased nor was the food removed. Instead, the boy was told to walk across the room and sit in a chair each time he emitted a self-destructive response. If no self-destructive responses occurred on the way to the chair, the trainer immediately went to the boy and reinforced his behavior by saying "Good" and giving him food. Otherwise, the subject was again instructed to walk across the room. This procedure was continued until he had walked from one chair to another without a self-destructive response.

After the second experimental period, the trainer instituted a reversal period in which the subject was instructed to walk from one chair to another, not because a self-injurious response had occurred but until such a response occurred. When it did occur, the trainer immediately reinforced the behavior and this kind of reinforcement gradually became intermittent. The reversal lasted for only three sessions and was designed to study the effects of the changed contingency on self-destructive behavior.

During the third experimental period, reinforcement contingencies were the same as those of the second experimental period. The entire program concluded at the end of 80 sessions.

Results of the first experimental period showed that there was a decrease in self-injurious behaviors but also considerable variability, with response rate ranging from 5.3 to 24.6 per minute (mean 14.2). The second experimental period, beginning with session 28, brought a reduced response rate which remained stable for six sessions and then became extremely variable. Then the rate of self-destructive behaviors gradually decreased and disappeared. The reversal period (sessions 64, 65, and 66) evoked a high level of response almost immediately (from a rate of 9.5 in session 64 to 23.2 in session 66). When the third experimental period was initiated in session 67, the response rate dropped to 3.2 responses per minute and remained at or near zero thereafter. After the program was concluded, ward attendants reported that the subject was less self-destructive and spent more time with other children.

Imitative Sign Training as a Facilitator of Word-Object Association with Low-Functioning Children (Bricker, 1972). When children cannot communicate, an initial step in helping them understand meaning is to teach them the ability to name or respond to the names of objects in their environment. This study describes a method for determining the effect of imitative-sign, sign-word, and sign-object training (explained below) on such children's ability to use labels as discriminative stimuli for choosing between objects.

The subjects were 32 severely handicapped residents of Parsons State Hospital and Training Center in Parsons, Kansas. These children were under 15 years of age, had severely limited language skills, no severely disruptive behavior, and hearing within normal limits. The objects used for training were small, three-dimensional toylike items mounted on wooden squares, chosen because they could easily be associated with motor movements or signs (for example, a rake), because they had phonetically different names, and because low-functioning children would probably not be familiar with them. A Wisconsin General Test Apparatus (WGTA) was used to present the stimulus objects. (WGTA is a large box-like structure with a movable door in the front, an open back, and movable trays with food wells located on its floor.)

Throughout the study, ice cream, soda, and candy were provided as reinforcement for each correct response or successive approximation of the correct response. Training sessions lasted approximately 20 minutes on consecutive weekdays until all training was completed.

In the pretest portion of the study, 30 toylike items were used, each appearing as a labeled object of a pair three times and as a distractor or nonlabeled object three times, for a total of 90 trials. After these 90 trials, the objects were divided into three groups in which each item appeared once as the named object. In each trial, the experimenter placed a small amount of food or drink in one of the WGTA wells and placed the named stimulus over that well. The distractor was placed over the empty well. Then the door of the WGTA was opened, the name of the correct object was given by a tape recorder, the experimenter pushed the tray forward, the child selected one of the objects, the door was lowered, and the experimenter recorded the selection and trial time.

After the pretest, the subjects were divided equally into a control group which received no training and an experimental group which received imitative sign training, sign-word training, and sign-object training. In imitative-sign training, the experimenter performed the motor movement or sign while saying "Do this" and, if necessary, shaped the child to imitate the motor movement by using physical prompts and fading. Each training segment was composed of five signs.

In sign-word training, the experimenter repeated the name of one of the training objects, followed by the sign for that object, and continued to use physical prompts, if necessary. In sign-object training, the object was presented to the subject and he was asked to use it to perform the motor movement or sign he had previously learned. Shaping procedures were continued if the child did not produce the correct sign.

Following each training phase, a 10-item probe test was given to subjects in both groups. At the conclusion of training for all subjects, a posttest was given in the form of a repetition of the pretest.

Analysis of the change scores from pretest to posttest showed a reliable difference in favor of the experimental group, indicating that the training facilitated the development of word-object association. Although a few of the children gained only slightly after several hours of training, many made large gains after only a few hours of training. This not only points out the heterogeneity of severely handicapped children as a group, but also shows that the training procedures are effective for many of them and should be considered in the education of low-functioning children.

Employing Paraprofessional Teachers in a Group Language Training Program for Severely and Profoundly Retarded Children (Phillips, Liebert, & Poulos, 1973). The training of severely handicapped children in language and other skills involves problems related to the amount of professional time needed to develop specific programs and problems related to training and supervising nonprofessionals to carry out these functions. To address these problems, a programmed language training approach involving minimal professional time was devised for training severely and profoundly handicapped children in language use.

The trainers in this study were ward aides who had previously been trained in behavioral techniques and were also given orientation to this program; they were supervised by a psychologist. The subjects were 42 severely and profoundly retarded children in a state institution who were divided into four groups based on their performance on a pretest. In the pretest, the subjects were first asked to identify objects corresponding to a label provided by the trainer (identification) and then to verbalize a label provided by the trainer (verbalization). Subjects in Group 1 were those who gave no response (mean correct identifications = 3.6%; verbalizations = 0%). Group 2 consisted of those children who identified a small number of items (20%) but gave virtually no verbalizations (3.3%). Group 3 identified about half the items (63.8%) but displayed very few verbalizations (10.4%), while Group 4 performed well (identification = 79.6%; verbalization = 51.7%). The groups were then divided into Experimental Group 1 and matched Control Group 1, Experimental Group 2 and matched Control Group 2, and so on.

For training, the four experimental groups were randomly assigned to a 45-minute daily class; control group children did not attend classes but engaged in the same activities as the experimental group for the rest of the day. Each class worked through 24 "Clothes We Wear" lessons. The first 12 lessons focused on the identification of items of clothing. An item would be displayed, the class would be told its name, and then they would be asked to identify it. The most competent student would be asked first to provide modeling for the others. Various discriminative features of the items were emphasized, and children were encouraged to try the clothing on and make comparisons with their own clothing, manipulating the clothing in various ways. The second part of each lesson used projected pictures rather than the items themselves. All correct responses were reinforced with food and praise, and various activities were introduced to prevent boredom.

Lessons 13 through 24 were of the same general format but the children were required to verbalize correct labels of the objects. Shaping of successive approximations was done with completely nonverbal children.

A posttest was administered at the end of training. Children in Groups 1 and 2 made more significant improvement than did children in Groups 3 and 4—children who had scored highest on the pretest. However, all the children showed improvement and some of these gains were quite dramatic, as in the case of children speaking for the first time during this 2-month training experience. In addition to the increases in language usage, the children learned to participate in classes, began interacting with each other as well as with staff members, and learned some self-help skills. Finally, the study also showed that aides were able to conduct classes of this type with little assistance.

Operant Conditioning of Grooming Behavior of Severely Retarded Girls (Treffry, Martin, Samels, & Watson, 1971). Self-grooming skills are among the self-help skills necessary for independent or semi-independent living. This study describes a program for teaching 11 severely retarded girls to wash and dry their hands and faces. The program was carried out at a cottage unit of the Manitoba Training

School, and the training staff consisted of eight male and female nurses and aides who had been trained in operant conditioning.

The washing and drying tasks were broken down into 12 steps, from pointing to the hot or cold water tap on command to drying the face after washing it. All sessions took place in a washroom containing all the necessary facilities and materials. During the first week, baseline data were recorded to determine basic performance patterns on a scale from excellent to very poor.

When training began, the trainer first taught step 1 and gave candy and social reinforcement for each correct response. Then the subject was guided through the entire 12 steps and received additional candy at the completion of washing. This pattern was continued in all sessions until the subject had mastered step 1. In the next session the subject would perform step 1 for candy, then receive training in step 2, and then be guided through the rest of the steps. The major technique used was fading while substituting new stimuli so that the response eventually occurs with a new set of cues. In this case, the physical guidance was gradually diminished until the subject could perform each task when given only verbal prompts.

When the program began, none of the girls could perform all steps without physical guidance. By the ninth week, seven could completely wash themselves without physical guidance. All made considerable gains in the acquisition of this self-grooming skill.

A Technique for Programming Sheltered Workshop Environments for Training Severely Retarded Workers (Crosson, 1969). Crosson believes that sheltered work environments should provide ways to train the retarded rather than limit their efforts to finding work to match current skills. Thus, this study reports procedures evolved through task analysis to increase the chance that the trainee will perform the proper task sequences at the proper rates. The trainers used pretraining on those components of the task which required more teaching and gave more prominent cues for those parts which were most difficult for the workers to recognize. With the use of demonstration of the task and continuous reinforcement until the appropriate response was achieved, the natural incentives in the work environment become reinforcing.

Evidence to support the effectiveness of these procedures was gathered at Fairview Hospital and Training Center in Salem, Oregon.[11] A randomly selected group of seven severely retarded adult males were trained to operate a drill press to manufacture wooden pencil holders and to use a hammer to assemble flower boxes. Each task was broken down into approximately 100 components, and the training procedures were developed according to the principles described above. The subjects acquired the drilling machine tasks rapidly, requiring an average of 18 trials to reach a criterion level of two errorless trials. Ten percent of the subjects required intensive shaping and/or discrimination training before they could accurately execute the task.

All subjects learned to perform the task at a very acceptable rate. Fifty percent attained this level of performance after 1 hour and 40 minutes of training, and all were able to do it with less than 3 hours' training. In a 2-month follow-up study, approximately 99% of the subjects' discriminations remained intact, and an average of only one trial was required to regain criterion level. In a 12-month follow-up, the percentage of intact discriminations remained in the midnineties or higher for all subjects with an average of four trials required to regain criterion level.

[11] Crosson, J. E., & DeJung, J. E. The experimental analysis of vocational behavior in severely retarded males. Unpublished manuscript, University of Oregon, 1967.

MEETING SPECIAL NEEDS

Without training, the severely handicapped can't do even the simplest things that other people can do. Their excessively inappropriate behaviors interfere with their acceptance and functioning. But they do learn.

These general guidelines should be followed in the management strategy for the severely handicapped. In addition, see the listing on page 250 as there is considerable overlap of program strategies for the severely and the profoundly handicapped.

1. *Plan for severely handicapped children where they are and teach them as effectively as possible. Don't plan an intervention program based on the limiting concept that they won't be able to do this or that.*

2. *It's crucial to start the instructional programming at, or shortly after, birth and arrange instruction based on reflexes and automatic responses. A good basis for infant curriculum is the Brazelton Neonatal Assessment Scale.*

3. *Assume that the severely handicapped will achieve a certain level of skills in academic areas. The preschool curriculum should develop preacademic tasks.*

4. *The severely handicapped are more likely to develop self-stimulating activities if they don't have planned programs and regular adult attention. Without intervention to prevent autistic, self-stimulating activity, it will increase and occupy the individual's attention. This intervention involves systematic programming, consistent presenta-*

tion of appropriate cues for responding, and insistence that the severely handicapped respond to cues correctly and repeatedly.

5. With the severely handicapped, it is absolutely essential to have precision in teaching for full achievement in performance. Precision teaching is:

1) Assessing performance in each class of behavior in an individual, direct way.
2) Establishing long-term and short-term instructional objectives.
3) Selecting curriculum and performing task analysis where it is indicated.

4) Measuring performance directly and continuously.
5) Refining the program and instructional procedures based on the analysis of measurement data.
6) Evaluating progress completely at 3-month intervals.

6. Communication is the single most important intervention target. The severely handicapped must be able to exchange information with the other people in their environment. Try for speech, then symbols and signs; don't leave out any effective options.

FOR MORE INFORMATION

Most of these resources are textbooks that are readily available. Check your instructor, the education library, or the general library at your school.

Haring, N.G. (Ed.). *Developing effective Individual Education Programs.* Washington, D.C.: Bureau of Education for the Handicapped, U.S. Department of Health, Education and Welfare, 1977.

Haring, N.G., & Brown, T.J. (Eds.). *Teaching the severely handicapped.* New York: Grune & Stratton, Vol. 1, 1976; Vol. 2, 1977.

Snell, M.E. (Ed.). *Systematic instruction of the moderately and severely handicapped.* Columbus, Ohio: Charles E. Merrill, 1978.

Sontag, E., Smith, J., & Certo, N. (Eds.) *Educational programming for the severely and profoundly handicapped.* Reston, Va.: Division on Mental Retardation, Council for Exceptional Children, 1977.

Thomas, M.A. (Ed.) *Hey! Don't forget about me: Education's investment in the severely, profoundly, and multiply handicapped.* Reston, Va.: Council for Exceptional Children, 1976.

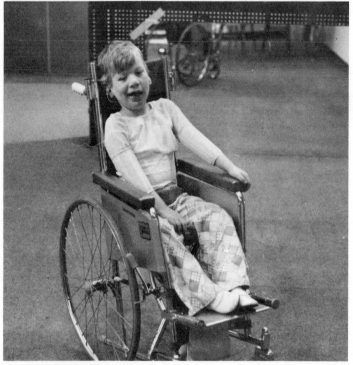

9

The Profoundly Handicapped

Norris G. Haring
Judy Smith

These are the major topics covered in this chapter. You may want to use them as a checklist when you review.

- *The unique behavioral characteristics ordinarily seen among the profoundly handicapped.*
- *Diagnostic categories contributing to profound handicaps.*
- *Problems and considerations currently facing special educators in providing appropriate services.*
- *Research contributions to management of the profoundly handicapped.*

The profoundly handicapped are the most seriously impaired of all disabled people. The nature, number, and severity of their handicaps are so great that, without training and therapy, they might be considered incapable of intelligence. Without instruction, they exhibit few of the purposeful behaviors of normal human activity; they cannot spontaneously orient themselves to the environment or to other people. Acquiring those skills basic to survival in any culture—skills like communicating, dressing, playing, feeding oneself—may be an abrupt threshold in human development (Wills, 1973). For the noncultural retardate, that threshold is so difficult to cross that few people in the helping professions have tried to teach them.

In the past, the profoundly handicapped were traditionally offered only basic life-sustaining services in institutions, because it was generally accepted that they could not learn. Educators have not, therefore, had to be concerned with planning programs for them, and only a few behavioral researchers have investigated programs designed for intervention with them. For all of these reasons, we know less about the profoundly handicapped, their learning processes, and their potential than we know about any other group of handicapped people.

The number of profoundly handicapped infants and young children is low. The incidence of profoundly handicapping conditions is estimated at less than one-tenth of one percent, or about one in every thousand people. These individuals, however, make up 40 to 50% of the total population of institutions (Bensberg, 1965), where their own impairments are often compounded by lack of stimulation, lack of movement, and restricted opportunities for interaction with the environment (Norton, 1975)—all of which can be modified by appropriate educational procedures. Medical science is helping these individuals live much longer than once was the case. As the profoundly handicapped become adults, crib care is not only more difficult for the staff but it is also less acceptable from a humanitarian viewpoint—particularly because we now know that the profoundly handicapped can learn to help themselves. They benefit from teaching, and they can be taught throughout their lives.

Many of our urban centers have the beginnings of excellent early intervention programs for profoundly handicapped children. Other services should be initiated as we have increasing numbers of trained professionals in this field.

BEHAVIORAL DESCRIPTIONS

In the broadest sense, the profoundly handicapped have a complex combination of most sensory and motor handicaps, with a high incidence of severe vision and hearing problems, cerebral palsy, and physical malformation. Their estimated IQs are less than 20.

Their handicaps are caused by the same factors that produce severe handicaps

His beanbag chair helps Ira, who has cerebral palsy, learn to sit up.

(see chapter 8), but the profoundly handicapped are disabled to a far greater degree. Some display only a minimal response level and few reflexes. In extreme cases, only respiration and digestion appear to be intact. Without instruction and therapy, some cannot suck, swallow, or chew, and many have no intelligible speech or self-help skills. Many cannot walk (nonambulatory), and all lack the capacity to learn spontaneously by imitation (Stainback, Stainback, & Maurer, 1976). These children may eat with their hands or have bizarre feeding patterns, may crawl instead of walk, and may communicate their needs by crying, grunting, or pointing. Behaviorally, the profoundly handicapped perform at a lower level than they might be able because it is physiologically and intellectually easier for them.

In the following descriptions of three profoundly handicapped children (Norton, 1975), the behaviors shown indicate acutely limited response repertoires. However, these are the very behaviors that can be improved significantly through appropriate instruction and are, therefore, the best targets for intervention.

Female, 4 years, 2 months. This child suffered diffuse brain damage due to encephalitis at 16 months, which also left her with seizures. Her muscle tone is deficient, and she has frequent severe spasms in her arms and mild spasms in her legs. She has poor head control and no hand function. Although she utters an occasional sound, she does not babble and has no speech. She is not alert, and she does not make eye contact. Her most active behavior is some rocking when tied in a chair. She shows no comprehension, and her highest level of spontaneous function is less than 4 months.

Male, 4 years, 9 months. This boy has mixed cerebral palsy and mental-motor retardation. The cause is unknown. Three days after birth, he began to have seizures.

His muscle tone alternates between *hypotonicity* (too little tension) and *hypertonicity* (too much tension). He has spasms in his upper left arm, his left hand is in a permanent fist, his shoulders are drawn back, and he has a stiff spine. He has no voluntary hand functions, and his head control is inadequate. He communicates by grunting, has no speech, and makes minimal eye contact. Although he engages in no purposeful activity, he is always moving, and he hurts himself repeatedly. He shows no comprehension, and his highest spontaneous level of function is less than 7 months.

Male, 3 years, 1 month. This child has cerebral degeneration, an abnormally small head, and low-pressure hydrocephaly, repaired by shunt. The cause unknown. His muscle tone is hypertonic. His upper arms are spastic, and his shoulders are drawn back and together. His hands and feet are deformed, he has no head control, shows no awareness of his environment, has no comprehension, and does not make eye contact. Behaviorally, he cries constantly and mutilates himself. His highest spontaneous level of function is less than 4 months.

In almost all instances, the profoundly handicapped are identifiable at or very shortly after birth. In addition to observable abnormalities, they usually have low birth weight and very low scores (below 4) on the Apgar scale (a test of reactions given to infants immediately at birth). They often require incubation and other life-sustaining assistance for some period after birth. Comprehensive management should begin with an infant learning program so that the child can reach his fullest potential. Further, some investigators (Hayden & McGinness, 1977) believe that early intervention of high quality can lessen the effects of profound handicaps in later life.

The profoundly handicapped differ quite significantly from the severely handicapped in terms of educational programming. Whereas teaching the severely handicapped require precise and systematic individualized programs by which they may learn to direct their behavior, the profoundly handicapped may not respond predictably to even the most carefully designed instructional program. Indeed, it may often appear that they lack the ordinary facility for responding. It has, however, been shown that even the most profoundly handicapped person can develop a consistent response pattern in the presence of repeated stimulation, although this response may be increased whining, intensified self-stimulation, or an effort to avoid the stimulus. In other words, while regular cueing eventually evokes responses in the profoundly handicapped, their behavior in reaction to cueing may be unpredictable and quite different from the constructive response that would ordinarily be desired. Current research efforts are accordingly being directed towards the systematic analysis of the learning processes of the profoundly handicapped and towards the discovery of instructional principles that will increase the predictability of appropriate responses to instructional cues.[1]

Another characteristic that makes these children somewhat different from other handicapped children is their need for constant comprehensive care, which can be somewhat reduced only through effective instruction in language or other forms of communication, self-help skills, and mobility skills. Until intervention has been achieved, the profoundly handicapped will

require the highest quality of comprehensive management from well-trained professionals, including:

● Individual attention during mealtime provided by an individual trained to feed, prevent choking, and resuscitate if necessary.

● Regular and appropriate exercising of muscles under the supervision of a competent therapist;

● Assistance in dressing, toileting, bathing, and personal hygiene;

● Instruction in language and alternate forms of communication;

● Comprehensive medical management.

TRENDS IN PERSONNEL AND PROGRAMS

The people who are presently most experienced in providing for the profoundly

Nadine, a physical therapist, is stretching Lisa's muscles to keep her joints supple.

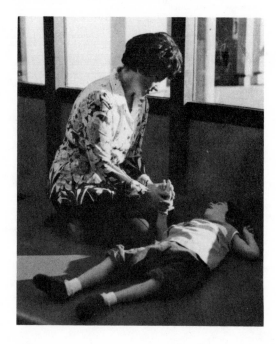

[1] Haring, N. G., White, O. R. & Liberty, K. Research being currently conducted at the University of Washington, Seattle. Funded by the Department of Health, Education and Welfare, Bureau for Education of the Handicapped, Division on Innovation and Development.

handicapped are on the staffs of residential centers where these individuals have traditionally been placed. However, because of the large number of institutionalized persons in comparison with the small number of qualified staff members, the quality of care in many of these facilities has been severely criticized (Blatt & Kaplan, 1966; Rivera, 1971). Federal legislation now requires that the profoundly handicapped receive appropriate education in the least restrictive environment, and this mandate of P.L. 94–142 places great responsibility on public education for establishing programs that will provide the quality of service needed by these children. This responsibility has had an enormous impact on the schools, on programs of personnel preparation, and on communities.

Public School Service Delivery

Although the incidence of the profoundly handicapped in the general population is small, the problems related to their care, education, and management in the least restrictive environment are great. In the relatively rare case where a profoundly handicapped child remains at home with his parents, the burden of his care can be heavy, and appropriate education is seldom available even in the most metropolitan communities. The use of systematic instructional procedures has, however, shown that it is possible to teach the profoundly handicapped, and efforts are being made in many school districts to establish comprehensive programs for them through a combination of systematic instruction and health management.

The focus of most programs currently in operation is early intervention, with its accompanying parent training, parent participation in infant education, and use of many disciplines in educational programming. For the infant and toddler, developmental goals include the *stimulation* of:

● Sight, hearing, touch, smell, and muscular response;

● Physical development, through correct positioning, mobility training, balancing exercises, purposeful use of hands, and the like;

● Preself-care, such as drinking from a cup and finger feeding, passive dressing and bathing, toilet regulation;

● Language, via procedures for increasing attention to sounds, encouraging vocalization;

● Interpersonal responses, including recognition of familiar persons, requesting attention, playing with toys (Luckey & Addison, 1974).

As children progress through preschool programs, they need to advance to intermediate classes, which in the majority of school districts have yet to be developed and implemented. As the principle of not excluding any child from appropriate education becomes the reality that federal legislation intends that it be, several levels of service delivery will be necessary to return institutionalized children to their communities. At the school-aged level, the profoundly handicapped child needs instruction that leads to the *development* of:

● Sensorimotor skills, through experiences in identifying shapes, colors, sizes, locations, sound patterns, textures, and so forth;

● Physical mobility and coordination, through practicing ambulation, overcoming obstacles, playing;

● Self-care, including self-feeding, dressing and undressing with supervision, partially bathing, using the toilet with supervision;

● Language, in terms of recognizing names of persons, objects, and body parts, responding to simple directions, imitating speech, using gestures;

● Social behavior, such as requesting attention, cooperating with others, using self-protective skills (Luckey & Addison, 1974).

A major cause of delay in producing uniform educational services for profoundly handicapped children has been an almost universal lack of professional experience with these individuals either in private or public settings. Few school administrators and teachers have had direct contact with a profoundly handicapped pupil because training institutions did not prepare professionals to work with this population until the early 1970s. The average person has never seen a profoundly handicapped person. Despite court actions dating from 1971 and the Education of All Handicapped Children Act of 1975, few of these individuals have thus far been deinstitutionalized; and par-

---

profile **THE DEBBIE SCHOOL, MAILMAN CENTER FOR CHILD DEVELOPMENT**

The University of Miami's model centers program for severely and profoundly handicapped infants and preschoolers was initiated in 1975. Its goals included developing:

● A comprehensive model program for the target population.

● Effective methods of parent education and delivery of family services.

● Language, motor, and sensorimotor curricular materials, and a program for their dissemination.

● Technical assistance for programs serving a similar preschool population, through consultation and visits to the model program.

This project has four major components. Its model classroom program consists of a center-based preschool for 25 children, staffed by two teachers, two assistant teachers, and two aides. In addition, it has consistent input from a nutritionist, physical therapist, nurse practitioner, and communication specialist. This staff has the responsibility of assessing each child initially and developing an appropriate IEP (see chapter 1) on the basis of the assessment data. The direct intervention staff, along with family members working in the classroom, implement the individualized plan and collect systematic data on each child's progress in language, sensorimotor development, and social, self-help, and motor skills.

Because of their handicaps, many of these children cannot do anything without direct assistance. Thus, a significant portion of their education must be individual, and much time is spent organizing and arranging the environment to maximize each child's learning when there is no adult available to work directly with him.

The parent involvement program is a comprehensive approach to parent education and counseling, carried out by a professional who works with preschoolers' families on eduational intervention strategies, social services and community resources, counseling, and child advocacy. Through a structured framework of learning experiences, the parents participate in individualized programs designed for each specific family. Training is both didactic and practical, group and individual. The goal is to have parents attend all workshops and training sessions, work regularly in the preschool classroom, and carry out planned educational activities with the child at home.

ents in many states continue to receive advice to place their profoundly handicapped newborns in state hospitals. Public education is struggling with radical changes in the concept and structure of education. Some school districts have done little to pave the way for these changes. Others, however, are initiating programs and, equally important, are establishing contact with institutions so that profoundly hand-

The third component, the development of curricular materials, focuses on creating programs for training preschool children in language, motor, and sensorimotor skills. First, a theoretical model is chosen from which to generate the content and sequence of instruction. On the basis of the model selected, a lattice is built to show essential training tasks and the sequence in which they should be taught. When the lattice is completed, a series of activities is developed. The activities are examples of potentially useful strategies for achieving specific objectives. In addition, methods for monitoring the child's progress on the training tasks are devised.

Technical assistance is provided through opportunities for professionals to observe the program and discuss their observations with staff members. When observers can remain for several days, they participate in the classroom to gain additional information and first-hand experience.

This program is already producing valuable results. The staff is accumulating data on population characteristics, causes, and the environments of severely and profoundly handicapped preschoolers. Procedures and materials to enhance their growth are being developed. Moreover, effective strategies for involving parents in their child's education are being developed, and spread to other professionals.

icapped children may be prepared for the transition to their homes and communities.

To compound the problem, the profoundly handicapped require extensive one-to-one instruction and attention as well as physical care and management, and their families need considerable training and support. These requirements call for a student-teacher ratio of no more than five to one, with the assistance of paraprofessional workers. Also, the need for the expertise of professionals from other disciplines—mainly medicine, nursing, social work, physical therapy, occupational therapy, and communication training—is probably nowhere more crucial than in the education of the profoundly handicapped. These professionals, the parents, the educator, and the paraprofessional work together as a team to determine a child's level of functioning, share findings, and develop an individualized educational plan. Ideally, one or a few professionals, specifically including the teacher, maintain direct contact with the child, while the team provides consultation. When team specialists do work directly with the child, they do so

This infant, who is blind and severely delayed, is already in a public day school program. She will stay there until she can succeed in a less restrictive placement.

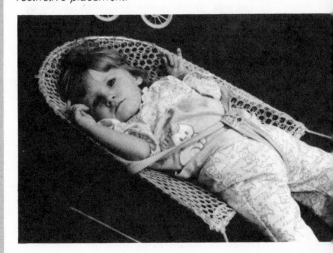

THE UNIVERSITY OF NEW MEXICO'S SPECIAL EDUCATION TRAINING PROGRAM

The University of New Mexico's Special Education Training Program prepares professionals to fulfill a variety of needs of exceptional children in the state. One important and immediate priority is training people to work with the severely and profoundly handicapped in areas that are rural and sparsely populated, within a population that is multicultural, bilingual, and often of very low income.

Through the New Mexico program, 10 bachelor's level teachers are trained and certified each year to serve the severely and profoundly handicapped. To do so, the existing program for training teachers of the mildly and moderately mentally retarded has been modified and extended.

In addition, through the Rural Master's Training Program, 10 teachers in rural sites are selected each year as candidates for a master's degree in special education. Priority is given to special education teachers who have roots in the rural community, who are bilingual, and who are familiar with a multicultural environment. These candidates are required to study on the university campus for only limited periods of time. Their program begins with an intensive 6-week summer session that includes 3

credit hours of practicum work with severely and profoundly handicapped children and 6 hours of coursework. During the following school year, the trainees return to the campus for a 1-week intensive course each semester, thereby gaining another 6 hours of credit toward the degree. Each workshop session is followed by readings and assignments to be completed and returned to the university for evaluation. Although requirements and assignments are geared to meet the needs of the rural teacher, the academic expectations are the same as those for resident master's students.

Students return to the campus for a second 6-week summer session, adding support courses such as Parent Counseling according to individual needs. During the second year, they come to the campus again for a workshop session and 3 hours of field experience, which allows university personnel to work with the trainees to develop very specific programs to meet individual requirements. The third summer is available to any student who may need to make up deficiencies in his program.

A crucial component of this program is a rural site coordinator who visits the master's candidates two to four times each semester. Not surprisingly, many of the rural teachers have no other specialists to assist them, no other special education teachers to talk with, and often minimal support for their programs. Thus, the site coordinator not only supervises the

within the child's regular home or classroom environment so that therapy is incorporated continuously and naturally into the child's daily activities (Perske & Smith, 1977). This kind of teamwork is new to public education and calls for the wise use of extensive personnel.

Thus, although there are few profoundly handicapped persons, their education has created the need for many trained workers,

with the kind of skill and understanding that few in the profession have been able to acquire. This need has, in turn, been felt by those who prepare professionals on both preservice and inservice levels.

Personnel Preparation

Teachers of the profoundly handicapped must have a number of competencies not

teacher, but also provides needed personal support.

The university also trains full-time resident master's students. Trainees who are already certified in special education are given priority in admission, because they can substitute for the rural master's candidates in their classrooms when the rural teachers come to workshops at the university. This experience with rural populations is intended to encourage some of the campus-based trainees to look for jobs in rural schools. It also provides a necessary link between rural and resident master's students. Moreover, rural administrators have had a very positive response to this aspect of the program.

A final component of the New Mexico training program is the Southwest Materials Center to house various materials relating to the severely and profoundly handicapped. The Center will house commercial and teacher-made instructional materials, resource books, pamphlets, monographs, working papers, training materials, and any other appropriate materials. It will also support the training program and serve as a resource for a wide variety of professionals in the Southwest. As part of the Materials Center, training packages to introduce administrators and others to the needs of the severely and profoundly handicapped are being prepared. A package on physical facilities, one on basic instructional materials, and another on general curriculum development are all being developed.

customarily expected of the special educator. Among these are the skills necessary for teaching the severely handicapped, including expertise in all aspects of behavioral technology and systematic instruction, the ability to teach basic life skills, interdisciplinary teamwork, diverse work with parents, and community coordination (Perske & Smith, 1977). Teaching the profoundly handicapped, however, requires

even more specialization and precision. Personnel must be prepared to give physical care, to feed, to resuscitate, to carry out positioning and mobility training, and to operate the prosthetic devices and life-saving equipment that are often essential to the profoundly handicapped. Also, the special educator in this field must be able to train parents for and support them in their role as primary program managers of their child's educational plan.

Dealing with the profoundly handicapped requires competencies in respondent, as well as operant, procedures. This means that the professional must be highly skilled not only in those behavioral procedures designed to shape and change behavior, but also in the techniques that bring out responses in children who appear to have almost no initial reactions. Achieving the smallest degree of progress with these children may involve lengthy, intensive, precise, and well-documented assessment, with repeated trials and applications to determine exactly what stimuli and reinforcers work (Block, 1971). For example, after many days of directly stimulating the stomach of a vegetative child, this procedure may begin to produce a response such as arm-raising (Piper & MacKinnon, 1969). This laborious process of causing responses in children is the fundamental competency which trainees must develop. Only after the child begins to respond can the professional begin to shape responses into productive behavior with emphasis on attending, compliance, response acquisition, and response maintenance.

The level of precision necessary for teaching the profoundly handicapped can be acquired only through lengthy hands-on experience with these children. Reaching these competencies depends on extensive, structured, well-supervised practicum work; yet in many areas profoundly handicapped children are not in the community and are not involved in training programs. The difficulty of placing trainees in adequate practicum settings has stimulated some universities to provide technical assistance to school districts and to set up demonstration programs where the profoundly handicapped may attend classroom programs and where trainees may learn to work with them.

Training institutions are also faced with the dilemma of trying to meet the demand for personnel in a field where no one has until recently been prepared for this kind of education while also producing the range of skills necessary for teaching the profoundly handicapped. In most training programs, it has been a policy to recruit only the most highly qualified, talented, and dedicated people to this area of special education.

> The single most important prerequisite for all professionals working with the severely and profoundly handicapped is the belief that all individuals can learn, and that their rate of learning is not a justifiable basis for judging the worthwhileness of an individual nor the importance of teaching him. If the professional or trainee has any question regarding the worth of an individual because he is severely or profoundly handicapped, it will be difficult for him to respond productively to his students. There must be a shared belief that the education of these people is very worthwhile indeed—that, for example, a movement from 2 to 4 responses is just as much a 100% gain as is the movement from 50 to 100 responses. (Perske & Smith, 1977)

Selectivity and high training standards are the foundation of the ultimate success of public education of the profoundly handicapped. Unless professionals can bring about change in profoundly handicapped children, they will be unable to help change society to allow these people to retain their rights and freedoms. This level of personnel preparation makes many demands on university resources and necessarily involves many programs and professions in a manner not known before in teacher training.

Simultaneously, higher education is called on to train public school administrators and community leaders whose support and understanding are essential to the successful reintegration of the profoundly handicapped.

Community Cooperation

The end result of any educational program is the achievement of the greatest possible independence by the student. With the profoundly handicapped adult, this achievement represents the *integration* of the skills and capacities that are stimulated in early childhood programs and developed during intermediate education. To expand on the list already presented:

● Sensorimotor integration, seen in such activities as sorting, transferring, folding; responding to music, signals, and warnings; making personal choices; discriminating among sizes, colors, locations, and so on;

● Physical dexterity and recreation, including using transportation, participating in gymnastic-like activities, marking with a pencil, using scissors, using community parks and other recreational resources;

● Self-care, as manifested in eating a varied diet in normal dining situations, using silverware, selecting foods, dressing and bathing with partial assistance, using the toilet independently with occasional supervision;

● Language and speech, involving listening skills, use of gestures, words, or phrases, following directions;

● Self-direction and work, including using protective skills, cooperating and collaborating with others, waiting for instructions, traveling with supervision, completing tasks, participating in a work activity center program (Luckey & Addison, 1974).

Many of these educational goals for the profoundly handicapped adult can be

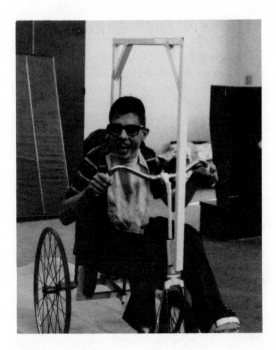

Jimmy Joe's father made this special bicycle and harness for him. It provides Jimmy Joe with a chance to exercise, to be mobile, and to have fun.

gained only through actual practice in the community. Once these skills are gained, they may be lost unless he continues to practice them in an accepting community which is oriented to his unique capabilities and needs. Because the profoundly handicapped are not capable of complete independence, they need community support systems to sustain them throughout their adult lives, if they are to remain outside institutions when their parents or guardians can no longer supervise them.

Although American communities were never designed to accommodate profoundly handicapped persons, there is currently a trend toward awareness of their needs. In some areas, experimental projects are being designed to keep these individuals in their home towns. Model communities intended to include profoundly handicapped people are being designed.

These efforts have been planned to gain information about how to solve the many problems associated with fully including all citizens in the community.

QUESTIONS OF PROVIDING EDUCATIONAL SERVICES

More controversy surrounds the problems of providing educational services to the profoundly handicapped than any other group of exceptional children. In spite of mandatory legislation, many professionals and nonprofessionals feel that it is relatively useless to spend the necessary human resources, expensive facilities, and sophisticated equipment required for the education of these individuals. Also at issue is the question of whether or not life should be maintained if life-sustaining equipment is required for a profoundly handicapped person. Some, too, question the point at which functioning can be considered so low that educational service does not need to be provided. Finally, there is the issue of whether the programs that are appropriate for these children do, in fact, constitute education.

What Is Education?

The first answer to these questions lies in the true meaning of education:

> Education is the process whereby an individual is helped to develop new behavior or to apply existing behavior, so as to equip him to cope more effectively with his total environment. It should be clear, therefore, that when we speak of education, we do not limit ourselves to the so-called academics. We certainly include the development of basic self-help skills. Indeed, we include those very complex bits of behavior which help to define an individual as human. We include such skills as toilet training, dressing, grooming, communicating, and so on. (Roos, 1971, p. 2)

profile MICHAEL

Michael is a 10-year-old enrolled at the Experimental Education Unit in a classroom for hearing impaired, multiply handicapped children. The cause of his problems are unknown; there is no history that his mother had problems during pregnancy or complications at birth. However, he is neurologically impaired, exhibiting slow, involuntary wormlike movement of his hands and feet from severe athetoid cerebral palsy and a profound hearing loss. Because of his cerebral palsy, he can't walk and has virtually no self-care skills or expressive communication without the aid of prosthetic devices. He is almost totally dependent on others for his existence. Before he was enrolled at the EEU, he appeared to be retarded, but as a result of more comprehensive programming he appears to function within the normal range of intelligence.

When he entered the program 3 years ago, Michael had no expressive language, but he did show some understanding (receptive communication) of about 50 words of a manual sign language. His physical condition was greatly limited. He had very poor head control and negligible eye contact. He was totally dependent on others to move him either in or out of his wheelchair and to move his wheelchair to another location. Because he could not communicate, people largely had to guess if and where he wanted to move. He required complete feeding, dressing, toileting, and movement by other people. In academic areas he had few skills; he was able to recognize about 60 words with questionable comprehension and to recognize sets of objects to about 50. He had no spelling or other observable academic skills.

In the past 3 years Michael has progressed dramatically. His receptive sign vocabulary now exceeds 600 words with greater comprehension. Using a communication board or other devices, he can express more than 150 words—he uses at least 30 daily to express practical needs, wants, and information. He has good eye contact and his head control has improved at the same time. He is able to move about using an electric wheelchair with a control specifically designed to accommodate his spastic movements. He feeds himself using a sandwich holder and a soup spoon, although he does spill some things.

He has enlarged his vocabulary in reading to more than 250 words and has greatly expanded the complexity of words that he can read and understand. He can perform basic addition and subtraction skills through 10, can tell time to the minute, and can count money in any combination up to 25 cents. He can spell 10 words, most of which he uses in his everyday life.

The major strategies for programming for Michael included carefully analyzing, verifying, and strengthening those skills he already had; teaching elemental skills to a high level of consistency; enlarging his response repertoire both through teaching and the use of prosthetic devices; and using a large amount of primary, tangible, and social reinforcement to increase his motivation to perform. At all times the emphasis has been on developing functional skills which Michael can use in his everyday activities, which help him to interact more with those around him, and which give him greater control over his environment.

Initially Michael asserted little control over his environment. Because he couldn't

When education is properly seen as the teaching and learning of all skills, then we can say that some profoundly handicapped individuals are already being educated and that all of them are capable of being educated. It is true that they have enormous

hear, couldn't move, and couldn't tell people what he wanted, he experienced extreme deprivation of sensory and social input. This resulted in his inability to generalize information. For example, he recognized an egg only in its original form; he couldn't recognize a fried or poached egg. His great lack of information was hidden by his smiles. Anytime someone came near him he broke into a winning smile, which made him appear more competent than he was. When he was enrolled at the Experimental Education Unit his teacher went beyond the smile and assessed every response she could, sorting out what Michael did and didn't know. She immediately enlarged his responses by teaching him to signal yes and no. She "filled in the blanks" by teaching him many instances of the same information. She worked on tasks he already performed consistently until he performed them reliably. She enlarged his repertoire by making or getting prosthetic devices such as a communication board, sandwich holder, spoon, number indicator (a "math spindle"), adapted typewriter, and electric wheelchair. In sum, she greatly broadened his repertoire, although he already had behavioral options that allowed him to communicate and to learn.

Learning is still often exhausting work for Michael. He must use greater energy to accomplish tasks that most people perform easily. He needs a lot of prompting, encouragement, and reinforcement. He still earns stars, points, prizes, notes home, and huge amounts of teacher praise. But his progress has been remarkable and he now functions at a vastly higher level than when he began 3 years ago.

learning difficulties and will always have severe limitations even if they learn to their full potentials. Despite this fact—indeed,

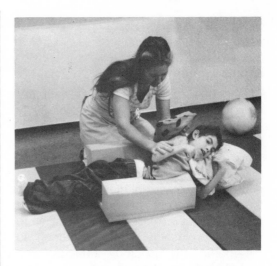

Lisa, whom we saw exercising on page 234, lies in a side-lying wedge to straighten her curved spine.

because of it—they should have the best possible education.

Is the Expense Worth It?

A second consideration involves the expense of educating the profoundly handicapped in terms of personnel, time, funds, and outcomes. Although the per capita cost of this education greatly exceeds that of educating a normal child in public school, it is still considerably less than the per capita cost of hospitalizing the profoundly handicapped in state institutions. Even if those costs were in balance, the cost-effectiveness of public school education is greater in that the quality of instruction, together with the availability of stimulation and normalization experiences, brings greater progress. In addition, many of the services, devices, and programs developed for this population can be used in other areas of special education, and the public accommodations provided for them benefit many other groups of handicapped people in the community.

Should Life Be Maintained?

Perhaps the most serious issue is whether life should be maintained in profoundly handicapped newborns who could not survive without life-sustaining equipment. While our society has begun to give thought to the right of the person who has a terminal and painful illness to die, and also has legalized the right to abortion, we must consider what is implied in the decision to allow a profoundly impaired person to die—particularly, government decisions on who should live and who should not. That issue would threaten the security of every member of society.

Special education must provide intelligent advocacy for the rights and privileges of the profoundly handicapped. Admittedly, the functional level of many profoundly handicapped individuals is very low. But, just as there cannot justifiably be selectivity regarding which infants survive, there cannot be selectivity regarding which children are educated. Regardless of their levels of functioning, all children can benefit trom, and have a right to, an appropriate education,

> *because they are human.* Our country was founded on the principle of respect for the dignity and rights of the individual. Any program which treats the retarded as being human, and which seeks to enable the handicapped person to walk upright, to feed himself, and to keep clothing on, is justified under this ethic. For society and for us to accept anything less should be an affront and a torment to our conscience.
>
> The second reason for providing the best care and training to this group is a more practical one. Individuals who have learned a skill such as toilet training have many advantages which those who are not trained do not have. For example, they are less likely to get disease from contact with their

feces. They require less care because they can do things for themselves. Finally, they are more readily accepted by others and may even be able to live in the community if parental-type care is available. (Bensberg, 1965, pp. 26–27)

NEEDS IN SERVICE DELIVERY

Because so much remains for professionals to discover about educating the profoundly handicapped, and because professionals and lay people have had so little experience with these children, there are unmet needs in practically every aspect of service delivery from research to programs.

Research

Very little research has been done to investigate the learning processes of profoundly handicapped individuals or to determine the intervention strategies that succeed best with them. Members of the profoundly handicapped population are very dissimilar—no two are alike and disability clusters, sensory deficits, response levels, and behavior patterns vary enormously from individual to individual. Therefore, an appropriate method for studying their behavior is a single subject ($n = 1$) research design in which each child's performance is compared with his past performance record, rather than with the progress of other children. Investigations should focus on one individual and compare that individual only with himself, over time and under varying contingencies. As public school programs are instituted, special educators and helping professionals will be in an excellent position to carry out investigations, provided that their work is well-documented and data-based.

Prime research targets should be detailed methodological studies involving stimulation of each sensory system through a variety of techniques, both manual and

The handicapped adult's greatest challenge is to live as independently as possible, in as normal an environment as possible. Even for severely handicapped adults like Eddie (top left), the sheltered workshop offers regular employment, a chance to earn money, and opportunities to learn new skills. With a carefully designed program of systematic instruction, Eddie learned to make plastic bags for seedling strips in only a few days. In a special education class in a regular high school, Lisa is learning such important daily living skills as cooking, sewing (top right), and housekeeping. Glenn, a visually handicapped high school senior (left), lived by himself in an apartment for several weeks to practice the skills necessary for full independence. For Beth, a physical disability means that special equipment, including special controls on her car, are needed for daily mobility.

Dennis and Lynn are both visually handicapped, while their 8-month-old son Peter is fully sighted. Despite his impairment, Dennis drives with the aid of special eyeglasses (called a *bioptic telescope*). Lynn, who is totally blind, uses a wide variety of aids—tactile aids like Braille cookbooks, labels, and writing devices, and auditory aids like bells on Peter's shoes to tell her where he is. For both Dennis and Lynn, the combination of special aids, special training, and their own ingenuity make them not merely independent but prosperous and happy.

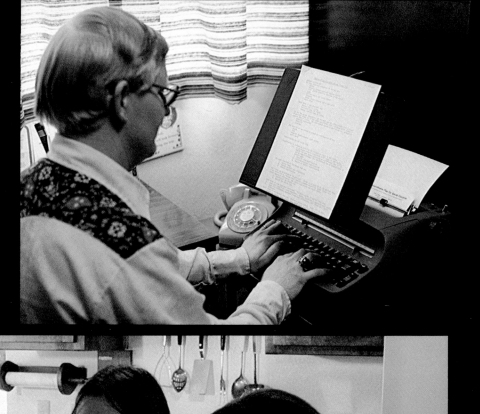

The six women who live in this three-bedroom home are special indeed. They are all retarded — some moderately, some severely. But supervised by the family of four who live in the adjoining half of their duplex, they live more normally than most of their counterparts in institutions. Events as commonplace as a room of one's own, a family-style breakfast, or a game with friends (here it's Candyland with the kids from next door) make each day special.

mechanical, with verification of procedures including numbers of profoundly handicapped children. As more and more techniques for the stimulation of responding are developed, the time required to reach these children will be reduced and their overall progress will be helped.

The technology of applied behavioral analysis must also be refined to include a variety of strategies for teaching those behaviors that are necessary to all skill development: attending, compliance, acquisition, and maintenance. (Chapter 1 has a more detailed discussion of these phases of learning.) Many profoundly handicapped children lack even the ability to make eye contact, so researchers should test many techniques for teaching this response, as well as teaching the many other responses that comprise attending behavior. Task analysis and teaching of compliance are still relatively unexplored, although the ability to comply, cooperate, follow simple directions, and collaborate must be mastered before a child is ready to learn the mobility, communication, and self-help skills that he needs for survival. We need to know much more about the procedures that lead these individuals to acquiring and maintaining skills.

Although these studies involve individualized programs with profoundly handicapped children, adolescents, and adults, studies which follow the long-term effectiveness of these programs and group comparison studies are still needed. For example, data are needed to substantiate the effectiveness of infant intervention programs, and this evidence can only be obtained if we follow the progress of the students as they advance through their educational experiences. We also need research in areas such as parent training, attitude change, effective advocacy tactics, procedures for deinstitutionalization and community reintegration, validation of professional competencies, and uniform

These roller boards are the only way Allison and Chris have to get around on their own.

measurement and assessment systems. Also, there is a pressing need for research that leads to the development of cost-effective adaptive and prosthetic equipment that helps the profoundly handicapped overcome some of their disabilities and that helps their families maintain them at home.

With such enormous research priorities, it is obvious that all professionals concerned with this population should receive training or retraining in research techniques and, equally important, in the skills that will help them share their findings with the whole profession. We cannot wait for scientists to do this job for us. We must become scientific and make classroom research part of our programming with the profoundly handicapped.

Service Delivery in Natural Settings

The least restrictive environment advocated by federal legislation should mean the natural community environment. With the profoundly handicapped, service delivery in the natural setting means changes and adjustments in attitudes and physical arrangements.

"There is little evidence to support the premise that we cannot provide for the more severely (or) profoundly handicapped child in the regular school building" (Sontag, 1976, p. 111). This is not, however, to say that we have the models and plans that will aid the integration of these children. First, we have no uniform and comprehensive system of deinstitutionalization, which should include counseling and preparing parents, working with the child in the institution to bridge the transition, and developing school and community services to meet the child's needs. Such programs would not only provide for the gradual reintegration of the profoundly handicapped and other handicapped individuals into their communities but would also do much to influence parents to keep their handicapped children at home.

Although programs are available for the profoundly handicapped in a few metropolitan areas, we do not have the programs that prepare administrators and educators for the entry of these children into school and methods for keeping these and other professionals informed about the profoundly handicapped. We also need to determine the best ways to develop positive attitudes of acceptance and assistance in normal people who encounter these children in school and in the community. A vital step here is to develop comprehensive instructional programs that focus on teaching the profoundly handicapped to become as physically and behaviorally acceptable as possible (normalization). Parallel is the need for greater use of plastic and cosmetic surgery to correct their disfigurements as much as possible and improve physical appearance.

In terms of the barriers in school buildings and other public pleas, as well as in transportation systems and recreational facilities, city planners, architects, and educators in most communities have yet to sit down together to determine the modifications that can and should be made to enable not only the profoundly handicapped but various other handicapped persons to be mobile in their immediate environment and to function in the community. Communities generally have not made a coordinated effort to provide the support services needed by this population or to encourage common services. Housing for them is usually available at two extremes: either at home or in hospitals. Alternative living arrangements, including group home living, which is most appropriate for the profoundly handicapped, by and large are not architecturally prepared, adequately staffed, or adequately equipped to accept the profoundly handicapped. Funding that would make this possible is needed.

For those families who keep a profoundly handicapped individual at home, no model system of support services has been developed to ensure the counseling, relief care, and in-home services and equipment that make family care possible. Even though some organizatons such as the Muscular Dystrophy Association and March of Dimes provide wheelchairs and other equipment and medical services to afflicted children, there are few resources that provide services or equipment to the profoundly handicapped.

One solution to some of these problems is increased numbers of trained personnel, particularly in supporting positions. Personnel preparation programs should give increased attention to recruitment and training of paraprofessionals to function not only as teacher aides, but also as child care workers, in-home aides, and group home attendants.

All efforts in education, community reintegration, and normalization should center on making the profoundly handicapped individual as self-sufficient as possible and making our communities capable of sustaining that individual throughout life.

REVIEW OF SELECTED RESEARCH STUDIES

The research studies described are a few of the projects that have shown that profoundly handicapped children and adults can learn and can develop skills that make their management simpler. Most educational work with this population has been done in institutional settings, but the procedures used have wide applications to public school settings.

Training Profoundly Handicapped Children to Stop Crawling (O'Brien, Azrin, & Bugle, 19/2). Although most profoundly handicapped children learn to crawl, few spontaneously learn to walk, probably because their physiological problems and slower learning rate make walking slower and more difficult than crawling. The authors of this study sought to make walking easier and faster for such children by providing practice and intervening to decrease the ease and speed of crawling. Instructional procedures were based on restraint from crawling and priming for walking.

The subjects were four profoundly handicapped children enrolled in a day-care nursery school program 6 hours daily, 5 days a week. They could not achieve any score on the Stanford-Binet Intelligence Test, were not toilet trained, had no self-help skills, and had no speech. All had been observed to walk with difficulty on occasion, but their primary mode of ambulation was crawling.

The experimenters first defined walking and crawling and arranged for automatic recording of both behaviors. The initial phase of the program was carried out in a large room with two chairs in diagonal corners. An adult would place himself in one of the corners with a chair, call the child by name, and encourage the child to come to that corner. When the child arrived, by walking or by crawling, the adult gave social praise, affectionate touches, and edible reinforcements. The adult then moved to the opposite corner and repeated the procedure until the end of the session. This phase of the program was intended to provide motivation to the child for moving from one corner of the room to the other.

When training was instituted, a second adult started each trail with the child in an off-feet position. The chairs made it possible for the child to raise himself if he wanted to. Thereafter, four different training procedures were used:

1. *No training.* The procedures used in the first phase;

2. *Restraint.* After 3 seconds of crawling, the trainer held the child from behind by the waist for 5 seconds; the child could make crawling motions but not move ahead;

3. *Response priming.* After 3 seconds of crawling, the trainer raised the child to standing to allow him to walk in the direction he was crawling;

4. *Restraint and response priming.* After 3 seconds of crawling, the trainer held the child by the waist for 5 seconds and then positioned him to stand.

These procedures were sequenced as follows: no training, restraint, restraint and priming, no training, priming, no training, restraint. Three 10-minute sessions were conducted daily, 1½ hours apart.

After the conclusion of the structured portion of the program, the nursery program teachers began training through restraint and priming, although they did not provide edibles or other contrived reinforcements. As a result, all four children crawled less and walked more. During the final phases of training, they crawled no more than once daily, or less than 10% of the time spent in ambulation—a level acceptable for children of their age level. When training was discontinued, some permanent improvement was noted in all four children. For the two whose physical impairments interfered with walking, further training with focus on restraint from crawling resulted in their walking almost exclusively 18 months after training.

An Analysis of Behavior During the Acquisition and Maintenance Phases of Self-Spoon Feeding Skills of Profound Retardates (Song & Gandhi, 1974). The four profoundly retarded children in this study were children whom aides had tried repeatedly to teach spoon-feeding but who had failed to learn this skill. The subjects had no speech and no self-help skills. When food was presented, three of them would reach for it with their hands or mouth; the fourth made no voluntary movement to reach for food.

The target behavior was the child's scooping up food with a spoon and bringing it to his mouth without guided assistance for more than 50% of the time during one meal. Training was conducted by aides, who had been instructed in a shaping technique, with reinforcement, and in fading procedures. For every undesirable behavior, the trainers removed the food tray from the child's table for 1 minute or until the child was properly seated for eating. The child's nonspoon hand was restrained to the chair to prevent his grabbing for food with his free hand. For each positive response, social reinforcement such as "Good boy," or a pat on the shoulder was given, frequently paired with food. For one child, who was distracted when the trainer's hand was in front of him, a hand-to-shoulder technique was used; the trainer would sit behind the child and push his elbow and his shoulder, rather than his hand. Another child who was prone to finger-feed was handled by placing a sock over his free hand with a spoon tied to it to prevent finger feeding.

For one child, the seven steps were successfully completed in 198 meals; for the second in 241 meals; for the third in 318 meals. The fourth child did not progress beyond the first step of the program. This was the child who had manifested no voluntary movement toward food, and her readiness for this type of training was thus in question throughout the study.

Decelerating Undesired Mealtime Behaviors in a Group of Profoundly Retarded Boys (Henriksen & Doughty, 1967). Inappropriate mealtime behaviors are often difficult to correct because they are immediately self-rewarding; for example, eating with hands may bring food into the mouth faster than awkward use of a utensil.

To deal with these problems, this study was conducted with four boys in a cottage setting. Their ages were between 11 and 14, and their Vineland social ages (see the appendix) were from 1 year 3 months to 2 years 4 months. Their common mealtime behaviors included eating too fast, eating with their hands, stealing food from others' trays, hitting others, and throwing trays of food on the floor. Two of these boys had speech and two did not; three manifested stereotyped behavior; all were hyperactive at times and presented problems such as smearing feces, tearing clothing, biting, pushing, and hitting. Only one was toilet trained. All of them could feed themselves with a spoon.

For training, the children were placed along the sides of a small square table in the dayroom, and two trainers were seated on diagonal corners of the table. Each child's misbehavior was reflected to him by a trainer's facial and verbal disapproval. If misbehavior continued, the child's movement was interrupted by means of holding his arm down. When a child displayed proper eating behavior, he was given verbal and facial approval. This training was conducted 3 meals a day, 7 days per week, for 13 weeks.

After 11 weeks, a fading process was begun. The boys were moved back to the original cottage setting for meals, and the trainers stood behind them at progressively increasing distances. As a result of training, inappropriate behaviors were considerably reduced. The boys also learned to discriminate among utensil foods and finger foods. Moreover, a wide generalization effect was noted, in that they became easier to train in other self-help areas.

Evaluation of Self-Help Habit Training of the Profoundly Retarded (Colwell, Richards, McCarver, & Ellis, 1973). The Columbia State School in Louisiana is a new residential training institution for the severely and profoundly retarded. Children aged 4 to 16 years (mean IQ, 16.1) are accepted for periods of 2 to 12 months, during which they are trained in a number of skills. Intensive training, which is conducted for approximately 15 hours per day in living quarters, dining room, playground, and training center, is based on operant procedures, with tangible rewards (edibles) gradually faded and replaced with social praise as instruction progresses. Major emphasis is placed on bringing toileting, dressing, and feeding behavior under verbal control, and training is also given in communication and motor skills.

Performance in each area is measured by checklists developed at the school. The scale for dressing contains 27 items, ranging from putting on and taking off clothes to buttoning, zipping, hooking, and so forth, which require fine motor skills. The feeding scale indicates how well a child can drink from a glass, use silverware, and eat appropriately. Toileting behaviors are measured in terms of the frequency of day and night wetting and soiling.

Of the 47 children who have been admitted to this institution, 24 have been discharged. Substantial improvements in feeding, dressing, and toileting behavior have occurred in 3 to 12 months. Reliability of agreement by independent raters has been quite substantial in showing that 42 of the children gained in mental age scores, 44 gained in dressing, 36 gained in feeding, and 33 gained in toileting. This indicates that, with the use of intensive training procedures, most profoundly handicapped children can become far better able to cope with their environments.

Using Attendants to Build a Verbal Repertoire in a Profoundly Retarded Adolescent (Wheeler, 1973). In this study, the subject was a 16-year-old profoundly retarded female at a state school. Her vocal repertoire consisted of screaming and singing recognizable tunes without distinguishable words. Her behavior included self-injury and aggression, including biting and spitting at attendants and residents, for which she was frequently restrained and tranquilized. To initiate intensive individualized behavior modification procedures, the subject was removed to a special unit. Sessions took place in a bare room at breakfast and lunchtime. Portions of her meal were used as reinforcers at the beginning of training, and later a token exchange system was used.

During the first 12 sessions of phase 1, the examiner made simple sounds for the subject to imitate. If the subject did a correct imitation, she received food. Otherwise, the prompts were repeated until she did imitate. During the next six sessions (phase 2), the procedure was the same, but words known to be in the subject's receptive repertoire were used, and reinforcement changed from food to tokens. In the seven sessions of phase 3, the attendant took over training, recording events of the session on a tape recording to be scored later by a technician. For the final 121 sessions of phase 4, more structure was incorporated. Five words were selected for each session, each presented three times during a session, for a total of 15 reinforcements. When the subject responded correctly to a particular word at the first discriminative stimulus each time it was presented for two sessions in a row, the word was dropped and a new word was added, on the basis of its functional value to the subject. Attendants and professional staff demanded that the subject use the newly learned words in appropriate situations outside of the training setting.

It became clear that the subject had previously learned to bite in order to gain the opportunity to be left alone. Through training, she learned to say "Go" to the attendant when she wanted to be left alone. Also, during all parts of the day, a time-out contingency was applied for instances of aggressive behavior. While aggression diminished, the subject's functional word list expanded to well over 100 words by the end of training.

MEETING SPECIAL NEEDS

The profoundly handicapped are handicapped in almost all areas. They have sensory impairments, extreme deficits in processing information, poor retention of information, and impaired motor performance. Even so, they can learn and they will learn more if they are systematically taught. Teaching and daily management of the profoundly handicapped are more difficult than with any other children. The teacher of these individuals must have the greatest competence.

While there are many basic procedures to follow, these general principles should be considered first in the management strategy for the profoundly handicapped.

1. The profoundly handicapped can be identified at birth or very shortly afterward. The most important time to begin systematic intervention is during the first few months of life.

2. The most essential behaviors must be attended to first and management strategies must be designed to achieve these behaviors. The primary concern is independent functioning, including dressing and undressing, toileting, eating, mobility, and communication.

3. The profoundly handicapped are subject to the same behavioral laws as all other individuals. The learning manager must know these and apply intervention procedures consistent with these laws.

4. The profoundly handicapped must comply with instructions as the first step in their instructional program. Predictable compliance behavior is difficult to achieve, but necessary.

5. An intervention program requires the competent application of skills of several professional disciplines, such as developmental therapists, communication disorder specialists, and medical specialists.

6. Parents are equal partners in the management plan. The more they know about all aspects of teaching, the better. Regular planning communication sessions provide the continuity and consistency that's essential to the success of the management plan.

7. It is essential that teachers and parents of the profoundly handicapped be systematic, consistent, firm, and insistent.

8. These children learn as long as they live, so it is important that a plan of instruction provides for formal teaching through adulthood.

FOR MORE INFORMATION, see p. 229 in chapter 8.

Perspectives on Children with Other Special Needs

Our focus in this book, as its title suggests, is the *behavior* of children with special needs. I have also tried to point out in these occasional *Perspectives* that it is useful to look at children from several points of view: in terms of their developmental progress, their educational needs, the severity of their handicaps, their potential to achieve vocational and career goals. These various points of view, when taken together, give us a fuller and more realistic picture of the exceptional child in school, at home, and in the community.

For the most part, these different points of view complement each other rather than conflict. And the same is true of the categories and labels traditionally used to describe and classify handicaps. As we have seen in several chapters already, labels like *retarded, emotionally disturbed,* or *learning disabled* can be overly restric-

tive if they are used as explanations for children's behavior or as the sole bases for placing them in programs. But when used in combination with other points of view, the categorical labels can be useful for classifying information about exceptional children, for funding research or providing services for them, or for better understanding their educational and vocational needs.

The next five chapters describe five categories of children with special needs we have mentioned so far only in the context of developmental delays, learning and behavior problems, or severe handicaps. We concentrate on those categories in separate chapters because of the extensive information we have about each, because of the history of programs and services organized for each, and because of the special instructional techniques and materials that have been developed over the years to meet the unique needs of each group.

In chapter 10, Jim McLean describes children with communication disorders, including both the speech-impaired child and those who have greater, more complex language and communication deficits. In chapter 11, Sheila Lowenbraun and Carolyn Scroggs introduce you to hearing impaired children, for whom language and communication are also major problems. In chapter 12, Dick DeMott surveys the visually handicapped. He describes the history of efforts to educate the blind, and he also reports the latest advances in educational techniques and materials. In chapter 13, June Bigge and Barbara Sirvis give you an overview of children with physical disabilities, including children who have multiple handicaps that involve a physical problem and some other disability as well. Finally, in chapter 14, Tom Stephens and Joan Wolf describe the gifted child, whose differences from normal children often require special attention to help them achieve their full potentials.

In many cases, the special needs of the children described in the next five chapters may seem clearer, if not necessarily easier to meet, than those of the other children we have already met. Often the use of special prosthetic devices, adaptive equipment, or other carefully designed materials can help the sensory and physically handicapped overcome their handicaps. (For a sampling of these, turn to the color photo essay that appears in these chapters.) In other instances, children with these special needs must learn new or different behaviors to compensate for deficits (manual language or other nonverbal symbols for children without speech, or reading and writing braille for blind children, for example). Whatever their handicaps, though, most of the children you will meet in the next five chapters are learners who can succeed in regular public schools, very often in the mainstream of the regular classroom, if their individual needs are met as early as possible.

10

Language Structure and Communication Disorders

James E. McLean

These are the major topics covered in this chapter. You may want to use them as a checklist when you review.

- *The components of the English language system.*
- *The motivation and functions of human language.*
- *The stages of linguistic development in normal children.*
- *Categories of communication disorders.*
- *Categories of speech impairments.*
- *Trends in treatment for communication disorders, including disorders in both language and speech.*

Children who are exceptional come to us with a wide range of behavioral problems which require a wide range of treatment. But, among most of these exceptional children, there is one kind of behavior which marks the child's other problems—his language behavior. A child's oral language reflects, in one way or another, all of the physical and environmental factors which influence him.

So often, when we think of communication disorders, we think of the stutterer whose struggle for speech is dramatic and painful. Or we think of the child whose physical development was affected in his early prenatal weeks and who, as a result, now speaks with the nasality and snorting caused by a cleft palatal structure of his mouth. Sometimes the term *communication disorder* makes us think of the first grader whose teacher cannot understand her because she misuses the sounds of our language and says "I taw da tun" instead of "I saw the sun."

These behaviors are, most certainly, communication disorders. Children with problems like these require special attention to bring their speech behavior as close to standard forms as possible. Communication disorders, however, take many forms other than the speech impairments we most often think of. Communication is carried out through a complex language system; therefore, disorders occur at the level of language as well as at the level of speech production. Speech is just one *mode* in which we use language.

Thus, before we can fully understand communication disorders, we must first understand our culture's language system. Only when we understand this code by which we communicate can we begin to understand the impact of various physical and environmental factors, to assess deviant behavior realistically, and to plan effective treatment goals and procedures.

THE NATURE OF LANGUAGE BEHAVIOR

It is strange, but most people know very little about the language they speak. Somewhere around 12 months of age, most infants say their first real "word," showing that they are beginning to learn the language of their home culture. The process includes some extremely complex learning tasks; it normally takes about 4 years before a child is producing a language anything like his adult language. Even after 5 or 6 years, a child makes many mistakes and has much more to learn. As adults, we continue to work on and refine our language, but most of us cannot describe what we have learned about our native language. Indeed, most of us can more easily discuss a second language we have learned than we can our native language.

Why this seeming ignorance of a behavior we use in every aspect of our lives? The explanation seems to be that native speakers really do *know* their language; they simply cannot state their knowledge about it at a conscious level. To understand our language, we must study the work of professionals who study and describe languages. These professionals are called *descriptive linguists*.

The first things they ask us to understand about *any* one language system are that: (1) it is, most basically, oral; (2) it is a complex system; and (3) it is essentially arbitrary.

Orality

All languages are created by people *talking* to one another. Other forms, such as writing, develop after an oral language has been created. Written languages are simply oral languages transcribed into another mode. Symbols are created to transcribe the sounds of a language, and then the spoken terms can be written down. Even today, there are languages which have no written form, and, of course, there are many people who cannot read or write. In spite of a language not having a written form or a person not being able to read, the language can continue to function. People can talk to others without being able to read, and a language which cannot be transcribed in written form can still be used in oral communication between speakers of that language.

Language as a System

In whatever forms it is available, a language is highly systematic, with definite rules for its formation. In its initial oral form, each language has its own set of specific sounds. Although some languages may share some of the same sounds, no distinct language has exactly the same sound system as another language. In all languages the number of sounds is finite; that is, there are just so many sounds acceptable in that language. In addition, each language has

rules about how these sounds can be put together. That is why it is difficult for a native English-speaking person to say a word like *Pfunt* in the German language, which combines sounds according to a different set of rules. According to most modern analyses, English uses 36 different sound families, called **phonemes.** The nature of these sounds are identified and described later in this chapter.

In addition to a sound system, each language has a system for combining sounds into units which have meaning. We usually think of units of meaning in terms of words, but meaning is carried in units smaller than words. In fact, it is really not accurate to think of words as the basic unit of meaning because many words are made up of several units of meaning. For example, the word *farm* has only one meaning unit, but by adding other sounds—or clusters of sounds—we can produce more single words which have several meaning units. For example, *farm, farmer,* and *farmerish*

Chapter ten

have one, two, and three meaning units, respectively. Each element of a word which carries meaning is called a **morpheme,** discussed in slightly more depth later in this chapter.

In addition to a sound system and rules for producing units of meaning, languages have definite rules for stringing units of meaning together so that other users of the language can quickly comprehend a message. The rules by which units of meaning are combined into utterances which carry a certain message are called the **syntax** of a language. The word **syntax** means "coming together." The syntactic rules of a language control the coming together of all of its parts—the sounds and the meaning units—into the long strings which carry messages. Like the sound system and the meaning units, the syntactic structures of English are discussed in more detail later.

Arbitrariness

The arbitrariness of language means that for no inherent reason certain forms or structures are advocated over other forms and structures in a language system. There is no direct relationship between events or objects and the sounds and sound arrangements we use in talking about them. An example of this concept appeared in the comic strip "B.C.," which is about cave dwellers. In one episode, the character Peter was advising his fellow cavemen about their importance to the world and to the future. He pointed out that they had to attach names to everything so that future generations would know what to call them. Showing them a uniquely striated rock, he asked, "What would be a good name for this rock?" One of his culture mates responded "How about *Irving?*" Indeed, why not?

To expand, there is nothing inherent in the word *farm* which necessarily relates it to a piece of land used to produce food or to the activities of producing that food, except

that a culture has chosen to use it that way. However, once arbitrary signs are accepted, they relate to other signs in the language and still other arbitrary signs can be added to them to form new signs, without changing the meaning of the original sign. And as in *farmer* and *farming,* the signs added to the original word *farm,* in this case *-er* and *-ing,* can be combined with other words with approximately the same meaning, for example, dri*ver* and dri*ving.*

This arbitrariness occurs throughout the structure of a language. Thus, we have very different words to represent the same thing in different languages, for example, *pencil/Bleistift.* Just as words differ among languages so does word order. In an English declarative sentence, the subject comes first, followed by the verb and then the direct object and prepositional phrase. In a comparable German sentence, the verb may be in two parts, with one part coming at the end of the sentence: *The student found the pencil in the class./Der Student hat den Bleistift in der Klasse gefunden.* In English, noun modifiers precede the noun; in French, the modifier follows the noun: *the red house/la maison rouge.*

After you recognize the basic arbitrariness of language, it is probably best to forget it. Because once the arbitrary decisions have been made by a language culture, the rules which emerge become fixed. Although many users of a language have little formal knowledge of their language and usually cannot state its rules, speakers "know" when another speaker is violating the structure of their language. In other words, the users of a language are able to *follow* the rules of their system even though they cannot *give* the rules.

Language and Communication Modes

Although a language is developed in the *oral mode,* it can be adapted to several other modes for transmission and comprehension. In oral language, we transmit through the *vocal mode* and receive in the *auditory mode*; that is, people talk to and hear one another. Our alphabet and a somewhat standardized spelling system allow us to put our oral language into a *written mode*. Most people receive written symbols through the *visual mode*. In braille, the symbols are patterned bumps in paper. These symbols are then received through the *tactile mode* as people feel the impressions with their fingertips. (See chapter 12 for more detail on communication systems used by the visually handicapped.)

Still other modes are used in transmitting and receiving language: the *manual* sign language of the deaf has characteristic hand postures which communicate meaning elements. Deaf persons also use a manual system called *fingerspelling* in which the alphabet is translated into certain finger positions and words are spelled out and put into sentence structures just as they are in the written mode of language. (Chapter 11 discusses manual and other communication systems used by the hearing handicapped.)

Note, however, that these alternative modes are all still based on the syntax of the original oral language. They are translations of an oral language into nonoral modes for transmission and reception.

Speech and Language

There is an important distinction between **speech** and **language.** Language is the structure of the specific patterns which underlie a particular communication system; speech is a mode in which the language is transmitted. Even remembering that speech is the most basic mode in which a language develops and that it is the most efficient mode for language, it is important to realize that they can be separated—language being the system and structure and speech being a mode for

its production. This distinction has important implications when we look at communication disorders.

THE STRUCTURE OF ORAL LANGUAGE

If we are to understand *communication disorders,* we must understand the normal, undisordered system.[1] Language structures include **phonology, morphology,** and **syntax.** *Phonology* relates to the sounds of oral language. *Morphology* is the structural level at which meaning units are created from the sounds. *Syntax* covers the rules and patterns by which the meaning units must be strung together within specific languages.

The Sound System of English

The anatomy of the human being has much to do with our ability to talk. Compared to

[1] In preparing this section, I have been heavily influenced by two books used in my classes on language of exceptional children. These books will also help the reader to investigate in further detail the structure of the English language. They are Norman C. Stageberg, *An Introductory English Grammar* (2nd ed.); New York: Holt, Rinehart and Winston, 1971; and Dwight Bolinger, *Aspects of Language;* New York: Harcourt Brace Jovanovich, 1968.

Finding out what's in the gift box is an interesting way to stimulate language disordered students to talk and ask questions.

other mammals, we have an elaborate mechanism for producing sounds. As air-breathing mammals, we must chew our solid food before we swallow it. Because we stand and walk upright, we need an effective mechanism to prevent solids and liquids from entering our lungs. We also have a motor system that allows us to control voluntarily the movement of certain parts of this mechanism, particularly the tongue but also the lips, soft palate, and the relative position of the laryngeal folds. The larynx, which acts as a fast and powerful closing valve to protect the lungs from foreign matter, can also be made to produce the vocal tone. We produce vocal tones by causing the larynx to vibrate with air from the lungs pushing through the closed vocal cords. The open spaces in the pharynx (the space just above the larynx), the oral cavity, and sometimes the nasal cavity act as resonators of the rather thin laryngeal voice tone and, in the process, add intensity and timbre to the tone. By putting the tongue in different positions, the size and the shape of the mouth or oral cavity are changed and, when changed, create different qualities in the tone emitted by the larynx. By placing the tongue in contact with different structures within the mouth, in effect, interfering with the breath stream, we can modify our vocal tones. Different types of interferences produce different sounds. Thus, by using the structures basic to breathing and feeding, we can produce a wide variety of vocal noises. Figure 10.1 shows these structures.

The sounds of a particular language are only a small set of all of the noises a human being can make. English, for example, uses a set of only 36 basic sound families. We say sound families because English really uses more than 36 different sounds. Some of the sounds it uses, however, are related to each other. Thus, instead of talking about each and every sound English users produce, we refer to the family to which they belong. We call these sound families **phonemes.**

The 36 families of sounds in English are shown in Table 10.1, along with the phonemic symbol used to identify each fam-

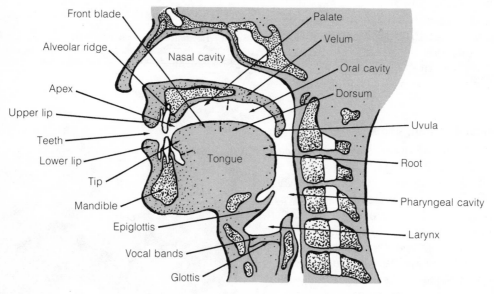

Figure 10.1
The human vocal tract

ily. We use phonemic symbols because the English alphabet does not represent variations in *sound*. We need a system that is consistent and accurate in specifying each sound of the language. For example, the /k/ sound can be *c* in *can*, *ch* in *chaotic*, and can even be a part of a sound *x* as in the word *box*. By specifying /k/ we can mark all members of that sound family more consistently.

Determining the number of phonemes which occur in a language is a laborious process carried out by the linguist. In this process, the linguist determines what sounds make differences in meaning to a speaker of the language. For example, the words *pin* and *bin* are identical except for the initial sound in each. This difference in sound at the beginning of each word causes speakers of English to assign different meanings to these two words. When sounds which occur in similar environments make a difference of meaning in a language, they are considered to be phonemes of that language. The sounds listed in Table 10.1 are those shown by linguists to signal differences in meaning to users of the English language. They are the phonemes of spoken English.

In any language the phonemes are limited in number. They also seem to be limited in type. We will look at English phonemes in terms of (1) manner of articulation, (2) place of articulation, and (3) use of voicing.

Manner of Articulation

Vowels

The most common distinction between speech sounds is that between vowels and consonants. The basis of this distinction is the amount of interference introduced into the vocal tract to modify the sounds being produced. In vowels, the interference is minimal. It consists of placing the tongue in certain positions within the mouth and producing a voicing sound at the larynx. The laryngeal sound comes through the pharynx and into an oral cavity which has been shaped by a certain tongue position. This particular oral shape produces sounds of a certain character. For example, positioning the tongue high and in the front of the mouth produces the vowel sound *ee* as in *beet*. Positioning the tongue low and in the middle of the mouth produces the vowel sound *ah* as in *father*. The 12 vowels of English are classified in terms of the position of the tongue which produces them. Figure 10.2 shows these vowels and their relative tongue positions.

Consonants

Consonant sounds are produced by creating more interference in the breath stream than is created by positioning the tongue for vowels. The interference is of two basic types: complete stoppage of the air or some other kind of interference which seriously impedes but does not stop the pas-

Consonants				Vowels	
/p/ peep	/k/ cook	/v/ valve	/ǰ/ judge	/i/ beet	/u/ boot
/b/ bib	/g/ gig	/s/ cease	/r/ rear	/I/ bit	/u/ book
/m/ maim	/ŋ/ singer	/z/ zones	/l/ lull	/ɛ/ bet	/ə/ buck
/t/ toot	/θ/ ether	/š/ shoe	/h/ hail	/e/ bait	/ɔ/ bought
/d/ deed	/ð/ either	/č/ church	/w/ wail	/æ/ back	/o/ boat
/n/ noon	/f/ fife	/ž/ azure	/y/ you	/a/ bother	/ər/ burr

Table 10.1
The phonemes of English

	front	central	back
High	i (b<u>ea</u>t) I (b<u>i</u>t)		U (m<u>oo</u>n) u (p<u>u</u>ll)
Mid	e (s<u>ay</u>) ε (s<u>e</u>t)	ə (<u>u</u>p)	o (<u>o</u>ver)
Low	æ (s<u>a</u>t)	a (f<u>a</u>ther)	ɔ (f<u>a</u>ll)

Figure 10.2
Relative tongue position for English vowel phonemes

sage of the breath stream. Sounds of English in which the breath stream is stopped completely include the *p, t, k, b, d,* and *g* sounds. If you make these sounds, you will see that the breath stream is stopped for an instant and then released.

If the air is not stopped to produce a consonant sound it is seriously interfered with. In one type of interference, the tongue is used to form small openings (apertures) through which the breath stream is forced under relatively intense pressures. Air passing through these apertures creates a friction noise. Sounds like *f, θ, s, š, v, ð, z,* and *ž* are produced this way. (Refer to Table 10.1 for the sounds which are represented by these phonemic symbols).

Some consonant sounds require a combination of air stoppage and small apertures. The initial consonants in *cheap* and *judge* are sounds of this type. The symbols for these sounds are *č* and *ǰ* (as in *chop* and *jump*); they are produced by first stopping the air and then releasing it into small, friction-producing apertures formed by the front part of the tongue's contact against the front part of the hard palate.

These three ways of creating interference produce certain types of consonants. These different types of consonants are named according to the *manner* in which their interference is produced. Thus,

sounds in which the air is stopped completely are called *stops*. Sounds in which air is pushed through small apertures to create friction noise are called *continuant fricatives*. Sounds which combine these two types of interference are called *affricates*.

In addition, there are two other ways to produce consonant sounds: *resonants* and *glides*. Resonant consonants are very much like vowel sounds in that their primary characteristics are the shape of the oral cavity formed by putting the tongue in certain positions. Resonants are classed as consonants, however, because of their distribution in English preceding and following vowels. The oral resonants in English are /l/ and /r/ sounds. Three nasal resonants are discussed later.

The glide sounds, too, are closely related to vowels; in fact, they begin as vowels. From their beginning as vowels, however, they move rapidly to another vowel and are, therefore, named after this gliding movement which gives them their characteristic quality. The glide consonants are /y/ and /w/. The /y/ begins as the high front vowel /i/ and the /w/ begins as the high back vowel /u/. As they glide to a following vowel they take on their primary quality—for example, in the words *yes* and *wing*.

Place of Articulation

When consonants are classified by the manner in which they are produced, there are several sounds in each of the classifications. The /p/, /t/, /k/, /b/, /d/, and /g/ are all stops, for example. The /f/, /θ/, /š/, /s/, /v/, /ð/, /z/, and /ž/ are fricatives and, to differentiate each of these from the other, another classification factor is used. This factor is a sound's *place of articulation*.

Again, all consonants are created by producing interference of the breath stream. This is done by placing one or more of the movable elements of the speech mechanism into contact with elements that do not move. The movable elements are called the *articulators* and include the lower lip and the tongue. The nonmoving parts of the articulatory mechanism are the upper lip, the upper teeth, the gum ridge above the upper teeth (alveolar ridge), the hard palate, and the soft palate (velum). These are called the *points of articulation.* These parts of the speech mechanism can be reviewed in Figure 10.1.

Consonant sounds, then, are classified by specifying the immovable structure and the movable articulator which contacts it to create the point at which interference occurs. If the tongue is the movable articulator, most linguists specify the specific *part* of the tongue involved. If it is the tip of the tongue which makes contact with the immovable structure, the term *apico* is used. If the part of the tongue immediately behind the tip makes contact, the term *fronto* is used. The back part of the tongue is referred to as *dorso.* Thus, the /t/, which is made by bringing the tip of the tongue into contact with the alveolar ridge above the upper teeth, is called an *apico-alveolar.* The /k/, which is produced by bringing the back part of the tongue into contact with the soft palate (velum) is a *dorso-velar* sound.

The stop /p/ is produced by bringing the movable lower lip into contact with the more immobile upper lip and is called a *bilabial* sound. By adding the point of articulation, we can better specify the differences between sounds which are made by the same manner of articulation. If we return to the stops, we can see that the /p/ is a bilabial stop; the /t/, an apico-alveolar stop; the /k/, a dorso-velar stop. All three sounds are produced by stopping the air completely, but for each the stoppage occurs at a different place in the articulatory system.

Voicing

Let us look further at the other stop sounds. If we were to give the point of articulation and manner of /b/, we would classify it as a bilabial stop—the same as the /p/. The /d/ would be an apico-alveolar stop like the /t/; and the /g/, a dorso-velar stop like the /k/. Obviously, these are different sounds, and their full differences are not explained just by describing their manner and their place of articulation. In addition to place and manner, then, we must determine whether a sound is made while the vocal cords are closed and vibrating or are open and allowing the air to pass through without producing a voice tone.

The /p/, /t/, and /k/ are voiceless sounds. The /b/, /d/, and /g/ sounds are identical to voiceless sounds but are produced with

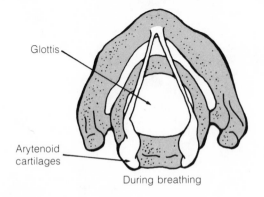
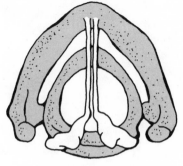

During breathing   When producing voice

Glottis

Arytenoid cartilages

Figure 10.3
Action of the laryngeal folds (vocal cords)

Chapter ten

voicing. Such pairs of sounds are called *cognates* and, while this difference may seem trivial, there are some languages where voicing or nonvoicing of a sound does not make a difference in the meaning of two words. In some languages, voicing does not make a difference in the phonemes of the language. It does in English, however, and the stop, fricative, and affricate manners of articulation all contain matched pairs of voiced and voiceless sounds, for example, /s/ and /z/, /f/ and /v/, /š/ and /ž/, /θ/ and /ð/, and /č/ and /ǰ/. Table 10.2 is a chart of the 24 English consonants. It indicates both their *place* of articulation and the *manner* in which their characteristic qualities are produced.

There is one feature in Table 10.2 not covered to this point. The /m/, /n/, and /ŋ/ are identified as *nasal* resonants. These three sounds contrast to all other consonants and vowels in that their distinctive quality depends not only on the place of articulation but also on the voiced breath stream being resonated in the nasal cavity instead of the oral cavity. In most English sounds, the soft palate is raised into contact with the pharyngeal wall and blocks the

breath stream from access to the nasal cavity. For the nasal sounds, however, the velum is not elevated, and the breath stream has easy access to the nasal cavity. The difference in these conditions can be easily observed by placing your index fingers on either side of your nose and saying alternately the bilabials /b/ and /m/ combined with one of the vowels. For example, say *bow* and *mow.* On *mow,* your fingers should detect the vibrations of sound in your nasal cavity; on *bow,* they will not detect vibration. (It may be easier to detect the difference by placing your fingers on another person's face while he says the words.)

Allophonic Variation (Sound Families)

Only the first principles of the sound system of English can be presented here. However, we need to discuss briefly the basis of the identification of sound families in English. It was mentioned earlier that English has 36 sound families which are used to produce all the words. However, more than 36 individual sounds are used. The basis of this distinction is carried in a process tech-

	Bilabial	Labiodental	Dental	Alveolar	Palatal	Velar	Glottal
Stops							
Voiceless	p			t		k	
Voiced	b			d		g	
Fricatives							
Voiceless		f	θ	s	š		h
Voiced		v	ð	z	ž		
Affricates							
Voiceless				č			
Voiced				ǰ			
Oral Resonants							
Voiced only				l	r		
Nasal Resonants							
Voiced only	m			n		ŋ	
Glides							
Voiced only					y	w	

Table 10.2
Consonants of English by place and manner of articulation

nically called *allophonic variation.* This term means that sounds are affected by their environment, that is, the other sounds preceding and following them, and thus may vary somewhat from one utterance to another.

For example, the /k/ in the words *kin, skin, baker,* and *walk,* as most speakers of English say these words, are all slightly different sounds. The /k/ in *kin* is an aspirated sound; when it is completed, a small puff of air is released. The /k/ in *skin* does not produce a puff of air at the end. This /k/ is called *unaspirated.* The /k/ sound in *walk* does not produce a puff of air and, in fact, there is no really hard contact between the tongue and the palate. If you say the word *walk* in a natural way, you will move your tongue up to a slight contact with the velum, stop the air gently, and go on to the next word without the little explosion of air found in the aspirated /k/ in *kin* or the forceful move into the vowel produced by the /k/ in the word *skin.* The /k/ in *walk* is called an *unreleased* /k/. Each of the three types of /k/ are written differently phonetically if you want to describe exactly what sound is used. The aspirated /k/ is written [k']; the unaspirated is written [k]; and the unreleased is written [k-]. Since, however, the way the sound is said makes no difference in the meaning assigned to the word, all these sounds are classed as members of the /k/ family. The /k/ phoneme has several members because some word environments make one way of making a /k/ easier than another way.

It is not possible here to go into all of the details of these variations of sound production. However, phonemes are affected by the sounds which precede and follow them though most people never hear the differences because the variations do not signal a change in meaning. It is only when differences in sounds signal a difference in meaning that most of us discriminate among them.

The Meaning Units of English

We will now look at the ways the sounds are put together to produce meaning in oral English. Remembering that language forms are arbitrary, you must realize that all words were "made up" by someone and accepted by a language community as meaning something. We know that we have taken words made up for other languages and made them part of ours. However, we may not be fully aware that we follow rules and processes in producing words which have the specific meaning we wish our listener to receive.

Free and Bound Morphemes

Any language has a large group of distinctive clusters of phonemes which mean something to a listener. As stated earlier, the clusters which carry meaning are called *morphemes.* These morphemes vary from clusters which refer to objects or events (like *ball, car, party, election,* and *rain*) to sound clusters which describe states or actions (*hit, walk, talk, sleep,* and *is*). These units of meaning, however, can also be clusters of sounds which are *less* than words—*un-* means something, and so does *-er, -ize,* and *-s.* These sounds and sound clusters do not mean much of anything alone, however. The words that stand alone with meaning are referred to by linguists as *free morphemes,* while the clusters which do not carry meaning by themselves are called *bound morphemes.* When we bind a bound morpheme to another morpheme we get clusters like *un*known, farm*er,* standard*ize,* and duck*s.* Each of these bound morphemes has added meaning to the word it was joined to. In addition, they can add the same meaning to other words—*un*washed, teach*er,* familiar*ize,* and cat*s.* These bound morphemes carry meaning just as powerfully and consistently as the bigger free morphemes.

Source and System Morphemes

In addition to being classified in terms of their ability to stand alone, morphemes are also classified in terms of what nature of meaning they carry. In the bound morphemes shown above, the morpheme /s/ does something slightly different than the other bound forms do. In this case, the /s/ indicates that the referent of the free morpheme (*duck, cat*) is plural. Compare this to the other bound forms in the examples above: *un-, -er,* and *-ize;* these morphemes actually change the referent of the morpheme. Adding an *er* to *farm* to make the word *farmer* changes the referent from the act of tending to the raising of crops or tending livestock to a person who carries out this act. Similarly, when we change *standard* to *standardize,* we no longer refer to something which is "in common use" or "a criterion reference" but rather to the act of making something "standard." Thus, adding some bound morphemes changes the dictionary meaning of words and, in many cases, even changes the way a word can be used in a sentence, that is, the part of speech. For example, *standard* changes from an adjective to a verb with the addition of the suffix *-ize,* and *teach* changes from a verb to a noun with the addition of *-er.*

On the other hand, the addition of the morpheme /s/ does *not* change the dictionary meaning of the words to which it is added; the referent of both *duck* and *ducks* is still a particular type of fowl. There are other morphemes that, like the plural morpheme form, add information about the reference of the word to which they are applied but do not change the basic referent itself. The /t/ which is added to *walk* to form *walked* does not change the basic meaning or reference of the word; it simply indicates that the action took place in the past. (Do not be confused by our example; remember we are talking about spoken language and the past tense of *walk,* even

though it is spelled *walked,* is spoken as /wawkt/. Whenever you see a letter set off by slash marks, you are looking at the written symbol for a spoken sound.)

These two kinds of bound morphemes are examples of *source* morphemes and *system* morphemes. The morphemes that change the referent meaning of a word are called *source morphemes.* They are among the primary sources of meaning for a word. The *system morpheme,* on the other hand, provides not so much a primary meaning as it provides meaning which is critical for the particular system of the language being spoken. Let us look at this function in more detail by examining the English past tense form.

It is possible to indicate that something has occurred in the past in several ways. A little child, for example, might say "I go to the lake, yesterday," when she means that sometime in the past she went to the lake. Deaf people who use a manual sign language sometimes produce the sign for a verb and then make a hand movement much like throwing something back over the shoulder. Figuratively, they are throwing this verb into the "past," and the audience receives the message. In spoken English, however, we have a set of morphemes to add to the ends of verbs to indicate their tense. If we want to indicate past tense, we add a /t/ to verbs like *walk, talk, wash, kiss,* and *type.* Verbs such as *cruise, move, mug,* and *nudge* do not take a /t/ to form the past; rather, they take a /d/. (Remember, *say* these words aloud to hear the difference.)

Why do some verbs take a /t/ and others a /d/? The key is the last sound in the verb which is being put into the past tense. If the last sound of a word is voiced, the /d/, another voiced sound, is added. If the final sound is unvoiced, the sound which is identical to the /d/ in manner and place of articulation but which is unvoiced, the /t/, is added. If a verb ends in a /t/ or a /d/, obviously the addition of another /t/ or /d/ is physically impossible. What do we do when this happens? Try putting these verbs in the past tense: *bat* (the ball); *bed* (the horse down); *rate* (the new employee). In making these past, you should have found that you added /əd/. Since you cannot add a /t/ or /d/ to another /t/ or a /d/, you add a vowel; and since the vowel is voiced, you finally add the /d/, the voiced sound used for many other verbs which end with a voiced sound.

If you describe all of this behavior, you see that it can be viewed as a set of "rules" to follow for making many past tense indicators in our language. Verbs ending in /t/ or /d/ take /əd/; verbs ending in unvoiced sounds other than /t/ take /t/; verbs ending in voiced sounds other than /d/ take /d/.

However, all verbs are not made past in this way. Some verbs change completely (*is/was; go/went*); still others require no change between their present and their past form (*hit/hit*).

The point is that some of our morphemes do not so much do things that are important for primary meaning but rather do things that are important to the language. In the English language system, tense, possession, and plurality are indicated by these system morphemes. English also compares its adjectives by adding system morphemes, such as sweet, sweet*er*, sweet*est*, and sour, sour*er*, sour*est*. In this sense, the morphemes also show relationships between the things and/or states which are being referenced.

This point leads to a consideration of another type of system morpheme. You recall that morphemes in general can be parts of words or whole words that can stand by themselves. System and source morphemes, thus, can be either whole words or parts of words. So far, we have looked at these morphemes as parts of words. We have seen that source morphemes change the actual referent of a word (*standard/standardize*) and that system morphemes change only some aspect of the referent but not the referent itself (*cat/cats*). System morphemes, however, can exist as whole words as well as parts of words. In this state, they still function in basically the same way. System words do not have a meaning in the dictionary sense as much as they have a duty to perform for the language system itself. These system words are sometimes referred to as *function* words in contrast to the *content* word label given source morphemes. System or function morphemes in English are words like *the, a, an, that, there, where,* and *for.* They are free morphemes which do not carry meaning in the same way that source words like *man, walk, sweet,* and *quick* do. While this distinction between content and function words might seem subtle here, we study them a little later as we discuss syntax, and, hopefully, their relationship will become a little clearer.

In this section, we have seen how English language users take their 36 bits of sound and put them together to form clusters which have meaning for a listener. We have seen that the English language user creates little bundles of sounds to use over and over to refer to certain things, actions, and events. He also has some smaller bundles of sounds that he adds at the beginning or end of other bundles to make new words or to add important information such as, "This is plural," "This is past," "This is more so than the other word" (*sweet/sweeter*). We have also learned that he makes some little word bundles which relate basic, dictionary-type meanings and other little word bundles which indicate meanings which are important but which are less easily defined in a dictionary sense.

We have outlined the sound system and we have discussed the derivation of meaning units. We can now look at how a language user puts all these together to produce standard, conversational language. Bolinger (1968) likens the sound and meaning units to prefabricated units from which larger language structures are built. This analogy properly indicates that the sound units and basic meaning units of our language have been developed and agreed on in the arbitrary sense we discussed earlier. Bolinger states that in the process of talking, the prefabricated units are used to build the larger structures of phrases and sentences. In a very real sense, the larger units of language usage are ad-libbed rather than prefabricated. Many times, we utter sentences that we have never uttered before. In fact, we may never have even heard them uttered before. We are saying something we need or want to say about a specific situation, and we have no previous model for the sentence. In this situation, we take the prefabricated units and build our intended utterance.

Naturally, prefabricated units of sound and meaning cannot be put together in just any old way. Rather, they are combined in terms of the syntactic rules of our language. There are about nine patterns of sentences in English, and these patterns are adapted to say what we want to say. The syntactic patterns of English cannot be analyzed completely in this chapter. However, some basic elements can be described. These elements are *word order* and the so-called *operators of syntax.*

Word Order

Perhaps the best way to realize the importance of word order is to look at the following sentence, which is a classic of linguistic literature:

The iggle squiggs trazed wombly in the harlish goop.

Most people have little difficulty "feeling" that this is a sentence which fits an English syntax pattern. For example, if asked what part of speech *squiggs* is, you would prob-

ably answer, a noun. Students often justify their selection of *squiggs* as a noun by indicating that it precedes a verb—*trazed.* The fact that no one has ever heard or used a verb *trazed* seems to make little difference. Similarly, most speakers of English identify *iggle* as an adjective, *goop* as a noun, and *harlish* as another adjective. The word *wombly* is, obviously, an adverb.

Now, if the sentence read differently—*The wombly iggle trazed harlishly in the squiggy goop*—a speaker of English would reclassify most of the words into different parts of speech. The reason is that English syntax patterns have certain places for words which do certain things. A noun, as you recall from elementary school days, "names persons, places and things. . . ." A verb specifies an "action or state. . . ." Adjectives modify nouns, and adverbs modify verbs. In an English declarative sentence in the active voice, these parts of speech occupy certain places in the sentence and certain places in relationship to each other. In more complex sentences, phrase structures follow similar "slot-class" correlations in that certain classes of words go into certain slots in the sentence structure.

Let's look at one more sentence and its implication for the function of word order in English syntax.

The iggle was hit by the wombly squigg.

In this sentence, the native speaker of English would have no difficulty identifying the part of speech of the various nonsense words. Neither would he have any difficulty understanding that it was *squigg* who hit the *iggle.* Yet we know that this is a different kind of sentence than the first in that it is in the passive voice. Given the verb form which signals the passive, the functions of the slots in a sentence call for different words than they do in the active voice. By comparing two sentences, we can see two of the syntactic patterns in our language, and we can see that a sentence slot requires more than just a word of a certain class, like a noun or a verb.

The iggle hit the squigg.

The squigg was hit by the iggle.

Both of these sentences describe the same event. Both sentences have the same nouns and same main verb. But using different syntactic patterns, each sentence orders these words in different ways. The *actor,* the *action,* and the *acted-upon* have specific slots in each of the sentences, and it is important to get the correct nouns and verbs in those slots.

Other changes in the word order can be used to further modify the basic meaning of an utterance. When you use the elements of our passive construction example but "front-shift" the auxiliary verb, you have *Was the squigg hit by the iggle?* This time, the utterance requests information. Thus, by altering the order of words, an English user can change the meaning relationships among the elements being used.

Hopefully you can see from these examples how word orders and slot-class correlations function in this process of building complex, ad-libbed utterances from the prefabricated units of sound and meaning.

Syntactic Operators

In addition to word order, interpretation and parts-of-speech identification of the sentences have support from another source—the syntactic operators. Bolinger (1968) identifies several aspects of language as traffic signals and names them *operators.* These operators include intonation and stress in our speech, and they also include the little morphemes or meaning units previously referred to as *system morphemes.* You recall that system morphemes are meaning units which do not have dictionary-type meanings like source

morphemes. They can be less than word size (bound morphemes) or whole words (free morphemes). The whole words are small words like *the, an, of, on,* and *after.* It is these system morphemes which act as the traffic signals of syntax and indicate the relationships we need in our language structures.

To see these operators in action, take another look at the nonsense sentence.

The iggle squiggs trazed wombly in the harlish goop.

There are seven operators in this sentence. Five of them are system morphemes; two are source morphemes of a special type. To see how they work, we can look at the identification of *squiggs* as a noun and see that, besides the word order, there were two other morphemes which helped us identify it as a noun. The letter *s* added to *squiggs* is one system morpheme which indicates plurality when added to a noun. Thus, it makes this word seem like a noun. In addition, the word *the* is called a *determiner,* and its primary function in English is to shout to a listener (or reader) "Hey, there's a noun coming soon!" Other determiners like *a* and *an* do the same thing. Other *inflectional endings* act as the *s* on *squiggs* does; the *ed* on *trazed* is one of the inflectional endings used to indicate past tense of verbs. Thus, its presence here indicates that *trazed* is probably a verb. As we look at the sentence again, we see another *the* and another function word—*in.* Familiar as we all are with the form of a prepositional phrase, we can predict that the last word in the phrase *"in the . . ."* will be a noun as the object of the preposition. So the *s* on *squiggs,* the *ed* on *trazed,* the two *the*'s and the *in* all act as operators in making the syntactic structure of this sentence clear to us even though the sentence is total nonsense. They are, remember, morphemes which carry important information about the relationships and functions within our language system and, as such, allow us to build messages which indicate exactly what we are trying to say in terms of the referents and the relationships among the referents.

In addition to the system morphemes, there were two other operators in our sentence. These are the *derivational morphemes ly* on *wombly* and *ish* in *harlish*. These two morphemes are source morphemes which are very often used to form adverbs and adjectives, respectively. Thus, we have the added cues that *wombly* is an adverb and that *harlish* is an adjective. When you consider all of these operators and add the information about English contained in the word order of the sentence, you realize that the ability to analyze such nonsense sentences is not remarkable.

Language is a complex system. It is not, however, a system which cannot be analyzed, partitioned, and thus understood in its form and structure. How human beings learn such a complex system, how we use it, and what goes wrong to disrupt the learning and use of it are discussed next.

LANGUAGE DEVELOPMENT AND DELAY

Given the complexity of sound and structure required, it seems miraculous that children ever acquire language without formal teaching. But most children *do* acquire language. What is more, they acquire it within fairly predictable time periods and broad patterns. Those times and patterns have already been outlined in chapters 3 and 4, but now that you have a more complete picture of the structure of our oral language system, let's briefly review the major phases in the normal development of language.

Why Children Acquire Language

A 1-year-old infant does not embark on a task that he perceives as learning 36 speech sounds which can be combined into hundreds of thousands of meaning units which can, in turn, be strung together into utterances of great length and variety. What motivates a child is better explained if we look at language as a tool the child uses to "awaken a response" in other humans and to "influence their attitudes and acts" (DeLaguna, 1963, p. 19). Thus, a young child begins to make noises *to attain responses* from the caregivers around him. As chapter 4 points out, language develops in the context of *communicative interaction*. The child's development of phonemes, morphemes, and syntax is motivated by his desires and needs to communicate effectively and efficiently with those who make up his social environment.

Prelinguistic Development

Since children do not usually say their first words until they are about a year old, the activities of that first year are considered *prelinguistic*. Instinctive cries and reflexive noises give way to experimentation, though, and *babbling* gradually takes the form of extended periods of sound production that seem to give children joy. During the babbling phase, children show more and more awareness of the sounds around them and begin to reflect the general patterns of the noises they hear. In this stage, sometimes referred to as *vocal play,* they begin to show patterns of inflection and phrase-like patterns of sound.

At this time, too, children begin to discriminate at least small parts of the stream of speech around them. They *respond* to the speech they hear. "Bath!" may bring squeals of anticipation, or "Where's the ball?" can prompt a full-scale search. In addition, children are themselves evoking many responses from those around them, through gestures like pointing, reaching, tugging, and producing gross noises which parents quickly learn to interpret. Children at this time also are extremely busy acquiring the bases for the *content* of their eventual language. As chapter 3 points out, they are learning about their world by acting upon it and receiving feedback information through their senses of touch, sight, and hearing.

Linguistic Development

From the time a child utters his first words, he is, in a real sense, a linguist. He is listening to language, deducing its meaning, and in the process learning its rules. He does not identify rules as such, of course; even as adults we have seen how difficult that is. Rather, it appears from research that he is deducing the ways in which different meanings are encoded in his native language (MacNamara, 1972). In the early stages of figuring things out, a child makes some rather gross guesses and produces some relatively gross language forms. As the process continues, however, the forms and structures of his language become closer and closer to the final, adult language system he will eventually attain. This process is fascinating, and, while there is still much to be learned, there are some interesting and provocative research data which describe many aspects of the stages involved in this developmental process. One of the most provocative accounts of the emergence of a child's early language content and forms has been provided by Lois Bloom (1970). It is largely her research findings that form the basis for this general discussion of linguistic development.

The initial, one-word stage of a child's language production, often called the *holophrastic* stage, occurs at 12 to 18 months. During this time, the child utters many single words and one-word phrases which are actually combinations of several words (*go-bye-bye, roll-ball, horsie-ride*). After a few months of building a small repertoire of such utterances, children begin producing what Bloom calls *topic-comment* utterances. These are two-word combinations which seem to be just what Bloom's term implies—a sequence beginning with something the child selects as a topic followed by some comment on it (*coat daddy, door open,* and *man hat,* for instance). Shortly after this stage, children enter what Bloom considers the *grammatical* stage. During this time they begin to produce two-word utterances which represent the rudiments of English syntax, especially correct word order (like *sweater chair*—the sweater is on the chair; *mommy sock*—mommy's sock; *mommy sock*—mommy, put on my sock; *mommy lipstick*—mommy is putting on lipstick). With time, children begin to add function words (*more milk; this a doggie; here cookie; light on*) and to produce longer and longer sequences.

Between 2½ and 3, children begin to produce three- and four-word phrases that begin to resemble adult English syntax. From this point, children between 3 and 4 work diligently to acquire the basic structures of grammar, a huge repertoire of basic words, and the structures to modify these words, to form tenses, to indicate plurals and possessives, and to compare adjectives. By about age 4, children have developed control of some extremely important aspects of their adult language. Between 4 and 6, they are busy learning some of the refinements which assure functional communications with others. They learn that words can get many things done for them, both by family and by friends, if the words are in sequences which are constructed carefully and appropriately. They learn, too, that most things that happen in their world can somehow be put into this "code"—and shared with others.

Problems in Language Acquisition

To acquire a behavior as complex as language, a child needs as much working for him as possible. To produce the necessary motor responses, he must have a neurological and motor system which functions optimally. To figure out the "code" around him, he must be able to hear and discriminate its parts. To deduce the code's rules and begin to produce his own matching version, he must use adequate intellectual functioning. Finally, to master language in all of its nuance and style, he must have a rich and realistic conceptual knowledge about the relationships of things and events in his world.

Since it demands so much, language learning is vulnerable to any problem which affects the child. A child who is emotionally ill does not perceive his world and the relationships in it accurately enough to put forth appropriate language. A child whose hearing is severely impaired cannot perceive and, thus, acquire the spoken language of her environment without a great deal of help—and, perhaps, not even then. A child whose motor system has sustained damage to the degree that he cannot move his tongue and lips with precision and speed cannot produce speech patterns which sound "normal" to his listeners. Thus, the condition of the child's most basic sensory and motor systems has much to do with the adequacy of his language repertoire.

The child's environment also affects language acquisition. Language learning takes a long time, and it must entail quite a bit of frustration. Unless the work pays off, a child might not work very hard at it. Happily, in all but the most extreme cases, language learning does pay off for children. Caregivers reward the cries for "More milk," the demands "Look mama," and the explanations "He hitted me first." Sometimes, however, language learning is not rewarded appropriately, and the process is inhibited somewhat. Some parents act in ways that keep their children from needing language: the milk is there before a child asks for more; mother is looking with interest before being requested to do so; or father is so protective that a child never needs to explain that he didn't do it first.

Other environmental factors can affect language learning. The parents' language

structure may be extremely poor, and the child's deductions made from poor models result in language which is also poor in comparison to more standard language forms. Homes in which no one listens to anyone else can also frustrate language learning. Talking does not have much effect in these homes and so physical action may be learned faster than language.

We must also recognize the effect of a child's general intellectual functioning level on language learning. Language seems to "map" a child's knowledge of the things, events, and relationships in his world. This knowledge might be most clearly recognized in terms of constructs developed to describe knowledge—like cognitive functioning and/or concept formation. If we think about a child's early language, we can see a few of the concepts which require such language maps; for example, existence of things (*here doggie*); nonexistence of things (*no doggie* or *doggie all gone*); attributes of things (*big truck*); agent-action relationships (*mommy read*); action-object relationships (*read book*); agent-action-object relationships (*daddy go car*); spatial relationships (*car in garage* or *hat on doll*); temporal relationships (*yesterday, I go to church*). Each of these language structures requires a child to know something about his world. A child whose intellectual functioning is so profoundly deficient that he cannot perceive or organize the relationships in the world around him does not have a wide enough knowledge base to sustain language acquisition of much substance.

We must be extremely careful, however, in making assumptions about a child's intellectual ability to acquire significant language behavior. There are relatively few children, even among those classified as severely/profoundly mentally retarded, who do not have knowledge enough for at least some language responses. Most moderate, severely, or profoundly retarded children are seriously delayed in language development but many eventually acquire some relatively complex language repertoires. In fact, it appears that many retarded children follow the same general patterns of speech and language development as normal children except that they are much slower to develop. Most adolescent retarded children have a language system which is adequate for at least basic communication with peers and with adults.

Any discussion of the relationship between "mental retardation" and language is dangerous. Because it is relatively easy to establish the correlation between *mental* retardation and *language* retardation, it is also easy to describe a cause-and-effect relationship between the two, that is, mental retardation causes language retardation. The problem is that the correlation can be easily reversed—if a child is retarded in language, he is most apt to be labeled mentally retarded. While it is totally rational to assume that some degree of intellectual ability is necessary to acquire language, it is not as rational to assume that any child who has not acquired language must be mentally retarded. We have seen that there are many other problems which can cause language learning to be less than optimal. Many cases of "mental retardation" turn out to be cases of severe hearing loss or severely depriving environment.

Thus, while we cannot rationally reject the need for intelligence to acquire the complex behaviors which make up human language, we cannot simply say that lack of intelligence is the "cause" of language learning problems among children.

There are many factors which can disrupt language acquisition and language production, and their effect can be either complete or partial, as we have discussed here and in chapter 4. Because language is learned behavior, it can be affected by all the factors which affect any learning. Factors like intellectual ability, motivation, and good models all affect language acquisition. Because language models are received in the auditory mode, the auditory sense is critical to natural language learning. Because the natural mode of producing language is motor, disrupted or diminished motor systems can affect language acquisition. Because language is connected with the child's world and learned within relationships in that world, a child's emotions can be a factor. Language carries the marks of whatever problems have affected a child.

COMMUNICATION DISORDERS

Because language has so many dimensions and complexities, identifying and classifying language behaviors that should be considered disordered or deviant is difficult. Judgments of which children should be considered to have a *communication disorder* requiring special educational or clinical programming are made from two basic comparisons. The first is a comparison of the child's language with the standard language form of the culture. The second is a comparison of the child's language with the language of other children at the same age level. The *difference* between a particular child's language and the language he will eventually need to be an accepted member of his language community and the degree of *deviance* between the child's progress towards the standard forms compared with other children of his relative age level are both considered.

Language Differences

There may be many differences between an individual's language and the standard structure of English. These differences may include regional or ethnic dialects which, although not standard English, are totally acceptable, even desirable, within the child's language community. Although these differences may become problems if a child moves out of his language community, it would be presumptuous to label them "disorders" and try to change them to conform to some standard. Consequently, dialects and ethnically based language forms are usually not treated as communication disorders. Sometimes speakers of different dialects or different language forms want to learn more standard forms of English. In this case, training programs to reduce the differences between a nonstandard language form and the more standard forms can be undertaken. The standard forms are then a second language for the individual. In this context, everyone has several languages. For example, people use slightly different vocabulary and syntactic structures talking with family and friends than with business or professional colleagues. While most of these variations occur in what might be called our *style* of language usage, there are times when even the phonemes used in words vary, for example, "Whatcha doing?" versus "What are you doing?"

While some degree of variance in language form is prevalent and acceptable, there are limits. For example, some differences in the sound system of children and even adults can be accepted. The child (or adult) who says "Look at the wabbit wun," probably will be understood by her listener. If, however, the phonological system is violated to the degree that this sentence is uttered "Wu a da wabi wa," understanding will be severely reduced and there will be a true communication problem. The same problem of degree of difference exists within the syntactic structures of language.

A speaker can only be so different and still be understood in his language community.

In summary, communication disorders are specified in terms of the differences between a standard form of the language and an individual's language behaviors. There is a basic language system for every culture, and its forms and structures must be acquired. Some differences are not considered a problem. The wider the differences become, however, the more they attract attention and identify the speaker as one who does not belong to the language community. Such a speaker must be considered to have a disordered, defective, and/or variant language system.

Deviance from Developmental Norms

Determining whether or not the differences in a child's language are communication disorders that require special treatment is usually done on the basis of the relative degree of language development. Wide differences between a child's language and standard language structure can be accepted and not considered communication disorders. As before, however, there are limits. If the differences in a child's language are relatively greater than those of other children of his approximate age level, that child is considered to have a language problem, or in this context, a communication disorder.

TYPES OF COMMUNICATION DISORDERS

Differences which have significance as communication disorders can occur in any or all of the dimensions of language. Language problems can be divided into three gross categories in order to analyze the most common communication disorders. Each of these categories are discussed here: (1) nonspeaking children, (2) lan-

lems, he appears to have set the stage for the development of the learning and behavioral dimensions of the field.

Travis and his work at Iowa, then, paralleled West and his work at Wisconsin in training professionals in the new discipline. Iowa's early graduates of the 1930s are famous in this field, as they opened new training programs in major colleges and universities throughout the midwest.

The contrasting approaches of West, strongly medical, and Travis, just as strongly psychological, were most important to the field and its development. Both men were extremely scholarly, and both were instrumental in developing the association that eventually became the American Speech and Hearing Association. The independent academic discipline we know today brings together physiological, psychological, educational, and physical science theories and practices. As such, it clearly reflects the strong influences of two of its earliest contributors and the academic programs they developed. Robert West and Lee Edward Travis will always be among the top in any list of pioneers in speech and hearing.

guage-disordered children, and (3) speech-impaired children.

Nonspeaking Children

A child may not acquire standard vocal language for any one of a number of reasons. Some children may have hearing impairments so profound that they cannot adequately hear the language of their culture. Other children may have behavior disorders so severe that their interactions within their social world are both restricted and deviant. In these cases, the basic communication functions for language are affected, and both the language learning motivation and process are significantly impaired or nonexistent. In still other cases, children who are profoundly developmentally delayed may lack both knowledge of the world and the basic symbolic abilities required.

In cases where the overall disabilities are not profound, highly specialized disabilities may hinder the language acquisition processes. Certain brain injuries can interfere with the interpretation or creation of the auditory-vocal modes needed for normal language. In some brain-injury cases, both the intellectual and basic symbolic processes *may* be adequate for language, but the child may not be able to encode language in an aural-oral mode.

Obviously, the various disabilities have different implications for language development. More profoundly affected children may be able to master only primitive symbolic communication. Children with highly specialized problems may communicate through nonstandard modes like

Some of these retarded students had no expressive language at all until they were taught to sign. Now they can follow their teacher in "singing" a favorite Christmas carol.

manual signs, communication boards using pictures, or various symbol languages (see Vanderheiden & Harris-Vanderheiden, 1976; chapters 11 and 13 in this book).

Whatever the cause of the child's not speaking, it should be clear that it is significant. The need to communicate is powerful, and a child who cannot speak has a serious deficiency. While in some cases, treatment or compensatory programming are effective (such as in profound hearing loss), more often than not a nonspeaking child is manifesting the effects of a profound and comprehensive problem which requires comprehensive special educational considerations.

Language-Disordered Children

Children in this general category are language users, but their language structure is not comparable to that of their peers. The symptoms of these disorders appear in their use of our language system at the phonological, morphological, semantic, or syntactic levels. Since all of these levels of language are mutually interacting and mutually dependent, it is probably more accurate to think of language disorders as developmental differences at all of these levels.

Causes of Language Disorders

The general causes for such disorders are, of course, many and varied. In many cases, children have just mislearned or not learned various structures of language. Such learning might be related to poor language models in the environment, inadequate motivation, or faulty hypotheses about various language structures. These children make some mistakes in hearing, analyzing, and developing their language forms; or their environment does not provide them with appropriate examples and enough rewards for proper language learn-

ing. These language disorders are usually mild to moderate.

In some cases, language learning can be severely inhibited by less-than-inadequate sensory perception or intellectual functioning. In these cases, the language may be severely deficient, and the child may not be able to use his language at anywhere near a satisfactory level. Children with these severe language disorders are often classified as mentally retarded, brain damaged, or severely learning disordered. For whatever reasons, they have not been able to bring together the physiological and/or intellectual resources necessary to acquire language structures as complex and subtle as the ones children of similar age have been able to acquire.

There is an important comparison between children in this category and children classified as nonspeaking. Language-disordered children, no matter how severe their problem, have demonstrated an awareness that their culture has developed a formal oral symbolic code with which to represent objects, relationships, and events. Nonspeaking children have not demonstrated such an awareness. Thus, regardless of the severity of the language problem, the child who has at least some oral language and who had become a language user had demonstrated something important. He is at least somewhere on the normal developmental track. Any child who is past 3 or 4 and has failed to attain this basic level of development is telling us that he has some severe problems in the most basic of human integration and learning areas.

Implications of Language Disorders

Whether language deficiencies occur at the phonological, morphological, semantic, and/or syntactic levels is significant in regard to the depth of the problem. Problems which exist only at the *phonological* level (forming the sound families) are, generally,

Although she can count and understand numbers, Danielle has trouble producing the word "seven" in response to the "7."

considered speech impairments. We deal with such problems more extensively later in this chapter. These problems relate to the production of oral language only and are usually the result of motor problems or learning problems which can be compensated for in some degree, except in the most extreme cases.

Problems at the *morphological* (creating words) and *syntactic* (combining words) levels are difficulties in acquiring the basic rule systems of a language. Such deficits may be related to environmental problems, like poor models, or they may indicate serious developmental deficits in intellectual processing. In still other cases, for example, the learning disability problems, dysfunctions in basic auditory and central processing affect the morphology and syntactic structures of a child's language. Some children simply cannot adequately decode the spoken elements of their language and effectively use them to express their own ideas and feelings. Such problems are usually related to highly specialized brain damage. In moderate to severe

learning disabilities, the phonology of the language may be a problem along with morphology and syntax. The overall effects on spoken language can be quite severe. Such problems, as we will see, require intensive clinical and educational programs to bring the child's overall language processing abilities to a point where he can use appropriate linguistic structures.

Semantic deficiencies occur in children who do not have adequate knowledge about their world or, for some reason, have not learned to represent available knowledge in their language. More often than not, significant deficits in the semantic content of language represent developmental delay related to overall intellectual functioning. There is, of course, a wide range of possible reasons for semantic deficiencies, ranging from relatively mild problems of poor environmental experience and language models to those severe deficiencies which are associated with severe mental retardation.

Children whose psychological and physiological mechanisms are intact will learn spoken language if they have anything resembling a normal environment. If, however, a child's intellectual functioning, psychological adjustments, or speech processing or production mechanisms are less than optimum, his language learning process will be affected. In many cases, mild to moderate deviations from optimum conditions do not completely prevent language acquisition. These deviations do, however, bring about slight to moderate differences in a child's language. As deviations in all of the human behavioral and physiological systems become more severe, so too do language deficiencies become more pronounced.

Speech-Impaired Children

Another source of communication disorders lies in disruptions of the primary and most efficient mode of learning and transmitting language—oral speech. Problems which disrupt the encoding and transmitting of speech create serious communication disorders. The primary serious speech impairments are articulatory disorders, stuttering, and voice problems.

Articulation Problems

Articulation problems are the most prevalent communication disorders of children. An articulation problem may be either a speech problem or a language problem; in some cases it is both. To understand this, it is necessary to review briefly our sound system. English has 26 consonant phonemes which are classified in terms of their (1) manner of articulation and (2) place of articulation. (See page 262.) Many of these phonemes are closely related. For example, each stop interrupts the airstream completely and then releases it to produce a sound, sounds like /p/, /t/, /k/ and their voiced cognates /b/, /d/, /g/, respectively. Furthermore, the primary difference among these stop sounds is that each is produced with a different *place of articulation.*

Children learning language often do not realize that phonemes which sound so much alike and which are produced so similarly are really different sounds. A child might select one of the unvoiced stop sounds, /t/ for example, and use it whenever the words call for /k/ or even /p/. He is substituting one stop sound for all stop sounds. In a sense, he has mislearned the sound system of his language. This mislearning very often is extended to other sounds of the language. For example, if he is substituting a /t/ for a /k/, he may also substitute voiced cognates, a /d/ for a /g/. Children who make one such mistake in their sound learning often make others, too. Thus, children with this articulation problem often make errors on three, four, or more phonemes in their sound system.

Sometimes children substitute one sound for another sound produced in or near the same place of articulation. A child might substitute an apico-alveolar stop /t/ for an apico-alveolar fricative continuant like /s/ even though these sounds are very different in their manner features and in the ways we hear them (their acoustics). In other cases, children *omit* sounds which are difficult to say. In still other articulation errors, a child does not produce the sound accurately and, while she does not substitute another sound ot the language, she does *distort* the sound. Articulation errors are, therefore, either substitutions, omissions, or distortions within the sound system of the language.

In most cases, children who make these errors have simply mislearned the English sound system. Often these children can produce the sounds they are misarticulating. In other cases, they may need some instruction in how to produce a /k/, an /r/, or an /s/, for example. In either case, many children with this problem usually have no demonstrable physical, intellectual, or perceptual problems. Their problems are simply problems in learning the language system, often referred to as *functional* articulation problems. Their treatment, while quite demanding, is usually successful.

Other articulation problems are not so successfully treated. Included here are children whose basic motor functioning makes it impossible to produce the rapid movements of the tongue, velum, and lips necessary to produce oral language accurately and rapidly enough for normal speech. Another serious articulation problem occurs when the structure of the oral mechanism is inadequate. A cleft in the hard palate, for example, makes it impossible to close off the nasal cavity from the air stream passage. The result is excessive nasality and also lack of air pressure to produce many of the consonant sounds with full value.

Still other articulation problems are caused by deficits in sensory perception. An auditory perception problem can prevent the discriminations necessary to learn sounds. A problem in perceiving sensations within the mouth may prevent a person from properly using the tongue, lips, gum ridge, and velum in producing speech.

Articulation problems caused by body structure or perceptual or motor ability are considered to be *organic* speech problems. In many cases, they are associated with primary medical problems. Cleft palates, for example, require medical and dental care including surgery and/or prosthetic appliances to restore proper mouth structure for feeding and speech learning. Cerebral palsy also requires medical management, sometimes including orthopedic surgery. Physical therapy is used to develop muscle strength for sitting, standing, and walking, as well as reaching and manipulating. The severe speech impairments found in some cerebral-palsied children may be treated by the speech pathologist.

Within the area of articulation disorders, then, are mislearned sound structures, damaged motor systems, structural deficiencies in the mouth and palate, and disrupted sensory systems which interfere with the learning and production of sounds. The treatments of these problems are generally complex and most often involve several professional disciplines, including medicine, dentistry, speech pathology, physical therapy, and education.

Stuttering

Of all speech impairments, **stuttering** is probably the most dramatic, perplexing, and frustrating. Although stuttering is a speech disorder, much stuttering behavior is not speech at all. Rather, severe stuttering consists more of gasps, eye blinks, facial contortions, and general struggles for breath. The popular concept of stuttering as simply repeating sounds or syllables usually applies only to the young child who

is exhibiting the normal nonfluencies which are common to everyone's speech.

Speech pathologists generally classify two types of stuttering to differentiate the early, repetition type from the severe types which usually involve little repetition of syllables or words. *Primary stuttering* is the term to describe the repetitious type, and *secondary stuttering* is applied to stuttering which has the added nonspeech behaviors. Evidence indicates that many young children, particularly boys, go through a stage of primary stuttering. Nonfluencies, repetitions, and false starts are all common in the speech of most adults. It

To help overcome his disfluency, this pupil makes up a story to tell his speech therapist.

seems logical, then, that a child who is still immature physiologically and neurologically and who is working hard to learn how to produce all of the language units and structures will make some mechanical mistakes. It has been the general counsel of speech pathologists to consider primary stuttering in young children (3 to 5 years old) as normal behavior.

The reasons that some children become severe stutterers with all of the added secondary symptoms are still unknown. There is evidence, however, to suggest that much of the secondary behavior stems from attempting *not* to stutter. A child may try to avoid stuttering by taking a little breath before he attempts the word. Gradually, this little breath must become longer and longer, and, finally, he may need a series of gasps to avoid stuttering. We cannot prove that this is what happens, but observations of and discussions with stutterers provide evidence of the fear and anticipation of stuttering and the planning of ways to avoid it. In addition, there has been no conclusive evidence which indicates that stutterers have any physiological or neurological differences from normal speakers. Thus, stuttering is generally considered to be learned or acquired behavior, and attempts to avoid it seem to prompt the secondary behaviors. There are many other explanations of this behavior, including those which are based on the theories of Freud and other psychoanalysts. Also, there are still those who are convinced there are physical reasons for stuttering behavior. The search goes on for the full explanation of this speech behavior.

Voice Disorders

While voice problems are not often thought of as speech impairments, they are included here because voicing is part of transmitting language. **Voice disorders** consist of inappropriate intensity, pitch, or quality of the vocal tone produced at the larynx and resonated in the pharynx, oral cavity, and sometimes the nasal cavity. Thus, voice problems can be either problems of vocal tone production or problems of the resonation of this tone. The most common resonance problem is excessive nasality. Nasality is strictly a problem of being unable to keep the voiced air stream from entering the nasal cavity. There are only three sounds in English that require nasal resonance (m, n, ŋ). All other English sounds require that the nasal cavity be shut off from the breath stream. This shutting-off is accomplished by raising the velum (soft-palate) so that it makes contact with the back wall of the throat (pharyngeal wall; see Figure 10.1). With the velum in place, air coming up from the lungs through the larynx is blocked off from the nasal cavity. Following the laws of physics and taking the path of least resistance, the air stream moves into the oral cavity and is shaped into the needed speech sounds. In the case of the sounds which require nasal resonance, the velum is not raised and the proper, nasalized /m/ or /n/ is produced by the air stream moving into the nasal cavity.

Excessive nasality occurs because the child cannot accomplish the velar-pharyngeal closing. This can be a result of a paralysis of the velum. Sometimes, however, nasality is a result of maldevelopment of the hard or soft palates. Clefts in the palatal structure can begin at the lip and run the entire length of the mouth from the alveolar ridge through the velum. In some cases, however, the clefts are not "complete" and affect a smaller area. Incomplete clefts sometimes only include the velum. Whatever the degree of cleft, however, there is no way to avoid excessive nasality in the voice unless the cleft is repaired, and the nasal cavity is separated from the oral cavity and pharynx. Clefts can be repaired surgically. It is becoming increasingly popular to close off minor clefts with appliances built by dental specialists.

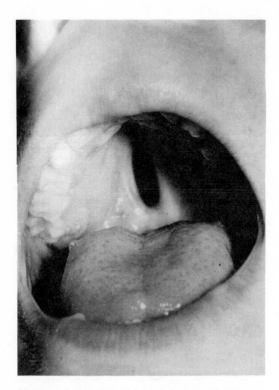

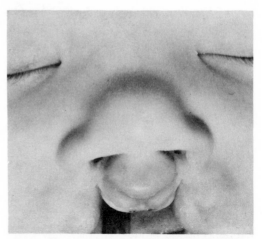

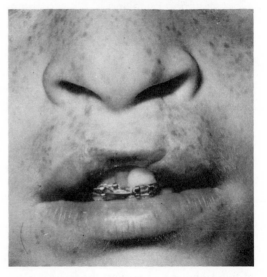

A cleft palate before repair (above left). A bilateral (two-sided) cleft lip before repair (top right) and another bilateral cleft lip after repair (bottom right).

These appliances are called *dental prostheses* and sometimes include protuberances of carefully shaped plastic which extend into the pharynx and which can be brought into contact with the pharyngeal wall to shut off the nasal cavity for normal voice quality.

Some children's soft palates are too short to reach the pharyngeal wall in the back of the throat. In these cases, another type of surgery is done. A flap of the pharyngeal wall tissue is sewed to the upper surfaces of the velum. Other methods of velar-

pharyngeal closure are being developed, including implanting silicone pads in the pharyngeal wall to allow a short palate to make contact. Recent continued refinement of both surgical and dental techniques has transformed the cleft palate problem from one in which a child was doomed to facial deformities and unintelligible speech into one in which minimal disfiguration and normal speech is more the rule than the exception. Children who have had clefts repaired require careful speech training to learn to use their new structures.

This is most often true of those with dental appliances and the pharyngeal - flap surgery.

In addition to the nasality problems associated with cleft or inadequate palate structures, there are cases of nasality with no physical cause. Faulty use of the velum is one of these. It can be corrected by learning better vocal production habits.

Voice problems that originate in the larynx generally have some physical base. The physical problems may be caused by misuse and abuse of the larynx by children (or adults) who use their voices inappropriately. For example, a man who talks loudly and forcefully may actually cause ulcerating of the vocal cords. Or a woman who talks in an extremely high pitch and with constant tension in her voice may create small nodules on her vocal cords. As a result of these ulcers or nodules on the vocal cords, the voices of these individuals become extremely hoarse or harsh. They may sound breathy and, in extreme cases, the person may lose his voice completely. These voice problems always require medical treatment. Without intensive training on how to use the voice after treatment, the

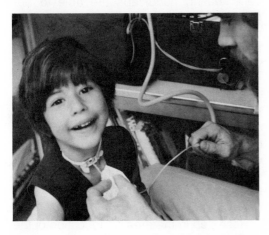

Although she is only 6, Adreana stands patiently while an aide suctions her tracheotomy. The "trache" has made her voice small and raspy.

problems may recur. Anyone with a consistently hoarse, harsh, breathy voice probably has some abnormality of the vocal cords. Such voice problems should always be examined by a physician, preferably a specialist in laryngology. This goes beyond just the treatment of vocal nodules or ulcers; there are other growths which occur on the vocal cords and bring about voice problems—carcinomas or cancers. Most often, when cancerous growths appear on the vocal cords, the entire larynx is surgically removed.

Surgical removal of the larynx is called a *laryngectomy*. With the larynx removed, a person is mute. She cannot produce a voice tone in the natural way. There are several compensatory alternatives for this situation. One is a mechanical vibrator which produces a steady tone. With this vibrator held to the throat just under the lower jaw, the tone is transmitted into the oral cavity, where it can be articulated into speech sounds. The sounds are not exactly like normal speech, but they are usually adequate for communication. Other mechanical devices to produce a substitute vocal tone are also available.

Another alternative in the case of laryngectomy is to teach the person to produce a vocal tone with structures still in his throat even after the larynx has been removed. A technique for trapping air in the esophagus and then bringing it back up through narrow strictures formed near the top of the esophagus has proved extremely successful for thousands of people. The voice is actually created by a process much like burping. With practice, many people can produce a voice of extremely good quality and can speak with phrasing patterns and articulation which are nearly normal. Of all of the alternatives, *esophageal speech* is the most desirable because there is no need for mechanical devices and it sounds most like natural speech. Not all people can learn this technique, however.

The human voice production mechanism is vulnerable to all kinds of abuse and trauma. When it is affected, its product can be made to sound hoarse, harsh, or nasal, or may be stopped altogether. When voice is so affected, human communication is obviously reduced, and medical treatment and voice therapy are critical to restore the person to full effectiveness.

TREATMENT AND RESEARCH

Communication disorders are so numerous and varied that a discussion of treatments could be quite lengthy. In this section, we comment only on the general principles involved in treatment of the major disorders and briefly discuss current research trends.

Nonspeaking Children

Children who do not have language have some severe problem, either psychological or physiological. The emphasis in treatment

Bruce and Annette are both hearing impaired. Although they use lip reading and auditory training to converse with friends, they often mouth words silently when they are alone.

is to overcome the problem to the degree that the child becomes a communicator in at least some basic way. Obviously, the treatment varies with the nature of the problems.

The deaf child cannot hear language, and, thus, cannot learn it unaided. Treatment for these children is increased auditory stimulation and intensive, early training. Such activity can begin in infancy. For many years, there has been a polarization in education of the hearing handicapped. Some educators insist that these deaf children be taught a mode of communication which can be learned without hearing—a manual sign or fingerspelling mode. Others, insisting that acquiring a manual language will inhibit the development of speech, concentrate on working for speech and oral language and specifically discourage the use of manual signs and even gestures. The *oralists* fit children with powerful hearing aids to let them use any hearing they have. At the same time, they use visual and tactile cues to show the children how to produce speech sounds. There has been some extremely fine work done in this area. Some children with severe hearing handicaps are able to become oral language users and, using lip reading plus whatever hearing they might have, they can receive spoken language with some success. The percentage of profoundly hearing impaired children who can accomplish this level of functioning in the oral mode is, unfortunately, limited. The current trend seems to be moving toward a *combined method* of language learning in which these children are taught both oral and manual modes of communication. Chapter 11 has more on this debate and the *total communication* method.

Research in the area of education of the hearing handicapped is extensive and includes experimental programs in both the oral and the combined methods. A great deal of research is being carried out in the area of developing speech and lip-reading ability in infants. Other research describes programs in which children are taught early communication in both the manual modes and oral speech.

While we have little trouble understanding why hearing handicapped children do not develop language normally, the problem is not so clear-cut with other children. The autistic child, the child with severe cognitive deficits, and the severely perceptually handicapped child present a rather cloudy picture for treatment. The most basic question is, "Can such children learn to use a set of symbols to represent objects and events in their world?" This basic question has recently generated some innovative research. The research by a psychologist who has been teaching a chimpanzee to use a language is particularly interesting. Knowing that a chimpanzee does not have a vocal and articulatory mechanism which can produce anything like the human speech sound system, David Premack (1970) decided that he would construct the "words" for Sarah, his chimpanzee. He created plastic "names" for fruits and objects up on a magnetic board. He taught her to describe certain events which were connected with these fruits and objects. She learned to use symbols to describe actions like giving, cutting, and inserting (in a pail). She learned still more symbols to indicate whether things were the same or different and to answer such questions as "Apple same as banana?" (yes/no). Sarah became able to look at the small blue triangle which was the symbol for apple and, through her language forms, tell Premack that it was round, red, and had a stem.

Premack's research findings prompted others to probe a nonverbal child's ability to use symbols. Research by a speech pathologist working with the mentally retarded (Carrier, 1974) has shown that many severely retarded children can learn language in this form. Additional work with autistic children (McLean & McLean, 1974) has demonstrated that even some of these totally nonverbal children can be trained to use a nonspeech language in simple sentence forms.

The implication of this work is important. In some cases at least, nonspeaking children using nonspeech modes can behave symbolically and actually be language users. Such discoveries raise the possibility that some children may simply be overwhelmed by oral language and, therefore, not able to make the discoveries that are necessary to begin to learn this complex code. They are capable of learning a code which is seen rather than heard and tangible rather than intangible as spoken symbols are.

While we cannot cite all research and clinical program developments with nonspeaking children, we can note a few to indicate their range and variety. One psychologist (Lovaas, 1966) is experimenting with the application and withdrawal of punishing stimuli contingent on speech. Systematically structured programs which begin with gross motor imitation and progress through discrimination responses, receptive language, and then speech imitation are being developed by psychologists (Bricker, Dennison, & Bricker, 1976) and speech pathologists (Kent, 1974). Another speech pathologist is working on a systematic program to help deaf, retarded children discriminate among attributes of objects and actions and use manual signs, writing, and then, if possible, speech to describe them (Berger, 1972). MacDonald (1976; MacDonald & Horstmeier, 1978) and his colleagues have developed an extensive program of assessment and parent-assisted programs aimed at the young child with severely delayed language. MacDonald's work stresses the content of language between child and caretaker and teacher. From this *semantic* base, programs are structured around activities in the nonspeaking child's environment. Since the process of language learning is normally begun in mother-child interactions (Bruner, 1974/75; Mahoney, 1975), this approach is both appropriate and long overdue in its formal development.

Other work is being carried out in hospitals, institutions for the retarded and the emotionally disturbed, and schools all over the country. The answers to all problems are not yet available; perhaps they never will be. But the treatment techniques which are being developed and validated hold great promise for nonspeaking children.

Language-Disordered Children

Probably no area of research and treatment is more active and productive than programming for children with language problems. The treatments for these children have a deceptively simple goal—to teach children the linguistic structures of our language system. Despite the straightforward goal, no area, is more fraught with controversies and polarized attitudes than that of training language responses in children. It is impossible to review the controversies and the competing programs in this chapter. We will indicate the trends in language training which appear to hold the most promise at this time.

The work of Bloom (page 269), of Premack (page 283), and of MacDonald (page 283), as well as research by Olson (1970), Slobin (1973), and Miller and Yoder (1972, 1974) all point to one important fact—children talk because they have something to say! While this may seem simplistic, somehow many people working in training language seem to have missed this point. Now, however, language structure is being taught in the context of the events, experiences, and relationships in a child's world, the things that seem to be important for him to know. This attention to the real world

means, however, that to talk about his world a child must know something about it. As all of the researchers listed above have said in one way or another, children use language to make maps of their knowledge about their world.

Training children to understand and verbalize about their world seems simple enough; however, it really is not a simple task. Somewhere, somehow children whose language is deficient have not learned how to map their knowledge about their world linguistically. Why? Is it because they lacked knowledge or because they lacked the resources to learn the linguistic structures necessary to talk about what they know? The trainer must discover which problem he is dealing with. If it is only the linguistic structures, he can begin to evoke and reinforce the language structures on the basis of what the child knows. This training includes all aspects of language from learning vocabulary (morphemes) to learning word order and other syntactic necessities.

If it is the child's knowledge of his world which is retarding his language development, we must teach the concepts and the linguistic forms which map this knowledge. We must help a child discover the code and the manner in which the code is used.

Work by psycholinguists, psychologists, speech pathologists, and special educators is growing in this area. New programs are being developed, tested, and disseminated regularly. Some important new models and programs are being developed (MacDonald, 1976; MacDonald & Horstmeier, 1978; McLean & Snyder-McLean, 1978; Miller & Yoder, 1972, 1974; Stremel & Waryas, 1974; Waryas & Stremel-Campbell, in press). These programs stem from a theoretical base extended from past bases; their approach to treatment is far more pervasive than past efforts.

Speech-Impaired Children

The greatest responsibility for treatment of speech-impaired children has traditionally fallen to speech pathologists, who traditionally have had more basic knowledge about training in the areas of articulation, stuttering, and voice problems than any other of the behavioral disciplines. The treatment is traditionally symptom-specific. That is, in articulation disorders, speech pathologists seek to develop conversational use of specific phonemes. They also work to reduce disruptive stuttering symptoms. After appropriate medical treatment of voice disorders, the speech pathologist can help the individual break the vocal habits which brought about the ulcers or the nodules. They also train the laryngectomized person to produce esophageal speech.

The primary trend in research in the training of the speech impaired seems to be more systematic procedures and wider application of the basic behavioral modification procedures (see chapter 1). This trend is most apparent in the areas of articulation therapy and stuttering. There are some limited cases of articulation programs offered by paraprofessionals under the guidance of professionals. However, stuttering still seems to be regarded as a problem which must be carefully monitored by highly trained professionals. Treatment of voice problems also remains a clinical problem which must be served by speech pathologists and physicians.

In articulation therapy, the trend is to train the child to produce the problem phoneme correctly and then work on increasing the child's fluency in producing the correct sound in context. It is surprising that, even though many children can correctly produce their defective sound in imitation or in certain words, consistent correctness in conversation takes careful programming over literally hundreds of training trials. Typical of the newest trends in systematic articulation therapy are the programs developed by Weston and Irwin (1971) and McLean, Raymore, and Long (1976).

In stuttering, the trends are to find conditions which help the stutterer gain speech fluency and then to maintain that fluency when the facilitating conditions are gradually faded out of use. One treatment consists of fitting a stutterer with headsets and delaying the feedback of his own voice to him by a few hundredths of a second. In attempting to talk under these conditions, a stutterer often can gain fluency. Since most stutterers have forgotten what talking fluently feels like, talking under these conditions apparently helps them establish some awareness which helps them relearn fluent patterns. In experiments, many stutterers can maintain fluency attained under special conditions even after the special conditions have been discontinued.

There are, of course, many other experimental approaches to stuttering. Programs of this type probably can only be applied by speech pathologists and psychologists highly experienced in this particular area.

Summary

Treatment and research in communication disorders has always been of high interest for behavioral scientists. Today is no exception; there are literally hundreds of new and promising research efforts. Training techniques for nonspeaking children are being pursued by every behavioral discipline. Language training in general is also the subject of research in psychology, speech pathology, psycholinguistics, and special education. The area of speech impairments, however, remains the speech pathologist's, and, in some cases, the psychologist's (stuttering) or the psycholinguist's (articulation).

Radically new trends with high promise for producing effective and efficient treatment procedures for communication-disordered children are apparent. Certainly, such programs are desperately needed. There is something particularly demeaning in not being able to communicate with fellow humans. Considering the complex system that we have developed for communication, it will take the very best efforts we can muster to meet the needs and the challenge of those who cannot now use this system adequately.

DELIVERY OF TREATMENT SERVICES

The needs of the child with a communication disorder tax not only our theoretical knowledge and clinical skills but also our personnel and service delivery systems as well. If we return to the three gross classifications of these disorders, we can take a brief look at the primary resources for treatment for (1) nonspeaking children, (2) language-disordered children, and (3) speech-impaired children.

Nonspeaking Children

Traditionally, many nonspeaking children have been placed in residential institutions for the emotionally disturbed or mentally retarded. If they have remained with their families, rarely have they attained a place in the everyday world. They have not been accepted in public schools or in the standard preschool programs, and, as a result, their treatment has been extremely spotty. Most residential institutions do not have the professional staff to provide the needed intensive treatment for such children. There are only a few nonresidential programs to serve them, and they are generally private and expensive.

Today the trend is toward early treatment programs for obviously handicapped chil-

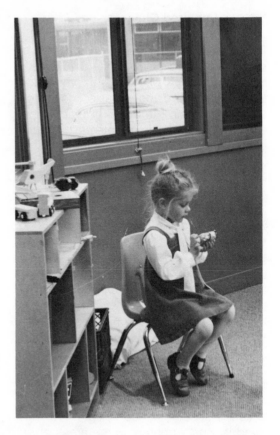

Via, who is able to speak but does not voluntarily use speech to communicate, attends a public day school program.

dren. With intervention beginning as early as possible, even in the first few months of life, many children who would ordinarily remain without language can be put on more productive tracks towards higher levels of functioning. While there are still significant financial, social, and political problems in providing the necessary services to the very young, this is the goal being sought.

Recent federal laws (see the chapter 1 discussion of P.L. 94–142) and state laws require appropriate treatment and educational programs for handicapped children in environments which are less removed from the normal mainstream of our culture. As a result of these sweeping new laws, alternatives to institutionalization are being developed for all types of handicapped children. Some alternatives are community-based units for treatment and education of hearing handicapped children, severely and profoundly retarded children, and seriously behaviorally disordered children.

Such far-reaching changes in our overall educational and clinical treatment resources require much change in our society. The number of trained people who can provide appropriate educational programming must be increased. The work in this area is far from glamorous, but it seems to be attracting excellent young people into special education and speech pathology training programs which prepare teachers and clinicians for work with both the very young and the severely to profoundly handicapped child.

Language—Disordered Children

The treatment resources in this area appear to be growing but they are not yet sufficient. Public schools are providing language therapy through their speech pathology programs. Community resources such as the Easter Seal programs and the community and university speech and hearing clinics also provide services for children with moderate to severe language disorders.

The trend towards increased training for special educators in language development, structure, and treatment is clear and means more attention to the language problems of children in public school classrooms and resource programs. Many special education program goals can be specified and quantified in terms of the adequacy of the child's language structure and language responses. Preschool programs being offered through public schools or other state and federal service systems are attacking language problems of both the handicapped child and the so-

cially disadvantaged child early in their lives.

All in all, sensitivity to language and language problems is occurring across the entire educational and clinical spectrum. Research in this area is relatively extensive. Programs in language training are becoming available in forms which are useable by well-trained professionals in many disciplines (Bricker, Dennison, & Bricker, 1976; Guess, Sailor, & Baer, 1974; Kent, 1974; MacDonald, 1976; MacDonald & Horstmeier, 1978; Miller & Yoder, 1972, 1974; Stremel & Waryas, 1974; Waryas & Stremel-Campbell, in press).

Speech-Impaired Children

The primary deliverers of services to speech-impaired children are speech pathologists. Their services are available within many different settings. Speech pathologists are employed by most school systems throughout the country. In addition, clinicians practice in community and university speech and hearing clinics and, in larger metropolitan areas, in private clinics. Most large hospitals with treatment services for the cerebral palsied or cleft palate child have speech pathologists on their treatment teams for these children.

Summary

There are definite trends to extend the scope and accessibility of special treatment services to communication-disordered children. These trends are highly visible in local, state, and federal educational programs for children. It is also clear that professionals in several service disciplines are gaining competencies for working with nonspeaking and language-impaired children. These professionals include speech pathologists, special educators, and psychologists. The trends of today also indicate the increasing availability of services to the communication-disordered child in his early years.

Given the complexity of their problems and the penalties communication-dis-ordered children suffer, the advances toward more, better, and earlier services are overdue.

FOR MORE INFORMATION

Most of these resources are textbooks that are readily available, many from Charles E. Merrill, the publishers of this text. Check your instructor, the education library, or the general library at your school.

McLean, J.E., & Snyder-McLean, L.K. *A transactional approach to early language training.* Columbus, Ohio: Charles E. Merrill, 1978.

Mowrer, D.E. *Methods of modifying speech behaviors.* Columbus, Ohio: Charles E. Merrill, 1977.

Schiefelbusch, R.L., & Lloyd, L.L. (Eds.). *Language perspectives—Acquisition, retardation and intervention.* Baltimore: University Park Press, 1974.

Van Riper, C. *Speech correction: Principles and methods* (6th ed.). Englewood Cliffs, N.J.: Prentice-Hall, 1978.

Wiig, E.H., & Semel, E.M. *Language disabilities in children and adolescents.* Columbus, Ohio: Charles E. Merrill, 1976.

11

The Hearing Handicapped

Sheila Lowenbraun
Carolyn Scroggs

These are the major topics covered in this chapter. You may want to use them as a checklist when you review.

- *How we hear.*

- *Causes of hearing handicaps.*

- *Assessment of hearing impairments.*

- *The probable effects of severe hearing loss before language development on a child's language, cognitive development, and social growth.*

- *Advantages and disadvantages of residential school placement, day school placement, and day classes in public schools.*

- *The aural/oral, manual communication, and total communication approaches to building communication skills for the hearing handicapped.*

- *Special competencies needed by teachers of the hearing handicapped.*

- *Working in the classroom with the hearing handicapped.*

Chapter eleven

We use vision, taction, **olfaction, gustation,** and audition to explore and understand our environment. Of these senses, audition and vision allow us to remain in contact with events occurring at a distance from ourselves. When either of these senses is faulty, the entire structure of the sense hierarchy is different, and the world is perceived differently.

Unlike vision, hearing cannot be turned off by a normal voluntary action. Hearing functions in the dark. Hearing allows us to be aware of auditory events in a 360-degree field; it is nonlinear. Audition serves us as a warning sense; hearing an unexpected sound such as a fire engine siren, we visually scan the environment to see the reason for the auditory signal.

Audition has an additional, even more vital function for us. Hearing is the sense used by the normally developing infant to assimilate the communication patterns of the people around him. It is primarily through this communication structure that human beings become socialized, gaining access to the language, accumulated knowledge, customs, and mores of their societies. Equally important, we use language internally, in our thoughts; we use it to promote abstract thought.

Deprived of the auditory sense, and without compensatory education, a hearing impaired infant grows up silent (mute), unable to communicate except perhaps by using a primitive gesture system, understood only by a few, and unable to function independently in adult society. Given appropriate education, a hearing impaired person acquires the communication skills necessary to function successfully as an independent individual, socially and economically.

SOUND AND THE EAR

Sound waves are produced by the extremely rapid motion of particles of matter, producing waves of *alternate condensation and rarefaction.* One compression and one rarefaction together make up one cycle. The frequency of a sound is the number of cycles that occur per second. The term used to designate cycles per second is **hertz** (Hz). 100 Hz means the frequency of the sound is 100 cycles per second. The human ear is sensitive to frequencies between 20Hz and 20,000 Hz (Davis & Silverman, 1970). A change in the frequency of the vibration is perceived as a change in pitch; the higher the frequency, the higher the pitch. Middle C, for example, has a frequency of 256 Hz. Doubling the frequency produces a perceived pitch change of one octave. While people are sensitive to sounds in a wide range of frequencies, the most important band is the range between 500 and 2,000 Hz, where most of the energy of speech sounds is concentrated. The intensity of a sound is measured in logarithmic units called **decibels** (dB). An increase in the intensity of a sound is thought of as an increase in loudness.

The normally functioning ear accepts sound waves and transforms them into neural impulses that are decoded in the temporal lobes of the brain. Hearing impairment occurs when there is a breakdown in one or more facets of this transmitting process. Hearing losses may cause a restriction in the range of frequencies received by the ear or in the intensity necessary for a sound to be perceived, or both.

Three variables of educational importance are generally used to describe the nature of the impairment: (1) the site in the ear where the impairment occurs, (2) the age at which the hearing loss originated, and (3) the extent to which hearing **acuity** is impaired.

Site of Impairment

Impairment in the mechanical transmission of sound waves through the outer ear and middle ear gives rise to **conductive hearing**

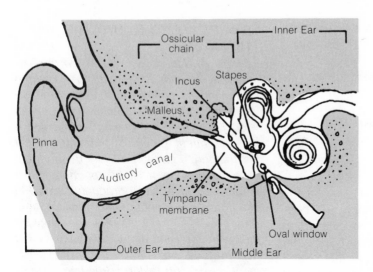

Figure 11.1
The human ear

losses. The outer ear consists of the external ear *(pinna)* and a passage about an inch long and a quarter inch in diameter (the *auditory canal*), which terminates at the eardrum *(tympanic membrane)* (Figure 11.1). Infrequently a child is born with missing or undeveloped pinnae and auditory canals. These conditions materially interfere with sound conduction, and a substantial conductive hearing loss results. In people with normally formed ears, if there is excess accumulation of ear wax or a foreign object lodged in the canal, sound waves are prevented from reaching the neural end organ. These conditions are usually easily corrected and special educational placement is not needed.

The middle ear is a cavity between 1 and 2 cubic centimeters in volume connected to the naso-pharynx by the Eustachean tube. It contains three tiny bones, the *malleus, incus,* and *stapes;* these bones, the *ossicular chain,* form a bridge between the tympanic membrane and the entrance to the inner ear *(oval window)*. Sound waves are carried by the ossicular chain to the inner ear. The footplate of the last bone in the chain, the stapes, is embedded in the oval window.

The most common cause of conductive hearing loss originating in the middle ear is inflammation of the middle ear *(otitis*

media) (Davis & Silverman, 1970). Another conductive disorder of the middle ear, *otosclerosis,* is a genetically based condition in which new bony growth occurs in the bone capsule surrounding the middle ear (Davis & Silverman, 1970). In approximately 10% of the cases where this occurs, the stapes is fixed firmly in the oval window by the new growth, inhibiting sound conduction. In many instances, the condition can be corrected surgically. In most cases, children with a short-term conductive hearing impairment do not require special educational services. If the condition is chronic, special help in speech reading and speech and the use of amplification usually allows the child to remain in a regular class. Even a slight hearing loss, however, can cause educational problems (Quigley, n.d.). In a study of school children in Illinois, Quigley found that a loss of as little as 15 dB reduced school performance.

In the inner ear, sound waves are converted into neural impulses which are then transmitted via the eighth cranial nerve to the temporal lobes of the brain. The vast majority of children enrolled in programs for the hearing handicapped have **sensori-neural hearing losses,** resulting from impairment of the inner ear or the eighth cranial nerve. Unlike conductive impairments, sensori-neural losses cannot generally be reversed surgically or medically. Because they originate in the neural mechanism, such losses not only reduce the intensity of the signal but may also distort the sounds which are perceived.

Age of Onset of Impairment

The age at which a hearing loss occurs is extremely important psychologically and educationally. Educationally, losses occurring after the child has begun to acquire oral language (*postlingual* losses) are considered less damaging than *prelingual* losses. Postlingually impaired children have had considerable aural input, and have begun acquiring language and speech. The later in life the impairment occurs, the more vocabulary and linguistic concepts the child is likely to have acquired. Primary goals for such children are

FOR YOUR INFORMATION . . .

Children with prelingual hearing losses need special educational provisions to acquire a communication system. Out of 38,898 hearing impaired special education students for whom the age at onset of hearing loss is known, 36,652 (or 94.2%) suffered the loss before age 3. These figures come from the Annual Survey of Hearing Impaired Children and Youth, Office of Demographic Studies, Gallaudet College, Washington, D.C., for the 1975-76 school year.

Age at onset	Frequency (n)	Relative frequency (%)
At birth	29,846	60.4
Under 3 years	6,806	13.8
3 years to 5 years, 11 months	1,702	3.4
6 years and older	544	1.0
(Not reported or unknown	10,529	21.3)
Total	49,427	99.9

profile EDWARD B. NITCHIE (1876–1916)

Edward B. Nitchie, who was hard of hearing, was influential in modifying lipreading instruction as well as in establishing services for deaf adults. Nitchie was born in Brooklyn in 1876. He planned to become a minister, but at the age of 14 he rapidly lost his hearing. Although initially despondent over his hearing loss, he returned to his studies and eventually graduated as a Phi Beta Kappa student from Amherst College. After graduation Nitchie had considerable difficulty obtaining a job because of his hearing loss. After finally gaining employment, he began taking lipreading instruction. The method used was analytical; lipreading was considered a process of understanding words by analyzing each individual lip movement. In 1903, when Nitchie was 26, he opened his own school for teaching lipreading. Eventually his

keeping their existing speech and language and using speech reading, and reading to acquire new information.

Prelingually deaf children are those who have never had normal hearing or who acquired a hearing loss before they had developed oral language. These children cannot acquire language by the normal processes, and special educational provisions must be made to help these children acquire a communication system. The child who is severely impaired depends heavily on vision to acquire language; as language inputs, he uses the lip movements of ordinary speech, the printed word, and perhaps some type of language using the hands (manual language system).

Extent of Impairment

Hearing impairment ranges in severity from slight to extreme. Impairment may occur in both ears (bilateral) or in one ear (unilateral). Some frequencies may be more af-

method evolved to one in which the lip-reader was to try to understand the message through grasping the whole idea rather then through an analysis of the individual movement.

Many of the students at Nitchie's school faced serious economic and social difficulties. Nitchie, who from the beginning was concerned with the total well-being of hearing handicapped people, instituted what became the New York League for the Hard of Hearing. The League provided lipreading scholarships, opened a handcraft shop, and had an employment bureau. Eventually associated leagues were established in nearly every major city in the United States. Today the New York league primarily serves adults in the New York City area. Nitchie also started a magazine for the hard of hearing, entitled Courage.

fected than others. The amount of hearing loss and the frequencies at which the loss occurs are important in decreasing loss of language reception. Most mildly and moderately hearing handicapped children—those with losses of 25 to 70 dB in the speech frequencies 500, 1,000, and 2,000 Hz—benefit from the use of amplification and may receive all or part of their education in the educational mainstream, with extra help in speech reading, speech, and language development. Children with severe and profound losses, who also benefit from using amplification, may need special class placement for most of their schooling. For some, spoken instruction may be aided by some form of manual communication. For these children, integration into regular classes must be carefully supervised.

CAUSES OF HEARING LOSS

Hearing loss in children may be caused by a number of different conditions. Losses may come from conditions originating within the developing organism, such as genetic anomalies; these are **endogenous** causes. Or a hearing loss may originate outside the organism, from disease or trauma; these are **exogenous** causes. Losses may occur before birth, during birth, or after birth.

Endogenous Causes

Hearing loss may be inherited as a genetic trait either alone or as part of a syndrome along with other abnormalities such as the skeletal deformities of Treacher-Collins syndrome or the abnormal pigmentation of the Waardenburg syndrome. Treacher-Collins syndrome is a genetic syndrome whose symptoms include facial bone and cartilage irregularities, cleft palate, cleft lip, and missing or malformed external ears, auditory canals, and middle ear bones. Because of the ear anomalies, Treacher-Collins causes a conductive hearing loss.

Waardenburg's syndrome is a genetic syndrome whose symptoms appear in varying combinations and with varying degrees of severity in those affected. These symptoms include a shock of white hair, usually growing from the front part of the head, bushy eyebrows that meet over the bridge of the nose; two different colored eyes, usually one blue and one brown; mild mental retardation; symptoms of emotional disturbance; sensori-neural hearing loss; and abnormal folds of the eyelids (epicanthus).

Deafness may be inherited as a dominant trait (14%), recessive trait (84%), or as a sex-linked disorder (2%). At the present time more than 50 genetic syndromes have been identified in which hearing loss may occur. It is estimated that genetic causes may account for 50% of all cases of deafness in children (Nance, 1976, pp. 6–7). It is common in residential schools for the deaf to find children who are the second or third generation of their families attending that school. A strong deaf subculture, with most marriages occurring between deaf people, may partially account for the high incidence of genetic hearing loss.

Exogenous Causes

The two types of exogenous causes of hearing handicaps are disease and injury.

German measles, or **rubella,** is a mild viral infection; however, when it is con- tracted by a woman during pregnancy, especially during the first three months, the developing fetus may be infected. This in- fection may cause the baby to be born with a hearing loss, and/or with defective vision, heart anomalies, and nervous system anomalies such as those associated with mental retardation and cerebral palsy. Dur- ing the rubella epidemic of 1963 to 1965, a substantial number of hearing handi-

---

profile PAUL

Paul was born in June, 1970. He is the third child in a middle-class family living in sub- urban Maryland. In contrast to her two pre- vious, rather easy pregnancies, Paul's mother had been sick during most of the months she had carried him. She had had several bouts with the flu and one alarming near-miscarriage which had led to hos- pitalization.

Paul was born 3 weeks prematurely after a difficult delivery. His mother remembers looking at her newborn son and thinking "for such an ugly little thing, he surely has caused a great deal of trouble."

Paul's first year was stormy. As with many other premature children, he could not tolerate cows' milk and proved to be allergic to several common grains. He also cried incessantly during most of the time he was awake. Paul developed slowly during his first year; while able to sit alone, he showed no signs of crawling, pulling him- self up to stand, or developing speech.

The concerned parents began a long series of trips to doctors, clinics, and hospi- tals, which ended when, at the age of 2, Paul was diagnosed as moderately re- tarded. The family was sent home to wait for his fifth birthday, when he could be ad- mitted into a special education program.

It was not until Paul was 5 and was seen by the school district diagnostic team that his severe bilateral hearing loss was dis- covered. The loss was probably due to a maternal viral infection during pregnancy.

At this age, Paul was walking, could coop- erate in dressing but not dress himself, and would finger-feed himself. He had no ex- pressive language but communicated his wants by pulling, tugging, screaming, and pointing. He was still sleeping badly and was throwing long and noisy tantrums whenever he did not get his way. The whole household revolved around Paul.

Paul has been placed in an experimental classroom for multiply handicapped hear- ing impaired children at a university labora- tory school. A behavior modification pro- gram is being used to get his tantrums and screaming under control. He responds well to positive reinforcers such as cereal and sips of juice. His mother attends a parent- ing class to learn to cope with him at home. Paul has been started on self-help pro- grams in dressing, feeding, and toileting and is slowly acquiring a sign language vocabulary with which to communicate his needs.

The future is uncertain for Paul; except for the experimental class, there is no ap- propriate placement for Paul in his school district; neither the classes for the retarded nor the classes for the hearing impaired meet his specific needs. However, under P.L. 94–142, he is guaranteed a free, ap- propriate public education in a setting as close to normal as possible. If such an education is provided, Paul should be able to lead a semi-independent, useful, self- satisfying life.

capped and multiply handicapped children were born who are now enrolled in educational programs. Of 16,037 students enrolled in programs for the hearing handicapped in 1970–71 (when the children born during 1963 to 1965 reached school age), 6,077 (37.9 percent) were known or presumed to have hearing losses caused by maternal rubella. In 1968 a vaccine which immunizes against rubella was produced and widely given to school-age children. This seems to have effectively prevented a rubella epidemic expected in the early 1970s. Other prenatal causes of hearing loss include viral infections such as mumps and influenza and toxemias of pregnancy.

Hearing impairment may also occur at or around the time of birth. Various complications in the birth process, such as prolonged labor, premature or abruptly caused birth (such as by an accident), or difficult delivery requiring obstetric instruments have been given as causes of deafness. One common cause of deafness is *prematurity,* said to be responsible for 13.8% of the cases of childhood deafness reported to the Office of Demographic Studies at Gallaudet College in 1970–71. *Rh incompatibility* was listed as the causal factor in 8.7% of the cases reported. Failure to breathe readily during or immediately after birth (*apnea*) is another commonly reported cause of hearing loss.

Following birth, hearing loss may be caused by viral infections such as mumps, measles, and meningitis. *Otitis media,* if chronic, may produce a permanent loss. Trauma, accidents, and high fevers are responsible for a small percentage of reported losses.

EVALUATION OF THE HEARING IMPAIRED
Audiological Assessment

The precise evaluation of the nature and extent of a hearing loss and the prescrip-

tion of appropriate medical, surgical, and/or prosthetic remediation is the province of the otologist, a medical doctor specializing in disorders of the ear, and the **audiologist,** a certified professional. Most audiologists hold a master's degree or doctorate in hearing science.

Hearing is measured in informal and formal ways. Gross evaluations may be done using Watch Tick and Coin Click tests as well as by noticing children's responses to a variety of noisemakers. Precise measurement of hearing loss, necessary for educational diagnosis, uses an *audiometer,* a machine which generates pure tones of known frequency and intensity. The client, seated in a soundproof chamber, wears a headset which allows the audiologist to test each ear separately. The client is asked to indicate, usually by raising a finger, each time he hears a sound. The audiologist then attempts to establish the client's hearing threshold. The hearing threshold is the intensity for each frequency at which the sound is heard one-half the

The audiologist uses colorful toys to help test this 3-year-old's hearing.

Chapter eleven

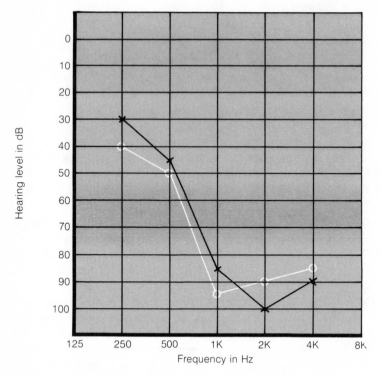

Figure 11.2

Pure tone audiogram of a child with a bilateral sensori-neural hearing loss that is more severe in the higher frequencies

time it is presented. This information is plotted on a chart called an *audiogram*.

The reference level of 0 dB is that point for each frequency at which a reference group of normally hearing people had their median threshold. Deviations from 0 dB indicate the added intensity—in dB—necessary for an individual to barely hear the sound at that frequency. Figure 11.2 shows the pure tone audiogram of a child with a hearing loss in both ears, which is more severe in the higher frequencies. Figure 11.3 shows the audiogram of a child with a conductive loss.

In *air conduction testing,* the sound waves pass through the outer and middle ears to the inner ear. But by placing a vibrator directly on the bone behind the external ear, an audiologist can bypass the outer and middle ears by allowing sound to be conducted through the bones in the skull directly to the inner ear. If an individual

has a conductive hearing loss, his *bone conduction threshold* is normal, while his *air conduction threshold* is raised. If the hearing impairment is in the neural mechanism, his bone conduction and air conduction thresholds are approximately the same. Other specialized audiometric techniques have been developed which can specify even more narrowly the site of the problem within the auditory mechanism. A relatively new technique is called *impedence audiometry*. It can determine precisely the condition of the tympanic membrane and middle ear. This technique does not require a voluntary response from the client and can be effectively used even with infants.

Small children or those with additional handicapping conditions may not respond to traditional pure tone audiometric techniques. Wesley Wilson, at the University of Washington, is currently pioneering work in behavioral audiometry; he conditions a

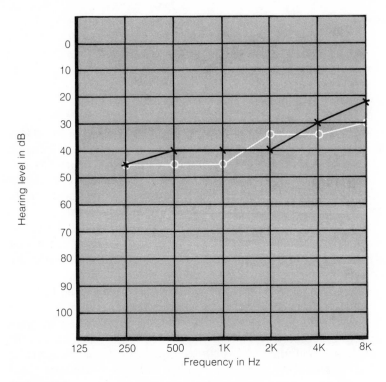

Figure 11.3
Pure tone audiogram of a child with a bilateral conductive hearing loss.

child to respond to sound by using rein-forcers such as food and animated toys (Lloyd & Dahle, 1976).

In addition to pure tone tests, the au-diologist may administer a number of speech tests to determine the extent of im-pairment of speech perception and phonemic discrimination.

Data from the audiometric assessment and medical and psychological information help the audiologist recommend appropri-ate amplification. Most hearing handi-capped children benefit from the use of personal amplification instruments. These hearing aids receive sound through a mi-crophone that may be worn on the body or at ear level. The sound is electronically amplified by a battery-powered, transis-torized system and is presented to the ear through a receiver, which transforms the electronic signals back to amplified sound. Hearing aids may be selected which

amplify certain frequencies more than others to mirror a specific hearing loss. In cases of sensori-neural loss, even the most powerful hearing aid cannot restore normal hearing because the neural mechanism it-self is faulty. However, amplification is con-sidered if even a slight improvement in au-ditory ability is possible. Instruction in the use of remaining hearing is considered es-sential in educating all hearing handi-capped children.

Intellectual Assessment

The intellectual assessment of hearing handicapped children is complicated by the fact that most intelligence tests are largely verbal tests. This makes them un-suitable for use with hearing impaired chil-dren. With school-age children, the test most generally used is the Wechsler Intelligence Scale for Children—Performance Scale (WISC-P) (Wechsler, 1949). This scale yields a performance IQ based on norms derived from a normally hearing population. Scores for hearing handicapped children are based on performance on the five nonverbal subtests of the WISC: Picture Completion, Picture Arrangement, Block Design, Object Assembly, and Coding. While the required responses to the items are nonverbal, the standardized directions for administration are presented orally. Despite this limitation, hearing handicapped children tend to obtain the same score distribution as normal children (Myklebust, 1964).

Several tests have been specifically designed for or standardized on a hearing-impaired population. The Hiskey-Nebraska Test of Learning Aptitude (Hiskey, 1966), which contains twelve nonverbal subtests measuring such things as bead pattern memory, memory for color, picture identification ability, and spatial reasoning, was standardized on a deaf population, the majority of whom came from state residential schools for the deaf. Not only do the items on the list require only nonverbal responses but standard pantomime directions for administration are provided. Other nonverbal tests, such as the Leiter International Performance Scale (Leiter, 1969) and the Goodenough-Draw-A-Man (Goodenough & Harris, 1963) have also been used. (See the appendix for more information on these and other tests.)

While there is no significant difference between the scores of normal hearing and deaf children on the nonverbal portion of the WISC-P, the question remains whether this type of test is suitable for predicting the achievement potential of deaf children. These tests are nonverbal while the vast majority of school tasks demand verbal facility.

Be sure to note that, although intelligence testing of hearing handicapped children is difficult, the results of nonverbal testing indicate that hearing impaired children exhibit the same range of intelligence as normal children.

Assessment at an Early Age

Early identification of infants with hearing losses is essential if parent and infant are to be appropriately trained as quickly as possible. However, early identification has proved difficult. It would be ideal if screening were performed at the place of birth—usually a hospital where screening is possible. However, the mass screening devices now available are either too expensive to use or else identify too many children as having hearing losses who do not have such a loss. Recognizing these problems, many hospitals are establishing high-risk registries rather than conducting mass screenings. Lists of children with high risk of hearing loss are compiled. These children are observed over a period of time to determine if they really do have a hearing loss. Among the reasons a child might be placed in the registry are a history of maternal rubella during pregnancy, history of early deafness in the family, or difficult or prolonged delivery.

Identifying the child makes it possible to obtain educational, audiological, and medical services early. In large metropolitan communities, privately funded speech and hearing clinics generally provide educational and audiological services. Audiological services include testing the infant's hearing and making recommendations concerning the fitting and adjusting of a hearing aid. Educational services for the infant in the clinic or at home usually emphasize training parents to develop the child's communication skills—especially aural/oral skills and language. In some instances, the parents are instructed in sign language. Often parent counselling is included. Sometimes services are provided by the public school system, where identified hearing handicapped children may be immediately eligible for help. In general, however, public school services are not available until the youngster reaches the age of either 3 or 5 years. Under P.L. 94–142 a free, appropriate public education must be provided for all handicapped children, including the hearing handicapped, from age 3 through age 21.

Parents living in rural areas have more difficulty receiving services for infants with hearing impairments and frequently have to travel hundreds of miles to get help. One service that is available to these parents, however, is provided by the John Tracy Clinic in Los Angeles. The clinic sends a correspondence course to parents of hearing handicapped children. The course provides essential information concerning hearing loss in children and lessons in helping the hearing handicapped child develop aural/oral skills and language. Recently several states, including Utah and Washington, have taken as a state function the provision of home instruction, parent counseling, and (where appropriate) sign language instruction to parents of hearing impaired infants. Children receiving such early training should develop more adequate communication skills than those whose education is delayed to age 3 or beyond.

EDUCATIONAL PLACEMENT OPTIONS

Deaf students are educated in environments ranging from public and private self-contained residential schools to integrated resource rooms in schools for normal children. Placement of a deaf child in one or another of these settings often determines the cultural environment in which the child is raised, the friends and social contacts she has, the method of communication she uses, and the curriculum she follows.

Residential Schools

Most states maintain at least one public residential facility for deaf children. In 1975–76, 17,795 pupils were enrolled in residential schools (Karchmer & Trybus, 1977). Of this total, 80 to 85% lived at the schools; the remainder lived at home and attended on a day-school basis. Public residential schools for the deaf are generally self-contained, providing programs from preschool or elementary level through the secondary level. While in some schools pupils may go home each weekend, in others students live at the school for the entire academic year, going home only on major holidays and for summer vacation. Generally, students whose homes are in the immediate vicinity of the residential schools are served by the school as day pupils.

A residential facility provides several important advantages. Since deafness is a low-incidence handicap, a residential school draws together children from a large area with other children of similar age and ability. Usually a full schedule of extracurricular activities, such as sports within the

Missy, a profoundly deaf preschooler, comes with her mother to the John Tracy Clinic to work with a teacher and get ideas to carry through at home.

school and with other schools, clubs, scouting, and religious instruction, is available. There is a fairly large peer group, which allows the child wide selection of companions. Also, often some teachers and cottage parents are role models of deaf adults.

Private residential schools generally use the aural/oral method of communication. They provide all the advantages of public residential schools in addition to a structured program backed by many supportive professional services.

One disadvantage of residential placement is the child's limited relationship with the rest of her family, who she sees only rarely and who may treat her as a guest rather than as a family member. Another disadvantage is that students who live in a closely supervised institutional environment may not have the chance to develop independent living skills such as using public transportation, cooking, cleaning, and budgeting. Residential facilities also usually do not provide many opportunities for educational and social contacts with normally hearing children. The high cost of private school tuition, which in some cases is borne by the parents and in other cases by the state, is another disadvantage.

Day Schools

Public day schools for hearing handicapped children are usually located in urban or suburban areas and admit only hearing handicapped. Generally, little or no academic mix with hearing children is provided. Advantages of these facilities include the possibility of placing a child according to his age and grade or ability level, the likelihood of a sequential program with adequate teacher supervision, and maintaining close pupil contact with family and community. Some extracurricular activities might be provided by the school for the deaf child. He may also have the opportunity to participate in recreational activities with normal peers in his home community. In 1975–76, some 5,150 students were served in day schools (Karchmer & Trybus, 1977).

Day Classes

Public day classes refer to one or more self-contained or resource room classes for hearing impaired children, located on or adjacent to the campus of a public school for normal children. In 1975–76, public day class programs served 10,314 hearing impaired pupils (Karchmer & Trybus, 1977). *Public day class* may apply to one class of preschool children in a single school district or to a well-defined multiclass program for children aged 3 to 21, serving several school districts on a contractual basis. The nearness to normal children allows some academic and social integration. The opportunity to place a child in a hearing impaired class according to his age and grade or ability level varies with the size and philosophy of the program. In some smaller programs, one class serves children of a wide range of ages with a single teacher providing all education on an individualized basis. In larger systems there may be enough children to have graded classes at some or all age levels. Some programs go only up through the preschool, elementary, or junior high levels, with pupils either transferring to the state residential school or totally integrating into the regular schools when their program ends. The public day class option allows children to be served close to normally; all or most extracurricular activities would be with normal children.

In addition to these options, many systems operate special classes for multiply handicapped hearing impaired children. In the 1971–72 school year, schools and classes for the deaf reported that of 40,849 students surveyed, 10,452 had at least one additional handicap. Not included in that survey were hearing impaired children served in programs primarily for children with other handicaps.

COMMUNITY MANAGEMENT

Community management is designed to provide services to help hearing handicapped people be independent, self-supporting adults, suitably employed, with a fulfilling personal and social life. There is a large, loosely coordinated service system at local, state, and national levels. Various organizations provide services ranging

profile KAREN

Karen is a first child born in December, 1963, while her parents were on military duty in Germany. Karen was eagerly awaited by her parents and proved to be a happy, alert child who responded avidly to affection. From the time she could roll over, she was busy exploring her world with arms, hands, feet, and mouth. When Karen was 9 months old, the family returned to the United States and settled in a suburban community where her father, a skilled engineer, obtained an excellent position. It was anticipated that Karen would be moving frequently as her father worked his way up the corporate ladder.

Her mother began suspecting a problem when Karen showed no sign, at 10 months old, of babbling as her neighbor's child had done at 9 months. At this time Karen's worried mother took her to her pediatrician for a check-up. A preliminary check indicated that Karen had a moderate binaural sensori-neural hearing loss, probably congenital of unknown cause. Further testing confirmed the loss and Karen's mother, after a period of initial shock and disbelief, began exploring the resources available to them in the big city.

By 15 months of age, Karen had been evaluated at a speech and hearing clinic associated with a large university hospital and fitted with hearing aids for both ears. Both of her parents were enrolled in a training program, and Karen was being seen once a week by a home teacher to work on auditory training, language, and speech.

Karen's father's company was notified of her special needs; and since he was a valued employee, they agreed to let the family
remain at their present location for the duration of Karen's school years. In the city, public education for hearing impaired children was available from age 3 to 21. When she entered school, Karen had a nonverbal IQ of 122. Her speech, while not normal, was intelligible, and she had a substantial receptive vocabulary and was using two- and three-word sentences.*

Because of Karen's moderate hearing loss, she was taught by the aural-oral approach (see p. 306 for a description). Her mother made sure Karen had opportunity for social contacts with hearing children by enrolling her in church school and park department sponsored play camps. By this time, Karen had two younger siblings who were normally hearing. They chattered incessantly to Karen and anyone else who would listen.

Karen is now spending 3 hours every day in an integrated open-concept classroom for second and third graders. She is with other children for all nonacademic periods such as lunch, recess, art and music, and for arithmetic, social studies, and science. A special class teacher works with her 2 hours daily on language development, reading, auditory training, and speech.

Karen is well aware that she is hearing handicapped. While she has normally hearing friends, her very best friend is a hard-of-hearing girl about a year younger than herself. Karen's parents are trying to accept the fact that their daughter will grow up being a member of two societies—the world of the hearing and the world of the hearing impaired. It looks now as if they and their daughter will succeed.

from parent counseling and infant training through geriatric care. Local agencies provide basic services for hearing handicapped children and adults and their families.

There are speech and hearing centers in many large metropolitan areas. These facilities may operate independently or as a part of other public agencies such as universities or hospitals. They provide a wide range of services, including audiological evaluation, preschool and parent education, and lip-reading instruction for people who have lost their hearing as adults. Also some centers provide complete client evaluation, psychological counseling, training programs in living skills, vocational counseling and job placement, and instruction in oral and manual skills.

The state assumes primary responsibility for the education of hearing handicapped children of common school age. Recently,

FOR MORE SUPPORT

For the most part, these professional organizations do not supply direct services to hearing impaired persons. Rather these organizations function primarily to serve the needs of those who are providing services to the hearing impaired individuals.

Conference of American Instructors of the Deaf (CAID)

CAID is an organization for all persons engaged in teaching the hearing impaired. The CAID philosophy does not commit itself to any one particular method, stating as its motto: "Any method for best results; all methods, and wedded to none" (Council Membership Directory, 1971).

The American Annals of the Deaf *is the official publication of the Conference of American Instructors of the Deaf and the Conference of Executives of American Schools for the Deaf. The journal is published bimonthly, with the April issue being a comprehensive directory of programs and services for the deaf in the United States. The other issues contain reports of research and other articles of interest to educators of the hearing impaired.*

Conference of Executives of American Schools for the Deaf (CEASD)

The CEASD consists primarily of people in management positions in schools for the deaf. The stated purposes of the organization are to "promote the management and operation of schools for the deaf along the broadest and most efficient lines, to further and promote the welfare of the deaf, and to promote professional growth of all those who work closely with the deaf" (Council Membership Directory, 1971). CEASD and CAID publish the American Annals of the Deaf.

The Alexander Graham Bell Association for the Deaf

The A.G. Bell Association was organized in 1890 for the purposes of promoting "speech, speechreading, and the use of residual hearing" in the hearing impaired. Its membership is open to all those interested in "improving the education, professional and vocational opportunities for hearing-impaired persons." Organizations affiliated with the A.G. Bell Association are the International Parents' Organization (IPO), the Oral Deaf Adults Section (ODAS), and the American Organization for the Education of the Hearing Impaired (AOEHI).

The official publication of the A.G. Bell Association is the Volta Review. *Typical contents include research articles, news notes of ODAS and IPO, and informational articles for parents and teachers.*

Council on Education of the Deaf

The Council on Education of the Deaf is an umbrella organization whose membership consists of professional organizations concerned with deaf children. CED has de-

most rehabilitation services have been provided jointly through state and federal rehabilitation programs. The purpose of the state programs, as stated by the Vocational Rehabilitation Administration (which is part of the Department of Health, Education and Welfare), is to "rehabilitate to employment people with mental or physical disabilities. The programs correct or reduce the handicapping effects of disability, provide training, and help the disabled person find the right job" ("Opportunities for the hard of hearing and the deaf," n.d.). Most services provided by state rehabilitation agencies are free. They include individual counseling and guidance; medical, surgical, hospital, or other services needed to lessen or correct handicapping conditions; training for employment; living expenses and transportation during the training period; placement in a suitable job; and follow-up to ensure satisfaction on the part of both the em-

termined national certification standards for teachers of the hearing impaired and monitors ongoing teacher education programs to assure their compliance with certification standards.

The Deaf Community

As adults, most deaf persons become part of what is known as the deaf community. While deaf adults generally have jobs within the hearing community, their social life tends to be centered around other deaf persons. Usually deaf persons marry one another, belong to clubs for deaf persons, and have as their social group other deaf people.

At the present time, there appears to be a growing political awareness among members of the deaf community. Hearing impaired adults are no longer content to have the "experts" make all the educational and legislative decisions. As a result, the organizations for the hearing handicapped adult have attained a more prominent position than they had had. Hearing handicapped adults now insist that they should be part of committees and organizations that make decisions affecting the lives of hearing-impaired persons, including the right to have a voice in educational decisions affecting hearing impaired children.

National Association of the Deaf

One of the most prominent organizations nationally is the National Association of the Deaf (NAD). NAD states that it is "the only national civic organization run solely by and for the deaf." The purpose of the NAD is to insure that "the rights and privileges of citizenship are maintained for the deaf" (Council Membership Directory, 1971). To carry out its purpose, NAD supports research concerning the deaf, studies social problems of the hearing handicapped, and investigates ways for working with all agencies associated with hearing handicapped persons. Moreover, NAD states that it "seeks to provide parents, employers, and others with realistic truths about deafness by people who, themselves, have lived with it."

NAD issues three publications, the Deaf American on a monthly basis, the NAD Newsletter, bimonthly, and the Junior Deaf American, quarterly.

Religious Organizations Serving the Deaf

There are several religious groups throughout the United States that have as their primary purpose meeting the "spiritual, moral, social, and cultural needs of the deaf and hearing handicapped." Among these organizations are the Board for Missions, Ministry to the Deaf, the Lutheran Church-Missouri Synod; the Department of Urban Ministries, the Board of Missions, the United Methodist Church; the Ephphatha Missions for the Deaf and Blind; the Episcopal Conference of the Deaf; the International Catholic Deaf Association;

ployer and employee. Some rehabilitation services have also been made available through other agencies, such as local welfare departments.

GOALS AND OBJECTIVES FOR HEARING HANDICAPPED STUDENTS

Educational goals for hearing handicapped students have traditionally been based on normalization; the emphasis was on language, speech reading, and speech training so that the child would be prepared for entry into the "normal" world. Curricula in areas such as mathematics, social studies, and science generally paralleled regular classes. Frequently the same tests with the same goals were used. However, because most hearing handicapped children are de-

ficient in language, their education could only be a weak version of regular curricula. A survey by the Advisory Committee on the Education of the Deaf (1964) indicated that the average achievement level of students completing secondary level programs was below the seventh grade.

Recently, however, there has been a move to develop special curricula for hearing handicapped students. These have the primary goal of developing in each student the competencies needed for independent fuctioning as an adult. It is now recognized that many hearing handicapped adults live in two societies. Their vocational lives are spent in the hearing world of competitive industry, but most of them rely on other hearing handicapped adults for a great portion of their social and emotional interactions. Education of hearing impaired chil-

and the National Congress of Jewish Deaf (NCJD).

The services provided by the individual organizations vary. However, many strive to provide religious services for the hearing handicapped members of their congregations, usually using manual communication. Several of the organizations provide publications for their hearing impaired members. Among these are The Deaf Catholic and the NCJD Quarterly.

Registry of Interpreters for the Deaf

RID was formed to encourage persons capable of being interpreters to serve in that position and to raise the function of interpreters to professional status. RID also has as its goals to "put into existence a developed body of knowledge, a list of specific skills to be attained and a formal means of evaluating or certifying such skills" (Council Membership Directory, 1971).

As hearing handicapped adults have attempted to gain a more active position in

official decision-making concerning themselves, the function of the membership of RID has changed from merely interpreting the hearing world to the hearing impaired. Members are more and more frequently being asked to help the hearing world understand the world of the hearing impaired.

Media Services for the Handicapped

Media Services for the Handicapped, a part of the Bureau for Education of the Handicapped, provides many services for deaf clients. These include captioned educational and recreational films for deaf adults and children which are available free to eligible groups. Media Services also sponsors workshops on media production and use for professionals in the field. Media Services is currently pioneering work in closed captioning for TV programs so that the deaf, by using a special decoder attached to their set, will be able to receive captions for many commercial and PBS TV broadcasts, as well as captioned news broadcasts and notification in case of emergencies.

Using a telephone independently is as important to a deaf teenager like Nancy as to any other 14-year-old (see the color close-up of Nancy's phone).

dren can now be aimed at promoting each child's skills and attitudes for maximum flexibility in selecting the society to which he wants to belong.

Goals listed here reflect those basic, minimum competencies needed by hearing handicapped adults to function independently. The maximum goals would be identical to those for a normally hearing person, perhaps with the addition of knowing some form of manual communication to allow the handicapped person to converse freely with deaf peers.

Communication

A hearing handicapped person should have sufficient command of English to:

1. identify her needs and express them to other nonhearing handicapped speakers of English, either through a written or spoken communication;

2. correctly interpret written or spoken communication directed to her by nonhearing handicapped persons;

3. correctly interpret common written materials such as newspapers, signs, and maps; to achieve minimal literacy.

Social Skills

Since most social skills, mores, and folkways of society are transmitted by people communicating with one another, people with hearing problems learn appropriate social behaviors only if they are deliberately sequenced into the curriculum. Minimally, a hearing handicapped person should be able to:

1. behave appropriately, according to the norms of society, in all common social settings;

2. interpret correctly the actions and motivations of people around her;

3. function as a full citizen of her community, state, and country.

Vocational Skills

Many skills and attitudes necessary for vocational success are transmitted through language. Therefore, for hearing-impaired, language-handicapped children, these skills must be incorporated into the curriculum. Minimally, a hearing handicapped person should be able to:

1. function independently as an adult by assuming overall responsibility for her conduct;

2. have sufficient vocational skills to enable her to obtain and keep employment.

Cognitive Development

Language is an essential tool for developing concepts and solving problems. A person with normal hearing may define a problem and then try to think of all the possible answers. He might discuss the alternatives with someone else. But the hearing handicapped person, not having as many terms or as complete an understanding of certain concepts, may not have enough information to develop adequate problem-solving skills. Lacking information, she may choose a poor solution repeatedly, even if it had proved unsatisfactory before. Therefore, any curriculum for the hearing handicapped should include problem-solving skills. As a minimum, the hearing handicapped individual should be able to:

1. acquire enough information to be able to arrive at a reasonable and rational solution to a problem;

2. make a choice by comparing alternatives and predicting their possible consequences.

MODES OF COMMUNICATION

In the United States there has been an ongoing debate between educators of deaf children who advocate the use of some form of manual communication along with speech (the **manualists**) and those who oppose the use of any form of communica-

tion except speech (the **oralists**). This conflict began almost with the first efforts to educate hearing handicapped children during the Renaissance. Differing circumstances have determined which method has been used where, but the arguments supporting each method have not substantially changed during the last 300 years. The controversy has both pragmatic and moral bases.

Oralists believe that deaf children should aspire to become as normal as possible and to be integrated into the hearing society. To do this requires the deaf person to speak and read lips. These skills are hard to learn; and, according to the oralists, if the child is given the choice of an easier, manual, form of communication, he will select that and never develop his oral communication skills.

Manualists believe that deaf people should not be faced with the impossible goal of becoming normal. Rather, they should be given the communication skills necessary to live in the deaf social subculture as well as the hearing world of work. Further, they believe that the enormous amount of time spent in teaching young deaf children to talk could be much more usefully spent in teaching them language skills and reading, areas in which the deaf have traditionally been deficient.

The Aural/Oral Approach

The aural/oral approach (Simmons-Martin, 1972) stresses the primary reception of language through the auditory channel, through the use of amplification prescribed for each person. Reception of sound through the defective auditory mechanism is aided by speech reading, the use of taction to decode speech, and the development of a kinesthetic feedback system for self-monitoring of speech. Children are taught to speak using analytic and synthetic approaches. Reading and writing are introduced as additional approaches to acquiring language. Underlying the aural/oral approach is the philosophy that it is desirable to totally integrate a hearing impaired child into normal society, that auditory reception of language and speaking ability are vital. This approach says that alternative modes of communication such as fingerspelling or sign language are crutches which get in the way of normalization.

Auditory Training

In almost all cases of hearing impairment, the loss is less than total; that is, some amount of residual hearing at one or more frequencies remains. This residual hearing, if appropriately amplified, may be used as

Chrissy's school uses a strictly oral approach. Jane is covering her mouth with a card to prevent Chrissy from lip reading, to force her to use her residual hearing.

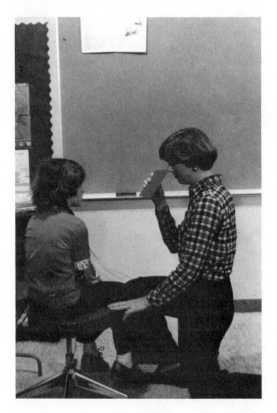

an aid in receiving and producing speech. An individualized program of auditory training is considered basic to the success of oral education. Children are taken through an instructional sequence which begins with recognizing the environmental and nonspeech sounds such as animal noises, musical tones, and sounds made by mechanical objects such as doorbells, train whistles, and jet engines. It culminates in the ability to discriminate words such as *pet* and *bed* through the auditory sense alone and to discriminate features such as stress and phrasing.

Speech Reading

Since hearing handicapped children cannot receive all necessary information via the auditory channel, speech reading is used to supplement auditory input. Speech reading has been defined as "the correct identification of . . . thoughts transmitted via the visual components of oral discourse" (O'Neill & Oyer, 1961). Speech reading is complicated because some sounds, called *homophonous sounds* (Jeffers & Barley, 1971), look alike on the lips. Examples include /p/, /b/, and /m/; /t/, /d/, and /n/; and /s/ and /z/. Another complication is that many speech sounds are hard to see. Jeffers and Barley (1971) estimate that when the speaker is talking naturally and making no attempt to produce highly visible speech, the viewer usually gains approximately 20% of the information he would gain if he could hear.

Two methods have been used in lipreading instruction. The analytic method teaches the student how each sound appears on the lips and asks him to identify each individual sound. The synthetic method instructs the student to attempt to determine as many words as possible in a spoken message and then fill in the words he did not understand through his linguistic competency and through his knowledge of the subject being discussed. Many teachers combine both the analytic and synthetic methods in speech-reading instruction.

Taction and Kinesthetic Feedback

Some information unavailable through speech reading may be obtained by feeling the movements of a speaker (taction). By feeling the cheek and nose of the speaker, you receive information on how the sound is made, for example, whether it is voiced, unvoiced, or voiced-nasal. While taction, combined with audition and speech reading, is useful for speech teaching in a classroom situation, it is not generally used to acquire information in social situations.

Normal individuals actually monitor the speech they produce—for correct articulation, volume, and pitch. This is possible because a small amount of the speech sound is returned to the auditory system of the speaker (this process is called an *auditory feedback loop*). A hearing impaired individual must substitute a kinesthetic awareness of the feel of the speech mechanism to correct her own speech pro-

duction. That is, the major feedback mechanism available to the hearing handicapped is the internal feeling of her own movements.

Manual Communication Methods

Manual communication uses sight to allow the receiving and sending of messages by manipulating the fingers, arms, and upper torso. Thus, the defective auditory-vocal channel is bypassed in favor of the intact visual-motor system. Those who believe in these approaches feel that general communication rather than any one form of language competence should be the goal for hearing handicapped children.

Fingerspelling

Fingerspelling is the use of the one-handed manual alphabet to form symbols for each letter of the English language, the ordinal numbers, and some punctuation. Finger positions are discrete and may be easily learned (see Figure 11.4). After having mastered the code, a person may send and receive any message that can be written.

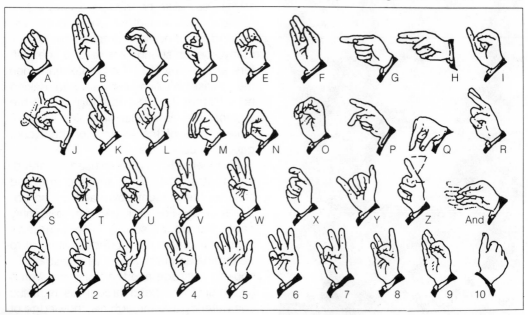

Figure 11.4
The fingerspelling code

An expert in fingerspelling can send and receive spelled messages at or near the speed of normal oral communication. A method referred to as the *Rochester Method,* for its origin at the Rochester, New York, School for the Deaf in 1878 (The Rochester Method, 1972; Scouten, 1964), uses fingerspelling simultaneously with speech in the education of hearing handicapped children. Fingerspelled words do not present the ambiguities of lip reading.

American Sign Language (ASL)

American Sign Language (ASL) is a manual communication system in which the fingers, hands, arms, and upper torso are used in rapid communication of ideas. American Sign Language, with several thousand signs, has a unique syntax (Bergman, 1972) which usually leaves out definite and indefinite articles, prepositions, forms of the verb *be,* participles, and cases. To some extent, verb tenses are also omitted. While ASL is the communication system most often used in the adult deaf community and appears to be adequate as a communication system, many educators do not consider it suitable for use with school-age children because of its syntactic difference from English, which might interfere with learning reading and writing.

Manual English

Within the past 10 years, as interest increased in sign language systems, a number of new, modified sign systems have been established which supplement and attempt to correct the deficiencies of ASL as a teaching method. ASL is seen as deficient in two ways in conveying the English language. First, its syntax does not at all correspond with that of English; second, its limited vocabulary does not permit full expression of the nuances of English meaning—For example, the words *hotdog, frankfurter, wiener,* and *knockwurst,* which all have slightly different meanings in English, share one common sign in ASL.

Though she attends a regular junior high, Nancy meets with a tutor to work on language skills and manual communication.

Manual English uses many of the signs of ASL and adds signs for inflectional endings, pronouns, articles, and other structural elements. However, manual English does sign by ideas—as does ASL—rather than by morphemes (see chapter 10). Other forms of Manual English such as Signing Exact English (SEE) (Gustason, Pfetzing, & Zawolkow, 1972) use signs by morphemes rather than by ideas. In selecting a SEE sign, the spelling, sound, and meaning of a word are considered. If any two of these are the same, the words are signed the same. Thus the word *right* in "turn right," "right to life," and "right answer" would be signed the same, but *write* and *rite* would be signed differently, for a total of three signs. In ASL and Manual English five different signs would be used for the five ideas. In all Manual English systems signs are modified, usually by the fingerspelling position of the hand(s), to allow for expression of synonyms.

Total Communication

The most major change in education of the hearing handicapped in the United States within the last 10 years has been combining the aural/oral approach with manual communication to form total communication. Garretson (1976) states that the term *total communication* as applied to the education of deaf children originated in the late 1960s with Roy Holcomb, a deaf teacher of the hearing handicapped who is himself the parent of two deaf children. Advocates of this approach believe that any and all means of communicating with a hearing impaired child should be used as early as possible. The goal is not to establish a specific language system but to establish basic communication pathways as quickly and efficiently as possible. In practice, total communication uses primarily auditory training, speech reading, fingerspelling, variations of the language of signs (usually SEE or Manual English), reading, and writing as ways of communicating. Advocates of total communication share the philosophy that it is the "moral right of the hearing impaired, as with normally hearing bilinguals, to maximal input in order to attain optimal comprehension and total understanding in the communication situation" (Garretson, 1976, p. 89).

Language

Severely hearing handicapped children rarely learn the English language communication system correctly. There are some serious problems in evaluating a deaf child's receptive and expressive language, but with the kinds of measures that have been used it is quite clear that most prelingually profoundly hearing impaired children have serious deficiencies in their knowledge of the English language. (Chapters 4 and 10 deal with language development, language disorders, and the effects of language disorders in much more detail.)

Only recently have young hearing handicapped children had formal instruction in the use of some kind of manual language. It is not yet known whether this instruction will in fact aid a child in the process of acquiring English, although there are some indications that children with early exposure to

a manual language do acquire English faster than those who are taught by the oral approach alone (Quigley, 1969).

Some professionals feel that even if a child does not acquire English, he should be allowed to acquire some language system. Exposure to some type of manual language may in fact help the child acquire a language early in life, giving him a means of getting needed information and communicating with others.

Language Instruction

It has long been known that the prelingually hearing impaired child does not acquire language in a normal way. Educators of the deaf have attempted to remedy language deficits through intensive programs of formal language instruction. There are two primary methods of language instruction: one historically known as the *grammatical method* and the other known as the natural language method (Miller, 1964).

The grammatical method. The underlying theory of the grammatical method is that since hearing handicapped children have been deprived of the opportunity to learn language naturally, another method must be used. The grammatical method teaches language by presenting children with specific grammatical rules for putting sentences together and then having them construct sentences using those rules.

The most widely used grammatical approach is based on *Straight Language for the Deaf* by Edith Fitzgerald (1937). A key—a linear representation of sentence patterns—is used to establish grammatical language. Children learn the parts of speech, represented as headings on the key, and are taught to visualize the grammatical relationships between words, phrases, and clauses (*Language*, 1972). Beginning steps in building the key are classifications of nouns under the key headings of "who" and "what." Later, words and phrase classifications include such key headings as "whose," "from," "how much," and "when." Symbols are used to designate parts of speech for which there are no simple question words. When sentences are taught, the words of a sentence are written in sequence under their key headings. Thus the sentence "John saw the dog" would be written under the key headings "Who = What" (" = " is the key symbol for a verb).

Recently language instruction curricula have been developed which use rules based on transformational grammar rather than more traditional grammatical systems.

> Transformational grammar is based upon a series of rules or a set of directions for producing or generating sentences. The term *transformational* refers to the division of American English sentences into two classifications: (1) basic sentences and (2) the transforms, or variations, of these basic sentences. The basic or kernel sentence is composed of two parts, the noun phrase and the verb phrase. (Lamb, 1977, p. 100).

Sentences can be diagrammed to show how the one-word noun and verb phrases make up the sentence. One transformational grammar curriculum is that of James McCarr (1973).

The natural method. Advocates of the natural language method do not feel that children can learn language by being taught its rules. They feel that hearing handicapped children should learn language by going through the same procedures as normal children; that is, through the process of formulating hypotheses and testing them.

"Natural language" programs generally use the most up-to-date sequence of language development for normal children. They have been called the *mother's method,"* and have been advocated by such educators as Buell (1954), Groht (1958), and Van Uden (1970). Language constructions and new vocabulary are used extensively in natural, meaningful situations. The situations may still be carefully structured; but the grammatical structure to be acquired is in the mind of the

When Jamie is not in class, her mother works with her to get her to listen. Living with a deaf child means constantly "feeding" language to her.

teacher, and the child is not consciously aware of it (Hart, 1964).

RESEARCH

Measuring Receptive Language

Before sign language systems were accepted in the schools, when lipreading was the primary mode of communication, it was very difficult to assess a child's knowledge of receptive language. It was impossible to determine whether a student's inaccurate response to a task was because of an inadequate knowledge of English or poor lipreading skills. Assessments were made by checking the performance of hearing handicapped children on standardized achievment tests.

It was also difficult to evaluate the expressive language of these children because the speech of hearing handicapped children is frequently difficult to understand. While it is usually possible to understand in general what a child is trying to say, it is not possible to record precisely the individual morphemes the child uses. As a result, nearly all expressive language development studies were based on writing behaviors. Admittedly this is an inadequate measure of true performance level.

Results of studies such as those of Heider and Heider (1940), Templin (1950), Simmons (1962), Myklebust (1964), Fusfeld (1965), and Quigley, Wilbur, Power, Montanelli, and Steinkamp (1976) indicate that the written language of deaf children is, in general, inferior to that of normally hearing children of similar chronological age. Considering quantity, deaf children tend to write shorter sentences than normal children. As to quality, their productions tend to be less complex, less flexible, more stereotyped, more inclined to include fixed repetitive phrases, and less grammatically correct than those of their normally hearing peers. Simmons (1962) and Myklebust (1964) found many nouns and verbs and relatively few pronouns, prepositions, adverbs, adjectives, and conjunctions in the samples.

These studies, while providing clues as to what the deaf child was not doing, gave little insight into the processes that the child was using to produce language.

Sign Language and Nonverbal Communication Systems

Until recently, there has been little examination of sign language *as a language.* In fact, sign language was not considered a language separate from English (Bloomfield, 1933); it was just another means of expressing English just as writing is a means of expressing English. The conclusions drawn from this point of view were that differences between English and American Sign Language were the result of signers having an inadequate understanding of English. However, work by Stokoe (1958) and later by researchers such as Bellugi and Fischer (1972) has shown that American Sign Language is a distinct language and not just an inadequate representation of English. A considerable amount of research is now being done to try to describe the linguistic features of ASL.

Research is also being carried out to describe the features of sign language systems used in other countries (for instance, see Dyer, 1976). And linguists have been interested in describing systems that use gestures developed by hearing handicapped people when they are not exposed to sign language and the systems the hearing handicapped use to communicate with each other when they are native speakers of two different sign language systems (Battison & Jordan, 1976).

With the acceptance of sign language in the educational setting, language acquisition studies have analyzed hearing handicapped children's expressive and receptive signing skills. These studies are more accurate and can provide information about the hearing handicapped child's process of language acquisition from the earliest stages. Limited studies have indicated that the stages of development in sign language acquisition are similar to the stages of normal language acquisition—at least in the earliest stages (Schlesinger & Meadow, 1972). Both the process and content of language acquisition appear to be similar when comparing the early expressive language of normal children and hearing handicapped children using sign language (Bellugi & Klima, 1972). There is even some evidence that young hearing handicapped children who are not exposed to sign language develop gestural systems in which the similarities expressed are, at least in the early stages, similar to those semantic relationships of both hearing and signing children (Goldin-Meadow & Feldman, 1975). Work is now in progress concerning the later stages of language development of the hearing impaired.

Social Development

There are drawbacks to studies on the social development of hearing handicapped children. Most studies have compared the behaviors of hearing impaired children with those of hearing children. A major weakness is that the instruments generally used to evaluate social development after the children reach a certain age are based partly on language behaviors. This factor makes the instruments less accurate with hearing impaired children.

Another confounding factor is that behaviors which may appear to be immature in a hearing person may not be immature in the same sense for a hearing handicapped person. For example, fairly early in life hearing children may verbally express anger or hostility toward another child. The hearing handicapped child, who may feel the same anger or hostility, does not have the same verbal tools as the hearing child—and these verbal tools would not be as effective for hearing handicapped recipients. Thus, the hearing impaired child, who may resort to some physical behavior such as shoving to express anger, might be considered immature.

Another drawback to studies using hearing handicapped children is that, in the past at least, a large segment of hearing handicapped school-age children were in residential schools. It is difficult for observers to determine the effect of institutionalization on the children's behavior.

A lot of information concerning social development comes from informal observations of hearing handicapped children (John Tracy Clinic). Studies that have been done do not agree whether the hearing impaired child shows different social development patterns than the hearing person. For example, a study conducted by Bradway (1937) concluded that the 6-to-7-year-old child is socially retarded by 1 year and 9 months. However, a study conducted by Springer (1938) using the *Haggerty-Olsen-Wichman Behavior Schedules* indicated that hearing handicapped children of this age differ very little from their hearing peers in terms of social behavior. Myklebust (1964), using the *Vineland Social Maturity Scale* with children who were 9 to 10 years old, found that hearing handicapped children were ap-

proximately 10% inferior to the hearing group, falling in the lower limits of normal in the social quotient.

A study by Bobrove reported in Research Trends in Deafness (1970) indicated that the social adjustment of deaf adolescents compared favorably with that of hearing adolescents. There did appear to be some adjustment problems for hard-of-hearing adolescents as they scored lower on the measures used to evaluate adjustment.

If a hearing handicapped person is to realize his full potential as an adult, educators need to be well-informed of his social development problems. But at this point, research cannot provide the educator with the kinds of information needed.

Cognitive Development

Some investigators of cognitive development feel that studying the hearing impaired can provide information about the relationship between cognitive development and language. Because of the very low reading level found in studies of the hearing handicapped, they are sometimes regarded as language deficient.

There have been no significant differences found between the performance of the hearing handicapped and of normal populations on most tests of cognitive functioning, although some slight differences—particularly for younger people—have been found. Moreover, there is no consistent pattern to explain why there are differences on some tests but not others, although Furth (1966) feels there is some evidence associating inferior performance with tasks which require the discovery of a principle. Furth attributes this to the drill-like educational methods used with the hearing handicapped. Furth, and other investigators who consider the hearing handicapped to be language-deprived, conclude, therefore, that language does not play an important role in cognitive development.

However, as Blank (1965) has pointed out, there is some question about considering the hearing handicapped a nonlanguage group. Young hearing impaired children, even when taught in oral programs, develop a system of gestures to communicate with each other. Tervoort (1961) suggests that, while this gesture system might vary from one situation to another, it is still capable of providing language symbols for words like *big* and *two* and opportunities for experience with these concepts.

Most children who are not successful in oral programs are usually placed into programs with a manual component so that, by the time a child reaches high school, he has at least been exposed to a manual language and has probably begun acquiring it. Therefore, it is questionable whether the hearing handicapped can be considered a nonlanguage group for the purposes of examining the relationship between language and cognitive development. To adequately explore this relationship, the language characteristics of the hearing handicapped populations being studied must be carefully determined.

INSTRUCTIONAL PROCEDURES AND PROGRAMS

Elementary Education

Class Size
Usually a class of severely hearing handicapped children is limited in size to five to

seven children. Because communication is limited to the range of vision of a particular child, the child must be able to see every child in the classroom easily and as soon as communication has begun. With many children in a room, it is difficult for the hearing impaired child to follow communication interactions as the interchange moves from one student to another. The primary goal in a class for the hearing handicapped is to develop communication skills. If the child is in a large class, she has relatively little opportunity to practice her communication skills with the teacher. This would decrease the opportunities she has to go through the process of hypothesis formation and testing needed to develop language.

Room Arrangement
An appropriate class arrangement is essential because of the visual requirements for communication. Each child must be seated so she easily can see both the instructor and all the other children. The usual arrangement is to place the children in a semicircle, with the teacher facing them so that no child sits with her back to windows. The teacher and children also sit fairly close to one another to help the speech-reading process.

Auditory Training Systems
Many classrooms for hearing handicapped children are equipped with auditory training systems. The systems were designed to provide the hearing impaired child in the classroom with high quality amplification across the range of frequencies necessary for speech reception. There are basically four types of auditory-training systems. They are hardwire, portable desk trainer, loop induction (magnetic and radio frequency—RF), and FM-radio frequency.

These four youngsters, their teacher, and a master teacher comprise one class in this oralist school.

Hardwire trainers. The hardware, or conventional group aid, consists of an audio power amplifier with many earphone sets connected to it. The earphones are wired to control units on each child's desk and permit individual adjustment of the volume controls. The teacher's microphone is connected to an amplifier which also is wired to each child's desk. The hardwire system is not popular with most teachers because it restricts the movement of the children and teacher.

Portable desk trainers. Portable desk trainers are units which can be hand carried, allowing the student greater freedom within the classroom. This trainer is similar to a hearing aid in that it picks up environmental sounds and is subject to varying sound pressure levels, depending on the child's physical location in relation to the teacher.

Loop induction system. The audio induction loop system consists of a wire placed around the classroom with an audio signal from an electronic amplifier passing into the loop. The electric current flowing through the wire loop creates a magnetic field within the room. The student uses her own hearing aid by switching to the telephone position, which allows the hearing aid to pick up the magnetic signals and convert them into sound. The induction loop provides the child freedom of movement within the area enclosed by the loop.

FM radio frequency system. The wireless FM radio frequency system consists of a teacher's microphone FM transmitter which broadcasts directly on frequency modulated or FM carrier waves to the child's and trainer's FM receivers. The acoustic energy is converted to electrical energy and then back to acoustic energy. The system provides complete freedom to the teacher and students, both inside and outside the classroom.

In addition to the amplification equipment, many classrooms also have other teaching aids. Most classrooms for the hearing handicapped have overhead projectors provided by federal funds through Captioned Films for the Deaf, now expanded to Media Services for the Handicapped. Many educators consider it important to have an overhead projector available. It allows the teacher to provide visual input to his students without having to turn his back to them as he would if he were using a chalkboard.

Other equipment available in many classrooms includes 16 mm projectors, slide or filmstrip projectors, and filmstrips. Other specialized equipment might include a Language Master tape recorder, record player, and auditory training equipment such as percussion instruments and pianos.

Secondary Education

Both regular and residential programs realize that the students will soon be entering the adult world. Some students in both residential and day programs will attend college. Students in secondary day programs frequently attend regular classes with the intention of preparing themselves for a college for normally hearing students. These students, and those who plan to continue in vocational education, are sometimes assisted by the use of either an interpreter or a note-taker in the classroom. Most hearing handicapped students are helped by a teacher of the hearing handicapped who may either tutor them or give instruction in those areas in which they are not able to participate in the regular classroom. Some residential schools usually provide precollege and prevocational and vocational training within the residential campus. Other programs place their students in actual work sites in the community to provide them with more adequate vocational preparation.

Postsecondary Institutions

Gallaudet College was founded in 1864 to provide higher education opportunities for the hearing handicapped. Located in

Washington, D.C., Gallaudet receives its funds from the federal government. It provides a 4-year, liberal arts program with majors in 20 different areas, ranging from social philosophy to physical education. Total communication is used in all classes. Personal and social counseling, speech and hearing therapy, vocational placement services, and manual communication training are available. A preparatory remedial precollege program is available for students who are admitted with deficiencies in academic skills.

However, many deaf students do not qualify for admission to Gallaudet College. And Gallaudet's curriculum, for the most part, is limited to those areas generally offered in a liberal arts college. As a result, the National Technical Institute for the Deaf (NTID) was established as part of the Rochester Institute of Technology in Rochester, New York. The first class of students was enrolled in 1968.

The major objective of NTID is to provide qualified deaf students with technical education in science, business, engineering, and applied arts, leading to well-paying and satisfying jobs. This objective is accomplished through a combination of the regular classes at NTID along with many supportive services, including tutoring and counseling, note-taking, and interpreting. A second objective of NTID is to determine methods appropriate for teaching hearing handicapped adults.

Other vocational-technical education programs at the community college level have developed within the last 10 years. These programs are exploring the feasibility of providing vocational-technical instruction to the hearing impaired at the community college level. Typically these programs start with a preparatory program, which gives students an opportunity to explore the programs offered by the community college as well as to improve their basic skills. The student then selects a training program. The special services provided by the community college include interpreters, note-takers, tutors, and counselors.

TEACHERS OF THE HEARING HANDICAPPED

All teachers need certain knowledge and skills. However, there are some areas of expertise that must be acquired by teachers of hearing handicapped students that are unique to them.

Knowledge of the Speech and Hearing Mechanisms

To be able to correctly diagnose and prescribe programs for their students, a teacher of hearing impaired children must have a comprehensive knowledge of the structure of the speech and hearing mechanisms and diagnostic procedures related to speech and hearing processes. The teacher should be able to interpret audiological and medical information in terms of expected performance.

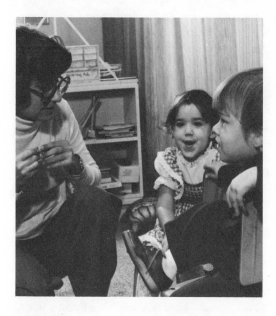

Before beginning instruction every day, Linda and Sean check the battery in his hearing aid. Jamie's have already been checked.

Developmental Areas

Because hearing loss has such serious effects on development, it is imperative that the teacher be well-informed about the effects of hearing loss, particularly in the areas of communication, academics, social and vocational growth, and assessment procedures. From assessment information, the teacher should be able to develop acceptable goals and objectives, keeping in mind the long- and short-term needs of each student.

Once the teacher has selected the goals and objectives for each program, he must either design or adapt a program to fit those goals. Often the teacher should develop his own materials, as it is difficult to find materials that fit both the needs and skill levels of the students.

Manual Communication

Every teacher who works with hearing handicapped children in a total communication setting must have proficiency in the sign language system used by his program. Moreover, his skills in sign language should be such that he can communicate easily with hearing impaired adults.

Classroom Management

The teacher must have a repertoire of behavioral management systems which can be used with hearing handicapped children. (See chapter 1 for a discussion of systematic instruction.) The teacher also needs to develop skills in organizing her classroom for maximum use of time and space. Even with such a small class, the children are by no means uniform in their levels of achievement. Therefore, the teacher must develop a wide range of individual or very small group programs for the students. Scheduling can most effectively be done with instructional assistants, teacher aides, and volunteer assistance.

Professional Setting

These teachers must be prepared to work in a variety of administrative arrangements ranging from a regular public school setting with extensive mainstreaming to a residential school which provides only for self-contained classrooms.

As in other areas of special education, the teacher of the hearing impaired must work as part of an interdisciplinary team, using information provided by psychologists, audiologists, otologists, speech therapists, and other specialists.

Skills Outside the Classroom

The teacher must be able to relate effectively to the parents of his students, provid-

---

MEETING SPECIAL NEEDS

Integrating the hearing handicapped into regular classes

Many professionals think that placing hearing handicapped children in classes for normal children is beneficial both academically and socially. Hearing handicapped children should be integrated for a specific subject area only if they are at approximately the same chronological age, mental age, and grade level as the class they enter, and if there is an individualized educational program as prescribed by P.L. 94–142. The child, his parents, special education personnel, and other professionals who have been involved in the child's assessment must be consulted before the child is placed, and provision for repeated follow-up should be made. Children with mild hearing losses or excellent language skills may spend a major part or all day in regular classes, perhaps receiving additional help through speech therapy or academic tutoring. More profoundly affected children, whose primary enrollment is in a special class or resource room, may be integrated for some specific academic subject areas or for social contact during nonacademic periods.

Using the following guidelines should help the teacher deal with the hearing handicapped child, while making only minimal adaptations of regular classroom procedures.

1. Seat the child where he can see your lip movements easily. Avoid seating him facing bright lights or windows.

2. Speak naturally, in complete grammatical sentences. Do not overemphasize lip movements or slow your rate of speech. Do not speak too loudly, especially if the child is wearing a hearing aid.

3. Avoid visual distractions such as excessive make-up and jewelry that would draw attention away from your lips.

4. Do not stand with your back to a window or bright light source. This throws your face in a shadow and makes speech reading difficult.

5. Try not to move around the room while speaking or to talk while writing on the

ing them with necessary support but with the understanding that he is a teacher and not a counselor.

The teacher should have extensive knowledge of the resources available to the hearing impaired child and her family. Also, the teacher should have an up-to-date knowledge of state and federal laws and rules and regulations that apply to handicapped persons and to teaching the handicapped (again, see chapter 1).

One of the most crucial skills the teacher needs is the ability to relate effectively to hearing handicapped adults. The teacher may have a great deal of difficulty selecting appropriate educational goals for his students if he is not familiar with the situations his students are likely to face as an adult. Much of this information can be obtained only through a great deal of social and professional interaction with deaf adults.

board. If possible, use an overhead projector, which allows you to speak and write while keeping eye contact with the children.

6. During class discussions encourage the hearing handicapped child to face the speaker. Allow him to move around the room if necessary to get a better view.

7. In some cases, a manual interpreter will be assigned to the child. Allow the interpreter and child to select the most favorable seating arrangements. The manual interpreter should interpret everything said in the classroom as precisely as possible. The interpreter may also be asked to interpret the child's oral or signed responses to the teacher and class. Interpreters are not tutors or classroom aides but rather professional personnel who are facilitators of classroom communication.

8. When possible, write assignments and directions on the chalkboard or distribute

mimeographed directions to the class. If assignments are given orally, a hearing student may be asked to take notes for the hearing handicapped child.

9. Ask the handicapped child to repeat or explain class material to make sure he has understood it. Embarrassed by his handicap, a hearing impaired child might learn to nod affirmatively when asked if he understood, even though he may not have understood the instructions at all.

10. If the child has a hearing aid, familiarize yourself with its operation and ask the child or his special teacher to demonstrate it to the class. The child should assume responsibility for the care of his aid.

11. Maintain close contact with the other professional personnel who have responsibility for the child's education. If possible, regularly exchange visits with the special class teacher or therapist to observe the child in his other educational settings.

Chapter eleven

FOR MORE INFORMATION

Most of these resources are textbooks that are readily available. Check your instructor, the education library, or the general library at your school.

Furth, H.G. *Deafness and learning: A psychosocial approach.* Belmont, Calif.: Wadsworth, 1973.

Newby, H.A. *Audiology* (3rd ed.). Englewood Cliffs, N.J.: Prentice-Hall, 1972.

12

The Visually Handicapped

Richard M. DeMott

These are the major topics covered in this chapter. You may want to use them as a checklist when you review.

- *Developmental delays frequently observed in children who are born blind.*
- *Alternative plans for educating visually handicapped children.*
- *Areas of current emphasis in the education of the visually handicapped.*
- *Curricular areas that are unique for visually handicapped children.*
- *Some procedures and aids used for instruction.*
- *Areas of emphasis or need which should receive special attention in the future.*
- *Major contributors to the education of the·visually handicapped.*

Chapter twelve

VISION AND VISUAL IMPAIRMENT

The Eye

The eye is an extremely complex organ whose primary function is to focus light on internal light-sensitive receptors that convert it into electrical impulses and send it to the brain (Gregory, 1966). Specific functions of the eye include:

1. Central vision, the perception and discrimination of object forms,

2. Accommodation, adjustment of focus for distant and near vision,

3. Binocular vision, the coordination of the two eyes so that a single object is perceived,

4. Peripheral vision, reception of small amounts of light in the periphery of the visual field, and

5. Color vision, the perception of color (National Medical Foundation, 1959).

The parts of the eye make vision possible. Light entering the eye is focused by the cornea and crystalline lens to form an inverted image that comes to a clear focus on the retina. Slight changes in the shape of the lens alter the angle of refraction of light entering the eye from objects at different distances. Thus a clear image is focused on the retina as the distance of an object from the eye changes. The amount of light entering the eye is regulated by the iris, which, through the relaxation or contraction of its many muscles, increases or decreases the size of the pupil through which light passes. Vitreous humor, a liquid or gelatin-like substance in the inner chamber of the eye, helps give the eye its shape. The sclera forms the outer protective covering of the eye and the point of attachment for muscles which turn and coordinate the two eyes (Vaughn, Asbury, & Cook, 1971). The retina is a thin layer of light-sensitive receptors made up of cones, daylight color-sensitive cells, and rods, which distinguish shades of gray and function in low illumination (Gregory, 1966).

Vision

The eye functions as an extension of the brain. The light-sensitive portion of the eye, the retina, is connected to the optic nerve, which transports electrochemical impulses

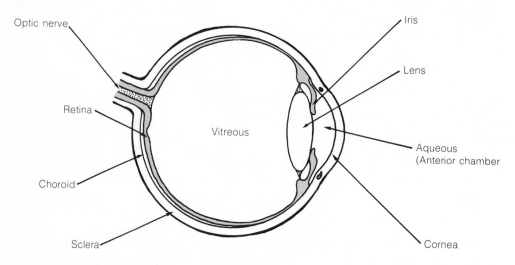

Figure 12.1
Cross section of the human eye

directly to the vision center in the brain. These electrochemical impulses do not take the form of images but function instead more like a code. The code carried to the brain by the optic nerve is translated into vision in the brain itself. While sensitivity to light is a function of the eye, vision is a function of the brain (Gregory, 1966).

Visual Impairment

Visual impairment results from a reduction in any of the five visual functions when a part of the eye stops working properly because of malformation, injury, or disease.

Among the most common visual impairments are those affecting central vision, or more specifically, accommodation and refraction (National Medical Foundation, 1959). Two common problems are myopia and hyperopia. Myopia, or nearsightedness, results when light is focused on a point in front of the retina, resulting in a blurred image. Hyperopia, or farsightedness, results when the image is focused at a point behind the retina. Clarity of central vision can likewise be impeded by a clouding of the lens (cataract) or through imperfections in the curvature or thickness of the cornea (astigmatism), either of which can result in a distorted, blurred, or incomplete image. Coordination problems include strabismus (cross-eye or wall-eye), where muscles fail to coordinate the two eyes together, and nystagmus, where the two eyes do not fixate on a single point but make jerking movements. Interference with peripheral visual can result when the normal flow of aqueous within the eye is interrupted. If aqueous is not removed at the same rate it is produced, there is a gradual increase in pressure within the eye. Such an increase in pressure, associated with glaucoma, can damage the retina and gradually reduce the field of vision. Complete interruption of vision results when either the retina or optic nerve fails to function. This interruption results from disease,

such as optic atrophy, retinal detachment, retinitis pigmentosa, or retrolental fibroplasia (a condition resulting from excess oxygen given to premature babies).

The most common visual impairments are impairments of central vision or visual acuity, such as myopia, hyperopia, and astigmatism. Strabismus is also of concern and occurs in about 2% of the total population (Gunderson, 1970; Lipton, 1971; Nawratzki & Oliver, 1972). This condition is particularly critical for children because, if it is not caught before the age of 7, it can result in amblyopia, a condition in which the brain represses the image received from one eye. Eventually that eye does not function. If caught soon enough, the condition can be corrected.

Most severe visual impairments result from problems caused by malfunctions of lens and retina (National Society for the Prevention of Blindness, 1966). Major causes are retrolental fibroplasia, glaucoma, and cataract. Studies concerned directly with children and adolescents indicate major problems were from optic nerve atrophy, retrolental fibroplasia, and congenital cataract, most of which were present at birth (Hatfield, 1963, 1972; National Society for the Prevention of Blindness, 1966). In fact, influences before birth were a cause in approximately half of all cases.

TERMS AND DEFINITIONS

The terminology used to describe people with defective vision has been changing recently. Not long ago, all individuals with defective vision were labeled *blind*. But new terms have become popular, *including blind, visually impaired, visually handicapped, partially seeing,* and *low vision.* Barraga (1971) defines **visually handicapped** children as the "total group of children who require special educational provisions because of visual problems"

(p. 13). Within this group, she describes three categories—blind, low vision, and visually limited.

Blind is used to refer to children who are totally without vision or who have light perception only. A blind child is described educationally as one who learns through the use of braille or related media without the aid of vision, even though she may be able to perceive light and use it for orientation or movement.

Low vision is used to describe children "who have limitations in distance vision but are able to see objects and materials when they are within a few inches or at a maximum of a few feet away" (p. 14).

Visually limited refers to children

> who in some way are limited in their use of vision under average circumstances. They may have difficulty seeing learning materials without special lighting, or they may be unable to see distant objects unless the objects are moving, or they may need to wear prescriptive lenses or use optical aids and special materials to function visually. (p. 14)

Legally blind people have **central visual acuity** of 20/200 or less in the better eye after correction (they can see at 20 feet what the average person could see at 200 feet), or have peripheral vision that is reduced to a total angle of 20 degrees or less in the better eye. Those less handicapped in vision but whose educational programs need to be modified because of visual loss are sometimes called *partially seeing*. Only the legally blind are eligible for materials from the Americal Printing House for the Blind.

Before 1946, when programs for the visually handicapped were being developed in local communities, most had separate classes for the blind and the partially seeing. However, the trend since the mid-1950s has been to educate blind and partially seeing children together (Jones & Collins, 1966).

IDENTIFICATION AND ASSESSMENT

Identification of Visual Handicaps

Some eye problems can go unnoticed by teachers and parents. Since many impairments can be corrected or their deterioration halted, it is important that visually handicapped children are identified as soon as possible so treatment or correction can start. The National Society for the Prevention of Blindness suggests the following signs of possible eye problems in children:

- *Behavior*
  Rubs eyes excessively.
  Shuts or covers one eye, tilts head, or thrusts head forward.
  Has difficulty in reading or in other work requiring close use of the eyes.
  Blinks more than usual or is irritable when doing close work.
  Holds books close to eyes.
  Is unable to see distant things clearly.
  Squints eyelids together or frowns.

- *Appearance*
  Crossed eyes.
  Red-rimmed, encrusted, or swollen eyelids.
  Inflamed or watery eyes.
  Recurring styes.

- *Complaints*
  Eyes itch, burn, or feel scratchy.
  Cannot see well.
  Dizziness, headaches, or nausea following close eye work.
  Blurred or double vision.

While these indicators do not offer conclusive evidence of significant eye problems, they do suggest further observation and examination. Conditions can change, making periodic reevaluations or eye examinations for visually handicapped children essential.

The most important initial screening device for detecting potential eye problems is one which measures central visual acuity—such as the Snellen Scale (Cunningham, 1963). (See Figure 12.2.) With the support of the National Society for the Prevention of Blindness (NSPB), periodic vision screening of children in public schools is becoming more common. By law, many states require annual vision screening of children in selected grades or ages and of all incoming students.

There also is greater emphasis on vision screening for preschool children. Many schools and public health departments conduct preschool vision screening, often with the assistance of local or state chapters of the NSPB and service clubs. To encourage early screening of vision, NSPB has developed a preschool vision screening instrument that can be given by the parent at home and mailed in for an interpretation of results (National Society for the Prevention of Blindness, 1972).

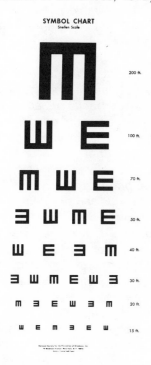

Figure 12.2
Snellen Scale symbol chart

If vision screening should reveal problems, the person is referred for an eye examination. **Optometrists** or **ophthalmologists** examine the eyes more closely by looking at the various visual functions. Glasses (corrective lenses) may be prescribed. If there are indications of injury, disease, or malfunction of the eye that cannot be corrected by lenses or that requires treatment in addition to lenses, an ophthalmologist may provide surgical treatment or medication.

Many otherwise serious visual impairments can be corrected by lenses, medication, or surgery. There still are, however, serious visual impairments which cannot be corrected; the condition causing visual impairment can be stabilized at best. It is this group that makes up the majority of the children receiving special education services for the visually handicapped.

Educational Assessment

Two major problems with the assessment of visually handicapped children by means of tests are accuracy of the results and interpretations of those results. First, it is often difficult to get accurate results from a test when some or all of the items depend on sight or visual experience for an answer. A child who cannot see to use a pencil or who has never seen a sunset has a disadvantage when asked to draw a figure or to describe sunsets on a test. Second, educators have grappled with questions of interpretation but have not reached any agreement. Should a blind child be expected to achieve at the same level or function in the same way as a sighted child? Are there other more relevant abilities to be measured? Should blind and sighted children be compared? What standard is appropriate? What is average or typical for blind children? Most have resolved the questions by adapting standardized tests (see the appendix). For tests with time limits, visually handicapped children are usually given more time. Tests that require reading have been transcribed in braille or large type or are read to the students. Inappropriate items, such as those that ask the child to draw a figure, name a color, or relate a response that depends on vision might be deleted for the blind child and be modified or interpreted for the visually limited child.

More and more, tests are being used to measure progress as shown by change over a period of time and are being used less to compare test performance with a predetermined standard. There is also more emphasis on measuring special skills

FOR MORE SUPPORT

American Association of Workers for the Blind, Inc. (AAWB)

An organization promoting work for the blind and prevention of blindness programs, AAWB is supported by member's dues, special grants, and contributions. Membership is open to anyone interested in the welfare of blind persons. AAWB publishes an annual, Blindness.

Association for Education of the Visually Handicapped (AEVH)

With its primary role to improve teaching of visually handicapped individuals, AEVH has memberships open to persons professionally involved in education or rehabilitation of the visually handicapped. The association is supported by dues, grants, and contributions. It publishes a journal, Education of the Visually Handicapped, *and the informative periodical,* Fountainhead.

American Foundation for the Blind (AFB)

Supported by voluntary contributions and endowments, AFB serves as a national clearinghouse for information on blindness. Among its services are providing a special reference library, promoting and conducting research on blindness and problems associated with blindness, consultating and lobbying for legislation beneficial to visually handicapped persons, and publishing numerous pamphlets, books, and monographs. Among its publications is the Journal of Blindness and Visual Impairment. *A list of agencies serving the visually handicapped is provided in the publication* Directory of Agencies Serving the Visually Handicapped in the United States, *available from AFB.*

National Society for the Prevention of Blindness, Inc. (NSPB)

NSPB supports research on eye diseases, surveys causes and incidence of blindness, distributes information on eye safety and low vision aids, and assists with vision screening and glaucoma detection. With the participation of people from the medical and education professions, NSPB provides considerable public service and information. It publishes the journal Sight Saving Review.

American Printing House for the Blind (APH)

Through an annual appropriation from Congress and special project funds, APH conducts research on educational materials and provides educational materials for distribution to legally blind children in the United States. Materials include books in large type, braille, and recorded form, and instructional aids and devices not commercially available.

APH houses the Instructional Materials Reference Center for the Visually Handicapped, which provides resource materials for teachers and reference services to volunteer-produced textbooks for the visually handicapped.

Free catalogs of aids, appliances, apparatus, and publications in large print or braille are available to teachers working with visually handicapped children. Periodic supplements and new items are sent to people who ask to be on the APH mailing list.

and abilities, such as roughness discrimination, body image, orientation and mobility, and visual efficiency.

BEHAVIORAL DESCRIPTIONS

Early Development

Research and experience have shown that being without sight does not directly affect any of the other senses or systems of the body—despite some beliefs to the contrary. Blindness does not prevent a person from hearing well nor does it make a person hear any better. Muscular coordination and strength are neither helped nor hindered by being without sight. Blind people cannot sing, play musical instruments, recognize sounds, or perceive by touch any better or worse because of their blindness. The child who is without sight from birth does not have special sensory advantages, although he may use or practice his other senses more than seeing children.

The inability to see does place some direct limitation on a person's sensory experience, however. Children's development is delayed relative to their vision and their total base of experience. A visually handicapped child shows developmental delays in at least three general areas; the amount of delay depends on how much vision the child has. The areas affected are movement, conceptual understanding, and self-awareness.

Movement

Children born blind are capable of the range and variety of movements common to any child. They progress through the same sequence of steps in their motor development as sighted children do (see chapter 3 for a description of the sequence). However, they are handicapped by their lack of vision in the perceptual aspects of movement. The blind child does not have the opportunity to reach out to objects when seeing them; only when he

develops to where he reaches towards sounds does he reach out to objects (Fraiberg, Siegel, & Gibson, 1966). The blind child has no chance to be motivated to move towards objects or to interact with them because they are not within his field of vision.

Conceptual Understanding

Sounds, unlike visual images of objects, give little concrete information about the characteristics of the objects making the sounds. Therefore, a blind child is at an early disadvantage in recognizing objects in his environment beyond his immediate grasp. The child is limited, too, in his ability to perceive relationships between objects or to perceive objects as wholes, particularly when the objects are large, some distance away, or moving—think of buildings, clouds, or birds in flight. Since blindness interferes with the child's perception of many objects and their interrelationships, his conceptual understanding can also be impaired.

Self-Awareness

Finally, the child's self-awareness is interfered with since he cannot make the kinds of visual checks that a sighted child makes regarding other people as models and his self-image in relation to others. For example, facial expressions that accompany verbal expressions, gestures, relative heights and sizes that are always within view, and general physique and appearance are all outside the blind child's repertoire of experiences. Even though some of these experiences can be acquired through touch, opportunities for the child to obtain them tactually are often socially prohibited.

Social Development

Visually handicapped children and youth face some problems with social interactions that are only indirectly caused by the visual impairment. Other people's attitudes

Chapter twelve

Will, a mobility instructor, follows Amy across the school yard to give her verbal cues and remind her to keep her head up.

and reactions to them are likely to shape the way a visually handicapped person perceives himself, as well as the way he relates to others. Parents who react emotionally and negatively to the birth of a handicapped child can easily project attitudes of low self-esteem or rejection. Children who are not included in playground games because they may not be able to catch or throw a ball or perform as well as the others are bound to have difficulty in building attitudes of self-confidence and worth.

Many people, including parents, feel unsure in caring for or relating to the visually handicapped. They may be offended when a low vision friend does not recognize them on the street. They may be afraid to offer assistance because they are afraid to do something wrong, or they may insist on helping when no help is needed or wanted. Blind children often learn at an early age that they must take the initiative by setting the sighted person at ease. Yet, the blind child may also permit attitudes of guilt or pity which result in unnecessary gifts or privileges.

Mobility is another limitation on social contacts. The difficulties of moving freely by foot, having to depend on others for transportation, and having people present without knowing it combine to place the visually handicapped individual at a disadvantage in initiating social contacts.

The Body and Movement

Lack of sight has its most severe and lasting effects in the area of posture and movement. Blindness prevents eye contact. Without that, a blind child does not need to hold her head erect, since a drooping head does not interfere with hearing or smelling. Unless she has had some visual sensation to attract the gaze of her eyes, a child's head and therefore her entire posture are commonly affected. Thus many blind children tend to slouch, which is not socially acceptable to a visually oriented society. Slouching can also eventually interfere with healthy growth or easy mobility. And without being able to see facial expressions in others, the blind child has no basis for developing expressive gestures of her own.

Finally, the critical area for a blind child is physical movement. Major difficulties in traveling are detecting objects and avoiding obstacles. The ability to travel safely makes it possible to get to and obtain further information about the environment.

Restricted travel means limited social contacts, fewer general experiences, and possibly a reduction in overall physical coordination and health.

Visual Handicaps and Learning

Visual handicaps affect the experiences to which a person can be exposed because they limit sensory input. Incidental learning that occurs as a result of everyday visual observations frequently does not occur in a blind child. Also, blindness can directly interfere with self-care and the ability to organize a person's environment. Grooming, locating lost or misplaced objects, and selecting clothing or furniture are visual experiences for most people. Judgments of quality and taste are beyond the direct experience of many of the visually handicapped.

Despite their lack of vision, the visually handicapped are able to learn to function effectively in most areas. However, they must be exposed early to a wide variety of experiences, given opportunities to explore objects thoroughly, and whenever possible have largely visual experiences in nature explained or translated into another sensory modality.

Parents and teachers cannot leave much to incidental learning but must instead watch for skills and little facts or information to introduce to the child so that he develops as completely as possible.

The variety of personality traits and ability levels among those who are categorized as visually handicapped are illustrated by these pieces of correspondence—a letter to a rehabilitation counselor, a referral to a local school placement committee, and a summary report of an annual administrative review. The children the correspondence describes are classified as *blind, low vision,* and *visually limited,* respectively.

profile **LETTER TO A REHABILITATION COUNSELOR**

Re: Carolyn   Age: 16 years, 10 months
Blind

Dear Ms. Karl:

Following my conference of last Wednesday with Carolyn and her parents, I am forwarding the following information at their request. This should help with an orderly transition to your caseload when Carolyn graduates and provide you some background to plan for your work with her this summer. I also would like to request your assistance in evaluating her vocational aptitudes and in helping her explore vocational alternatives.

Carolyn, a totally blind student, is presently in her junior year at West Morland High School, which she has attended since the beginning of her sophomore year. Prior to her coming here she attended a residential school for the blind for 3 years. Her earlier schooling was in the local public schools of California, Massachusetts, and Maryland. She is the older of two children.

Her father is stationed locally as a military recruiter and her mother is employed as a teller with a city bank. Her parents have been extremely cooperative with the schools and give every evidence of providing Carolyn with a stable, supportive home environment.

Carolyn is very involved in school activities. She is presently a member of the forensics team, treasurer of the Junior class, and chairperson of the prom committee. She has shown herself to be a capable leader and an active participant as well as a good student. She has remained on the B+ honor roll all but one quarter since coming to West Morland.

Carolyn is an attractive young woman who shows a positive, out-going personality. She makes friends quickly. As for her plans for the future, she has been reluctant to consider alternatives but on occasion has stated an interest in exploring the possibility of a business school or perhaps college. She has good typing skills and a fine command of braille. She uses tapes effectively for her lessons and organizes both time and materials well. She travels well with the cane, has excellent orientation, and uses public transportation effectively.

We have not been able to explore vocational opportunities with her to any extent. Your assistance in exploring appropriate vocational choices and more fully evaluating her aptitudes would be most valuable. While Carolyn has been a most successful student, her parents and I both feel that considerable attention should now be given to her future in terms of vocational alternatives.

I truly appreciate the excellent assistance you provided in our efforts with Paul and certainly look forward to the possibility of working again with you for the benefit of this fine young lady.

We have a signed copy of the Parental Release of Information Form granting release of our records to you. Please let me know about the records you need and we will forward them to you.

Cordially,

T. C. Collins, Counselor

profile REFERRAL TO LOCAL SCHOOL PLACEMENT COMMITTEE

To: Placement Committee

From: R. Moore, S. Tainner

Re: Robert   Age: 8 years, 4 months
Low vision.

This youngster is being referred to the local placement committee by Robert's classroom teacher and the itinerant teacher of the visually handicapped for more ap-

propriate placement. Because of the need for concentrated instruction in the areas of orientation and mobility, daily living skills, and preacademic and academic skills, it is felt that full-time placement in a class for the visually handicapped represents the least restrictive alternative. Consideration might be given to placement at the state school for the blind. Local schools have only itinerant services available in addition to the federally funded early childhood programs for handicapped children in which Robert has been enrolled for the past 2 years. Because of age he no longer qualifies for placement there.

The following Referral Information Summary is being sent to you, along with his school, medical, and social records in response to your request which accompanied the signed Parental Release of Information form.

Referral Information Summary

Medical: Robert was diagnosed as having congenital cataracts in infancy. Cerebral palsy was diagnosed by Handicapped Children's Clinic at age 6 months. The C. P. affects only the left side and is noticeable mainly in his use of the fingers of his left hand. At 3 years of age cataracts were removed through a needling procedure at University Hospital with only partial success. Corneal clouding has subsequently developed, along with some retinal deterioration. Prognosis is guarded.

Visual acuity is 20/400 OS [left eye]; hand movements only OD [right eye].

Psychological: The Hayes-Binet intelligence test administered when he was 8 years, 1 month old yielded a mental age of 7 years, 2 months. Based upon these results, Robert should benefit from formal education.

Administration of the Roughness Discrimination Test resulted in demonstrating very little ability to discriminate between roughness samples. One would predict only limited success with formal instruction in braille at this time.

Social History: Robert was born fourth of six children. The family, while remaining in the same general area, has had frequent moves. The father is frequently unemployed, and the family have often been welfare recipients. The parents refer to Robert as their "blind child" and commonly behave toward him as though he were totally blind. The kind of support and assistance afforded Robert in the home environment would be considered marginal at best. He spends considerable time in the home of the maternal grandparents, an environment in which he receives only minimal stimulation. The grandparents take pride in doing things for Robert; as recently as last summer they continued to feed him at meals and dress him each day.

Educational Functioning: Robert was first enrolled in school when he was 6. Initial enrollment, where he has continued since, was in the early childhood class for handicapped children. In addition he has received regular services of an itinerant teacher of the visually handicapped.

Initially, Robert behaved as though he were totally blind. He gave no evidence of having useable vision, would walk into objects in the room, and constantly explored his environment with his hands. He exhibited numerous mannerisms and rocking behaviors. At first, he refused food unless it was fed to him and showed neither interest nor ability to feed himself.

With behavior modification techniques, the early childhood specialist was able to develop skills in dressing and self-feeding. The vision teacher has used a planned sequence of activities to foster increased visual efficiency. Robert can identify primary colors, differentiate between geometric shapes, and responds to the movement of individuals about the room. The mannerisms, too, have been reduced, although

he still occasionally rocks and shows some self-stimulatory behaviors. Social and academic progress have not kept pace with his physical growth or indicated intellectual abilities. Progress for this child has been considerable over the past 2 years; however, there was noticeable regression in social behavior and academic skills between last spring and his return to school this fall.

profile SUMMARY OF AN ANNUAL ADMINISTRATION REVIEW

To: J. Brown

From: D. Bornstien

Re: Andrew   Age: 7 years, 8 months
Visually Limited

The annual administrative review conducted in the spring of last school year indicated that Andrew's progress in school was quite satisfactory. As a result of that review it was recommended that he be placed in the third grade class at St. Catherine Elementary and that he be carried on the caseload of the itinerant teacher as a "consultation only." Monthly to quarterly visits to the class should provide sufficient observation and information to monitor his progress.

The following summary report should provide you some basis for adding him to your caseload. Additional medical, psychological, social, and educational information is on file at St. Catherine Elementary School and at the Special Education Office in the County School Board Building. You have access to any of these records.

Summary Report

Medical: Medical history shows a normal delivery and birth with no abnormalities reported during pregnancy or following birth. He was born second of three children.

At 3 years of age a high fever accompanied by convulsions is reported, but no reference is made to later episodes or to any eye problem at that time.

At age 7, he was seen by Albert McBride, M. D., who diagnosed high myopia and presence of cataracts. Lenses were prescribed but no other treatment was indicated. Visual acuity following correction was given as 20/80, OS and 20/100 OD.

Social History: Andrew was born in Madison County, Virginia, where the family lived until their move to the local community. At age 6 he was enrolled for the first time in the first grade. The father is a laborer and the mother a homemaker. The home environment appears accepting and supportive. Discipline is commonly handled by resorting to physical punishment. Until recently, the parents have had rather negative feelings toward the public schools.

Psychological: Recent evaluation shows a youngster who is gaining in his ability to make social relationships and improved self-concept over that reported just 2 years before.

Administration of the WISC yielded a verbal IQ of 112 and a performance IQ of 98. Andrew's intellectual functioning is in the average range.

Educational Functioning: Andrew was enrolled at Weston Elementary School when he was 5½. His initial enrollment was in the first grade; however, after 6 weeks he was placed back in the kindergarten. Following his enrollment in first grade, Andrew had shown immature social behavior and was described by his first grade teacher as inattentive, easily distracted, immature, and a "loner." His academic skills were very low; he usually responded to requests to identify letters or match objects, which that teacher stressed, with disinterest or open rebellion.

At the teacher's request, the school recommended placement in kindergarten, where he could obtain instruction in preacademic skills and social develop-ment. The parents objected and overtly opposed the change. Andrew was unofficially withdrawn from school after a long string of colds. After pressure from school authorities he was again enrolled in school, but this time at St. Catherine, where he was placed in the first grade.

When he was 7, Andrew failed the vision screening conducted by the health department, which eventually resulted in his parents arranging an appointment with Dr. McBride.

Once identified as visually handicapped, Andrew received itinerant teacher services. Through these services Andrew learned to make use of a hand-held lens for some reading and to use some enlarged type materials. Both your predecessor and his classroom teachers report rapid gains for Andrew in social behavior and in academic skills over the past year and a half.

Progress reports and achievement tests indicate that Andrew is within 5 to 8 weeks of performing at age and grade level in most areas of mathematics, reading, and language arts.

EDUCATIONAL PROGRAMS AND SERVICES

Reading

While walking the streets of nineteenth century Paris, Valentin Haüy came across a group of blind men who were being ridiculed so that people would pay to see them. The event changed Haüy's life, motivating him to begin a school for blind people. Quite by accident, one of Haüy's students discovered one day he could feel some of the printed letters formed by heavy ink from a printing press. His descovery led to development of embossed printing for the blind, including publication of entire books with raised letters in Roman style print.

Earlier attempts to use wax tablets, series of knots on a string, or carved wood symbols had never had more than limited personal success. Embossed printing opened up the possibility that many blind people would have access to books to read. However, reading embossed materials presented difficulties. The process was slow and laborious, and many never fully mastered it. And there was no means of handwriting available to the blind with this system. Some blind readers proposed or encouraged competing systems, but educators were concerned about further isolating the blind from the rest of society. Educators also preferred a system which

instructors already understood. So embossed systems with Roman letters continued to be used.

Early competitors did have some success. Louis Braille, a student of Haüy, developed a system of dots to help blind people read. At first condemned, his system gained official status at Haüy's Paris school in 1845. Braille's system later came to the attention of people throughout the world, and in 1860 was officially accepted at the institution for the blind in Missouri. The success pupils at the Missouri school had in learning to read by this system prompted William Wait, teacher and superintendent at the New York Institution

profile VALENTIN HAÜY

Born in 1745, Haüy lived in the thick of social and educational revolution. His motivation to make education available to blind children may have been affected by the writers and philosophers of those years which preceded the French Revolution. Haüy was a younger contemporary of Jean Jacques Rousseau. In 1760, Abbé de l'Epee had started a school for the deaf in Paris. Abbé de l'Epee's successor, Abbé Sicard, impressed many people, including Haüy, when he taught a deaf boy to communicate through sign language. While these were all potential motivators for Haüy, a particular event prompted him to start his school (Farrell, 1956).

While walking the streets of Paris one evening Haüy was drawn to a café. There he found several blind men dressed in ugly robes, wearing large pasteboard spectacles, dunce's hats, and donkey's ears, and playing stringed instruments with crude stringless bows. It was an abuse of handicapped persons for the purpose of entertaining customers. It so upset Haüy that it led him to a life-long resolve: to teach the

blind to read. It was a noble ambition, but years passed before it was realized.

During the time between this distressing experience and the start of his school, Haüy had several opportunities to observe or hear about successes of handicapped people. When he finally did take steps to start the school, he first located a promising pupil and began teaching him. To gain recognition and provide support for the school, Haüy would take his pupil for demonstrations before various groups. After the demonstrations, appeals were made or collections taken on behalf of the school.

So far as reading was concerned, Haüy had no successful approach at first; when it did come, it was quite by accident. His student discovered one day that he could feel some of the printed letters formed by heavy ink from the printing press. From this discovery Haüy worked with the idea of embossing large letters from the back side of the page so that they could be felt by the reader's fingers. Haüy developed his embossed writing, where blind readers traced Roman style letters with their fingers. He was convinced that education of the blind should parallel the education of the sighted.

Chapter twelve

profile LOUIS BRAILLE

Born in 1809 to the family of a harness-maker in Coupvray, France, Louis Braille was blinded by an accident when he was 3 years old. His parents had him attend school in his local village for several years. When he was 10, Braille obtained a scholarship to attend the Paris school founded by Valentin Haüy, known then as the Royal Institution for Blind Youth. He entered as the school's youngest pupil and as a student was exceptional. He completed his studies and, while still a teenager, became an instructor at the same institution.

During the time he was at the school, Braille grew increasingly interested in developing a means for reading which was less difficult and cumbersome than the embossed type developed by Haüy. At that time Haüy's system was the officially accepted system at the school. Fortunately, a military officer who had devised a code system using dots and dashes on cardboard came to the institution with an adaptation he proposed for use by the blind. His system was enthusiastically accepted by the blind residents at the school, including Braille. Braille worked to perfect the system and eventually completely redid it by developing a code composed of combinations of six embossed dots. At just 15, Braille had devised a means whereby the blind could both read and write, and only 5 years later he published his dot system.

Despite the fact that his system was preferred by those who read by touch, Braille's dot system was not permitted to be used by the pupils to do their lessons. While he was encouraged to continue with developing his system, it was not accepted as the official means of reading for the blind even at the Paris school. Louis Braille died in 1852 without knowing if the system would ever be used.

for the Blind, to experiment with dot systems. His efforts led to the publication in 1868 of his improved dot system, known as New York Point.

In 1871, when directors and teachers from several institutions for the education of the blind gathered for the first convention of the American Association of Instructors of the Blind (AAIB)—which later became the Association for Education of the Visually Handicapped (AEVH)—there was stiff competition for the Roman style embossed systems. In fact, AAIB endorsed New York Point. The American Printing House for the Blind in Louisville, Kentucky, which had been chartered in 1858, had by then been embossing materials in several systems. In time the dot systems gained precedence. During this same period, the federal government made its first commitment to providing embossed books for the blind.

Books for the Blind

Samuel Gridley Howe, a pioneer American educator of the blind, was quite successful in getting educational institutions established in several states. His appeals to Congress for support of publishing books for the blind did not, however, meet with immediate success. But in 1879, Congress did pass legislation allowing interest from bonds to be used by the American Printing House for the Blind in producing embossed books and other tactile apparatus for the blind.

A Resolution for Reading Problems

In 1892 Frank Hall, superintendent of the Illinois School for the Blind, invented a braille writer which made adapting Braille's system, "American Braille," easier and more rapid.

In 1895 a second organization joined the ranks of AAIB in pressing for better conditions for blind citizens. The American Blind Peoples Higher Education and General Improvement Association opened its membership to anyone involved in or interested in the welfare of the blind. Among their early concerns was resolution of the conflict between competing systems of embossed reading for the blind. The American Association of Workers for the Blind (AAWB)—as the organization was renamed in 1905—appointed a Uniform Type Committee to research the various dot systems. Ten years later they were joined in this research by AAIB.

The system devised by Braille had begun to replace other embossed types in Great Britain so that by 1905 the British had incorporated his basic code into three levels or "grades." Grade one braille was a fully spelled out system in which each cell represented only one letter or symbol. Grade two braille incorporated a moderate

profile SAMUEL GRIDLEY HOWE

Born 8 years before Louis Braille, Samuel Gridley Howe, an American, made his greatest contribution to special education after the age of 30. He was trained as a physician, but rather than establish a practice, he sailed for Europe to participate in the fight for Greek independence. After 6 years' absence from the United States, Howe returned. His return followed closely the establishment of the first educational institution for blind children in the United States and almost by sheer accident he became its first director.

Another physician, John Fisher, who had returned from medical studies in France, had generated interest in establishing an institution like those he had observed in Europe. In 1829 the New England Asylum for the Blind was founded in Boston. Samuel Howe was appointed director in 1831. Howe immediately returned to Europe, where he observed several institutions for the blind, including the one at Paris. While both Fisher and Howe had contact with the institution at Paris, there is no indication that either had any association with Braille or his system of reading for the blind.

Although Howe was quite critical of what he saw in the European institutions he visited, he transported many of their ideas and policies back to the New England Asylum

for the Blind, even to the extent of bringing two teachers with him. Among the practices Howe picked up was to take his pupils on tours for demonstrations. In these demonstrations the pupils showed their skills before audiences. These demonstrations were so impressive that they frequently brought legislators to tears (Farrell, 1956), and helped Howe influence legislation and obtain financial support for institutions for the blind.

Influenced by Howe's touring demonstrators, Ohio established the first state supported institution for the education of the blind in 1837. A graduate of the New England Asylum for the Blind became its teacher.

The influence of Samuel Gridley Howe goes well beyond his efforts to persuade legislators and establish institutions for the blind. In the same year that he assisted in the start of the institution in Ohio, he took in a deaf-blind girl, Laura Bridgman, to live at the New England Asylum for the Blind. With the aid of Howe's tutoring, she eventually became the first deaf-blind person known to acquire the use of language.

Along with other pioneer educators and reformers of his day, Howe made significant contributions to the education of the "feeble minded," care of the insane, and oral education of the deaf.

Chapter twelve

Figure 12.3
This sample of grade two braille reads "Braille uses many contractions."

number of representations of several letters or an entire word by a single braille cell (contractions). The use of contractions had the advantage of saving space on the page and therefore saving reading time. Grade three braille was a highly contracted system.

In 1923 the newly established American Foundation for the Blind was given responsibility for solving the embossed type problem. The use of contractions in the British system of braille had distinct advantages. During the following years there was a concerted effort to work with English Braille until finally in 1932 an international code was developed. It had as its basis the British grades of Braille's system. This resolution has been called the *Treaty of London*.

As the Treaty of London was approaching, the United States Congress enacted legislation in 1931 which gave the Library of Congress funds to provide books for the use of adult blind persons. With final agreement on a uniform braille code, federal legislation providing for production of embossed books by the American Printing House for the Blind, and distribution of books to adult blind by the Library of Congress, access to touch reading was becoming available to increasing numbers of blind U.S. citizens.

Further access to reading materials was made possible when, in 1934, recorded materials in the form of "talking books" were introduced. Eventually talking books and talking book players were distributed by the Library of Congress. The blind had available reading materials not only in the medium of touch but hearing as well.

Alternative Plans for Educating the Visually Handicapped

Responding to parental pressure, attempts were made in 1900 to establish schooling for the blind closer to Chicago area residents. Efforts resulted in establishing a cooperative plan in which blind students attended a special class, but, whenever possible, attended classes with sighted children. Over a 10-year period, day school classes for the blind were established in Cincinnati, Cleveland, and New York City. An alternative to residential institutions for educating blind children was emerging.

At the same time, examinations of children in London schools for the blind revealed that some were not blind but instead were extremely nearsighted. The physician's report recommended that these children should not be educated with blind children but should be provided separate education. As a result, the first school for partially seeing children was established in 1908. This idea was brought to the United States, and in 1913 classes for children with defective eyesight were started in Boston and Cleveland. As classes were started in other parts of the United States they became known as *sight conservation* or *sight saving* classes. A distinction between classes and teaching procedures for children who were blind and those who had defective but useable vision was a developing pattern.

When the controversy over type style or system for reading was finally resolved, the task of educating visually handicapped children gained priority. Old ways and inadequacies were challenged. Ideas and plans advocated a century before by Johann Klein, a pioneer advocate of the blind, were being put into practice.

Walking canes were modified and a series of special techniques developed to teach independent foot travel to the blind largely because of Richard Hoover and his staff, who worked with blinded veterans in the U.S. Army and Veterans Administration programs. By 1963, this training had become an area of specialization requiring college training. The first college programs for orientation and mobility specialists were offered at Boston College—where these specialists were named *peripatologists*—and at Western Michigan University.

Use of dog guides has never proved appropriate for children. The responsibility and strength required to work effectively with a dog guide has restricted its use to adults. Foot travel with the aid of the travel cane, on the other hand, has direct application and use by children. At least two residential schools for the blind had introduced

orientation and mobility training with the travel cane before 1950.

Three Patterns of Programs

The day school classes for visually handicapped children first used at the turn of the century were widespread by 1950. *The Pine Brook Report* (American Foundation for the Blind, 1957) identified the three patterns of programs for educating the blind with the sighted most frequently found to be used by schools in the United States. (1) In the cooperative plan, most instruction is given in a special class. By cooperating with regular classroom teachers, some instruction for the handicapped child was provided in regular classrooms with sighted children. (2) In the **integrated plan**, the visually handicapped child is enrolled in a regular classroom with sighted

Orientation and mobility are key skills

profile JOHANN WILHELM KLEIN
There is no evidence that Johann Klein was even aware of Haüy's school when in 1804 he established the Imperial Royal Institute for the Education of the Blind in Vienna, Austria. Klein was an educator and, probably more than anyone in his time, operated his school on sound pedagogical principles. Within 2 years of the start of his school he was attempting to get visually handicapped children admitted to schools for the sighted. Although operating a residential institution for the blind, Klein advocated raising and educating blind children in their own homes.

Klein was the first person to write a book on the education of the blind. Long before there was any systematic use of dog guides, he published a description of how to train dogs as guides for blind persons.

classmates. The student has available to him a special teacher and a resource room where he can go for special assistance or specialized instruction when needed. This plan is frequently referred to as a *resource plan.* (3) A third pattern is the **itinerant teacher plan.** In this plan educational needs of the visually handicapped child are served by the regular classroom teacher in the local school where he is enrolled. Special instruction is provided by a special teacher who travels from school to school.

Enough interest was being shown in educating visually handicapped children in their local communities that by 1960 there were more children registered with the American Printing House for the Blind attending school in their local communities than there were attending residential schools (Jones & Collins, 1966). This trend has been aided by changes in legislation permitting more children enrolled in local schools to receive aids and appliances from the American Printing House for the Blind.

Perhaps the largest single cause of increased use of local schools was the increasing number of children suffering from retrolental fibroplasia. **Retrolental fibroplasia (RLF)** is caused from excessive oxygen given to premature infants, resulting in the eventual destruction of light receptor cells in the eye. It frequently causes total blindness. In the past premature infants often were given oxygen to help them survive but without appropriate controls on the amount of oxygen administered. Not until after 1950 was there routine monitoring of the oxygen given so that the child could survive without the chance of destroying his eyes in the process. Between 1940 and 1955 thousands of children were blinded by this cause alone. When these children reached school age, their parents pressured local schools to provide educational programs for visually handicapped children.

The 1963 to 1965 german measles (rubella) epidemic resulted in the birth of many multiply handicapped children. As mentioned in chapter 11, when a pregnant woman contracts rubella, her child may be born with visual impairments, hearing impairments, mental retardation, and heart ailments (Selman, 1972). Like the RLF influx of the 1940s, the rubella epidemic of the 1960s had profound effects on increased attention and programs for educating the multiply handicapped. Since children with rubella syndrome frequently function at relatively low levels or show serious delays in development, they require individualized educational programs, specially trained staff, and special procedures. This usually means small, self-contained special classes. There has been a decided change in the populations residential schools have served over the last decade. Some are rapidly becoming institutions for educating the multiply handicapped.

Other Current Trends, Issues, and Needs

Many of the topics discussed in this chapter show current trends, issues, and needs in education of the visually handicapped. In 1976, 72% of the 27,000 visually handicapped children registered with the American Foundation for the Blind were in public day school classes (mainstreamed) rather than in residential schools (Hooper, 1976). Public Law 94–142 has caused local schools to look more seriously at the alternatives and decide to provide direct services. (See chapter 1.) As we have seen, more residential schools for the blind are being converted to serve the multiply handicapped. By 1975 federal support of regional centers had helped 3,312 of 5,502 identified deaf-blind people in the United States receive services (Dantona, 1975). This trend has also led to a shift from academic classes to basic instruction in sensory development, motor training, communication, and socialization.

Two other issues should be mentioned: the use of senses and education for life and employment.

Use of Senses

There was a time when it was thought that using defective eyes could injure them further and that the eyes should be used no more than absolutely necessary. Recent medical evidence has stressed the opposite. Research clearly indicates that many youngsters with limited functional vision still can use that remaining portion for learning. Many children who are classified as blind can read printed books and materials (Jones, 1961). Research by Barraga (1964) demonstrated that following a period of specific training, children with severe visual handicaps were able to improve use of their limited vision. They were able to learn to use their vision more effectively or efficiently.

There is growing emphasis on using any remaining vision to the maximum (Sykes, 1972; Fonda, 1970). By using the vision that remains, a child has access to that much more information or experience. Educators are emphasizing maximum use of other available senses. Sensory training in listening, smelling, touching, and taste are all important and are increasingly a part of the special teacher's repertoire. Also, these skills are regularly taught along with or before formal orientation and mobility training.

Education for Life and Employment

Unfortunately, too many visually handicapped children still are being educated in the academic subjects, but are not getting specific skills training which would let them find jobs themselves and manage their personal lives. All too frequently otherwise capable, intelligent people have assumed dependent lives, remaining unemployed or returning to their parents' homes following graduation from high school or college.

Educators are increasingly stressing career education (Wolfe, 1973).

TEACHING AND TEACHERS

Primary Goals of the Educator

Bateman (1967) has identified three primary goals of the educator of blind children. These are:

1. Help the child get to information in the environment by giving mobility training,

2. Teach the child to use all senses to their maximum, and

3. Translate unuseable visual stimuli into a form that can be used.

These goals dictate to some extent desirable teacher characteristics.

Teacher Characteristics

The characteristics a teacher of the visually handicapped needs depend somewhat upon whether he serves in a residential, resource room, or itinerant setting.

Residential School Teacher

Normally, a residential school teacher is certified to teach at the elementary level or to teach a specific subject at the secondary level. These teachers should have a healthy attitude toward visually handicapped children and an understanding of their needs. Visually handicapped children frequently come up against negative, debasing, cruel, unduly sympathetic, or patronizing attitudes. The teacher should help foster healthy attitudes and self-images and help the children deal with other people's reactions toward them.

Teaching a child social skills to help establish healthy relationships with others also falls among teacher responsibilities. The simple ability to request assistance or decline unnecessary or undesirable aid can be a critical survival skill in some cir-

Touch, hearing, and sight are all used to help visually handicapped children acquire information.

cumstances. Talking with another person, exercising acceptable behavior in a public place, or acting appropriately as a host or hostess are other important skills.

Teachers in residential settings must also have a working knowledge of braille codes for science, math, and literature. This lets the teacher work with the child who depends on a tactile medium for reading and writing. Skills in teaching children to effectively use any and all remaining senses are also important. Teachers need to understand listening, hearing, and the **tactile-kinesthetic sense** as well as taste and smell, and should be able to assist the child in getting information and gaining conceptual understanding through these senses. The child must learn to pay attention to and interpret information which comes to her by way of a variety of senses, or else she misses many of the experiences available to her.

The teacher also should be able to use materials effectively as instructional tools and representational models to help the children acquire experience and develop essential concepts. Finally, the teacher

should know special techniques to help visually handicapped children move safely in their environment. Teacher creativity in helping the child organize her own environment so that she can function well in it is essential. Arranging space and locating materials where they can be easily found; identifying and avoiding dangers; developing skills in handling, measuring, and obtaining accurate information from reliable sources—all are critical skills for the visually handicapped. They are therefore vital skills for the teacher.

Resource Room Teachers

In the resource room setting, the special teacher functions within a day school environment. This teacher commonly provides supplementary or special instruction while the instruction in standard school subjects is conducted by the regular classroom teacher. The teacher must have some special skills and understandings.

He typically relies on special skills such as:

1. Skills in alternative approaches such as an understanding of the braille code or knowledge of availability of large print or recorded materials,

2. Aptitude in teaching listening skills,

3. Techniques for teaching typing for the pupil to use in school work,

4. Instruction in skills needed for basic orientation and mobility and sensory training,

5. Knowledge of special devices or media used by the visually handicapped child to gain information or interpret sensory data.

Itinerant Teacher

Perhaps more is demanded of the itinerant teacher than the others. While the itinerant teacher is employed as an educator, she often must function as a public relations specialist. The itinerant teacher works directly with a number of adults—classroom teachers, counselors, specialists, principals, and parents. She must work with teachers and administrators who may feel the handicapped child is an undesirable, added burden to their school or classroom. It takes skill to foster acceptance of and confidence in a handicapped child when a teacher or administrator is apprehensive or resentful. The itinerant teacher must often serve as the child's advocate and must change unhealthy attitudes towards the child by the child's parents, peers, or teachers. Parents who may feel guilt-ridden or teachers who are insecure about their ability to work with visually handicapped children may need assistance and support. The itinerant teacher must also counsel the handicapped child and may need to modify the child's attitudes about himself and to develop self-worth and realistic confidence.

During periodic visits to the child's school, the itinerant teacher may be in a position to recommend a pupil for special services beyond those the school can provide directly. Thus the itinerant teacher must know about a variety of services available to visually handicapped children

These visually impaired boys attend a resource room for part of each day.

and be prepared to initiate referrals and obtain services when the need arises or the request is made. Furthermore, an itinerant teacher may find herself the only specialist working with the child and must therefore provide the child necessary social skills or skills of daily living. Much as the resource room teacher, the itinerant teacher should be able to cope with infinite problems and should be well-rounded in education and well-balanced in her outlook on life.

Other Teachers Who Work with the Visually Handicapped

Other Special Educators

Teachers with special training and experience in other areas of special education are assuming increasingly important roles in teaching visually handicapped students who have reading, spelling, orientation, or coordination problems. A visually handicapped child with mild academic deficiencies may have a learning disability as his primary handicap. (See chapter 7 on learning disabilities.) At the least, the diagnostic/prescriptive approach of teachers of the learning disabled may apply to teaching many visually handicapped children.

With an increase in programs for the multiply handicapped, personnel with experience and training in areas such as hearing impairment, mental retardation, and emotional disturbance are becoming more important in education of visually handicapped children. Those with experience and expertise in a variety of other disciplines are especially in demand.

Orientation and Mobility Instructor

Today, most schools and adult rehabilitation agencies employ only specially trained personnel to teach how to travel with the cane. The orientation and mobility instructor teaches the visually handicapped person to use the travel cane for safe and independent travel. A variety of special techniques are used to let the person follow a safe path, detect objects, and negotiate routes of travel indoors and out. Special stress is placed on using all the senses in combination with the cane to gain the important information about the environment needed for traveling safely.

The orientation and mobility instructor does more than teach cane travel skills. He also teaches basic concepts such as distance and direction, how to use all available senses, and how to effectively use public and private transportation.

RECENT RESEARCH AND DEVELOPMENT IN VISION

Research in the Use of Vision

When thinking about the visually handicapped, most lay people and professionals emphasize the absence rather than the presence of sight. But most visually handicapped people have partial vision and can use it in most situations. The extent of this remaining vision and how useful it can be was demonstrated by Barraga (1964). She studied visually handicapped children with partial vision whose instruction had previously been restricted to tactual and auditory materials. An experimental group was instructed in using their vision through daily practice sessions with reading readiness materials. Comparison with a control group after 2 months showed significant differences in visual discrimination in favor of the experimental group. While there was no improvement in the children's visual acuity or in their eye condition, there was significant improvement in their ability to use their vision efficiently.

Since this research, there has been an increased tendency for students in programs for the visually handicapped to use print rather than braille as a medium for reading. While in 1960, 58% of those registered with the American Printing House for the Blind were listed as braille readers and 38 percent as print readers (Jones, 1961), the figures for 1975 were 24% braille readers and 44% print readers (Hooper, 1976).

Low Vision Aids

In recent years there has been an increase in both the attention given to and the availability of low vision aids for better use of remaining vision. Low vision clinics provide services ranging from prescription of low vision aids to special training in their use. The aids available range from hand-held magnifiers and telescopic lenses for seeing at a distance to glasses. Eyeglasses can have a wide variety of attached lenses or specially ground-in surfaces (facets) for focusing at various distances. (Fonda, 1970).

There is growing evidence that with low vision aids more visually handicapped children can use printed material effectively and in many instances do not have to resort to specially produced materials with enlarged type sizes (Sykes, 1971). These children can save considerable time and

Dennis is using a telescopic lens to read a regular print book.

effort if they do not have to buy or make large type materials.

Technology and Aids

Development of technological hardware is perhaps the most significant advancement in educating the visually handicapped. A number of aids and devices have been under development for years, but only recently has this research resulted in practical help.

Many visually handicapped people still rely on touch as a medium for reading despite the availability of auditory media such as records and tapes. In terms of time, listening is considerably more efficient than braille. Considering the amount of material a student must read in the course of a year, the braille reader has a distinct disadvan-

tage which can be reduced if listening is substituted for touch. Through special recorders and devices now available, it is possible to obtain time-compressed tape recordings which permit readers to "read" the tapes faster than braille or normal recordings without significant loss in comprehension (Foulke, Amster, Nolan, & Bixler, 1962; Tuttle, 1972).

There are reading materials which are not available in braille or recorded form, such as newspapers. Until recently, the only alternative for the person who could not see to read was to ask a person with sight to read to him. With the aid of the Optacon, a new device that translates printed visual symbols into tactual configurations that can be perceived by touch, blind users are able to read newspapers and other printed materials.

The Kurzweil Reading Machine is a very recent device for translating print images into a mode that severely visually handicapped individuals can use. A prototype model was introduced in 1976. This reading machine reads printed material and translates it into computer speech. This is the first device that has been able to translate directly from print to auditory output successfully.

For some individuals with limited but useable vision, a special adaptation of closed circuit television (CCTV) has proved to be helpful (Turner, 1976). By displaying an enlarged image on a screen, the visually handicapped reader can read materials that might otherwise be unreadable because of type size. The CCTV systems available include special features such as the ability to reverse the image to show white on black or black on white, change magnification, and focus for clarity.

Working mathematical problems that require memory or complex operations is difficult for someone who cannot see to use pencil and paper. Setting up and calculat-

Kelly places her left hand on one part of the Optacon while she runs a sensor over a printed page. The device also includes a visual display monitor.

ing a multiplication or division problem in braille is extremely laborious. The Cranmer Abacus, an adaptation of the Japanese soroban, is a valuable calculating device for the severely visually handicapped (Nolan & Morris, 1964). It is inexpensive, small, easily carried, and a person can readily learn to operate it.

In the last few years, pocket calculators have made calculating easy for most people. But because they use visual displays, calculators were unuseable by many visually handicapped. However, the new talking calculators are convenient for those without sight. Using a limited vocabulary, the talking calculator "speaks" by saying the number or operation entered and the answer that appears.

Technology has also provided potential benefits in mobility. A number of special mobility aids are being developed to supplement the travel cane and dog guide (Farmer, 1975). Most are a form of electronic detection device which translates reflected signals into a tactile or auditory signal. They range from hand-held instruments to devices worn like glasses or carried like a cane. Through practice the visually handicapped have been successful in using these devices to detect objects and negotiate routes of travel (Farmer, 1975; Thornton, 1975).

Electronic devices have been helpful when used by knowledgeable people, but they are not the answer for everyone. They are expensive, usually require special training, and most are still experimental. But some have proved helpful as supplementary aids, and the outlook for further improvements is good.

FUTURE CONSIDERATIONS AND NEEDS

The future of educating the visually handicapped probably will be affected more by public attitudes towards them than any

Closed circuit television can be helpful for some students with limited or low vision.

other factor. Public attitudes are reflected in financial support for special education and legal or legislative demands placed on general and special education. More than technology or procedures, legal and financial limitations affect education because they determine the environment where that education takes place.

There are several current needs or trends that should be considered.

1. If the visually handicapped are to function well socially and economically, the people around them must have positive attitudes. If never given the opportunity to try, the most capable person is ineffective.

2. More research is needed to determine if being visually handicapped affects only the quantity of sensory information available or if the visually handicapped use a fundamentally different thinking process than the nonhandicapped.

3. Data are needed on the most effective sequence for teaching braille to beginning

Glenn's calculator looks like any other until it talks.

readers. Most teachers use commercially produced materials designed for sighted children and merely have them reproduced in braille word for word, line by line. These materials frequently refer to pictures which are not in the braille texts. They rely on some phonic or phonetic analysis. Unfortunately, the braille code using contractions does not lend itself to such analysis. Current materials fail to consider the design or complexity of braille in introducing new vocabulary. Teaching braille reading to beginning readers continues to be a serious problem.

4. Listening may be more efficient than reading by touch. Technology has made it possible for visually handicapped people to be exposed to much more information much quicker than in the past. Educators must use electronic hardware if visually handicapped children are to have maximum educational opportunities.

5. Vocational education and employment is an increasing concern of the school program. Before graduation, the student must learn the skills he needs to get a job and must be aware of available job opportunities.

6. Skills in personal management and daily living are often slighted in the visually handicapped child's education. Frequently it is these skills rather than academic skills that determine a person's success as an adult.

7. We need to emphasize the low-vision child in research and educational practice. Research, teacher education programs,

Being a blind homemaker and parent requires resourcefulness and optimism. Lynne carries a slate and stylus in her purse for jotting down notes (like phone numbers) when she is out. She labels her cannisters in braille with plastic tape, and labels canned goods and staples with plastic-coated paper. Like other parents, she and Dennis have "baby-proofed" their home to prepare for the time when Peter is walking and getting into everything.

and inservice delivery systems have stressed blindness. Relatively little is known about the visually handicapped who have some vision. But there are far more persons who have some vision than have none. Most visually handicapped children can see; they just do not see well.

8. There is a need to understand more clearly the ways that handicaps interact or combine to influence development and behavior. Today, there is professional disagreement about and little understanding of the ultimate goals for programs for multiply handicapped children.

9. The concept of mainstreaming and the role of the residential school deserve careful attention by educators of the visually handicapped. While mainstreaming as a concept appears valid, in practice it can be less than desirable. To place visually handicapped children in regular classrooms with infrequent or inadequate special services does not serve their best interests. While some excellent local programs exist, there are also local schools that provide only minimum services and do not let the visually handicapped participate fully in the school program.

The future role of residential schools should also be weighed carefully. Residential schools are becoming institutions for multiply handicapped by default. More planning should go into designing the overall educational delivery system. We cannot claim to be serving handicapped children well when residential schools are treated as dumping grounds for other people's problems.

10. Educators are concerned about the future of existing programs for the visually handicapped. Few school-age children have severe visual handicaps. As a group they have faired relatively well in receiving benefits and funding from federal and state governments. These funds may be cut back as emphasis on special education shifts to local public schools and as programs for more and more handicapped children become mandated. Spreading limited funds around could destroy the efforts that have gone into developing present programs.

MEETING SPECIAL NEEDS

Teachers who are faced with a newly arrived visually handicapped pupil may experience feelings of self-doubt, apprehension, or even fear— the same feelings some parents have. A mature, creative teacher has the basic skills for successfully working with visually handicapped children. Teachers increase their effectiveness through experience or outside help. Here are some suggestions for classroom teachers that may aid the new teacher until he gains experience or help comes. The successful teacher of visually handicapped children concentrates his attention on identifying ways for students to contact, interact with, and derive meaning from the environment.
1. The successful teacher helps the visually handicapped child learn ways to
contact the environment. A pupil must be able to move within the environment and successfully reach objectives. Take time to orient visually handicapped children to the school environment. A little time and attention here can do much to make the child independent and help her effectively use the school and its resources.

If possible, introduce the child to school before the other children arrive in the fall. This allows time to explore, ask questions, or go over details. Walk the visually handicapped student through the route from the main entrance to each class. She should also be taught alternate routes and emergency exit procedures. In teaching a new route to a child, familiarize her with adjoining hallways and location of doorways, lockers, and fountains or other per-

manent objects that can help her indentify direction or location in a route.

Have a child walk the length and width of a classroom to grasp its size. Using the door as a point of reference, have her explore the perimeter of the room and identify objects or features such as the chalkboard, windows, and pencil sharpener. Then identify furniture such as her desk, the teacher's desk, tables, or learning centers in relation to the door and to each other.

A blind student should be able to effectively use the sighted guide technique— simply grasping the guide's arm at the elbow and walking with him. This permits the pupil to be easily guided and not awkward or unnecessarily conspicuous. Sighted classmates should know how to serve as guides and to offer help if needed and accepted by the visually handicapped person.

2. The successful teacher helps the visually handicapped child learn ways to interact with the environment he has contacted.

Every available sense should be used to its maximum potential. When vision is impaired, other senses can take its place or supplement what vision there is.

Hearing is vital to those who cannot see. Teach listening skills— to recognize important information and distinguish it from background noise. Eliminate unnecessary noises so they will not be a distraction. At times a quiet room without distractions significantly aids learning.

Touch is another way to learn. There is no braille counterpart for pictures. The only substitutes are verbal descriptions or actual contact with objects or participation in events. Encourage the blind child to handle objects as a part of his learning.

Help children with some remaining vision explore the lighting and seating arrangements to find those that best meet their needs. Some may see and participate better when they are seated near the front or focal center of the room. Some can use their vision more efficiently with the aid of an extra light, while others work better with less light.

3. The successful teacher helps the visually handicapped child learn ways to derive meaning from his interactions with the environment. Many things that are learned incidentally by the normally sighted child are not learned by the child who is visually handicapped. His learning cannot be left to chance. Expose the child to as many practical experiences as possible; take nothing for granted. For each new event or encounter give a running dialogue for any part of the situation that the child cannot experience directly. While walking with a blind child, describe the objects or events that make the sounds he hears and describe the things observed only by the sighted. This can help a child's conceptual understanding of the environment to exceed his limited sensory experience.

4. Structuring your environment is important to understanding it and to using it effectively. Having specific places for things, such as shelves for books or personal belongings, envelopes or drawers for papers, organized work space, and established routines or schedules is important, especially to the handicapped. But don't forget, even routines occasionally should be altered to expand learning potential.

5. Finally, successful teachers make the best possible use of all the available resources for teaching visually handicapped children. Having a visually handicapped child in your class doesn't mean you automatically obtain braille or large type materials. Some students can read standard-size type with little adaptation, while others can read it with a hand-held lens or other device. If special education consultants are available locally, ask them to help you find materials and consult with them on ways to *better approach instruction. It is not good use of the special education teacher's skill or time to request or expect that he tutor a visually handicapped child in academic or content areas. It is better to have his assistance with those areas that apply directly to the handicap, such as instruction in braille, use of special devices or aids, materials, or consultation in alternative methods.*

Most states have educational or rehabilitation services available through a commission or bureau for the visually handicapped, a state department of education, or a residential school for the visually handicapped. Any or all of these agencies are available to provide direct services, consultation, lend materials, or provide valuable information.

FOR MORE INFORMATION

Most of these resources are textbooks that are readily available, many from Charles E. Merrill, the publishers of this text. Check your instructor, the education library, or the general library at your school.

Barraga, N.C. *Visual handicaps and learning.* Belmont, Calif.: Wadsworth, 1976.

Hanninen, K.A. *Teaching the visually handicapped.* Columbus, Ohio: Charles E. Merrill, 1975.

Jan, J.E., Freeman, R.D., & Scott, E.P. *Visual impairment in children and adolescents.* New York: Grune & Stratton, 1977.

Lowenfeld, B. *Our blind children (3rd ed.).* Springfield, Ill.: Charles C Thomas, 1971.

Lowenfeld, B. (Ed.). *The visually handicapped child in school.* New York: John Day, 1973.

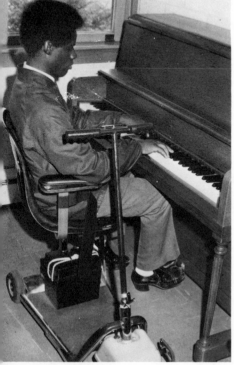

13

Children with Physical and Multiple Disabilities

June Bigge
Barbara Sirvis

These are the major topics covered in this chapter. You may want to use them as a checklist when you review.

- *Major medical information on certain physical handicaps.*

- *Considerations for the teacher in dealing with physical handicaps.*

- *Physical management and educational modifications which may be necessary to include the physically handicapped child in the regular classroom.*

- *Questions used to get the information necessary to design appropriate educational programs for children with physical or multiple handicaps.*

- *Special intervention and management procedures.*

Several terms are applied interchangeably to the population of children generally referred to as *crippled and other health impaired* (COHI), *physically handicapped,* and *physically disabled.* Although the Bureau for Education of the Handicapped in the United States Office of Education uses COHI consistently, professionals, parents, and disabled people themselves do *not* seem to use any one term consistently. (Chapter 1 discusses the distinction between *disability* and *handicap.*) Further confusion arises because the term *physically handicapped* is also used by some people to describe visual or hearing impairments. Hearing or visual impairments are not considered in this chapter unless they are associated with other physical disabilities. See chapters 11 and 12 for in-depth discussions of the hearing and the visually handicapped.

The crippling and other health impairing conditions found in the physically disabled vary in cause as well as in needs for physical management and educational modifications. In addition to their actual physical handicaps—which may or may not be visible—the physically disabled may, at the same time, have learning handicaps. These problems, often related to speech, vision, hearing, and/or behavioral disorders, are not easily recognized but impede function as well as learning. The multiple handicapping conditions of these youngsters make a categorical definition of this group difficult, if not impossible.

Wald (1971) reported the following composite definition of the crippled and other health impaired:

> The COHI population appears to be seen in three dimensions: physical definition, functional problems, and programmatic modifications. The population is comprised of those children and adults who as a result of permanent, temporary, or intermittent medical disabilities require modifications in curriculum and instructional strategies. Fre-

quent separation from family and a lack of adequate parental guidance contribute to secondary emotional problems of the COHI population. The child's physical limitations are often the basis of functional retardation as well as sensory, perceptual, and conceptual deficits. The development of realistic expectation levels requires the identification of additional and unique instructional materials, equipment, and strategies for evaluation. (p. 95)

HISTORICAL PERSPECTIVES

Historically, educational programming for the physically disabled population began with those children who were hospitalized with disabilities resulting from diseases such as polio and tuberculosis. Gradually, however, children with more severe disabilities such as cerebral palsy began to alter the direction of special education programs. While early programs had been merely supplements to extensive medical treatment in hospitals, a team approach to treatment gradually evolved. It recognized the importance of educational intervention as well as medical services and gave equal status to educational programming. Although a variety of disciplines supported and contributed to the development of extensive educational programming for physically handicapped children, the roots of this programming lay in medicine and the related health professions; physicians, physical rehabilitation specialists, physical and occupational therapists, nutrition and rehabilitation engineers got involved.

Moreover, educational programming emerged from a realization that the major focus should be on compensation for physical disabilities. Elise Martens was a pioneer in building national acceptance of the concept of education for the physically handicapped, and Romaine Mackie's survey (1955) established the need for special education programming. Henry Viscardi and Earl Carlson, both disabled, have become advocates for educational programming and vocational training for the physically disabled, pointing out the positive effects of these services. University personnel have provided substantive material on the nature and educational needs of the physically handicapped student, and teacher preparation specialists have led the way in developing special education programs to prepare qualified, competent classroom teachers for this population. Other university personnel such as Frances P. Connor also have become advocates for the disabled in the community; they have provided leadership at the national level by testifying for major legislation and leading national special study institutes exploring education and rehabilitation programming for the physically disabled. And a major

contribution has been made by all the educators and other specialists who provide direct instructional services to meet the individualized needs of this multiply handicapped population, all around the United States.

In addition, parent groups have organized various agencies to meet the needs of specific physically disabled populations, for example, the Easter Seal Society for Crippled Children and Adults, the United Cerebral Palsy Association, the Muscular Dystrophy Association, and the National Hemophilia Foundation. Cain (1976) noted that parent groups have been significantly influential in improving services and educational programming for the disabled. Such groups often evolve into agencies that provide national advocacy for legislative efforts and research and training related to the disabled. In addition, local branches and affiliated parent groups provide financial support for treatment, home care referral services, and research.

Currently educational programs serve children from infancy through young adulthood. With programs for early identification of disabilities and potential problems, infant stimulation programs, early childhood education, and vocational education for the physically and multiply handicapped, it is difficult to determine the number actually being served or who need special education services and programrning. However, the National Advisory Committee on the Handicapped (1976) identified 255,000 crippled and other health impaired children between birth and 19 years old who were served in special education programs; in addition, it noted 73,000 who are yet unserved. The committee estimates that approximately 9% of the total number of handicapped children served have a crippling or other health impairing condition.

NATURE OF DISORDERS

Following are some of the major disabilities of the physically disabled population. This information is brief and general; see the end of the chapter for suggestions for more information. In addition, remember that some students with crippling conditions and other health impairments *may* be multiply handicapped and, thus, may have accompanying problems related to learning, sensory input, social-emotional adjustment, or other areas.

Note that some of these disabilities are *acquired* after birth rather than present at birth (**congenital**). The difference in onset may, in fact, lead to different commonly associated emotional and psychological problems. Those with congenital disabilities may have a *sense of difference,* of not being like other people; those with acquired disabilities may experience a *sense of loss*, of having lost something they once had. The ways people deal with these conditions are quite different for the two groups and may also lead to the differences commonly seen in their approaches to problem solving and socialization. For example, newly disabled adults often become vocal advocates for their needs because they have just acquired a disability. In contrast, congenitally disabled children may become tired of "fighting" by the time they reach adulthood and thus may become condescending.

Crippling Conditions

Plegia refers to a paralysis while **paresis** refers to a partial paralysis. These two suffixes are often used with any number of prefixes to refer to the specific area of paralysis: **mono-** (one limb), **para-** (both lower extremities), **hemi-** (both extremities on the same side), **quad-** (all four extremities), and **di-** (all four extremities with greater involvement in the lower limbs). For example, a person with *hemiplegia* would have paralysis of both limbs on the same side of the body while a person with *monoparesis* would have partial paralysis of one limb.

Cerebral Palsy

Cerebral palsy accounts for the largest percentage of physically disabled children in special education programs. It is caused by damage to or improper development of the brain. *Cerebral palsy* refers to a general category of motor handicaps which have "in common an impairment of the coordination of muscle action with an inability to maintain normal postures and balance and to perform normal movements and skills" (Bobath & Bobath, 1975). The amount of physical disability varies greatly; some youngsters have slight fine motor coordination problems while others are severely involved. Several types of cerebral palsy are recognized, including those with the following characteristics:

1. Spasticity, referring to increased muscle tone (overactive, tight muscles);

2. Athetosis, characterized by uncontrolled, jerky, and irregular movement patterns;

3. Ataxia, lack of coordination related to balance; and

4. Mixed, indicating various combinations of the other types (Denhoff, 1976).

For example, a child with spastic cerebral palsy has excessive muscle tone which makes her muscles tight and resistant to movement, while a child with athetosis may have flailing limbs which are difficult for him to control for even gross movements; a child with ataxia has considerable difficulty in maintaining balance.

Often associated with cerebral palsy are problems related to sensory deficits, convulsive disorders, intellectual function, behavioral disturbance, learning, and emotional coping (Denhoff, 1976). The cause

profile
WINTHROP M. PHELPS, M.D.

Before 1900, little was done to encourage and rehabilitate persons with cerebral palsy and other physical disabilities. In the few years since then, much has happened to rehabilitate these individuals. About 1900, people first began to realize that children were not necessarily feebleminded if they were born with palsies that originated in the brain (cerebral). Before this time, Dr. William J. Little, an English surgeon, defined a group of clinical characteristics which became known as Little's Disease. *These characteristics covered:*

> the whole group, of which a typical example was the feebleminded, drooling child, with scissors gait and marked general spasticity. But further study has shown that there are many physically handicapped types, with or without mental deficiency. (Phelps, 1932, pp. 9–10)

Phelps, a surgeon, further explained that:

> These individuals may often be wrongly classified as mentally deficient because of lack of motor control of the facial muscles, or physical inability to speak or perform the usual intelligence tests. (1932, p. 10)

Phelps had recognized that there are many children with varied patterns of motor dysfunction due to apparent cerebral disorder

who may or may not be mentally deficient. He then organized his findings into descriptions of various types of motor dysfunction classified by state of muscle tone and presence or absence of involuntary movement, variabilities of etiologies or causes, and approaches to management. To this syndrome he applied the now universally accepted term cerebral palsy.

Dr. Phelps, assuming these handicapped individuals would be able to benefit from a treatment program, developed muscle training techniques. These basic principles of treatment are still being used. Using this positive approach, in 1937 he founded the Children's Rehabilitation Institute near Baltimore, which not only became a treatment center for handicapped persons but a training center for physical therapists, occupational therapists, and physicians. Parents became hopeful, and soon voluntary and public agencies, many spearheaded by parents, actively promoted the development of treatment centers.

By 1947, only 10 years after the Children's Rehabilitation Institute was opened as a treatment center, there was so much interest in rehabilitation of cerebral palsied persons that the American Academy for Cerebral Palsy was formed, with Phelps as

may be any number of factors which occur before, during, or after birth; risks of the child's having cerebral palsy are greater when there are problems related to prematurity, difficult labor, lack of oxygen at birth, and childhood trauma (Gordon, 1976).

In the classroom, students with cerebral palsy may need adaptive equipment to help them complete learning tasks. In addition, adaptive devices may be required to aid them in activities related to communication as well as in self-help activities such as toileting, dressing, and feeding. For some, physical tasks may be impossible even with adaptive aides and devices. When tasks are difficult, teachers and parents should encourage students to attempt as many as possible. They should avoid the temptation to overprotect children by doing tasks for them. Emphasis should be on increased independence. Physical, occupational, and speech therapists are active members of the team, providing assistance in physical improvement and developing adaptive approaches to help students function independently. Parents may help by continuing therapeutic treatment at home (Tyler & Kahn, 1976).

---

one of the four founding physicians. By 1957, 200 physicians specializing in cerebral palsy, including many trained by Phelps, had joined. Now the academy is called the American Academy of Cerebral Palsy and Developmental Medicine and has a membership of 900.

As Phelps was influencing the study and treatment of cerebral palsy throughout the United States and the world, he was also realizing that cerebral palsy was not only a medical and therapy problem. He collaborated with an educator and a parent of a handicapped child to write the first major book to help medically and educationally oriented lay and professional persons in their efforts to understand and rehabilitate persons with cerebral palsy. This book, The Cerebral-Palsied Child: A Guide for Parents *(Phelps, Hopkins, & Cousins, 1958), was the first and unfortunately one of the few comprehensive books in this field. In this book Phelps, a physician, helps parents understand their child's disability. He recognizes and addresses concerns related to medical and therapy matters and shows how collaboration is necessary among professionals (including teachers and psychologists), parents, and the disabled. Phelps saw that persons with cerebral palsy not only need treatment for motor problems but present other complex problems of rehabilitation:*

● How can those without speech or hand use show their intelligence?

● How can the child's self-help needs best be cared for?

● What can be done to help parental attitudes and adjustments towards children with such a handicap?

● How can these disabled students be helped to develop a desirable mental attitude and outlook?

● How can persons with cerebral palsy be helped to get along with other children and adults and to cope with reactions from able-bodied persons who don't understand the effects of cerebral palsy?

● What about schooling?

● Can cerebral-palsied individuals hope to work and lead useful lives?

Phelps opened the doors to understanding that most children with cerebral palsy—the largest group of physically disabled school-aged children can be taught to become contributing members of our society.

profile SUZANNE

Suzanne is in a primary class in a special education school. She is severely physically handicapped and confined to a wheelchair as a result of athetoid cerebral palsy. She is nonverbal because motor problems affect her speech. Lack of control of the muscles in her shoulders and arm make her unable to control a pencil for writing or coloring. An unspecified learning disability has prevented her from learning to read beyond a preprimer level, and she has very poor spelling skills. She does seem socially alert and appears to be aware of interactions and activities in class. Because she cannot talk or write, the school staff is trying to find different ways for her to communicate.

Muscular Dystrophy

Although **muscular dystrophy** has several adult forms, there is only one childhood form commonly found in special education classes—the Duchenne or pseudohypertrophic form. This disability causes an increasing (progressive) weakness of the skeletal muscles. Initial symptoms may include difficulty in running or climbing stairs; later, the child has difficulty in walking on a level surface. A characteristic "waddling gait" gives the impression of awkwardness or slowness; this sign usually appears before muscle weakness becomes so severe that the child is confined to a wheelchair. Weakness in the upper extremities may appear at the same time or somewhat later (Chutorian & Myers, 1974). This disease progresses fairly rapidly, with death usually occurring in the middle to late teens. It is generally caused by a sex-linked recessive gene transmitted through unaffected mothers to their sons; this hereditary disorder is rarely found in female children.

Physical treatment is limited to therapy to delay the development of muscle contractures. Teachers should remember that physical management of muscular dystrophy students includes allowing for the facts that they may tire easily, may be knocked down easily, and that their muscle weakness may cause them to be unable to complete tasks such as opening doors. Those who can still walk around the classroom may need wheelchairs for field trips.

Educational intervention is critical because the teacher can provide the psychological support the child needs to maintain a positive attitude, even though he has a terminal disability. Educational programming should provide for scholastic success with stress on development and accomplishment of attainable short-term goals. Overindulgence should be avoided at all costs; overprotection may foster negative attitudes and "whining" when reasonable demands for performance are made both at school and at home. In his emotional reactions, the child may be resentful and aggressive, and show signs of frustra-

profile ROY

Roy is a 9-year-old boy with muscular dystrophy who was enrolled in a special education program last year when he was no longer physically able to keep up with his regular school classmates. He often fell on the playground and in the classroom. He recently began to use a wheelchair for mobility, and he pushes it with his feet. Since then he has had many outbursts of anger and disruptive behavior in the classroom. Academically he is quite able, but his schoolwork seems to be affected by an increasingly negative attitude. His parents refuse to discuss the terminal nature of his disability with him or even with the teacher. The teacher has referred the family to the school social worker for discussions related to death, with the hope of increasing the quality of Roy's life, even though the amount of time he has left cannot be predicted.

tion, especially as he loses his independence and becomes nonambulatory. Educational programming should include preparation for sedentary but mentally active leisure-time and vocational training. In addition, the greatest problem for the teacher who works with muscular dystrophy students may be coping with their impending death. Death education is crucial for these students, their families, their peers, *and* their teachers.

Spina Bifida

Spina bifida takes several forms and, depending on its extent, it may also be called *meningocele* or *myelomeningocele;* students with myelomeningocele are most often found in special education classrooms because the disability is more complex and involved. A portion of the spinal cord is not enclosed by the vertebral neural arches, and a distortion of the spinal cord and nerve roots results in a neurological disorder and related deformities. Varying degrees of distortion of the spinal cord affect the neurological deficit; the neurological involvement may vary from minor sensory and/or motor loss to paraplegia with lack of bladder control (incontinence). There may be urinary tract disorders, orthopedic deformities, and problems related to skin sensitivity. In addition, many children with spina bifida may develop an abnormal blockage of cerebrospinal fluid in the cranial cavity (**hydrocephalus**), which, if not corrected by surgical implantation of a shunt, can cause mental retardation (Swinyard, 1966).

Children with spina bifida require considerable medical attention, often including physical therapy to help them develop walking (gait) patterns, usually with braces and crutches, and to help them become skilled in using a wheelchair. Classroom teachers should work closely with medical personnel to support treatment programs.

profile **KEVIN**

Kevin is a handsome young man born with spina bifida which left him paralyzed from the waist down, unable to move his legs and incontinent. The physician referred his parents to the local chapter of the Easter Seal Society for Crippled Children and Adults, where he was enrolled in a preschool program; the staff of the agency worked with his parents at home and at the agency to help him develop. Now 18 years old, Kevin is completing high school in a program which provides itinerant assistance from a special education resource specialist. Kevin has learned to drive, using a car with hand controls instead of pedals. He is almost totally independent in his physical care; only on occasion must he ask for help from others. He is writing to find out which 4-year colleges have barrier-free grounds and dormitory space. His expressed concerns are over his lack of confidence around women and his uncertainty about what he might investigate as a possible vocation.

Good personal hygiene, especially because of odor and infection caused by bladder and bowel control problems, should be part of the instructional program; self-care should be encouraged as early as possible. In addition to the physical problems which may be of major importance, especially in young children, teachers should be aware of the learning problems which may accompany hydrocephalus.

Spinal Cord Injury

Increasing numbers of students with **spinal cord injuries** and resulting paraplegia or quadriplegia owe their disability to traumatic injury—often bicycle or automobile accidents. Potential problem areas include urinary tract infections, respiratory infections, pressure sores from lack of movement which slows circulation (decubitus ulcers), contractures, and mobility problems.

Rehabilitation procedures are long and involved and never result in total return of lost function. However, using adaptive aids to complete activities, for example, wheelchairs for mobility, hand controls for driving, and button hooks for dressing, and developing alternative muscle groups to perform some activities may help the child recover maximum function.

The psychological trauma of any acquired disability may cause the greatest difficulty and hinder classroom performance; psychological support services may be necessary (Caywood, 1974). Students with higher level, and thus more debilitating, injuries (lesions) are more physically involved and may need more adaptive aids—for example, electric typewriters instead of pencils or pens, eating utensils with large handles—to complete tasks. Again, in all instances, independence should be encouraged in all activities; overprotection may foster unhealthy dependent relationships.

Osteogenesis Imperfecta

Osteogenesis imperfecta, or "brittle bones," is characterized by defective development in the quantity and the quality of bone. As a result, bones do not grow normally in length and thickness and are therefore very brittle. Dwarfism and deafness may be secondary associated disabilities.

Although learning is not affected by this disability, physical problems may be a major concern for classroom teachers. Students and teachers must be constantly aware of the student's fragility; simple activities such as stapling may even cause fractures. An early goal is the child's development of responsibility for self-protection. Teachers should try to supervise without hovering, allowing the student and classmates to develop a safe attitude. Activities, interests, and hobbies should focus on those skills which do not require much physical activity.

Limb Deficiency

Whether congenital or acquired, **limb deficiency**—absence of one or more limbs—may present a major obstacle to function and physical activity. In addition, the extent of the limb deficiency, for example, the level of functional loss, affects physical ability. Early intervention by rehabilitation personnel, including training in the use of an artificial limb (prosthetic device), is crucial to developing maximum function. Some students may choose not to use an artificial limb, relying instead on the use of the remaining portion of their deficient limb as a support limb. Student and parent perceptions of functional use of the artificial limb are a major consideration in a student's choice of whether or not to use it. Motivation may be a primary factor in determining if the child can better use her own limbs with the aid of a prosthesis. Therapists are essential members of the team, as they teach the child to use an artificial limb or the remaining portion of the natural limb most effectively and efficiently. Classroom teachers need to work with physical and occupational therapists to carry treatment over into classroom activities. Children with upper extremity involvement may need adaptive equipment for writing and feeding.

The kind or severity of psychological problems (related to the differences between congenital and acquired disabilities) may well depend on the age of onset, severity of disability, and the attitudes of parents and other significant people who work with the limb-deficient child.

Legg-Calve-Perthes Disease

Legg-Calve-Perthes disease, often referred to as Legg-Perthes or simply Perthes disease, usually occurs on only one side and involves a change in the density, or porousness, of the round end of the long thigh bone that fits into the hip socket (femoral head). The cause is unknown but may be trauma or genetics. Good to adequate return of function has been found in 80% of cases. Recovery depends on the amount of the femoral head which has been affected and the amount of permanent damage done during the course of the disease. Treatment often involves a brace which holds hips turned (in rotation) away from midline and prevents insult to the bone tissue normally caused by walking; some walking is possible with this brace (Katz & Challenor, 1974).

Although this disability does not affect learning potential, it may affect a student's attitude toward learning and the world in general. A negative attitude toward the sudden loss of independence may develop.

Arthrogryposis

The congenital disability **arthrogryposis** is characterized by stiff joints and weak muscles. Joints are usually deformed and stiff, with limited mobility; muscles of the limbs may be smaller than normal. Walking may or may not be possible, depending on the amount of hip and leg involvement. Adaptive equipment, such as hand splints for holding pencils and eating utensils, is often used to improve physical function, especially of the upper extremities.

In the classroom, students should follow a normal academic pattern. Vocational and leisure-time goals may need to include activities which do not require extensive hand skills or general mobility.

Juvenile Rheumatoid Arthritis

Juvenile rheumatoid arthritis is a chronic inflammatory disease of the joints and the tissues around them, usually developing between ages 2 and 5. Fever spikes, rash, and morning stiffness are characteristic symptoms and problems which often cause absences from school. Some children get relief from symptoms after a period of 10 years—as opposed to adults, who rarely get relief (Jacobs & Downey, 1974).

These students need some freedom to move in the classroom. If they sit for long periods of time, their joints may "gell." Alternative methods for completion of class assignments, for example, oral examinations or dictation on tape in lieu of written work, ease physical pain and allow for maximum academic function if the student's use of his hands is affected.

Spinal Muscular Atrophy

Spinal muscular atrophy is a hereditary disability which takes two separate forms: an infantile form called Werdnig-Hoffman's Disease and a juvenile form called Kugelberg-Welander Disease. Both forms are progressive neuromuscular disorders which cause muscular wasting (atrophy). The infantile form is characterized by rapid progression, usually resulting in death before school age. However, children with the juvenile form, which has a slower, more benign course, may be enrolled in special education programs. Initial atrophy in the juvenile form is usually in the leg muscles and progresses later to the muscle of the shoulder girdle, upper arms, and neck. Children with this form may live a normal life span and may be able to walk for as long as 20 years after they first have symptoms (Koehler, 1975).

The classroom implications for this disability are much like those for muscular dystrophy. Students may tire and fall easily; a wheelchair may be helpful for field trips. As the upper extremity muscles weaken, adaptation of long writing activities may be necessary. When students lose their physical independence, they may act resentful and frustrated.

Other Health Impairments

We have been discussing the common crippling disorders of the COHI population—the more visible disabilities. Following are other common health impairments. Many of these disorders are not visible, which may cause problems for the disabled person because the general public does not understand some of the unique behavior patterns which develop as a result of, or as an adaptation to, the disability.

Epilepsy

Epilepsy is a seizure disorder that may be a problem all to itself or a disability associated with another physical problem such as cerebral palsy. There are several types of seizures, all of which are caused by abnormal, excessive electrical brain discharges. Not all seizures are readily visible; only some involve a change in state of consciousness or obvious physical movement. No set form of classification of epilepsy has been recognized. However, Bruya and Bolin (1976) cite the work of Schmidt and Wilder (1968), adopted in 1970 by the International League Against Epilepsy, as a system which organizes seizures in a way that aids understanding of cause and treatment. They describe

---

profile MARGARET

Margaret is a seemingly normal second grader; however, she has generalized seizures, both grand mal and petit mal. Although the doctors have been relatively successful in controlling the grand mal seizures with medication, she occasionally has a seizure in class. She was terribly self-conscious after the first seizure, but the teacher helped her and her classmates by explaining to the class that Margaret could not help her actions and that they should not be afraid. Rather, they should try to understand a seizure and not dwell on it after it was over. In addition to grand mal seizures, Margaret has frequent petit mal seizures which have not been controlled with medication. As a result, Margaret's teacher is careful to note when Margaret misses words in dictation of spelling lists or suddenly stops reading aloud; both of these may be signs of petit mal seizures.

---

generalized, partial, and miscellaneous seizures.

Generalized seizures. Generalized seizures include grand mal, petit mal, myoclonic, and akinetic seizures. Generally, the person loses consciousness, and the seizures occur without warning. The *grand mal* is the most striking and involves extraneous, uncontrolled movement of all portions of the body, equally on both sides (symmetrical). Salivation increases; bladder and bowel control may be lost. Most grand mal seizures last only a few minutes, after which the student may sleep for several hours. During the seizure itself, the teacher should try to set a good example for the other students by remaining calm and should move furniture or other objects which may harm the student if he strikes them during the seizure. If possible, the student's head should be turned to the side so saliva does not accumulate and cause choking. *Petit mal seizures* may go unnoticed in the classroom because obvious behavior changes very little; sometimes the only clue may be a slight disorientation in the midst of an activity; for example, the student may miss a word during a dictation assignment. *Myoclonic seizures* involve a sudden, brief muscular contraction that may or may not be symmetrical and recurring; the "myoclonic jerk" involves upward jerk of arms and trunk bending (flexion), which may cause a student to fall to the ground from his chair. *Akinetic seizures* involve a sudden loss of muscle tone and postural control; this lack of control affects the student's ability to "break his fall" and thus he may injure his head or shoulder because of a fall, which suggests that the child should always wear a helmet to protect his head.

Partial seizures. Partial seizures may affect both motor function and behavior; they are often called *psychomotor seizures.* These seizures may appear in many patterns, ranging from brief loss of consciousness to extended periods of purposeless activity. For instance, the student who misbehaves or acts strangely during this type of seizure may appear to be conscious when, in fact, he is not at all conscious of the abnormal behavior, even, for example, running around the room. Another type of partial seizure is the *Jacksonian seizure*. It is often called a "marching seizure" because the motor movement begins in one extremity and progressively "marches" through the entire body until there is generalized body movement.

Miscellaneous seizures. Miscellaneous seizures include those which appear to be related to high fever in infants and young children, that is, *febrile seizures*. The seizure is usually of the grand mal type. The tendency toward this type of seizure is usually outgrown by the time the child reaches age 6.

Seizure disorders may present relatively few classroom management problems if antiepileptic drugs are successful. Teachers can provide physicians with vital information about the effect of medication changes or changes in classroom behavior which seem related to medication. An epileptic child's teachers should be aware of appropriate treatment and precipiting factors for seizure (Feldman, 1975).

In addition, teachers should be aware that the alteration of brain function associated with seizure disorders does not imply associated learning problems. Academic ability varies among those with epilepsy as it does among those in the normal population (Holdsworth & Whitmore, 1974). However, heavy medication may affect student learning; academic performance changes should be reported to the physician for consideration in medication management.

Juvenile Diabetes Mellitus

Juvenile diabetes mellitus is an often hereditary metabolic disorder characterized by the body's inability to use sugars and starches (carbohydrates) to create energy needed for normal functioning. The pancreas does not make enough insulin, which causes glucose—the energy provider—to disperse into the cells. Thus, the glucose level in the blood rises because it cannot get into the cells without insulin; without glucose, the body has no energy and cannot function (Christiansen, 1975).

The classroom teacher needs to be aware of the symptoms of insulin reaction (too much insulin) and ketoacidosis (not enough insulin), and notify medical personnel at the first sign of a problem. Improper identification of their symptoms and improper treatment may be fatal. The symptoms of insulin reaction are rapid onset of headache, nausea, vomiting, palpitations, irritability, shallow breathing, and/or cold, moist skin. The recommended treatment is to give orange juice, a candy bar, a sugar cube, or other sugar on which the insulin will react.

The symptoms of ketoacidosis are gradual onset of fatigue, drinking large amounts of water, producing large amounts of urine, excessive hunger, deep breathing, and/or warm, dry skin. The treatment is to give insulin (Christiansen, 1975).

Hemophilia

Sometimes referred to as "bleeder's disease," **hemophilia** is a blood disorder that is sex-linked genetically; the unaffected mother passes the disorder to her son. The disease is extremely rare in females. It is characterized by poor blood clotting ability; and, although there is great danger in case of massive blood loss, internal hemorrhage is the most difficult problem. Bumps which would cause normal bruising in a nonhemophiliac child may cause massive internal bleeding in the hemophiliac. Such bleeding may cause blood to pour into joints and surrounding tissues; accumulation of blood in these areas may destroy tissue, causing temporary immobility and pain, with the possible danger of permanent disability from degeneration of joints.

Treatment previously involved massive transfusions of whole blood, but modern technology has isolated the clotting factor of the blood which is missing in hemophiliacs, called Factor VIII. Factor VIII is frozen into a substance called *cryoprecipitate* which may be given intravenously to aid in clotting. Some students may be on regular doses of "cryo" in an effort to prevent bleeding (McElfresh, 1974).

Learning may be indirectly affected by hemophilia. Frequent, short absences from school due to internal bleeding may disrupt educational programming. The child needs to become responsible for protecting himself early in life, especially since this disability is invisible, and other people, therefore, have no "warning" to be careful with or to protect the hemophiliac. Students need to become responsible for establishing a safe but *not* distant attitude among their peers. In addition, teachers and administrators in the mainstream of regular education may need to be encouraged to accept the hemophiliac. Although children with hemophilia should be cautious, they should not be overprotected and sheltered from a normal learning environment because of physical considerations; only slight modifications in programming are necessary. Educational programming should include moderately modified physical activity.

Cystic Fibrosis

Cystic fibrosis is a terminal hereditary disorder found mostly in Caucasians and is characterized by chronic lung (pulmonary) disease, pancreatic deficiency, and high levels of sweat electrolytes, which cause a serum-like sweat. Respiratory symptoms, including a dry, nonproductive cough, susceptibility to acute infection, and bronchial obstruction by abnormal secretions, are a major problem. Recent medical advances have improved a once generally poor prognosis. Early diagnosis may extend life expectancy into adulthood; treatment may include taking antibiotics, replacing defi-

cient pancreatic enzymes, modifying diet, and doing breathing exercises (Committee for a Study for Evaluation of Testing for Cystic Fibrosis, 1976).

As with other fatal disabilities, educational programming may provide a major source of support and stability in these students' lives. Learning potential is not directly affected by this disability, so programming should include successful, challenging academic work. In addition, teachers should recognize the psychological implications of the treatment and prognosis. Activities should continue, but teachers should be aware that strenuous exercise beyond tolerance may be harmful. The student should be encouraged to cough to loosen thick coating on bronchial passages. Death education should be a consideration in helping the children develop a concept of *quality* in a limited lifespan.

Sickle Cell Anemia

Sickle cell anemia is a hereditary disorder more prevalent among, but not limited to, members of the black population. It is an abnormal blood condition in which the shape of the hemoglobin in the red blood cell is distorted into a crescent (sickle) shape. These cells do not pass easily through blood vessels and thus may abruptly cut off blood supply to some tissues, causing severe pains in the abdomen, legs, and arms; swelling of the joints; fatigue; and high fever. Periods when these symptoms occur are referred to as "crises." The potential damage to tissues due to loss of blood supply may cause degeneration of joints and related orthopedic problems. "Crises" are chronic and recur at irregular intervals (Walker, 1975).

Although academic programming is not directly affected by this disorder, frequent absence from school may affect academic performance. Classroom considerations include avoiding crisis-producing situations such as emotional stress, chilling, strenuous exercise, and infections.

Cardiac (Heart) Conditions

Cardiac conditions may be either congenital or acquired; if acquired, they usually result from some type of infectious disease, such as rheumatic fever. In addition, heart defects present at birth may not be detected until later; so even though they are congenital, they may seem to be acquired. Physical considerations and safe level of activity are recommended by the student's physician.

Essentially, cardiac patients may attend most regular school programs with or without minor modifications to regulate physical activity and rest periods. Motivation for academic performance may be difficult if physical activity must be severely limited. Students need to feel that they are part of the group and to develop skills which do not require excess physical exertion.

Cancer

Cancer is an uncontrolled irregular cell growth. Its causes and cure are still largely unknown. In children, leukemia (marrow failure) and tumors of the eye, brain, bone, and kidney are most common. Usually, the prognosis depends on early treatment; treatment choices include radiation, drugs (chemotherapy), and surgery. Side effects of the disease or treatment include emotional problems, fatigue, extreme weight loss or gain, nausea, susceptibility to upper respiratory infection, headaches, and baldness.

Although the educational program of the child with cancer need not necessarily be different, teachers need to accept the student's need for a flexible schedule that allows for time to rest. Time may be lost due to physical discomfort and irritability as well as hospitalization. In addition, the unique psychological needs of the child with a potentially terminal illness must be recognized. Motivation and performance may

profile ANGELA

Angela, once a very normal first grader, is now severely physically handicapped and profoundly retarded as a result of brain injuries sustained when she was struck by a car. She makes no attempt to move on her own, to reach for objects, or to move toward someone. Her parents could not tell if Angela could see or hear, but they knew very well she could not move without being physically guided. Devastated by the changes that resulted from the accident, they sought an education program which would help their child. Fortunately, they found an excellent one in a public school program for severely developmentally delayed children.

vary somewhat with both the child's mood and physical involvement.

Other Syndromes and Birth Defects

We have examined the major disabilities which are found in the COHI population. This list is not all inclusive. There are many syndromes and birth defects which occur infrequently but which may warrant major considerations in educational programming. See the reading list at the end of the chapter for references which might cover these other disabilities.

The psychological implications and other side-effects of crippling conditions and health impairments are as varied as the disorders themselves. Some notes on psychological problems related to specific disabilities have been made throughout this section. Anxiety, frustration, resentment, and poor self-concept are symptoms which are common within this population but which may be at least partially relieved by a psychologically supportive environment, both at school *and* at home (see Sirvis, Carpignano, & Bigge, 1976).

PROBLEMS REQUIRING INTERVENTION AND MANAGEMENT

Communication

Many children who have physical disabilities also have communication problems. Some disabled children are nonvocal; they have much to say but cannot say it because of a physical inability to produce intelligible speech. Some may have delayed language development or may have only limited, if any, ideas to express. Other children do know what they want to mark or write during their lessons but cannot do so because of their physical disability. (See chapter 10 for more details on communication disorders.)

Expressing Thoughts to Others

Expressing basic needs and conversing in spite of unintelligible or absent speech is a major problem for many children with physical disabilities. Few nonvocal physically disabled children can communicate in complex social situations. Many learn to convey only their basic wants and needs. They may never learn to use the seemingly simple concepts of yes and no. Those children, who do have something to say but cannot say it because of physical disability, need to establish some movements that can be used consistently as signals to indicate yes and no, at least. These are simple but vital responses. Signals vary from looking at the written word _yes_ applied to one wheelchair arm and the word _no_ on the other wheelchair arm to blinking the eyes to

profile THE TRACE RESEARCH AND DEVELOPMENT CENTER

The interdisciplinary research and development work of the Trace Center (Madison, Wisconsin) focuses on solving the communication problems faced by nonvocal persons with severe physical handicaps. All Center projects share the common goal of providing these individuals with meaningful and efficient means of communicating. The staff particularly encourages and welcomes information on methods and materials developed by teachers working with nonvocal handicapped children and adults.

Since 1972, the Trace Center has evolved several major projects. Communication Aid Research and Development _involves creating and refining simple, complex, and electronic communication aids, as well as the accessories and input/output modes that will maximize the usefulness of_ these aids. In Training and Communication Research, _the Center staff develops and conducts workshops on communication programs for the nonvocal severely physically handicapped, offering this training on both inservice and preservice levels. To expand the impact of this personnel preparation program, a series of application notes and a videotaped curriculum series for teachers are being produced._

Another major component of the Trace Center, the Research Integration and Information Dissemination Project, _finds information produced in the field and spreads it through reports, publications, and annotated bibliographies. In addition, through its_ Consultative Services Project, _Center staff members work with professionals or parents who are trying to develop communication for nonvocal severely handicapped children or adults._

These projects have produced written reports and tangible products, including:

communicate yes and dropping the head for no.

In addition to the use of basic signals like yes and no, many children. learn to use other systems of communication. Many use "communication boards" that contain displays of pictures, symbols, letters, numbers, words, and/or phrases to which they point directly. When it is impossible for physically disabled children to point with their hands, electronic communication aids can be activated by hand, elbow, tongue, or eye.

Children who rely on "yes/no," "I don't know," and "maybe" responses depend on others to use specific procedures in questioning. When given choices, these children must be given a chance to review the options and then to indicate yes or no to each option until their choice, or choices, becomes clear. The listener may need to repeat as much of the message as he has received and then ask if the interpretation is "exactly right." A reply of no should be followed by questions such as "Is there more?" or "Am I close?" If these techniques do not clarify the message, the listener

Peter uses his communication board to tell jokes, debate, and interact with his high school classmates.

should repeat each word individually until the disabled person in some way indicates the incorrect or misleading word.

Many nonvocal students are capable of using their skills to solve problems and to interact with others when those who work

- *The Autocom, an auto-monitoring communication board.*

- *The Versi-com, a similar aid that can be used by individuals who are so severely handicapped that they cannot point with a finger, arm, or hand.*

- *An easily operated scanning communication aid that can be used by the severely mentally and physically handicapped.*

- *A miniature data-recording system useful along with advanced electronic communication boards to provide language acquisition information.*

- *A state-of-the-art paper and synthesis of current issues and problems in providing effective communication avenues for non-*

vocal severely physically handicapped individuals.

- *A series of annotated bibliographies of currently available communication aids.*

- *A national workshop series on communication aids and techniques, including publications of workshop proceedings.*

- *A series of two-day workshops and a packaged workshop,* Where to Begin *in the development of communication programs for the nonvocal severely physically handicapped.*

- *A Bliss Symbol communication program at the Central Wisconsin Center for the Developmentally Disabled, which is providing the residents enrolled with a functional and effective means of communication.*

with them devise ways for them to communicate and show what and how much they are thinking. Their contributions and interactions are limited only the nonhandicapped communicator's ability to find ways to permit and foster two-way communication. On college campuses, on the streets, and in classrooms, physically disabled persons are often avoided because ablebodied persons are unsure of how, or how much, the obviously disabled person can communicate. This is a disadvantage to both of them; each is deprived of the opportunity to become acquainted and communicate with the other. When in doubt, people should feel free to approach disabled children and adults and talk with them as they would with anyone else. If it becomes evident that the disabled person has a problem in expression, others can ask: "Please show me the way you say yes and the way you indicate no." In most cases, disabled persons are more than happy to show their ways of communicating so that they can proceed with the conversation. Much too frequently people ask only simple questions, rather than pursue a more in-depth conversation such as they would with those who have speech. Often nonvocal people are anxious for more in-depth interactions.

Recording Answers and Ideas when Unable to Write

In almost any school situation, children work independently at their seats writing lessons. However, some physically disabled children cannot write because of poor motor control, a lost limb, or weak arms. They need other ways to record answers and write ideas. Tape recorders may be used to record answers or lessons. In addition, the physically disabled may be taught to use the typewriter, even though their disability may limit them to onehanded typing. Electric typewriters are the easiest for most disabled youngsters to

This template lets students type with a stick more easily.

handle. Metal guards placed over typewriter keys prevent students from hitting more than one key at a time. Typewriter keys may be used traditionally or struck in alternative ways, for example, with erasers on the end of pencils which are held in the student's hand, by dowel sticks attached to head gear, or by mouth sticks. Problems may be written on large sheets of paper and placed on an easel, so the child can

Merry is using a mouth stick to type.

Chapter thirteen

mark correct answers by stroking them with a large crayon attached to an extension from a helmet on his head.

It is difficult but possible to find ways some moderately and severely physically disabled children can have the opportunity to complete a task without aid from others. Using adaptive procedures and devices such as those suggested, students can learn to work independently on several lessons each day.

Positioning, Movement, and Mobility

Sitting posture may be difficult for some children with physical disabilities. Finnie (1975) explains that after analysis of each child's difficulties, one finds positions which "enable him to use his hands to the best advantage, that will be easiest for eye-hand coordination and will present the least difficulties for balance" (p. 229). There are several sitting positions that may provide a secure posture for the child during classroom activity periods: crossed-leg or "tailor" sitting, side sitting, and chair sitting. Straps and other props are sometimes added to improve posture. Medical personnel and therapists should be asked to recommend positions for each child to aid desired posture and movements and discourage undesirable ones.

Whenever possible, disabled persons should have the privilege of moving from place to place as independently as possible. Again, medical personnel and therapists can recommend procedures which do not negatively affect a child's physical condition.

If children cannot walk alone, they are often taught other means of mobility. They may begin to develop independence in moving from place to place by rolling or crawling. They may need crutches, walkers, or toy vehicles such as flexies or tricycles. Other students may learn to maneuver wheelchairs using one or two hands; still others use electric wheelchairs or other

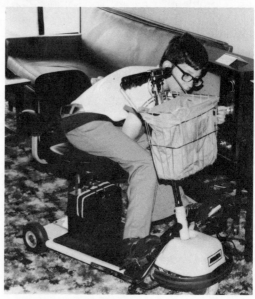

John is using an Amigo to get from place to place.

means of motorized vehicular travel such as the *Amigo*. A child should not use a motorized vehicle until he has enough motor control to maneuver the electric wheelchair carefully and he shows enough responsibility to operate it without hurting the people around him.

When students use vehicular travel, they must learn to transfer to and from a car or to be able to instruct others how to transfer them. They must depend on others to know and use proper lifting techniques, proper transferring techniques, proper positioning, and safe wheelchair pushing.

Physical Barriers and Inconveniences

Whether children are educated in special settings or in regular schools, modifications are often necessary to allow them to be physically independent. Advocates should take some responsibility to identify and remove possible barriers (Bigge, 1976c). Ramps enable children in wheelchairs or on crutches to enter buildings easily. In many older buildings, doorways must be expanded to allow wheelchairs to pass. In some cases, it is helpful to protect the bases of doors and door jambs so that the wheelchairs do not scar them. Toilet facilities, play areas, and drinking fountains must be located so that children in wheelchairs or on crutches have access to them. "Grab bars" alongside drinking fountains, in toilet stalls, and near sections of chalkboards are also helpful.

In the classroom, some furniture may need to be removed to make room for wheelchairs. Foot rests and adjustable seats that swivel to allow children with braces to sit down more easily and then

turn to face the desk may be helpful. Special adjustable tables, "cut-out" tables, and stand-up tables help children who have special problems in sitting or standing.

Adaptive Methods, Equipment, and Materials

Problems related to coordination, muscle weakness, paralysis and loss of sensation, low vitality, and limb deficiency often prevent children from completing tasks without aids. Special educators, therapists, parents, and rehabilitation specialists all need to assess the physical problems which make it difficult for a child to complete necessary tasks. Teachers may be catalysts in developing substitute ways for children to do things independently. Adaptations and designs of methods, equipment, and materials to assist with communication, completion of classroom tasks, positioning, body movement, and mobility have already been mentioned. Each adaptive procedure is designed to accommodate the learning abilities and characteristics of individual disabled children. Considerations for adaptive equipment and materials also include size, type of materials, and the child's kinds and limitations of physical movements. Often trial-and-error is necessary; only when an adaptive method is successful may everyone be convinced the choice of material, design, and method was justified.

Self-Help

Throughout their schooling and their interaction with parents and other helpers, physically disabled children need help in learning self-help skills to use in all of the other aspects of their lives: toileting, eating, homemaking, transportation, and solving all kinds of problems that pertain to their self-sufficiency (Bigge, 1976c; Connor, 1975; Cruickshank, 1976; Finnie, 1975). *Self-help* may not always mean actually

Robert's mother experiments with a cup adapted for him.

A wooden jig was designed so Suzie could stuff envelopes.

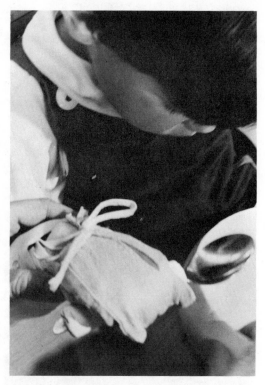

Shawn uses a spoon attached to a mitt to prevent him from constantly dropping it.

Emily has learned to tell others how they can help her.

doing the task independently, because that may be physically impossible. Here, *self-help* may mean that handicapped persons learn how to direct others in helping them complete such tasks.

Whenever possible, children should be taught to manage common classroom equipment such as pencils and papers. They may need to be taught to use special equipment such as special table tops, clamps which prevent their papers from slipping, cups with handles to prevent spilling, or special pencil holders. They must also learn early how to operate their own rehabilitation equipment—braces, wheelchairs, splints—as much as possible. If they cannot manage certain parts of their equipment, they should learn procedures to be used by helpers and be able to direct their helpers in using those procedures. They should learn simple maintenance and repair of their own equipment whenever possible.

Disabled persons or their advocates should be able to recognize the need for specialized rehabilitation equipment and help select it. They need to be aware of financing possibilities, criteria for eligibility for funding, commercial sources of equipment, and procedures for obtaining equipment that is not made commercially.

CURRENT NEEDS IN INSTRUCTIONAL PROGRAMMING

The degree of a child's physical disability is not always the same as the severity of the educational problems. Some children with only mild physical disability may have profound retardation; some confined to wheelchairs have accompanying learning problems that require special procedures and materials to help them learn; still others with a wide range of severity in physical disabilities can learn with their nondisabled peers. Educational programming for the physically handicapped may include early intervention, varied educational services, flexible personnel, and innovative curricula and instructional strategies.

Early Intervention

Early intervention is crucial to the development of physically disabled children's maximum potential. Some infants have obvious problems at birth while others' problems may not be recognized until they fail to develop as expected. Educational programming should begin in infancy, or as soon as the special needs are noticed. It should continue into preschool programming and throughout the school years to career education and sometimes even into extended adult education. Educational programming for some may be identical, or very similar, to educational programming for the nonhandicapped. Those with problems that require highly specialized help or a special environment may be taught in special settings.

Varieties of Educational Service

Educational programs for the physically disabled take many forms and are provided within a variety of administrative arrangements. Some programs serve primarily infants and preschoolers, while others serve school-age pupils and still others provide continuing educational opportunities for adults. Persons seeking appropriate educational services for disabled students should investigate city, county, regional, state, national, private, and social service agency resources. A wide variety of programs are available, including:

1. Agency programs for infant development, for example, United Cerebral Palsy Association programs for atypical infants;

2. Head Start, school district, and other programs which include handicapped children;

3. Regular classes with no supportive help, if none is needed;

4. Regular classes with needed supplementary instructional services and other resource services—specialists in education

of disabled students, specialists in helping students with visual and/or hearing impairment, physical therapists, occupational therapists, speech therapists, and perhaps services of psychologists and social workers;

5. Public school special classes in special education schools or in regular schools;

6. Private education programs;

7. Telephone teaching—"teleteaching";

8. Developmental centers for profoundly handicapped;

9. Community colleges with special education counselors;

10. Colleges and universities;

11. Regional occupational centers;

12. Sheltered workshops;

13. Continuing education programs; and

14. Combinations of any of the above plus innumerable other options.

Gromek and Scandary (1977) suggest considerations for special classroom placement and regular classroom placements.[1] They suggest that those students considered for classroom placement should have need for one or more of the following:

1. Intensive habilation or rehabilitation therapy:

"Intensive" implies that the child shall have two or more therapy treatments weekly for an extended period of time (time span consideration in *months* or *years*).

2. Extensive habilation or rehabilitation therapy:

"Extensive" implies the need for multiple therapy programs (i.e., occupational

---

[1] Guidelines for special class placement and regular class placement are used with permission of the authors. From "Considerations in the Educational Placement of the Physically or Otherwise Health Impaired Child" by I. Gromek and J. Scandary, *DOPHHH Journal*, 1977, *3*(1), 9–11.

Special equipment can lead to better learning for handicapped children, whether the equipment is for physical therapy, like gross motor training for Denise with the wedge (right), or mobility training for Randy with his walker (lower left). Or equipment can actually compensate for limits created by impairments, as with Diana's hand-powered wheelchair on the ramp (lower right) or Billy's motorized wheelchair (top left).

The occupational therapist uses a special piece of equipment to teach Diana the fine motor skills necessary for dressing herself (top left). A mirror and mat with a special cushion (lower left) help this child with cerebral palsy learn to raise his head and keep it up. With a spoon attached to his hand, Eddie is able to feed himself (top of opposite page). Because he does not have adequate arm and hand control, Randy types with a pencil which he holds between his toes (bottom of opposite page).

Special equipment is critical for individuals with sensory impairments. For the hearing handicapped, a hearing aid (top right) amplifies sound to take advantage of any residual hearing that is present. For those who cannot hear phone conversations at all, a Magsat telephone (top left) uses regular phone lines but has a keyboard and read-out for visual display of messages. For visually handicapped people who use Braille, a Perkins Brailler (center right) is a special typewriter that allows them to create their own Braille materials. For the partially sighted, a vast array of low vision aids are available. Some of these require no special optics but use large print, special lighting, and the like (lower left). Others (lower right) use some form of optical design — microscopic or telescopic — to aid vision.

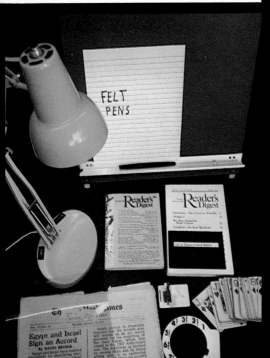

therapy, physical therapy, speech therapy, etc.) for two or more therapy treatments weekly for an extended period of time.

3. A protective environment for an extended period of time for one or more of the following reasons:

    a. Need for constant assistance in the performing of basic daily living activities (eating, toileting, dressing, etc.)

    b. Need for a limited environment for *safe* functioning of the child.

    c. Inability to communicate needs and responses in any understandable manner.

    d. When the "normal" school setting for the child would pose multiple educational barriers to the extent that the child's educational program would be too restricted (i.e., architectural barriers and curriculum offerings were too limiting for a full range of educational programming for the child.)

    e. The disability is so deforming that psychological abuse to the child in the "regular" educational setting must be considered.

    f. The child exhibits inabilities for coping with the "normal" educational atmospheres and pressures (has need for slower pace, fewer children, less change, etc.).

4. Parents or guardians who give support to a special classroom placement consideration and see it as most appropriate educational placement for the child at this particular time.

Gromek and Scandary (1977) further suggest guidelines for students considered for regular class placement. Students should have:

1. Sufficient mental ability to function within the range of intelligence within the classroom into which the child will be moving.

2. Sufficient mobility to move from place to place within the normal educational setting. This does not mean that such mobility must be totally independent of aid. Wheelchairs, push chairs, wagons, motorized chairs, crutches, canes, and walkers can be used to facilitate movement of the student.

3. Sufficient indication of ability to interact with peers in a variety of settings, classroom, recreation, and social events.

4. A desire to be with normal peers in a regular school setting.

5. Some exposure to or experiences in integrated activities whether through school, recreational, social or church settings.

6. Parents or guardians who express a desire for the child to be integrated and feel that the child can be successful in such a setting, or favorably consider such placement for a trial period.

7. The ability to function independently in most activites of daily living, i.e., feeding, toileting, dressing, etc. (It is understood that for particular handicapping conditions some of these skills may not be fully realized. However, careful analysis should be made as to the amount of help needed per individual child as well as the child's ability to communicate to get the necessary help when needed.)

8. Sufficient emotional stability to be able to cope with the normal educational setting and situations (doesn't panic under change of setting, personnel or scheduling).

9. Sufficient ability to communicate needs in some understandable [and quick] manner. This is not restricted to verbal communication ability. Written, typed, signs, gestures—when understandable to a receiver, are considered as adequate.

The decision to change an individual student's placement, of course, depends upon many factors: the responsibility shown by the personnel at the current school, the responsibility accepted by the personnel at the proposed new schools or program, the willingness of personnel from several disciplines to collaborate on programming, the availability of transportation and aides or volunteers, and architectural access outside and inside the school. A specific decision about the best course for a certain individual may not be consistent with broad guidelines. It is possible, for instance, to consider placing a student who has interests and "mental ability to function within the range of intelligence within the classroom" in a regular classroom. That student may, however, be totally dependent on others and may not have ability to "function independently in most activities of daily living."

Nor do some students have "ability to communicate needs (ideas or answers) in some manner which is understandable (and quick)." Chris, who is shown in the upper right photograph on page 350, fits this description. He can think on levels similar to his regular class peers but can not read enough to learn his lessons through reading. He learns his lessons by listening to lectures, listening to others read, and listening to tapes of textbooks provided by volunteer readers. He communicates his answers with head signals and an alphabet board slowly but accurately to resouce teachers who come "on call" to assist him.

Laura and her teacher discuss their plans for the day.

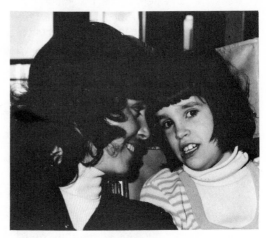

In whatever setting or settings students with disabilities receive their education, every effort should be made to help them become and remain a part of the group and prevent them from becoming and remaining apart.

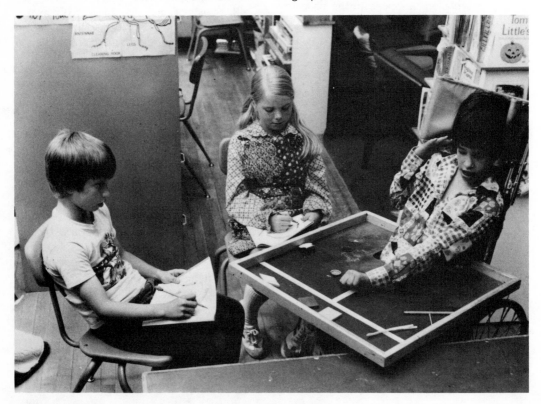

Laura enjoys being a part of regular classes.

Flexible, Discerning Professionals

Regardless of where physically disabled children are taught or by whom, questions must be asked to receive the accurate, relevant information needed to design appropriate educational programming. Teachers may ask questions about a variety of topics, including the following examples.

Communication Questions

1. In what ways, and with what clarity, can this child communicate:
    a. Intelligible speech?
    b. Gesture language?
    c. Consistent body movement or signals for yes and no?
    d. Pointing at symbols on a communication board?
    e. Handwriting?
    f. Using electronic communication device?

2. Does this pupil need extended time to respond?

Written Expression Questions

1. How are the pupil's understanding and skill levels assessed?

2. Can the child write or type?

3. If the child cannot write, type, or talk, in what other ways can he respond?

4. How can the pupil mark answers and record ideas?

Learning Questions

1. What adaptations are necessary to help the pupil manage classroom equipment and materials, for example, pencils, paper, books, and other materials?

2. What, if any, behavior management techniques are used?

3. How (through what mode) does this student best learn each different kind of task (auditory, visual, and so forth)?

4. What special procedures or materials help the child learn?

5. What are top priority objectives for learning?

Mobility Questions

1. What limitations, if any, are there on mobility?

2. How does the child move from place to place (crawl, roll, trike, wheelchair, and so forth)?

3. When, and how, should the pupil be physically assisted (lifting, transfers, pushing, in and out of walker, tied in wheelchair, and so forth)?

Self-Help Questions

1. What physical self-help activities can the pupil do for himself?

2. If he cannot complete some self-help tasks independently, what assistance does he require?

Questions about Accommodation for Physical Differences

1. Are there any restrictions on physical activities?

2. How can games and activities be adapted so he can participate?

3. What physical positions and postures are to be encouraged? Discouraged?

4. What special emergency procedures should be anticipated?

Interdisciplinary Planning Questions

1. Who else is, or ought to be, working with this student?

2. How can efforts of professionals and others be guided to benefit this child?

While teachers have a major responsibility for *education* of each preschool and school-aged student, a variety of rehabilitation specialists meet their therapy needs, evaluate them, and serve as resources. Generally, **physical therapists** (P.T.'s) concentrate on improving postures and movement patterns, recommend positions, and teach the use of rehabilitation equipment such as braces and wheelchairs. This help should begin at infancy—earlier than required academic education—and continue throughout life. **Occupational therapists** (O.T.'s) also work on improving postures and movements. They traditionally concentrate on self-help skills or activities of daily living, such as eating, dressing, and grooming. In many instances, physical therapists and occupational therapists take a major responsibility to help teach life experience skills such as use of public transportation, homemaking, mobility, and prevocational training.

Speech and language specialists help the many physically disabled children who also have speech problems or language delays. Psychologists, social workers, rehabilitation counselors, nurses, and agency personnel assist with special problems. It is imperative that whenever possible and helpful, teachers, rehabilitation specialists, parents, perhaps the disabled person herself, and others collaborate in education and rehabilitation of the disabled person.

Curriculum

Curriculum objectives for physically disabled students may be planned by educators, therapists, parents, vocational counselors, pupil service workers, medical personnel, and the disabled students themselves whenever appropriate. Academic learning as traditionally defined may or may not be among the priority curriculum objectives. Reading, writing, and arithmetic may never be priority objectives for those physically disabled persons who are also profoundly mentally retarded. Increasing self-care can be considered a universal curriculum objective for persons with physical disabilities. For those able to learn to function with some degree of independence in the home, school, and community, school curricula should include opportunities to learn life experience skills, work skills, and related social behaviors. The physically disabled need to learn to be advocates for their own interest. All should also have the opportunity to learn productive and satisfying leisure time activities.

Academic Learning

Academics should be taught to the highest degree possible for each individual. Curricula should reflect different goals for different individuals. Some students profit most from emphasis on practical aspects of academic subjects. Practical math, for instance, teaches the basic skills necessary for conducting personal business such as budgeting and spending money and measuring and following directions in cooking. When there is an indication that a pupil might be able to do more complex and theoretical operations in math or any other academic subject, these goals and objectives should be extended. Physically disabled persons should study the social sciences, biological sciences, mathematics, and other academic subjects to the degree possible for them.

Self-Care

Self-care is a priority for disabled persons of all ages. Young severely physically disabled and profoundly retarded persons need various combinations of program goals based on basic functional needs: eating and drinking, toileting, dressing and undressing, bathing, and nasal and oral hygiene. Physically disabled persons should strive to accomplish these functional skills throughout their lives, but they must first know *what* they need to learn to do.

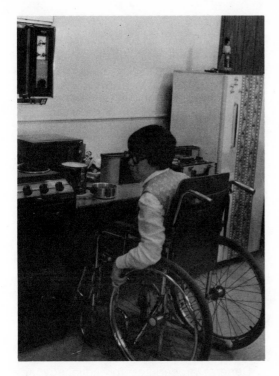

The classroom for the physically handicapped where Lisa is learning to cook is part of a regular high school.

Life Experience Skills

To help disabled individuals become more independent, some school curricula now include life experience skills (Life experience program, 1976). This program incorporates skills which apply not only at home and in school, but outside of school. For example, the program includes learning to find transportation, to find ways of getting in and out of transportation vehicles, to ask strangers for directions, and to locate and use community resources.

Work Skills

There should be opportunities for developing work skills or task completion skills and related social behavior throughout the curriculum. They are important even for those who may never work in sheltered or com-

petitive employment. Some of the most profoundly handicapped may be taught to complete a task in sequence. They may be taught to follow directions given by a single word command or a gesture. Knowing how to perform even the simplest work tasks reduces dependence—whether in custodial care, leisure time use, homemaking, or employment.

School-age children who are doing academic tasks must learn to work as quickly and accurately as possible—to complete tasks quickly, correctly, and perhaps within time limits. When one set of tasks is finished, they must be able to move on to another set of tasks without having to

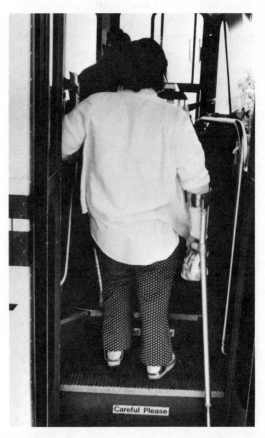

Cooperation between home and school helps students learn life experience skills.

be reminded; they must learn to get their materials ready for work and to put away materials when finished. Whenever possible, physically disabled students should learn to work independently, even though they may have problems with use of hands or mobility. Unless they learn to work independently, they will always have to wait until a teacher, volunteer, or parent is available to help them. But they may be able to work alone if materials and procedures are devised to allow them to solve problems and record their own thoughts. Even though they cannot write, they may use adaptive aids, materials, and procedures so that they can proceed during the time when no one is available to work with them.

Older students need skills and knowledge to do various jobs. Some skills depend on academic knowledge, such as knowing how to use correct punctuation so articles written for the school newspaper are correctly punctuated; others may be specific to a task, such as knowing how to measure the slats in making wooden planters. For any task, a pupil needs to compare his skills with those needed for the specific job. If his skills are not perfected, he needs to seek help to improve or find more realistic objectives.

Bachman (1971) tried to determine the economic status of 1964–1965 graduates of selected California school programs for orthopedically handicapped and other health impaired students. She identified hand use and independence in mobility as two variables which were significantly related to effective employment. The opportunity to become effectively employed also was related to work experience in school. Therefore, the more established these skills and behaviors become during the school years, the more prepared students will be for custodial care, homebound employment, sheltered work, competitive work, or professional training.

Advocacy

One part of a curriculum unique to individuals who are disabled is the study of advocacy. Disabled individuals, their parents, and other interested persons must learn what they can do to improve conditions for physically and multiply disabled citizens; they need to learn to deal with architectural barriers, inadequate housing, and poor transportation, while being involved in getting the government to act on these problems. If physically disabled persons themselves are unable to become advocates or to direct others in advocating for them, then teachers should give parents or others information about kinds of resources available from which to seek help on specific problems. If each person who reads this chapter would join as a citizen advocate to help get the disabled equal rights with nondisabled persons, our society could be proud.

General procedures for advocacy actions are described by Bigge (1976a). Citizen actions include:

1. Finding existing federal, state and local laws which pertain to specific problems by addressing requests to:

a. House or Senate Documents Room, U.S. Capitol, Washington, D.C. 20501. Request must be in writing and include the public law number, popular name title, or subject area description.

b. State Capitol, Legislative Billroom for state rules and regulations.

c. Local City Hall for local ordinances and regulations.

2. Communicating views to senators and representatives:

a. For current names and addresses, obtain *When You Write to Washington: A Guide for Citizen Action Including Congressional Directory,* League of Women Voters of the U.S.A., 1730 M Street N.W., Washington, D.C. 20036.

More specifically, there are some areas in which individuals with physical disabilities need our help: architectural barriers, housing, transportation, tax benefits and exemptions, Social Security benefits and supplemental security income, education, vocational training and employment, and other civil rights.

Leisure Time

Leisure time is another curriculum area which needs to be incorporated into goals and objectives for individuals with physical disabilities (Fairchild & Neal, 1975). Like nondisabled persons of every community, the physically disabled should have opportunities to learn leisure activities to enjoy both during the school years and later on. Curricula should expose students to a variety of leisure-time activities and should teach ways to adapt them for people with physical disabilities.

Rusalem (1973) studied the creative adaptation of severely disabled adults to unsheltered society. Based on his findings, he recommended that (1) special education needs to be more relevant to adult functioning and (2) special education should be extended into the adult years. He concluded also that:

> special education teachers will need to study the development of handicapped people throughout the life-span . . . to follow their students into the community and evaluate their programs. Special educators will need more adequate preparation in the teaching of reading at all age levels, career education, guidance and counseling, community involvement—especially in advocacy activities—and special education programming at the secondary level, with particular reference to work-study, recreation, and leisure programs. (p. 65)

Individualization

Instruction for the physically disabled student is based on individualized planning.

When they develop individual curricula, teachers need to ask:

● With infinite curriculum and instruction possibilities, what topics should be taught?

● What kind of learning is most functional, based on the severity of the individual's disability, his age, and his present and future educational needs?

Multiple Disabilities

Children with physical disabilities often have one or more other associated disabilities. A cerebral palsied person, in particular, may have problems related to learning, vision, hearing, speech, seizures, emotional adjustment, perceptual motor involvement, or retarded mental development (Cruickshank, 1976; Denhoff & Robinault, 1960). Conversely, a child may have one or more disabilities and function as gifted. Teachers should therefore be aware of the endless combinations of educational methods (many of which are mentioned in other chapters of this book) to better understand children with multiple disabilities. Some further adjustments may be necessary because the child is not just a child with a crippling condition or with a health problem; she may be a child who is physically disabled and who also has vision problems. A combination of disabilities may present more complex or unusual problems; specialists with expertise in different disabilities should collaborate to decide how to best help each child. Some youngsters who have the type of cerebral palsy that causes excessive involuntary movements and who also have a severe visual disability may not get the maximum benefit from wearing glasses because they are unable to hold their heads still to focus carefully. Ordinarily, children who cannot read print because of visual impairment learn to depend on braille as their major means of communication. Children with cerebral palsy often cannot read braille because they cannot control the gross uncoordinated movement of their hands or they do not have fine sensory discrimination in their fingertips. Also, those who might need hearing aids may have trouble wearing them and making them work functionally because of uncoordinated head movements that cause excess, irritating noise that is amplified by the hearing aids.

Individuals who are physically disabled as well as severely or profoundly retarded present yet undetermined abilities to learn. Referring to cerebral palsied individuals with severe or profound mental retardation, Shotick (1976) states that "Programming efforts are too new to even speculate on probable ultimate performance achievement. Present organization and delivery of services can be defined as a new beginning" (p. 454).

Teachers must help students find ways to surmount, accommodate to, and cope with any kind of problem which affects learning. They should provide instruction or seek help from others to reduce or correct every type of physical and educational disability a student may have. Teachers must help each individual establish and meet essential, priority objectives and then extend and enrich curricula for each person.

Task Analysis: A Basis for Instruction

Task analysis (see chapter 1, page 22) (Bateman, 1967; Bigge, 1976c; Wallace & Kauffman, 1978) is of special help to rehabilitation and education personnel in assessing pupil problems and deciding how and what to teach. Task analysis requires pinpointing subskills or segments of tasks. Task analysts assume that when disabled persons cannot accomplish a given task it is because of their inability to accomplish one or more parts of the task or problem.

Partial Task Completion

Some persons complete some parts of defined tasks but not others. Subsequent ob-

jectives for them may take one of three directions:

1. To teach the unperformed subtask so that the individual can perform the entire task in a usual manner;

2. To devise an alternative to a usual method of performing the uncompleted parts of the task either with or without special equipment or materials; or

3. To select a different task or goal to be accomplished.

Figure 13.1 is a model for studying and recording information about tasks tried but not accomplished.

For some persons, it may be possible to teach those subtasks that are not performed without devising an alternative method or using special equipment or materials. It might be possible to teach the child in the example to grasp her released crutch before the door closes and then move through the door.

Figure 13.1

Given the task of: Opening the classroom door and walking through it while using crutches, the student performed these parts of the task:

1. Walked to the door
2. Stood in position to open door
3. Released hand from crutch to reach for knob
4. Reached door knob
5. Grasped knob
6. Turned knob
7. Pulled door open
8. Released door knob

But did not perform these parts of the task:

1. Grasp the released crutch before the door closed
2. Walk through the door

Note: From J. L. Bigge, "Systems of Precise Observation for Teachers: Observation Guide to Accompany Film," Department of Health, Education and Welfare, U.S. Office of Education, Bureau of Education for the Handicapped, 1970.

Some people may be able to learn to complete a task independently and acceptably only by using an alternate or adapted method to deal with their disabilities. A boy who has control of only one hand because of cerebral palsy may open a thermos by holding it between his legs so that the thermos does not twist when he attempts to unscrew the lid with his only useable hand. Another student using prostheses may need to use a sandwich holder to eat a sandwich. A girl may need to complete classroom assignments by typing when her classmates are handwriting. In a workshop, a student may be using a jig because he does not have the fine hand coordination needed to hold a piece of wood in place while sawing at a certain angle.

Some persons never learn to complete all parts of particular tasks. For them, completion is not a realistic goal. Subsequent objectives are to establish new goals. For example, some people who are severely physically handicapped and profoundly retarded, or extremely physically handicapped but not mentally retarded, will never be able to feed themselves. In this instance, the objective may be to teach them to open their mouths voluntarily at the sight of the spoon, or to signal on a communication board that they need someone to help. In a work situation, when a person is completely unable to perform a task and it is unlikely that he will ever learn to do so, a completely different task should be found.

Completing Tasks in Usual and Functional Ways

At times a disabled student completes a task in a quite usual and functional way. The next objective can be an advanced task, a similar task, or an entirely different task. For instance, a student's physical disability may affect only the lower parts of the body and not affect hand use for eating. The emphasis in her instruction, therefore, should be placed on tasks other than those involving eating. Also, among the physically disabled are some people who can proceed through the curriculum with no more adaptations in materials or processes than are necessary for their nonhandicapped peers. Students may be able to write their lessons usefully even though they have hand coordination problems or hand weakness. In prevocational training or in job settings, some disabled individuals can function with no more adaptation than sitting in a wheelchair instead of a regular chair.

Completing Tasks Too Slowly

Some students can complete the task assigned but complete it so slowly that their performance is not really functional. A subsequent task objective is to increase speed with or without adaptations. A child may be able to feed himself, but feeding himself a whole meal may take over an hour. The next objective is to increase his speed, perhaps by placing sides on the plate so that as the child scoops the food, it will not go off the edge of his plate. Perhaps he should be provided a special spoon bent in a certain way so he can't spill the food as he brings it to his mouth. Perhaps it is possible to teach him to eat the way he is eating now, but merely to move faster. Another example may be the high school age youth who can complete math problems on a third grade level but takes several minutes to complete one problem. A later objective might be to teach her to use a calculator so that she can perform math skills needed for purchasing groceries and depositing money in a bank. Allowing a child to work math problems slowly and not functionally without trying to speed the process would be an injustice. People might well become very impatient with her if she attempted to do practical math while clerks and tellers were waiting.

In prevocational or career tasks, many people are paid hourly and by the piece. It would be to the disabled student's advantage to increase the speed of his work while maintaining necessary quality. A new goal might be to increase speed by cutting the number of movements needed to complete certain tasks.

Completing Tasks with Uncoordinated Movements

Still other disabled students can complete the task but do so with such uncoordinated movements that the results are not functional. Involuntary athetoid movements may cause a child to spill most of his milk as he tries to pick it up or moves it jerkily to his mouth. The next objective might be to decrease the effects of uncoordinated or clumsy movements with or without adaptations. The child might be taught to use a weighted glass or to use a holder to stabilize the glass on the table and then drink with a straw.

While performing common classroom writing tasks, one athetoid child decreased the amount of uncoordinated movements

by sitting on one hand, which allowed her to focus her attention on controlling the movements of the hand doing the writing. Another child might try to type but keep hitting two keys at once. His inexact movements could be reduced by giving him practice in localizing his stroke so that he increases the number of times he hits the intended letter on the first try. Some dis-

Cliff enjoys painting with a head pointer.

abled persons may walk with a very unstable gait and thus be easily knocked over by fellow workers who pass their work stations. For some, the effects of these clumsy and sometimes unsafe movements can be minimized if they use a wheelchair to move about in work situations.

Changes Necessary for Completing Tasks

Some individuals with weak, missing, or uncoordinated movements cannot attempt tasks without some kind of change in procedure, special supportive aids, adapted materials, adapted equipment, or other aids. An objective for these people is to devise alternatives to the usual methods of performing the task. A person who has been paralyzed to the degree that he is barely able to move his arms enough to feed himself needs some special arrangement. Wheelchair attachments providing moveable, ball-bearing arm rests may be a solution. If the person cannot hold a spoon, he is not even able to start to feed himself. A spoon could be sewed onto a mitt which fits on the hand. The spoon would remain in the correct position and would never be dropped because it is attached to the mitt.

Painting pictures is a common classroom task undertaken by many students. Some may not even attempt the task unless some-

Sound educational programming can give the handicapped the skills they need to be independent.

thing other than their hands can be used to hold and manipulate the paint brush. Many cerebral palsied or spinal-cord-injured people paint with head pointers—brushes attached to headbands. People who are completely paralyzed from the shoulders down can and do complete tasks such as operating computers which would never be possible without some adaptations in processes or in the equipment itself. Subsequent tasks would be to devise any other kinds of adaptations which would make even more complex computer tasks accessible to people with very little movement.

By using these guidelines to observe the ways a physically disabled person completes a task, a teacher can focus upon the specific subtasks the learner needs to master. Task analysis can be applied to a variety of situations. It is applied to help individuals with physical disabilities to improve performances in speech and language, self-care, leisure use, academic skills, and work (Bigge, 1976c). Task analysis also can be applied to academic subject areas, concept development, development of thinking skills, and social behaviors.

MEETING SPECIAL NEEDS

Communication

1. Assume—until evidence proves otherwise—that students with unintelligible speech understand at a higher level than they can express, and treat and teach them accordingly.

2. Invite students who cannot talk to show you how they answer yes, no, and I don't know.

3. Invite students to demonstrate for you all the ways they know for letting people know what they want to say.

4. Teach the most vital communication skills to students for whom learning communication skills is extremely difficult. Two important skills are using gestures to express a need to be taken to the bathroom, and smiling and saying "hi" as a greeting.

5. Invite students who talk to you but cannot be understood because of unintelligible speech to:
"Please repeat that again."
"Please say that in another way."
"Show me by gestures or pointing."
"Write, type, or point to the alphabet letters or words."

6. Repeat to students what you think they tried to communicate in order to clarify. "Is that exactly correct?"

7. Finds ways for students who cannot speak or write intelligibly to demonstrate increasingly difficult thinking skills. For instance, a student might classify and reclassify objects, pictures, or words mounted on blocks of cardboard by pushing them into groups.

8. Directly or indirectly encourage students to improve their speech as they study phonics, spelling, reading, and dramatic play.

9. Give students time to respond.

10. Find ways individuals who can not talk can contribute to class discussions.

11. Ask parents or speech and language specialists how to help students improve their speech and expressive language skills.

12. Model ways nondisabled students and adults can talk to and with disabled students.

Learning

1. If children understand, ask them what kind of adaptions, special equipment, or teaching procedures work best for them.

2. Ask parents, therapists, or special education specialists what, if any, special devices or procedures are needed to help children; for example, secure papers to desks with masking tape to keep them from slipping.

3. Ask parents, therapists, or the child what safety restrictions or cautions are necessary. Help the disabled students increase their responsibility for their own health and safety.

4. Unless otherwise recommended, give students the opportunity to do what their peers do even though they might walk awkwardly, fall often, or seem uncoordinated.

5. Realize that illegible writing and slowness in written or oral answers may not indicate that the students do not know their lessons.

6. Find ways for disabled students to evaluate their performances objectively so they will not be unrealistic about what they can learn and do.

7. Include all students in group learning experiences even if you have to phrase some questions so disabled students can give yes or no answers; even assist them physically when necessary.

Mobility

1. Ask disabled students, their parents, or therapists to demonstrate all the ways that the students can move from place to place.

2. Ask disabled students, their parents, or therapists when and how students should be physically assisted.

3. Have volunteers assist with physical management so whenever possible disabled students can go on field trips, participate in special events, and participate in special projects.

4. Arrange for elimination or reduction of architectural barriers.

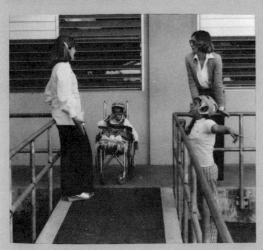

Schools for the physically handicapped should have ramps for easy wheelchair access.

Self-help

1. Encourage students to complete as much of every self-help task as possible.

2. Find what steps of tasks students cannot do and see if those parts can be taught with

or without adaption of material, equipment, or procedures.

3. Openly discuss any uncertainties as to when or how to aid a disabled student. You could say "I'm not sure if you would like my help. Would you?"

Attitudes

1. Ask doctors or parents about a child's understanding of his own illness and disabilities. Find out how they want teachers to respond to questions by the child and his peers.

2. Help nondisabled students and adults understand that such characteristics as drooling, unusual ways of talking, and physical awkwardness cannot be helped and are not to be ridiculed.

3. Prepare yourself and class for helping students with special needs. For example, provide a rest period for students who tire easily, remove furniture from students when they have seizures, arrange for a nondisabled child to make carbon copies of class notes for a classmate who cannot write.

4. Treat ill or disabled students as normally as possible; do not give them better grades than deserved.

5. Prepare classmates for students' return after long absences because of illness or accident (a student might be bald or wear a wig, because of cancer treatment; someone might have a missing arm or leg, or a body cast).

6. When organic deterioration affects learning, consider keeping the student with her peers even though she cannot continue to keep up in academic or physical activity.

7. Support the possible decision of children with potentially terminal diseases to cut the amount of school work and physical activities undertaken because of frequent absences, limited energy, or personal attitudes.

Resources

1. Ask the parents, school administrators, or special educators to suggest resources if and when additional help or ideas are needed. Whenever possible use disabled persons themselves as resources for ideas on how they can be helped.

2. Find ways disabled students can become resources for nondisabled persons.

3. Train and use volunteers to aid student learning and increase the independence of students who need extra help.

4. Use peers as teachers and helpers of their handicapped classmates.

5. Read articles and books on education of individuals with physical handicaps.

FOR MORE INFORMATION

Most of these resources are textbooks that are readily available. Check your instructor, the education library, or the general library at your school.

Bigge, J.A., with O'Donnell, P.A. (Eds.). *Teaching individuals with physical and multiple disabilities.* Columbus, Ohio: Charles E. Merrill, 1976.

Bleck, E.E., & Nagel, D.A. (Eds.). *Physically handicapped children: A medical atlas for teachers.* New York: Grune & Stratton, 1975.

Downey, J.A., & Low, N.L. (Eds.). *The child with disabling illness: Principles of rehabilitation.* Philadelphia: Saunders, 1974.

14

The Gifted Child

Thomas M. Stephens

Joan S. Wolf

These are the major topics covered in this chapter. You may wish to use them as a checklist when you review.

- *Definitions and characteristics of giftedness.*
- *Ways to identify gifted children.*
- *Educational provisions.*
- *Teacher competencies and instructional approaches.*
- *Major research studies on educating the gifted.*

Concern for gifted and talented students has waxed and waned throughout our history. Some authorities have attempted to account for educators' erratic interest in giftedness by comparing this interest with the politics and economics of different times (Trezise, 1973). Jefferson and his followers believed that trained leadership of the best minds was essential to the survival of a free world; Andrew Jackson's era was noted for its anti-intellectualism. Jacksonian democracy seemed to prevail in the U.S. in the 1960s (Huntington, 1975), which was a time when education of the gifted was at a low ebb. Other authorities feel that social incentives such as state and federal funding can account for peaks of interest in the academically gifted (Terman, 1954).

Marland (1972), in a report to Congress when he was U.S. Commissioner of Education, cited impressive statistics that a vast majority of our gifted and talented students have not been served. These students must be nurtured and supported in school to develop their potential for their own self-fulfillment as individuals and for making the best use of human resources for the welfare of our country and the world (Hildreth, 1966).

Gifted youngsters are found at every economic level in every strata of society, across all cultural, ethnic, and racial groups. These youngsters represent the potential leaders, scientists, and literary talents of tomorrow and need a rich, supportive educational environment to realize this potential. While many of them may become leaders regardless of their learning environment, the *quality* of their leadership performances may well depend on the quality of their schooling.

DEFINITIONS AND CHARACTERISTICS

Several definitions of giftedness have been proposed (Fliegler & Bish, 1959; National Society for the Study of Education, 1958; Witty, 1951). The one dominant definition since the late 1950s was contained in the 1958 Yearbook of the National Society for the Study of Education. It defined a talented or gifted child as one who shows *consistently remarkable performance in any worthwhile line of endeavor.* Since our society has a wide range of worthwhile activities, this definition includes performances not always identified with scholastic achievement, for example, performances in the arts and mechanical skills. In addition to being broad, this definition is unique in that it relies heavily on *performance* rather than *potential.*

Fliegler and Bish (1959) incorporated *potential* into their definition. They indicated that those with ability in the top 15 to 20% of the school population were gifted. And they also included creative ability as representing giftedness. Later, Lucito (1963) incorporated *innovators* and *powerful thinkers* into his statement.

Lewis Terman, whose work has been indelibly stamped upon programs for gifted children, defined the gifted as those who score at the upper end of the normal distribution of intelligence, the top 1% in the ability to acquire and manipulate concepts (Terman, 1954). He considered *giftedness* different from talent and from creativity. *Talent* was viewed by Terman as a promise of unusual achievement only when it is combined with high IQ scores. He considered *creativity* to be a personality factor and differentiated it from both giftedness and talent.

Current concern for the many aspects of giftedness is reflected in the definition used by the U.S. Office of Education (1972):

> Gifted and talented children are those identified by professionally qualified persons who, by virtue of outstanding abilities, are capable of high performance. These are children who require differentiated educational programs in order to realize their contribution to self and society.

Children capable of high performance include those with demonstrated achievement and/or potential ability in any of the following areas, singly or in combination:

1. General intellectual ability,
2. Specific academic aptitude,
3. Creative or productive thinking,
4. Leadership ability,
5. Visual and performing arts,
6. Psychomotor ability.

Today this definition is important because of its financial and policy-making potential. But no one definition is "correct." Definitions of giftedness reflect the attitude of the times, as Terman noted in 1954:

> But however efficient our tests may be in discovering exceptional talents, and whatever the schools may do to foster those discovered, it is the prevailing Zeitgeist [spirit of the times] that will decide, by the rewards it gives or withholds, what talents will come to flower (p. 227).

The trend is away from specific definitions of giftedness to broader and more general concepts. Since Terman's work, definitions have not been based on data or theory. Instead, they have simply evolved out of political and social movements. Perhaps that is as it should be, since giftedness will probably always be relative to a given society's values at certain times in its history.

Characteristics of Giftedness

One group of characteristics of giftedness often cited in the literature are those derived from the work of Terman and his associates under the general title of *Genetic Studies of Genius* (Burks, Jensen, & Terman, 1930; Cox, 1926; Oden, 1968; Terman et al., 1925; Terman & Oden, 1947; Terman & Oden, 1959). Among these characteristics are: fast learning, interest in reading biographies, scientific inclination, began reading prior to entering school, enjoys learning, good abstract reasoning, good command of language, poor hand-

writing, only child, eldest child, born of older parents, well-adjusted, physically healthy, high IQ, high scores on achievement tests, imaginative, and high energy level. These represent stereotypes characteristic of the academically gifted at the time of Terman's studies. It is unlikely, however, that these would be typical of individual gifted students today.

Some authorities present characteristics of giftedness based on experience. Clark (in press), for example, speculates that gifted students can be distinguished from their more normal peers through differential cognitive characteristics, affective characteristics, and physical characteristics. She lists the characteristics under each of these three major categories and then logically deduces examples of related needs and possible associated problems. For example, under differential physical characteristics, she identifies the unusual discrepancy between physical and intellectual development of the gifted. From this characteristic, gifted students presumably need "to find satisfying physical activity that allows for individualized progress." As an associated problem, Clark provides as an example those gifted children who stress mental activity to the detriment of their physical development.

Because there is no evidence derived under today's conditions, those charac-

Many gifted students enjoy doing research projects on their own.

Chapter fourteen

teristics of giftedness which are cited in the literature are often misleading and have questionable validity when universally applied. We believe that identifying the gifted in ways that rely heavily on lists of characteristics or traits screens out some bright students and screens in many non-gifted students. A more functional approach is to tie the identification of the students directly to appropriate school programs.

Step	
1	Establish Program Goals
2	Develop Objectives
3	Specify Requisite Student Characteristics
4	Locate Students
5	Assign Students

Figure 14.1

A functional approach to program development for the gifted

A functional approach to program development generally consists of the five steps in Figure 14.1. Typically, program goals are established by school personnel, with the community involved. The goals tend to be general, for example, "to identify potentially gifted primary grade students." Specific procedures for the program, in the form of objectives, are then developed in relationship to each goal. In the third step, those student characteristics which are required to achieve the objectives are specified. Students who possess the characteristics identified in step three are then located. The final step consists of assigning students, based on their characteristics, to the special education provisions which have been established to achieve the goals developed in step one. Such an approach results in identifying students for particular programs or services.

profile PHILIP

An only child, Philip was born when his parents were in their mid-30s. His mother was an executive secretary and his father a printer. They noted that he began to talk and walk at a normal age but began reading, without instruction, at 4 years old.

By the time Philip attended kindergarten he was already reading story books. He could tell time to the quarter hour, knew the names of coins, and could add and subtract simple problems. Philip's handwriting was poor, although his written ideas far exceeded his age.

His fourth grade teacher referred him to the school psychologist for individual intelligence testing when she noticed that he was bored in school. His Stanford-Binet IQ at 8 years of age was 166. He was, at that time, reading at the 12.8 grade level as measured by the Iowa Silent Reading Test and doing beginning algebra problems.

Philip expressed an early interest in science and, throughout his elementary school years, his teachers used that interest for enrichment activities. Since the local school policy did not permit grade skipping, Philip completed high school at the normal age. Throughout secondary school he was placed in the "fast track" which permitted him to take advanced courses. Upon graduation he had earned college credit through the Advanced Placement Program.

Philip obtained college scholarships which permitted him to major in science and at 21 completed his bachelor's degree. He is currently in graduate school majoring in computer science.

Had Philip been permitted to enter school earlier and accelerated during his elementary and secondary school years, he might now have obtained a Ph.D. in science and would be well established in his career by his mid-20s. Instead, he continues to take some courses he has already mastered, very much as he has been forced to do throughout his school life.

For a more detailed example, a program which has as its goal "to provide appropriate instruction for high-achieving elementary students" may have among its objectives:

1. To accelerate students in those subject areas where they demonstrate high achievement;

2. To accelerate students by skipping grades when they are achieving highly in all subjects; and

3. To arrange out-of-school experiences for students whose high achievement exceeds the school's provisions.

In step three, student characteristics are developed from those program objectives established in step two. For example, those characteristics needed to achieve objective (1) above may include:

1. Functioning beyond grade placement at least two grade levels on standardized achievement tests, and

2. Consistently high achievement in the classroom in a particular subject, as noted by teachers.

Step four simply involves looking for the students which show those characteristics.

This approach does not keep you from including underachieving gifted students. They may be included by establishing the necessary goal and by following the steps illustrated in Figure 14.2.

One serious omission of such a functional approach is that students for whom provisions are not available are often overlooked. Since the approach begins with establishing goals, students are selected to fit those goals rather than program goals being based on the characteristics of the students. School personnel can guard against overlooking gifted students by being aware of the strengths of individual students. Those who display superior thinking or talent should be referred for individual aptitude and achievement testing.

---

1. Program Goal: To provide assistance to low-achieving gifted students in grades 4 through 8.

2. Program Objectives:
a. Provide counseling in study skills where needed.
b. Provide encouragement for higher achievement.
c. Provide special tutoring if needed.
d. Provide assistance to teachers of identified students.

3. Student Characteristics:
a. IQ scores above 120 on an individual test of intelligence, and
b. Daily school achievement, as reflected on report cards, of grade C or lower, or
c. At least one grade level below placement on standardized achievement tests in any one subject.

4. Locate Students.

5. Assign Students.

Figure 14.2

Incidence and Prevalence of Giftedness

Data concerning the incidence and prevalence of giftedness are affected by the definitions and identification methods used. *Incidence* figures indicate the number of students identified as gifted at a specified time. *Prevalence,* however, refers to the total number estimated to be in the population at a given time.

The incidence of giftedness is higher now than it was in the 1920s, due to the broader definitions now used. When Terman used an IQ score of 130, only 2 to 3% of the population was identified as gifted. But the use of the Taylor Multiple Talent Model (Taylor, 1968) results in reported incidence figures from 1% to 90% of a school population.

Incidence studies of giftedness are rarely found in the literature. In a 1961 study (Stephens, 1962), 2% of all students enrolled in Ohio's public schools were identified as gifted. DeHaan & Havighurst

(1957) found 15% of students in Illinois to be gifted. Incidence figures differ from school to school and, as a general rule, more gifted children are identified in schools drawing from higher socio-economic groups.

Estimates of the prevalence of giftedness have varied widely, depending on criteria used and definitions. Marland (1971) estimated the prevalence to be about 3 to 5%. Hollingworth (1942), using an IQ cut-off of 180 in her study of the highly gifted, was considering only one child in a million. When an IQ cutoff of 115 is used, 15 to 20% of a school population are called gifted. But when an IQ score of 130 is considered as a minimum cut-off point, only 2 to 3% of students qualify as gifted. Using the broad definition of the U.S. Office of Education, the incidence of giftedness is between 3 to 5% of the population.

PROCEDURES FOR IDENTIFYING THE GIFTED

It is necessary to agree on the characteristics of giftedness to develop educational programs. These characteristics are often reflected in criteria for including students in special programs. Typically, criteria for placement are established after program goals and objectives have been clarified.

A variety of procedures have been used for identifying the gifted and talented, including standardized tests (see the appendix), teacher nominations, and behavioral checklists. Often a combination of these are used.

Standardized Tests

Standardized tests range from tests of mental ability to group and individually administered achievement tests. Achievement tests are often used as rough screening devices. They are used to identify children who are academically gifted or those

profile **JULIAN C. STANLEY**

A noted educational psychologist, Dr. Julian C. Stanley has authored or coauthored 10 books and more than 275 professional articles, technical notes, chapters, and reviews. He is Professor of Psychology and Director, Study of Mathematically and Scientifically Precocious Youth, The Johns Hopkins University. This project will produce at least five volumes of studies. The first volume, which Stanley identifies as his single most important contribution to the literature on intellectual talents, is edited by him, Daniel Keating, and Lynn H. Fox and is entitled Mathematical Talent: Discovery, Description, and Development *(1974). He and his associates have already demonstrated that "some 13-year-olds can do excellent full-time college work, quite a few of the top ½% of the age group can learn 4 or more years of high school mathematics in 2 hours per week during a single 13-month period, many can take college courses part-time and make excellent grades, many can skip one or more school grades to their advantage, and many can succeed in college before completing the usual kindergarten through twelfth-grade lockstep" (p. 19).*

whose are proficient in a specific skill area such as math, science, or language. Individual intelligence tests are useful to gain further information on those youngsters scoring high on group achievement tests.

Despite the criticisms of the use of individual intelligence tests, they still are important in identification. Competent clinicians can identify specific strengths and weaknesses of students which can have valuable instructional meaning to teachers. Unfortunately, many of the more meaningful findings of clinicians can be overshadowed by test scores. For that reason, the scores of individual intelligence tests should be accompanied by a report written by the clinician.

Although individual intelligence tests—such as the Stanford-Binet and the Wechsler Intelligence Scales—yield valuable clinical information, their use in identifying the gifted and talented has been criticized (Getzels & Jackson, 1958; Torrance, 1970). Too heavy reliance on intelligence test scores, it is claimed, restricts the definition of giftedness and makes it synonymous with high IQ scores. According to some authorities, a narrow definition of giftedness may deny opportunities to those who are not academic achievers or who, because of cultural differences, may not score at a high level on an intelligence test. Gallagher & Kinney (1974) point out that the IQ test focuses mainly on "the absorption of facts and the systematic processing of those facts in predetermined ways."

Much of the criticism directed at the use of IQ scores in identifying the gifted is based on studies of creativity. Getzels & Jackson's study (1962) is generally cited as the basis for using measures of creativity. In fact, subsequent studies by Torrance (1970) were based on their earlier work. The Getzel and Jackson study, however, has been criticized for its many serious weaknesses. Stephens (1964) found that the statistical procedure they used to obtain deviation IQ scores was questionable. They dramatized a difference in IQ which may not have existed to the extent reported. Thus, both groups in the study could appropriately have been termed *high IQ*. Stephens also pointed out that the Getzel and Jackson creative thinking tests were not used with entire school populations. Consequently, they did not discriminate students of less ability from those with more potential.

Other Instruments Used to Identify the Gifted

As a reaction to the critics, measures in addition to or in place of IQ scores have been developed and used to identify gifted students. (Also see page 401 for recent research on alternative ways to identify the gifted.) One measure being used, often for screening, is teacher nomination of gifted students. Today there are instruments available for teachers to use in selecting their gifted students. Many of these focus on observable characteristics, which seem to be a more reliable measure than teacher inference. Early research in teacher nomination revealed that junior high school teachers did not locate gifted children effectively enough to place much reliance on them for screening (Pegnato & Birch, 1959).

Behavioral checklists are one type of instrument teachers can use. For example, the Scale for Rating Behavioral Characteristics of Superior Students (Renzulli, Hartman, & Callahan, 1971) is designed to obtain teacher estimates of a student's characteristics in the area of learning, motivation, creativity, and leadership. Separate, weighted scores are obtained on each dimension, and the student's traits can be ranked. Checklists like this deal with observable characteristics and appear to be useful for identifying students with particular strengths.

Another checklist lists learning characteristics of gifted children and identifies some potential problems children with specific characteristics might have. For example, a gifted child might be extremely capable verbally with a large vocabulary and facility in verbal expression. But the child might use this ability to escape into verbalism and glibness. Other characteristics with both positive and possibly negative connotations are included in the checklist.

Lucito (1974) compiled a summary of traits generally associated with creative students. Many of the characteristics listed are observable and behavioral and could be useful to teachers. Another listing of general characteristics directed to teachers for the identification of gifted children was developed by Plowman and Rice (1971). Their list consists of 15 characteristics of behavior in the classroom and on the playground.

LEGISLATIVE AND PROGRAM TRENDS

There has been a strong surge of interest in the education of the gifted and talented during the 1970s. This revival of interest represents a third major trend in this direction. Terman's studies (1925 through 1959) at the beginning of the century focused attention on this population and succeeded in dispelling many myths concerning social and physical characteristics of the gifted. While some of his research methodology has been questioned, the studies served a valuable function as the first comprehensive longitudinal studies of giftedness.

Another upsurge of attention was directed towards the gifted in the post-sputnik era of the late 1950s, when accelerated programs in science and math

---

profile LISA

Not only is Lisa classified as academically gifted, but she is also talented in music. Her musical genius manifested itself at a very young age. Lisa's mother noticed that she was able to sing on key at approximately 14 months old. She sang harmony as a pre-schooler and, by the time she was in the first grade, could sight read alto notes of a musical score. At age 6, Lisa started violin lessons and she progressed rapidly on this instrument. She added piano lessons at age 8. Lisa attended summer music camp, sang in the chorus in elementary school, played in the orchestra, and presently, as an eighth grader, is in the district-wide honors orchestra, a select group of young musicians in her school district.

Lisa is an unusual gifted child in that she is talented across many areas in addition to music. She has achieved at an extremely high level academically, and achievement test scores have consistently placed her well above grade level in reading and math skills. In first grade, her Stanford Achievement Test scores ranged from 2.9 to 5.5 (grade level equivalents) with a battery average of 3.6. Again at sixth grade, she scored high on the Stanford Achievement Test with a range from 8.8 to 12.0, displaying a twelfth grade level in no less than five

areas: reading comprehension, listening comprehension, language, social science, and science. Her test battery average at sixth grade was 10.6.

Lisa's grades also reflect her high level of achievement with almost all A's throughout her school career and up to her present eighth grade placement.

Lisa is an outgoing, friendly, sociable, independent girl who gets along well with her peers. She is well-rounded with diverse interests. Although music is a great love, she is not consumed by it and is determined "to have music enrich my life, not dominate it." Lisa's early development gave some clues of her giftedness, especially in the area of music. The times at which she started walking and talking were within normal range; however, Lisa wrote all the letters of the alphabet before she went to school and as a kindergartner taught herself to read. Her ability to reproduce musical sounds accurately and to sight read musical notations at an early age was remarkable. Some of Lisa's teachers recognized her outstanding ability and made attempts to individualize her instruction. Others were not able to deal effectively with her rapid progress and insisted she submit to drill, rote learning, and repetition of much material which she had al-

received funding and support. However, many of these programs lost their state and federal dollar support in the middle and late sixties as national priorities were directed to other areas of concern.

Governmental Support

The third wave of interest in the education of the gifted and talented received impact from Marland's Report to Congress (Marland, 1972). As United States Commissioner of Education, Marland provided a comprehensive status report to document the neglect of the gifted throughout the na-

ready mastered. Because Lisa is basically patient and conforming, she coped with these situations simply by repeating the work, even though it was often far below her instructional level. She was anxious to fit in with the other students and so never behaved in such a way as to call attention to her superior knowledge or abilities. As a junior high school student, Lisa is enrolled in several advanced courses, notably science, algebra, and French. She continues her violin studies and her career goals are focused on music.

It is interesting to note that Lisa's family has had several members who have attained very high levels of achievement in the field of music. Her grandmother was a well-known opera singer, an uncle had a career as a renowned accompanist and self-taught teacher of voice at a prestigious institution, and her father was the first flutist for the symphony orchestra of a major city. On the basis of Lisa's school career to date, it appears that she could be successful in a number of areas in addition to music. Opportunities for accelerated courses and opportunities to interact with other gifted youngsters would be of benefit to her as she continues to explore career options and to develop her varied talents on higher levels.

tion. He urged Congress to support the development of educational programs for gifted and talented students. The 93rd Congress passed Title IV, Section 404, Gifted and Talented Children, in 1974. From this legislation, the Office of Gifted and Talented Children was established, under the sponsorship of the Office of Education. Although $12,250,000 was requested for the development of services to gifted and talented students across the nation, less than $3,000,000 was allocated.

The Office for Gifted and Talented, together with the National/State Leadership Training Institute (N/S LTI), has led in developing programs and assisting states to develop state plans. N/S LTI is an agency funded through the U.S. Office of Education with offices in California and Virginia. The Institute has been involved in activities related to training of key leadership in gifted education at local, state, and national levels.

State teams comprised of state education agency representatives of higher education, consultants, local school district personnel, and parent advocates have projected needs in developing state plans for serving the gifted. The National Clearinghouse on the Gifted and Talented is a valuable resource for providing materials for professionals involved in determining needs and developing programs.

There has been a significant growth of parent advocate groups in behalf of the gifted and talented. Representatives have participated as state team members in Leadership Training Institute meetings, in drafting state plans, as proponents of programs by encouraging state legislation, and by working with local school district personnel in planning for gifted and talented students.

Teacher preparation programs for the gifted and talented have increased. As interest in providing for educational needs of gifted children has grown, university per-

FOR MORE SUPPORT

National resources

Office of the Gifted and Talented, U.S. Office of Education
This office, established in response to Marland's report to the Congress, Education of the Gifted and Talented *(1972), coordinates leadership at a national level for the education of the gifted and talented.*

National Clearinghouse for the Gifted and Talented, The Council for Exceptional Children
The National Clearinghouse gathers and disseminates information about the education of the gifted and talented.

National/State Leadership Training Institute on the Gifted and Talented
This institute is a federally funded program designed to provide services to state agencies and local school districts in the education of the gifted and talented.

Professional organizations

● *The Association for the Gifted, The Council for Exceptional Children*

● *National Association for Gifted Children*

● *The American Association for the Gifted*

● *The Council of State Directors of Programs for the Gifted, Florida State Department of Education*

Student organizations

● *MENSA and Teen MENSA*

● *National Honor Society*

● *National Merit Scholarship Corporation*

sonnel have begun to prepare more teachers. Both preservice and inservice training programs are available through college and universities. As of September 1976, 34 colleges or universities were listed as providing training programs for teachers of the gifted (Johnson, 1976). These are at both the master and doctoral levels, and most involve certification for teaching the gifted. As local school districts develop increasing numbers of programs for the gifted and talented, the need for specific training in this area grows. Institutions of higher education are attempting to respond by seeking increased local, state, and federal support for preparing teachers and other educators in working with the gifted.

Program Modifications

Although few schools have no bright students, many have no special provisions for the gifted and talented. In those schools which do have special provisions, they may take several different forms. Getzels and Dillon (1973) listed 26 practices and programs which might be useful in meeting the educational needs of the gifted. A combination of four types of programs may be found:

1. Special services,

2. Administrative arrangements,

3. Instructional methods, and

4. Subject-matter modifications.

Special Services

Once bright students have been identified in a special services model, they may be directly or indirectly assisted by their teachers. Special services are those provisions beyond the regular scope of the school program. These services may be within the regular classroom or beyond it, within the child's home school or outside it. Sometimes special assistance is left to the discretion of the teacher. In such situations, teachers may provide special attention, extra assignments, enriched experiences, and other activities which go beyond the regular program. In some cases, provisions are made which reach beyond the teacher. These may be assignment to a resource teacher, accelerated classes, self-paced independent study, college-level courses, university instruction, and education from individuals in the community with specific expertise.

Direct services may be provided through special counseling, tutoring, and interest stimulation. Bright students typically need early career counseling to be aware of the variety of career options which may be open to them. They should have guidance beginning at early ages and extending throughout their school careers. Counselors should be careful not to encourage early career commitments; rather, they should inform students about qualifications for specific careers.

Tutoring may extend the range of selected subject matter or provide instruction which is not normally available to students in particular grades. This instruction can be conducted by teachers or by outside personnel.

Interest stimulation often takes the form of after-school interest clubs or groups which meet during school hours. Because gifted students frequently are curious, they have a wide range of interests. It is often necessary to draw on community resources in order to satisfy these diverse interests.

Other indirect services can be provided for classroom teachers. One common resource is consultants to provide suggestions, conduct or coordinate inservice training, and identify resources outside schools. Building principals and central district administrators need to make arrangements if special assistance is to be of value. Administrators can help consultants gain access to teachers, permitting them a place on parent/teacher programs and otherwise demonstrating the importance of services to gifted students. They can provide incentives to school personnel who are identifying and teaching the brighter students. These incentives may be additional funds for enrichment materials and for special field trips. They can also publish special bulletins focusing on instructional provisions for the gifted.

Administrative Arrangements

Three possible administrative arrangements for the gifted and talented are special grouping, grade acceleration, and early admission to school.

Grouping may consist of special class placement where all bright students at a particular age-grade level are assigned together. In smaller schools it is often necessary to form special classes across several age groups because of the number of students involved. Resource rooms, where children go to special teachers for portions of their school days, are another type of grouping.

At the junior and senior high school levels, special grouping is often seen in tracking programs; that is, programs in which a student is put in one of several tracts according to past achievement or suspected ability. A student may be in a special track for one, for several, or for all his classes.

These elementary school children attend a resource room for enrichment. Here they are doing a science lesson about air.

Parents can work as aides to hold literature discussions to supplement reading instruction.

Early admissions permit students to attend school at earlier than usual ages (Birch, 1954; Brage, 1971; Larson, 1963). These programs involve psychological testing and trial placements. In some programs students may skip kindergarten, entering directly into first grade. Or they may begin kindergarten one or more years early. Students are seldom permitted to skip more than one grade because that is believed to be detrimental to social adjustment.

There also may be grade skipping during the school years. Often this is only permitted after careful individual study of students. It is always done with parental approval. It is important that students are provided with any necessary supplemental instruction and personal assistance so that their transitions to an accelerated grade take place smoothly.

Advanced placement (Gerritz & Haywood, 1965) courses may be taken at the high school level. In this program, students take college-level courses and may apply the credit to certain colleges by passing an examination. In some schools with nearby colleges, selected high school students may take college courses on campus in combination with their high school work. In some systems students can skip one or more years of high school entirely and enter college earlier (Pressey, 1967, 1969; Stanley, 1974).

Instructional Methods

Sound instructional practices are necessary regardless of the special provisions used for gifted and talented students. Terman (Seagoe, 1975) believed that bright students should receive systematically differentiated instruction throughout their school lives because they learn differently. While the objectives for the gifted are similar to those for other students, the ways to meet them differ. Emphasis should be on creativity, intellectual initiative, critical thinking, social adjustment, responsibility, and leadership.

Gifted students should be taught through concepts and principles rather than concrete facts. They also learn inductively, responding to logic and reason instead of custom. Bright students thrive on many new ideas with minimal review and drill.

Teachers of the gifted and talented often use enriched experiences to encourage them to learn on their own initiative. Special projects and reports, community resources, and other such activities can be used. In some programs, students are encouraged to initiate and conduct class discussions under teacher direction. Often these discussions take the form of seminars with students inviting people from the community to serve as resources.

Subject Matter Modifications

Subject matter is often modified in the same ways instructional methods are. For instance, principles and concepts are emphasized. Students are encouraged to use deductive and inductive logic and other scientific tools, such as observation. Since most bright students are steeped in information, they are often taught scientific

Often gifted students can study alone or in small groups in the library.

methods early as a means of evaluating knowledge rather than merely assimilating it.

Gallagher (1975) advocates a special curriculum for gifted students. He points out that any attempt to provide total mastery of all available knowledge, even in one subject area, is not realistic, considering the rate at which our knowledge base is expanding. Thus, instructional objectives should stress advanced concepts and ideas that may not be readily learned by average students. He seems to agree with other authorities, who believe that gifted students' cognitive powers permit them to learn differently.

Gallagher stresses the importance of learning how to learn. At the lower grade levels, gifted and talented students should be taught research and self-study skills. Typewriting, shorthand, reference skills, and use of the library may be taught to them before the sixth grade. The rationale for teaching these skills is that they let a gifted child take the initiative in developing her own abilities.

TEACHER COMPETENCIES

Practically all teachers prefer students who learn quickly and who are interested in their studies. But though many gifted and talented students are eager learners, they also often challenge teachers and display other characteristics that require tolerance and maturity of the teachers. Successful high school teachers of the gifted have been characterized as mature, experienced, emotionally well-adjusted, and highly intelligent (Ward, 1961; Newland, 1962). One of the most significant variables is knowledge of giftedness and expressed support for special attention to the gifted (Bishop, 1968).

Teachers of the gifted and talented must be able to accept challenges from their students. They must be personally secure enough to accept the fact that their students may be more knowledgeable than they are in certain areas. In those cases, the teacher should help each student in his search for more knowledge.

Teachers should be excited about what they teach to the gifted; this fosters interest among bright students. At upper grade levels, teachers must be knowledgeable in subject matter, willing to learn with their students, and capable of providing guidance and direction to students as they explore their intellectual interests.

REVIEW OF RESEARCH

Evidence of the increase in research interest concerning the gifted and talented is reflected in the literature. The first major bibliography on giftedness (Henry, 1924) listed 450 references for the three decades preceding its issue. By 1961, Gowan published a bibliography listing nearly double that number covering the 1950s alone. The number and variety of articles concerning gifted education continue to increase.

Terman's studies (1925 through 1959), begun in the 1920s and continuing for more than 25 years, made highly significant contributions in specifying characteristics of the gifted. His goals were to find the traits which characterized children of high IQ and to follow these children through to adulthood. His sample of approximately 1,000 subjects with measured IQs of 140 or higher revealed that, in general, they were superior to unselected children not only intellectually, as measured by a battery of achievement tests, but physically, socially, emotionally, and morally. These studies did much to dispel traditional notions of the one-sided, physically frail, emotionally insecure, but highly intellectual youngster. Subsequent studies have confirmed Terman's findings (Gowan & Demos, 1964).

Creativity

Recent interest in characteristics other than high intellectual performances as measured by intelligence tests has led to studies on creativity. Some work has examined the relationship between creativity and intelligence (MacKinnon, 1962; Roe, 1953). Most findings indicate that the correlation between creativity and intelligence as measured by an intelligence test tends to be low. MacKinnon (1962) reported that the correlation between rated creativity of 60 eminent architects and scores on an adult intelligence test was low. Getzels and Jackson (1962) found low correlations between intelligence test scores and creativity as measured by divergent thinking tests. Torrance (1962) reported the same results regarding correlation of intelligence test and creativity scores. A review of the literature by Taylor and Holland (1962) revealed that most studies report positive but low correlations between the two factors for the

profile **JAMES J. GALLAGHER**

Director of the Frank Porter Graham Child Development Center at the University of North Carolina since 1970, Dr. James J. Gallagher has also held administrative positions in the U.S. Office of Education. For 14 years he was a faculty member at the University of Illinois. He has been an active researcher in giftedness and wrote, with Aschner and Jenne, a Council for Exceptional Children research monograph on productive thinking of gifted children (1967). He has edited and authored many other books and articles on gifted, including Teaching the Gifted Child *(1975) and* Talent Delayed—Talent Denied *(1974).*

Gallagher is a past president of The Association for the Gifted as well as the Council for Exceptional Children. Perhaps Research Summary on Gifted Child Education *(1966) is his most important publication, because it provided impetus to other states' programs for the gifted.*

general population but little or no correlation at the higher ability levels.

Fostering Creativity

There is little definitive information on how to encourage creativity or factors which influence children's creativity. Barron (1965) suggests that much potential creativity is discouraged by the unfavorable climate both in the classroom and in society at large, where divergent, creative behavior is often punished.

Heilbrun (1971) examined the relation of creativity in boys to maternal child-rearing patterns. He concluded that sons who perceived their mothers as controlling and hostile were judged as less creative than those who perceived their mothers as low in control and high in nurturance.

Teachers may play an important role in developing creative behavior in their students. Zimmerman and Dialessi (1973) examined the influence of a model on creative behavior of 120 fifth grade children. In four treatment situations they measured the effects of a model high or low in fluency on the children's fluency and flexibility. The students were required to perform both a similar task and one that was different than that modeled. High model fluency significantly increased child fluency and flexibility on a similar task. On the task which was not modeled, the children's fluency was slightly increased after they observed increased model fluency. However, increased flexibility in the model produced decreases in children's fluency and flexibility. These results may, however, have been influenced by the model's evaluation of the students, which has been shown in other studies to inhibit fluency.

It seems that modeling with the gifted may be especially significant. These students often indicate that mentors or teachers greatly influenced their development (Maugh, 1974). Desirable models have been people who either achieved extremely high levels in their chosen fields or those who inspired their proteges with an extreme love and commitment to their area of interest.

However, we still do not know very much about the role of modeling in fostering creativity. So far, modeling techniques have been studied most often with exceptional populations with disabilities or specific handicaps. Modeling is used to facilitate responses, to inhibit responses, or to increase response acquisition. This technique may have important implications for use with gifted populations.

Alternative Achievement Tests

Dissatisfaction with conventional procedures of identifying gifted students through formal intelligence and achievement tests has led to the development of alternative methods. Renzulli (1973) designed the Sub-Cultural Indices of Academic Potential, which requires students to assess their reactions to everyday situations and yields a profile of student preferences and learning styles. Meeker (1969) attempted to

This class of sixth graders is trying to decide what to do if another ice age comes—an exercise in fluency and flexibility.

identify and test for specific types of gifted-ness using Guilford's structure of intellect model (1959).

Bernal (1972) has tried to identify gifted-ness among Chicano students in Texas. And Bruch (1972), in her development of the ABDA (Abbreviated Binet for Disadvan-taged), has attempted to create a bias in favor of disadvantaged black youngsters. Grant and Renzulli (1975) developed an inventory to identify potentially successful college students from minority cultures who might be missed by conventional identifica-tion procedures. Their final instrument con-sists of a pool of 30 items designed to be used in conjunction with other methods for evaluating student performance. Attempts to develop alternative methods for identify-ing the gifted are relatively recent and un-doubtedly will receive continued and in-creased attention.

Administrative Procedures

Numerous studies on administrative pro-cedures applicable to the gifted have been reported. These include early entrance, acceleration, enrichment, grouping, and variations of these (Laubenfels, 1978). Gal-lagher (1966) categorized programs for the gifted as administrative, instructional, and adjunctive. The administrative program changes the educational world around the child, the instructional program changes the content or style of subject matter pre-sented, and the adjunctive program pro-vides special services beyond the usual program.

We do not have extensive evaluations of various administrative practices. By con-trast, data on acceleration have been avail-able for some time, and the research find-ings are consistently favorable. In an early study, Keys (1938) compared the perfor-mance of 348 students who entered the university at age 16½ or younger with a group entering at 17 years or later. The accelerated students had superior academic performance as reflected in grade point average and scholarships earned. Terman and Oden's follow-up of their sample (1947) revealed that the ac-celerated did better than the nonacceler-ated in educational achievement, physical health, marital adjustment, and vocational success. Justman (1953, 1954) and Wor-cester (1956) confirmed these results.

Despite the consistent evidence in sup-port of acceleration, it is not widely prac-ticed, although early admission to school is one form that *is* practiced. Studies by Lar-son (1963) and Braga (1971) found positive results of this practice. Lehman (1953) pre-sented powerful evidence that the most productive period of life is early adulthood. By giving the gifted an early start, they are able to make significant social contributions earlier than if they were made to proceed through school at a normal rate. Pressey (1949) cited this argument for accelerating the gifted. However, the use of early en-trance, like other forms of acceleration, is not widely practiced.

Special grouping has been the subject of much heated debate through the years. Arguments in favor of ability grouping indi-cate that it allows the gifted to be stimulated more (Ward, 1961). It also encourages new leaders to emerge and be identified (Barbe, 1962). Opponents of ability group-ing claim that it encourages elitism and is contrary to principles of equality. In this age of emphasis on individualization, one solu-tion may be to group youngsters for the skill areas according to their current achieve-ment so that they can go through sequen-tial programs in the basic skills. Thus, stu-dents may be grouped by ability and achievement for academic skill learning and grouped by age for other activities, particularly where the prime objective is socialization.

profile **WALTER B. BARBE**
Since 1950, Dr. Walter B. Barbe has been involved directly in educational programs and research on gifted children. He is currently editor of the magazine Highlights for Children *and is also Adjunct Professor of Education at The Ohio State University. He has lectured extensively throughout the United States, taught courses on the gifted in more than 50 colleges and universities, and served as consultant to numerous school districts. Dr. Barbe has written more than 100 publications on giftedness. He identifies as his single most important contribution the monograph* One In A Thousand: A Comparative Study of Moderately and Highly Gifted Elementary School Children *(1964). He followed his adviser, noted authority Paul A. Witty, in specializing in the teaching of reading and using it to enrich the education of the gifted.*

Needed Research

The number of studies and authoritative opinions published on the subject of the gifted have increased greatly over the past 50 years. But there are areas in which practically no good research has been reported.

Perhaps the most carefully conducted research has been in grade acceleration. Yet this provision is not popular in the United States. Since resistance to its use appears to be rooted in attitudes of school personnel and perhaps parents, research studies should be directed at those attitudes. By finding out why people oppose grade acceleration, it might be possible to refute those reasons that are false and to correct any true drawbacks of this approach.

Applied behavioral analysis has been used more and more widely in the United States during the last decade. (See chapter 1.) The gifted population, however, is generally not included in those studies reported in the literature. Apparently, high-achieving gifted and talented students are internally motivated to learn. Because of this inner drive, these students should be prime subjects for using self-monitored behavior analysis (McLaughlin, 1976). A fruitful area of research would be the affects of teaching gifted students self-recording and self-control procedures.

Underachieving bright students would appear to be good subjects for research using social modeling, token economy, contingency contracting, and other operant conditioning approaches. There are almost no studies using these methods with gifted students to increase their interest in school learning.

A careful analysis of enrichment activities for gifted children has yet to be reported. If these activities for both gifted and non-gifted groups are similar and result in no significant differences when certain factors (such as IQ) are controlled, we could dismiss enrichment as special instruction. Contrary findings would, of course, establish enrichment as a valuable instructional approach for the gifted and talented.

MEETING SPECIAL NEEDS
Once students have been identified and placed in specially designed educational situations, it is their teachers who make the major contributions to their schooling. By encouraging students, making special provisions, and carefully choosing teaching methods, teachers can develop better instructional approaches to the gifted.

Encouragement

Highly motivated bright students often need little encouragement. Some students, however, may have not yet developed their motivation for learning. With these children, teachers may:

1. Provide recognition for their efforts.

2. Provide extra credit for novel ideas or products.

3. Stress positive comments in all teacher-pupil exchanges.

4. Offer special privileges for specified performances.

5. Permit high-achieving students to be "teacher."

6. Encourage student-initiated projects and activities for those who have completed assignments.

7. Make special arrangements for high-achieving students to take selected subjects in higher grades.

8. Introduce elementary age students to research methods.

9. Teach debating skills and encourage students to sponsor and participate in debates on topics of their choice.

10. Have high-achieving math students create mathematical puzzles.

11. Encourage students to write scripts for TV and radio programs and "participate in" the programs.

12. Have students present a synopsis of a magazine or newspaper article to the class in a way that is interesting and understandable.

13. Have a "crazy idea" session where only unusual notions can be discussed.

14. Conduct a traditional brain-storming session.

15. Let them express themselves in art forms such as drawings, creative writing, and role playing.

16. Have them dramatize their readings.

17. Have a great books seminar to introduce students to the classics.

Special provisions

No one teacher can provide instruction to gifted children in all of their interests and subject areas. This problem is particularly difficult in elementary school self-contained classrooms. Some of the following ideas can be helpful.

1. Make library services available to them. If the school library is inadequate, take them on regular trips, if possible, to a public library. Arrange to secure hard-to-get materials from state or university libraries.

2. Try to guide the children to the resources they need. Refer them to encyclopedias, dictionaries, and other reference sources.

3. Develop a catalog of other resources which students can use, possibly containing addresses of agencies providing free and inexpensive materials or local community resources.

4. Form interest clubs with students as officers.

5. Identify people in the community who are available to work with individual gifted students. Help those who are knowledgeable in their fields but do not know how to manage or teach children.

Teaching methods

Sometimes gifted students are discouraged from risk taking in academic learning; their thinking is often trained to focus on the right answer. When they are faced with tasks in which there are no clear answers or in which there may be a variety of possible correct answers, they may be confused or feel threatened with failure. Try some of these tactics.

1. Use a questioning technique rather than giving information.

2. Use hypothetical questions beginning with "What if . . . ?"

3. *Ask students to develop situations where no one answer is correct.*

4. *In subjects such as arithmetic, where specific answers are required, encourage students to estimate their answers.*

5. *Have students check your written work for errors; let them see that all adults are fallible.*

6. *Instead of information only, emphasize concepts, theories, ideas, relationships, and generalizations.*

7. *Provide opportunities and assignments which rely on independent reading and research.*

8. *Have students give reports on their individual research and experimentation; this helps them acquire a sense of sharing their knowledge.*

9. *Provide foreign language materials—books, periodicals, recording, newspapers—for young gifted children.*

FOR MORE INFORMATION

Most of these resources are textbooks that are readily available. Check your instructor, the education library, or the general library at your school.

Gallagher, J.J. *Teaching the gifted child* (2nd ed.). Boston: Allyn & Bacon, 1975.

Gold, M.J. *Education of the intellectually gifted.* Columbus, Ohio: Charles E. Merrill, 1965.

Newland, T.E. *Gifted in socio-educational perspective.* Englewood Cliffs, N.J.: Prentice-Hall, 1976.

15

Conclusion: Classroom Two

Norris G. Haring

Our goal in the last fourteen chapters has been two-fold: both to introduce you to exceptional children and to show you something of the field of special education. Over the course of these chapters you have, no doubt, picked up much of the language by which the field describes children's needs and the programs and services set up to meet those needs. We hope that, in learning these categories and terms, you've also come to understand the complex but unavoidable difficulties of labelling groups of individuals. To some extent, we have organized this book to reflect that different systems of categorizing children can be useful, depending on whether you are most concerned with their age, level of development, severity of handicap, or the type of programming needed. And while there are some real differences from category to category that must be accommodated for, we have stressed throughout that the individual child's behaviors and learning characteristics are the critical variables in any decision we make about him or her.

In fact, throughout its relatively short history, the profession of special education has been primarily concerned with the individual child. Research in special education has consisted not only of classical research procedures (using experimental and control groups), but also of the applied analysis of the behaviors of single subjects (using direct and repeated observations and experimental control). In the classroom, special educators have emphasized individual assessment and carefully planned individualized instructional programs. In effect, the need to be the most competent of all educators has directed the special educator to focus on the individual differences and special needs of each child. Now, with the legal mandate of P.L. 94–142 for an *individually planned* education for every handicapped child in the United States, the demands on special education are greater than ever.

FUTURE TRENDS

The most immediate demand P.L. 94–142 places on the public schools is to provide services for those half million or more children who have up to now been denied any educational opportunity at all. These "priority one" children, as the law describes them, must be located, identified, assessed, and placed in educational programs that are appropriate for their needs. Of almost equal urgency is the need to provide full services for the "priority two" children, those who are receiving only *some* of the special educational help or other services they need to succeed. Providing for these two groups of children represents one of the most important goals of the Bureau of Education for the Handicapped, and for special education in general. In addition, the Bureau's three other highest priorities indicate directions for the near future: increased education of young handicapped children, full educational opportunity for the severely handicapped (including deaf-blind and multiply and profoundly handicapped), and career and vocational education for children with handicaps.

We have dealt extensively in this book with young handicapped children, partially because of the increasing national focus on this population. We have seen that it is crucial to identify handicaps early in life and to devise programs to prevent or reduce further developmental delays. The majority of profoundly handicapped children can now be identified at birth (with Apgar scores of 4 or below), the majority of severely handicapped during the first few weeks of life, and the majority of moderately handicapped before they reach 2 years of age. With this information, it is possible to establish infant intervention and parent education programs very early in a child's development. It is reasonable to believe that, with early identification and teaching,

Her involved parents, loving brothers, and early education promise Jennifer a good chance to overcome her delays.

we can avoid some of the serious problems of later adaptation of the environment.

Despite our current programs in early identification, however, we have much to do. The need for even better procedures, and particularly for more systematic and widely applied infant assessment, is absolutely critical. According to the National Advisory Committee on the Handicapped (1976, p. 2), almost three-quarters of a million handicapped children between birth and age 5 are still unserved. The Consortium on Adaptive Performance Evaluation (CAPE) and its Committee on Infant Assessment (CIA) have been created to assess young severely handicapped children. Organized national efforts like these, along with better education and training for parents, physicians, preschool and day care staffs, and all others who interact with very young children, offer much hope for great advances in both identification and intervention as early in life as possible.

As our responsibility for educating all handicapped children increases, governed and monitored by federal and state legislation, professionals in special education are becoming more responsive to the moderately, severely, and profoundly handicapped. This trend, begun only very recently, is taking the shape of a national commitment to offer full educational services to those historically denied them. Here, too, this book has dealt in depth with current research and systematic instructional procedures that are proving effective for these individuals.

Perhaps for the first time in history, we are beginning to see severely handicapped persons as capable of learning. And we are beginning to realize that many behaviors of severely handicapped that seem unproductive or valueless—self-stimulation, so-called "blank" stares, and the like—are in fact *learned*. Behaviors such as these result from the lack of systematically applied stimuli that might promote learning; they seem to be responses learned to compensate for lack of stimulation from the environment (DeLissavoy, 1964; Lovaas, 1967; Provence & Lipton, 1962; Berkson, 1967). Their eventual effect is to impair an already impaired person. Nowhere is this more clearly seen than in our own work with Down's children (Hayden & Haring, 1976). These children, because of their delays in responding to their mothers' communication attempts (which would evoke communication responses from an ordinary child), actually decreased the numbers of attempts the mothers made. This extinction of the mothers' communication efforts served only to lessen the stimuli acting on the children and to delay them further. Thus, more than ever before, the children in special education will demand the most carefully researched and refined assessment and instructional procedures.

While space hasn't allowed us to cover other advances in detail, like those in non-vocal communication, the use of Blissymbols, the teaching of sign language, and the development of equipment like the Auto-Com and the Porta-Printer have greatly increased the abilities of the severely physically handicapped to communicate with those around them (Vanderheiden & Grilley, 1976). Technological advances like these often result only through the combined efforts of professionals in several fields. More and more, we are coming to realize the crucial need for close and continued teamwork by many professionals, in medicine, nursing, occupational and physical therapy, communication disorders, psychology, social work, and community services. If we are to succeed, the problems of teaching the severely handicapped must be shared by all of these intervention and management disciplines.

As we pointed out, these new concerns for more severely involved children are requiring regular educators to become more responsive to mildly handicapped children. In a recent report, *Training Educators for the Handicapped* (1976), the Government Accounting Office urged HEW to:

- Provide a major emphasis on programs for training the Nation's regular classroom teachers to effectively deal with the handicapped, in cooperation with State and local agencies and institutions of higher education . . . .
- Emphasize the need for applying individualized instruction techniques to the handicapped by supporting projects— such as those for preparing and using paraprofessionals—designed to extend the regular classroom teacher's ability to reach individual students. (p. ii)

To insure the success of regular education's responsibility to the mildly handicapped, the roles of special educators as consultants and resource specialists must increase. Evidence of this shift in roles can be seen in data gathered for the Government Accounting Office report mentioned above. In the school districts sampled for the report, most of the teachers the districts had hired in the 1974–75 school year were for self-contained special education clas-

ses. In contrast, most of the teachers they planned to hire for the 1975–77 school years were either resource room or itinerant teachers. No doubt much of the work of these new specialists will be to assist regular education personnel to identify and individualize programs for the special needs of the children they serve.

Finally, the goal of providing career education and vocational training for handicapped persons is a clearly developing demand which special education must help to meet.

> One of the factors working against placing the handicapped in regular vocational education classrooms is the regular vocational educators' lack of training in working with the handicapped. Most vocational teachers do not have such training and so are reluctant to accept the handicapped in their classes . . . . Vocational educators' lack of sensitivity and skill in dealing with the handicapped is a major barrier to integration into the regular vocational education programs. (*Training Educators for the Handicapped,* 1976)

The development of vocational education programs for mildly and moderately handicapped students has been a concern of special education for several years.

In sheltered workshops, many handicapped adults learn skills to transfer to the outside world.

Kolstoe's work (1965, 1975) resulted in a three-phase program of work-training for retarded adolescents, including initial work experience, on-the-job training, and permanent job placement. More recently, Brolin and his associates in PROJECT PRICE (Brolin, 1976; Brown, McIntosh, & Tuoti, 1974) have developed a competency-based career education curriculum for mildly and moderately retarded students, with emphasis on daily living skills, personal-social skills, and occupational guidance and preparation.

Several special educators have responded to the need for prevocational and vocational education for the more severely handicapped. Gold's work (1972) has recognized the potential of severely handicapped adults to develop vocational skills. His training sequences for assembling bicycle brakes, printed electronic circuits, and gas cap locks for automobiles are effective demonstrations in training severely handicapped adults. Bellamy (1976) has followed with training sequences to develop a variety of marketable skills. Mithaug (Mithaug & Haring, 1977) has developed prevocational programs concentrating on establishing criteria for success in a sheltered workshop, particularly with severely handicapped adolescents. Finally, we are coming to see that severely handicapped adolescents and adults are able to achieve a certain amount of financial independence and success in the job market.

PREPARING PROFESSIONALS

These priorities, expressed in federal legislation, court rulings, state laws, and BEH policies, and echoed by leaders throughout the field, all point to one direction. These conditions demand, and will continue to demand, higher levels of competence in special educators than the field has ever

seen before. More than ever, professional training programs must respond with more competency-based and applied experiences for their students.

> Higher functioning special education disability areas allow student teachers to transfer much that they know about normal child development and much that they have learned in the college classroom about special education to the instruction process with their students. This is unfortunately not often the case for teachers of the severely/multiply handicapped child. These teachers must learn teacher–child interactions that may be totally different from anything they've ever done before. These students should have intense and durable experiences with severely handicapped children from their first week of the college training program. (Sailor & Haring, 1977)

One of the most important findings of those professionals who work closely with the severely handicapped individual is the need for more intensive training. If the severely handicapped are to succeed, the professional educator who works with them must develop the same kind of rigorous confidence as has been developed in other helping professions—medicine, nursing, physical therapy, and communication disorders.

At the outset of this book, we spoke of developing a view of teaching as managing and arranging the information, the resources, and the total learning environment so that children learn. Let us add to that view of teaching *the continual need to become even more effective*. Like any scientist, the special teacher must change, to deal with new information and new procedures, by continually evaluating and refining our best efforts in assessment, instruction, and curriculum design. In other words, special educators at all levels must assess *themselves*. We must collect information not only about our children's progress but also about the effectiveness of the instructional plans we have written to insure that

Teaching Kelly requires firmness and consistency, as well as concern.

growth. Special educators must, then, learn from their own teaching.

As a final analysis, we could offer a list of things to do to work for greater effectiveness, but lists are often too long and almost as often incomplete. Instead, then, let us consider three areas of professional growth in teaching handicapped children.

Competence

We have said on several occasions that special children are those who require special arrangements and special instructional procedures or materials in order to learn successfully. To perform not only proficiently, but almost automatically in the way a skilled surgeon does, the special teacher needs carefully refined and well-practiced skills. Among these are the ability to observe, to analyze, and to record behaviors critical for instruction. Beyond this, the ability to predict trends in a child's performance—to anticipate difficulties as well as sustained growth—is critical. Without this skill in "formative" measurement as it is called (measurement used to formulate new teaching interventions), a teacher may condemn a child to an inappropriate or ineffective instructional plan.

In addition to these basic skills in observing and analyzing information about how children perform, the competent special education teacher must be fully familiar with the laws of behavior. This involves both an understanding of the events in the environment which generate behaviors and the principles by which we can bring about changes in behaviors. The competent special teacher must be able to identify the phase or level at which a child is learning (acquistion, fluency, maintenance, generalization, or application) and to specify an instructional procedure (shaping, molding, demonstration, modeling, cueing, drill, practice) appropriate to that phase.

Horner, Holvolt, and Rinne (1976) have identified and listed the following competencies for teachers of severely/multiply handicapped:

1. Techniques for managing severe behavior problems;

2. Procedures for developing teacher-made instructional materials;

3. Engineering physical properties of a classroom;

4. Basic principles of the acquisition of operant behavior;

5. Basic principles and techniques of measurement;

6. Basic principles of imitation training, generalization, discrimination, and maintenance;

7. Basic principles of task analysis;

8. Development and implementation of instructional programs; and

9. Procedures used to develop curriculum sequences.

A teacher of the severely handicapped must be flexible and prepared to handle surprises.

For the most part, this list is as useful a summary of skills necessary for any special educator as for teachers of severely handicapped.

Beyond these skills, special educators must understand the principles and roles of all the other professionals who work with children: the occupational therapist, the physical therapist, the communication disorders specialist, the pediatrician, the school nurse, the building principal, the school psychologist, the counselor, the regular classroom teacher. And perhaps most important, special educators must learn to support, to work with, and to ask for help from the parents of the children with whom they work. Not only do legislation and the forces of parent advocacy demand this interaction, but so does the awareness that a handicapped child's educational needs do not end at the classroom door.

Staying Informed

Special education training is both a process of acquiring and building skills and of expanding one's knowledge about handicapped children, programs and services, and curricula and methods. But there is another kind of information that is often too dynamic to be learned from books or perhaps even from formal courses in colleges and universities. That information, like specific local procedures for observing due legal process in referring or placing a child in special education, or procedures for maintaining confidentiality and for legitimate release of information about a child, varies somewhat from locale to locale and year to year. On the other hand, the obligation to become informed about such issues and responsibilities is no less important. The procedures for due process and confidentiality, for instance, are now legal issues; and at least certain minimum requirements are in force in every state. But they were ethical issues long before the laws were passed, and informed teachers have paid careful attention to such rights for just as long. Like any profession, the profession of special education demands careful attention to the issues of the day and enduring responsibilities to handicapped children and their families.

Social Responsiveness

Perhaps one of the basic motives a person has for entering special education is the desire to serve. Perhaps without this motivation a career in the field would not be rewarding at all. Certainly, making the decision to serve society and searching out the best means of service are difficult enough. But the philosophical decision to work in special education because of humanitarian efforts to serve those in need is soon met with the weight of professional training that is both scientific and technological.

In practice, the humanitarian motivation is necessary but hardly enough. Being effective, helping children learn and grow *despite their handicaps,* requires the kinds of competence we have just outlined and the determination to accept small but successively better approximations of the targets we have chosen for instruction.

The handicapped child's environment, in the small world of the classroom or the larger world of the community, is social, of course. And the eventual goal of any special educational program must be to move a child as close to the normal, "natural" environment as he can successfully move. But such a goal is demanding in time, in patience, and sometimes in what goes occasionally for sympathy or humanitarian concern.

> Classroom One . . . operates on the theory that severely/multiply handicapped children need warmth, love, relaxation, and stimula-

tion. . . . A glance at Classroom One at nearly any time will show children being held, rocked, and cooed at by members of the teaching staff . . . The staff all *feel* that the children are learning, but come and look again in 6 months and what do you see? The same activities with the same children. . . . The students are probably enjoying the activities, but they aren't learning.

> Consider Classroom Two. The students are also enjoying the activity, which is also warm, nurturing, and loving. The only difference is that the children in Classroom Two are learning as a function of the consequences for their actions. Action is required . . . In Classroom Two, we might see a teacher supporting a child in a sitting position, listening to music from a radio or record player. However, the difference from Classroom One might be that the radio stops when the child's head slumps from midline and starts when he raises it again to midline. Music to this child is a pleasurable *consequence* of an action he is learning to make in his environment . . . . In Classroom Two, when you return in 6 months to observe, you will see the same children engaging in *different* activities—activities which are more complex and more demanding of the child than 6 months before, and which build on those earlier activities . . . . Learning to exercise control over one's environment is a rewarding experience for all children. (Sailor & Haring, 1977, pp. 75–76)

Being too soft brings no change. Without change, which can be specified and observed and noted as it was in Classroom Two, the handicapped child has no future, only an endless present.

It is not possible, in a sentence or a paragraph, or even a page, to summarize adequately the mass of facts which so many have collected, written, revised, checked, and rewritten for this book. It is only left for me to say that you the reader, as a future teacher of handicapped children, have choices and challenges before you. If you can strive for these characteristics we have just discussed—competence, awareness of professional issues and responsibilities, and a responsiveness to the social and emotional demands of this field, your classroom can, like Classroom Two, be one where change takes place.

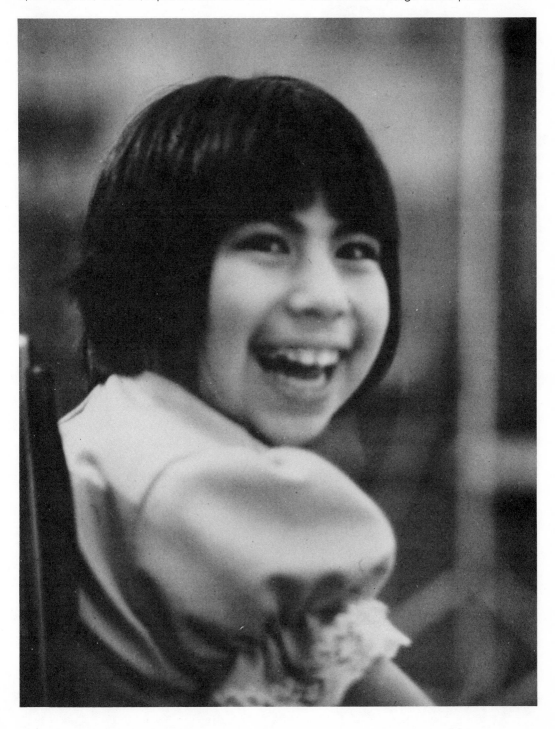

The tests and rating scales listed here are widely used to classify children, both handicapped and nonhandicapped. Their presence here does not reflect any endorsement on the part of the editor or the publisher.

AAMD Adaptive Behavior Scale

This scale is intended to provide objective descriptions and evaluations of how effectively an individual copes with environmental demands. Part One relates to personal independence in daily living; Part Two focuses on maladaptive behaviors related to personality and behavior disorders. An informed observer fills out the scale or obtains information through an interview. A profile rather than a single score is obtained.

Apgar Test

The Apgar test is used to evaluate newborn infants at 1 minute and again at 5 minutes after delivery is complete. An observer gives the infant a score of 0 to 2 on five criteria: heart rate, respiratory effort, muscle tone, reflex response, and color. A score of 4 or less indicates a need for immediate attention. Approximately 70% of newborns achieve a score of 7 or better.

Bayley Scale of Infant Development

This standardized test evaluates infants on 163 items, most of which involves sensorimotor or perceptual functioning, although some involve language. It is designed to evaluate overall intelligence, based upon the individual infant's performance on the items.

Bender Visual-Motor Gestalt Test

Originally designed to test the visual-motor responses of children from 5 to 10 years old, this test asks the subject to copy patterns. The testor, a trained psychologist, rates the child's mode of attack, efficiency, and success. This test is intended to evaluate psychological processes rather than specific skill areas. It is widely used to help diagnose learning disabilities.

Denver Developmental Screening Test

This scale is designed to evaluate children from age 2 weeks to 6 years on personal-social, fine motor, language, and gross motor development. An inexpensive and easily administered test, it is often used to predict future learning problems.

Durrell Analysis of Reading Difficulty

This is a series of individual subtests in oral and silent reading, listening comprehension, word recognition and word analysis, visual memory, auditory analysis, and learning rate. Tests in phonics, spelling, and handwriting are also available. It may be used with nonreaders through the sixth grade.

Frostig Developmental Test of Visual Perception

This test can be used with preschool children for screening or with school-age children for diagnosis. It evaluates five areas of visual perception: eye-motor coordination, figure-ground discrimination, constancy of shape, position-in-space, and spatial relationships. An overall perceptual quotient and a perceptual age for each of the subtests are obtained. The test may be given to individual children or in small groups.

Gates-McKillop Reading Diagnostic Test

This test includes subtests in oral reading, flashed presentation of words, untimed presentation of words, flash presentation of phrases, knowledge of word parts, recognition of the visual forms of sounds, and auditory blending. It has supplementary tests in spelling, oral vocabulary, syllabification, and auditory discrimination. This test is intended to be used with children with severe reading and spelling disabilities.

Gesell Schedules of Development

This was the first infant intelligence test developed. Basically a test of sensorimotor and perceptual functioning, it can be administered as soon as a few months after birth.

Goodenough-Harris Drawing Test

This test requires the child to draw a person. It is essentially a nonverbal intelligence test, often used to evaluate perceptual functioning. The number of details the child includes detemines the score, which is compared to the number of

Appendix A

details on a "normal" scale to find the child's mental age. From the mental age, an IQ can be derived.

Hiskey-Nebraska Test of Learning Aptitude

This is a nonverbal intelligence test with several subtests, including bead pattern memory, color memory, picture identification, spatial reasoning, picture association, paper folding, block patterns, puzzle blocks, memory for digits, visual attention span, and completion of drawings. Standardized on a deaf population, it can be used with children from age 3 on up through high school age.

Iowa Silent Reading Test

This is an early test of reading achievement, which yields a grade-level score.

Illinois Test of Psycholinguistic Abilities (ITPA)

This is an individually administered diagnostic test for children from age 2 years 4 months to 10 years 3 months. It involves three dimensions—levels of organization, psycholinguistic processes, and channels of communication—that give a profile rather than a single score. The 12 subtests include auditory reception, visual reception, auditory association, visual association, verbal expression, manual expression, grammatic closure, visual closure, auditory sequential memory, visual sequential memory, auditory closure, and sound blending.

Leiter International Performance Scale

This test evaluates behavior rather than verbal skills, and thus can be used with children with communication disorders or hearing impairments.

Peabody Individual Achievement Test (PIAT)

This individually administered test provides scores for mathematics, reading recognition, reading comprehension, spelling, and general information, and a total test score. It can be used with children from kindergarten through age 12.

Pupil Rating Scale

This is a standardized rating scale with five behavioral categories: auditory comprehension, spoken language, orientation, behavior, and motor skills. Each category includes several specific items, and the classroom teacher rates the student from 1 to 5 on each item.

Purdue Perceptual-Motor Survey

This standardized scale was designed for children from age 6 to 9, but can be used with older, retarded students. It assesses balance, postural flexibility, laterality, body image, rhythm, translation of an auditory stimulus to motor response, symmetrical control of the body, directionality, eye-foot coordination, ocular control, form perception, figure-ground relationships, muscular fitness, and gross motor coordination.

Scale for Rating Behavioral Characteristics of Superior Students

This scale is designed for use by classroom teachers. Students who are thought to be gifted are rated from 1 to 4 on specific characteristics, grouped into learning characteristics, motivational characteristics, creativity characteristics, and leadership characteristics.

Stanford Achievement Test

This is a group-administered achievement test appropriate for all grade levels. Originally published in 1923, it was the first wide-range battery of standardized achievement tests.

Stanford-Binet Intelligence Scale

This is an individually administered intelligence test which yields an IQ. The subject answers items until he or she misses a certain number of consecutive items, thus reaching a "ceiling." The 1960 revision of the Stanford-Binet included minorities in the standardization population in an effort to combat cultural bias.

Sub-Cultural Indices of Academic Potential

This scale is designed to help identify gifted youngsters by assessing their behavior in everyday situations. It yields a profile rather than a single score.

Sequenced Inventory of Communication Development

This assessment tool is used to evaluate a preschool child's language development in receptive language, expressive language, grammar, and speech.

Vineland Social Maturity Scale

This standardized scale is administered through an interview with a person who knows the subject well. The examiner determines basal and ceiling ages from which a social quotient is derived. The tasks studied are divided into six areas: self-help, self-direction, locomotion, occupation, communication, and socialization. It can be used with subjects from infancy through adulthood.

Washington Guide to Promoting Development in the Young Child

This assessment tool is used to evaluate preschool children on such measures as motor skills, feeding, and play.

Wechsler Intelligence Scale for Children (WISC)

In its revised edition (WISC-R), this standardized intelligence test gives separate IQ scores for a verbal scale, performance scale, and total scale. The verbal scale includes six subtests: information, comprehension, arithmetic, similarities, vocabulary, and digit span. The performance scale also includes six subtests: picture completion, picture arrangement, block design, coding, object assembly, and mazes. The test can be used with children from age 6 through age 17.

Wide Range Achievement Test (WRAT)

This achievement test includes two subtests which can be administered to a group, covering spelling and mathematics, and one covering reading recognition that must be individually administered. It can be used for people of all ages. Three kinds of scores are available: grade ratings, percentiles, and standard scores.

Academic Therapy
1539 Fourth Street
San Rafael, CA 94901
This is a quarterly journal with international readership. It is dedicated to the interdisciplinary study and remediation of learning disabilities. Articles include case studies and current topics in education.

American Annals of the Deaf
This bimonthly journal is the official publication of the Conference of American Instructors of the Deaf and the Conference of Executives of American School for the Deaf. It focuses on education of the deaf or hearing handicapped.

American Association for the Education of the Severely/Profoundly Handicapped Review
1600 W. Armory Way
Seattle, WA 98195
The Association's official publication, this quarterly publishes research reports dealing with the population named.

American Journal of Mental Deficiency
5201 Connecticut Avenue NW
Washington, D.C. 20015
This bimonthly journal publishes studies and discussions of the behavioral and biological aspects of mental retardation. It is the official publication of the American Association of Mental Deficiency.

ASHA
10801 Rockville Pike
Rockville, MD 20852
The readers of this monthly journal are the members of the American Speech and Hearing Association—audiologists, teachers of the deaf, and language, speech, and hearing therapists. It includes articles and organization information.

Association for Children with Learning Disabilities Newsletter
P.O. Box 3303
Glenstone Station
Springfield, MO 65804
A monthly newsletter published by the Association for Children with Learning Disabilities, it contains reports of news from local chapters, recent developments in the field of learning disabilities, conventions, and other events of interest to parents and professionals.

American Annals of the Deaf
5034 Wisconsin Avenue N.W.
Washington, D.C. 20016
This journal, published six times a year, provides book reviews and questions and answers about clinical problems. It offers an annual directory of programs and services for the deaf.

Education of the Visually Handicapped
919 Walnut Street
Philadelphia, PA 19107
This is the quarterly publication of the Association for Education of the Visually Handicapped. It emphasizes teaching ideas and programs, and is not particularly technical, although research studies are included.

Educational Horizons
4101 East Third Street
Box A 850
Bloomington, IN 47401
This is the official publication of Pi Lambda Theta, the National Honor and Professional Association in Education. It regularly devotes part or all of an issue to education of the handicapped. Published quarterly.

The Exceptional Parent
20 Providence Street
Boston, MA 02116
This is a magazine published six times a year for parents and educators of all types of exceptional children. It focuses on informal reports rather than scientific research findings.

Focus on Exceptional Children
Love Publishing Company
6635 East Villanova Place
Denver, CO 80222
This is a monthly newsletter dealing with children with special needs. Each issue contains a single article on a topic dealing with exceptional children, plus a short section for teachers called "Classroom Forum."

Appendix B

The Gifted Child Quarterly
217 Gregory Drive
Hot Springs, AR 71901
This quarterly is published by the National Association for Gifted Children.

Journal for Special Educators
179 Sierra Vista Lane
Valley Cottage, NY 10989
This journal, which is published three times per year, deals with guidance, rehabilitation, psychology, and education of exceptional children, with emphasis on the retarded.

The Journal of Applied Behavior Analysis
Department of Human Development
University of Kansas
Lawrence, KS 66044
This quarterly journal of the Society for the Experimental Analysis of Behavior publishes reports of experimental research involving the application of behavior analysis. Although it is not exclusively a special education publication, it focuses heavily on the use of behavior analysis with the handicapped.

Journal of Learning Disabilities
101 E. Ontario Street
Chicago, IL 60611
This multidisciplinary journal is published bimonthly 10 times a year. In addition to articles on educational, medical, and psychological topics, regular columns on current research and curriculum materials are included.

Journal of Rehabilitation
1522 K Street NW
Washington, D.C. 20005
This is the official bimonthly publication of the National Rehabilitation Association. Its articles are practical rather than research-oriented, covering rehabilitation education, social work, employment, programs, and techniques.

Journal of Special Education
3515 Woodhaven Road
Philadelphia, PA 19154
This quarterly publishes articles dealing with every aspect of special education, many of them research studies of high quality. It also deals with critical issues in the field.

Journal of Speech and Hearing Disorders
10801 Rockville Pike
Rockville, MD 20852
Another publication of the American Speech and Hearing Association, this quarterly publishes articles dealing with communication disorders. It includes research reports.

Mental Retardation
5201 Connecticut Avenue NW
Washington, D.C. 20015
This is another publication of the American Association on Mental Deficiency. Published for any professional person who works with the retarded, it includes research, case studies, essays on topical issues, and descriptions of programs.

New Outlook for the Blind
American Foundation for the Blind
15 W. 16th St.
New York, NY 10011
This is the official publication of the American Foundation for the Blind. Published monthly except July and August, it covers all aspects of dealing with the blind of all ages.

The Volta Review
3417 Volta Place NW
Washington, D.C. 20007
This journal is the official publication of the Alexander Graham Bell Association for the Deaf. It is published monthly except in the summer, and is intended to "encourage the teaching of speech, speechreading, and use of residual hearing to deaf persons."

In addition to these publications, the following are published by the Council for Exceptional Children, 1920 Association Drive, Reston, VA 22901, or its divisions.

Exceptional Children
Published eight times a year, this journal includes articles dealing with "problems, research, findings, trends, and practices in educational programs" for all types of exceptional children. It particularly focuses on broad problems that cross categorical lines and affect large numbers of children.

TEACHING Exceptional Children
This is a quarterly journal intended for classroom teachers of all kinds of children with special needs, from preschool through adolescence.

Behavioral Disorders
This quarterly is the publication of the Council for Children with Behavioral Disorders. It includes articles dealing with research and current issues, as well as containing regular columns and departments.

Career Development for Exceptional Children
This journal is the publication of the Division on Career Development. Its articles cover vocational and self-help training for the handicapped, as well as the overall concerns of helping the handicapped lead fulfilling, independent lives.

DOPHHH Journal
This is the publication of the Division on Physically Handicapped, Homebound, and Hospitalized.

Education and Training of the Mentally Retarded
This quarterly is the publication of the Division on Mental Retardation. It is directed towards educators and other professionals working with the mentally retarded from preschool through secondary school.

Teacher Education and Special Education
This is the quarterly publication of the Teacher Education Division. It focuses on preparation of teachers and other professionals to work in the field of special education of the handicapped.

acuity—keenness of the senses; reception of external stimuli.

adapative behavior—behavior that meets the standards of personal-occupational independence consistent with one's age and culture.

aggression—behavior that may take forms of tantrums, verbal abuse, opposition, physical assault, noncompliance, destruction, and so on.

Applied Behavior Analysis (ABA)—a system of studying behavior and intervening to modify it, based on behavioral principles; involves direct daily measurement and experimental control in the intervention of targeted behavior.

arthrogryposis—congenital disability characterized by stiff joints and weak muscle.

articulation—the accurate sound production of a language's phonemes.

ataxia—lack of coordination of voluntary muscles, symptomatic of one variety of cerebral palsy.

athetosis—involuntary, irregular movement patterns of the extremities, symptomatic of one variety of cerebral palsy.

audiologist—a person certified in identification, measurement, and study of hearing and hearing impairments; recommends rehabilitative procedures.

autism—a disorder (appearing by age 2) characterized by noncommunication, lack of social skills, withdrawal, developmental delays, and stereotypic behavior.

behavior—overt response to a stimulus emitted voluntarily or elicited involuntarily.

behavior modification—the systematic environmental arrangement of cues or consequences to produce desired frequency of overt responses.

bilateral hearing loss—hearing impairment occurring in both ears.

biophysical model—model of emotional disorders based on "disease" model, wherein the pathology is within the individual; the disorder may be manifested at any time, but environmental stresses may be necessary to activate disturbance.

blind—totally without vision or having light perception only.

cancer—uncontrolled irregular cell growth.

cardiac—relating to the heart.

central visual acuity—impairment of vision such as myopia (nearsightedness), hyperopia (farsightedness), and astigmatism (imperfection in the thickness or curvature of the cornea).

cerebral palsy—a disorder that is the result of damage to or maldevelopment of the brain; *cerebral palsy* refers to the general catagory of neuromuscular disorder.

classical conditioning—changing behavior by repeatedly pairing an unconditioned stimulus with a neutral conditioned stimulus, until the conditioned stimulus acquires the response originally elicited by the unconditioned stimulus.

cognitive behavior modification—alteration of thought processes by techniques based on operant or respondent conditioning.

communication—the whole spectrum of visual and auditory stimuli—facial expression, gestures, sounds, words, phrases—used to convey interpersonal messages.

competency-based program—a program in which a teacher is expected to demonstrate a particular level of competency in mediating and manipulating the learning environment that will result in altering specific student progress outcomes.

conductive hearing loss—impairment in the mechanical transmission of sound waves through the outer and middle ear.

Glossary

congenital—present at birth.

contingency—a temporal and/or physical condition in which a response is followed by a positive or negative reinforcing stimulus or the removal of either.

criterion of ultimate functioning—a criterion based upon the behaviors required for the greatest degree of independent functioning, used for selecting information and skills to be taught to an individual.

cue (cueing)—use of a specific stimulus to evoke a desired response.

cystic fibrosis—hereditary disorder characterized by chronic pulmonary disease, pancreatic deficiency, and high levels of sweat electrolytes that cause a serum-like sweat.

decibels (dB)—units of sound intensity that are perceived as loudness or softness.

diparesis—partial paralysis in all four extremities with greater involvement in the lower limbs.

diplegia—paralysis in all four extremities with greater involvement in the lower limbs.

Down's syndrome—a chromosomal disorder in which there is an extra chromosome in each somatic cell; a syndrome associated with characteristic flat facial features, mental retardation, and other congenital defects. Also called *mongolism.*

dyslexia—a disorder characterized by failure to attain adequate reading skills.

educable mentally retarded (EMR)—description for people who are mildly mentally retarded, who achieve academically about 2 years slower than normal children during school age, and who have a high probability of vocational independence.

electroencephalograph (EEG)—an instrument that measures and graphically records changes in the electrical energy generated by the brain.

emotionally disturbed—description for individuals who frequently display maladaptive behavior such as temper tantrums, hyperaggressive behavior, or withdrawn behavior. Same as *behaviorally disordered.*

endogenous—describing conditions of which the origins are inherent in the organism.

epidemiological study of emotional disturbance—study in which disturbance is compared across cultures and social classes or in which such factors as social change are examined to determine how they might contribute to the disorder.

epilepsy—seizure disorder caused by abnormal, excessive electrical brain discharges.

etiology—origins or causes of a disease or condition; some are organic, others are environmental.

exceptional children—children who deviate from the average sufficiently to require special consideration.

exogenous—describing conditions which originate outside the organism.

fetus—a developing organism in the latter stages of development in uterus; in humans, from third month to birth. Prior to the third month, the organism is called an *embryo.*

fine motor skills—small muscle actions such as those involved in eye-hand coordination, reaching, grasping, and object manipulation.

functional definition—a definition that states what the cause of the problem appears to be, generally in physical or genetic terms, and is based upon more than behavioral observation.

genetics—when pertaining to handicapped children, the study of hereditary factors having a causal relationship with an exceptionality.

grammatical method—method of teaching language to hearing impaired children by presenting them with specific grammatical rules for putting sentences together and then having them construct sentences using those rules.

gross motor skills—large muscle actions such as sitting, crawling, standing, and walking.

gustation—act of tasting

handicap—a disadvantage that results from a disability and may vary for people with identical disabilities.

hemiparesis—partial paralysis on one side of the body.

hemiplegia—complete paralysis on one lateral half of the body or part of it.

hemophilia—a sex-linked, blood disorder characterized by a deficit in one or more of the factors which cause the blood to clot.

hertz (Hz)—a frequency measurement of sound based on the number of cycles per second.

high-risk (infants)—infants who, for socioeconomic, health, physiological, or genetic reasons, face likely developmental delay.

humanistic approach—in education, emphasis on individual's dignity and encouragement of interests; concentrates on enhancing individual's internal motivation, emotional involvement, and self-evaluation.

hydrocephaly—abnormal blockage of cerebrospinal fluid in the cranial cavity; if not corrected, spinal fluid accumulates in the cranial cavity, enlarging the head and damaging the brain, usually causing mental retardation.

imitation—matching a modeled behavior, or behaving similarly to what is observed.

individualized educational program (IEP)—an educational program mandated by federal legislation in P.L. 94–142, designed and signed by parents, teacher(s), and any additional professionals who will be needed to implement the program, reflecting short- and long-term goals for the child for a year. It insures confidentiality, placement in the least restrictive environment, and appropriate, individualized education.

initiating behaviors—one person's cueing, modeling, physically prompting, or mandating an event that serves as a stimulus for initial responses from another person.

integration plan—a model program designed to integrate handicapped with nonhandicapped students.

interdisciplinary team—a group of professionals representing relevant educational and management specialties who combine their individual expertise in providing comprehensive services for the education, treatment, and development of a child

IQ—stands for "intelligence quotient"; quantity derived in some systems by dividing chronological age into mental age and multiplying by 100 [(MA/CA) × 100]

intervention—design for changing the behavioral, medical, or health status of an individual, or a change program itself.

itinerant teacher—a special teacher who serves several schools. Children usually leave their regular classroom to work with the itinerant teacher.

juvenile diabetes (diabetes mellitus)—often hereditary, metabolic disorder characterized by the body's inability to manufacture sufficient insulin to metabolize sugars and other food substances.

juvenile rheumatoid arthritis—chronic inflammatory disease of the joints and the tissues around them; usually develops between ages 2 and 5.

kinesthetic—describing neuromuscular sensing of the body parts' position in space.

labeling—categorizing individuals by some group of like characteristics.

language—arbitrary system of vocal symbols providing people with a way to interact and communicate. Nonverbal language involves signing and using physical symbols, to enable individuals to communicate.

Legg-Calve-Perthes disease—disability that usually occurs on only one side and involves a change in the density, or porousness, of the femoral head.

limb deficiency—absence of one or more limbs, either as the result of postnatal disease or injury, or of a congenital problem.

Glossary

low vision—condition characterized by limitations in distance vision but ability to see objects and materials when within a few inches or, at maximum, a few feet.

mainstreaming—a system for integrating handicapped children into regular classes, providing for their special needs through individualized instruction, tutoring, or their spending a portion of their day with a resource or special teacher.

manualist—one who believes that, for the hearing impaired, oral communication should be replaced by or supplemented with some form of manual communication not in common use by normal hearing persons.

microcephalus—cranial abnormality of low cephalic index, or small head.

modeling—a procedure that uses demonstrations to prompt an imitative response.

mongolism—see Down's syndrome.

monoparesis—partial paralysis in one limb.

monoplegia—complete paralysis in one limb.

morphemes—smallest meaning-carrying units of language.

morphology—the study of the structure level at which meaning units are created from phonemes (sounds).

multisensory disorders—deficits in more than one sense; usually hearing and visual impairments that occur together.

muscular dystrophy—disability that causes a progressive weakness of the skeletal muscles; generally caused by a sex-linked recessive gene.

natural method—system of teaching language to hearing impaired children in carefully structured situations so they can learn through the process of hypothesis formulation and testing in sequences that closely follow language development of normal children.

neonatal—pertaining to the newborn's first 4 weeks of life.

neurological disorder—an abnormal functioning of the central nervous system.

nonverbal (nonspeaking) person—one who has not acquired or cannot acquire standard, vocal language system for any reason.

observational learning—patterning behavior after an observed model; encompasses attention to and retention of observed behavior and motoric response. Same as: imitative learning.

occupational therapist—a person registered and/or licensed to apply knowledge of the effects of occupation upon human beings to facilitate the integration of biological, social, and psychological systems to help them attain or maintain maximum functioning in their daily life tasks.

olfaction—act of smelling.

operant conditioning—changing behavior by altering its consequences; affecting the future probability of a response by providing positive or negative reinforcement as a consequence of its occurrence.

ophthalmologist—a physician specializing in diagnosis and treatment of diseases and defects of the eye.

optometrist—a certified professional who examines, measures, and treats certain eye defects by methods not requiring a medical license.

osteogenesis imperfecta—congenital disability characterized by defective development of bone tissue, both in quantity and quality.

perinatal—pertaining to or occurring at the time of birth.

phonemes—the smallest units of sound in a language.

phonology—the science of the sound system of oral language.

physical therapist—a person registered or licensed to apply knowledge or neurodevelopmental techniques to problems of feeding, positioning, ambulation, and the development of other gross motor and fine motor skills.

pinpoint—to specify an observable behavior.

postnatal—pertaining to or occurring after birth.

Precision Teaching—instructional procedure involving (1) pinpointing behaviors to be changed, (2) measuring frequency of behaviors, (3) designing instructional plan or intervention procedure, (4) measuring performance continuously and directly, and (5) graphing data to analyze trends and insure that aims are met.

prenatal—pertaining to the period before or occurring before birth.

prompt—an auxiliary stimulus selected to cue a desired response.

prosthetic device—an artificial device that replaces an absent body part.

psychodynamic model—a system of psychotherapeutic procedures as conceived by Freudian and neo-Freudian therapists.

psychoeducational approach model—a combination of psychiatric and educational inputs in developing an instructional program for an individual.

psycholinguistics—the psychological study of language and its effect on the way in which the individual receives, processes, and expresses information.

psychologically disordered—see *emotionally disturbed.*

psychosis—a severe behavior disorder marked by a break from reality and excessively frequent inappropriate behavior.

psychotherapy—any type of treatment relying primarily on verbal and nonverbal communication between patient and therapist rather than medical and/or behavioral procedures.

quadriparesis—partial paralysis in both arms and both legs.

quadriplegia—complete paralysis in both arms and both legs.

reinforcement—the operation of arranging a consequential event in order to increase the rate of desired behavior. A consequence is called a *reinforcer* when it increases the behavior immediately preceding it.

residential school—a school, usually self-contained, where students live, going home only on major holidays or summer vacation; many provide programs for preschool or elementary grades through secondary level.

residual sensory acuity—the limited but useable portion of a sense which is affected after an acquired or congenital sensory loss.

resource room—place where a teacher is available to work with individuals or small groups of students who have specific learning difficulties.

response—a behavior following and resulting from a presented stimulus.

retrolental fibroplasia (RLF)—a disorder caused by excessive oxygen given to premature infants, resulting in the eventual destruction of light receptor cells in the eye.

rubella syndrome (German Measles)—a syndrome involving hearing loss and/or defective vision, heart anomalies, and nervous system anomalies as a result of the mother's contracting rubella (a mild viral infection) during pregnancy, expecially during the first trimester.

schizophrenia—a severe behavior disorder characterized by distortion of thinking, abnormal perceptions, and frequent strange behavior.

sensorineural hearing loss—impairment of the inner ear or the eighth cranial nerve; not only reduces intensity of signal but may also distort the sounds received.

shaping—reinforcing successive approximations of a desired behavior not present in the repertoire.

sickle cell anemia—hereditary disorder characterized by abnormal blood condition in which the shape of the red blood cell is distorted into a sickle (crescent) shape; appears predominantly in black people.

sociological model—a model for treating emotional disorders which may take two forms: 1) epidemiological factors are examined to determine how they may contribute to disordered behavior; or 2) emotional disturbance is viewed simply as social rule-breaking or "deviance."

Glossary

spasticity—excessive tension of muscles and resistance to extension or flexion, as in cerebral palsy.

speech—vocal transmission of language.

spina bifida—a disorder in which a portion of the spinal cord is not enclosed by vertebral arches; usually a distortion of the spinal cord and roots results in a neurological disorder and related deformities.

spinal cord injury—traumatic injury to the spinal cord, often from a bicycle or automobile accident; may result in paraplegia or quadriplegia.

spinal muscular atrophy—hereditary disability involving progressive neuromuscular disorders that cause muscular wasting (atrophy).

stimulus—anything that serves to evoke a response, such as, sound, light, shape, or sight.

stuttering—a speech disorder characterized by severe nonfluency.

syntax—the rules and patterns by which the meaning units (morphemes) must be strung together within a specific language.

systematic instruction—a process of instruction characterized by: 1) systematic arrangement of the conditions for learning; 2) initial assessment; 3) specification of objectives; 4) continuous measurement of a child's performance; 5) instructional decisions based on performance measured; and 6) evaluation of overall effects of instructional conditions.

tactile-kinesthetic sense—sensory awareness of touch in the fingers; awareness in the sensory organs in the tendons, joints, and muscles stimulated by movement.

tactile mode—a means of receiving meaning from stimuli by using touch, for instance, using braille.

task analysis—breaking down a task (job) into the finest response components.

technology—the application of scientific findings to education, psychology, or any other professional discipline.

total communication—an approach to teaching language to hearing impaired children that combines the aural-oral approach with manual communication.

trainable mentally retarded (TMR)—a description no longer widely used for people who generally have an IQ of 25 to 50; will have a low rate of development; will be semidependent throughout life; have the potential for learning self-care and adjusting socially to the family and neighborhood; are not capable of profiting from a program for educable mentally retarded people; may have physical and/or motor impairments; and may have sensory deficits.

unilateral hearing loss—hearing impairment occurring in one ear.

visually limited—individuals who in some way have limited vision under average circumstances; they may need special lighting or may be unable to see distant objects unless the objects are in motion, or may need to wear prescriptive lenses or use optical aids.

vocal mode—oral language that individuals transmit (express) through speaking (vocal mode).

voice disorders (voicing)—inappropriate intensity, pitch, and/or quality of vocal tone produced at the larynx and resonated in the pharynx, oral cavity, and sometimes the nasal cavity.

written mode—oral language transcribed into symbols that represent the spoken terms; transcription of symbols onto paper.

References

Abeson, A. Movement and momentum—government and the education of handicapped children. *Exceptional Children,* 1972, *39,* 63–66.

Abeson, A. Movement and momentum: Government and the education of handicapped children—II. *Exceptional Children,* 1974, *41,* 109–115.

Achenbach, T.M. The classification of children's psychiatric symptoms: A factor analytic study. *Psychological Monographs,* 1966, *80* (1, Whole No. 615).

Achenbach, T.M. *Developmental psychopathology.* New York: Ronald Press, 1974.

Advisory Committee on the Education of the Deaf. *A report to the Secretary of Health, Education and Welfare by his advisory committee on the education of the deaf.* Washington, D.C.: U.S. Department of Health, Education and Welfare, 1964.

Aldrich, R.A., & Wedgwood, R.J. Examination of the changes in the United States which affect the health of children and youth. *Educational Horizons,* 1970, *48*(4), 110–16.

Allen, K.E., Rieke, J., Dmitriev, V., & Hayden, A.H. Early warning: Observation as a tool for recognizing potential handicaps in young children. *Educational Horizons,* 1972, *50*(2), 43–55.

Altman, R., & Talkington, L.W. Modeling: An alternative behavior modification approach for retardates. *Mental Retardation,* 1971, *9,* 20–23.

American Foundation for the Blind. *The Pine Brook report: National work session on the education of the blind with the sighted.* New York: Author, 1957.

American Psychiatric Association. *Diagnostic and statistical manual of mental disorders* (2nd ed., DSM-II). Washington, D.C.: Author, 1968.

Apgar, V., & Beck, J. *Is my baby all right?* New York: Trident, 1972.

Ayllon, T. Intensive treatment of psychotic behaviour by stimulus satiation and food reinforcement. *Behaviour Research and Therapy,* 1963, *1,* 53–61.

Azrin, N.H., Kaplan, S.J., & Foxx, R.M. Autism reversal: Eliminating stereotyped self-stimulation of retarded individuals. *American Journal of Mental Deficiency,* 1973, *78*(5), 241–248.

Bachman, W. *Influence of selected variables upon economic adaptation of orthopedically handicapped and other health impaired.* Unpublished doctoral dissertation. University of the Pacific, 1971.

Bandura, A. *Principles of behavior modification.* New York: Holt, Rinehart & Winston, 1969.

Bandura, A. *Aggression: A social learning analysis.* Englewood Cliffs, N.J.: Prentice-Hall, 1973.

Barbe, W. Administrative aspects of gifted programs. In W. Barbe & T.M. Stephens (Eds.), *Attention to the gifted a decade later.* Columbus: Ohio Department of Education, 1962. pp. 15–19.

Barbe, W. *One in a thousand: A comparative study of moderately and highly gifted elementary school children.* Columbus: Ohio Board of Education, 1964.

Barnard, K.E., & Powell, M.L. *Teaching the mentally retarded child.* St. Louis: Mosby, 1972.

Baroff, G.S. *Mental retardation: Nature, cause, and management.* New York: Wiley, 1974.

Barraga, N. *Increased visual behavior in low vision children.* New York: American Foundation for the Blind, 1964.

Barraga, N. *Visual handicaps and learning: A developmental approach.* Belmont, Calif.: Wadsworth, 1976.

References

Barron, F. The psychology of creativity. *New Directions in Psychology.* New York: Holt, Rinehart & Winston, 1965.

Barton, E.S. Operant conditioning of appropriate and inappropriate social speech in the profoundly retarded. *Journal of Mental Deficiency Research,* 1973, *17,* 183–191.

Bateman, B.D. Three approaches to diagnosis and educational planning for children with learning disability. *Academic Therapy Quarterly,* 1967, *2*(4), 215–222.

Bateman, B.D. Visually handicapped children. In N.G. Haring & R.L. Schiefelbusch (Eds.), *Methods in special education.* New York: McGraw-Hill, 1967. pp. 257–301.

Battison, R., & Jordan, L.K. Cross-cultural communication with foreign signers: Fact and fancy. *Sign Language Studies,* 1976, *10,* 53–68ff.

Beck, R., Adams, G., Chandler, L, & Livingston, S. The need for adjunctive services in management of severely and profoundly handicapped individuals: A view from primary care. In N.G. Haring & L.J. Brown (Eds.), *Teaching the severely handicapped* (Vol. 2). New York: Grune & Stratton, 1977.

Becker, R.D. Minimal brain dysfunction. *Journal of Learning Disabilities,* 1975, *8,* 429–431.

Becker, W.C. Consequences of different kinds of parental discipline. In M.L. Hoffman & L.W. Hoffman (Eds.), *Review of child development research* (Vol. 1). New York: Russell Sage Foundation, 1964.

Beez, W.V. *Influences of biased psychological reports on teacher behavior and pupil performance.* Unpublished doctoral dissertation, Indiana University, 1969.

Bellamy, G.T. (Ed.). *Habilitation of severely and profoundly retarded adults: Reports from the Specialized Training Program* (Vol. 1). Eugene, Ore.: University of Oregon, 1976.

Bellugi, U., & Fischer, S. A comparison of sign language and spoken language. *Cognition,* 1972, *1,* 173–200.

Bellugi, U., & Klima, E.S. The roots of language in the sign talk of the deaf. *Psychology Today,* 1972, *6,* 61–76.

Bensberg, G.J. Helping the retarded grow and learn. In G.J. Bensberg (Ed.), *Teaching the mentally retarded.* Atlanta: Southern Regional Education Board, 1965.

Berger, S.L. A clinical program for developing multimodal language responses with atypical deaf children. In J.E. McLean, D.E. Yoder, & R.L. Schiefelbusch (Eds.), *Language intervention with the retarded: Developing strategies.* Baltimore: University Park Press, 1972.

Bergman, E. Autonomous and unique features of American sign language. *American Annals of the Deaf,* 1972, *117*(5), 20–24.

Berkowitz, I. Control of aggression. In B.M. Caldwell & H.N. Ricciuti (Eds.), *Review of child development research* (Vol. 3). Chicago: University of Chicago Press, 1973.

Berkowitz, P.H., & Rothman, E.P. *The disturbed child: Recognition and psychoeducational therapy in the classroom.* New York: New York University Press, 1960.

Berkson, G. Abnormal stereotyped motor acts. In J. Zubin & H.F. Hunt (Eds.), *Comparative psychopathology: Animal and human.* New York: Grune & Stratton, 1967, *55,* 76–94.

Bernal, E. *Assessing assessment instruments: A Chicano perspective.* Paper prepared for regional training program to serve the bilingual/bicultural exceptional child. Montal Educational Associates, Sacramento, February 1972.

Berry, K.E., & Buktenica, N.A. Berry-Buktenica Developmental Test of Visual-Motor Integration. Chicago: Follett, 1967.

Bettelheim, B. *Love is not enough.* New York: Macmillian, 1950.

Bettelheim, B. *The empty fortress.* New York: Free Press, 1967.

Bettelheim, B. Listening to children. In P.A. Gallagher & L.L. Edwards (Eds.), *Educating the emotionally disturbed: Theory to practice*. Lawrence, Kans.: University of Kansas, 1970.

Bigge, J.L. Systems of precise observation for teachers: Observation guide to accompany film. Produced under contract for Media Services and Captioned Films Branch of the Bureau for Education of the Handicapped, U.S. Office of Education, 1970.

Bigge, J.L. Advocacy. In J.L. Bigge with P.A. O'Donnell (Eds.), *Teaching individuals with physical and multiple disabilities*. Columbus, Ohio: Charles E. Merrill, 1976. (a)

Bigge, J.L. Self-Care. In J.L. Bigge with P.A. O'Donnell (Eds.), *Teaching individuals with physical and multiple disabilities*. Columbus, Ohio: Charles E. Merrill, 1976.(b)

Bigge, J.L. Task analysis. In J.L. Bigge with P.A. O'Donnell (Eds.), *Teaching individuals with physical and multiple disabilities*. Columbus, Ohio: Charles E. Merrill, 1976. (c)

Bigge, J.L. with O'Donnell, P.A., (Eds.). *Teaching individuals with physical and multiple disabilities*. Columbus, Ohio: Charles E. Merrill, 1976.

Bijou, S.W. Behavior modification in teaching the retarded child. In C.E. Thoresen (Ed.), *Behavior modification in education*. Chicago: University of Chicago Press, 1973.

Bijou, S.W., & Cole, B.W. The feasibility of providing effective educational programs for the severely and profoundly retarded. In *Educating the 24-hour retarded child*. Arlington, Tex.: National Association for Retarded Citizens, 1975.

Birch, J.W. Early school admission for mentally advanced children. *Exceptional Children*, 1954, *21*, 84–87.

Birch, J.W. *Mainstreaming: Educable mentally retarded children in regular classrooms*. Minneapolis: Leadership Training Institute, University of Minnesota, 1974.

Bishop, W. Successful teachers of the gifted. *Exceptional Children*, 1968, *39*, 317–325.

Blank, M. Use of the deaf in language studies: A reply to Furth. *Psychological Bulletin*, 1965, *63*(6), 442–444.

Blatt, B., & Kaplan, F. *Christmas in purgatory: A photographic essay on mental retardation*. Boston: Allyn & Bacon, 1966.

Block, J.D. Operant conditioning. In J. Wortis (Ed.), *Mental retardation: An annual review*. New York: Grune & Stratton, 1971.

Bloom, L. *Language development: Form and function in emerging grammars*. Cambridge: MIT Press, 1970.

Bloomfield, L. *Language,* New York: Holt, 1933.

Blue, M.C. Education of the mentally retarded in residential settings. In A.A. Baumeister & E. Butterfield (Eds.), *Residential facilities for the mentally retarded*. Chicago: Aldine, 1970.

Bobath, K., & Bobath, B. Cerebral palsy. In P. Pearson & C.E. Williams (Eds.), *Physical therapy services in the developmental disabilities*. Springfield, Ill.: Charles C Thomas, 1975.

Bolinger, D. *Aspects of language*. New York: Harcourt Brace Jovanovich, 1968.

Bornstein, P.H., & Quevillon, R.P. The effects of a self-instructional package on overactive preschool boys. *Journal of Applied Behavior Analysis*, 1976, *9*, 179–188.

Boshes, B., & Mykelbust, H.R. A neurological and behavioral study of children with learning disorders. *Neurology*, 1964, *14*, 7–12.

Bower, E.M. *Early identification of emotionally handicapped children in school* (2nd ed.). Springfield, Ill.: Charles C Thomas, 1969.

Bower, E.M., & Lambert, N.M. *A process for in-school screening of children with emotional handicaps*. Princeton, N.J.: Educational Testing Service, 1962.

References

Bradway, K.P. The social competence of deaf children. *American Annals of the Deaf,* 1937, *82,* 122–140.

Braga, J. Early admission: Opinion vs. evidence. *The Elementary School Journal,* 1971, 35–46.

Braud, L.W., Lupin, M.N., & Braud, W.G. The use of electromyographic biofeedback in the control of hyperactivity. *Journal of Learning Disabilities,* 1975, *7,* 420–425.

Bricker, D.D. Imitative sign training as a facilitator of word-object association with low functioning children. *American Journal of Mental Deficiency,* 1972, *76*(5), 509–516.

Bricker, D.D. Educational synthesizer. In M.A. Thomas (Ed.), *Hey! Don't forget about me: Education's investment in the severely, profoundly, and multiply handicapped.* Reston, Va.: Council for Exceptional Children, 1976.

Bricker, D.D., Dennison, L., & Bricker, W.A. A language intervention program for developmentally young children. *MCCD Monograph Series,* Mailman Center for Child Development, University of Miami, 1976 (No. 1).

Bricker, D.D., & Iacino, R. Early intervention with severely/profoundly handicapped children. In E. Sontag, J. Smith, & N. Certo (Eds.), *Educational programming for the severely and profoundly handicapped.* Reston, Va.: Division on Mental Retardation, Council for Exceptional Children, 1977.

Brolin, D.E. *Vocational preparation of retarded citizens.* Columbus, Ohio: Charles E. Merrill, 1976.

Bronfenbrenner, U. Is early intervention effective? In B.Z. Friedlander, G. Sterritt, & G. Kirk (Eds.), *Exceptional infant* (Vol. 3). New York: Brunner/Mazel, 1975. Pp. 449–475.

Brown, G., McIntosh, S., & Tuoti, L. *Career education materials for educable retarded students.* Working paper no. 2, Project PRICE, University of Missouri–Columbia, December 1974.

Brown, L.J., et al. Effects of consequences on production rates of trainable retarded and severely emotionally disturbed students in a public school workshop. *Education and Training of the Mentally Retarded,* 1972, *7*(2), 74–81. (a)

Brown, L.J., et al. The development of quality, quantity, and durability in the work performance of retarded students in a public school prevocational workshop. *Training School Bulletin,* 1972, *69*(2), 58–69.(b)

Brown, L.J., Nietupski, J., & Hamre-Nietupski, S. Criterion of ultimate functioning. In M.A. Thomas (Ed.), *Hey! Don't forget about me: Education's investment in the severely, profoundly, and multiply handicapped.* Reston, Va.: Council for Exceptional Children, 1976.

Brown, L.J., & York, R. Developing programs for severely handicapped students: Teacher training and classroom instruction. *Focus on Exceptional Children,* April 1974.

Bruch, C. *The ABDA: Making the Stanford-Binet culturally biased for disadvantaged black children.* Paper presented at Southeastern Invitational Conference on Testing Problems, University of Georgia, Athens, December 1972.

Bruner, J.S. From communication to language—A psychological perspective. *Cognition,* 1974/75, *3,* 255–287.

Bruya, M.A., & Bolin, R.H. Epilepsy: A controllable disease. *American Journal of Nursing,* 1976, *76*(3), 388–397.

Buell, E.M. *Outline of language for deaf children,* (Book 1). Washington, D.C.: Volta Bureau, 1954.

Burchard, J.D., & Haring, P.T. Behavior modification and juvenile delinquency. In H. Leitenberg (Ed.), *Handbook of behavior modification and behavior therapy.* Englewood Cliffs, N.J.: Prentice-Hall, 1976.

Burks, B., Jensen, D., & Terman, L.M. *The promise of youth.* Stanford, Calif.: Stanford University Press, 1930.

Cain, L.F. Parent groups: Their role in a better life for the handicapped. *Exceptional Children,* 1976, *42*(8), 432–437.

Campbell, P.H., Green, K.M., & Carlson, L.M. Approximating the norm through environmental and child-centered prosthetics and adaptive equipment. In E. Sontag, J. Smith, & N. Certo (Eds.), *Educational programming for the severely and profoundly handicapped.* Reston, Va.: Division on Mental Retardation, Council for Exceptional Children, 1977.

Carter, J.L., & Synolds, D. Effects of relaxation training upon handwriting quality. *Journal of Learning Disabilities,* 1974, 7, 236–238.

Cavan, R.S., & Ferdinand, T.N. *Juvenile delinquency* (3rd ed.). New York: Lippincott, 1975.

Caywood, T. A quadriplegic man looks at treatment. *Journal of Rehabilitation,* 1974, *40,* 22–25.

Chalfant, J.C., & Silkovitz, R.G. *Systematic instruction for retarded children: The Illinois program.* Danville, Ill.: Interstate Printers and Publishers, 1972.

Chaney, C.M., & Kephart, N.C. *Motoric aids to perceptual training.* Columbus, Ohio: Charles E. Merrill, 1968.

Christiansen, R.O. Diabetes. In E.E. Bleck & D.A. Nagel (Eds.), *Physically handicapped children: A medical atlas for teachers.* New York: Grune & Stratton, 1975.

Chutorian, A.M., & Myers, S.J. Diseases of the muscle. In J.A. Downey & N.L. Low (Eds.), *The child with disabling illness: Principles of rehabilitation.* Philadelphia: Saunders, 1974.

Clark, B. *Growing up gifted.* Columbus, Ohio: Charles E. Merrill, in press.

Cohen, M.A., Gross, P.J., & Haring, N.G. Developmental pinpoints. In N.G. Haring & L.J. Brown (Eds.), *Teaching the severely handicapped,* (Vol. 1). New York: Grune & Stratton, 1976.

Colwell, C.N., Richards, E., McCarver, R.B., & Ellis, N.R. Evaluation of self-help habit training of the profoundly retarded. *Mental Retardation,* June 1973, 14–18.

Committee for a Study for Evaluation of Testing for Cystic Fibrosis. Clinical aspects of cystic fibrosis. *The Journal of Pediatrics,* 1976, *88*(4), 712–713.

Connor, F.P. The education of children with crippling and chronic medical conditions. In W.M. Cruickshank & G.O. Johnson (Eds.), *Education of exceptional children and youth* (3rd ed.). Englewood Cliffs, N.J.: Prentice-Hall, 1975.

Connor, L.E. Reflections on the year 200. *Exceptional Children,* 1968, *34*(10).

Cott, A. Megavitamins: The orthomolecular approach to behavioral disorders and learning disabilities. *Academic Therapy,* 1972, *7,* 245–259.

Cox, C. *The early mental traits of three hundred geniuses.* Stanford, Calif.: Stanford University Press, 1926.

Crosson, J.E. A technique for programming sheltered workshop environments for training severely retarded workers. *American Journal of Mental Deficiency,* 1969, *13*(5), 814–818.

Cruickshank, W.M., Bice, H.V., & Wallen, N.E. *Perception and cerebral palsy.* Syracuse: Syracuse University Press, 1957.

Cruickshank, W.M. The false hope of integration. *The Australian Journal on the Education of Backward Children,* 1974, *21,* 70–72.

Cruickshank, W.M. (Eds. *Cerebral palsy: A developmental disability* (3rd ed.). Syracuse: Syracuse University Press, 1976.

Cruickshank, W.M., & De Young, H.G. Educational practices with exceptional children. In W.M. Cruickshank & G.O. Johnson (Eds.), *Education of exceptional children and youth* (3rd ed.). Englewood Cliffs, N.J.: Prentice-Hall, 1975.

Cruickshank, W.M., & Johnson, G.O. *Education of exceptional children and youth.* Englewood Cliffs, New Jersey: Prentice-Hall, 1967; 3rd ed., 1975.

References

Cunningham, F. The Massachusetts Vision Test Battery. New York: National Society for the Prevention of Blindness, 1963.

Dantona, R. Demographic data and status of services for deaf-blind children. *The National Advocate for Deaf-Blind Children,* 1975, *3,* 1–2.

Davis, H., & Silverman, S.R. *Hearing and deafness* (3rd ed.). New York: Holt, Rinehart & Winston, 1970.

DeHaan, R., & Havighurst, R. *Educating gifted children.* Chicago: University of Chicago Press, 1957.

Delacato, C.H. *Neurological organization and reading.* Springfield, Ill.: Charles C Thomas, 1966.

DeLaguna, G.A. *Speech: Its function and development.* Bloomington: Indiana University Press, 1927; 1963.

Delgado, J.M.R. *Physical control of the mind: Toward a psychocivilized society.* New York: Harper, 1969.

DeLissavoy, V. Head-banging in childhood: A review of empirical studies. *Pediatrics Digest,* 1964, *6,* 49–55.

Denhoff, E. Medical aspects. In W.M. Cruickshank (Ed.), *Cerebral palsy: A developmental disability* (3rd ed.). Syracuse: Syracuse University Press, 1976.

Denhoff, E., & Robinault, I.P. *Cerebral palsy and related disorders.* New York: McGraw-Hill, 1960.

Dennison, G. *The lives of children.* New York: Random House, 1969.

Deno, E. Special education as developmental capital. *Exceptional Children,* 1970, *37,* 229–37.

DesLauriers, A.M. & Carlson, C.F. *Your child is asleep: Early infantile autism.* Homewood, Ill.: Dorsey Press, 1969.

Devin-Sheehan, L., Feldman, R.S., & Allen, V.L. Research on children tutoring children: A critical review. *Review of Educational Research,* 1976, *46,* 355–385.

Dietz, S.M., & Repp, A.C. Decreasing classroom misbehavior through the use of DRL schedules of reinforcement. *Journal of Applied Behavior Analysis,* 1973, *6,* 457–463.

Doll, E.A. The essentials of an inclusive concept of mental deficiency. *American Journal of Mental Deficiency,* 1941, *46,* 214–219.

Doll, E.A. *Vineland Social Maturity Scale: Condensed manual of directions* (1965 ed.). Circle Pines, Minn.: American Guidance Service, 1965.

Dollard, J., Doob, L.W., Miller, N.E., Mowrer, O.H., & Sears, R.R. *Frustration and aggression.* New Haven, Conn.: Yale University Press, 1939.

Donnellan-Walsh, A., Gossage, L.D., LaVigna, G.W., Schuler, A., & Traphagen, J.D. *Teaching makes a difference: A guide for developing successful classes for autistic and other severely handicapped children.* Albany, N.Y.: National Society for Autistic Children, 1976.

Down's Syndrome Performance Inventory. Experimental Education Unit, College of Education and Child Development and Mental Retardation Center, University of Washington, Seattle, 1976.

DuBard, E. *Teaching aphasics and other language deficient children.* Jackson, Miss.: University Press of Mississippi, 1974.

Dunn, L.M. Special education for the mildly retarded—Is much of it justified? *Exceptional Children,* 1968, *35,* 5–24.

Dunn, L.M. (Ed.). *Exceptional children in the schools: Special education in transition* (2nd ed.). New York: Holt, Rinehart & Winston, 1973.

Dunn, L.M., & Smith, J.O. *Peabody language development kits.* Circle Pines, Minn.: American Guidance Service, 1965.

Dyer, E.R. Sign language agglutination: A brief look at ASL and Turkish. *Sign Language Studies,* 1976, *11,* 133–148.

Eames, T.H. Physical factors in reading. *The Reading Teacher,* 1962, *15,* 427–432.

Eaton, J.W., & Weil, R.J. *Culture and mental disorders: A comparative study of Hutterites and other populations.* Glencoe, Ill.: Free Press, 1955.

Elashoff, J.D., & Snow, R.E. *Pygmalion reconsidered.* Worthington, Ohio: Charles A. Jones, 1971.

Elgar, S. Teaching autistic children. In J.K. Wing (Ed.), *Early childhood autism: Clinical, educational and social aspects.* New York: Pergamon, 1966. Pp. 205–237.

Ellis, N.R. Foreword. In J.M. Kauffman & J.S. Payne (Eds.), *Mental retardation: Introduction and personal perspectives.* Columbus, Ohio: Charles E. Merrill, 1975.

Englemann, S., & Bruner, E. *DISTAR Reading I and II: An instructional system.* Chicago: Science Research Associates, 1969.

Englemann, S., & Osborn, J., & Englemann, T. *DISTAR Language I: An instructional system.* Chicago: Science Research Associates, 1969.

Ennis, B.J., & Friedman, P.R. (Eds.). *Legal rights of the mentally handicapped* (Vol. 2). New York: Practicing Law Institute, 1973.

Fagen, S.A., Long, N.J., & Stevens, D.J. *Teaching children self-control.* Columbus, Ohio: Charles E. Merrill, 1975.

Fairchild, E.L., & Neal, L. (Eds.). *Common unity in the community: A forward looking program of recreation and leisure services for the handicapped.* Eugene, Ore.: Center of Leisure Studies, 1975.

Farber, B. *Mental retardation: Its social context and social consequences.* Boston: Houghton Mifflin, 1968.

Farmer, L.W. Travel in adverse weather using electronic mobility guidance devices. *The New Outlook for the Blind,* 1975, *69,* 433–439, 451.

Farrell, G. *The story of blindness.* Cambridge: Harvard University Press, 1956.

Feingold, B.F. Hyperkinesis and learning disabilities linked to the ingestion of artifical food colors and flavors. *Journal of Learning Disabilities,* 1976, *9,* 551–559.

Feldman, Robert G. Patients with epilepsy. *American Family Physician,* 1975, *12*(4), 135–140.

Fenichel, C. Psychoeducational approaches for seriously disturbed children in the classroom. In P. Knoblock (Ed.), *Intervention approaches in education emotionally disturbed children.* Syracuse: Syracuse University Press, 1966.

Fenichel, C. Carl Fenichel. In J.M. Kauffman & C.D. Lewis (Eds.), *Teaching children with behavior disorders: Personal perspectives.* Columbus, Ohio: Charles E. Merrill, 1974.

Fernald, G.M. *Remedial techniques in basic school subjects.* New York: McGraw-Hill, 1943.

Finch, S.M. *Fundamentals of child psychiatry.* New York: Norton, 1960.

Fine, M.J. Consideration in educating children with cerebral dysfunction. *Journal of Learning Disabilities,* 1970, *3,* 132–142.

Finnie, Nancie R. *Handling the young cerebral palsied child at home.* New York: Dutton, 1975.

Fitzgerald, E. *Straight language for the deaf: A system of instruction for deaf children* (3rd ed.). Austin, Tex.: Steck Company, 1937.

Fliegler, L., & Bish, C. Summary of research on the academically talented student. *Review of Educational Research,* 1959, *29,* 408–450.

References

Fonda, G. *Management of the patient with subnormal vision.* St. Louis: Mosby, 1970.

Foulke, E., Amster, C.H., Nolan, C.Y., & Bixler, R.H. The comprehension of rapid speech by the blind. *Exceptional Children,* 1962, *29,* 134–141.

Foxx, R. M., & Azrin, N. H. Restitution: A method of eliminating aggressive-disruptive behavior of mentally retarded and brain damaged patients. *Behavior Research and Therapy,* 1972, *10,* 15–27.

Foxx, R.M., & Azrin, N.H. *Toilet training the retarded: A rapid program for day and nighttime independent toileting.* Champaign, Ill.: Research Press, 1973.

Fraiberg, S., Siegel, B.L., & Gibson, R. The role of sound in the search behavior of a blind infant. *The Psychoanalytic Study of the Child,* 1966, *21,* 327–357.

Frampton, M.E., & Gall, E.D. (Eds.). *Special education for the exceptional* (3 vols.). Boston: Porter Sargent, 1955.

Frostig, M., & Horne, D. *The Frostig program for development of visual perception* (Rev. ed.). Chicago: Follett, 1973.

Frostig, M., Lefever, W., & Whittlesey, J.R.B. *The Frostig Developmental Test of Visual Perception.* Palo Alto, Calif.: Consulting Psychologists Press, 1964.

Fusfeld, I. The academic program of schools for the deaf. *Volta Review,* 1965, *57,* 63–70.

Furth, H.G. *Thinking without language: Psychological implications of deafness.* New York: Free Press, 1966.

Gallagher, J.J. *Research summary on gifted child education.* Springfield, Ill.: Department of Program Planning for the Gifted, 1966.

Gallagher, J.J. The special education contract for mildly handicapped children. *Exceptional Children,* 1972, *38,* 527–536.

Gallagher, J.J. *Talent delayed—Talent denied.* Reston, Va.: Council for Exceptional Children, 1974.

Gallagher, J.J. *Teaching the gifted child* (2nd ed.). Boston: Allyn & Bacon, 1975.

Gallagher, J.J., Aschner, M.J., & Jenne, W. Productive thinking of gifted children in classroom interactions. Reston, Va.: Council for Exceptional Children, 1967.

Gallagher, J.J., & Kinney, L. *Talent delayed—Talent denied: The culturally different child.* Reston, Va.: Foundation for Exceptional Children, 1974.

Gallup, G.H. Seventh annual Gallup poll of public attitudes toward education. *Phi Delta Kappan,* 1975, *57,* 227–240.

Gardner, W.I. *Learning and behavior characteristics of exceptional children and youth.* Boston: Allyn & Bacon, 1977.

Gardstrom, M., & Lovitt, T.C. Creative writing rates of second graders: Effects of reading their stories and seeing their performance graphs. In T.C. Lovitt & N.G. Haring (Eds.), *The classroom application of precision teaching.* Seattle: Special Child Publications, forthcoming.

Garretson, M.D. Total communication. *Volta Review,* 1976, *78*(4), 88–95.

Gelfand, D.M., & Hartmann, D.P. *Child behavior: Analysis and therapy.* New York: Pergamon, 1975.

Gerritz, E., & Haywood, E. Advanced placement: Opinions differ. *NEA Journal,* 1965, *54,* 118–123.

Getzels, J., & Dillon, J. The nature of giftedness and the education of the gifted. In N. Gage (Ed.), *Handbook of research in education,* 1973. Pp. 689–731.

Getzels, J., & Jackson, P. The meaning of giftedness: An examination of an expanding concept. *Phi Delta Kappan,* 1958, *40,* 75–77.

Getzels, J., & Jackson, P. *Creativity and intelligence.* New York: Wiley, 1962.

Gesell, A., & Amatruda, C.S. *Developmental diagnosis.* New York: Harper & Row, 1969.

Gilhool, T.K. Education: An inalienable right. *Exceptional Children,* 1973, *39,* 597–609.

Gillingham, A., & Stillman, B.W. *Remedial training for children with specific difficulty in reading, spelling, and penmanship* (7th ed.). Cambridge: Educators Publishing Service, 1966.

Glavin, J.P. *Cross-cultural development of the field of emotional disturbance: Implications for special education.* Unpublished manuscript, Temple University, 1973.

Glidewell, J.C., Kantor, M.B., Smith, L.M., & Stringer, L.A. Socialization and social structure in the classroom. In L.W. Hoffman & M.L. Hoffman (Eds.), *Review of child development research* (Vol. 2). New York: Russel Sage Foundation, 1966.

Glim, T.E. *The Palo Alto reading program: Sequential steps in reading.* New York: Harcourt, Brace & World, 1968.

Gold, M.W. Stimulus factors in skill training of retarded adolescents on a complex assembly task: Acquisition, transfer, and retention. *American Journal of Mental Deficiency,* 1972, *76*(5), 517–526.

Gold, M.W. Factors affecting production by the retarded: Base rate. *Mental Retardation,* 1973, *11*(6), 41–45.

Goldin-Meadow, S., & Feldman, H. The creation of a communication system: A study of deaf children of hearing parents. *Sign Language Studies,* 1975, *8,* 225–234.

Goldstein, H., Arkell, C., Ashcroft, S.C., Hurley, O.L., & Lilly, M.S. Schools. In N. Hobbs (Ed.), *Issues in the classification of children* (Vol. 2). San Francisco: Jossey-Bass, 1975.

Goodenough, F.L., & Harris, D.B. Goodenough-Harris Drawing Test. New York: Harcourt Brace Jovanovich, 1963.

Goodwin, D.L., & Coates, T.J. *Helping students help themselves.* Englewood Cliffs, N.J.: Prentice-Hall, 1976.

Gordon, N. *Pediatric neurology for the clinician.* Philadelphia: Lippincott, 1976.

Gowan, J. *An annotated bibliography on the academically talented.* Washington, D.C.: National Education Association, 1961.

Gowan, J., & Demos, G. *The education and guidance of the ablest.* Springfield, Ill.: Charles C Thomas, 1964.

Grant, J., & Renzulli, J. Identifying achievement potential in minority group students. *Exceptional Children,* 1975, *40,* 255–259.

Graubard, P.S. Children with behavioral disabilities. In L.M. Dunn (Ed.), *Exceptional children in the schools* (2nd ed.). New York: Holt, Rinehart & Winston, 1973.

Gregory, R.L. *Eye and brain the psychology of seeing.* New York: McGraw-Hill, 1966.

Grieger, T., Kauffman, J.M., & Grieger, R.M. Effects of peer reporting on cooperative play and aggression of kindergarten children. *Journal of School Psychology,* 1976, *14,* 307–313.

Groht, M.A. *Natural language for deaf children.* Washington, D.C.: Volta Bureau, 1958.

Gromek, I., & Scandary, J. Considerations in the educational placement of the physically or otherwise health impaired child. *DOPHHH Journal,* 1977, *3*(1), 8–11.

Grossman, H.J. (Ed.). *Manual on terminology and classification in mental retardation, 1973 revision.* Washington, D.C.: American Association on Mental Deficiency, 1973.

Group for the Advancement of Psychiatry, Committee on Child Psychiatry. *Psychopathological disorders in childhood: Theoretical considerations and a proposed classification* (Vol. VI). Report No. 62, June 1966.

Guess, D., Sailor, W., & Baer, D. To teach language to retarded children. In R.L. Schiefelbusch & L.L. Lloyd (Eds.), *Language perspectives—Acquisition, retardation and intervention.* Baltimore: University Park Press, 1974.

Guess, D., Sailor, W., & Baer, D.M. *Functional speech and language training for the severely handicapped.* Lawrence, Kans.: H & H Enterprises, 1976.

References

Guilford, J.P. Three faces of intellect. *American Psychologist,* 1959, *14,* 469–479.

Gundersen, T. Early diagnosis and treatment of strabismus. *The Sight-Saving Review,* 1970, *40,* 129–136.

Gustason, G., Pfetzing, D., & Zawolkow, E. *Signing exact English.* Rosemoor, Calif.: Modern Sign Press, 1972.

Hall, G.S. *Educational problems,* (Vol. 1). New York: Appleton, 1911.

Hallahan, D.P., & Kauffman, J.M. *Introduction to learning disabilities: A psycho-behavioral approach.* Englewood Cliffs, N.J.: Prentice-Hall, 1976.

Hallahan, D.P., & Kauffman, J.M. Categories, labels, behaviors: ED, LD, and EMR reconsidered. *Journal of Special Education,* 1977,*11,* 139–149.

Hammill, D.D., Goodman, L., & Wiederholt, J.T. Visual-motor processes: Can we train them? *Reading Teacher,* 1974, *27,* 469–478.

Hamre, S. An approximation of an instructional model for developing home living skills in severely handicapped students. *American Association for the Education of the Severely/Profoundly Handicapped Review,* March, 1974.

Hanna, P.R., Hanna, J.S., Hodges, R.E., & Peterson, D.J. *Power to spell Spelling Series, Levels 1–6.* Boston: Houghton Mifflin, 1970.

Haring, N.G. *A program project for the investigation and application of procedures of analysis and modification of behavior of handicapped children.* U.S. Department of Health, Education and Welfare, Office of Education, Bureau of Education for the Handicapped. Final Report of Grant No. OEG-0070-3916(607), 1972.

Haring, N.G. Norris G. Haring. In J.M. Kauffman & C.D. Lewis (Eds.), *Teaching children with behavior disorders: Personal perspectives.* Columbus, Ohio: Charles E. Merrill, 1974.

Haring, N.G. Introduction. In N.G. Haring (Ed.), *The experimental education training program* (Vol. 1, *Systematic instruction*). Seattle: University of Washington, Experimental Education Unit, 1977.

Haring, N.G., & Cohen, M.A. Using the developmental approach as a basis for planning and sequencing different kinds of curricula for severely/profoundly handicapped persons. In *Educating the 24-hour child.* Arlington, Tex.: National Association for Retarded Citizens, 1975.

Haring, N.G., & Phillips, E.L. *Educating emotionally disturbed children.* New York: McGraw-Hill, 1962.

Haring, N.G., & Schiefelbusch, R.L. (Eds.). *Teaching special children.* New York: McGraw-Hill, 1976.

Haring, N.G., & Whelan, R.J. Experimental methods in education and management. In N.J. Long, W.C. Morse, & R.G. Newman (Eds.), *Conflict in the classroom.* Belmont, Calif.: Wadsworth, 1965.

Harris-Vanderheiden, D., & Vanderheiden, G.C. Basic considerations in the development of communicative and interactive skills for non-vocal severely handicapped children. In E. Sontag, J. Smith, & N. Certo (Eds.), *Educational programming for the severely and profoundly handicapped.* Reston, Va.: Division on Mental Retardation, Council for Exceptional Children, 1977.

Hart, B.O. A child-centered language program. In *Report of the proceedings of the International Congress on the Education of the Deaf.* Washington, D.C.: U.S. Government Printing Office, 1964. Pp. 509–514.

Hatfield, E.M. Causes of blindness in school children. *The Sight-Saving Review,* 1963,*33,* 218–233.

Hatfield, E.M. Blindness in infants and young children. *The Sight-Saving Review,* 1972, *42,* 69–89.

Hayden, A.H., & Haring, N.G. The acceleration and maintenance of developmental gains in Downs syndrome school-aged children. In *Proceedings of the International Association for the Scientific Study of Mental Deficiency symposium, August 1976, Washington, D.C.* Baltimore: University Park Press, 1976.

Hayden, A.H., & McGinness, G.D., Base for early intervention. In E. Sontag, J. Smith, & N. Certo (Eds.), *Educational programming for the severely and profoundly handicapped.* Reston, Va.: Division on Mental Retardation, Council for Exceptional Children, 1977.

Hayden, A.H., McGinness, G.D., & Dmitriev, V. Early and continuous intervention strategies for severely handicapped infants and very young children. In N.G. Haring & L. J. Brown (Eds.), *Teaching the severely handicapped,* (Vol. 1). New York: Grune & Stratton, 1976.

Heber, R.F. A manual on terminology and classification in mental retardation (Rev. ed.). *Monograph Supplement American Journal of Mental Deficiency,* 1961, *64.*

Hedrick, D.L., Prather, E.M., & Tobin, A.R. *The sequenced inventory of communication development.* Seattle: University Press, 1975.

Heider, F., & Heider, G. A comparison of sentence structure of deaf and hearing children. *Psychological Monographs,* 1940, *50,* 40–103.

Heilbrun, A. Maternal child rearing and creativity in sons. *Journal of Genetic Psychology,* 1971, *119,* 175–179.

Henriksen, K., & Doughty, R. Decelerating undesired mealtime behaviors in a group of profoundly retarded boys. *American Journal of Mental Deficiency,* 1967, *72,* 40–44.

Henry, T. Annotated bibliography on gifted children and their education. In G. Whipple (Ed.), *The education of gifted children. The Twenty-Third Yearbook of the National Society for the Study of Education, Part I.* Bloomington, Ill.: Public School Publishing, 1924.

Heston, L.L. The genetics of schizophrenic and schizoid disease. *Science,* 1970, *167,* 249–256.

Hewett, F.M. *The emotionally disturbed child in the classroom.* Boston: Allyn & Bacon, 1968.

Hewett, F.M., & Forness, S.R. *Education of exceptional learners.* Boston: Allyn & Bacon, 1974.

Hildreth, G.H. *Introduction to the gifted.* New York: McGraw-Hill, 1966.

Hingtgen, J.N., & Bryson, C.Q. Recent developments in the study of early childhood psychoses: Infantile autism, childhood schizophrenia, and related disorders. *Schizophrenia Bulletin,* 1972, No. 5, 8–54.

Hiskey, M.S. The Hiskey-Nebraska Test of Learning Aptitude. Lincoln, Neb.: Union College Press, 1941; Rev. ed., 1966.

Hobbs, N. Helping the disturbed child: Psychological and ecological strategies. *American Psychologist,* 1966, *21,* 1105–1115.

Hobbs, N. Nicholas Hobbs. In J.M. Kauffman & C.D. Lewis (Eds.), *Teaching children with behavior disorders: Personal perspectives.* Columbus, Ohio: Charles E. Merrill, 1974.

Hobbs, N. *The futures of children.* San Francisco: Jossey-Bass, 1975(a)

Hobbs, N. (Ed.). *Issues in the classification of children* (Vols. 1 & 2). San Francisco: Jossey-Bass, 1975.(b)

Holdsworth, L., & Whitmore, K. A study of children with epilepsy attending ordinary schools. 1: Their seizure patterns, progress, and behavior in school. Developmental Medicine and Child Neurology, 1974, *16,* 746–758.

Hollingshead, A.B., & Redlich, F.C. *Social class and mental illness: A community study.* New York: Wiley, 1958.

Hollingworth, L. *Children above 180 IQ.* Yonkers-on-Hudson, N.Y.: World, 1942.

Hooper, M.S. Notes from American Printing House. *Insight,* 1976, *1,* 6–8.

Horner, R.D., Holvolt, J., & Rinne, T. *Competency specifications for teachers of the severely and profoundly handicapped.* Unpublished manuscript, University of Kansas, 1976.

Horner, R.D., & Keilitz, I. Training mentally retarded adolescents to brush their teeth. *Journal of Applied Behavior Analysis,* 1975, *8,* 301-309.

References

Huntington, S., The United States. In M. Crozier, S. Huntington, & J. Watanuki (Eds.), *The crisis of democracy: Report on the governability of democracies to the trilaterial commission.* New York: New York University Press, 1975. Pp. 59–118.

Iannone, R. Current orientations in teacher education. In S.E. Goodman (Ed.), *Handbook on contemporary education.* New York: Bowker, 1976.

Itard, J.M.G. [*The wild boy of Aveyron*] (G. Humphrey & M. Humphrey, Eds. and trans.). New York: Appleton-Century-Crofts, 1962. (Originally published, 1894.)

Jacobs, J.C., & Downey, J.A. Juvenile rheumatoid arthritis. In J.A. Downey & N.L. Low (Eds.), *The child with disabling illness: Principles of rehabilitation.* Philadelphia: Saunders, 1974.

Jeffers, J., & Barley, M. *Speechreading (Lipreading).* Springfield, Ill. Charles C Thomas, 1971.

Johnson, B. Master's and Ph.D. programs in gifted education. *National/State Leadership Training Institute for Gifted and Talented,* 1976, *3.*

Johnson, J.L. Special education and the inner city: A challenge for the future or another means for cooling the mark out? *Journal of Special Education,* 1969, *3,* 241–251.

Jones, J.W. *Blind children: Degree of vision mode of reading.* Washington, D.C., U.S. Government Printing Office, 1961.

Jones, J.W., & Collins, A.P. *Educational programs for visually handicapped children.* Washington, D.C.: U.S. Government Printing Office, 1966.

Jordan, T.E. *The mentally retarded* (4th ed.). Columbus, Ohio: Charles E. Merrill, 1976.

Justman, J. Personal and social adjustment of intellectually gifted accelerants and nonaccelerants in junior high schools. *School Review,* 1953, *61,* 468–478.

Justman, J. Academic achievement of intellectually gifted acceleratants and nonaccelerants in junior high schools. *School Review,* 1954, *62,* 143–150.

Kaiser, C., & Hayden, A.H. Education of the very, *very,* young. *Educational Horizons,* Fall 1977.

Kanner, L. *A history of the care and study of the mentally retarded.* Springfield, Ill.: Charles C Thomas, 1964.

Karchmer, M.A., & Trybus, R.J. *Who are the deaf children in "mainstream" programs?* Series R, No. 4. Washington, D.C.: Gallaudet College Office of Demographic Studies, 1977.

Katz, J. F., & Challenor, Y.B. Childhood orthopedic syndromes. In J.A Downey & N.L. Low (Eds.), *The child with disabling illness: Principles of rehabilitation.* Philadelphia: Saunders, 1974.

Kauffman, J.M. Nineteenth century views of children's behavior disorders: Historical contributions and continuing issues. *Journal of Special Education,* 1976, *10,* 335–349.

Kauffman, J.M. *Characteristics of children's behavior disorders.* Columbus, Ohio: Charles E. Merrill, 1977.

Kauffman, J.M., & Hallahan, D.P. Control of rough physical behavior using novel contingencies and directive teaching. *Perceptual and Motor Skills,* 1973, *36,* 1225–1226.

Kauffman, J.M., & Hallahan, D.P. Evaluation of teaching performance. In W.M. Cruickshank & D.P. Hallahan (Eds.), *Perceptual and learning disabilities in children* (Vol. 1). Syracuse: Syracuse University Press, 1975.

Kauffman, J.M., & Hallahan, D.P. (Eds.). *Teaching children with learning disabilities: Personal perspectives.* Columbus, Ohio: Charles E. Merrill, 1976.

Kauffman, J.M., & Lewis, C.D. (Eds.). *Teaching children with behavior disorders: Personal perspectives.* Columbus, Ohio: Charles E. Merrill, 1974.

Kauffman, J.M., & Payne, J.S. (Eds.). *Mental retardation: Introduction and personal perspectives.* Columbus, Ohio: Charles E. Merrill, 1975.

Kazdin, A.E., & Bootzin, R.R. The token economy: An evaluative review. *Journal of Applied Behavior Analysis,* 1972, *5,* 1–30.

Kenowitz, L.A., Gallaher, J.J., & Edgar, E. Generic services for the severely handicapped and their families: What's available. In E. Sontag, J. Smith, & N. Certo (eds.), *Educational programming for the severely and profoundly handicapped.* Reston, Va.: Division on Mental Retardation, Council for Exceptional Children, 1977.

Kent, L.R. *Language acquisition program for the severely retarded.* Champaign, Ill.: Research Press, 1974.

Keogh, B.K. Optometric vision training programs for children with learning disabilities: Review of issues and research. *Journal of Learning Disabilities,* 1974, *4,* 219–231.

Keys, N. *The underage student in high school and college.* Berkeley: University of California Press, 1938.

Kirk, S.A. *Educating exceptional children.* Boston: Houghton Mifflin, 1962; 2nd ed., 1972.

Kirk, S.A. Behavioral diagnosis and remediation of learning disabilities. In S.A. Kirk & J.M. McCarthy (Eds.), *Learning disabilities: Selected ACLD papers.* Boston: Houghton Mifflin, 1975.

Kirk, S.A., & Kirk, W.D. *Psycholinguistic learning disabilities: Diagnosis and remediation.* Urbana, Ill.: University of Illinois Press, 1971.

Kirk, S. A., McCarthy, J. J., & Kirk, W. D. The Illinois Test of Psycholoinguistic Abilities (rev. ed.). Urbana, Ill.: University of Illinois Press, 1968.

Kirk, W.J. Juvenile justice and delinquency. *Phi Delta Kappan,* 1976, *57,* 395–398.

Knoblock, P. Open education for emotionally disturbed children. *Exceptional Children,* 1973, *39,* 358–365.

Koehler, J. Spinal muscular atrophy of childhood. In E.E. Bleck & D.A. Nagel (Eds.), *Physically handicapped children: A medical atlas for teachers.* New York: Grune & Stratton, 1975.

Kolstoe, O.P. *Mental retardation: An educational viewpoint.* New York: Holt, Rinehart & Winston, 1972.

Kolstoe, O.P. Secondary programs. In J.M. Kauffman & J.S. Payne (Eds.), *Mental retardation: Introduction and personal perspectives.* Columbus, Ohio: Charles E. Merrill, 1975.

Kolstoe, O.P., & Frey, R. *A high school work-study program for mentally subnormal students.* Carbondale, Ill.: Southern Illinois Press, 1965.

Komoski, P.K. The continuing confusion about technology and education of the myth-ing link in educational technology. *Educational Technology,* 1969, *4,* 70–74.

Kreger, K.C. Compensatory environmental programming for the severely retarded behaviorally disturbed. *Mental Retardation,* 1971, *9*(4), 29–33.

Krim, M. Scientific research and mental retardation. *President's Committee on Mental Retardation Message* (No. 16.) Washington D.C.: U.S. Government Printing Office, 1969.

LaBrant, L. A few suggestions about language learning. *Educational Horizons,* 1972, *50*(3), 105–108.

Lamb, P. *Linguistics in proper perspective* (2nd ed.). Columbus, Ohio: Charles E. Merrill, 1977.

Lambert, N.M., Windmiller, M., Cole, L., & Figueroa, R. *AAMD Adaptive Behavior Scale: Public school version 1974 revision.* Washington, D.C.: American Association on Mental Deficiency, 1975.

Lane, H. *The wild boy of Aveyron.* Cambridge: Harvard University Press, 1976.

Language. Curriculum Series, 1972. Northhampton, Mass.: Clarke School for the Deaf, 1972.

Larsen, S.C. The learning disabilities specialist: Role and responsibilities. *Journal of Learning Disabilities,* 1976, *9,* 498–508.

Larson, A.R. A study of early entrance to school. In T.M. Stephens & A. Gibson (Eds.), *Acceleration and the gifted.* Columbus, Ohio: Ohio Department of Education, 1963. Pp. 17–23.

Laubenfels, M. (Ed.). *The gifted child: An annotated bibliography.* Westport, Conn. Greenwood Press, 1978.

References

Lehman, H. *Age and achievement*. Princeton, N.J.: Princeton University Press, 1953.

Lehrman, N.S. Precision in psychoanalysis. In T. Millon (Ed.), *Theories of psychopathology*. Philadelphia: Saunders, 1967. Pp. 235–242.

Leiter, R.G. The Leiter International Performance Scale. Chicago: C.H. Stoelting, 1969.

Leland, H., & Smith, D.E. *Mental retardation: Present and future perspectives*. Worthington, Ohio: Charles A. Jones, 1974.

Lent, J.R. The severely retarded: Are we really programming for their future? *Focus on Exceptional Children*, 1975, 7(1).

Lerner, J.W. *Children with learning disabilities*. Boston: Houghton Mifflin, 1976.

Levy, S.M. The development of work skill training procedures for the assembly of printed circuit boards by the severely handicapped. *American Association for the Education of the Severely/Profoundly Handicapped Review*, 1975, 1(1).

Lieghton, A.H., & Hughes, J.M. Cultures as causative of mental disorder In *Causes of mental disorders: A review of epidemiological knowledge*. New York: Milbank Memorial Fund, 1959. Pp. 341–365.

Life experience program: An alternative approach in special education. San Jose, Calif.: Office of the Santa Clara County Superintendent of Schools, 1976.

Lily, M.S. Special education: A teapot in a tempest. *Exceptional Children*, 1970, 37, 43–49.

Linder, R. Diagnosis: Description or prescription? A case study in the psychology of diagnosis. *Perceptual and Motor Skills*, 1965, 20, 1081–1092.

Lindsley, O.R. Direct measurement and prosthesis of retarded behavior. *Journal of Education*, 1964, 147, 62–81.

Lippman, L., & Goldberg, I.I. *Right to education: Anatomy of the Pennsylvania case and its implications for exceptional children*. New York: Teachers College Press, 1973.

Lipton, E.L., Remarks on the psychological aspect of strabismus. *The Sight-Saving Review*, 1971, 41, 129–138.

Litow, L., & Pumroy, D.K. A brief review of classroom group-oriented contingencies. *Journal of Applied Behavior Analysis*, 1975, 8, 341–347.

Lloyd, L.L., & Dahle, A.J. Detection and diagnosis of a hearing impairment in the child. *The Volta Review*, 1976, 78(4), 12–22.

Long, N.J. Nicholas J. Long. In J.M. Kauffman & C.D. Lewis (Eds.), *Teaching children with behavior disorders: Personal perspectives*. Columbus, Ohio: Charles E. Merrill, 1974.

Lovaas, O.I. A program for the establishment of speech in psychotic children. In J.K. Wing (ed.), *Early childhood autism*. London: Pergamon Press, 1966.

Lovaas, O.I. A behavior therapy approach to the treatment of childhood schizophrenia. In J.P. Hill (Ed.), *Minnesota symposia on child psychology*. Minneapolis: University of Minnesota Press, 1967.

Lovaas, O.I., & Koegel, R.I. Behavior therapy with autistic children. In C.E. Thoresen (Ed.), *Behavior modification in education*. Chicago: University of Chicago Press, 1973.

Lovaas, O.I., & Newsom, C.D. Behavior modification with psychotic children. In H. Leitenberg (Ed.), *Handbook of behavior modification and behavior therapy*. Englewood Cliffs, N.J.: Prentice-Hall, 1976.

Lovitt, T.C. Self-management projects with children with behavioral disabilities. *Journal of Learning Disabilities*, 1973, 6, 138–150.

Lovitt, T.C. Applied behavior analysis technique and curriculum research: Implications for instruction. In N.G. Haring & R.L. Schiefelbusch (Eds.), *Teaching special children*. New York: McGraw-Hill, 1976.

Lovitt, T.C. *In spite of my resistance.* Columbus, Ohio: Charles E. Merrill, 1977.

Lovitt, T.C. & Cardell-Gray, D. *An evaluation of the Slingerland method with LD youngsters: The report of a summer program.* Unpublished manuscript submitted to the State Department of Public Instruction, Olympia, Washington, 1976.

Lovitt, T.C., & Curtiss, K.A. Effects of manipulating an antecedent event on mathematics response rate. *Journal of Applied Behavior Analysis,* 1968, *1,* 329–333.

Lovitt, T.C., & Hurlbut, M. Using behavior analysis techniques to assess the relationship between phonics instruction and oral reading. *Journal of Special Education,* 1974, *8,* 57–72.

Lovitt, T.C., Lovitt, A.O., Eaton, M.D., & Kirkwood, M. The deceleration of inappropriate comments by a natural consequence. *Journal of School Psychology,* 1973, *11,* 148–154.

Lovitt, T.C., & Smith, J.O. Effects of instruction on an individual's verbal behavior. *Exceptional Children,* 1972, *38,* 685–693.

Lowenfeld, B. History of the education of visually handicapped children. In B. Lowenfeld (Ed.), *The visually handicapped child in school.* New York: John Day, 1973. Pp. 1–25.

Lucito, L. Gifted children. In L.M. Dunn (Ed.), *Exceptional children in the schools.* New York: Holt, Rinehart & Winston, 1963.

Lucito, L. The creative. In R. Martinson (Ed.), *Identification of the gifted and talented.* Ventura, Calif., June 1974. Pp. 21–23.

Luckey, R.E., & Addison, M.R. The profoundly retarded: A new challenge for public education. *Education and Training of the Mentally Retarded,* October 1974, *9,* 123–130.

Lynch, V., Shoemaker, S., & White, O.R. Training needs survey. *American Association for the Education of the Severely/Profoundly Handicapped Review,* 1976, *1*(4), 1–16.

MacDonald, J.D. Environmental language intervention: Programs for establishing initial communication in handicapped children. In F. Withrow & C. Nygren (Eds.), *Language and the handicapped learner: Curricula, programs and media.* Columbus, Ohio: Charles E. Merrill, 1976.

*MacDonald, J.D., Horstmeier, D.S. *Environmental Language Intervention Program.* Columbus, Ohio: Charles E. Merrill, 1978.

Mackie, R.P. *Directors and supervisors of special education in local school systems* (Bulletin 13). Washington, D.C.: U.S. Office of Education, 1955.

MacKinnon, D. The nature and nurture of creative talent. *American Psychologist,* 1962, *17,* 484–495.

MacNamara, J. Cognitive basis of language learning in infants. *Psychological Review,* 1972, *74,* 1–13.

Madsen, C.H. Jr., Becker, W.C., & Thomas, D.R. Rules, praise, and ignoring: Elements of elementary classroom control. *Journal of Applied Behavior Analysis,* 1968, *1,* 139–150.

Madsen, C.H., & Madsen, C.K. *Teaching/discipline* (2nd ed.). Boston: Allyn & Beacon, 1974.

Mahoney, G. An ethological approach to delayed language acquisition. *American Journal of Mental Deficiency,* 1975, *80,* 139–148.

Mahoney, M.J. *Cognition and behavior modification.* Cambridge, Mass.: Ballinger, 1974.

Mainstreaming: Helping teachers meet the challenge. Washington, D.C.: National Advisory Council on Education Professions Development, 1976.

Marland, S. *Education of the gifted and talented: Report to the Congress of the United States by the U.S. Commissioner of Education* (Vol. 1). Washington, D.C.: 1971.

Marland, S. *Education of the gifted and talented* (Vol. 1). Washington, D.C.: U.S. Government Printing Office, 1972.

Martin, B. Parent-child relations. In F.D. Horowitz (Ed.), *Review of child development research* (Vol. 4). Chicago: University of Chicago Press, 1975.

References

Martin, E.W. Breakthrough for the handicapped: Legislative history. *Exceptional Children,* 1968, *35,* 493–503.

Martin, E.W. Individualism and behaviorism as future trends in educating handicapped children. *Exceptional Children,* 1972, *38,* 517–525.

Marx, J.L. Learning and behavior: Effects of pituitary hormones. *Journal of Learning Disabilities,* 1976, *9,* 223–224.

Maslow, A.H. *Toward a psychology of being.* New York: Van Nostrand, 1962.

Maugh, T.H. Creativity: Can it be dissected? Can it be taught? *Science,* 1974, *7,* 1273.

Mayo, L.W. *A proposed program for national action to combat mental retardation.* Report of the President's Committee on Mental Retardation. Washington, D.C.: U.S. Government Printing Office, 1962.

McCarr, J.E. *Lessons in syntax.* Lake Oswego, Ore.: Dormac Publishing, 1973.

McClearn, G.E. Genetics and behavior development. In M.L. Hoffman & L.W. Hoffman (Eds.), *Review of child development research* (Vol. 1). New York: Russell Sage Foundation, 1964.

McCracken, G., & Walcutt, C.C. *Lippincott's basic reading.* Philadelphia: Lippincott, 1965.

McDaniels, G. Successful programs for handicapped children. *Educational Horizons,* Fall 1977.

McElfresh, A.E. What is hemophilia? *The Journal of Pediatrics,* 1974, *84*(4), 623–624.

McLaughlin, T. Self-control in the classroom. *Review of Educational Research,* 1976, *46,* 631–663.

McLean, J.E., Raymore, S., & Long, L. *Stimulus shift articulation program.* Bellview, Wash.: Edmark-McLean, 1976.

McLean, J.E., & Snyder, L.K. *A transactional approach to early language training.* Columbus, Ohio: Charles E. Merrill, 1978.

McLean, L.P., & McLean, J.E. A language training program for nonverbal autistic children. *Journal of Speech and Hearing Disorders,* 1974, *39,* 186–193.

Meeker, M. *The structure of intellect: Its use and interpretation.* Columbus, Ohio: Charles E. Merrill, 1969.

Meichenbaum, D.H. The effects of instructions and reinforcement on thinking and language behaviors of schizophrenics. *Behavior Research and Therapy,* 1969, *7,* 101–114.

Meichenbaum, D.H., & Goodman, J. Training impulsive children to talk to themselves. *Journal of Abnormal Psychology,* 1971, *77,* 115–126.

Menninger Foundation, Children's Division. *Disturbed children.* San Francisco: Jossey-Bass, 1969.

Menninger, K. *The vital balance.* New York: Viking, 1963.

Mercer, C.D., Forgnone, C., & Wolking, W.D. Definitions of learning disabilities used in the United States. *Journal of Learning Disabilities,* 1976, *9,* 376–386.

Mercer, J.R. Sociocultural factors in labeling mental retardates. *Peabody Journal of Education,* 1971, *48,* 188–203.

Merwin, M.R. *The effects of pretraining upon training and transfer of circuit board assembly skills of retarded adults.* Unpublished doctoral dissertation, University of Illinois, 1974.

Michigan Department of Education, *Michigan special education code.* Lansing: Michigan State Department of Education, October 10, 1973.

Miller, J.F. Practices in language instruction. *Exceptional Children,* 1964, *30,* 355–358.

Miller, J.F., & Yoder, D.E. A syntax teaching program. In J.E. McLean, D.E. Yoder, & R.L. Schiefelbusch (Eds.), *Language intervention with the retarded.* Baltimore: University Park Press, 1972.

Miller, J.F., & Yoder, D.E. An ontogenetic language teaching strategy for retarded children. In R.L. Schiefelbusch & L.L. Lloyd (Eds.), *Language perspectives: Acquisition, retardation and intervention.* Baltimore: University Park Press, 1974.

References

Mithaug, D.E., & Haring, N.G. Community vocational and workshop placement. In N.G. Haring & L.J. Brown (Eds.), *Teaching the severely handicapped* (Vol. 2). New York: Grune & Stratton, 1977.

Montagu, M.F.A. (Ed.). *Man and aggression*. New York: Oxford University Press, 1968.

Montessori, M. *The Montessori method*. New York: Stokes, 1912.

Morse, W.C. The "crisis teacher" public school provision for the disturbed pupil. *University of Michigan School of Education Bulletin, 1962, 33,* 101–104.

Morse, W.C. William C. Morse. In J.M. Kauffman & C.D. Lewis (Eds.), *Teaching children with behavior disorders: Personal perspectives*. Columbus, Ohio: Charles E. Merrill, 1974.

Morse, W.C. The education of socially maladjusted and emotionally disturbed children. In W.M. Cruickshank & G.O. Johnson (Eds.), *Education of exceptional children and youth* (3rd ed.). Englewood Cliffs, N.J.: Prentice-Hall, 1975.

Morse, W.C. The helping teacher/crisis teacher concept. *Focus on Exceptional Children, 1976, 8,* 1–11.

Morse, W.C., Cutler, R.L., & Fink, A.H. *Public school classes for the emotionally handicapped: A research analysis*. Washington, D.C.: Council for Exceptional Children, 1964.

Myers, D.G., Sinco, M.E., & Stalma, E.S. The right to education child. Springfield, Ill.: Charles C Thomas, 1973.

Myers, P.I., & Hammill, D.D. *Methods of learning disorders*. New York: Wiley, 1969.

Myklebust, H.R. *The psychology of deafness* (2nd ed.). New York: Grune & Stratton, 1964.

Nance, W.E. Studies of hereditary deafness: Present, past, and future. *Volta Review, 1976, 78(4),* 6–11.

National Advisory Committee on the Handicapped. *The unfinished revolution: Education for the handicapped* (1976 Annual Report). Washington, D.C.: Department of Health, Education and Welfare, United States Office of Education, 1976.

National Medical Foundation for Eye Care. *Identification of school children requiring eye care*. Washington, D.C.: American Association of Ophthalmology, 1959.

National Society for the Prevention of Blindness. *Estimated statistics on blindness and vision problems*. New York: Author, 1966.

National Society for the Prevention of Blindness. *Home eye test for preschoolers*. New York: Author, 1972.

National Society for the Study of Education. *Education for the gifted*. Fifty-seventh Yearbook, Part II. Chicago: University of Chicago Press, 1958.

Nawratzki, I., & Oliver, M. Screening for amblyopia in children under 3 years of age. *The Sight-Saving Review, 1972, 42,* 14–19.

Nelson, C.M. Techniques for screening conduct disturbed children. *Exceptional Children, 1971, 37,* 501–507.

Neufeld, G.R. Deinstitutionalization procedures. *American Association for the Education of the Severely/Profoundly Handicapped Review, 1972, 2(1),* 15–23.

Newland, T. Some observations on essential qualifications of teachers of the mentally superior. *Exceptional Children, 1962, 29,* 111–114.

Nicholls, K., Dmitriev, V., & Oelwein, P. Mark. In A.H. Hayden (Ed.), *Selected case studies*. Seattle: Experimental Education Unit, Child Development and Mental Retardation Center, University of Washington, 1972. Pp. 47–50.

Nietupski, J., & Williams, W. Teaching selected telephone related social skills to severely handicapped students. *Child Study Journal, 1975, 6(3),* 139–153.

References

Nihira, K., Foster, R., Shellhaas, M., & Leland, H. AAMD Adaptive Behavior Scale (1974 rev.). Washington, D.C.: American Association on Mental Deficiency, 1974.

Nolan, C.Y., & Morris, J.E. The Japanese abacus as a computational aid for blind children. *Exceptional Children,* 1964, *31,* 15–17.

Norton, Y. Neurodevelopment and sensory integration for the profoundly retarded multiply handicapped child. *American Journal of Occupational Therapy,* 1975, *29*(2), 93–100.

O'Brien, F., Azrin, N.H., & Bugle, C. Training profoundly retarded children to stop crawling. *Journal of Applied Behavior Analysis,* 1972, *5,* 131–137.

Oden, M. The fulfillment of promise: 40-year follow-up of the Terman gifted group. *Genetic Psychology Monographs,* 1968, *77,* 3–93.

O'Leary, K.D. The assessment of psychopathology in children. In H.C. Quay & J.S. Werry (Eds.), *Psychopathological disorders of childhood.* New York: Wiley, 1972.

O'Leary, K.D., & Drabman, R.S. Token reinforcement programs in the classroom: A review. *Psychological Bulletin,* 1971, *75,* 379–398.

O'Leary, K.D., Kaufman, K.F., Kass, R.E., & Drabman, R.S. The effects of loud and soft reprimands on the behavior of disruptive students. *Exceptional Children,* 1970, *37,* 145–155.

O'Leary, K.D., & O'Leary, S.G. Behavior modification in the school. In H. Leitenberg (Ed.), *Handbook of behavior modification and behavior therapy.* Englewood Cliffs, N.J.: Prentice-Hall, 1976.

Olson, D. Language and thought: Aspects of a cognitive theory of semantics. *Psychological Review,* 1970, *77,* 257–273.

O'Neill, J.J., & Oyer, H.J. *Visual communication for the hard of hearing.* Englewood Cliffs, N.J.: Prentice-Hall, 1961.

Opportunities for the hard of hearing and the deaf. Washington, D.C.: U.S. Department of Health Education and Welfare, Vocational Rehabilitation Administration, n.d.

Orton, S.T. *Reading, writing and speech problems in children.* New York: Norton, 1937.

Ousley, O., & Russell, D.H. *The Ginn basic readers.* Boston: Ginn, 1961.

Parke, R.D., & Colmer, C.W. Child abuse: An interdisciplinary analysis. In E.M. Hetherington (Ed.), *Review of child development research* (Vol. 5.). Chicago: University of Chicago Press, 1975.

Patterson, G.R. *Families.* Champaign, Ill.: Research Press, 1971.

Patterson, G.R., Cobb, J.A., & Ray, R.S. Direct intervention in the classroom: A set of procedures for the aggressive child. In F.W. Clark, D.R. Evans, & L.A. Hammerlynck (Eds.), *Implementing behavioral programs in schools and clinics.* Champaign, Ill.: Research Press, 1972.

Patterson, G.R., Reid, J.B., Jones, R.R., & Conger, R.E. *A social learning approach to family intervention* (Vol. 1, *Families with aggressive children*). Eugene, Ore.: Castalia, 1975.

Pegnato, C.W., & Birch, J.W. Locating gifted children in junior high schools: A comparison of methods. *Exceptional Children,* 1959, *25,* 300–304.

Perske, R., & Smith, J. (Eds.). *Beyond the ordinary—The preparation of professionals to educate severely and profoundly handicapped persons: Toward the development of standards and criteria.* Document Developed through Grant No. HEW-105-76-5001 from the Research and Development Division, Developmental Disabilities Office, U.S. Department of Health, Education and Welfare, 1977.

Peterson, R.F., & Peterson, L.R. The use of positive reinforcement in the control of self-destructive behavior in a retarded boy. *Journal of Experimental Child Psychology,* 1968, *6,* 351–360.

Phay, R.E. (Ed.). Mentally retarded and other exceptional children. *Yearbook of school law 1973.* Topeka, Kans.: National Organization on Legal Problems of Education, 1973.

References

Phelps, W.M. Cerebral birth injuries: Their orthopaedic classification and subsequent treatment. *Clinical Orthopaedics and Related Research,* 1966, *47,* 9–17. (Reprint of paper read at the Section of Orthopaedic Surgery, New York Academy of Medicine, January 15, 1932.

Phelps, W.M., Hopkins, T.W. & Cousins, R. *The cerebral-palsied child: A guide for parents,* New York: Simon & Schuster, 1958.

Phillips, S., Liebert, R.M., & Poulos, R.W. Employing paraprofessional teachers in a group language training program for severely and profoundly retarded children. *Perceptual and Motor Skills,* 1973, *36,* 607–616.

Piper, T.J., & MacKinnon, R.C. Operant conditioning of a profoundly retarded individual reinforced via a stomach fistula. *American Journal of Mental Deficiency.* 1969, *71,* 42–47.

Plowman, R., & Rice, J. Some general characteristics of gifted children. In *Education of mentally gifted minors.* California State Department of Education, 1971.

Premack, D. A functional analysis of language. *Journal of the Experimental Analysis of Behavior,* 1970, *14,* 107–125.

Preschool training pays off. *Report on Preschool Education,* June 7, 1977.

Pressey, S.L. *Educational acceleration: Appraisals and basic problems.* Columbus, Ohio: The Ohio State University, Bureau of Educational Research, 1949.

Pressey, S.L. "Fordling" accelerates ten years after. *Journal of Counseling Psychology,* 1967, *14,* 73–80.

Pressey, S.L. Education's (and psychology's) disgrace: And a double dare. *Psychology in the Schools,* 1969, *6,* 353–358.

Provence, S., & Lipton, J. *Infants in institutions.* New York: International University Press, 1962.

Provus, M. *Discrepancy evaluation for educational program improvement and assessment.* Berkeley, Calif.: McCutchan, 1971.

Quay, H.C. Patterns of aggression, withdrawal and immaturity. In H.C. Quay & J.S. Werry (Eds.), *Psychopathological disorders of childhood.* New York: Wiley, 1972.

Quay, H.C. Classification in the treatment of delinquency and antisocial behavior. In N. Hobbs (Ed.), *Issues in the classification of children* (Vol. 1). San Francisco: Jossey-Bass, 1975.

Quigley, S.P. *The influence of fingerspelling on the development of language, communication, and educational achievement in deaf children.* Urbana, Ill.: Institute for Research on Exceptional Children, University of Illinois, 1969.

Quigley, S.P. *Some effects of hearing impairment upon school performance.* State of Illinois, Division of Speech Education Services, n.d.

Quigley, S.P., Wilbur, R.B., Power, D.J., Montanelli, D.S., & Steinkamp, M. *Syntactic structures in the language of deaf children.* Arlington, Va.: United States Department of Health, Education and Welfare, National Institute of Education, 1976.

Reed, E.W., & Reed, S.C. *Mental retardation: A family study.* Philadelphia: Saunders, 1965.

Reger, R. Schroders, W., & Uschold, D. *Special education: Children with learning problems.* New York: Oxford University Press, 1968.

Renzulli, J. Talent potential in minority group students. *Exceptional Children,* 1973, *39,* 437–444.

Renzulli, J., Hartman, R., & Callahan, J. Teacher identification of superior students. *Exceptional Children,* 1971, *38,* 211–214.

A report on the achievement of specific language disability children. Cambridge: Educators Publishing Service, 1974.

References

Research trends in deafness: State of the art. Washington, D.C.: Department of Health, Education and Welfare, Social and Rehabilitation Service, Office of Research and Demonstrations, 1970.

Restak, R. Jose Delgado: Exploring inner space. *Saturday Review,* August 9, 1975, 21–25.

Rhodes, W.C. Curriculum and disordered behavior. *Exceptional Children,* 1963, *30,* 61–66.

Rhodes, W.C. The disturbing child: A problem of ecological management. *Exceptional Children,* 1967, *33,* 449–455.

Rhodes, W.C. A community participation analysis of emotional disturbance. *Exceptional Children,* 1970, *37,* 309–314.

Rhodes, W.C., & Head, S. (Eds.). *A study of child variance* (Vol. 3, *Service delivery systems*). Ann Arbor: University of Michigan, 1974.

Rhodes, W.C., & Tracy, M.L. (Eds.). A study of child variance (Vol. 1, *Theories*). Ann Arbor: University of Michigan, 1972. (a)

Rhodes, W.C., & Tracy, M.L. (Eds.). A study of child variance (Vol. 2, *Interventions*). Ann Arbor: University of Michigan, 1972. (b)

Richardson, E.L. *MR 71: Entering the era of human ecology.* Report of the President's Committee on Mental Retardation. Washington, D.C.: U.S. Government Printing Office, 1971.

Rimland, B. *Infantile autism.* New York: Appleton-Century-Crofts (Prentice-Hall), 1964.

Rimland, B. Psychogenesis versus biogenesis: The issues and the evidence. In S.C. Plog & R.B. Edgerton (Eds.), *Changing perspectives in mental illness.* New York: Holt, Rinehart & Winston, 1969. Pp. 702–735.

Rimland, B. The differentiation of childhood psychoses: An analysis of checklists for 2,218 psychotic children. *Journal of Autism and Childhood Schizophrenia,* 1971, *1,* 161–174.

Rivera, G. *Willowbrook.* New York: Random House, 1971.

Roach, E.G., & Kephart, N.C. The Purdue Perceptual-Motor Survey. Columbus, Ohio: Charles E. Merrill, 1966.

Robbins, M., & Glass, G.V. The Doman-Delacato rationale: A critical analysis. In J. Hellmuth (Ed.), *Educational Therapy* (Vol. 2). Seattle: Special Child Publications, 1969.

Roberts, H.A. A clinical and metabolic reevaluation of reading disability. In *Selected papers on learning disabilities, fifth annual convention, Association for Children with Learning Disabilities.* San Rafael, Calif.: Academic Therapy Publication, 1969.

Robins, L.N., West, P., & Herjaniz, B. Arrests and delinquency in two generations: A study of urban families and their children. *Journal of Child Psychology and Psychiatry,* 1975, *16,* 125–140.

Robinson, H.B., & Robinson, N.M. (Eds.), *International monograph series on early child care.* New York/London: Gordon and Breach, 1973.

Robinson, N.M., & Robinson, H.B. *The mentally retarded child: A psychological approach* (2nd ed.). New York: McGraw-Hill, 1976.

The Rochester Method as a vehicle for improving the education of deaf children. Rochester, N.Y.: Rochester School for the Deaf, August, 1972.

Roe, A. A psychological study of eminent psychologists and anthropologists and a comparison with biological and physical scientists. *Psychological Monographs,* 1953, *67,* 1–55.

Rogers, C. *Freedom to learn.* Columbus, Ohio: Charles E. Merrill, 1969.

Ronayne, A.M., Wilkinson, P.A., Bogotay, N., Manculich, K., Sieber, L., & McDowell, M. *Perceptual motor development curriculum guide.* Pittsburgh, Penn.: Allegheny Intermediate Unit, 1974.

Roos, P. Current issues in the education of mentally retarded persons. In W.J. Cegelka (Ed.), *Proceedings: Conference on the education of mentally retarded persons.* Arlington, Tex.: National Association for Retarded Citizens, 1971.

Rosenthal, R., & Jacobson, L.F. *Pygmalion in the classroom.* New York: Holt, Rinehart & Winston, 1968.

Ross, A.O. *Psychological disorders of children.* New York: McGraw-Hill, 1974.

Ross, S.L., Jr., De Young, H.G., & Cohen, J.S. Confrontation: Special education placement and the law. *Exceptional Children, 1971, 38,* 5–12.

Rusalem, H. Continuing education. In F.P. Connor & M.J. Cohen (Eds.), *Leadership preparation for education of crippled and other health impaired multiply handicapped populations.* New York: Teachers College Press, 1973.

Rutter, M., & Bartak, L. Special educational treatment of autistic children; A comparative study—II. Follow-up findings and implications for services. *Journal of Child Psychology and Psychiatry, 1973, 14,* 241–270.

Sailor, W., & Haring, N.G. Some current directions in education of the severely/multiply handicapped. *Review, 1977 2*(2), 67–87. *American Association for the Education of the Severely/Profoundly Handicapped*

Sameroff, A.J., & Chandler, M.J. Reproductive risk and the continuum of caretaking casualty. In F.D. Horowitz (Ed.), *Review of child development research* (Vol. 4). Chicago: University of Chicago Press, 1975.

Sartain, H.W. Instruction of disabled learners: A reading perspective. *Journal of Learning Disabilities, 1976, 9,* 489–497.

Scarr-Salapatek, S. Genetics and the development of intelligence. In F.D. Horowitz (Ed.), *Review of child development research* (Vol. 4). Chicago: University of Chicago Press, 1975.

Schalock, R., Ross, B.E., & Ross, I. *Basic skills remediation manual and basic skills screening test.* Hastings, Neb.: Mid-Nebraska Mental Retardation Services, 1974.

Schlesinger, H., & Meadow, K.P. *Sound and sign: Childhood deafness and mental health.* Berkeley, Calif.: University of California Press, 1972.

Schmidt, R.P., & Wilder, B.J. *Epilepsy.* Philadephia: Davis, 1968.

Schultz, E.W., Salvia, J.A., & Feinn, J. Prevalence of behavioral symptoms in rural elementary school children. *Journal of Abnormal Child Psychology, 1974, 2,* 17–24.

Scouten, H.L. The place of the Rochester method in American education of the deaf. *Report of the Proceedings of the International Congress on the Education of the Deaf.* Washington, D.C.: U.S. Government Printing Office, 1964, Pp. 429–433.

Seagoe, M. Some learning characteristics of gifted children. In R. Martinson (Ed.), *Identification of the gifted and talented.* Ventura, Calif.: June 1974. Pp. 20–21.

Seagoe, M. *Terman and the gifted.* Los Altos, Calif.: William Kaufmann, 1975.

Selman, J.E. Rubella: Medical aspects. *Education of the Visually Handicapped, 1972, 4,* 22–25.

Shearer, D. *Portage guide to early education.* Portage, Wisc.: Cooperative Educational Service Agency #12, 1972.

Shotick, A.L. Mental retardation. In W.M. Cruickshank (Ed.), *Cerebral palsy: A developmental disability* (3rd ed.). Syracuse: Syracuse University Press, 1976.

Simches, R.F. The inside outsider. *Exceptional Children, 1970, 37,* 5–15.

Simmons, A. A comparison of the type-taken ratio of spoken and written language of deaf and hearing children. *Volta Review,* September 1962, *64,* 417–421.

Simmons-Martin, A. The oral-aural procedure: Theoetical basis and rational. *Volta Review,* December 1972, *74,* 541–551.

Sirvis, B., Carpignano, J.L., & Bigge, J.L. Psychosocial aspects of physical disability. In. J.L. Bigge with P.A. O'Donnell (Eds.), *Teaching individuals with physical and multiple disabilities.* Columbus, Ohio: Charles E. Merrill, 1976.

Skinner, B.F. *Science and human behavior.* New York: Free Press, 1953.

References

Skinner, B.F. Critique of psychoanalytic concepts and theories. In T. Millon (Ed.), *Theories of psychopathology.* Philadelphia: Saunders, 1967. Pp. 228–235.

Slingerland, B. *Screening tests for identifying children with specific language disability.* Cambridge: Educators Publishing Service, 1964.

Slingerland, B.H. *A multi-sensory approach to language arts for specific language disability children: A guide for primary teachers.* Cambridge: Educators Publishing Service, 1971.

Slingerland, B.H. *Preventive teaching programs in the classroom: A general education responsibility.* (Bulletin). Towson, Md.: Orton Society, 1972. (Reprint # 50.)

Sloane, H.N., Johnston, M.K., & Bijou, S.W. Successive modification of aggressive behavior and aggressive fantasy play by management of contingencies. *Journal of Child Psychology and Psychiatry,* 1967, *8,* 217–226.

Slobin, D.I. Cognitive prerequisites for the development of grammar. In D.I. Slobin & C. Ferguson (Eds.), *Studies of child language development.* New York: Holt, Rinehart & Winston, 1973.

Smith, D.D., & Lovitt, T.C. The use of modeling techniques to influence the acquisition of computation arithmetic skills in learning disabled children. In E. Ramp & G. Semb (Eds.), *Behavior analysis: Areas of research and application.* Englewood Cliffs, N.J.: Prentice-Hall, 1975.

Smith, D.D., & Lovitt, T.C. The differential effects of reinforcement contingencies on arithmetic performance. *Journal of Learning Disabilities,* 1976, *9,* 32–40.

Somerton, M.E., & Myers, D.G. Educational programming for the severely and profoundly retarded. In N.G. Haring & L.J. Brown (Eds.), *Teaching the severely handicapped* (Vol. 1). New York: Grune & Stratton, 1976.

Song, A.Y., & Gandhi, R. An analysis of behavior during the acquisition and maintenance phases of self-spoon feeding skills of profound retardates. *Mental Retardation,* February 1973, 25–28.

Sontag, E. Zero exclusion: Rhetoric no longer. *American Association for the Education of the Severely/Profoundly Handicapped Review,* 1976, *1*(3), 105–114.

Sontag, E., Burke, P., & York, R. Considerations for serving the severely handicapped in the public schools. *Education and Training of the Mentally Retarded,* 1973, *8*(2), 20–26.

Speech, language, and hearing program: A guide for Head Start personnel. Washington, D.C.: Office of Child Development, U.S. Department of Health, Education and Welfare, Pub. No. (OCD) 73–1025, 1973.

Spooner, F., & Hendrickson, B. Acquisition of complex assembly skills through the use of systematic training procedures: Involving profoundly retarded adults. *American Association for the Education of the Severely and Profoundly Handicapped Review,* 1976, *1*(7), 14–25.

Spring, C., & Sandoval, J. Food additives and hyperkinesis: A critical evaluation of the evidence. *Journal of Learning Disabilities,* 1976, *9,* 509–519.

Springer, N.N. A comparative study of a group of deaf and hearing children. *American Annals of the Deaf,* March 1938, *83,* 138–152.

Stainback, S., Stainback, W., & Maurer, S. Training teachers for the severely and profoundly handicapped: A new frontier. *Exceptional Children,* 1976, *42*(4), 203–212.

Stageberg, N. *An introductory English grammar* (2nd ed.). New York: Holt, Rinehart & Winston, 1971.

Stanley, J. Intellectual precocity. In J. Stanley, D. Keating, & L. Fox (Eds.), *Mathematical talent: Discovery, description, and development.* Baltimore: Johns Hopkins University Press, 1974. Pp. 1–22.

Stanley, J., Keating, D., & Fox, L. (Eds.), *Mathematical talent: Discovery, description, and development.* Baltimore: Johns Hopkins University Press, 1974.

Stein, A. Strategies for failure. *Harvard Educational Review,* 1971, *41,* 158–204.

Stephens, T.M. *A look at Ohio's gifted.* Columbus, Ohio: Ohio Department of Education, 1962.

Stephens, T.M. An analysis of creative thinking tasks as measures of academic potential with special reference to the work of Getzels and Jackson. In T.M. Stephens & A. Gibson (Eds.), *Pathways to progress*. Columbus, Ohio: Ohio Board of Education, 1964. Pp. 132–140.

Stick, S. The speech pathologist and handicapped learners. *Journal of Learning Disabilities,* 1976, *9,* 509–519.

Stokoe, W. Sign language structure. In *Studies in Linguistics.* Occasional Paper No. 8. Buffalo: University of Buffalo, 1958.

The story of the White House Conferences on Children and Youth. Washington, D.C. U.S. Dept. of Health, Education and Welfare, Social and Rehabilitation Service, Children's Bureau, 1967.

Strauss, A.A., & Lehtinen, L.E. *Psychopathology and education of the brain-injured child.* New York: Grune & Stratton, 1947.

Strauss, A.A., & Werner, H. Disorders of conceptual thinking in the brain-injured child. *Journal of Nervous and Mental Disease,* 1942, *96,* 153–172.

Stremel, K., & Waryas, C. A behavioral-psycholinguistic approach to language training. In L. McReynolds (Ed.), Developing systematic procedures for training children's language. *ASHA Monograph No. 18,* 1974.

Sullivan, M.W. *Sullivan Reading Program.* Palo Alto, Calif.: Behavioral Research Laboratories, n.d.

Sulzbacher, S.I. Behavior analysis of drug effects in the classroom. In G. Semb (Ed.), *Behavior analysis and education.* Lawrence, Kan.: University of Kansas Press, 1972.

Swinyard, C.A. (Ed.). Comprehensive care of the child with spina bifida manifesta. *Rehabilitation Monographs,* 1966, *31,* 1–147.

Sykes, K.C. A comparison of the effectiveness of standard print and large print in facilitating the reading skill of visually impaired students. *Education of the Visually Handicapped,* 1971, *3,* 97–105.

Sykes, K.C. Print reading for visually handicapped children. *Education of the Visually Handicapped,* 1972, *4,* 71–75.

Tarver, S., & Hallahan, D.P. Children with learning disabilities: An overview. In J.M. Kauffman & D.P. Hallahan (Eds.), *Teaching children with learning disabilities: Personal perspectives.* Columbus, Ohio: Charles E. Merrill, 1976.

Tawney, J. Personal communication with the Education Committee, National Association for Retarded Citizens, regarding teacher certification, July 27, 1976.

Taylor, C. Multiple talent approach. *The Instructor,* 1968, 27ff.

Taylor, C., & Holland, J. Development and application of tests of creativity. *Review of Educational Research,* 1962, *32,* 91–102.

Templin, M.C. *The development of reasoning in children with normal and defective hearing.* Minneapolis: University of Minnesota Press, 1950.

Terman, L.M. The discovery and encouragement of exceptional talent. *American Psychologist,* 1954, *9,* 221–230.

Terman, L.M., et al. *The mental and physical traits of a thousand gifted children.,* Stanford, Calif.: Stanford University Press, 1925.

Terman, L.M., & Merrill, M.A. The Stanford-Binet Intelligence Scale (3rd rev.). Boston: Houghton Mifflin, 1973.

Terman, L.M., & Oden, M. *The gifted child grows up.* Stanford, Calif.: Stanford University Press, 1947.

Terman, L., & Oden, M. *The gifted group at mid-life.* Stanford, Calif.: Stanford University Press, 1959.

Tervoort, B.T. Esoteric symbolism in the communication behavior of young deaf children. *American Annals of the Deaf,* 1961, *106*(5), 436–480.

References

Thomas, A., Chess, S., & Birch, H.G. *Temperament and behavior disorders in children* New York: New York University Press, 1968.

Thornton, W. Four years' use of the binaural sensory aid. *New Outlook for the Blind,* 1975, *69,* 7–10.

Torrance, E.P. *Guiding creative talent.* Englewood Cliffs, N.J.: Prentice-Hall, 1962.

Torrance, E.P. Broadening concepts of giftedness in the '70s. *Gifted Child Quarterly,* 1970, *4,* 199–208.

Training educators for the handicapped: A need to redirect federal programs. Report to the Congress by the Comptroller General of the United States, HRD-76-77, 1976.

Tredgold, A.F. *A textbook of mental deficiency.* Baltimore: Wood, 1937.

Treffry, D., Martin, G., Samels, J., & Watson, C. Operant conditioning of grooming behavior of severely retarded children. *Journal of Applied Behavior Analysis,* 1971, *4*(4), 283–290.

Trezise, R. Are the gifted coming back? *Phi Delta Kappan,* 1973, *54,* 687–688.

Turner, P.J. The place of CCTV in the rehabilitation of the low vision patient. *New Outlook for the Blind,* 1976, *70,* 206–214.

Turnure, J., & Zigler, E. Outerdirectedness in the problem solving of normal and retarded children. *Journal of Abnormal and Social Psychology,* 1964, *69,* 427–436.

Tuttle, D.W. A comparison of three reading media for the blind: Braille, normal recording, and compressed speech. *Education of the Visually Handicapped,* 1972, *4,* 40–44.

Tyler, N.B., & Kahn, N. A home treatment program for the cerebral palsied child. *The American Journal of Occupational Therapy,* 1976, *30*(7), 437–440.

The unfinished revolution: Education for the handicapped. Annual report of the National Advisory Committee for the Handicapped. Washington, D.C.: 1976.

U.S. Department of Health, Education and Welfare. *Mental retardation and the law: A report on status of current court cases.* Washington, D.C.: U.S. Government Printing Office, 1975.

U.S. Office of Education. *Education of the gifted and talented.* Subcommittee on Labor and Public Welfare, U.S. Senate, March 1972.

U.S. Office of Education, Bureau of Education for the Handicapped. Definition of severely handicapped children. *Code of Federal Regulations,* 1974, Title 45, Section 121.2.

U.S. Office of Education. *Estimated number of handicapped children in the United States, 1974–1975.* Washington, D.C.: U.S. Office of Education, 1975.

Vanderheiden, G.C., & Grilley, K. *Non-vocal communication techniques and aids for the severely physically handicapped.* Baltimore: University Park Press, 1976.

Vanderheiden, G., & Harris-Vanderheiden, D. Communication techniques and aids for the nonvocal severely handicapped. In L.L. Lloyd (Ed.), *Communication and assessment and intervention strategies.* Baltimore: University Park Press, 1976.

Van Uden, A. *A world of language for deaf children.* Rotterdam, Netherlands: Rotterdam University Press, 1970.

Vaughan, D., Asbury, T., & Cook, R. *General ophthalmology* (6th ed.). Los Altos, Calif.: Lange Medical Publications, 1971.

Vernon, M. *Myths about the education of deaf children.* Communication Symposium, Maryland School for the Deaf, Frederick, Maryland, March 13, 1970.

Wald, J.R. Crippled and other health impaired and their education. In F.P. Connor, J.R. Wald, & M.J. Cohen (Eds.), *Professional preparation for educators of crippled children.* New York: Teachers College Press, 1971.

References

Walker, H.M., & Buckley, N.K. *Token reinforcement techniques*. Eugene, Ore.: E-B Press, 1974.

Walker, J. What the school health team should know about sickle cell anemia. *Journal of School Health,* 1975, *45*(3), 149–153.

Wallace, G. Interdisciplinary efforts in learning disabilities: Issues and recommendations. *Journal of Learning Disabilities,* 1976, *9,* 520–526.

Wallace, G., & J.M. Kauffman. *Teaching children with learning problems* (2nd ed.). Columbus, Ohio: Charles E. Merrill, 1978.

Ward, V. *Educating the gifted*. Columbus, Ohio: Charles E. Merrill, 1961.

Warren, J. *Early and periodic screening, diagnosis and treatment. Educational Researcher,* May 1977.

Waryas, C., & Stremel-Campbell, K. Grammatical training for the language delayed child. In R.L. Schiefelbusch (Ed.), *Language intervention strategies*. Baltimore: University Park Press, in press.

Wechsler, D. Wechsler Intelligence Scale for Children. New York: The Psychological Corporation, 1949; rev. ed., 1974.

Wechsler, D. Wechsler Preschool and Primary Scale of Intelligence. New York: Psychological Corporation, 1967.

Wehman, P. Vocational training of the severely retarded: Expectations and potential. *Rehabilitation Literature,* 1976, *37*(8), 233–236.

Weinberger, C.W. *MR 72: Islands of excellence.* Report of the President's Committee on Mental Retardation. Washington, D.C.: U.S. Government Printing Office, 1972.

Weinberger, C.W. *Silent minority.* Report of the President's Committee on Mental Retardation. Washington, D.C.: U.S. Government Printing Office, 1973.

Weinberger, C.W. Memo informing public of Executive Order #11776, 1974.

Weiner, B.B. Assessment: Beyond psychometry. *Exceptional Children,* 1967, *33,* 362–370.

Werry, J.S. Organic factors in childhood psychopathology. In H.C. Quay & J.S. Werry (Eds.), *Psychopathological disorders of childhood.* New York: Wiley, 1972.

Weston, A., & Irwin, J.J. *The paired stimuli technique kit.* Memphis: National Educators Service, 1971.

Wheeler, A.J. Using attendants to build a verbal repertoire in a profoundly retarded adolescent. *Training School Bulletin,* November, 1973, *70*(3), 140–144.

Whelan, R.J. The relevance of behavior modification procedures for teachers of emotionally disturbed children. In P. Knoblock (Ed.), *Intervention approaches in educating emotionally disturbed children.* Syracuse: Syracuse University Press, 1966.

White, B.L. *The first three years of life.* Englewood Cliffs, N.J.: Prentice-Hall, 1975.

White, O.R., & Haring, N.G. *Exceptional teaching: A multimedia training package.* Columbus, Ohio: Charles E. Merrill, 1976.

Whitman, T.L., Zakaras, M., & Chardos, S. Effects of reinforcement and guidance procedures on instruction-following behavior of severely retarded children. *Journal of Applied Behavior Analysis,* 1971, *4*(4), 283–290.

Williams, C.D. The elimination of tantrum behavior by extinction procedures. *Journal of Abnormal and Social Psychology,* 1959, *59,* 269.

Williams, R.J. The biological approach to the study of personality. In T. Millon (Ed.), *Theories of psychopathology.* Philadelphia: Saunders, 1967.

Wills, R.H. *The institutionalized severely retarded: A study of activity and interaction.* Springfield, Ill.: Charles C Thomas, 1973.

Wing, J.D., & Wing, L.A. A clinical interpretation of remedial teaching. In J.K. Wing (Ed.), *Early childhood autism: Clinical, educational and social aspects.* New York: Pergamon, 1966. Pp. 185–203.

References

Wint, J. Contrasting solutions for school violence: I. The crackdown. *Phi Delta Kappan,* 1975, *57,* 175–176.

Witty, P. (Ed.). *The gifted child.* Boston: Heath, 1951.

Wolfe, M.E. Career education: A new dimension in education for living. *New Outlook for the Blind,* 1973, *67,* 193–199.

Wolfensberger, W. *The principles of normalization in human services.* Toronto: National Institute on Mental Retardation, 1972.

Wolfensberger, W. Will there always be an institution? II: The impact of new service models. In M. Rosen, G.R. Clark, & M.S. Kivitz (Eds.), *The history of mental retardation: Collected papers* (Vol. 2). Baltimore: University Park Press, 1976.

Woody, R.H. *Legal aspects of mental retardation: A search for reliability.* Springfield, Ill.: Charles C Thomas, 1974.

Worcester, D. *The education of children of above average mentality.* Lincoln, Nebr.: The University of Nebraska Press, 1956.

Wunderlich, R.C. Treatment of the hyperactive child. *Academic Therapy,* 1973, *8,* 375–390.

Zimmerman, B., & Dialessi, F. Modeling influences on children's creative behavior. *Journal of Educational Psychology,* 1973, *65,* 127–134.

June L. Bigge is a Professor of Special Education at San Francisco State University. She received the Ed.D. with honors at the University of Oregon. Before she began university teaching, she taught regular first grade, classes of children with physical and multiple disabilities in a special education school, individuals with severe learning disabilities in regular classes, and physically disabled students who received most of their education in regular classes.

Bigge's publications focus on the physically handicapped. In 1976 she coedited a book, *Teaching Individuals with Physical and Multiple Disabilities*. During 1977 to 1978, she was President of the DOPHHH Division (The Division on the Physically Handicapped, Homebound, and Hospitalized) of the Council for Exceptional Children.

Richard M. DeMott is Superintendent of the Iowa Braille and Sight Saving School, Vinton, Iowa. He comes to this position with years of experience in teaching the visually handicapped, including positions as Associate Superintendent of the same school and as Principal of the Ohio State School of the Blind. DeMott has taught general science in the public schools, before moving on to teach at Michigan State University, Northwest Nazarene College, and the University of Virginia.

In addition to his experience in academic positions, DeMott has been involved in several projects to develop educational service delivery models for the visually impaired. He also serves as a book reviewer for *Education of the Visually Handicapped*.

A native of Michigan, Dr. DeMott received his B.S. in general science and M.A. in educational psychology from Michigan State University. He also received a Ph.D. in special education from the same university.

Valentine Dmitriev is currently the coordinator of the Down's Syndrome Programs at the Experimental Education Unit, Child Development and Mental Retardation Center, University of Washington. After twenty-five years of teaching everything from piano to nursery school in the Seattle area, with an emphasis on education of young children and their families, Ms. Dmitriev joined the University of Washington. She was awarded the M.Ed. there in 1967.

Ms. Dmitriev has worked extensively with the severely retarded, both at the University and as a consultant to developmental disabilities centers throughout the area. She is a member of several professional organizations, and has published extensively, with particular focus on early stimulation of infants with Down's syndrome.

Norris G. Haring, born in Kearney, Nebraska, in 1923, is currently Professor of Education, Lecturer in Pediatrics, and principal investigator of the Western Technical Assistance Region (WESTAR), a technical assistance project for early intervention, funded by BEH and located at the University of Washington in Seattle.

Dr. Haring received his Bachelor of Arts degree from Kearney State College in 1948; his Master of Arts degree from the University of Nebraska—with study at the Merrill-Palmer Institute and a Ford Foundation Fellowship in Child Development and Family Life—with a major in psychology in 1950; and his Doctor of Education degree in special education from Syracuse University in 1956.

As an educator, Dr. Haring has served as Instructor in Education at Syracuse University from 1954 to 1956; as Director of Special Education for the Arlington County Public Schools, Arlington, Virginia, from 1956 to 1957; as Associate Professor and Coordinator of Special Education at the University of Maryland from 1957 to 1960; and as Professor of Education, Associate Professor of

Pediatrics, and Educational Director of the Children's Rehabilitation Unit at the University of Kansas Medical Center from 1960 to 1965.

Dr. Haring has special interests in research in systematic instruction with both mildly and severely handicapped children. He is currently the President of the American Association for the Education of the Severely/Profoundly Handicapped.

Alice H. Hayden is a leading proponent and practitioner of early childhood education. She is currently Professor of Education at the University of Washington and Director of the Model Preschool Center for Handicapped Children at the Child Development and Mental Retardation Center.

Her experience includes membership on numerous state, regional, and national committees. She has been instrumental in developing state plans for the education of young handicapped children and has assisted many new early childhood projects. Her technical assistance and outreach work has contributed to the upgrading of skills and techniques among thousands of teachers of the young handicapped.

Dr. Hayden has published extensively in the area of early childhood education. Research conducted under her direction has resulted in new ways of teaching traditionally "unteachable" populations, such as Down's syndrome children. Her work has changed many traditional views toward the handicapped.

Dr. Hayden received her B.S. and M.S. degrees at Oregon State University and her Ph.D. degree at Purdue University. Purdue also awarded Dr. Hayden an honorary Doctor of Letters degree for her "dedicated leadership in the creation and application of educational theory" and her "pioneering work in the broad area of child development."

James M. Kauffman is an Associate Professor and Chairman of the Department of Special Education of the University of Virginia. His early education was in the field of elementary education, and he has taught both nonhandicapped and emotionally disturbed children. Since receiving an Ed.D. in special education from the University of Kansas in 1969, he has taught at Illinois State University, Normal, and the University of Virginia.

Dr. Kauffman has written extensively in special education. Of particular note is his already widely used introductory text, *Characteristics of Children's Behavior Disorders,* published in 1977. Kauffman is also interested in the history of special education services to the behavior disordered.

Thomas C. Lovitt is currently Professor of Special Education at the University of Washington. He received his B.A. and M.A. degrees in music education from the University of Kansas, and was awarded an Ed.D. degree in special education from that same university.

He began his professional career as a musician with the Kansas City Philharmonic and taught trumpet in several colleges in Kansas and Missouri. In 1962 he began his career in special education as a teacher in North Kansas City, Missouri. He taught the next 2 years at the Children's Rehabilitation Unit at the University of Kansas Medical Center. Lovitt continued at the University of Kansas as a student and faculty member until 1966, when he came to Seattle. Since that time he has taught special education courses, worked with doctoral students, and conducted research. His research specialty has been curriculum investigations with learning disabled youngsters.

In order to write the profiles of Josh and Ben which appear in chapter 7, Lovitt observed the boys several times, talked with them, their friends, and their teachers. He studied their test scores and the materials and techniques used to instruct them. He then put all that information together to describe a typical day in their lives.

Sheila Lowenbraun is an Associate Professor, Deptartment of Special Education, University of Washington. Her experience includes teaching deaf and multiply handicapped students at the New York School for the Deaf and serving as Assistant Professor of Education at the University of Northern Colorado. Dr. Lowenbraun has served as an educational consultant and has written scripts for films for hearing impaired children. She has also been a consultant for the Division of Personnel Preparation and Division of Program Planning and Innovation of BEH, and has conducted inservice courses on language development and programmed instruction techniques for teachers of the hearing impaired.

Dr. Lowenbraun received her B.A. at Barnard College, M.A. at Teachers College, Columbia University, and a Ph.D. in special education with an emphasis on education of the hearing impaired from Columbia University.

Contributors

James McLean is a speech pathologist with a wide range of experience in both speech pathology and special education. He served for 7 years as a speech clinician in public schools and was a state supervisor of public school speech and hearing programs in Kansas. He was a research coordinator in the U.S. Office of Education's Handicapped Children and Youth Branch and was Professor and Chairperson of the Department of Special Education at George Peabody College.

Dr. McLean is currently the Director of the Parsons Research Center, a component of the Kansas Center for Research in Mental Retardation and Human Development. He holds appointments as a Research Associate in the Bureau of Child Research of the University of Kansas and Professor of Speech and Drama. His primary research interests have been in articulation modification and the language problems of mentally retarded and young handicapped children. Dr. McLean received the B.S. in Speech Correction from Indiana University in 1951 and the M.A. in Speech Pathology from the University of Kansas in 1959. He also earned the Ph.D. in Speech Pathology and Audiology from the University of Kansas in 1965.

restaurant manager who hired and trained the retarded for 4 years in Topeka, Lawrence, and Kansas City, Kansas; he then spent 1 year as the proprietor of a custodial service employing the retarded. He was a vocational counselor, first for the Vocational Rehabilitation Unit, Topeka, and then for the Kansas Vocational Rehabilitation and Special Education Unit, University of Kansas Medical Center, for a total of 2½ years. Payne spent a year as planning director, Wyandotte County Schools and Sheltered Workshop, and 3 years as Director of the Kansas City, Kansas, Head Start preschool program.

Dr. Payne received his M.S. in 1967 and his Ed.D. in 1970, both in special education with an emphasis on mental retardation, from the University of Kansas. He is a member of many professional organizations, and has written extensively on mental retardation.

James S. Payne is Associate Professor of Education at the University of Virginia. Before he became a professional educator, Payne spent several years working with the retarded. He was a

Ronald E. Reeve is an Assistant Professor in the Foundations of Education Department at the University of Virginia. Before receiving his Ph.D. in education and psychology at the University of Michigan in 1976, he served as a school psychologist for 3 years. His experience in working with exceptional children includes serving as director of two summer camps and a summer academic program for special children. He has also been Program Associate in Psychology at the Institute for the Study of Mental Retardation and Related Disabilities at the University of Michigan.

therapist. In addition, she has been an instructor at the National College of Education and at Northwestern University. She received her A.B. from Capital University and her M.A. from Northwestern University.

Carolyn Lee Scroggs is an Associate Professor of Special Education at Northern Illinois University. She also has taught the deaf at the New York School for the Deaf, in the Seattle Public Schools, and in a preschool program in Tacoma, Washington. Scroggs has also been Assistant Professor at the University of Washington.

Dr. Scroggs received her B.A. at Reed College with a year of study as an exchange student at Keel University, England. She received her M.A. in Education of the Deaf at Teachers College, Columbia University, and her Ph.D. in special education at the University of Washington.

Jane Rieke is currently the coordinator of the Communication Programs at the Experimental Education Unit, Child Development and Mental Retardation Center, University of Washington. A member of both ASHA and CEC, Ms. Rieke has made presentations at state, regional, and national conventions dealing with the communication and language development of young children. She travels widely across the country, conducting workshops on the procedures that have been developed in her communication programs. She also serves as a consultant to school districts both in Washington and in other parts of the country where similar programs are being begun.

Ms. Rieke has taught in elementary and high schools, as well as serving as an itinerant speech

Contributors

Barbara Sirvis has a joint appointment to the faculties of the Departments of Special Education and Recreation and Leisure Studies at San Francisco State University. She taught previously at the University of Washington and has had adjunct positions at New York University and the University of California, Santa Cruz. She earned her Ed.D. at Teachers College, Columbia University.

While at Teachers College, Dr. Sirvis served as Administrative Assistant, Special Education Child Study Center. Before teaching at the university level, Dr. Sirvis spent several years teaching physically/multiply disabled high school students in a resource room program and preschool children in a self-contained class.

Dr. Sirvis has presented several workshops on death education for the Council for Exceptional Children Conventions. She was chairman of the CEC Institute on the IEP for the Physically and Other Health Impaired. Her publications include several articles and book chapters in special education and therapeutic recreation.

tor, for which she taught technical writing at various Navy installations, government agencies, and private industries on the east coast; as a free-lance writer and editor; and as public relations director for two hospitals in southern Virginia.

With an M.A. in Special Education, she joined a psychiatric group in Norfolk and was trained as a psychometrician and caseworker, dealing with private outpatients and in the psychiatric service of Norfolk General Hospital. When the group expanded to develop private hospitals, she established and administered Atlantic Academy, the school for severely disturbed adolescents that is an adjunct to the Tidewater Psychiatric Institutes, and worked there as teacher, adolescent therapist, and school administrator.

In 1974, she entered the doctoral program at the Department of Special Education, University of New Mexico, and in 1976, became a staff member of that Department's dissemination project, Teacher Education/Special Education, under a grant from the Bureau of Education for the Handicapped. Her publications emphasize education of the severely and profoundly handicapped.

With a B.A. in English, Judy Smith worked for a number of years in positions involving writing and media—as assistant sales promotion director of a national insurance company; on the staff of the Norfolk (Virginia) newspapers; as a teacher of high school English and as a writing instructor for the University of Virginia extension program; as chief editor and instructor for a defense contrac-

Thomas M. Stephens is Professor and Chairman of the Faculty for Exceptional Children at The Ohio State University. His professional experience includes teaching gifted children, and Stephens was the state of Ohio's first consultant for programs for the gifted. He has written and served as editor for 16 monographs on giftedness. In 1962-1963, Dr. Stephens served as the first President of the Council of State Directors of Programs for the Gifted.

In addition to his interest in the gifted, Stephens has been instrumental in developing the Directive Teaching Instructional Management System, a skills training approach to curriculum and assessment for mildly handicapped students.

Stephens is a native of Youngstown, Ohio, and received a B.S. from Youngstown College, an M.Ed. from Kent State University, and the D.Ed. from the University of Pittsburgh.

Ms. Thomas has taught retarded children in public school systems in Virginia and Alaska and has been a Head Start teacher. She also served for 2 years as school psychologist in the Pittsylvania County Public Schools, Chatham, Virginia, before entering the doctoral program.

Dr. Joan S. Wolf is presently a Clinical Assistant Professor in the Department of Special Education, University of Utah, Salt Lake City.

A native of Boston, Massachusetts, she began her career as an elementary school teacher in the Salt Lake City Schools. She completed her B.S. degree in elementary education at the University of Utah, an M.A. in School Psychology, and a Ph.D. in Exceptional Children at The Ohio State University in Columbus, Ohio. Dr. Wolf is certified as a teacher, a school psychologist, and a supervisor in the area of learning disabilities.

Her experiences have included working with learning disabled children in a variety of settings. She has worked as a research associate with The Ohio State University and the Ohio Department of Education in helping to develop programs for gifted/talented children. She has taught courses on the education of the gifted and has presented numerous workshops on various aspects of gifted education.

Carol Thomas is a Doctoral Fellow in Special Education at the University of Virginia. Her major emphasis is in mental retardation, with minors in the areas of learning disabilities and school psychology. While completing both the B.A. and M.S. degrees in psychology at Radford College, she spent summers working with retarded and handicapped children and adults in residential camp settings.

Name Index

Name Index

Name Index

Subject Index

Subject Index

Subject Index

Subject Index